A Companion to Aesthetics

Edited by

DAVID E. COOPER

Advisory editors

Joseph Margolis
and
Crispin Sartwell

BLACKWELL
Reference

Blackwell Companions to Philosophy

This benchmark student reference series offers a comprehensive survey of philosophy as a whole. Written by many of today's leading figures, each volume provides lucid and engaging coverage of the key figures, terms and movements of the main subdisciplines of philosophy. Each essay is fully cross-referenced and supported by a bibliography. Taken together, it provides the ideal basis for course use and an invaluable work of reference.

Already Published

1   The Blackwell Companion to Philosophy
     Edited by Nicholas Bunnin & Eric Tsui-James

2   A Companion to Ethics
     Edited by Peter Singer

3   A Companion to Aesthetics
     Edited by David Cooper

4   A Companion to Epistemology
     Edited by Jonathan Dancy and Ernest Sosa

5   A Companion to Contemporary Political Philosophy
     Edited by Robert E. Goodin and Philip Pettit

6   A Companion to the Philosophy of Mind
     Edited by Samual Guttenplan

7   A Companion to Metaphysics
     Edited by Jaegwon Kim and Ernest Sosa

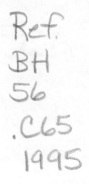
8   A Companion to Philosophy of Law and Legal Theory
     Edited by Dennis Patterson

9   A Companion to Philosophy of Religion
     Edited by Philip L. Quinn and Charles Taliaferro

10   A Companion to the Philosophy of Language
     Edited by Bob Hale and Crispin Wright

Copyright © Blackwell Publishers Ltd, 1992, 1995
Editorial organization © David E. Cooper, 1992, 1995

First published 1992
First published in USA 1992
First published in paperback 1995
Reprinted 1996 (twice), 1997

Blackwell Publishers Ltd
108 Cowley Road
Oxford OX4 1JF, UK

Blackwell Publishers Inc
350 Main Street
Malden, Massachusetts 02148, USA

British Library Cataloguing in Publication Data
A CIP catalogue record for this book is available from the British Library

Library of Congress Cataloging in Publication Data
ISBN 0–631–17801–5 (hd)
ISBN 0–631–19659–5 (pb)

Typeset in 9.5 on 11pt Lasercomp Photina
by Alden Multimedia Ltd, Northampton
Printed and bound in Great Britain by Hartnolls Ltd, Bodmin, Cornwall

This book is printed on acid-free paper

Contents

Paul Gaugin, *D'où venons-nous? Que sommes-nous? Où allon-nous?* a detail of which is used on the jacket (for further information please see jacket).

Introduction

DAVID E. COOPER

'Art, in my estimation, does not suffer discussion,' says a character in *Anna Karenina*. Until about twenty-five years ago, it seems that most English-speaking philosophers of this century shared that opinion. Few of them wrote on aesthetics at any length, and the notable exceptions – such as Collingwood and Dewey – did not subscribe to the 'analytic' fashions of their time. With the focus on the language and logic of evaluation, the predominant feeling seemed to be that whatever was worth saying about beauty and taste – still perceived as the two prime topics of aesthetic attention – could be quickly derived from a quite general discussion of evaluative discourse. Aesthetics, in fact, was a Cinderella of philosophy.

Today's scene is totally different. Aesthetics is one of the most popular student choices from the philosophy curriculum, and each year sees a flood of new publications in the area. Just a few of the factors responsible for this transformation are worth mentioning. First of all, there have been developments in other areas of philosophy helping to bring new, or newly formulated, questions about art into prominence. Work by philosophers of language on reference and meaning has challenged older views on the relations – notably representation – between an artwork and its object. Some epistemologists have challenged the status of propositions as the privileged conveyors of truth, opening up the possibility that artworks may, in their way, be vehicles of knowledge. Debates over cultural and moral relativism have inspired new interest in the criteria, if any, of good taste and beauty.

Second, and more widely, there has been a shift, favourable to aesthetics, in the general philosophical sensibility. This sensibility is a much more catholic one than that of a quarter of a century ago. For one thing, it is increasingly receptive to the work of 'Continental' philosophy. Here one could mention the growing appreciation of nineteenth-century German thought, which ascribed such a central place to art as a dimension of the human condition, and thence to aesthetics as the reflection of that place. For Schelling, Schopenhauer and the early Nietzsche, it was through art that man might best hope to articulate and express the realm of that ultimate reality which, since Kant, was held to be closed to conceptual understanding and rational discourse. More recent influences from across the English Channel have been the 'hermeneutic' inquiries of Heidegger and Gadamer into the problems of interpretation and art-historical understanding, and the writings of French structuralists and poststructuralists, whose radical claims have forced rethinking about the nature of texts and the relations between artists, their works and their audiences.

If geographical barriers have come down (and, here, one should not ignore a growing interest in 'the East'), so have those between the disciplines. Philosophers are much less shy than earlier in the century to engage in what might just as happily be called psychology, sociology, or literary criticism as philosophy. The effects of this kind of catholicity may be seen in recent work on the perception of music and paintings, on the role of art institutions and 'the artworld', and on the importance of metaphor and irony as something more than literary decoration.

It is not only developments within philosophy, however, that explain the revival of aesthetics. Developments in the arts themselves, clearly, have spawned new questions or lent special urgency to older ones. Abstract art, 'ready-mades', Dadaism, 'self-referential' works, the parodic products of 'postmodernism' and *musique concrète* have provided plentiful fodder for discussions of, *inter alia*, the function of art, the possibility that art is 'at an end', the definition of 'art', and the ontological status of artworks. (Is Duchamp's famous urinal only, if at all, a work of art while inside the gallery?) Finally, art now enjoys a place within society at large that is without precedent in history. Through television, reproduction and recording, artists can have an impact as never before on the general public. The totalitarian regimes of this century witness the massive and pernicious influence that the arts, when under unscrupulous control, can exert. Issues, therefore, of art and morality, of censorship and artistic responsibility, of 'popular' art and art's impact on the environment, and of the 'authenticity' of both the artist and his works, assume a new or enhanced importance.

Several of the developments cited are, of course, retrievals of themes discussed for many centuries; in some case, since the very beginning of philosophy. One has only to recall the worries of Plato, or Chuang-Tzu, about the moral impact of art; or ancient debates about representation and realism in connection with idolatry and iconoclasm. It is an irony that may of these topics disappeared from the philosophical purview at just the time, during the eighteenth century, when the label 'aesthetics' was first deployed as a philosophical term of art. Its coiner, Alexander Baumgarten, defined it as 'the science of sensible knowledge', which soon came to be understood as the 'science' of beauty and taste. Hegel was surely right to point out, at the beginning of his own *Ästhetik*, that 'aesthetics', so understood, was much too narrow to cover the range of the traditional reflections and concerns of philosophers in the realm of art. (This narrowness is still reflected in the *Oxford English Dictionary*'s definition of 'aesthetics' as 'the philosophy or theory of taste, or of the perception of the beautiful'.) But, as his use of the term as the title of his own work indicates, Hegel was also right to concede that 'aesthetics' had become too entrenched to get rid of, even if 'philosophy of art' would better register the proper range of the subject. (In one respect, though, both Hegel's and subsequent uses of the term are narrower than the eighteenth-century one, including Kant's: for the focus is on art and no longer on *natural* beauty.)

In this Companion, anyway, 'aesthetics' is used in the broader sense of philosophy of art, with 'art' itself taken broadly so as to include, for instance, literature. A quick glance at the list of headings will show the reader the wide range covered by the articles — of which there are more than one hundred and thirty, each provided with a bibliography (and a list of writings, in the case of biographical articles), and most of them with cross-references to related articles. The articles vary from 1200 to 4000 words in length, and one, 'theories of art', is much longer. Readers to whom aesthetics is a new area of interest are encouraged to read this article first, for it offers them a survey of the main directions taken by philosophers on the core issues of aesthetics. That the volume contains a large number of substantial pieces, some of them taking original and contentious lines, means that it is not simply a work of reference: it is also a repository of essays reflecting 'the state of the art' at the end of the twentieth century.

One hundred and thirty is a large number, but there is no pretence of providing an absolutely comprehensive coverage. While I hope that all the most important topics and concepts of aesthetics are dealt with, each reader will no doubt experience his or her individual disappoint-ment at this or that omission. In particular, the choice of philosophers and other writers covered was bound to be a partly personal matter. And at some point, a more or less arbitrary line had to be drawn between those who should count as philosophers of art and those who had to be excluded as 'mere' critics, historians or men of letters.

There are many people to whom I owe thanks for their help in the preparation of this volume. First, to the secretary of my department, Ann Walker, for putting on the word-processor a large number of contributions whose typographical quality fell well short of their scholarly merit. Second, to the ever helpful team at Blackwell – especially Richard Beatty, Alyn Shipton, Stephan Chambers and Steve Smith – and to Sue Philpott for her hawk-eyed copy-editing. Third, to the many contributors who also provided suggestions on the volume's contents, thereby repairing omissions in my original list. Finally, I owe special thanks to my two editorial advisers, Joseph Margolis and Crispin Sartwell. Their intimate knowledge of the American scene helped guarantee that, on their side of the Atlantic at least, the right people were commissioned for the right jobs.

David E. Cooper

Contributors

Thomas M. Alexander
Southern Illinois University at Carbondale

Douglas R. Anderson
Pennsylvania State University

George Bailey
East Carolina University

Robert Bernasconi
Memphis State University

Andrew Bowie
Anglia Polytechnic University

Entries written with the support of the Alexander von Humboldt Foundation

Malcolm Budd
University College London

Allen Carlson
University of Alberta

David Carrier
Carnegie-Mellon University

Noèl Carroll
University of Wisconsin-Madison

Wojciech Chojna
La Salle University

John Compton
Vanderbilt University

Steven Connor
Birkbeck College, London

David E. Cooper
University of Durham

Donald Cullen
Bowling Green State University

Nicholas Davey
Cardiff, UK

Stephen Davies
University of Auckland

Kenneth J. DeWoskin
University of Michigan

George Dickie
University of Illinois at Chicago

Martin Donougho
University of South Carolina

Richard Eldridge
Swarthmore College

Catherine Z. Elgin
Lexington, Massachusetts

David Freedberg
Columbia University

Patrick Gardiner
Magdalen College, Oxford

Alan H. Goldman
University of Miami

Timothy Gould
Metropolitan State College of Denver

R.A.D. Grant
University of Glasgow

Morris Grossman
Fairfield University

Kalyan Sen Gupta
Jadavpur University, Calcutta

John Haldane
University of St Andrews

Stephen Halliwell
University of Birmingham

Andrew Harrison
University of Bristol

Ronald W. Hepburn
University of Edinburgh

Kathleen Marie Higgins
The University of Texas at Austin

P.H. Hirst
Brighton, UK

John Hyman
The Queen's College, Oxford

David Jasper
University of Glasgow

Peter Kivy
Rutgers University

Michael Krausz
Bryn Mawr College

Samuel R. Levin
The City University of New York

Jerrold Levinson
University of Maryland

John Lippitt
University of Hertfordshire

Ann Loades
University of Durham

Renée Lorraine
University of Tennessee at Chattanooga

Colin Lyas
University of Lancaster

Laura Marcus
Birkbeck College, London

Joseph Margolis
Temple University

Paul Mattick, Jr
Adelphi University

Charles Molesworth
The City University of New York

Mary Mothersill
Columbia University

Stephen Mulhall
University of Essex

David Novitz
University of Canterbury, New Zealand

Anthony O'Hear
University of Bradford

Margaret Paton
Milton Bridge, Midlothian, UK

Dieter Peetz
University of Nottingham

Diane Proudfoot
University of Canterbury, New Zealand

Diana Raffman
Ohio State University

Jack Rillie
Glasgow University

Tom Rockmore
Duquesne University

Crispin Sartwell
Vanderbilt University

Roger Scruton
Stanton Fitzwarren, Wiltshire

Gary Shapiro
University of Richmond

Richard Shusterman
Temple University

Anita Silvers
San Francisco State University

Stuart Sim
University of Sunderland

Michael Smithurst
University of Southampton

John Sturrock
London

Michael Tanner
University of Cambridge

Paul Taylor
University of Cape Town

Dabney Townsend
University of Texas at Arlington

Andrew Ward
University of York

Patricia Waugh
University of Durham

Michael Weston
University of Essex

Michael Wheeler
University of Lancaster

David Whewell
University of Durham

John White
Institute of Education, University of London

Caroline Wilde
University of Bristol

Bernard Williams
Corpus Christi College, Oxford

Mary Wiseman
New York

Nicholas Wolterstoff
Yale University

Richard Woodfield
City University Nottingham

Julian Young
University of Auckland

Eddy Zemach
Hebrew University

A

abstraction Absence of representation. In painting and sculpture, pure abstraction consists in the absence of representative elements, elements which recognizably resemble items in the external world and which the work is intended to portray. Abstraction, however, admits of degrees. Extremely realistic works display a minimum of abstract elements. As the artist introduces distortions or generalizations or purely decorative elements, the work grows more abstract.

The history of abstract art is a long one. In various decorative arts (for example, carpet design, quilting, floor tiling), abstract designs have been employed since ancient times in many cultures. This is especially true in cultures which have strictures on the use of images (for example, in Judaic and Moslem societies). And music and architecture have always been predominantly non-representational. However, the use of pure abstraction in Western painting and sculpture is relatively recent, and as a widespread phenomenon dates from c.1910.

In the second half of the nineteenth century, impressionism was the dominant artistic style among 'advanced' painters in Europe and the Americas. Impressionists viewed their project as the perfectly accurate representation of visual impressions. Émile Zola addressed the impressionist Pissarro thus: 'Why the devil do you have the arrant clumsiness to paint solidly and study nature frankly? An austere and serious kind of painting, an extreme concern for truth and accuracy . . . You are a great blunderer, sir, you are an artist whom I like' (Zola, 1967, p. 45). Practically all the great practitioners of impressionism could be quoted to similar effect.

Nevertheless, impressionism is not today generally thought of as a realistic tradition, despite the claims of its proponents. What shocked the art world about the impressionist salon was not the strident realist declarations of the exhibitors, or even the subject-matter of their paintings. Rather, what was shocking was the way they handled paint: with bravura strokes of unmixed pigment applied with large brushes or even palette knives. Such devices were seen at first by those who employed them primarily as techniques for painting quickly, before the impression faded. But paradoxically, in their effort to efface paint and painter and to record the experience of an 'innocent eye' (to use Ruskin's phrase), they offended by making the paint itself so explicit, because it was so little worked. And whatever their declared programme, their technique began to exert its own seductions and its own demands. In Monet, for example, the image steadily receded; the painted surface insinuated itself more and more as a decorative object. Eventually, it became clear that in some ways the impressionists' method contradicted their professed programme. But this led not to a rejection of impressionist painting, but to a rejection of the realist tradition.

Thus, for the next generation of avant-garde painters, the manipulation of colours and forms for their own sake began to be seen as a central artistic challenge (this was true also of surviving first-generation impressionists such as Monet and Degas). The post-impressionists systematically introduced distortions and 'purely decorative' elements into their work, obviously pursuing ends that had little to do with realism. Seurat, for example, constructed forms out of points of pure colour. Seen as realistic from a distance, such 'pointillist' paintings dissolved into abstractions on closer approach. Van Gogh left realistic representation behind in a conscious search for intensity of emotional expression achieved through systematic distortion. Albert Pinkham Ryder (an American working outside 'mainstream' European art) dissolved land and seascapes into vague and disquieting generalities. The Fauves, including Matisse at an early stage of his career, heightened colours and deconstructed forms to achieve almost hallucinatory effects. And Gauguin employed broad expanses of plain colour surrounded by sinuous lines in a way that consistently drew attention away from the represented items and towards the mode of representation. The post-impressionist painter Maurice Denis famously enjoined his fellow-artists to 'remember that a picture, before being a battle horse, a nude woman, or some anecdote, is essentially a plane surface covered with colours' (Denis, 1930, p. 1).

The route from Denis' view to pure abstraction is direct and, in retrospect, obvious. In c.1910, such developments culminated in the almost simultaneous development of pure abstract painting by a number of artists in different parts of the world. Early abstractionists included the Swedish 'medium' Hilma af Klint, the Russian Wassily Kandinsky (who is sometimes held to have 'discovered' pure abstraction), the American Arthur Dove, the Dutchman Piet Mondrian, the Bohemian Frantisek Kupka, and the Italian Giacomo Balla. Many of the early works displayed 'hangovers' from representational art; Kandinsky's paintings, for example, often seemed to contain various amorphous entities deployed in what was still clearly three-dimensional space. But by the time Kasimir Malevich painted his 'suprematist' geometrical shapes in 1914–15, abstraction had become truly pure. And, of course, much of the great European and American art of this century, such as works by Georgia O'Keefe, Constantin Brancusi, Hans Hofmann, Jackson Pollock, Robert Morris and Martin Puryear, has been abstract.

The rise of abstraction has affected the philosophy of art primarily in two ways. First, it has motivated formalism as a theory of art and as a programme for its interpretation and criticism. Second, it has decisively refuted certain theories of art, especially the views that art is an imitation or an idealization of the world, both of which presuppose that all art is representational.

Let us take as representatives of formalism Clive Bell and Clement Greenberg. Bell claimed that works of art were items that displayed 'significant form', combinations of plastic elements (lines, masses, colours) that move us aesthetically. And he argued that 'to appreciate a work of art we need bring with us nothing from life, no knowledge of its ideas and affairs, no familiarity with its emotions. Art transports us from the world of man's activity to a world of aesthetic exaltation' (Bell, 1958, p. 27). Bell wrote that in 1913, and his view is only comprehensible in the atmosphere in which pure abstraction is possible. 'Let no one imagine,' he wrote, 'that representation is bad in itself; a realistic form may be as significant, in its place as part of a design, as an abstract. But if a representative form has value, it is as form, not as representation' (Bell, 1958, p. 27).

As an overall theory of art, Bell's view is incredibly impoverished. To pretend that, say, the religious content of the Ghent altarpiece is not relevant to its meaning as a work of art, is to miss most of what is aesthetically significant about it. And quite the same applies to all the traditional themes of painting, including still-life, landscape and (particularly) portraiture. At the very least, a fit of form to content must be relevant to the aesthetic effect, and Bell's view prohibits us from taking content into account in aesthetic interpretation. But furthermore, Bell's formalism, though it is evidently designed to account for and to celebrate abstract art, also yields an extremely truncated appreciation for such works. It is not true that to appreciate these aesthetically 'we need bring with us nothing of life.' Kandinsky, for example, wrote: 'The artist must have something to say, for his task is not the mastery of form, but the suitability of that form to its content . . . [the artist's] actions and thoughts and feelings, like those of every human being, constitute the spiritual atmosphere, in such a way that they purify or infect the spiritual air' (Kandinsky, 1982, p. 213). Many of the early abstractionists viewed their project as a spiritual exploration, and their works are largely incomprehensible without a sense of this purpose. Indeed, it is not hard to see how the development away from the realistic representation of actual objects might be seen as a development towards the spiritual (see Tuchman, 1986). Or consider the abstract expressionists. Here, the human gesture and its emotional content are absolutely key for interpreting the work; the work is a trace or record of the gestures that produced it, and cannot be understood except as part of a human emotional life. Thus, we may conclude that Bell's formalism, though inspired by the movement towards and into abstraction, does not adequately address that movement, let alone art as a whole.

Greenberg, in his 1939 essay 'Avant-garde and kitsch', formulates a very different formalist programme, but one that is also inspired by abstraction:

> It has been in search of the absolute that avant-garde has arrived at 'abstract' or 'non-objective' art . . . The avant-garde poet or artist tries in effect to imitate God by creating something valid solely on its own terms . . . something *given*, increate, independent of meanings, similars or originals. Content is to be dissolved so completely into form that the work of art cannot be reduced . . . to anything not itself. (Greenberg, 1961, pp. 5, 6)

In Greenberg's view, art has had to turn inward on itself, leaving behind references to the world; art has become the exploration of the physical aspects of its own mediums: paint, stone, and so forth. And indeed, as abstraction gained momentum, it seemed, as we have noted, that (in the case of painting) paint itself and the act of applying it became more and more explicit aspects of the final work. This is very evident, for example, in Pollock, whom Greenberg, in his capacities as dealer and critic, later championed.

But one must ask here what value art has for people once it is divorced from everyday human concerns, and what value the exploration of the physical qualities of paint could possibly have for those not engaged in its manipulation. Greenberg's 'avant-garde' would become more and more self-concerned, more and more involuted, and of less and less importance. And, indeed, this is just how 'modern' art was seen by many people. However, it is worth noting again that this view, which is at least as impoverished as Bell's, would also be rejected by the very artists whose work it is designed to explain. Again, think of Pollock. Here the work is, to repeat, incomprehensible outside of the gestures that produced it, and, more importantly, outside the full-fledged human context in which such gestures have significance.

There is one conspicuous service, however, that abstract art has undoubtedly performed for philosophy; it has dealt the death blow to the ancient views that art is the imitation or the idealization of the real world. For abstract art is precisely art that has no determinable and specific real-world object, that fails to represent. If abstract works can be art (which, I suppose, hardly anyone will at this point be perverse enough to deny), such works provide decisive counter-examples to the traditional theories. In fact, it is partly in response to such works that the characteristic twentieth-century theories of art – for example, Bell's formalism, the 'expression' theories of Croce, Langer and many others, and even Dickie's institutional theory – have been formulated. So despite the fact that initial responses by theoreticians to abstraction were over-enthusiastic and implausible, abstraction has had a profound effect on twentieth-century art theory.

See also BELL; FORM; REALISM; REPRESENTATION; RESEMBLANCE; THEORIES OF ART.

BIBLIOGRAPHY

Bell, Clive: *Art* (New York: G.P. Putnam's Sons, 1958).

Denis, Maurice: *Théories: 1870–1910* (Paris: 1930).

Greenberg, Clement: 'Avant-garde and kitsch',

Art and Culture (Boston, Mass.: Beacon Press, 1961).

Kandinsky, Wassily: *Über das Gerstige in der Kunst* (Munich, 1912); trans. as *On the Spiritual in Art*, in *Kandinsky: Complete Writings on Art*, trans. and ed. Kenneth C. Lindsay and Peter Vergo (Boston, Mass.: G.K. Hall, 1982).

Tuchman, Maurice, ed.: *The Spiritual in Art: Abstract Painting 1890–1985* (New York: Abbeville Press, 1986).

Zola, Émile: *Mon Salon* (Paris: 1866). Quoted in Phoebe Pool, *Impressionism* (New York and Oxford: Oxford University Press, 1967).

CRISPIN SARTWELL

Adorno, Theodor (Wiesengrund) (1903–69) German philosopher and musicologist; leading figure in the Frankfurt school of critical theory. Born into a wealthy family in Frankfurt am Main, Theodor Wiesengrund – he took his mother's name, Adorno, in 1938 – received his Ph.D. in philosophy in that city in 1924, but spent the following year studying composition in Vienna with Alban Berg. While remaining practically involved in the music world, he taught philosophy at Frankfurt University until Hitler's advent to power finally drove him to the USA in 1938, where he joined the Frankfurt Institute for Social Research in exile, working in New York and southern California. He returned to a professorship in Frankfurt in 1953, and succeeded his close collaborator Max Horkheimer as director of the institute, also reinstalled in that city, in 1964. His work, like that of the Frankfurt school associated with the institute generally, had great influence on the German student movement of the 1960s. By the time Adorno died, this influence had been weakened, however, by his intellectual antagonism to the movement as well as by his use of the police to evict student radicals from the institute.

Adorno's collected works run to twenty volumes, of which the majority are concerned with aesthetic questions. There are studies of Berg, Mahler and Wagner; numerous essays on literary and musical matters; an *Introduction to the Sociology of Music* (1962); and two central theoretical works: *Philosophy of Modern Music* (1948) and *Aesthetic Theory* (1970). Special mention should be made of the wide-ranging *Minima Moralia* (1951), perhaps Adorno's masterwork and one of the great books of the post-war period.

Central to Adorno's aesthetic thinking is the insight that art must be conceptualized as an 'historically changing constellation of aspects' (Adorno, 1970, p. 11). His primary interest is in the 'autonomous' art that emerged from earlier functional contexts at the end of the eighteenth century. This autonomy 'was a function of the bourgeois consciousness of freedom, which itself developed together with the social structure' (1970, p. 334); thus art expressed the autonomy of the individual subject *vis-à-vis* society. The fate of art in bourgeois culture is therefore identified by Adorno with the fate of subjectivity, as society became increasingly alienating and repressive.

Art's autonomy means a development of its own structures of meaning, independent of direct reference to the social world; hence Adorno suggests that the concept of art is strictly applicable only to music, since literature and painting always include 'an element of subject-matter transcending aesthetic confines, undissolved in the autonomy of form' (Adorno, 1974, p. 223). Paradoxically, according to him, it is the very tendency towards the elaboration of its own formal nature that constitutes art's social meaning. As the expression of a subjectivity engaged dialectically with a social reality at once repressive of its desires and defining its conditions of existence, art represents the demand for freedom from repression. Its autonomy, its functionlessness, allow it to stand as a critique of a society dedicated to the domination of nature in the interests of commercial profit: as the 'true consciousness of an epoch, in which the real possibility of utopia – that the earth, given the level of productive forces, could here and now be Paradise – is as great as the possibility of total catastrophe' (Adorno, 1970, pp. 55–6).

But also, as itself an element of the modern society to which it stands in this critical relation, aesthetic form is a sedimentation of social content, because 'artistic labour is social labour' (Adorno, 1970, p. 351; and see p. 14). Its history follows the pattern of social development generally: that of the progressive mastery of nature by humankind, described by Adorno (following Max Weber) as a process of rationalization. Nature is represented in music, to take Adorno's central example, by what he calls the musical 'material' confronting composers at any given time: sound as organized by historically evolved musical form. The drive to control over this material led first to the elaboration of the tonal system by the masters of Viennese classicism (above all, Beethoven) and then to the total control over the material achieved by Schoenberg. With the second Viennese school, no conventions force the composer 'to acquiesce to traditionally universal principles. With the liberation of musical material, there arose the possibility of mastering it technically' . . . The composer has emancipated himself along with his sounds' (Adorno, 1973, p. 52).

The emancipation achieved by modern art through its progressive denial of earlier conventions must be paid for. 'In the process of pursuing its own inner logic, music is transformed more and more from something significant into something obscure – even to itself' (Adorno, 1973, p. 19). For example, twelve-tone technique, which achieved the rationalization of the musical material, blocked the production of new large-scale forms to replace those made possible by tonality. Freedom turned into its opposite: 'The construction of truly free forms, delineating the unique nature of a composition, is prevented by a lack of freedom ordained by the row technique – by the continual reappearance of the same elements' (1973, p. 97).

From the artists' point of view, 'the progress in technique that brought them ever greater freedom and independence of anything heterogeneous, has resulted in a kind of reification, technification of the inward as such' (Adorno, 1974, p. 214). For the listener, music has lost its transparent meaningfulness and the satisfaction it once gave. Its meaning – what Adorno calls its

truth content – now requires, beyond 'sensory listening', aesthetic theory, which alone makes possible 'the conceptually mediated perception of the elements and their configuration which assures the social substance of great music' (Adorno, 1973, p. 130). Given the non-discursive character of art, theory is necessary to bring out the truth content of modern art, which resides precisely in its resistance to the ideological demand that experience be depicted as the achievement of harmonious totality.

Art that does not confront society in this way, and so point forward to a potential social transformation, is condemned by Adorno as regressive, both in the realm of high art, as with Stravinsky's primitivism and neo-classicism, and in that of the popular music mass-produced by the 'culture industry'. In either case music adapts itself to social reality: in the former by formally modelling the submission of the individual to social irrationality, in the latter by accepting completely the consequences of the commodity form for musical production. 'Classical' music as a whole is drawn into the system of commercialization, as its presentation is adapted to a mass listenership no longer capable of structural hearing but able only to wait for the appearance of beautiful melodies and exciting rhythms. In this, too, music bears a social meaning – that of the increasing domination of individual experience by the needs of industrial capitalism.

It follows from Adorno's conception of artworks as 'concentrated social substance' that a critical aesthetics must seek social significance in the formal properties of individual works. This is, of course, a difficult prescription to follow, and Adorno's studies of artworks are typically less convincing than his theoretical generalizations. Attempts at combining formal analysis with sociological decoding, such as the comparison of serial technique to bureaucratization, or of the relation between theme and harmony in sonata form to the dialectic of individual and society, are too often 'merely verbal analogies which have no basis in fact but owe their origin and a semblance of plausibility to a generously ambivalent use of words like . . .

"general and particular"' (Dahlhaus, 1987, p. 243). In addition, Adorno does not hesitate on occasion to subordinate matters of fact to his philosophical purposes (see Dahlhaus, 1970). His clearly inadequate dismissal of Stravinsky and his inexpert and unsubtle treatment of popular music have also come under much (not unappreciative) criticism. Nevertheless, his work remains an important achievement as an aesthetics of modernism, both for its general programme, the discovery of social meanings in artistic form, and for its many powerful observations and suggestions.

See also ART HISTORY; AUTONOMY, AESTHETIC.

WRITINGS

Ästhetische Theorie, in *Gesammelte Schriften* [Collected Works], vol. 7 (Frankfurt: Suhrkamp, 1970).
Philosophie der neuen Musik (Frankfurt: 1948); in *Gesammelte Schriften*, vol. 12 (Frankfurt: 1976); trans. A.G. Mitchell and W.V. Blomster, *Philosophy of Modern Music* (New York: Continuum, 1973).
Minima Moralia (Frankfurt: 1951); trans. E.F.N. Jephcott, *Minima Moralia* (London: Verso, 1974).
Einleitung in die Musiksoziologie (Frankfurt: 1962); 2nd edn, in *Gesammelte Schriften*, vol. 14 (Frankfurt: 1973); trans. E. B. Ashton, *Introduction to the Sociology of Music* (New York: Continuum, 1976).

BIBLIOGRAPHY

Dahlhaus, C.: 'Soziologische Dechiffrierung von Musik. Zu Theodor W. Adornos Wagnerkritik' [Sociological deciphering of music. On Theodor Adorno's critique of Wagner], *International Review of Music Aesthetics and Sociology*, 1 (1970), 137–47.
Dahlhaus, C.: *Schoenberg and the New Music*, trans. D. Puffett and A. Clayton (Cambridge: Cambridge University Press, 1987).
Gendron, B.: 'Theodor Adorno meets the Cadillacs', *Studies in Entertainment*, ed. T. Modleski (Bloomington, Ill.: Indiana University Press, 1986), pp. 18–36.
Paddison, M.: 'Review article: Adorno's *Aesthetic Theory*', *Music Analysis*, 6 (1987), 355–77.
Zuidervaart, L.: *Adorno's Aesthetic Theory. The Redemption of Illusion* (Cambridge, Mass.: MIT Press, 1991).

PAUL MATTICK, JR

aestheticism The doctrine that art should be valued for itself alone and not for any purpose or function it may happen to serve, and thus opposed to all instrumentalist theories of art. Historically, the idea of art for art's sake is associated with the cult of beauty, which had its roots in Kantian aesthetics and the Romantic movement, although its potential application is wider than that.

The phrase *l'art pour l'art* (art for art's sake) first became current in France in the first half of the nineteenth century as the rallying cry of the aesthetic movement, and was associated with such names as Théophile Gautier and Baudelaire, and later with Flaubert. The doctrine became fashionable in England in the second half of the nineteenth century under the influence first of Walter Pater and later of such luminaries as Oscar Wilde, Whistler, Aubrey Beardsley and A.J. Symons (author of *The Quest for Corvo*), among others. The movement is famously satirized in the Gilbert and Sullivan operetta *Patience*, where Wilde appears under the guise of the poet Bunthorne. In its earliest and most uncompromising form, the doctrine asserts not merely that a work of art should be judged only on its internal aesthetic properties, but that any extraneous purpose or function it may happen to serve must be counted a serious defect. Thus, in the preface to his novel *Mademoiselle de Maupin*, Gautier argues that 'nothing is truly beautiful except that which can serve for nothing; whatever is useful is ugly.' This was in part a reaction to the utilitarian and materialistic values of the new industrial age. It can clearly be seen to be an overreaction – to quote Harold Osborne:

As we survey the art work of the past from the earliest cave art onwards we find that, various as their uses were, by and large all works of art were made for a use . . . They were essentially utensils in the same sort of sense as a suit of armour, a horse's harness or objects of domestic service are utensils, though the purpose they served was not necessarily a material one. (Osborne, 1968, p. 13)

The very idea of 'the fine arts', arts such as painting, poetry, music, sculpture and ballet, in which the aesthetic properties are thought to be more important than the utilitarian ones, was largely an eighteenth-century innovation. By Gautier's criterion, beauty in its purest form simply did not exist in art prior to the eighteenth century. A far more sensible line is that taken by André Malraux, who has argued that by viewing the art of all times, all places, all cultures as pure aesthetic objects, divorced from their original purposes and functions, we have in effect entered into 'an entirely new relationship with the work of art', where 'the work of art has no other function than to be a work of art.' We have, he says, created for ourselves 'a museum without walls' (Malraux, 1974).

Clearly, to accept this contextless approach to art as a perfectly legitimate and even desirable one, is to adhere to one of the main tenets of the art for art's sake doctrine. The central core of truth in this doctrine can be summarized in the following way: aesthetic values depend on properties which are internal to the work of art on account of which it is valued for its own sake. In other words, aesthetic merit, thus narrowly defined, is a type of final value but clearly distinguishable from all other final values such as knowledge for its own sake, the love of God and doing one's duty. As the philosopher Victor Cousin said, 'we must have religion for religion's sake, morality for morality's sake, as with art for art's sake . . . the beautiful cannot be the way to what is useful, or to what is good, or to what is holy; it leads only to itself' (Cousin, 1854).

It is, then, a necessary condition of a work's being valued for its own sake that it be valued on account of its intrinsic properties and not on its relationship to anything external, such as nature, moral and political

systems, audience response and so on. We deem the internal properties of a work to be aesthetic not because they belong to a distinct class, like the class of colour concepts, but because of the way they contribute to or detract from its value. Properties commonly identified as aesthetic include beauty, elegance, grace, daintiness, sweetness of sound, balance, design, unity, harmony, expressiveness, depth, movement, texture and atmosphere. Not all such properties could accurately be described as formal properties – expressiveness, for example. This is important, because most of those who espouse the doctrine of art for art's sake do so on the basis of some sort of formalistic theory. Take, for example, E.M. Forster: 'Works of art, in my opinion, are the only objects in the material universe to possess internal order, and that is why, though I don't believe that only art matters, I do believe in art for art's sake' (E.M. Forster, 1951, p. 104). Since the aesthetic movement owed much of its inspiration to Kant's powerfully formalistic theory in the *Critique of Judgement*, it is perhaps not surprising that the two doctrines should be so closely associated.

A major drawback to a strict formalist approach is that whilst the form/content distinction is clear enough within the narrow confines of Kant's aesthetics, it has a tendency to break down when applied across the board, especially when applied to the literary arts. For instance, if expression in art is treated as an internal property and not defined in terms of self-expression or audience reaction, then no distinction can usefully be drawn between the particular feeling being expressed and the manner of its expression. Nevertheless, as Scruton has observed, 'aesthetic expression is always a value: a work that has expression cannot be a total failure, (Scruton, 1974, p. 213). Other non-formal aesthetic properties might include brilliance of colour, sweetness of sound, texture and felicity of language.

This leads to the question of whether the self-sufficiency of works of art, upon which the doctrine of aestheticism depends, is in any way undermined by the presence of affective properties – properties that express or reflect human response, such as those that render works of art moving, exciting, interesting, amusing, enjoyable. Clearly, these properties are not internal in the required sense. The attitude of the aesthete, typified by Oscar Wilde, is to regard their presence as aesthetically harmful, because 'all art is quite useless' and has no business with such external effects. As long as a thing affects us in any way, either for pain or for pleasure, or appeals strongly to our sympathies, then it is outside the proper sphere of art.

However, it is a mistake to treat the affective response to art as a specific state of mind that is produced by the object but that might be produced in other ways – as, for example, a relaxed frame of mind might be produced by tranquillizers, meditation, or by reading escapist literature. For the very identity of the affective response depends on the identity of the intentional object, and cannot be independently described. Thus it would be misleading to say that the purpose of a work of art is to interest, amuse or please, because to find it interesting, amusing or pleasing on account of its internal properties is, in effect, to value it for its own sake. It is, after all, the work itself that is interesting, amusing or pleasing, and not the state of mind produced by it. Thus, from the aesthetic point of view, a work of art is moving, interesting or enjoyable not because it does move, interest or please its audience, but because that is how the audience ought to respond whether it does so or not. This is the truth that lies behind Wilde's reply to the person who asked him at the first night of *The Importance of Being Earnest* whether the play was going to be a success: 'It is already a success; the only question is whether the audience will be a success!'. There is an analogy here with morality. To say of a brutal murder, for example, that it is a shocking deed, is to say that it ought to shock us even if we have become so insensitive that it fails to do so. This, of course, raises the problem of how there can be an aesthetic 'ought' as distinct from a moral 'ought'; however, this is not just a problem for the aesthete, but for anyone who believes in the objectivity of aesthetic judgement.

A related problem which more particularly concerns the aestheticist is how to justify the treatment of aesthetic values, not only as final values, but as ultimate values alongside truth and goodness. Some in the aesthetic movement, of whom Walter Pater is a prime example, see aesthetic values as actually overriding all other values, even moral ones. For Pater, the aesthetic quest is the highest way of life a man can follow. The possibility of such a 'philosophy of life' was anticipated and attacked by Søren Kierkegaard in his *Either/Or* (1843). Under the influence of Pater, Wilde's humour is sometimes aimed at subverting morality and elevating what may be broadly termed aesthetic values, as when he says that 'people will only give up war when they consider it to be vulgar instead of wicked', or, again, that it is better to be beautiful than to be good. Such remarks may sound flippant, but anyone who acknowledges the supremacy of aesthetic values is bound to take them seriously. Not surprisingly, few have been prepared to defend such an extravagant position, which is usually stigmatized as decadent.

Even if one adopts the less extreme position of treating aesthetic values as immensely serious, one encounters difficulties. It is not enough to say, as Harold Osborne (1968, p. 202) does, that aesthetic activity is a self-rewarding and therefore self-justifying activity, because many self-rewarding activities, like smoking and billiards, are relatively trivial. The high seriousness of aesthetic value could perhaps be established in two stages: first, by showing that aesthetic preferences are not merely private and personal but may be correct and incorrect; and second, by linking them, if only indirectly, to overriding moral values or some more general notion of the 'good life'. The second move would run counter to the spirit of aestheticism. However, if the aestheticists are right to claim that aesthetic values are ultimately important in and for themselves, that would in itself place us under a moral obligation to preserve them.

Whatever its other defects, the art for art's sake approach is surely too restrictive. The aesthetic standpoint is not the only possible standpoint from which one can approach a work of art, as is shown by the wide diversity of theories about the nature and purpose of art, all illuminating different aspects. To understand a work of art adequately, one may need to consider it from more than one aspect. For example, if one were to view a piece of medieval stained glass from a narrowly aesthetic standpoint, one would be unable to appreciate it as a *religious* work of art. To refuse to take account of that aspect, on the grounds that it is aesthetically irrelevant, would be to diminish rather than to enrich one's appreciation, and would be a kind of aesthetic puritanism.

See also ATTITUDE, AESTHETIC; BEAUTY; FUNCTION OF ART; KANT; WILDE.

BIBLIOGRAPHY

Beardsley, M.C.: *Aesthetics* (New York: Harcourt & Brace, 1958).
Bradley, A.C.: 'Poetry for poetry's sake', *Oxford Lectures on Poetry* (London: Macmillan, 1909).
Cousin, V.: *Lectures on the True, the Beautiful and the Good* (Paris: 1853); trans. O.W. Wright (New York: D. Appleton & Co., 1854).
Ellman, R.: *Oscar Wilde* (Harmondsworth: Penguin Books, 1987).
Forster, E.M.: 'Art for art's sake', *Two Cheers for Democracy* (London: Edward Arnold, 1951).
Gautier, T. *Mademoiselle de Maupin*, preface (Paris: 1835); trans. J. Richardson (Harmondsworth: Penguin Books, 1981).
Johnson, R.V.: *Aestheticism* (London: Methuen, 1969).
Malraux, A.: *Les Voix du Silence* (Paris: 1952); trans. S. Gilbert, *The Voices of Silence* (London: Paladin, 1974).
Osborne, H.: *Aesthetics and Art Theory* (London: Longman, 1968).
Pater, W.: *The Renaissance: Studies in Art and Poetry*, esp. conclusion (London: Macmillan, 1873).
Scruton, R.: *Art and Imagination* (London: Methuen, 1974).
Wilde, O.: *Complete Works of Oscar Wilde*, ed. Vyvyan Holland (London and Glasgow: Collins, 1983).

DAVID WHEWELL

Aquinas, Thomas (1225–74) Italian Dominican friar whose philosophy and theology ('Thomism') have decisively shaped Catholic thought. Born into an aristocratic Italian family, Aquinas disappointed his relatives by failing to enter the affluent Benedictine Order, instead becoming a friar of the newly founded Dominican Order of Preachers. Under the tutelage of St Albert the Great in Cologne, he began to study Aristotle and later became a major figure at the University of Paris and at the papal court. He died on his way to the Council of Lyons; and in 1323 he was canonized.

Aquinas is generally regarded as the greatest of the medieval philosophers. This estimate is hard to fault when one takes account of the scale and variety of his intellectual achievements, for he was the first medieval thinker to work out at length the new synthesis between Catholicism and philosophy. It is sometimes supposed that this just meant 'Christianizing' Aristotle. Even were that the limit of his achievement it would have been considerable, but in fact he went further. For, while he opposed unquestioning appeals to authority, he believed in the idea of cumulative philosophical and religious wisdom, and sought to integrate Neoplatonist, Augustinian and Anselmian ideas, as well as Aristotelian ones, with scripture, patristic teaching and evolving Catholic doctrine.

He was a prodigious writer on a multitude of topics. In its current (Latin/English) edition his unfinished *magnum opus*, the *Summa Theologiae*, runs to sixty volumes, and the ideas set out there and in other works of commentary and in original treatises have continued to guide Thomistic thinkers from the fourteenth century until the present day. With a few exceptions (such as Jacques Maritain and Armand Maurer), however, philosophers inspired by Aquinas have had little to say

9

about aesthetics. This reflects the character of his own writings, for while he offers remarks on the nature of beauty and of art-making, he has no treatises on these subjects or any well developed or extensive theory. All the same, it is possible to extract from his work ideas of enduring interest for philosophical aesthetics.

The two most important sources of these ideas are brief remarks in his *Commentary on the Divine Names* (*De Divinis Nominibus*) and in the *Summa Theologiae*. In the first of these he observes that something is not beautiful because we like it, but that our liking for it is due to its beauty (c. IV, *lectio* 10), having earlier remarked that anyone who depicts a thing does so for the sake of making something beautiful; and that each thing is beautiful to the extent that it manifests its proper form (c. IV, *lectio* 5). In the *Summa*, this notion of manifest form occurs implicitly within the famous Thomist analysis of beauty: 'Three things are required for beauty. First, integrity or perfection (*integritas sive perfectio*), for what is defective is thereby ugly; second, proper proportion or consonance (*proportio sive consonantia*); and third, clarity (*claritas*)' (*Summa Theologiae* 1 q. 39 a. 8; see also *Summa Theologiae* 1–2 q. 54 a. 1: 'Beauty is the compatibility of parts in accordance with the nature of a thing').

Before commenting on these ideas, it will be as well to introduce another of Aquinas' interesting claims. This is the suggestion that beauty is a *transcendental* quality identical in an entity to that thing's *being*, its *unity*, its *goodness* and its *truth*. Moreover, according to Aquinas, it is part of what it is to be a transcendental quality that everything possesses it. Thus, 'There is nothing which does not share in goodness and beauty, for according to its form each thing is both good and beautiful' (*De Divinis Nominibus* c. IV, *lectio* 5).

The key to understanding what otherwise appear obscure remarks is Aquinas' notion of *form* – more precisely, substantial form (*forma rei*). That which makes a thing what it is, constitutes its principle of organization and (in the case of something animate) of life. Carbon, cars and cats all have organizing forms – chemical, mechanical and biological, respectively. The form of a thing gives it exist-ence, and inasmuch as its being is an object of value for it or for others it has *goodness*. Equally, when that existence is affirmed in the mind of a thinker the thing has *truth*, and when it is viewed as an object of contemplation it takes on the character of *beauty*. In speaking of goodness and beauty (as of being and truth), therefore, one is not speaking of intrinsically different properties but of one and the same quality considered in relation to different concerns. In contemporary philosophical language the difference is one of sense or 'intension' and not of reference or 'extension'.

In short, beauty is only ascribable in the context of actual or potential contemplation of the form of a thing. This introduces an element of subjectivity but relates it directly to an objective ground, the nature of the object being contemplated. The earlier analysis of beauty now emerges as an account of the necessary conditions under which the meeting of an object and a subject gives rise to aesthetic experience. The thing in question must be possessed of the elements or aspects apt to something having the relevant form or nature (*integritas*), these elements must be properly related to one another (*proportio*), and these states must be manifest when the entity is perceived or contemplated (*claritas*).

This interpretation suggests parallels with Kantian aesthetics. For Aquinas is claiming that the experience of beauty arises directly as a type of intellectual satisfaction taken in the contemplation of elements apt for cognition, when one's present interest in them is neither practical nor scientific. Where Aquinas differs from Kant, however, is in regarding the contemplated forms as being structural elements of a mind-independent reality. On which, if either, of these philosophers this difference reflects greater credit is a matter beyond discussion here. It should be clear, however, that Aquinas has interesting ideas to offer to those who hope to integrate an account of beauty and aesthetic experience within a broadly realist epistemology and metaphysics.

See also BEAUTY; FORM; KANT.

WRITINGS

Summa Theologiae; trans. various, 60 vols (Oxford and London: Blackfriars with Eyre & Spottiswoode, 1963–75).

De Divinis Nominibus [Commentary on the Divine Names]: selected translations from this and other relevant works are to be found in *The Pocket Aquinas*, ed. and trans. V. Bourke (New York: Washington Square Press, 1969), and in *History of Aesthetics*, W. Tatarkiewicz, vol. 2 (The Hague: Mouton, 1970), pp. 257–63.

BIBLIOGRAPHY

Barrett, C.: 'The aesthetics of St Thomas re-examined', *Philosophical Studies* (Ireland), 12 (1963), 107–24.
Eco, U.: *Il Problema estetico in Tommaso d'Aquino* (Milan: 1970); trans H. Bredin, *The Aesthetics of Thomas Aquinas* (Cambridge, Mass.: Harvard University Press, 1988).
Maritain, J.: *Art et Scolastique et Frontières de la poésie* (Paris: 1935); trans. J.W. Evans, *Art and Scholasticism* (Notre Dame, Ind.: University of Notre Dame Press, 1974).
Maurer, A.: *About Beauty* (Houston: Center for Thomistic Studies, 1983).
Phelan, G.: 'The concept of beauty in St Thomas Aquinas', *G. Phelan, Selected Papers*, ed. A. Kirn (Toronto: Pontifical Institute of Mediaeval Studies, 1967), pp. 155–80.

JOHN HALDANE

Aristotle (384–322 BC) Greek philosopher, logician and scientist of immense and enduring influence; a pupil of Plato, he became tutor to Alexander the Great and founded the *Lyceum*. Often regarded as the first philosopher to develop a conception of the independent character of certain kinds of aesthetic activity and experience, and to have done so in direct reaction against the views of his teacher, Plato. Although there is some truth in this contrast, a more complex and qualified judgement of the relation between the two philosophers' positions is needed.

Like Plato, Aristotle's engagement with issues of aesthetic relevance occurs largely in his thoughts on a group of arts (poetry, painting, sculpture, music and dance), and above all on poetry. Again like Plato, Aristotle regards all these arts, with only slight exceptions, as essentially mimetic: by mimesis he understands artistic representation in its various modes and styles, including some things – for instance music's relation to the feelings – which might now be classed as expression (Halliwell, 1990). Unlike Plato, Aristotle also accepts all these mimetic activities as 'arts' in the full Greek sense of *technai* (plural of *technê*) – that is, as productive processes which follow controlled, intrinsically rational principles, and which do so in order to impose upon their particular materials a form which is consciously conceived by the mind of the maker (*Metaphysics* 7.7). It is because of its orderly and purposeful (or teleological) character that all 'art' – *technê* (including, for instance, medicine and carpentry), not just mimetic art – is said by Aristotle to 'imitate nature' (for instance, *Physics* 2.2, 2.8). This latter principle must therefore not be confused, as it was later in antiquity, with the idea of mimesis itself. All disciplined arts follow procedures which Aristotle takes to be analogous to the workings of nature; but only the mimetic arts have as their specific purpose to produce representations or fictional renderings of the world.

By admitting the fully artistic status of poetry and other forms of mimesis, Aristotle necessarily accepts something that Plato had often questioned – namely, their possession of a self-consistent, 'internal' rationale, whose standards and goals are capable of being explained and justified: it is just such systematic explanation which the *Poetics* seeks to provide for poetry. Moreover, Aristotle again diverges from Plato by refusing to lay down any strictly prescriptive rules for the content of artistic mimesis. According to *Poetics* 25, all the mimetic arts can represent any one of three things (as well as combinations of them): actual reality, past or present; (popular) conceptions of, or beliefs about, the world; or normative ideas of what 'ought' to be the case.

By recognizing the artistic legitimacy of these different kinds of material, Aristotle commits himself to fundamental aesthetic liberalism. In this same chapter of the *Poetics*, which is in poor textual condition yet includes some crucial points of basic principle, he makes a pronouncement that confirms this impression: 'Correctnesss in poetry is not identical with correctness in politics [including ethics] nor in any other art.' This statement should not, however, be taken as a formula for aestheticism, as though the values of poetry were completely separate from those of life and morality: 'not identical' is a denial of singleness or identity of values, not an assertion of radical dissociation. Aestheticism, in any of its strong senses, is something that Aristotle cannot subscribe to, and the reasons for this lie deep within his view of mimesis.

This view, as we have seen, allows for a large range of artistic materials, from the realistic to the highly imaginative. But Aristotle assumes that all mimesis is concerned to present and explore some idea of a *possible* world – a world whose sense the audience of art can grasp and evaluate in ways that are not sharply different from the ways in which they interpret the world outside art. He sometimes employs the language of 'likeness' to cover all mimesis, and a sentence in *Politics* 8.5 tells us that 'habituation to feeling pain and pleasure in the case of likenesses [that is, works of art] is close to being so disposed towards the truth'. The *Poetics* repeatedly insists on this point by its use of the criteria of 'necessity and/or probability' (the latter being the dominant consideration), criteria which call *both* for 'internal' consistency in the terms of an artistic representation, *and* for an underlying connection between these terms and the broad beliefs which people hold about reality. Although Aristotle nowhere fully works out an equivalent case for any other art, we have good reason to suppose that he assumes the application of similar criteria to, at any rate, the figurative arts: in this and in other connections, it is important that he regularly indicates the comparability of the mimetic arts (for example, *Poetics* 1, 2, 8, 25).

It is partly because of the required connection between the imagined world of an artwork and the regularities of reality which the audience of art knows from its experience as a whole, that Aristotle is able to say in *Poetics* 9: 'Poetry is more philosophical and more serious than history, for it deals more with universals, while history speaks of particulars.' Aristotle does not mean by this that poetry is abstract, or that it presents reductively typical specimens of people and events; good poetry, he knows, will contain vividly imagined particulars (cf. *Poetics* 17). What he appears to mean is that works of poetic art (and probably of other arts too) can possess a richness of significance which invites and rewards interpretation in terms of the larger conceptions which structure human experience and understanding. The potential to carry such significance is undoubtedly connected, in Aristotle's thinking, with the importance of unity. 'Just as in the other mimetic arts a unitary mimesis is a representation of a unitary object, so the plot-structure [of tragedy] . . . should be a representation of a unitary and complete action' (*Poetics* 8).

As this quotation suggests, Aristotle's notion of unity is not formalist in character. All order and beauty depend on concepts of the nature and function of the objects in which these qualities appear (*Politics* 7.4). Artistic unity reflects the intelligible content of a work of art; the criteria of wholeness and completeness which *Poetics* 7 sets out, with the formula of 'beginning, middle and end', cannot be detached from the coherence (according to probability) of the 'actions and life' (*Poetics* 6) which the poem portrays. And ch. 9's remarks, already quoted, follow directly from the discussion of unity: so unity, probability and quasi-universal significance are mutually reinforcing elements in a theory of poetry that allows artistic representations the capacity to endow their particular images with a deeper sense of human meanings.

Form and content are therefore intertwined in Aristotle's account of aesthetic objects; and his conception of aesthetic experience possesses matching features. *Poetics* 4 and *Rhetoric* 1.11 give an essentially cognitive explanation of the pleasure which arises from contemplation of mimetic works (we 'understand and infer each element' in the work). As the passage from *Politics* 8.5 quoted earlier confirms, aesthetic responses are closely aligned to the ways in which we react to people and events in the world. Yet Aristotle certainly recognizes one major qualification on this point, for *Poetics* 4 registers the operation of aesthetic pleasure even in cases where the subject-matter would in life be displeasing: our experience of mimetic works rests on an acceptance of their fictive nature, and this allows our appreciation of their artistic organization to transform part of what would be our response to raw reality of a similar kind.

But Aristotle is in no doubt, even so, that the central elements in our responses to these images entail the cognitive and affective components that structure our experience in general: here too his position eschews aestheticism. Where these views are worked out in some detail, in the *Poetics'* theory of tragedy, Aristotle's argument presupposes that we can feel richly ethical emotions towards the imagined characters and events of art. And however obscure his concept of catharsis remains, it is part of a perspective in which such emotions are occasioned by, and mediated through, active recognition of the nature of the realities dramatized by the artwork. Plato had feared that art could subvert reason by its power over the emotions; Aristotle believes that good art elicits responses in which these psychological elements are balanced and integrated.

The pleasure afforded by representational art, on Aristotle's reading, depends on a full grasp of the meanings embodied in art; as such, this pleasure is cognitivist and objectivist, in sharp contrast to the dominant Enlightenment interpretation of aesthetic experience. It is possible, therefore, to say that while Aristotle diverges from the Platonic movement towards absolutism of aesthetic standards, as well as the premiss of the unity of all value on which it rests, he does not seek to establish an outright autonomy for art. And that is because both the making and the reception of art are seen as modes of un-

derstanding. Art is thus vindicated within Aristotle's distinctive view of human nature (*Metaphysics* 1.1).

See also CATHARSIS; PLATO.

WRITINGS

The Poetics of Aristotle: Translation and Commentary, S. Halliwell (London: Duckworth, 1987).
Politics, trans. S. Everson (Cambridge: Cambridge University Press, 1988), bks 7, 8.
The Art of Rhetoric, trans. H. Lawson-Tancred (Harmondsworth: Penguin Books, 1991).

BIBLIOGRAPHY

Halliwell, S.: *Aristotle's Poetics* (London: Duckworth, 1986).
Halliwell, S.: 'Aristotelian mimesis re-evaluated', *Journal of the History of Philosophy*, 28 (1990), 487–510.
Rorty, A.O., ed.: *Essays on Aristotle's Poetics* (Princeton, NJ: Princeton University Press, 1992).
Schaper, E.: *Prelude to Aesthetics* (London: George Allen & Unwin, 1968).

STEPHEN HALLIWELL

'art for art's sake' *See* AESTHETICISM.

art history What a history requires is a narrative framework relating what comes earlier to what happens later. A culture could have art, and even a concept of art, without having any conception of art history. That culture might make art, and theorize about that activity, without thinking that its art had a history. Writing a history of art requires thinking of its development as having an historical structure.

The first extended history of European art appears in an odd place, bk 35 of Pliny's *Natural History*, between the discussion of medicinal drugs in bk 34 and the description of stones in bk 36. As modern commentators (Kris and Kurz, 1979) have observed, the anecdotes that Pliny presents about various

Greek painters recur frequently in accounts of Renaissance artists. Pliny's history of naturalistic art is told in terms of progress. Early, later, latest is good, better, best: such is the story of the development of naturalism. Art originates in the copying of shadow images; and when the tradition gets going, Pliny cites many figures who contribute innovations, such as Cimon, the first painter to invent foreshortened images, and Parrhasius, the artist who learned how to depict vivacious faces (Pliny, 1968 edn, pp. 303, 311).

Vasari's history of art of the Italian Renaissance from the time of Cimabue and Giotto to his own era, two and a half centuries later, employs a similar framework. The 'arts resemble nature as shown in our human bodies; and have their birth, growth, age and death' (Vasari, 1968 [1550], vol. 1, p. 18). In such a history, once image-making begins, it continues, this model suggests, until the tradition dies. Just as a person is born, develops and dies, so the same is true of the arts.

In one way, beginnings and endings have a certain symmetry. Whatever art comes before the beginning, like what comes after the end of the tradition, is not part of the history of art. In another way, however, endings raise special problems. Vasari explains that he judges each artist relative to the standards of that man's time: 'Although Giotto was admirable in his own day, I do not know what we should say of him or the other ancients if they had lived in the time of Michelangelo' (Vasari, 1961 [1550], vol. 4, p. 291). In so far as the claim of his account is that Michelangelo is an absolutely great artist, a figure whose work sums up the whole tradition, it is very hard to see what could come next. At earlier times, of course, great artists had successors, but given Vasari's narrative framework one has difficulty in imagining Michelangelo's successors.

Once the cycle is started, it is hard to see how it can conclude, except in decay which, after some interval, may be followed by a rebirth of the tradition. Vasari's working assumption is that the cycle of development in antiquity, as described by Pliny, repeats in his own time. That repetition is possible only because medieval art marks a break in the tradition, a gap between the development of illusionism in antiquity and the rebirth of that artistic tradition in the Renaissance. A modern historian of technology might think that indefinite progress is possible; when employing Pliny's and Vasari's organic model, such a view of history is hard to imagine. This, perhaps, is why Vasari found no immediate imitators, and artists of the next generation lost interest in aesthetics.

Here Winckelmann's *Reflections on the Imitation of Greek Works in Painting and Sculpture* (1987 [1755]) introduces an important conceptual complication. He both discusses the tradition which concerns him most deeply, the story of Greek sculpture, and explains its relationship to art of the Renaissance. In some ways, he admits, the modern artists are better: 'In the science of perspective modern painters are clearly superior ... Various subjects ... have likewise been raised to a higher degree of perfection in modern times, for example, landscapes and animal species' (Winckelmann, 1987 [1755], p. 59).

Gombrich has argued that 'rather than Winckelmann's *History of Ancient Art*... it is Hegel's *Lectures on Aesthetics* ... which should be regarded as the founding document of the modern study of art ... they contain the first attempt ever made to survey and systematize the entire history of art' (Gombrich, 1984, p. 51). While Winckelmann's account remains focused on Greek art, it is Hegel who provides a way of linking art of antiquity to painting of the Renaissance. For Hegel, it should be added, what constitutes 'the entire history of art' is defined by the concerns of early nineteenth-century European scholarship. He did not know much about Chinese and Indian art; he does not discuss Japanese painting or African sculpture.

Winckelmann shows how the distinct qualities of Greek art express the religious beliefs, culture and climate of the ancient world. In so far as Greek art is thus bound up with a culture which had disappeared, it is hard to see why the Renaissance would want to imitate Greek art. Hegel takes up precisely this point. Since the larger culture has changed, what follows is that Renaissance art must differ from sculpture of antiquity. Christian painting is superior to Greek sculpture because the Greek 'vision of human or divine affairs' did not make it possible to express 'such a depth of spirituality as was presented in Christian painting' (Hegel, 1975, p. 801).

Unlike Pliny, Vasari and Winckelmann, Hegel does not focus on the history of the development of illusionistic painting and sculpture within one culture. He explains how the art of quite different cultures is part of one continuous story, a universal history of art. In so far as each culture possesses its own values, it too may express them in its art. The goal of art history is to identify the relationship between a culture and its art. Thus, to understand Dutch art of the Golden Age, 'we must ask about Dutch history' (Hegel, 1975, p. 169). The Dutch struggle against Spanish rule, the feats of their maritime empire and their pleasure in communal festivities are all expressed in their art. A history of the art of any culture might be written in this way. The Japanese and the Africans can also express themselves in their art.

One consequence of Hegel's approach is to suggest that each culture must have its own independent artistic ideals. Wölfflin (nd [1908]) develops this idea. The classical and the baroque are distinct artistic cultures, each with its own values, but neither reducible to the other. The art historian's task is to explain how and why the classical evolved into the baroque without making value judgements. If the classical space must come earlier, that is only because it is easier for the artist to construct, and the viewer to grasp, than the space of baroque art. The classical and the baroque 'are like two languages, in which everything can be said, although each has its strength in a different direction' (Wölfflin, nd [1908], p. 12).

Vasari certainly implies that later art is better; Michelangelo can do things which Cimabue cannot. Wölfflin both claims that the baroque must succeed the classical, and implies that it is not superior, only different. Wölfflin's history employs a formalist approach, explaining the development of art as a self-contained process without much reference to the larger culture. Another development of Hegelian art history occurs in the diverse approaches of art historians who focus on the social history of art. As Hegel sees Dutch art as expressing the characteristic political, religious and social concerns of that culture, so these historians treat each culture as capable of expressing its own values in its art.

Both the formalist approaches and these social histories can describe the art of very diverse cultures. So, for example, American abstract expressionist painting of the 1940s can be understood formally as developing the flattened space found earlier in cubism, and in the early modernist art of Cézanne and Monet (Greenberg, 1961). But it may also be explained as an expression of post Second World War American culture. The formalist finds similarities between artists whose work looks different. Thus in Wölfflin's account, not only Rembrandt and Rubens, but also Vermeer and Bernini, must be linked under the rubric 'baroque'. If the danger of formalism is this need to appeal to such a fiction of a 'period style', the problem of a social history of art is that it may link art with the general society in all too facile a fashion. A formalist history tends to reduce all the different artists of a given time to their lowest denominator, as if all those works were painted by one super-individual; a social history must pretend that the culture of the time is more united than it really was. If the ideals of Holland of the Golden Age are expressed not only by Rembrandt and Vermeer, but also in the writings of the philosopher Spinoza, the political struggles of the time and every aspect of that society, then it is hard to know in what non-trivial way that culture expressed itself in its visual art.

These problems with both formalist and social histories become more pressing as we approach the present. It is difficult enough to identify the common features of the work of Bernini, Pietro da Cortona, Borromini and all the other artists working in Rome in the era of the baroque. But when we look at the culture of New York during the 1940s, then speaking of that as the era of American abstract expressionism really is problematic. We must connect work of quite diverse painters by reference to a period style; we must exclude from the account painters working in other styles; and we need to explain how American philosophy and the larger culture are related to that art. Doing that in a convincing way is not easy.

Recognizing that both formalist and social histories of art thus must employ fictions is only to acknowledge that they, like any history, must use such devices in order to tell a story (Carrier, 1991). It is important to recognize connections between the literary structures of art histories and those employed by creative writers. When Vasari treats the collective creation of artists from Cimabue to Michelangelo as akin to an organism which is born, develops to maturity, and dies, he is only using an analogy. Vasari's analogy has an important influence on how he thinks about art history. An organism must die, but there is, in principle, no reason why an artistic tradition might not continue indefinitely.

Any story must be selective. The art historian, like the creative writer, chooses to describe those events which he can fit into a plausible narrative. But in one essential way, literature and history are different. The stories of the novelist seek merely to be convincing; the narrative of the art historian aims for truth. This ideal of art history is complex. When the art historian reconstructs the original context of works from the past, he is concerned to present those works unanachronistically, as they appeared to the artist. At the same time, that writer's goal as historian is to place those works within a larger historical framework. Wölfflin wants to understand how Raphael's High Renaissance classicism anticipates the baroque, although Raphael could not think of his art in that way; Greenberg seeks to grasp the relationship between cubism and abstract expressionism, although the cubists could not imagine that later movement.

Can we both exercise our modern sensibility and simultaneously be aware that the artist whose work we study saw it differently?

When, for example, we see a Rubens crucifixion, may we apply to it 'some concepts derived from psycho-analysis – some such notions as the release of aggression with the displacement of guilt' (Podro, 1982, p. 214), which, though alien to Rubens' culture, express in our vocabulary how his contemporaries saw that work? These questions are unanswerable. Any translation of Christian ideas into a psychoanalytic vocabulary will be controversial. The best we can do is both understand Rubens' culture in its own terms, and interpret it as best we can in our modern vocabulary.

In general, in writing a history we cannot but reconstruct the past in terms which were in part unknowable to the actors. Rubens could have understood Wölfflin's idea that baroque artists of his time were building upon the achievement of the baroque, but Raphael could not have imagined the place he would have in that history, any more than Giotto could have foreseen how Vasari would describe his relationship to Michelangelo. Certainly, a historian is interested in how these artists thought of themselves, but when it comes to explaining their work he almost inevitably must supplement that information.

The development of art history by A. Riegl, Wölfflin and E. Panofsky out of the legacy of Hegel (Podro, 1982) requires pruning that theory of Hegel's metaphysics. For the modern art historian to say that a culture expresses itself in its art is only a manner of speaking, not a theory to be taken literally. Modern art historians work within the general framework established by these founding fathers of their discipline, collecting information about artists and periods not yet intensively studied by the precursors, yet without abandoning this historical framework itself. But when now we collect in our museums not only Greek and Italian Renaissance art, that Dutch painting which Hegel discusses and the baroque works Wölfflin deals with, but also Chinese and Japanese painting, Hindu sculpture, African artefacts, weaving and other decorative work from many cultures, and modernist and postmodernist art, then the claim that it is possible to write a general history of art seems increasingly questionable.

In so far as a history is a story in which all of these artworks are to be set within one narrative framework, the claim that there can be some general interpretative framework adequate to all art now seems highly problematic. In a way which would have surprised, and perhaps amused, that great dialectical thinker, Hegel, the seeming triumph of his universal art history has resulted in a loss of faith in our ability to tell a history of art.

Vasari could believe that his history showed that art had progressed because he knew so much less art than do we. He was uninterested in medieval art and, while he could understand some aspects of the baroque, he would have been baffled by modernist painting. Hegel knew more art than Vasari, but now his vision of art as an expression of its culture also seems problematic. His history seems to presuppose a confidence in the superiority of European culture which we have lost. Because we know more than Vasari or Hegel, we find their views of art history difficult to accept, or even to comprehend. But if the grand era of speculative universal art history has thus ended, the legacy of lasting value provided by Vasari, Hegel and their successors is these ideas about how to write histories of art, which now art historians can apply to art from every culture and any period.

See also GADAMER; GOMBRICH; HEGEL; MEDIEVAL AND RENAISSANCE AESTHETICS; MODERNISM AND POSTMODERNISM; TRADITION.

BIBLIOGRAPHY

Carrier, D.: *Principles of Art History Writing* (University Park and London: Penn State University Press, 1991).
Gombrich, E.H.: ' "The father of art history". A reading of the lectures on aesthetics of G.W.F. Hegel (1770–1831)', *Tributes. Interpreters of our Cultural Tradition* (Ithaca, NY: Cornell University Press, 1984), pp. 51–69.
Greenberg, C.: *Art and Culture* (Boston, Mass.: Beacon Press, 1961).
Hegel, G.W.F.: *Vorlesungen über die Ästhetik* (Berlin: 1835); trans. T.M. Knox, *Aesthetics. Lectures on Fine Art* (Oxford: Clarendon Press, 1975).
Kris, E. and Kurz, O.: *Die Legende von Künstler: Ein historischer Versuch* (Vienna: 1934); trans. A. Laing and L.M. Newman, *Legend, Myth, and Magic in the Image of the Artist* (New Haven, Conn. and London: Yale University Press, 1979).
Pliny: *Naturalis Historia* (AD 77); trans. H. Rackham, *Natural History*, 10 vols. Vol. 9 (London: Heinemann, 1968).
Podro, M.: *The Critical Historians of Art* (New Haven, Conn. and London: Yale University Press, 1982).
Vasari, G.: *Le Vite de' più eccellenti Architetti, Pittori e Scultori Italiani* (Florence: 1550); trans. A.B. Hinds, *The Lives of the Painters, Sculptors and Architects* (London: Dent, 1963).
Winckelmann, J.J.: *Gedanken über die Nachahnung der griechischen Werke in der Malerei und Bildhauerkunst* (Dresden: 1755); trans. E. Heyer and R.C. Norton, *Reflections on the Imitation of Greek Works in Painting and Sculpture* (La Salle, Ill.: Open Court, 1987).
Wölfflin, H.: *Kunstgeschichtliche Grundbegriffe* (Munich: 1908); trans. M. Hottinger, *Principles of Art History* (New York: Dover, nd).

DAVID CARRIER

artefact, art as Until recently, everyone had assumed without question that art is artefactual – that is, that a work of art is a manmade object. When ancient Greeks uttered the slogan, 'Art is imitation', or later philosophers made such claims as 'Art is expression' or 'Art is the creation of forms symbolic of human feeling', they assumed that the referents of their remarks were artefacts. Traditional philosophers of art attempted to defend their claims that art is expressive, symbolic or of some other nature, but it never occurred to them to defend their common view that art is artefactual. Of course, an object need not be physical in order to be an artefact; for example, a poem or a theory is a non-physical artefact.

Why, then, have philosphers of art become concerned in recent times with the question of whether artefactuality is or is not a necessary condition for being art? This concern has its origins in certain developments within the philosophy of language: namely, Ludwig Wittgenstein's view about how certain words apply to their objects. These words apply, Wittgenstein maintains, in virtue of 'family resemblances' among the objects to which they apply, rather than in virtue of the objects possessing properties that satisfy necessary and sufficient conditions.

Paul Ziff (1953), Morris Weitz (1956) and William Kennick (1958) were the first to attempt to apply this linguistic thesis to the philosophy of art. These three and subsequently other philosophers claimed that 'art' (or 'work of art') does not have any necessary and sufficient conditions that must be satisfied in order for something to be a member of the class of works of art. Rather, they maintain that the members of the class of works of art belong to that class in virtue of the 'family resemblances' that obtain among the members. Thus, work of art A is a member of the class of artworks because it shares a property with work of art B, and work of art B is a member of the class because it shares a property with work of art C, and so on. Work of art A and work of art Z, however, may not share any property and do not need to. Although work A and work Z do not share any property, they are related to one another through the property-sharing of other members of the class of works of art. Every member of the class of works of art will share a property with at least one other work (and probably many more), but a given pair of works need not share any property. If the members of the class of works of art do not need to share *any* property, then they do not need to share the property of artefactuality. And, in fact, these philosophers claim that there are works of art which are not artefacts, these non-artefacts having become works of art by sharing a property with a prior-established work of art. Weitz, for example, claims that a piece of driftwood can become a work of art when someone notices its resemblance to some sculpture and says, 'That driftwood is

a lovely piece of sculpture.' Driftwood, sunsets and other non-artefacts can become works of art in this way. Thus, according to Ziff, Kennick, Weitz and company, is the traditional assumption that every work of art is an artefact shown to be false.

There are several difficulties with what may be called 'the new way' of conceiving of art. First, if resembling a prior-established work of art is the basic way that something becomes a work of art, it is going to be virtually impossible to keep everything from becoming a work of art, for everything resembles everything else in *some* way. Second, 'the new view' gives the impression that sharing a property with, or resembling, a prior-established work of art is the only way that something can become a work of art. If, however, every work of art had to become art by resembling a prior-established work of art, then an infinite regress of works receding into the past would be generated and no work of art could ever have come into being. Some other way of becoming a work of art would be required to block the regress, and the only plausible way would be that the regress-blocking work or works came into being as a result of an artefact being created. Thus, this new view requires two distinct and different kinds of art – art as conceived of by Ziff, Weitz and Kennick and which may be called 're-semblance art', and what may be called 'artefactual art'.

Artefactual art has a temporal priority. Of course, it is not just that artefactual art is required to block the regress. Even given the new way of conceiving of art, much of the art that has been created has come into being as artefactual art. Thus, artefactual art, with its one necessary condition (artefactuality), forms an unacknowledged basis or core of the new conception of art. The two kinds of art required by the new conception have two very different bases: the one derives from acts of human creativity and the other from acts of noticing similarities. This striking difference suggests that it is the members of the class of artefactual art that we have in mind when we speak *literally* of works of art, and that the other class of objects is a metaphorical derivative.

Suppose, however, that both classes are literally art. This just means that it is and always was the class of artefactual art that philosophers from Plato to Danto have been interested in theorizing about. Traditional philosophers of art have sought to discover the essential nature of a particular class of human artefacts, and even if the members of this class of objects do not have any other interesting property or properties in common, they are all artefacts. Artefactuality is built into the philosophy of art because philosophers have always been interested in theorizing about a set of objects that are produced by human creativity. The fact that another class of objects can be generated by means of resemblance to the members of the class of artefactual art provides no reason to divert philosophers of art from their traditional task.

There is another apparent challenge to the artefactuality of art. How are philosophers of art to deal with things such as the urinal that Duchamp entered in that now famous art show under the title, *Fountain*? The urinal is an artefact of the plumbing trade, but is *Fountain* Duchamp's artistic artefact? Duchamp did not alter the urinal in any way – altering being the typical way in which artefacts are created. Consequently, some traditional philosophers think *Fountain* is not an artefact and, therefore, not a work of art. On the other hand, it can be argued that *Fountain* is an artefact, and a work of art, because it is a complex object made up of a urinal used as an artistic medium in a way analogous to the way that oil paints and marble are used to create paintings and sculptures. Although Duchamp does not alter the urinal, his *use* of the urinal within the domain of the artworld suffices to make it into a *minimal* artworld artefact.

See also DEFINITION OF 'ART'.

BIBLIOGRAPHY

Davies, S.: *Definitions of Art* (Ithaca, NY: Cornell University Press, 1991).
Dickie, G.: *The Art Circle* (New York: Haven, 1984).
Kennick, W.: 'Does traditional aesthetics rest on a mistake?', *Mind*, 67 (1958), 317–34.
Mandelbaum, M.: 'Family resemblances and generalization concerning the arts', *American Philosophical Quarterly*, 2 (1965), 219–28.
Weitz, M.: 'The role of theory in aesthetics', *Journal of Aesthetics and Art Criticism*, 15 (1956), 27–35.
Ziff, P.: 'The task of defining a work of art', *Philosophical Review*, 62 (1953), 58–78.

GEORGE DICKIE

'artworld' A term that has both a philosophical and an ordinary meaning. Philosophically, the idea of an 'artworld' serves as a device for analysing 'art' and the 'aesthetic'. Artworld theory makes these concepts the products of certain social practices so specialized that persons engaged in them appear to be operating in an autonomous world. In the vernacular, the 'artworld' is the actual society of persons whose interactions affect the valuation of works of art. What these meanings have in common is an understanding of art as being the consequence of institutionalized activities.

That art should be thought of as situated in a special world of its own is a notion of recent fabrication, and one quite alien to antiquity's robust idea of art as central to practical human life. Plato and Aristotle located artistic activity and appreciative experience among practices meant to promote the goals of cognition and conduct. But, subsequently, at least two lines of thought converged to drive art from this central location.

The first was triggered by Plato's pressing reasons for doubting how effectively art can realize vital practical functions. To the extent that these objections remain unanswered today, the concerns that they raise enervate theories which assign to art a pivotal role in attaining the benefits of the good life.

Moreover, where Plato's criticisms are challenged, art's apologists have tended to isolate it from everyday activities or experiences as a stratagem for defending its value. For instance, despite his commitment to art's being a natural route to learning, Aristotle attributes its success to the advantages of studying idealized imitations in protected circumstances. The art theories of the Enlightenment and the succeeding Romantic period further exacerbate this tendency to isolate art by locating its value in its disengagement from pragmatic concerns. These views typically define art (or the appropriate experience of it) as autonomous, arguing that art characteristically induces unique ways of feeling or thinking, or is the product of a unique kind of activity, or is at least a unique product of ordinary activities.

The result is to construe art as independent of practical contexts, and aesthetic value as irreducible. This strategy blunts Plato's complaints by removing art from the constraints usually associated with cognition and conduct, but it also threatens art's place in the everyday world.

A second line of thought which makes the notion of situating art in an environment of its own attractive is fuelled by the need to account for certain phenomena attendant upon the emphasis on originality in Western art. The customary readings of the development of art in the West depict it as driven by processes which systematically undercut all proposals about essential artistic or aesthetic properties. As Morris Weitz puts it in an influential essay (1956), not only is no discernible property both common and exclusive to all art, but to impose a substantive definition of art is to prevent the art of the future from essentially challenging the art of the past (cf. Gallie, 1956). But this being understood, it remains to be explained how objects impossible to imagine being called art in one time and place come to be thought of as art in another.

The difficulty in constructing an illuminating account of how radical innovations come to be accepted as art is magnified if one stands by the theoretical commitments to preserve art's autonomy and to avoid relativizing it to practical contexts. If we discern no essentially definitive properties in art objects themselves, then whatever warrants the identification of some objects as art must be found in the contexts in which these objects are situated. But if to recognize something as art is also to accept it as independent of contexts occasioned by the everyday world, being art must be conditional upon circumstances which obtain in a special artworld. Several late twentieth-century theorists, notably Arthur Danto and George Dickie, develop this thought by arguing that objects qualify as art in virtue of being the subject of practices characteristic of an irreducible world exclusive to art.

There are at least three importantly different influential contemporary philosophical accounts of what this artworld is. In Dickieworld$_1$, fully articulated in *Art and the Aesthetic* (Dickie, 1974), (almost) anyone can make (almost) anything art simply by subjecting it to status-conferring behaviour 'undertaken on behalf of the Artworld'. Dickie develops this theory to conform to the familiar story of the history of Western art, a narrative which emphasizes how unpredictable what will be counted as art has come to be. What separates Dickieworld$_1$ from the everyday world is the behaviour of its inhabitants; these engage in activities which give (some) objects the status of art by treating them as such. Whoever performs the right actions can elevate things to artistic status, but Dickie is not definitive as to what must be done to something to transform it into art.

An advantage of this account is that it in no way constrains art's future, for there is no way of predicting whether anyone will be inclined to treat any particular object as art. This satisfies Weitz's prohibition against over-determining the future of art. But the 'institutional' theory which informs Dickieworld$_1$ has also been criticized for being just so unrestrictive. This is because the account's basic plausibility depends to a great extent on construing actions executed in the artworld as performatives which have the power to transform things into art. But performatives are empowered by the practices in which they are embedded, and these practices characteristically are structured by certain restrictions as to their proper objects and agents. In contrast, in Dickieworld$_1$, agents need have no distinctive authorization or qualification to perform as long as they suppose themselves to be in the artworld, nor does Dickie specify kinds of objects which defeat the performance, with the exception that no natural object can achieve the status of art. So Dickieworld$_1$ seems to lack the systematization common to effective transformational practices.

Responding to his critics, Dickie creates Dickieworld$_2$ in *The Art Circle* (1984). In Dickieworld$_2$:

(1) An artist is anyone who participates with understanding in the making of an artwork.
(2) An artwork is any artefact created to be presented to an artworld public.
(3) An artworld public is any group made up of persons prepared to some extent to understand artworks presented to them.
(4) The artworld is the totality of all artworld systems.
(5) An artworld system is what constitutes the framework for presenting an artist's work to an artworld public.

These conditions form a circle, but an informative one which circumscribes the boundaries of the artworld. In Dickieworld$_2$, not everyone qualifies to be an artworld agent; only artists and audiences who are authorized by having mutual understandings about art do so. Moreover, their activities must be framed within a mutually accepted system.

But the artworld within this circle is static, not innovative. The constraints on who can act on behalf of the artworld in Dickieworld$_2$ require there to be expectations shared mutually between artist and audience. In this world, how can there be art which defies rather than satisfies the expectations of audiences? Yet surely the most original art is precisely that which is unanticipated. Moreover, Dickieworld$_2$ also appears to eliminate its own history and preclude its own future, for how can future audiences with evolved expectations be bound in mutual understanding with artists of the past, and how can artists make art for posterity, not just for contemporary audiences whose expectations arise within their shared artworld system? Art diffuses more insistently and thoroughly across classes, cultures and historical periods than is provided for by the philosophical

theory that informs Dickieworld$_2$, or, for that matter, by the sociological art theory of Pierre Bourdieu (1968), whose approach bears some interesting similarities to Dickie's later views.

Whereas both Dickieworlds are artefacts of the actions of their present-time artworld agents, Dantoworld is a by-product of something more abstract; within its framework objects qualify as art in virtue of their relation to the history and theory of art. Danto remarks: 'To see something as art requires something the eye cannot descry – an atmosphere of artistic theory, a knowledge of the history of art: an artworld' (Danto, 1964). That is, what makes an object art lies in how its properties connect with those of its predecessors, and, as well, whether there are art theories under which the object can be subsumed.

Concerning the artworld's past, Danto usually writes as if art's history is unilinear and verifiable. But postmodernist writers, among others, make much of the ultimate undecidability of art's history. And revisionist scholars make much of the multiplicity of readings of art's history. If the world of art objects cannot be distinguished from the world of everyday ones in virtue of having an identifiable, distinctive history, does Danto's account support the conception of a separate artworld (cf. Silvers, 1976, 1989)? Danto himself sometimes seems to suppose that this need not be the case, as when he contends that art may have no future because its evolutionary direction threatens to dissolve the distance between art and real things. Were this to occur, if it could occur, would there be no art at all, or would art instead recapture its intimate connection with cognition and conduct, as was presupposed in antiquity before the widening wedge between imitation and reality drove art and life apart?

Despite acknowledging that art made in the past influences the present artworld, Danto is inclined to treat predecessor works as somehow less immediate and vigorous than contemporary ones. In doing so, he appears to import the values of certain artistic periods such as the New York art scene of the last thirty years, or that of Paris between the World Wars, where fascination with the avant-garde devalued traditional art. Moreover, by declaring that those who work in the styles of the past make reproductions, not art, Danto (1981) ignores the facts of traditional art cultures where individualized departures from custom take second place to the respect accorded work within accepted stylistic standards.

Nevertheless, there is no overruling reason why the forces of tradition should be diminished in Dantoworld. Indeed, Danto's conception of an artworld 'atmosphere' somewhat resembles what Walter Benjamin (1955) has called the 'aura' with which tradition informed works of art in eras previous to our own. Danto's account also is not inimical to Benjamin's observation that traditional art furthers habitual conceptions of conduct and cognition and, in so doing, contributes to the persistence of the dominant sociopolitical system, while iconoclastic art destabilizes these familiar frameworks. But to understand the historical and theoretical systems of the artworld as being infused by cognitive and moral commitments in this way is to accept art as integrated with other aspects of life.

In sum, the contemporary philosophical conception of the artworld locates what is definitive of art in the application of some set of practices, whether these be activities which treat art organizationally, historically or theoretically. As an intellectual position, this view resembles those sociological theories which propose that institutions define 'reality'. To hypothesize an artworld is to explain that objects qualify as art by being 'institutionalized' – that is, by operating or being operated upon within a definitive institutional framework.

But the relevant institutions need not constitute an all-encompassing world which embraces all the kinds of human activities. So such questions as whether the artworld is democratic or elitist are not automatically relevant; they are germane only where there is reason to construe artworld systems as political. On the one hand, it seems parochial for philosophers to posit unique aesthetic practices when so wide a range of explana-

tions of institutionalized phenomena is available in the work of other disciplines. The more thoroughly the artworld is conceived in terms of principles which operate also in the world of practical life, the more misguided seems the drive to separate these worlds.

On the other hand, to operationalize the artworld in social scientific terms is to submit to reductionism. As Terry Eagleton points out (1990), postmodern thought resolves this problem by aestheticizing ethics and epistemology. A version of this solution is introduced in Martin Heidegger's 'The origin of the work of art' (1975), where artworks are described as actively making worlds rather than as being made by them. Heidegger proposes that works of art transform the way things look to us, including how humans look to themselves. This and related efforts, such as the writing of Jacques Derrida, transfer characteristics customarily used to mark our experience of art and extend them throughout domains once thought to be more firmly founded. But the details of how a work of art can make a world are even more obscure than accounts given by institutional theorists to explain how a world can make an artwork.

In the vernacular, to speak of the artworld is to refer to networks of persons engaged either vocationally or avocationally in activities which affect the buying and selling of art. But to recognize the power of such persons by no means solves the problem of whether their actions determine, or are determined by, aesthetic or other values. This brings us finally to the question of whether the conception of the artworld is simply another relativizing notion.

To what kinds of systematized circumstances is the identification of objects as art to be tied, and may these encompass, or must they exclude, systems which also are constitutive of the practical world? Are the art systems of different times and places frameworks to be thought of as begetting separate worlds? Fragmenting aesthetic contexts in this way makes it hard to explain the undoubted ease with which cultures adopt and appreciate each other's art. Or are the divergent systems to be incorporated into one complex artworld scheme so as to account for art's demonstrable ability to diffuse transculturally and trans-historically? If this latter alternative is the case, then how are we to decide which systems' values are to be marginalized? Thus, the most vexing disagreements about the interpretation and evaluation of art reappear, unresolved, within artworld theory.

Many philosophers have spent much time recently addressing these and other questions, while perpetuating a crucial ambiguity: is the artworld of philosophical theory meant as a real or as an idealized imitation world. Despite their failure to treat this matter decisively and unequivocally, however, it is possible that artworld theory commands sufficient interest to reverse a trend grown increasingly pervasive since the Enlightenment. By institutionalizing art, all three contemporary versions of the artworld retrieve it from the realm of private subjectivity, returning it to a publicly accessible because publicly constituted place. In doing so, artworld theory may also cancel the inherited biases about art which impelled its initial formulations.

See also ART HISTORY; AUTONOMY, AESTHETIC; DANTO; DEFINITION OF 'ART'; DICKIE; FUNCTION OF ART.

BIBLIOGRAPHY

Benjamin, Walter: 'The work of art in the age of mechanical reproduction', *Illuminations*, trans. Henry Zohn (New York: Harcourt Brace & World, 1955).

Bourdieu, Pierre: 'Outline of a sociological theory of art perception', *International Social Science Journal*, 20 (1968).

Danto, Arthur: 'The artworld', *Journal of Philosophy*, 61 (1964), 571–84.

Danto, Arthur: *The Transfiguration of the Commonplace* (Cambridge, Mass.: Harvard Universtiy Press, 1981).

Dickie, George: *Art and the Aesthetic: An Institutional Analysis* (Ithaca, NY: Cornell University Press, 1974).

Dickie, George: *The Art Circle: A Theory of Art* (New York: Haven, 1984).

Eagleton, Terry: *The Ideology of the Aesthetic* (Oxford: Basil Blackwell, 1990).

Gallie, W.B.: 'Art as an essentially contested concept', *Philosophical Quarterly*, 6 (1956), 97–114.

Heidegger, Martin: 'Der Ursprung des Kunstwerkes', *Holzwege* (Frankfurt: 1950); trans. A. Hofstadter, 'The origin of the work of art', *Poetry, Language & Thought* (New York: Harper & Row, 1971), pp. 17–75.

Silvers, Anita: 'The artworld discarded', *Journal of Aesthetics and Art Criticism*, 34 (1976), 441–54.

Silvers, Anita: 'Once upon a time in the artworld', *Aesthetics: A Critical Anthology*, ed. G. Dickie, R. Sclafani and R. Roblin (New York: St Martin's Press, 1989), pp. 183–95.

Weitz, Morris: 'The role of theory in aesthetics', *Journal of Aesthetics and Art Criticism*, 15 (1956), 27–35.

ANITA SILVERS

attitude, aesthetic The question of what it is to adopt a distinctively aesthetic attitude to objects is important in its own right, but also because of the role attributed to this attitude within wider issues. For example, the difficulties – much intensified by developments in 'modern art' – in defining 'art' in terms of a ubiquitous function or of intrinsic aesthetic qualities have prompted the attempt to define works of art as those towards which it is appropriate to adopt the aesthetic attitude. Some philosophers, including Schopenhauer and Heidegger, have discerned in the proper attitude to works of art a kind of stance which is more revealing of reality than our everyday manner of encountering the world.

By far the most popular approach is inspired by Kant's notion of 'disinterest'. Here is a typical example: 'I will define "the aesthetic attitude" as "disinterested and sympthetic attention to and contemplation of any object of awareness whatever"' (Stolnitz, 1960, pp. 34–5). (Strictly speaking, Kant himself did not employ 'disinterest' to distinguish the aesthetic from the non-aesthetic, but to distinguish, within the realm of what he called the 'aesthetic', judgements of beauty and sublimity from those of mere pleasantness.) Kant explains the 'disinterested' attitude as one where the subject is 'merely contemplative . . . indifferent as regards the existence of an object', and focusing rather upon its 'appearance' or 'representation' (Kant, 1966 [1790], p. 43). This is intended to capture the insight that when viewing something 'disinterestedly', and so aesthetically, will and desire are in abeyance. When so viewing an object, a person is unconcerned with its practical utility, including its role as a source of intellectual or sensuous gratification. From this Kant draws some dubious conclusions. Not only, he says, is emotion a 'hindrance' to 'pure' appreciation of beauty, but the subject must have no concern with the kind of object he is viewing – that is, with the 'concept' under which it falls.

There have been several significant variations on Kant's theme. For Schopenhauer, too, the aesthetic attitude is marked by a withdrawal from our usual practical, wilful engagement with things. It is, once again, a type of contemplation, but directed towards the Platonic ideas or forms which lie behind 'appearances' themselves. In contemplating a building, I am indifferent to, *inter alia*, its function, attending instead to the ideas of space, gravity, and so on. The psychologist Edward Bullough has characterized the aesthetic attitude in terms of 'psychical distance'. On a fogbound ship, the aesthete distances himself from the fears and practical concerns of the crew, and concentrates on the strange shapes and forms which the fog lends to things. Finally, a number of phenomenologists, elaborating on Kant's talk of 'indifference' to actual existence, have argued that the true object of the aesthetic attitude is not an actual object in the world but an 'intentional object', existing only for the perceiver. Strictly, therefore, there cannot be a single object to which both aesthetic and non-aesthetic attitudes may be taken, for in the two cases different kinds of object are being considered.

More dramatic are the implications which many twentieth-century artists and critics have drawn from Kant's notion of 'disinterest' for the proper ambitions and functions of art. One of these is a marked hostility to representational art. In 'pure' aesthetic experience, wrote Clive Bell (1947, p. 32), a painting must be treated as if it 'were not

representative of anything'. More generally, there should be no concern for content and meaning since this, it is held, would contradict the required indifference to matters of existence and conceptualization. A second implication drawn – also very much in the 'formalist' spirit – is that art should not aim to be expressive of emotion. The proper response to art is not an emotional one, but something like Kant's 'restful contemplation'. Finally, 'disinterest' has been invoked to support the aestheticist or 'art for art's sake' estimation of art. Since a person is not viewing something *as* art if he is interested in further benefits to be derived, no justification need, nor should, be offered for art beyond the satisfaction which aesthetic contemplation of it yields.

It is hard to be sure how far Kant would endorse such claims, since the bulk of his discussion is about the aesthetic attitude towards nature, not art. Extrapolation to a Kantian theory of art is uncertain. (What, for example, is the analogue in the case of painting to suspension of interest in a thing's actual existence? Indifference to the existence of the canvas and pigments? Or to that of whatever is depicted?) But some of his remarks indicate that he would not accept these alleged extensions of his idea. Thus, while he indeed insists that judgements of beauty should be 'independent of emotion', the feeling of the sublime – itself an aesthetic one – is an 'outflow of vital powers' and may be 'regarded as emotion' (Kant, 1966 [1790], p. 83). And, unlike the aestheticists, Kant is happy to offer extrinsic justifications for aesthetic experience. Most notably, it is 'purposive in reference to the moral feeling', since it 'prepares us to love disinterestedly' (Kant, 1966 [1790], p. 108).

Whatever Kant's response might have been, the formalist and aestheticist programmes are surely not entailed by the bare idea of 'disinterest'. That my concern with a painting must not be practical (pecuniary, say), nor a 'conceptual' one of classification (pre-Raphaelite, say), cannot imply that paintings should not be produced and appreciated as representations of things. Even less can it be implied that I should suspend all

too much a product of society's prescribed roles or ideological influences. Drawing a distinction between sincerity and authenticity, they would take the latter to imply not just honesty but a personally discovered and strongly felt sense of self that is distinctive of the person as an individual, and they would ascribe this quality to art when it embodies appropriate features of uniqueness and individuality. Let us consider, in turn, sincerity, and then authenticity in the latter sense, as qualities of art.

On one understanding of the concept, sincerity is not an interesting artistic quality or criterion of aesthetic worth. We may describe a person as sincere if what he or she says is not, or not consciously, a lie: what is said corresponds to what is inwardly believed. When we read a novel or poem we are aware of an authorial presence – an 'implied author' – and the work may reveal that the implied author has certain beliefs. We may now say that the work is sincere if these beliefs correspond to the beliefs of the actual author at the time when he or she wrote the work. But it is unlikely that a critic will be interested in whether a work is sincere in this sense. As it features in criticism, sincerity is a quality that is discernible *in* writing, and the notion is not applied or withdrawn in a way simply dependent on biographical facts, irrespective of the internal quality of the writing.

A more relevant kind of sincerity is displayed by someone whose beliefs or attitudes are deeply held, so that, for example, we would expect him or her to live by and make sacrifices for those beliefs and attitudes, and do so consistently. Sincerity of this kind shows itself in the way people live their lives in practice; it is frequently possible to detect it, or its absence, in the way people express their beliefs and attitudes in what they do and how they do it.

This kind of sincerity, judged according to the manner in which it expresses itself in art, is an important concern of critics of art and literature. Such a concern is displayed, for instance, in F.R. Leavis's judgement that Emily Brontë's poem 'Cold in the Earth' is insincere (Leavis, 1968). This poem invites us to identify the dramatic speaker with Brontë herself, and the writer presents herself as having suffered, with discipline and composure, a tragic and deeply felt loss. Leavis defends his judgement of insincerity on the grounds that the writing does not show evidence of being informed by real events and feelings – 'She is dramatizing herself', he writes, 'in a situation such as she has clearly not known in actual experience' – and he suggests that Brontë covertly enjoys the way the poem casts her in a noble and tragic role. The notion of insincerity that Leavis applies to her poem here is closely related to the concept of sentimentality as applied to works of art. A painting, piece of music or literary work is sentimental in this sense if it evokes an emotion that cannot be accounted for as a justified response to an external situation, but has been aroused to satisfy an ulterior need or motive.

The notion of authenticity has come to the fore in the twentieth century as an ethical ideal – celebrated, for example, in the writings of the existentialists. The ideal of authenticity prescribes a life which avoids externally imposed forms and standards of behaviour and requires that individuals discover through their personal circumstances how to live and what to value. This ideal differs from that of sincerity in that the latter is compatible with a life lived strictly according to codes prescribed by religion or a pre-existing moral or social order. Like sincerity, personal authenticity can be expressed in artistic activity and become embodied in works of art.

In fact, the virtues emphasized by the ethical ideal of authenticity appear to be taken for granted as virtues of artistic practice. We expect of the best art that it will avoid the clichéd response, the prevailing stereotype, the derivative plot, the predictable pattern of events, the all too familiar viewpoint, the 'academic' style. Authentic artists are supposed to have their own style and viewpoint; we look to them to 'make it new', to use their unique perspective and experience to confront us with the ambiguous and unexpected. When they succeed, their work offers a model of the alert and critical mentality required for a life lived according to the ethical ideal of authenticity – a life that is relatively uninfluenced by the standardized idioms and images in terms of which we are invited to see ourselves by the world around us.

One of the central problems confronting writers, composers and visual artists is that of expressing themselves in a way which accurately captures an experience, perception or vision which they wish to record for precisely the reason that, however subtly it differs from the commonplace, it is distinctive in some valued way. This task of expression is one which modernist writers, because of their special concern with language and its influence upon our experience, have written about illuminatingly and at length. It is a truism of modern aesthetics that language is not a neutral medium by means of which writers can simply describe reality as they experience it, since established associations of the language in which they must express themselves will place an imprint upon the experiences they attempt to represent and the accompanying attitudes they wish to express, influencing the reader's impression of those experiences and attitudes.

The difficulty that arises for writers in their attempt to portray characters, objects and situations in a way which does justice to the experienced uniqueness of those things is that language, as they find it, is laden with established associations and assumptions which tend to stifle our sense of the singularity of what is described. The originating experience, as Virginia Woolf complained, is falsified: it 'refuses to be contained any longer in such ill-fitting vestments as we provide' (Woolf, 1938, p. 148). The writer, some theorists have claimed, writes in vain: the words 'lie', failing to say what he or she wants to say but instead sounding like the words of many others. In striving to escape the falsifying effects of language – striving for what can be called authenticity of expression – writers must aim to pass beyond the stale associations of language as they find it.

Roland Barthes believes that writers will always fail in this aim (and here we have one of the foundations of Barthes' thesis of the impossibility of writing): the writer is 'unable to pen a word without taking a pose characteristic of an out-of-date, anarchic or imitative language' (Barthes, 1968, p. 84). While the problem of expression that Barthes is concerned with here deserves recognition, the extreme form in which he expresses the difficulty must contend with the fact that, though successful imaginative writing is not to be taken for granted, many writers have consistently achieved authentically individual forms of expression.

See also AUTHENTICITY OF THE ARTWORK; BARTHES; COMMITMENT AND ENGAGEMENT; PERFORMANCE; SARTRE.

BIBLIOGRAPHY

Barthes, R.: *Le Degré zéro de l'écriture* (Paris: 1953); trans. A. Lavers and C. Smith, *Writing Degree Zero* (New York: Hill & Wang, 1968).

Baugh, B.: 'Authenticity revisited', *Journal of Aesthetics and Art Criticism*, 46 (1988), 477–87.

Budd, M.: 'Belief and sincerity in poetry', *Pleasure, Preference and Value*, ed. E. Schaper (Cambridge: Cambridge University Press, 1983), pp. 137–57.

Davies, S.: 'Authenticity in musical performance', *British Journal of Aesthetics*, 27 (1987), 39–50.

Davies, S.: 'Transcription, authenticity and performance', *British Journal of Aesthetics*, 28 (1988), 216–27.

Josipovici, G.: 'The Balzac of M. Barthes and the Balzac of M. Guermantes', *Reconstructing Literature*, ed. L. Lerner (Oxford: Basil Blackwell, 1983), pp. 81–105.

Leavis, F. R.: 'Reality and sincerity', *A Selection from Scrutiny*, ed. F.R. Leavis (Cambridge: Cambridge University Press, 1968), pp. 248–57.

Trilling, L.: *Sincerity and Authenticity* (Oxford: Oxford University Press, 1972).

Wollheim, R.: *Art and its Objects* (New York: 1968); 2nd edn (Cambridge: Cambridge University Press, 1980).

Woolf, V.: *The Common Reader* (Harmondsworth: Penguin, 1938).

PAUL TAYLOR

authenticity of the artwork An artwork's

authenticity – its being *the* 'Midnight' by 'Major', for example – does not guarantee its originality, where 'originality' implies that the work has its own style, or presents something novel. It is equally obvious that a work's originality is no guarantee of its authenticity, as Van Meegeren's forgeries illustrate. Where authenticity is the dominant concern, philosophers have concentrated on three issues:

(1) Can there be aesthetic differences between perceptually indistinguishable artworks?

(2) If identifying, and perhaps locating, a work in art history is necessary in order to determine the work's aesthetic character, does it follow that copies or extensive restorations cannot be authentic instances of the works copied, and thus cannot share their aesthetic character?

(3) Is it incoherent to predicate aesthetic characteristics of unauthentic works, even when these are correctly identified? (Except when it would alter significantly the philosophical implications of what is being asserted, 'aesthetic' is used as if it were equivalent to 'artistic'.)

Nelson Goodman is perhaps the best-known of the defenders of a positive response to question (1). His argument is based on his belief that an artwork's aesthetic character involves unexhibited as well as exhibited characteristics. This belief derives from his holding that an artwork's aesthetic character depends upon how the work is perceived, in conjunction with his using a rather unusual aesthetic principle: that if a work may have aesthetically relevant characteristics that are not being perceived now but that someone may learn to perceive, this fact in itself constitutes an unexhibited, aesthetically relevant, characteristic of the work. This is not explicitly acknowledged by Goodman, but none the less it is the principle behind his discussion of two separate but very similar-looking works, when he argues that, no matter how similar-looking two works are, merely knowing that they are separate works establishes that someone may learn to perceive differences between them. The knowledge that we may learn to perceive differences between two works constitutes an unexhibited aesthetic difference between them.

What Goodman's argument overlooks is that the principle required to support its conclusion, if sound, also establishes that there is an unexhibited aesthetic difference between any artwork as it is perceived now, and the same artwork perceived at any later time. Because no one is omniscient with regard to any artwork's aesthetic character, we know now that there may be characteristics in any work that are not perceived now but that someone may learn to perceive. By Goodman's reasoning, this fact constitutes an aesthetic difference between what is perceived now, and the same object perceived at any later time. Since this reasoning applies to any aesthetically relevant characteristic perceived in any work at any time, his argument to show that there are aesthetic differences between even the most similar-looking works implies that every artwork's aesthetic characteristics differ from the aesthetically relevant characteristics that the work is perceived to have now, and thus that every artwork's aesthetic characteristics are permanently inaccessible to imperfectly informed human perception. A more reasonable alternative to accepting this conclusion is to reject the aesthetic principle required by the argument, and with it the widely influential view that Goodman has succeeded in showing that, no matter how similar two works are, there are aesthetically relevant differences between them.

The failure of Goodman's argument does not establish that all aesthetic characteristics are exhibited characteristics discernible by observers who may be entirely ignorant of the identity of the works they perceive. But if all aesthetic characteristics are exhibited, then, as Monroe C. Beardsley has insisted, while authenticity is relevant to an artwork's art-historical value, for example, it is not relevant to aesthetic value (Beardsley, 1983, pp. 26–7).

If some of an object's aesthetic characteristics are accessible only when the object is

31

correctly identified and located in art history, does this mean that copies or extensively restored works (copies, for simplicity) cannot be authentic instances of the works copied, and so cannot have their aesthetic character? One way to argue that a copy has the aesthetic character of the work copied, while at the same time accepting the view that some of a work's aesthetic characteristics depend upon its identity and place in art history, is to invoke the type–token distinction and maintain that the copy whose authenticity is in question is a token of the same work embodied by the authentic prototype (the first instance of the work).

This approach makes it possible to challenge the conditions on authenticity for a given art type that currently are taken for granted by many philosophers of art. For example, with paintings this approach makes it possible to question whether the first instance of a painting is the only possible authentic instance of the painting. If this first instance exemplifies a type (or 'megatype', as Joseph Margolis holds), it seems conceptually possible (at least in principle) that the works instantiated have multiple instances. Philosophers advancing theories of art that explicitly utilize the notion of a type–token distinction in accounting for art's ontology often attempt to defend the view that painting is one of the few art forms where works cannot have multiple instantiations. While such attempts aim at justifying a widely shared intuition, they are problematic because they run contrary to the basic metaphysical model used by their authors in explaining their theories of art.

If it is true that, in principle, copies of any artwork may be authentic instances of the work, this leaves unresolved the question of whether a copy that is not an authentic instance of the work copied can have its own aesthetic character. Reasons offered in support of the view that unauthentic works cannot have aesthetic characteristics often involve claims about various essential art-making roles that unauthentic works cannot fulfil. One of the more interesting of these alternatives has it that aesthetic characteristics can be predicated only of objects appro-priately linked with genuine art-making activities, such as discovering a solution to an artistic problem. Since copies are not appro-priately linked with any genuine art-making activities, making copies cannot be seen as working to solve artistic problems, and copies cannot be seen as marking an artist's success in these endeavours. Consequently, aesthetic characteristics cannot be predicated of copies.

The argument that only objects produced in an attempt to resolve artistic problems can be ascribed aesthetic characteristics focuses on the claim that none of the problems that someone faces in copying an existing work are artistic problems. If none of these problems are genuinely artistic problems, neither the activity of creating copies nor the results of this activity can have aesthetic characteristics (see Dutton, 1983, for example). This view had currency during the heyday of modernism, especially in areas that firmly rejected the centuries-old mimetic tradition, such as non-objective painting. In these postmodern times, however, mimesis (including even the complete appropriation of existing artworks) is once again acceptable.

From a philosophical perspective, however, even during the modern period the problems that have had to be solved in order to express or represent anything at all were the very same problems facing the artist who chose an existing artwork as his or her subject-matter. The reason such projects often fail to have aesthetically interesting results is because artworks themselves constitute art's most difficult subject-matter. Copies or reproductions rarely succeed in solving the problems inherent in attempting to express or represent what is aesthetically essential to the work copied in a work that manifests a unique aesthetic character of its own. Only someone who can resolve these most difficult of artistic problems can hope to copy another artwork successfully without merely producing another instance of the work copied. Since failed attempts to copy a work without merely producing it do represent failures to solve the same artistic problems facing all artists, even failed attempts have an aesthetic character of their own, albeit a negative one.

In any event, such failures are not necessitated by the nature of the artist's subject-matter.

In conclusion, the distinction between authentic and unauthentic works has not as yet provided a means for deciding whether any two separate objects can have the same aesthetic character, whether any given sort of artwork can have multiple instances, each with the same aesthetic value, or whether a copy of an artwork can have its own aesthetic characteristics.

See also ORIGINALITY; PROPERTIES, AESTHETIC.

BIBLIOGRAPHY

Beardsley, Monroe C.: 'An aesthetic definition of art', What is Art?, ed. Hugh Curtler (New York: Haven, 1983).

Currie, Gregory: An Ontology of Art (New York: St Martin's Press, 1989).

Danto, Arthur C.: The Transfiguration of the Commonplace (Cambridge, Mass.: Harvard University Press, 1981).

Dutton, Denis, ed.: The Forger's Art (Berkeley, Calif.: University of California Press, 1983).

Goodman, Nelson: Languages of Art (Indianapolis: Bobbs-Merrill, 1968).

Kennick, W. E.: 'Art and inauthenticity', Journal of Aesthetics and Art Criticism, 44 (1985), 3–12.

Margolis, Joseph: Art and Philosophy (Atlantic Highlands, NJ: Humanities Press, 1980).

Morton, Luise H. and Foster, Thomas R.: 'Goodman, forgery, and the aesthetic', Journal of Aesthetics and Art Criticism, 49 (1991), 155–9.

Sparshott, Francis: The Theory of the Arts (Princeton, NJ: Princeton University Press, 1982).

GEORGE BAILEY

autonomy, aesthetic The notion of aesthetic autonomy is central to the ongoing debate between the varying kinds of truth in philosophy, the natural sciences and art. Its implications have been most effectively worked out in the Kantian and post-Kantian tradition of German philosophy.

For Kant, a rational being is 'autonomous' by being able to 'give the law to itself', as opposed to being 'heteronomous' by accepting a pre-given law from a source external to its capacity for free decision. Seen in relation to art, this means that if religion, science or philosophy are perceived as being able to 'give the law' to art, by being able to explain art in non-aesthetic terms, then the autonomy of the aesthetic is an illusion. On the other hand, if what is essential to art is its radical separation from other kinds of truth, by virtue of its irreducibility to being judged in terms of anything but itself, then the truth that art can communicate threatens to become marginal to the central concerns of the present. The vital question, then, is the truth status of art, and its relation to other conceptions of truth.

The suspicion of art has a history which, of course, goes back to Plato. The lowly place assigned to art in philosophies orientated towards the mathematically based natural sciences is, therefore, not merely a result of the advance of science: it is a return to one of the oldest and most questionable of Western philosophical ideas – the idea that the truth is a representation or imitation of a pre-existing ideal reality. Seen in this way, art, as mimesis, is only a derivative form of a higher mimesis which is the goal of the sciences and of philosophy, an idea which is still implicit in aspects of Hegel's Aesthetics and is common currency in the dominant assessment of the relative merits of the arts and the sciences in the modern period.

The most important modern alternative to this idea is that, rather than truth being the revelation of a pre-existing reality, it is in fact a creative process of 'disclosure'. Artworks, in this view, reveal aspects of the world which would not emerge if there were no such disclosure; truth 'happens' – it does not imitate or represent. If we accept this conception of truth there can be no absolute division between art and science, because both are forms of disclosure. At the same time, the notion of a specifically aesthetic truth can thereby be eliminated, because any form of disclosure can be the happening of truth, and what happens in art is only one case of a more fundamental disclosure. The question is whether one particular form of disclosure does not lead to aspects of the world becoming hidden because the light from one direction, be it theology, natural science or art, prevents one from seeing in another direction.

Why, then, should the idea of the autonomy of art become so important in the modern period? The answer lies mainly in the fear that the scientific form of disclosure will usurp all other forms: in Gadamer's terms, that 'method' will consume 'truth'. Kant highlights the dangers of seeing the world only in cognitive and instrumental terms, giving great importance to the notion that rational beings are 'ends in themselves', and to the concept of 'dignity' as that which is without price. Works of art can, of course, command extremely high prices. The point is, though, that what determines the price is not a criterion of the *aesthetic* value of what is being bought. Consensual judgements of taste do not depend upon an appropriative relationship to the object. Furthermore, if the judgement is made in cognitive terms, by identifying the object as 'just a pile of bricks', or is made in relation to whether the meaning of a play is in accordance with morality, these will not be aesthetic judgements.

The aesthetic relationship to the object is a result of the play between our ability to constitute a world of objects and what our imagination enables us to make of that world that is not a result of identification of the objects in cognitive judgements. Conceptual language that identifies objects cannot, therefore, represent 'aesthetic ideas', which 'strive towards something beyond the boundary of experience'. Kant, then, tries to secure autonomy for aesthetic judgements by distinguishing them from cognitive or ethical judgements. Is this autonomy, though, an indication of art's higher status, or actually a way of excluding it from the dominant forms of truth in the present, in much the same way as mythology and theology were excluded?

The separation of spheres of judgement is not just a theoretical matter: it reflects the rationalization of modern societies into the separate value spheres of science and tech-

nology, law, and art. Autonomous art becomes possible when the truth of art ceases to be subordinated to theology; its emergence opens up the way to a new *aesthetic* understanding of non-autonomous art from the pre-modern period. The liberation of the aesthetic from heteronomy, however, sets in motion a process which threatens to destroy the very notion of art. Marcel Duchamp's signing and exhibiting of a urinal is the culmination of this process: is the urinal now an object that makes us strive beyond the boundary of experience, or does it remain just a urinal? If it is the former we have to accept that the aesthetic, as Kant already began to suggest, is in some way independent of the empirical medium in which it is manifested. What is now at issue is not so much whether one can assign art an autonomous status in its own value sphere, as whether the significance of art lies in its ability to reveal, *by its special status*, what nothing else can.

Implicit in this question is the thought that, despite all attempts to assign the aesthetic to its own sphere, it may actually be inherent in all the spheres, as that which prevents them from ever being absolute in their own terms (an idea first given extensive theoretical expression by Schleiermacher in his *Aesthetics* (see Bowie, 1990). Kant's conception of the imagination – *Einbildungskraft* – makes it constitutive of both cognitive and aesthetic relations to the object (see Frank, 1989; Bowie, 1990), which leads Novalis and others to see it is the basis of all cognitive acts. The centrality of judgement in any theory of truth is also evident in the consensus theory of truth; in the same way that Kant denies the possibility of validating judgements of taste except by consensus, consensus theories of truth deny the possibility of criteria for truth claims outside the process of intersubjective communication (see Bowie, 1990, on Schleiermacher). At this level the aesthetic becomes central to the very issue of truth, even in the cognitive sense. This should not conceal the fact that the correlate of the notion that the aesthetic is present in areas from which it initially appears absent is the thought that, quite simply, there may really be no such thing as art or the aesthetic, anyway.

The best – very serious, and very funny – consideration of this idea is Kafka's story, written very shortly before he died in 1924, called 'Josephine the Singer, or the Mouse People'. The story suggests that art – Josephine's 'singing', which, according to the narrator, is perhaps only the same noise the other mice make – is no different from anything else. By putting the very existence of art into question in a story about mice, Kafka has, though, written a masterly piece of ironic art. The meaning of the story results from the way 'form' and 'content' (which are only ever relative to each other – form, as Adorno puts it, is 'sedimented' content) negate each other. In doing so they give rise to something that can only be understood in the process of engaging with the story, not by analysing individual aspects of the story on the assumption that they will give the final answer to what the story means. There is no such final meaning.

Kafka's story is a classic example of what is meant by art in German Romantic philosophy. Most of the subsequent debate in modern philosophy about aesthetic autonomy can be understood via the contrast between the Romantic views of art present in the early work of Schelling, in the Schlegel brothers, Novalis, Solger and Schleiermacher (one of the least known but probably the greatest aesthetic theorist of the nineteenth century), and Hegel's interpretation of art as a form of *Geist* lower than philosophy in his system. The form of art which best illustrates the contrast between the Romantics and Hegel is, as was suggested by Josephine, music, particularly wordless music.

The question is whether music is deficient because it does not have conceptually determinable meaning, or whether it is most significant for that very reason. The same question can be asked about other arts: if a literary text's deviation from linguistic convention (think of Joyce) is wholly explicable via semantic rules (see Menke, 1991, pp. 69–82), then a correction of the deviations will have a higher truth status than the text itself. If the correction does not have this

status there can be no final way of analysing what is meant by the deviations.

It can be argued that this is what gives the text literary or aesthetic status. The fact that wordless music is inherently non-representational and non-referential (though it may involve elements which can be interpreted as representing something) means that there can be no symmetry between musical articulation and any attempt to reveal its *meaning*, as opposed to its formal structures, in discursive terms. The same will later apply to non-representational art, and ultimately, if this theory is valid, to any kind of autonomous art. Either this makes music merely the expression of 'subjective inwardness', a lower form of *Geist* which must be grasped at a conceptually higher level in philosophical language, as Hegel suggests, thereby subsuming the aesthetic into philosophy (see Danto, 1986), or it makes it the locus of the 'unsayable', as Romantic philosophy maintains. In the Romantic view, then, music is a means of access to the 'absolute'. What does this mean?

Hegel's account of the absolute relies on the demonstration that the attempt to arrive at cognitive certainty by defining something as true necessarily leads to the realization that every particular proposition negates itself by being dependent upon other propositions. This realization ultimately leads to the claim that the truth is itself a process of negation: this insight is 'absolute knowledge' – that is, it is what emerges as the truth of the process, which is only possible by going through the logic of the process. Philosophy, then, already knows what truth is, and its job is to articulate its highest forms. A dynamic conception of the negativity of individual aspects of the empirical world is not, however, limited to Hegel's philosophy. Both Romantic philosophy, even before Hegel had worked out his system, and, later, Adorno use such a conception in order to reveal the philosophical importance of art. They both, though, share a fundamental difference from Hegel.

Hegel's conception of the absolute retains a Platonic sense that any finite appearance will only achieve its truth by being articulated in philosophy. The Romantic view is that the aesthetic is precisely that which resists philosophical articulation: it refutes the idea that there could be a conceptual articulation of the absolute. The art object, as a product of freedom, points to the absolute because it only achieves aesthetic status when what could be explicable in scientific terms – the measurable frequencies and amplitudes of the sound waves in music, and the cognitive processes in the listener, for instance – is transcended into the meaning of the music, by a process which cannot be described in scientific terms. Whilst there may be a semantics of natural languages, there cannot be a semantics of music.

Hegel's view presupposes the ability to demonstrate the ultimate identity between the means of signification and what is signified, as aspects of *Geist*. Music, though, does not give one any conceptual grounds for assuming such an identity. Precisely because the meaning of the work relies upon the negation of its elements as conceptually identifiable phenomena, by understanding them in their configuration in the specific work, the meaning cannot be finally determinate. Each reinterpretation of the meaning of the elements, each re-configuration, must confront the fact that the work's continued manifestation as material object will subvert any attempt to make its meaning final. It is this experience of inherent incompleteness, of 'longing' (Schlegel, Novalis), whose condition is a sense of what makes us aware of that incompleteness, that is meant by the absolute in Romantic philosophy (this conception is echoed in aspects of poststructuralism; cf. Bowie, 1990; Menke, 1991). As Adorno suggests, the absolute is not present in the work: works of art are not symbols, in the manner of sacred objects. It is the impossibility of reducing artworks to the final assertion of *what* they mean, along with the certainty *that* they do have meaning, that gives them their potential for truth.

This position leads to the fundamental problem in contemporary aesthetics. A 'negative aesthetics' of the kind offered by Adorno is able to sustain the idea of aesthetic autonomy against the Hegelian idea that art comes to an end when it is philosophically understood. At the same time it relies upon the notion of the *work* of art which can be clearly demarcated from what is not art. Adorno's theory is most convincing at this level when dealing with the continuing power of the great works of autonomous bourgeois art. Such art is, though, put in question by the avant-garde attack on the notion of the work exemplified in Duchamp. One response to this is the idea that, by returning the semantic potential of art to the contexts of everyday life, the aesthetic can be introduced into spheres from which it has come to be excluded (see Bürger, 1974; 1983). The result, though, is the loss of the specific power of the aesthetic to resist any attempt to reduce it to something else. By contributing to the overcoming of repressions in the other spheres, the aesthetic contributes to the development of modern rationality: Hegel beckons.

The problem of trying to assimilate the aesthetic becomes apparent, though, if one considers at what level judgements about the assignment of something to one or other of the value spheres are made. Such judgements cannot be made within a particular value sphere: there was, as we saw, no cognitive way of assigning aesthetic status. Habermas, for instance, wishes to insist on the difference between world-disclosing and problem-solving, upon keeping the spheres separate. As has often been argued, though, many cognitive discoveries, particularly at the level of fundamental 'paradigm shifts', are the result of aesthetic acts, because they rely on opening up a world which was hidden by existing forms of articulation. At the same time the aesthetic can be the reminder that any such disclosure is also a hiding of some other possibility. In psychoanalysis, for instance, it is clear that problem-solving is often achieved by the use of metaphor to disclose in a new way what it is that is causing the problem. This process can be seen either as already having a solution which the theory of analysis has already found, or – and this reintroduces the aesthetic moment – as being dependent on meanings which are not within the existing economy of meanings of the analysand, or even, more importantly, of the analyst. There can be no final meaning of this kind (see Bowie, 1987). Such meaning is part of a process analogous to the experience of autonomous art, which subverts any final attempt at determination.

The crucial fact is that in the process of actual engagement with cognitive and ethical issues, as opposed to the reconstruction of the results of such process in theory, one comes up against irreducible aspects of the aesthetic which are not just factors that can be filtered out by better methodology. This fact depends upon the same issues as were outlined above, in the tension between the Hegelian and the Romantic positions. The period of the production of great autonomous art may, as Hegel's *Aesthetics* prematurely suggested, have come to an end. However, the inability of theory to circumscribe the meanings that were revealed, and continue to be revealed, by autonomous art is not an issue which disappears when that particular form of aesthetic production is no longer dominant.

See also AESTHETICISM; 'END OF ART'; GADAMER; HEGEL; INEFFABILITY; KANT; METAPHOR; SCHELLING; TRUTH IN ART.

BIBLIOGRAPHY

Adorno, T. W.: *Ästhetische Theorie* (Frankfurt am Main: Suhrkamp, 1970); trans. C. Lenhardt, *Aesthetic Theory* (London: Routledge, 1984).

Bowie, Andrew: *Aesthetics and Subjectivity: from Kant to Nietzsche* (Manchester: Manchester University Press, 1990).

Bowie, Malcolm: *Freud, Proust and Lacan: Theory as Fiction* (Cambridge: Cambridge University Press, 1987).

Bürger, Peter: *Theorie der Avantgarde* (Frankfurt am Main: Suhrkamp, 1974); trans. Michael Shaw, *Theory of the Avant-Garde* (Minneapolis: Minnesota University Press, 1984).

Bürger, Peter: *Zur Kritik der idealistischen Ästhetik* (Frankfurt am Main: Suhrkamp, 1983).

Danto, Arthur C.: *The Philosophical Disenfranchisement of Art* (New York: Columbia University Press, 1986).

Frank, Manfred: *Einführung in die frühromantische Ästhetik* [Introduction to early Romantic aesthetics] (Frankfurt am Main: Suhrkamp, 1989).

Gadamer, Hans-Georg: *Die Aktualität des Schönen* (Stuttgart: 1977); trans. N. Walker, *The Relevance of the Beautiful and Other Essays* (Cambridge: Cambridge University Press, 1986).

Kafka, Franz: *Werke* (Frankfurt am Main: Suhrkamp, 1976); *The Complete Short Stories* (Harmondsworth: Penguin, 1983).

Menke, Christoph: *Die Souveränität der Kunst, Ästhetische Erfahrung nach Adorno und Derrida* [The sovereignty of art. Aesthetic experience following Adorno and Derrida] (Frankfurt am Main: Suhrkamp, 1991).

Schleiermacher, Friedrich Daniel Ernst: *Vorlesungen über die Ästhetik* [Lectures on aesthetics], ed. C. Lommatzsch (Berlin and New York: De Gruyter, 1974).

Shusterman, Richard, ed.: *Analytic Aesthetics* (Oxford: Basil Blackwell, 1989).

ANDREW BOWIE

B

Barthes, Roland (1915–80) French semioticist and literary and cultural critic; a leading representative of structuralism. At the Pavillon des Arts in Paris in 1986 there was an exhibition called *Roland Barthes: Le texte et l'image*. It consisted of paintings, photographs and posters, accompanied by Barthes' writings about them blown up large enough to be comfortably seen from the viewing distance called for by the images. The words overpowered the images, which in turn became illustrations of them, in a fitting exhibition for one for whom words, written or spoken, sounded or seen, were material, physical, affecting each other and whatever encountered them as do all material things. Words had for Barthes a power akin to that of tribal carvings or icons and to the power he found in certain photographs. It was the power of the past and of the form without which nothing could work or take effect or make its mark, including the brute, dumb, blind energy of the unconscious and its instincts.

Barthes was a writer for whom writing was the quintessential human activity, because through it the individual participates in the production of sense and experiences the limits of the intelligibility hard won by productive labour; through it she imbricates herself in the structure of birth and death common to meaning and nature alike. By the death of meaning or sense is meant escape from the systems of difference that alone create sense, a leap beyond the limits of the intelligible, cultured world into the raw, the intractable real, the primitive. The experience of the primitive is possible only as an irruption of the cultured; it is, therefore, not the primitive raw that is experienced but the opposition between cultured and raw, between what Barthes calls in his last book, *Camera Lucida: Reflections on Photography* (1980), 'the tame and the mad'. To appreciate the opposition is to be struck, shaken by the collision of the opposing terms, by the catastrophe that befalls the hitherto privileged term. A successful opposition is as violent or forcible as what it opposes is entrenched, and when the privileged is the set of culturally endorsed beliefs, its unsettling is cataclysmic. The cataclysm occurs in the individual whose beliefs are undone by the incursion of the primitive.

This is the poststructural deconstruction of precisely those received meanings explained by structuralism in terms of Ferdinand de Saussure's linguistic model. Barthes was a pre-eminent scriptor of this deconstruction, which appears full-blown in *S/Z* (1970), his reading of a Balzac short story fragmented along the lines of language, money and sex that organize Michel Foucault's *The Order of Things* (1966). Barthes' career is intimately connected with the rise and fall of structuralism in Paris in the 1960s and the scepticism born of the end of what he called 'the dream of scientificity' to which structuralism had given rise. A structuralist, Barthes tell us in his primer, *The Elements of Semiology* (1964), is simply one who uses words like 'sign', 'signifier', 'signified' and finds the models of language of Saussure and Hjelmslev helpful in classifying the elements of signification, which are taken to be signs, arbitrarily connected with that of which they are signs, not meanings, whose connection with the things whose meanings they are is thought to be necessary. His interest was in the structuring activity, which he described as fragmenting the given and encoding the fragments in a variety of codes – as many as imagination could devise. It was the freedom of the activity of structuring that he sought, not the structures that it produced.

Freedom appears as a value in Barthes' first book, *Writing Degree Zero* (1953), as the freedom of the writer to choose his forms. This is a high modernist tract that identifies writing in its difference from both style, a writer's utterly personal signature born in the depths of his body, and language, an algebra-like system of rules, impersonal and abstract. The modern writer, refusing to inherit tradition's forms of literature, bears the responsibility of choosing the forms in which he shall write. The necessity of positioning himself with respect to the tradition follows from the historicism to which modernism is committed. By the time of *S/Z* (1970), however, Barthes' focus turns from the modern writer's choice of forms to 'writerly' reading, and the opposition between classic and modern yields to that between 'readerly' and writerly.

Each is a way of reading that can be used indifferently on classic or modern texts, and the reader is free to choose between the ways. The readerly is the comfortable, familiar way of reading, whereas the writerly is what unsettles all that the readerly assumes: it undoes the reader's 'historical, cultural, psychological assumptions, the consistency of his tastes, values, memories, [and] brings to a crisis his relation with language' (Barthes, 1974, p. 93). The readerly brings pleasure, the writerly bliss, where bliss is an ecstasy in which are dissolved all familiar conceptions, including those along whose lines the reader's identity is drawn. The reader, then, loses herself in the act of reading in the writerly way.

This distinction appears in the last book as the distinction between a photograph's *studium*, what in it is culturally coded, and its *punctum*, what, unbeckoned, rises out of it to pierce, touch, wound its viewer. The *punctum* connects the viewer with the object whose light-drawn image the photograph records, proving the past reality of the object and putting the viewer in touch with the past as nothing else can. Barthes calls light a 'carnal skin' enveloping the photographed object and its viewer, thereby carrying the viewer back to the time of the photograph's taking. The ecstatic dissolve of the viewer into the past made present in the photograph can bring madness, madness being the other side of the tame, the civilized – that exists, however, only as an encroachment upon the tame, the sane. Culture and its systems of meanings are always already there, therefore, and the work of Barthes' last five years consists of efforts to trick, outwit, outplay, evade these delimiting systems. Identity questions are raised, only to be shown to be impossible of answer, especially questions about the identity, completeness and consistency of the self. *A Lover's Discourse* (1977) characterizes a discourse warranted neither by the speaker's intentions or by the rules of language and, driven 'into the backwater of the "unreal" . . . has no recourse but to become the site, however exiguous, of an *affirmation*' (Barthes, 1978, p. 126). This discourse is pure act, the site of the affirmation of itself, not of its speaker.

For Barthes the subject, the speaker, vanishes into acts of writing, reading, speaking, as in *Camera Lucida* material objects vanish into their photo-recordable traces of light. Language is put into motion as each word becomes a step along a path to all the other words to which it can be connected by resemblance, by difference, by contiguity, with the result that the materiality of words themselves vanishes into the gathering speed of writerly reading. At the end of *Camera Lucida* Barthes says of whether to view the matter in this mad way or in a manner more familiar: 'The choice is mine.'

See also DECONSTRUCTION; STRUCTURALISM AND POSTSTRUCTURALISM.

WRITINGS

The Elements of Semiology; trans. A. Lavers and C. Smith (New York: Hill & Wang, 1967).
Writing Degree Zero; trans. A. Lavers and C. Smith (New York: Hill & Wang, 1967).
S/Z; trans. R. Miller (New York: Hill & Wang, 1974).
The Pleasures of the Text; trans. R. Miller (New York: Hill & Wang, 1975).

A Lover's Discourse: Fragments; trans. R. Howard (New York: Hill & Wang, 1978).

Camera Lucida: Reflections on Photography; trans. R. Howard (New York: Hill & Wang, 1981).

BIBLIOGRAPHY

Culler, Jonathan: *Barthes* (New York and Oxford: Oxford University Press, 1983).

Thody, Philip: *Roland Barthes: A Conservative Estimate* (Atlantic Highlands, NJ: Humanities Press, 1977).

Wiseman, Mary Bittner: *The Ecstasies of Roland Barthes* (London: Routledge & Kegan Paul, 1989).

MARY BITTNER WISEMAN

Baumgarten, Alexander (Gottlieb) (1714–62) German philosopher and logician; a significant influence on Kant's aesthetics. The 'father' of aesthetics and the first to employ the term in a distinctly philosophical context; his pseudonym was Aletheophilus, 'friend of truth'. Baumgarten's principal doctrines were:

(1) that aesthetics comprises a science of sensitive knowing (*scientia cognitionis sensitivae*);

(2) that such knowing is not, as Spinoza and Leibniz believed, solely subordinate to logical knowledge but possesses an autonomy of its own;

(3) that aesthetic knowledge exhibits its own perfection, here understood in the eighteenth-century manner as a specific activity achieving its fruition (*per-facere*). Baumgarten accordingly conceived of the task of aesthetic knowing as the translation of an obscure sensuous manifold into a clear perceptual image.

A professor of philosophy at Frankfurt and Halle, Baumgarten was known as a formidable logician, theological hermeneuticist, astute critic and a follower of the rationalist Christian Wolff. Rather unjustly, Baumgarten is remembered solely for his definition of aesthetics as 'the science of sensitive knowing' (*Aesthetica*, § 1), a science that touches neither on the nature of art *per se* nor on its social import but on the direct sensuous apprehension of actuality. The context and purpose of his argument is, regrettably, hardly remembered. But given the vehement contemporary debate over the perception of meaning in postmodern aesthetic and hermeneutic theory, his works have much to offer.

Baumgarten's philosophy is shaped by the rationalist conviction, *cognitio vera est realitas*: the world is considered an intelligible totality constituted by the relations of greater and lesser wholes, the logical key to which is the form of the subject–predicate proposition. Just as reality is the greatest unity and variety of its actual states (predications), so, Baumgarten believed, sensuous perfection attains the greatest unity and variety of perceptions within a singular image. Aesthetics springs from a 'dark faculty' of the soul, an *ars combinationis*, which intuitively fuses a perceived sensuous manifold into a coherent whole, the perfection of which lies in the degree of its 'intensive and extensive clarity' – an argument that cleverly reworks the Cartesian terms, 'clear and distinct'.

Descartes insisted that, though we may perceive the sea before us 'clearly', we may not know those defining properties which make it 'distinct' from other types of water. We might, equally, 'know' sea-water's distinct properties and yet never have 'clearly' seen the sea. Baumgarten departs from this juxtaposition (specially Leibniz's version of it) with his insistence that, though remaining logically indistinct, sensitive knowledge has a perfection of its own which cannot be reduced or dissolved by conceptual knowing. With an ingenious word-play, Baumgarten names the sensuously perceived realm 'confusion's field' (*campus confusionis*), which, though it appears to abide by the rationalist conviction that the sensuous is logically confused (indistinct and muddled), in fact breaks with it by displaying the perceptual world as confluence, convergence and synthesis (con-fusion), a world in which indiscernible particulars (Leibniz's 'dull perceptions') are combined to produce a distinctly 'clear' image. The argument is worked out in the *Metaphysica* (1739) and in the incomplete two-volumed *Aesthetica* (1750, 1758), but its basis stems from his earliest work, *Meditationes philosophicae de nonnullis ad poema pertinentibus* (1735). In a manner close to Gadamer's, he suggests that poetic words have both an intensive and an extensive clarity – intensive in so far as they invoke a highly particular object, and extensive in as much as the richness of poetic allusions involves making all the implicit associations of an image explicitly clear. Baumgarten's understanding of semiotics was such that he believed there to be no difference between the functioning of visual signs and of poetic words.

It is unclear whether he appreciated the extent to which his insistence upon an irreducible perfection proper to aesthetic knowledge disrupted the rationalist programme of knowledge as a logically unified science. And yet his merit is that, though by no means a deprecator of reason, he reveals how any transition from the phenomenological experience of the sea's immediacy to an analysis of salt-water involves a great diminishment of the experiential world. The transition might facilitate an advancement of 'distinct' knowledge, but only at the cost of weakening our aesthetic sensibility. Baumgarten was one of the first moderns to defend the autonomy not only of aesthetics but also of immediate experience against the encroachments of theory, whilst his suggestion that sensuous appearance is art's proper terrain opens a line of thinking which leads to Nietzsche, Heidegger and Gadamer.

Once Kant steered aesthetics towards a transcendental study of the objective preconditions of judgements concerning the beautiful, Baumgarten, despite the proselytizing efforts of G.F. Meier and the admiration of Moses Mendelssohn and J.G. Herder, was fated to fall into obscurity. His location of the aesthetic in the realms of the 'sensitive' condemned him in Kant's eyes as an apologist for sensationalism and subjectivism. In the *Critique of Pure Reason*, Baumgarten is referred to as that 'admirable thinker' who 'attempted to bring the critical treatment of the beautiful under rational principles, and to raise its rules to the rank of a science'. Yet Kant dismissed the attempt because 'the said rules . . . [are] empirical and . . . can never serve as determinate *a priori* laws by which our judgement of taste must be directed' (Kant, 1970 [1781], p. 66). However, it is now Kant's star that is waning, for since Gadamer has forcefully undermined the estranged intellectualism of Kant's aesthetic and reasserted the truth claim of the aesthetically immediate, the virtues of Baumgarten's initial position are apparent. Contemporary debates about the distinctness of aesthetic as opposed to scientific knowledge, recent appeals to an intuitive sense of aesthetic wholeness to mitigate between opposing interpretations, and attempts to defend perceptions of unitary meanings in artworks against deconstructive criticism, all indicate that Baumgarten's aesthetics remains not merely relevant, but ripe for serious philosophical reappraisal.

See also AUTONOMY, AESTHETIC; GADAMER; IRONY; KANT.

WRITINGS

Meditationes philosophicae de nonnullis ad poema pertinentibus (Halle: 1734); trans. K. Aschenbrenner and W. Holther, *Reflections on Poetry* (Berkeley, Calif.: University of California Press, 1974).
Texte zur Grundlegung der Ästhetik, ed. H.R. Schweizer (Hamburg: Felix Meiner Verlag, 1983). This contains a dual Latin and German text of extracts from Baumgarten's *Metaphysica* (Halle: 1739), §§ 501–623; *Philosophia generalis* (Halle: 1770), § 147; and the *Aesthetica* (Frankfurt: 1750/58) § 1.
Theoretische Ästhetik: Die grundlegenden Abschnitte der 'Aesthetica' ed. H.R. Schweizer (Hamburg: Felix Meiner Verlag 1983). This text is an edited collection of extracts from Baumgarten's *Aesthetica* (Frankfurt: 1750/58).

BIBLIOGRAPHY

Cassirer, E.: *The Enlightenment* (New Haven, Conn.: Yale University Press, 1969), pp. 338–53.
Davey, N.: 'Baumgarten's aesthetics: a post-

Gadamerian reflection', *British journal of Aesthetics*, 2 (1989).

Kant, I.: *Critique of Pure Reason* (Riga: 1781); trans. N.K. Smith (London: Macmillan, 1970).

Wessel, L.: 'Alexander Baumgarten's contribution to the development of aesthetics', *Journal of Aesthetics and Art Criticism*, 30 (1972), 335.

NICHOLAS DAVEY

Beardsley, Monroe C. (1915–85) American philosopher of art and literary criticism. While having contributed importantly to the philosophy of action, Beardsley developed extensively and defended articulately the twentieth century's most influential aesthetic theory since John Dewey. Growing out of the desire to provide a philosophical foundation for the New Criticism as well as a sense that the arts have a distinctive social and cultural place, the body of Beardsley's aesthetic theory is supported at the heart by a conception of aesthetic experience or an experience having aesthetic character (whatever other character it may have too) and aesthetic value.

The latter notion is to be understood in terms of the former, aesthetic value being, in Beardsley's most considered view, a value owing to a potentiality of artworks and other relevantly similar objects to afford experiences that, through cognition, characteristically involve 'attention firmly fixed on a perceptual or intentional object; a feeling of freedom from concerns about matters outside that object; notable affect that is detached from practical ends; the sense of exercising powers of discovery; and integration of the self and of its experiences' (Beardsley, 1981, p. lxii). Objects which have such value provide experiences with aesthetic character in virtue of their formal unity and/or the 'typically human as well as formal' regional qualities of a complex whole' (Beardsley, 1982, p. 22). The interpolation is worthy of special note, since Beardsley was intent upon separating himself from formalist views such as those of Clive Bell and Roger Fry (Beardsley, 1981, p. xvii). An artwork itself is to be understood as an arrangement of conditions in such an object intended to afford such an experience.

Now, while 'intention' plays an important part in Beardsley's notion of an artwork, his best-known doctrine is that it is a fallacy to hold that appeal to information about the artist's intention is indispensable for determining the meaning or aesthetic character of an artwork (Beardsley and Wimsatt, 1946). Whatever the peculiar causal conditions entering into the creation of art, the artist's intentions being among them, the aesthetic features of the work are themselves independently perceivable. This gives the work a critical autonomy.

A central aspect of the theory here, taking the especially difficult case of a literary work, is that the work *as such* be understood to be not itself a speech act but, rather, the imitation or representation of a speech act (Beardsley, 1970). (An analogous point could be made concerning any theory of art that considers the work *qua* work to be an expressive act.) However, that we need not know the intentions of Wordsworth in order to fully appreciate 'A Slumber did my Spirit Seal' does not mean that we do not need to know the meanings of words as they were used when Wordsworth was writing. Thus, it would be unreasonable to think that an author could write successfully a piece that is ironical if an educated reader of the author's time could not be reasonably expected to catch the irony in virtue of knowing how the language works (Beardsley, 1982, pp. 188–207). That a later reader should be helped in appreciating the irony by reading the author's private correspondence is compatible with it not being necessary that such help be generally provided for a full appreciation of the work. Any residual indeterminacy of meaning is simply a matter of strict ambiguity.

The artwork, though admittedly often a very complex object, is an object none the less, and our reasoning about its value and character is not logically different from other sorts of reasoning about values. Beardsley resists both relativism and Kantian subjectivism in his account of aesthetic judgement.

And while artworks can be judged from other points of view – as we can judge literature for its truth value, for example – properly critical judgement is judgement which addresses the work from the aesthetic point of view. It manifests an interest in the aesthetic value of the work and defends its judgements by referring to the aesthetic qualities of the work. These qualities are condition-governed (Beardsley, 1982, pp. 99–110). That is, they are causally generated by the non-aesthetic perceptual or intentional qualities of the work in the way that a *Gestalt* is causally conditioned by perceptual and semantic features which constitute the local qualities of a figure. Beardsley thus wants to set strict limits on the contextual determination of the character of the artwork.

The artwork, then, does have contextual and causal conditions, some of which might be called institutional, but Beardsley resists the institutional definition of art most saliently represented in the work of George Dickie. He worries that in gathering a sense of all the cultural dependencies that enter into the practice of art, we will lose a sense of what makes art special (Beardsley, 1982, p. 356). Art is not, he says, *essentially* institutional (1982, pp. 125–43). An essentially institutional act is one that could not take place independent of the existence of an institution – for example, depositing a pay cheque in a bank account. Beardsley does not deny that the creation of many artworks takes place within institutions: that is, as part of the day-to-day activity of those institutions. Rather, his point is that art does not require such institutions.

Think of Sunday painters, or children's art. It may be the case that some properties of some artworks – for instance, belonging to a genre – are institutionally conditioned, but that does not make the writing of a poem essentially institutional. Nor is the existence of art essentially dependent upon the presence of some theory of art which allows or disallows one to ascribe entitlement to art status, though some artists create with theories in mind about what they are doing. Are there certain normal kinds of aesthetic qualities that are essentially institutional?

Beardsley leaves open the possibility that there may be. If so, then art would perhaps turn out to be essentially institutional in certain ways in the normal case (which is perhaps a peculiar kind of essence). But even so, it would not follow that we should not look for how art functions quite generally to satisfy certain basic human needs and interests – that is, aesthetic interests. An answer to the question 'What things are called "art" by artistic establishments?' is no substitute for an answer to the question 'what is art?'

Whether or not there is a special aesthetic dimension that is basic to human life depends, it would seem, on whether the aesthetic is *distinctly* present in the experience of persons trans-historically and cross-culturally. That is, the roughly 'transcendental' (not to say universal and necessary) conditions which constitute the categories under which persons belonging to a particular culture experience their world should *cut* out *within consciousness* a distinctively aesthetic character to that experience, one that is enjoyed for its own sake. Beardsley's view requires at least that much.

A priori there is little reason to think that there must be such a distinctly aesthetic character to experience. And that *we* look at a Cycladean fertility figure with delight in its sculptural qualities does not entail that it has a potentiality to be so enjoyed no matter who is looking at it. It might be argued that taking the aesthetic attitude towards such a figure is the most reasonable stance to take up, once one discards the superstitious belief that was associated with such an object – a frankly invidious expression of desacralization and parochialism. In short, if such a case is exemplary, cultural context matters with respect to how one appropriately reacts to objects that we call 'artworks'. And it matters with respect to whether these objects are simply aesthetic objects *at all or even in part* – whether or not it matters with respect to *the way* in which an aesthetic object is experienced as such.

Now, this criticism might be construed as merely an argument for replacing Beardsley's aesthetic realism with some form of epistemological contextualism, relativizing aesthetic experience and aesthetic concepts to particular forms of life and social practices. Influenced more by Nietzsche than by Hume, recent 'deconstructive' or 'postmodern' criticism would go further. Contextualism often looks like an argument for conservatism, for leaving categories and concepts as they are when one might well seek to develop alternative 'economies of meaning', different paradigms, metaphorically speaking. Binding the aesthetic to the erotic as do some recent French feminist critics, modernist aesthetics looks in general like a depersonalization, even a desacralization, of art – alienating and objectifying at the same time – a phallocentric supersensualism. If cultural context is not authoritative for how we experience art, then let us recreate the context and thereby our experience. Let us not simply 'redescribe – to evoke Richard Rorty's recent contribution to these discussions – but 'rewrite' the meaning of, the feeling of, the doing of, art. Whether or not contextualism or these more radical Nietzschean moves will defeat aesthetic realism remains to be seen.

See also 'ARTWORLD'; ATTITUDE, AESTHETIC; 'INTENTIONAL FALLACY'; MODERNISM AND POSTMODERNISM.

WRITINGS

(And Wimsatt, W.K.) 'The intentional fallacy', *Sewanee Review*, 54 (1946), 3–23.
The Possibility of Criticism (Detroit: Wayne State University Press, 1970).
Aesthetics: Problems in the Philosophy of Criticism (Indianapolis: Hackett, 1981).
The Aesthetic Point of View, ed. Michael Wreen and Donald Callen (Ithaca, NY: Cornell University Press, 1982).

BIBLIOGRAPHY

Rorty, Richard: *Contingency, Irony, Solidarity* (Cambridge: Cambridge University Press, 1989).

DONALD CALLEN

beauty Beauty is a topic of great philosophi-cal interest and one that is relatively unexplored. Few would deny its importance, and yet the mere suggestion that it be defined drives intelligent people to witless babble. They suppose that the first and obvious requirement is to prove that beauty is 'objective'; that it is not, as they like to say, 'in the eye of the beholder'. They assume that the burden of proof lies on those who maintain that utterances of the form 'O is beautiful' are either true or false, and they also assume that no proof will be forthcoming, that only very unsophisticated persons think that such judgements are 'objective'. The suggestion is that until what is assumed to be impossible has been achieved, there is no point in talking about beauty.

But this is all pretentious nonsense: the unhappy metaphor in which a complex epistemological problem is presented as a question about what is or is not 'out there' is multiply ambiguous. As a remedial first step, consider the following: beauty is linked with appreciation, so if all human beings died, then there would be no one to do the appreciating and no claim that something was beautiful would be true. But under such circumstances, no claim of *any* kind would be true since there would *be* no claims – no sentences uttered. If that is the idea, then truth, as well as beauty, is 'in the eye of the beholder'. On the other hand, if beauty being in the eye of the beholder is supposed to mean that everything is equally beautiful or that nothing is beautiful, then the hypothesis needs the backing of a developed theory, since in an ordinary way of thinking it is false. Beauty is not more equally distributed than is height or intelligence. Perhaps there are people to whom nothing is beautiful: they are either deprived or very depressed.

Even if it were cleaned up, the inside–outside question would be premature. How the taking of something to be beautiful fits into our overall scheme, whether the cognitive idiom is appropriate to such takings – these are questions that presuppose some understanding and interpretation of the phenomena. Reductive analyses are empty without a clear conception of what the candidate for reduction is. To prove that *thinking* something beautiful is, so to speak, all there is, or that what we take to be aesthetic pleasure is some other kind of gratification in disguise, we have to be able to characterize the alleged illusion, to explain what it is that people mistakenly take to be the case.

Those who think that beauty is undiscussable have another familiar objection: tastes, they observe, differ, and of two incompatible judgements it is impossible to prove that one is right. This is an idea that has haunted the literature since the eighteenth century. I believe it comes from assuming that to define a term is to offer a criterion for its application. A definition of *x* is thought of as answering the question, 'By what marks can I recognize a case of *x*?' Three observations:

(1) If what is wanted is a test, then beauty is indefinable, but so are most terms of everyday language. (This is Wittgenstein's point in *Philosophical Investigations* where he speaks of the futility of attempts to define game.) Definitions that tell me how to recognize an *x* are found in legal textbooks, in formal logic, in the physical sciences, but rarely elsewhere.

(2) A definition presents two terms as equivalent, but equivalent with respect to what? Do they apply to the same items? Do they have the same meaning? Is the equivalence something discovered, or something stipulated? It all depends on what you want to use the definition for, what function it plays in your inquiry. Developing a philosophical theory is not like putting together a manual for beginners. When Russell and Frege argue about how to define number, they are not thinking about helpful clues that will help the layman *recognize* a number when he comes across one.

(3) A term of everyday language – beauty, say, or game – is indefinable in the sense of lacking criteria for application. You can make up a definition if you want to and perhaps force everyone to adopt it. But then you will have to invent another term to do the job that had been done by game or by beauty. This is a general

point, but it is important for the theory of the beautiful since we are often tempted to look for rules or principles that would bolster our particular preferences. Kant was the first philosopher to see how empty such attempts must be.

A final and inconsequential obstacle: it is said that 'beauty' is not the right *term* to focus on because it carries the suggestion of something mildly pleasing and non-strenuous, thereby excluding much great art. (How many times have we been told that neither the ceiling of the Sistine Chapel nor *King Lear* nor late Beethoven quartets are 'beautiful'?) This is just pedantry: in eighteenth-century critical parlance where, in accord with the now forgotten theory of genres, the beautiful was divided from the 'sublime', the 'picturesque', the 'pathetic' and so forth, it had a point, although even then it was one known only to insiders. Non-experts then and now apply the term 'beautiful' across the board, and the same is true for its cognate in other languages. Anyone who thinks 'aesthetic value' is an improvement is free to adopt it – but then it has to be explained: beauty is a good, so 'value' is appropriate, but what do you say about 'aesthetic'?

Once we set aside the questions that have been supposed to block inquiry, we are free to consider the role that aesthetic considerations play in our lives. We care a *lot* about good appearance: to be beautiful, to have good-looking children, nice clothes, a fine house – these are accounted blessings. People work long and hard, inspired by the hope that what they achieve may be beautiful – and not just the artists, but gardeners and industrial designers. Our perceptions of beauty are deeply intertwined in the complexities of our affective lives. Why does a mere house inspire in me feelings of pride? 'Because it is mine and because I think it beautiful' is an answer that anyone can understand. Think further of the role that 'because it is beautiful' plays in explanations of such emotions as envy, love, ambition, solicitude. It is not only in theory of affect that such considerations figure. No account of deliberation or practical reason that did not allow them their proper weight could be adequate. What is at issue in particular cases may be momentous (Which one shall I marry?) or minor (Where shall we spend our vacation?) or trivial (Shall I buy this pot-holder?). But there is no decison in which what Kant calls 'the judgement of taste' may not play a role, and in some contexts it is decisive. So there is every reason to recognize that beauty is a basic and indispensable concept in whatever sense one could say the same of knowledge, belief, wrongdoing, logical validity or virtue.

To say of beauty that it is relatively unex-plored is just to observe that many great philosophers treat it in a perfunctory manner or not at all. None of the system-builders of the seventeenth century – not Descartes, Locke, Spinoza, Berkeley, Leibniz – has anything much to say about the beautiful. Who, then, have made significant contribu-tions? Plato, for one, Aquinas and some of the medievals, Hume, Kant; and, in the present century, Dewey, Santayana and a handful of later writers. The popular conception – that there is a vast literature, many theories, as many as there are theorists – is false. It is also a mistake to assume that the views that we *do* have are in conflict with one another. On questions of ontology, theory of knowledge and ethics, Plato, Hume and Kant represent very different positions, and such differences emerge in their analyses of the beautiful. But with respect to what it is that *needs* analysis, the characterization of the data, their views converge. There are differences of emphasis but, by and large, these are complementary rather than competitive. Furthermore, the philosophers' consensus is in accord with common sense – that is, with the opinion of reflective laymen.

Certain propositions are taken to need no argument: they are not axioms or *a priori* truths but commonplaces derived from ex-perience and observation. Some examples:

(1) Beauty is a kind of good, a 'positive value'.
(2) Beauty is linked with pleasure: what we take to be beautiful we enjoy. The converse does not hold, since we enjoy things that we do not think beautiful or even seemly.
(3) Beauty inspires love and thus acquires its power as an element of motivation.
(4) Appreciation of beauty depends on per-ception or, if abstract entities are in question, on some other form of ac-quaintance. Hence our findings are, as one might say, all first-personal, and dis-cussions of a piece of music that is des-cribed but never heard are necessarily vacuous.
(5) The claim, when it is serious, that a par-ticular item is beautiful brings into play a kind of judgement that is distinctive – not to be subsumed under the heading of practical or theoretical judgement. Kant was the first to make it explicit and recognize its importance.

The five propositions listed provide a basis to build on. Taken together, they suggest a number of further propositions. Thus, if, as according to proposition 4, ascription of beauty to an individual, O, requires that the ascriber be acquainted with O, then it appears that, whatever the warrant for the ascription may be, it cannot depend on infer-ence from general principles. A major premise for a syllogism that had 'O is beauti-ful' as its conclusion would have to be of unrestricted generality, like 'All roses are beautiful', which, in contrast with 'All the roses in this vase are beautiful', requires com-mitment with respect to an indefinitely large number of hitherto unexamined roses – and this is incompatible with proposition 4.

When it comes to determining what is beautiful, no interesting, law-like generaliza-tions are available. Kant puts it plainly: there are no principles of taste. Kant takes his claim to be self-evident, but it is not – as appears from the manifest convictions of many to the effect that *unless* there are principles of taste, the judgement of taste must be 'merely sub-jective'. Kant's greatest contribution is his recognition that what is posed as a dilemma is not a dilemma; that while there is some-thing to be explained, there is no forced option; and that the singular judgement of taste, 'O is beautiful', despite lack of principled support, is (sometimes at least) a valid judgement. Although Kant puts his negative thesis with respect to principles as an *a priori* truth that needs no argument, it is perhaps helpful to see that his point can be derived from, or at least supported by, proposition 4. What proposition 4 amounts to is the claim that the judgement of taste is, in a radical sense, an empirical judgement.

The virtual consensus among historical authors with respect to the phenomenal characteristics of the beautiful should not stand in the way of our noting that none of the traditional accounts is wholly adequate. Plato, for instance, appears to believe that spiritual progress, anchored in a love of the beautiful, moves (if all goes well) from appreciation of the particular – as might be, a handsome youth – to the more general – what handsome youths have in common – thence to the beauty of social institutions (the 'just state'), and finally to a grasp of the form of absolute beauty. If we grant the five propositons listed above, then beauty belongs only to individuals, and Plato's second step is a false step. Moreover, Plato's account is full of apparent incoherences: earthly items become beautiful by 'participating' in the form, beauty, and that form is said to be itself the most beautiful of all. But the good is also said to be the most beautiful of all forms, and if the good has to 'participate' in beauty, then – well, you can see the difficulties. Maybe the story of the progressive ascent from handsome youth to absolute beauty is not really Plato's considered view; the account comes from the *Symposium*, where it is attributed by Socrates to Diotima, a prophetess.

Or consider Kant, so clear and persuasive on the main points; yet he has the weird idea that when I judge something beautiful, I am focusing not on the *thing* but on what Kant sees as a command (something like the categorical imperative) that every human being must assent to my claim. Admittedly, it is true that if I think I am right, I will *expect* competent peers to concur in my judgement, but to *demand* that everyone agree with me seems a most illiberal and anti-Enlightenment requirement. Here again, there may be a way of squaring Kant's docrine with com-

mitment to freedom of thought and expression, but what way has yet to be made out.

Hume's mistake was fairly basic: he is probably the originator of the idea of a dilemma – that only if there are principles of taste can we grant that some judgements of taste are true and others false. Hume believed that there was some conflict between holding on the one hand that a speaker, in making a judgement of taste, manifests not his beliefs but his 'sentiments' and recognizing, on the other, that some judgements – such as the judgement that Ogilby (a forgotten poet) is the equal of Milton – are not merely false but absurd. Hume tries to solve the problem by proposing that there *are* principles of taste, but very elusive ones, difficult to discern and impossible to formulate. (This is like claiming that there are moral principles but that it is not possible to cite any examples.) Hume's epistemological commitments lead him to a kind of waffling that Kant was careful to avoid, although when Hume forgets his theories, he is as clear-sighted as anyone has ever been.

In fact, the conflict that worried him need not have arisen: it depends entirely on his assumption that the *motive* of an utterance is decisive in determining its claim to have a truth value. He is therefore led to believe that, given their provenance, judgements of taste, like moral judgements, are beyond the reach of reason and hence neither true nor false. Hume offers no arguments for this claim, one which surely needs defence. It would have astonished Plato and Aristotle. (In a fit of passion, I shout out, 'Socrates is a Greek!'; in a moment of cool reflection, I murmur, 'Alcibiades is beautiful.' There may be questions about truth claims, but they are not questions that are settled by discovery of my emotional state at the time of utterance.)

The preceding observations about Plato, Kant and Hume are meant to suggest that the philosophers who have contributed most to the analysis of the beautiful have raised issues of consequence and have left us with many problems to solve. They present a challenge to anyone who takes the topic seriously. Why has the discussion languished?

You might think that philosophical aesthetics is the study of the beautiful, but that is not how things have turned out. From its mid-eighteenth-century beginnings when it first became an academic subject in German universities, aesthetics has been mainly concerned with the fine arts. Kant's *Critique of Judgement* (1790) is the first work that can be said to offer a systematic theory of beauty, but Kant was the last philospher to consider nature on an equal footing with the arts. Indeed, because of his precoccupation with the 'sublime' as a bridge between aesthetics and ethics, and his hope of preserving what he felt was valuable in the 'Argument from Design', he pays more attention to natural phenomena than to works of art.

The shift of focus from the concept of beauty to the idea of a unitary enterprise called 'Art' happened gradually, and can escape notice because works of art were always among the items taken as exemplars of the beautiful. The expression 'work of art' itself is an honorific title that belongs not just to any old poem or painting but to those that are deemed notably beautiful. But works of art can be studied from many different points of view, and are interesting for reasons other than their aesthetic value. Plato was the first to see that because drama, music and poetry have powerful emotional effects, statesmen and educators can put the arts to work in support of political goals, worthy or unworthy. Plato also thought that what later ages were to call the 'fine arts' were essentially mimetic; that, for instance, melancholy music causes hearers to feel melancoly by 'imitating' melancholy feelings. For reasons connected with his metaphysical doctrines, he supposed such music to be doubly hazardous: first, because it arouses negative emotions, and, second, because what it imitates or represents is not part of true reality but an aspect of the bungled world of appearance and becoming. The practice of the arts, he argues, must be strictly controlled because art is both deceptive and demoralizing.

Aristotle is another who is less concerned with the beauty of the arts than with their psychological effects which, in contrast to Plato, he takes to be mainly benign. To be moved by an imitation of wrongful action or bad feeling is good: vicarious satisfaction of our own antisocial wishes makes us less rather than more likely to model ourselves on the doomed characters depicted on the Attic stage. Medieval authors, drawing on what was available to them from the classical tradition, take beauty seriously but show a kind of ambivalence about the arts. The delight we take in pageantry, music, ornamentation and sculpture is seductive and may lead us away from our spiritual vocation. On the other hand, the arts, by way of fable or allegory, prefigure for simple folk truths of faith that are abstract and difficult to grasp. Manifest physical beauty is a clue to and a reminder of the beauty that is higher but less obvious – namely, the beauty of the virtuous soul secure in its faith.

Another persistent theme is that the world as a whole is an object for admiration and pleasure. The creator in Plato's *Timaeus* had wanted to make a *kosmos*, fine in every detail and beautiful as a whole. One article of the Manichaean heresy was the claim that the world is in a constant state of strife between good and evil. Scholastic philosophers bent on refutation of that view found it helpful to emphasize the intimate connection between the beautiful and the good. In the face of the facts, it is harder to argue that God is benevolent and just than to argue that God is an artist who needs contrasts – shadows to make brightness more striking, discords that can be harmoniously resolved.

What properties of the universe as a whole make it beautiful? The answer is going to have to be fairly abstract and not susceptible to disconfirmation, since we have only our own world to appreciate and nothing to compare it with. Thus the notion of 'unity in variety' comes to the fore, often embellished with fanciful doctrines of ratio and proportion. Presumably Pythagorean in origin, these doctrines exercise a strange fascination over theorists and artists alike; by the time of the Renaissance they are a familiar obsession. As for the beauty of the *kosmos*, you can appreciate it without being a believer or thinking of the *kosmos* as a work of art.

Because of the size and duration of the universe, you cannot *grasp* it as a whole, but this is not fatal: it can be seen as a limiting case of the difficulty of getting a fix on extremely long novels or operas. None the less, it is a thought that impressed the medievals more than subsequent generations. It is perhaps echoed on a smaller scale in the reflections of philosphically unpretentious astronauts who have found our planet, seen from afar, fragile, solitary and beautiful.

The story of the progressive institutionalization of the arts and of their elevation to a social status comparable with that of the professions has been told by historical scholars. Out of the miscellany of crafts and techniques – some messy and manual like painting and sculpture, some intellectual and gentlemanly, like music and poetry – there emerged the notion of art as a unitary enterprise, and with it the belief that it was important to determine what the essential characteristics of art may be. The arts are obviously very different, and yet there does seem to be some bond. A straightforward and seemingly uncontentious suggestion is that works of art are artefacts that are beautiful; and that suggestion, although rarely accepted as adequate, lurks in the background of traditional theories of beauty. This explains the fact that, until the early nineteenth century, there is no sharp distinction between explications of beauty and explications of what we might call artistic excellence or merit. The big break came with Hegel, although the way was prepared by his German predecessors, who worked on such questions as that suggested by a passing remark of Horace's – namely, how much of an affinity does narrative poetry have with painting? What does the medium dictate? Is it or is it not illuminating to think of architecture as 'frozen music'? Hegel's contribution was to propose that, while common people characterize as 'beautiful' landscapes or plants or animals that happen to please them, this is a loose way of speaking. The only true beauty is that which is 'born again of the mind', and hence is to be found only in human beings and in the works of art that they relate.

Hegel was the first to recognize that, although artistic beauty may be timeless, to understand a work from an alien or bygone culture requires research: you have to learn about the social, economic and ideological context in which the work was produced. Conversely, once you get the point, you can use the work as a key to what Hegel refers to as 'the spirit of the age'. To the extent that 'the philosophy of x' is conceived as an attempt to discover the meaning of x, then Hegel's insight is the discovery that the philosophy of art, rather than being an independent subject, is identical with the history of art – or at any rate its history seen through the eyes of a philospher. Hegel's own version is interesting, although the elaborate system in which each of the arts is supposed to speak for the spirit of one or another of various historical eras such as the classical, the Christian, the Romantic and so forth is apt to strike us as rather arbitrary. Some of his more extravagant claims can hardly be stated without a review of his system as a whole. Hegel believed, for example, that all history is at bottom a sort of psychobiography of 'absolute spirit', in the course of which the subject undergoes dialectical vicissitudes; conflicts and contradictions are resolved and the resolution generates new contradictions. Hegel also puts forward the peculiar hypothesis that art is about to come to an end and to be replaced by a yet higher and more evolved spiritual form: namely, philosophy.

Academic aesthetics has accepted and absorbed one part of Hegel's legacy and ignored another part. If this was a choice, it was an unfortunate choice. What was accepted was the view that mere nature is aesthetically defective and just sits there in its dumb way as subject-matter for the creative artist. This assumption, although understandable, has had some bad consequences for aesthetic theory. On the other hand, few aestheticians have appreciated the merit of Hegel's claims about the importance of history – which is why much of the best work in the philosophy of art has been done not by professional philosophers but by philosophically minded art historians and scholars.

What is wrong with taking philosophical aesthetics to be the study of art as distinct from such items as landscapes or persons or the universe as a whole? In a way, there is nothing wrong: when we believe of something that it was marvellous that it was made by another human being, our admiration and interest acquire added dimensions: we raise questions about technique, intentions, motives, feelings that would be inappropriate were the item in question taken to be the accidental product of natural forces. Besides, it may be that some works of art are more beautiful than any such product. Plato did not believe this and neither did Kant, but it still might be true. There does appear to be some perpetual fascination with the idea of magical changes: think of the myth and folklore that turn on the idea of statues suddenly coming to life or of persons transformed into works of art (or trees or animals).

The difficulty lies deeper, and has to do with our grasp of what it is to find something beautiful. There are works of art that you cannot appreciate or understand without some background and knowledge of the relevant conventions (Hegel's point): polyphony is chaotic to someone unfamiliar with counterpoint; Picasso looks primitive (or crazy) to someone who has never encountered anything other than anecdotal nineteenth-century painting. And yet, as one might put it, everything that is there *is there*. Acquaintance with 'Row, row, row your boat' or with the preoccupations of cubist artists may lead you to notice features that you had not noticed before, but beliefs about a picture are not visual properties of the picture, and knowing how a fugue is supposed to work is not like adding a fourth voice. If you look and listen and are patient enough, then, even without instruction, you will eventually see what Picasso or Bach is up to. And then there are cases where you really do not *know*. John Dewey asks us to imagine an interesting little piece of stone that is first classified as a geological accident, then as an artefact, a tool, and then as an artefact that has a symbolic or aesthetic function – asks us to consider how it is moved from one museum to another and how we look at it in different ways depending on how it is described. Changes of belief may, but need not,

affect appreciation: if I like the way the little thing looks or how it feels when I hold it in my hand, then my state is one of appreciation and I am on the threshold of a judgement of taste.

To say that only works of art are beautiful is paradoxical in the way in which it would be paradoxical to say that only wrongful actions are bad. A terrible catastrophe occurs: someone says, 'I can't say whether it was bad or not until I know whether it as deliberately brought about by an agent.' We find ourselves in an alpine meadow bright with wild flowers: I say, 'I can't tell you whether this is beautiful or not until I know whether it is a garden.'

In one respect Hegel's influence is on the wane: some forty years ago, aestheticians under the influence of Wittgenstein began to disparage the attempt to find what is essential to art. The end of the trail was marked by the emergence of the so-called institutional theory of art, according to which something is a work of art only if a person of authority in the 'artworld' says it is a work of art. At the time, the boundaries of the 'artworld' were being extended to allow in what had been thought of as mere crafts and to admit a variety of 'anti-art' productions, known as 'statements'. The conception of an 'authority' was itself becoming quite thin, and while you can see why the institutional theory was congenial, it does not seem like a contribution to philosophy but rather a sociological echo or reflection of the market-place.

However that may be, aesthetics as currently practised is unstructured and decentralized. An issue of the *Journal of Aesthetics and Art Criticism* will print an article on the *auteur* theory of film, an historical essay, a piece on dance notation, a review of a current exhibition and an essay on metaphor. The work is often interesting; the question is why put it under one cover? Many people would find it enough to say that aesthetics covers any question that is directly or indirectly connected with criticism or the arts. All right – but then was not Baumgarten mistaken in thinking that he had discovered a new subject? Perhaps he was, but perhaps not. One suggestion: works of art do have something in common, but it is not peculiar to works of art. Works of art are man-made items that are pre-eminently beautiful. They exhibit a kind of goodness, although possibly in higher degree, that is also manifest in particular persons, rivers, mountains, animals and plants. If this is so, then philosophical aesthetics needs to return to the question of the nature of beauty and to try to develop the insights of past philosophers in a systematic way.

See also ATTITUDE, AESTHETIC; HARMONY AND SYMMETRY; 'END OF ART'; HEGEL; HUME; JUDGEMENT, AESTHETIC; KANT; PLATO; SUBLIME; TASTE.

BIBLIOGRAPHY

Aristotle: *Poetics*, in *The Basic Works of Aristotle*, ed. McKeon (New York: Random House, 1941).
Dewey, J.: *Art as Experience* (New York: Minton, Balch, 1934).
Hegel, G.W.F.: *Philosophy of Fine Art*, trans. Osmaston, 4 vols (London: 1920).
Hume, D.: *A Treatise of Human Nature*, ed. Selby-Bigge (Oxford: Clarendon Press, 1960).
Hume, D.: *Of the Standard of Taste*, ed. Lenz (New York: Bobbs-Merrill, 1965).
Kant, I.: *Critique of Judgement* (1790); trans. J.C. Meredith (Oxford: Clarendon Press, 1964).
Mothersill, M.: *Beauty Restored* (Oxford: Clarendon Press, 1984).
Osborne, H.: *Theory of Beauty* (London: Routledge, 1952).
Plato: *Ion, Symposium, Phaedrus, Republic*, trans. Jowett (New York: Random House, 1920).
Santayana, G.: *The Sense of Beauty* (New York: Scribner, 1902).

MARY MOTHERSILL

Bell, (Arthur) Clive (Heward) (1881–1964) British art critic; an early champion of post-impressionist and abstract art. Convinced that little had been so far achieved in aesthetics, Bell proposed a fresh start: a return to basic personal experience of authentic works of art. In his book *Art* (1914), he took as basic a distinctive 'kind of emotion',

'aesthetic emotion', and a quality 'common and peculiar to all the objects that provoke it'. In visual art, Bell's main concern, this quality must arise from certain 'forms and relations of forms', 'relations and combinations of lines and colours'. Why these arouse aesthetic emotion we do not know: we have to postulate 'unknown and mysterious laws' whereby particular forms constitute for us 'significant form', as Bell labels it.

Creating and responding to significant form is a very different matter from furnishing and receiving *information* through purely descriptive, illustrative painting (William Powell Frith's *Paddington Station*, for example); different, too, from evoking and reliving the varied emotions of human life. In authentic art, the painted forms are themselves the objects of our (aesthetic) emotion, not the 'means of suggesting emotion and conveying ideas'. The proper goal of art is not the perfecting of mimetic accuracy through technical virtuosity. For imitation, we now, in any case, have the camera. Where painting is concerned, if 'a representative form has value, it is as form, not as representation'.

What we should look for and hope to experience in art, then, is what we seldom experience in life outside art – the aesthetic thrill, rapture or ecstasy. For all the inexhaustible variety of styles, idioms and media throughout the history of art, the same thrill that testifies to significant form is the vital constant feature of genuine art. It is common to Sumerian sculpture, archaic Greek art, sixth-century Byzantine art, to Giotto, Poussin and Cézanne, with his 'insistence on the supremacy of significant form'. But from the High Renaissance to the impressionists, Bell sees numerous highly regarded painters as failing in the crucial respect. His aesthetic theory supported radical revisions in the estimation of artistic achievement, and in particular gave a theoretical warrant to the efforts of Roger Fry and Clive Bell himself to win acceptance for the artists of the first and second post-impressionist exhibitions, in 1910 and 1912. (It is worth adding that much later in life, in his preface to the 1949 edition of *Art*, Bell allows that he spoke 'absurdly and impertinently of the giants of the High Renaissance'.)

With some diffidence, he now ventures a 'metaphysical hypothesis'. To experience the purely formal, we have to strip off the everyday human significance of objects in the world and abandon seeing them merely as means to our practical ends. To contemplate them as pure forms, as 'ends in themselves' or 'things in themselves', is to reach a vision of 'ultimate reality', to become aware of 'the God in everything . . . the all-pervading rhythm'. Here 'the chatter and tumult of material existence is unheard'. Not surprisingly, Bell sets together 'art and religion as twin manifestations of the spirit', two roads 'to ecstasy'. Similarly, there is no special problem, for Bell, in relating the values of art and the values of morality. In fulfilling its proper task of facilitating aesthetic experience, an intrinsically excellent state of mind, art ministers directly to one of the fundamental forms of goodness. Bell explicitly models his thinking here on G.E. Moore's *Principia Ethica* (1903).

Clive Bell's bold, unitary, simple theory of art has been a tempting target for criticism by analytical philosophers, sceptical of speculative systems as such. They have seen it as failing to present a genuinely informative verdict about human experience of art. His main concepts ('work of art', 'aesthetic emotion', 'significant form') constituted, rather, a self-supporting set, defined in terms of one another: they achieved no triumph of comprehensive explanation, since they were not really open to empirical confirmation or falsification. The analytical philosopher tended thus to dismiss Bell's theory as metaphysical in a bad sense, as simplistic or, indeed, vacuous. Nevertheless, there is some reason to see these critics as themselves simplifying and distorting Bell's position.

Bell certainly believed his theory to be anchored in individual experience – experience of one characteristic type evoked by art from primitives to post-impressionists. He cannot give a formula for what evokes it; but he knows that formal structures, not narrative or sentimental matter, are its source. Many readers of Bell, again, deny that there exists any distinctive aesthetic emotion. Should we not speak, instead, of the 'aesthetic attitude', contemplatively disengaged from practical concerns (Dickie, 1965)? But surely that would be too remote from what Bell meant by 'aesthetic emotion', for we can take up an aesthetic attitude to an object which (because of its lack of satisfying formal unity) does not in the event sustain or reward that attitude. Closer to Bell might be a response of admiration, delight and wonder to an individual achievement of formal unity. That would capture the essential receptivity, without insisting on a specific aesthetic emotion – though that too cannot be dogmatically denied (see Meager, 1965).

Art was an eloquent and much needed reappraisal of sentimental, literary and moralizing painting. Did it, however, react excessively against the according of aesthetic value to representation as such? Bell himself came to realize that there were complexities that he had shied away from in *Art*. More basically, though, the very distinction of 'form' and represented 'content' cannot be sharply maintained – a fact of high importance to aesthetic theory. In countless paintings, the way we apprehend the represented subject-matter – its overall expressive quality – is a function of the design, pattern and textures in and through which the subject-matter is represented. So, too, the emotions, attitudes and appraisals evoked by the *form* are inseparable from our awareness of what these same forms are representing. Those are, in fact, crucial strategies by which art intensifies and extends human experience. Again, where we perceive formal unity as being won from heterogeneous or conflictful materials, we can appreciate that triumph of the formal only if we also, and first, respond to the diversity and the tensions. We must experience the recalcitrance, the near-refusal, of some (perhaps chaotic, or tragic) represented material to be contained and assimilated within any form, before we can appreciate fully the fact that a work of art *has* ordered and subdued it. In a word, the interplay and 'fusion' of formal and representational elements need a more complex and balanced exploration.

There is no doubt that aesthetic experience and religious experience can be very near neighbours: for instance, a contemplative withdrawal of ordinary concepts and categories may feature in some mystical states of mind. Yet Bell is not a clear-headed guide in this area: he slides, rather than convincingly argues, from talk of non-utility perception to perception of objects as ends in themselves, as things-in-themselves, as reality and as God in everything.

Bell should not be judged on one book alone. In later writing 'significant form' became a more elusive quality, and art criticism correspondingly more difficult and more fallible a task. Significant form may manifest itself in a shock or sudden thrill to the passive spectator, yielding a judgement that subsequent study in detail and depth cannot properly modify or overlay. Conversely, an analytical grasp of a work's form cannot reverse an unfavourable holistic emotional response. Form is 'significant' in later Bell if, but only if, it cannot be further worked upon, refined, simplified and intensified by an artist in an artwork. Nature's forms are therefore not in the strong sense significant. They become so only when an artist realizes their potentiality (see also Elliott, 1965).

See also ATTITUDE, AESTHETIC; FORM; RELIGION AND ART.

WRITINGS

Art (London: 1914); 3rd edn, with intro. by J.B. Bullen (Oxford: Oxford University Press, 1987).
Since Cézanne (London: Chatto & Windus, 1922).
Enjoying Pictures (London: Chatto & Windus, 1934).

BIBLIOGRAPHY

Dickie, G.T.: 'Clive Bell and the method of Principia Ethica', *The British Journal of Aesthetics*, 2 (1965), 139–43.
Elliott, R.K.: 'Clive Bell's aesthetic theory and his critical practice', *The British Journal of Aesthetics*, 2 (1965), 111–22.
Lake, Beryl: 'A study of the irrefutability of two aesthetic theories', *Aesthetics and Language*, ed. W. Elton (Oxford: Basil Blackwell, 1954), pp. 100–13.
Meager, R.: 'Clive Bell and aesthetic emotion', *The British Journal of Aesthetics*, 2 (1965), 123–31.
Osborne, H.: 'Alison and Bell on appreciation', *The British Journal of Aesthetics*, 2 (1965), 132–8.
Read, Herbert: 'Clive Bell', *The British Journal of Aesthetics*, 2 (1965), 107–10.

RONALD W. HEPBURN

Benjamin, Walter (1892–1940) German philosopher and cultural and literary critic; influenced as much by Jewish mysticism as by surrealism and Marxism. Born in Berlin and commmitted suicide at the age of forty-eight on the Franco-Spanish border; generally recognized to be one of the most important literary critics and aesthetic theorists that Germany has produced in the twentieth century.

Such recognition was belated, however; it was only after Theodor Adorno's 1955 publication of selections from his work that Benjamin became known to a wider public. After decades of intensive commentary, and supported by a scholarly *Gesammelte Schriften* (Complete Works), Benjamin's position in the intellectual firmament of our time is assured – assured, but hardly clear. Indeed, his thought is famous for an obscurity that stems from the denseness of its expression, the fragmentary nature of even the published works, and the apparent inconsistency of positions he was drawn to in what he once called 'the economy of my existence'.

One problem in interpreting Benjamin lies in deciding how far he should be considered an aesthetic theorist at all. He saw art as subservient to theological, philosophical and political concerns; he also claimed, in effect, that art is at an end. The ambiguity of his utterances may be seen in their varied reception. For example, he was brought to the attention of the English-speaking world by the 1968 publication of *Illuminations*, Hannah Arendt's selection of his essays (the volume was supplemented in 1978 by a second, *Reflections*). Implicitly – and openly in her introduction – Arendt denominates Benjamin a literary critic and 'poetic thinker', thus taking issue with other perspectives that would view him as primarily a philosopher (as does Adorno), a proponent of a metaphysics with messianic overtones (as does Gershom Scholem), or as a political theorist whose engagement with historical materialism was (as Terry Eagleton has it) more than 'a contingent peccadillo or tolerable eccentricity'.

It is not just Benjamin's legacy that is ambiguous; in his own lifetime, too, he was different things to different friends and interlocutors. Moreover, the bewildering array of sources from which he drew inspiration – from Kant to surrealism – makes it especially difficult to characterize his thinking. Benjamin was a collector of both objects and quotations. Yet he refused to follow any fashion or *Fach* (speciality): it is no accident that his intended doctoral dissertation on baroque *Trauerspiel* (tragic drama) was rejected as incomprehensible by the faculties of both philosophy and German literature at the University of Frankfurt. Benjamin's preferred method of 'immanent criticism' – any theoretical principles were to emerge from the material or work being studied – was really no method at all.

Nevertheless, there are certain motifs running through his writings, which can be treated as falling into two phases. The first, more metaphysical or theological, phase would extend as far as his *Trauerspiel* work; and a later phase, more political and materialist in orientation, would run from 1925 almost to the end of his life, and would include the enormous and unfinished *Passagenwerk*, or 'Arcades' project (several hundred pages of which are now available in Ralph Tiedemann's scholarly edition of 1982).

BENJAMIN'S EARLY AESTHETICS

Benjamin's theory of art was all along a theory of *experience*. In his first essays he opposed what he saw as the neo-Kantians' reduction of experience to empirical terms,

their refusal to allow the suprasensible as a possible object of knowledge. He viewed language as originally unified but, after the fall into profane temporality, fragmented and wholly separate from the divine realm of law. At first he thought that metaphysics could imitate the divine power of creative naming (the essence of language, for Benjamin), so redeeming human experience. By the time of his 1919 thesis on German Romantic art criticism (*Kritik*) he had given up the notion that a philosophic system could accomplish this. He suggested that art, however, could do so – or, at least, art completed by a criticism that would reveal its animating form, or 'idea'. Benjamin remained faithful to the romantics' principle of 'immanent criticism'.

The principle found immediate application in a brilliant, still untranslated, essay of 1922 on Goethe's *Elective Affinities*. Only in and through the historical specificity of the novel would its inner truth emerge – a truth not unconnected to Benjamin's own fundamentalist, or Kantian, ethics. Art occupies a fragile place between regression to a mythic nature and election to moral grace. It can offer no more than an *image* or 'semblance' (*Schein*) of human unity with the divine, and hence a measure of hope: it cannot 'create'.

Such ambivalence towards art is found also in the work that sums up Benjamin's early career, *The Origin of German Tragic Drama* of 1924–5. At times this reads as if it were a parody of the dissertation it was meant to be, scholarly footnotes jostling darkly brilliant insights and generalizations. 'Generalization' is the wrong term, however, for Benjamin wishes to avoid a universal aesthetics of tragedy. Instead, he wants to rehabilitate a specific historical genre, that of seventeenth-century *Trauerspiel*. Only after this specificity has been grasped can he enlarge on its universal significance, its 'truth content': historical commentary must precede interpretative criticism. Yet the converse also holds for him: the historicity of works of art (he wrote, in a letter of December 1923) emerges not via art history but only in interpretation.

The so-called 'epistemo-critical prologue' to the work – one of the densest pieces of prose anywhere – offers a unique reflection on Benjamin's own method. In brief, he aims at the presentation (*Darstellung*) of the material in such a way that the timeless and monadic 'ideas' shine through. 'Ideas are to objects as constellations are to stars' he suggests (Benjamin, 1977a, p. 34). The metaphor of 'constellation' supplies one of his main concepts: the arrangement of phenomena is what 'saves' them and at the same time presents the truth. The first or more historical part, though, is taken up with the description of Protestant *Trauerspiel*. Benjamin notes that this was taken to be historical fact as well as theatrical device: what appears dramatic in history is its fallen state. History is transposed to spatial form, the self-enclosed world of stage or of court; it is petrified into nature, as Benjamin puts it. *Trauerspiel* tells sad stories of the death of monarchs, whether tyrants or martyrs. Compared with the setting of ancient tragedy, death is radically contingent; the bodies pile up with the ruins of the world. In the second part of his treatise Benjamin shifts beyond the externals of the work towards its inner truth or idea – namely, allegory. This is understood not as conventional expression but as the 'expression of convention': that is, a reflection on the finitude of a world that has lost the wholeness of Greek tragedy. In turn, allegory will become the emblem of a modernity now understood as secularized and mortified history; here we glimpse the 'smuggler's path' that preserves an esoteric past within present concerns. Moreover, Protestant and melancholic contemplation is revealed as an historico-political practice – and, again, a secret path leads us towards the political tendency in Benjamin's work.

THE TURN FROM THEORY

The *Trauerspiel* book contains the seeeds of much that follows. Benjamin celebrates, yet also delimits, the momentary 'semblance' of salvation that art offers us. The question he grappled with for the remainder of his life was this: how could such an essentially theological model of interpretation be transposed into historical materialist terms? While finishing the dissertation he had begun reading Lukács, which along with his meeting the revolutionary Asja Lakis (who later introduced Benjamin to Bertolt Brecht) helped make him a committed Marxist. Around this time too he came upon the work of the surrealists, whose play upon contingent juxtapositions of objects of ordinary life and on dream logic left a deep impression. The essay 'Marseilles' carries an epigraph from André Breton which could apply to much that followed: 'The street . . . the only valid field of experience' (Benjamin, 1978, p. 131).

Marxism and surrealism are essential to an understanding of Benjamin's ultimate project, the intended book called 'Paris, Capital of the Nineteenth Century' (also known as the 'Arcades' work, after the glassed-in shopping streets that he took as emblematic of emergent modernity). Here a 'montage' of quotations – 'citing without citation marks' (Benjamin, 1982, p. 572) – was to take over the function that 'criticism' had previously performed. Benjamin called its principle one of 'dialectical image' or 'dialectics at a standstill': 'When thinking reaches a standstill in a constellation saturated with tensions, the dialectical image appears. The image is the caesura in the movement of thought' (Smith, 1989, p. 67). In its initial conception, the 'Arcades' work was to have juxtaposed representative personages (Fourier, Grandville, Louis-Philippe, Baudelaire, Haussmann) with a physiognomic description of the cityscape (World Exhibition, street, *intérieur*, arcade), taken as a commodified and technologized life-world, a phantasmagoria of nature. Later, perhaps influenced by the Institute for Social Research that was supporting him, he made Baudelaire the central figure. The two essays he wrote (translated in *Charles Baudelaire*) are a small but brilliant precipitate from a mass of notes. Benjamin's overall procedure remains controversial, however. Adorno criticized it as being too reductively materialist, suspended between 'magic and positivism'. Marxists have found it too metaphorical in its imaginative montage of material and cultural phenomena.

During the 1930s Benjamin wrote several

essays of remarkable originality on, for example, Proust, Nikolai Leskov and Kafka (to whom he felt especially close). From the association with Brecht came a number of important studies of 'epic theatre'. Benjamin's 'materialism' is also evinced in the essays 'The author as producer' and 'The work of art in an age of reproducibility'. This last has become a classic of sorts, and it illustrates his concern with the technology of aesthetic reception. Technology could be seen as an extension of the human life-world, but also as a congealing or mortification of history. Photography and cinema have supplanted the 'aura' of traditional art with communal experience and the 'shocks' of montage; yet Benjamin considers that they might be of use in 'politicizing' aesthetics, instead of Fascism's 'aestheticizing' of politics. This, too, brought down Adorno's censure; he rejoined that Benjamin had overestimated the potential of mass media, while ignoring the critical function of an autonomous art.

Benjamin's last word and testament (though he may not have thought it ready for publication) is the 'Theses on the philosophy of history', eighteen runic fragments shored against a disastrous time (the Hitler–Stalin pact, the occupation of Poland). Its meaning and interpretative context are more than usually controversial, as Benjamin seems to return to his initial messianic views and invokes a mystic 'now-time' blasting through the continuum of ordinary history. What remains constant, however, is his anti-historicism, his commitment to rescuing the past in the name of the future, and the conviction that (to cite his Goethe essay) 'only for the sake of those without hope is hope given us' (Benjamin, 1974, p. 201).

See also AUTONOMY, AESTHETIC; MARXISM AND ART; RELIGION AND ART.

WRITINGS

Illuminations, trans. H. Zohn (New York: Harcourt Brace & World, 1968).
Charles Baudelaire: A Lyric Poet in the Era of High
Capitalism (Frankfurt: 1969); trans. H. Zohn (London: New Left Books, 1973).
The Origin of German Tragic Drama, trans. John Osborne (London: New Left Books, 1977a).
Aesthetics and Politics, ed. R. Taylor (London: New Left Books, 1977b).
Reflections: Essays, Aphorisms, Autobiographical Writings, trans. E. Jephcott, ed. Peter Demetz (New York: Harcourt Brace Jovanovich, 1978).
Gesammelte Schriften, 7 vols (Frankfurt: Suhrkamp, 1974–82); vols 1–4 (1974), vols 5–7 (1982).

BIBLIOGRAPHY

Adorno, T.W.: 'Portrait of Walter Benjamin', *Prisms* (London: Neville Spearman, 1977), pp. 227–41.
Habermas, Jürgen: 'Walter Benjamin: consciousness-raising or rescuing critique' (Frankfurt: 1972), *Philosophical–Political Profiles* (Cambridge, Mass.: MIT Press, 1983), pp. 129–63.
Roberts, Julian: *Walter Benjamin* (London: Macmillan, 1982).
Smith, Gary, ed.: *Benjamin: Philosophy, Aesthetics, History* (Chicago, Ill.: University of Chicago Press, 1989).
Wolin, Richard: *Walter Benjamin: An Aesthetics of Redemption* (New York: Columbia University Press, 1982).

MARTIN DONOUGHO

Burke, Edmund (1729–97) Irish lawyer, politician and, through his criticism of the French Revolution, a founder of modern conservative thought. Born and educated in Ireland, Burke graduated from Trinity College, Dublin. His reputation chiefly rests upon his political career and writings: elected a Member of Parliament for the first time in the 1760s, he was the author of various trenchant political books and pamphlets, including the famous *Reflections on the Revolution in France* (1790). These have tended to overshadow his early *Philosophical Enquiry into the Origin of our Ideas of the Sublime and Beautiful*, a contribution to aesthetics which was originally published in 1757 and reissued two years later in an enlarged edition. Some of the views it contains were anticipated by Joseph Addison's 1712 *Spectator* articles on 'the pleasures of the imagination', and the introduction that Burke added to his second edition seems also to have been partly prompted by Hume's essay, 'On the standard of taste', which had recently appeared. None the less, the *Enquiry* was of importance in its own right. It attracted considerable attention in England, and an extended review by Moses Mendelssohn was instrumental in arousing a comparable interest in the book in Germany, where it impressed both Lessing and Kant.

In common with much eighteenth-century British work on aesthetics, Burke's investigation is essentially explanatory and genetic in character. A notable feature of his approach, however, lies in the manner in which he seeks to interpret aesthetic reactions in terms of certain universal instincts and sentiments that are basic to human nature. Drawing upon a division that had already acquired a limited currency but whose appeal his own essay did a great deal to strengthen, he distinguishes between pleasures of the kind intrinsic to the experience of beauty and the specific form of 'delight' that he attributes to experience of the sublime. The source of the former is to be found in the 'social passions', predominantly that of sex but also ones involving friendship and sympathy with others: the latter, by contrast, originates in our instinctual preoccupations with self-preservation, and turns 'mostly on pain and danger'. The *Enquiry* is largely taken up with showing how such primal proclivities operate to induce the two types of aesthetic response in question.

So far as the experience of the sublime is concerned, it is requisite that its objects be apprehended as being in some way 'terrible' and hence capable of instilling fear or awe. Burke recognizes, however, that it seems paradoxical to suggest that we can derive satisfaction from phenomena that threaten our lives or well-being. The answer he gives is that the experience is typically confined to situations in which we are not ourselves placed in dangerous circumstances and only have an 'idea' of these. Our sense of the fearful, in other words, is felt at a safe remove from the real thing; in consequence, it is able to tense and set in play 'the finer parts of the system' in a fashion that is stimulating and invigorating without being noxious. As opposed to cases where we suffer actual terror, we are here conscious of a 'sort of delightful horror', this being principally produced by images evocative of immense power or unfathomable dimensions.

Similar considerations are adduced when Burke comes to connect the awareness of beauty with such fundamental passions as love and sexuality. Just as the sublime is experienced when there is no question of our having to ward off or avoid a present danger, so experiences of the beautiful are distinguishable from those of 'desire or lust' which 'hurry us on' to the possession of certain coveted objects. Instead, the relevant sentiments are transposed to, and modified within, a setting where they exert no active influence; we are caused to respond to particular things in a purely contemplative frame of mind, the pleasure involved – unlike that of the sublime – deriving from their tendency to relax the 'fibres' and 'solids' of the whole system. As might be expected, the qualities Burke identifies as being especially well suited to effecting this happy outcome carry erotic overtones: he refers, for example, to smoothness (something explicitly attributed to the skins of 'fine women'), gradual variation of the kind exemplified by 'waving' and 'serpentine' lines, and delicacy or fragility.

In his treatment of beauty Burke is insistent that it requires 'no assistance from our reasoning' to appreciate it, and he goes to considerable if sometimes implausible lengths in denouncing classical theorists who invoked mathematical criteria of measurable proportion; proportion is 'a creature of the understanding', and as such it has no share in what properly belongs to 'the senses and imagination'. And a comparable emphasis upon the crucial importance of perceptual immediacy and imaginative potential is also apparent in his account of the sublime. At the same time, however, he is at pains to stress the distinctive role these play in the latter context. For there it is not formal grace and elegance, together with their sensuous associations, that elicit a psycho-physiological reaction. On the contrary, it is characteristic of sublime objects or works of art that they should often be dark in tone and rugged or indistinct in outline; so presented, they are experienced as mysterious and obscure, conveying intimations whose full import eludes our conscious grasp and whose very indeterminacy is apt to arouse sensations of uncertainty or apprehension.

In making such claims, Burke helped to alter and enlarge the boundaries implicit in the taste and critical canons of his period: he may be regarded, furthermore, as on occasions anticipating themes that were to figure prominently in the subsequent development of Romantic modes of thought. When he insists at one point in the *Enquiry* on the failure of clear ideas or imagery to communicate impressions of grandeur, and when he asserts at another that 'it is our ignorance of things that causes all our admiration and chiefly excites our passions', his remarks seem far removed in spirit from that of an age which – in art as elsewhere – put a premium on the ideals of perspicuous representation and rational intelligibility.

See also BEAUTY; SUBLIME.

WRITINGS

A Philosophical Enquiry into the Origin of our Ideas of the Sublime and Beautiful (London: 1757); 2nd edn, with intro. and notes, J.T. Boulton (London: Routledge & Kegan Paul, 1958).

BIBLIOGRAPHY

Ayling, S.: *Edmund Burke: His Life and Opinions* (London: John Murray, 1988).
Engell, J.: *The Creative Imagination: Enlightenment to Romanticism* (Cambridge, Mass.: Harvard University Press, 1981).
Monk, S.H.: *The Sublime* (Ann Arbor, Mich.: University of Michigan Press, 1960).
Wood, N.: 'The aesthetic dimension of Burke's political thought', *Journal of British Studies*, 4 (1964), 41–64.

PATRICK GARDINER

C

canon The *Concise Oxford Dictionary* defines a canon as 'n. Church decree; canon law, eccl. law; general law governing treatment of a subject; criterion; list of Bible books accepted by Church; list of recognized genuine works of a particular author' (5th edn). This discussion will focus primarily on the last definition.

It will be useful, first, to return to the etymological origins of the term, for the issue of the formation of canons, a highly contested area in aesthetic debate in the late twentieth century, continues to raise questions about the foundations of value, if not of truth. Engaged here, on the one hand, are critics who claim that aesthetic values are essential and universal and thus self-evidentially reflected in a broadly stable canon of great works of art. Some of them might argue that such values may be intuited in a subliminal way, but in their transcendence of or resistance to the categories of conceptual thought they must finally remain outside that which can be described. For others, aesthetic values arise out of modes of formal and structural complexity peculiar to works of high art and which guarantee the possibility of their endless interpretability. Although a range of divergent meanings may be attributed to such works in different ages, their essential trans-historical aesthetic value remains stable. Moreover, if it is a property of form it may be described through the vocabulary of close rhetorical analysis.

More recently, however, there has been a burgeoning challenge to such essentialist readings. The development of feminist, Marxist, postmodernist and post-colonial approaches to art, the sense of an increasing commodification of the aesthetic in Western societies, the notion of a multicultural society, of new artistic forms arising out of technologies such as video, computers and television, have all contributed to a new 'explosion' of the traditional identities of high art. These changes have given rise to a variety of arguments which represent the canon as an ideological formation bound up with relations of power within those institutions which are seen to regulate cultural value and notions of taste: the academy, the publishing industry, arts councils, schools, ministries for the arts.

These challenges to the earlier definition of the canon arise from a variety of ethical, political and epistemological positions, but tend to share certain broad perspectives. The canon is seen to function as an instrument of exclusion, through the construction of a value system which legitimates as good those artefacts which mediate or represent the identities of those with cultural power. According to this argument it is significant, for example, that the canon of English literature contains so few texts that do not represent black people as primitive savages: Caliban, the silent natives in Conrad's 'Heart of Darkness', the self-deluding Othello, appear in this guise. Even when the canon seems to be constructed in the terms of a liberal, representative democracy (the argument runs), the apparent pluralism is really a politically shaped consensus where dissenting voices are dealt with either through forms of incorporation (Brecht's Marxian 'epic theatre' being staged as bourgeois musical comedy) or strategies of exclusion through non-recognition.

One example here might be the tendency to establish the value of the aesthetic through some notion of disinterestedness or non-utilitarian 'purposeless purpose', and then to demote to the category of 'craft' those cultural forms such as ceramics or needlework which do not conform to this definition (and which tend to be practised by women). Feminist discourses have been powerful in exposing varieties of exclusion and devaluation, and also in revealing the ways in which discrimination has historically condoned the notion expressed by Charles Tansley in Virginia Woolf's novel *To the Lighthouse* (1927): 'Women can't write; women can't paint.' Henry James saw the contemporary flabbiness of the novel as bound up with the rise of the woman novelist and her gender-based inability to respond to the requirements of form. A feminist response to this might argue that women writers are thus excluded from the canon on the basis of non-aesthetic judgements disguised as aesthetic ones, or claim that the notion of form as an impersonally crafted structure is in itself a patriarchal construction which devalues feminine modes of expression.

The ecclesiastical use of the term 'canon' dates back to the fourth century, when it was the means of establishing which books of the Bible and writings of the Early Fathers were to be preserved as bearing the fundamental truths about Christianity. In the sense, the word was developed from the Greek term for a rod, reed, or instrument of measurement. In its aesthetic use, as already described, it is still bound up with the construction of an orthodoxy which keeps out heretics, but is no longer seen to provide a measurement of absolute truth. In its specific literary critical use, the term started to acquire its modern meanings in the eighteenth century with the establishment of a vernacular English literature, the appearance of scholarly editions of English writers, the rediscovery of Chaucer, and the publication of anthologies of English poets (most of them now unheard of). One current view is that the 'public sphere' which established literary value in the eighteenth century (the gentleman critic, the non-academic cultural journals such as the *Tatler* and the *Rambler*, the coffee house culture) has collapsed and that the legitimation of cultural value and the establishment of canons have now passed to the educational institution, and in particular to the academy and its professionalized body of critics.

The literary canon provokes so much debate because, since the nineteenth century, it has been viewed as the place where the language achieves its finest expression, so that questions about the canon are bound to involve issues concerning the construction of national identities, national supremacy, the spread of literacy and the possibility that, in an increasingly secular age, literary works may provide that cultural unity previously established through religion. Literary commentaries on texts become as important as the texts themselves in this process, for a work which appears to express the harmonic properties of organic form may be seen to provide a model for social and political consensus. What appear to be purely aesthetic reasons for designating canonical value may turn out to be political ones after all.

Debates about the canon emerged powerfully in the early part of this century. In 1919, T.S. Eliot published his essay 'Tradition and the individual talent', which tried to construct a notion of canon as both timeless and temporal. The argument is, in fact, close to the contemporary hermeneutic view that what we experience as valuable in the present has arisen through the values of the past, and therefore allows us not only to understand past works of art but to experience a continuity of value, even when we cannot step out of our own temporal situation to find universal terms for the *description* of this experience of value. A related idea was formulated by the formalist critic Roman Jakobson through the notion of 'shifting dominants': the idea that there is an entity called an aesthetic function, which is a timeless formal value inherent in all great works of art and which he understands in post-Kantian terms as a message focused on itself for its own sake. This function always coexists with other non-aesthetic functions, however, which situate the work in the historical world and may come to dominate at particular times. Thus, a work canonized in one age for formal aesthetic qualities may be regarded by a later age as more valuable for what it reveals about history or the life of its author. If such functions (referential, expressive) are seen as dominant, then the work's aesthetic function may not be recognized. Accordingly it may cease to be canonized, though it will not intrinsically lose its aesthetic value.

Throughout this century the canon has been reshaped and reformulated: Eliot, for example, included for the first time the metaphysical poets, F.R. Leavis excluded Shelley and was attacked by René Wellek for disguising his presuppositions and claiming to devalue Shelley on aesthetic grounds when really he was simply out of sympathy with the philosophical idealism of romanticism. But it was not until the 1960s that the most severe challenges to the canon as an ideological construction or conspiracy theory began to emerge. The impetus from this came from three broad areas: New Left interest in art and ideology, work on institutions developed by Michel Foucault, and the gathering poststructuralist critique of mimetic or expressive accounts of art which undermined notions of great art as reflecting permanent truths about human nature. The first and second together produced some powerful feminist analyses, which showed how women had been excluded from the means of production of art (barred from the academies, forced to publish under pseudonyms, prevented from participation in those modes of public life which provide important material for art, such as the new modes of citizenship represented in modernist art). They also revealed how academically formulated critical discourses of aesthetics had functioned to marginalize the experience of women, who had rarely thought of themselves in terms of 'autonomy' or 'impersonality' or even Romantic subjective creative genius.

The extent to which these challenges have undermined not only a sense of stable aesthetic value but even consensus about what constitutes literature is comically expressed in David Lodge's novel *Changing Places*, where his academic protagonist Philip Swallow imagines the publication of a volume of his examination papers – a work imagined to be of such high aesthetic value that it must totally confound all distinctions between art as a 'world-disclosing' discourse

and criticism as a 'problem-solving' one. It would be a work of 'totally revolutionary form . . . questions that would be miracles of condensation, eloquence and thoughtfulness, questions to read and re-read, questions to brood over, as pregnant and enjoyable as haikus, as memorable as proverbs, questions that would, so to speak, contain within themselves the ghostly, subtly suggested embryos of their own answers. *Collected Literary Questions*, by Philip Swallow' (Lodge, 1975, p. 12).

Lodge looks forward, uncannily, to the current postmodern preoccupations which have added a new dimension to debates about the canon: if ordinary language can be shown to be as dependent on rhetorical tropes as literary languages, are both not equally concerned with the construction of fictional worlds? If this is the case, how can the aesthetic be distinguished from the nonaesthetic? If the latter is collapsed into the former, how can any hierarchy of value be perceived within or imposed upon the aesthetic itself?

See also FEMINIST CRITICISM; MODERNISM AND POSTMODERNISM.

BIBLIOGRAPHY

Baldick, Chris: *The Social Mission of English Criticism 1848–1932* (Oxford: Clarendon Press, 1987).
Eagleton, Terry: *The Function of Criticism* (London: Verso, 1984).
Kermode, Frank: *The Classic* (London: Faber & Faber, 1975).
Lodge, David: *Changing Places* (London: Secker & Warburg, 1975).
Wolff, Janet: *The Social Production of Art* (London: Macmillan, 1975).

PATRICIA WAUGH

catharsis Greek: 'cleansing'; the term used by Aristotle for part of the psychological experience and effect of tragedy, and the most striking instance of an aesthetic concept whose history has proved utterly disproportionate to its origins. Its interpretation is fraught with acute difficulties. The final clause of the definition of tragedy in *Poetics* 6 describes the genre as 'achieving through pity and fear the catharsis of such emotions'. But the term 'catharsis' is not discussed or explained elsewhere in the work. In *Politics* 8.7, however, Aristotle says of music that it should be used 'both for education and for catharsis', and adds: 'What I mean by catharsis I shall state simply now, and will discuss it again more clearly in my treatment of poetry.'

He proceeds to refer to variations in the degree to which people are susceptible to emotions such as pity, fear and 'frenzy', and he notes how, in the case of the latter, there are religious ceremonies in which special music is used to arouse the emotion and to allow those gripped by it to find 'as it were a cure and a catharsis'. Other people can experience something of the same kind ('a certain catharsis and pleasurable alleviation'), to the extent to which they are given to the emotion. Whichever treatment of poetry is referred to in this passage of the *Politics* (part of the lost second book of the *Poetics* is a common hypothesis), it seems very likely that in his early (now lost) dialogue, *On Poets*, Aristotle discussed catharsis, stressed that it was an answer to Plato's qualms about the emotional experience of art, allowed for its occurrence in relation to comedy as well as tragedy, and linked it to an idea of a psychological balance or 'mean' (Janko, 1987, pp. 181–6).

The term 'catharsis' belongs to a word family which has many applications, among them the following: ritual purification from guilt or pollution, or for purposes of initiation; physiological evacuations and medical purges of various kinds, usually directed towards restoring a balance of humours; the physical cleansing or refinement of almost any object or entity that calls for it; the purification of soul or mind – for example by philosophy.

The common element in all these uses can be summed up by a phrase of Plato's (referring to one kind of catharsis): 'removing the bad, and leaving the good' (*Republic* 8.567c). But these facts about general Greek usage provide no ready solution to the problem of catharsis in Aristotle's *Poetics* 6; indeed, they have served to exacerbate argument over the source and nature of his metaphor. Above all, there has long been polarized disagreement between proponents of the translations 'purification' and 'purgation', the former mostly insisting on the religious uses of the term, the latter on the medical. But this sharp dichotomy is unprofitable: these two areas of practice are not wholly distinct in Greek culture, and Aristotle refers to *both* of them in *Politics* 8; in any case, the concepts of purgation and purification are not mutually exclusive.

The pertinence of the *Politics* passage is itself a cause of dispute. Two reasonable suppositions, disregard for either of which produces unattractively extreme interpretations, are: first, that the cross-reference to a treatment of poetry clearly shows that the passage has *some* relevance to the catharsis of the *Poetics*; second, that the particular context in the *Politics* rules out any simple equation between the two texts. What the two passages do have in common is a principle of psychological 'homeopathy': it is precisely *through* the experience of emotions that something happens *to* the emotions. This at once suggests that a crude sense of purgation or discharge, a mere outlet for the emotions, can hardly be Aristotle's point where poetry is concerned (though it may be closer to the pathological cases mentioned in the *Politics*).

This observation can be reinforced by the wider principle that the emotions are not intrinsically suspect for Aristotle; they are, in their proper function, a necessary and appropriate part of human responses to the world. The *Poetics* is predicated on the premise that tragedy arouses certain emotions in an intense yet justifiable form. Moreover, the experience of pity and fear, in this aesthetic context, is pleasurable (*Poetics* 14), and Aristotle's notion of aesthetic pleasure rests on a strongly cognitivist basis. It is still hard to be sure how catharsis was meant to be related to these factors of aesthetic understanding, emotion and pleasure (Lear, 1988), but there are grounds for integrating the concept into this larger configuration of ideas, rather than treating it as an appendage to the theory of tragedy. If we also accept the link between catharsis and the mean, we can infer, albeit sketchily, that Aristotle took the emotional experience of tragedy, and probably of epic and comedy too, to entail processes of psychological adjustment and refinement: art arouses powerful feelings that are motivated by, and grounded in, apt perceptions of the (fictional) world. And such refinement, in its implications at least, could not but have been a matter of ethical significance for a philosopher with the moral psychology of Aristotle.

The problems of evidence and interpretation that I have indicated make it unsurprising that catharsis has been so variously understood (Halliwell, 1986, appendix 5). From most sixteenth- and seventeenth-century neo-classicists the idea received a heavily moralized, somewhat Stoic reading: catharsis, mediated by the 'lessons' of tragedy, involved either an extirpation of dangerous passions, or an acquisition of emotional fortitude. But movement closer to the idea of psychological moderation or refinement was made by, among others, Heinsius and Lessing. It was against such views that Jacob Bernays reacted, in an immensely influential monograph of 1857: insisting on the idea of quasi-medical purgation, he treated catharsis as no more than a discharge of feeling. Catharsis as purgation consequently became an academic orthodoxy (now waning); it was even adhered to by, among others, Nietzsche, in a series of dismissive references to Aristotle's *Poetics*. Bernays' influence also encompassed the psychologist Breuer, and, partly through Breuer, Freud (who married Bernays' niece) (see Sulloway, 1979, pp. 55–7). It is the entanglement of catharsis with psychoanalytic ideas that has helped to give the term a ubiquitous currency in the present century: one word in the *Poetics* has been transformed into a shibboleth of both popular aesthetics and popular psychology; and in the process it has acquired a bewilderingly protean character.

See also ARISTOTLE; PLATO.

BIBLIOGRAPHY

Aristotle: *The Poetics of Aristotle*, trans. S. Halliwell (London: Duckworth, 1987).

Aristotle: *Politics*, trans. C. Everson (Cambridge: Cambridge University Press, 1988).

Halliwell, S.: *Aristotle's Poetics* (London: Duckworth, 1986).

Janko, R.: *Aristotle Poetics* (Indianapolis: Hackett, 1987).

Lear, J.: 'Katharsis', *Phronesis*, 33 (1988), 297–326.

Nussbaum, M. C.: *The Fragility of Goodness: Luck and Ethics in Greek Tragedy and Philosophy* (Cambridge: Cambridge University Press, 1986), pp. 378–91.

Plato: *Republic*, trans. H. D. P. Lee (Harmondsworth: Penguin, 1955).

Schaper, E.: *Prelude to Aesthetics* (London: George Allen & Unwin, 1968), pp. 101–18, 158–67.

Sulloway, F.J.: *Freud: Biologist of the Mind* (London: André Deutsch, 1979).

STEPHEN HALLIWELL

Cavell, Stanley (1926–) American philosopher of language, literature, and film at Harvard University. Cavell's contributions to aesthetics move in two directions: (1) towards his own guiding project of diagnosing and undermining scepticism, which he characterizes as an issue not only for philosophy but also for poetry, drama and film; and (2) towards issues and problems within specific fields of criticism and within works of art or literature. These directions in turn contain prospects for a unity that helps to structure – though it cannot eliminate – the inveterate plurality of Cavell's investigations. Ultimately, this unity derives from the possibility that the various versions of scepticism are, in fact, various guises of a single, self-inflicted threat to human existence. He characterizes the threat of scepticism as the most recent and perhaps the most destructive version of the ancient wish to escape the human being's situation within language and history. What philosophy knows as Cartesian or Humean scepticism is only the most intellectually refined expression of this sceptical wish.

63

Cavell's most detailed effort to undermine epistemological scepticism takes the form of a reading of Wittgenstein (Cavell, 1979). As in Wittgenstein, the terms of Cavell's investigations bear obvious affinities to some of the crucial enterprises and concepts of aesthetics. He inherits and modifies the enormous weight that Wittgenstein attaches to the possibilities and necessities of human judgement, including features of what other philosophers take to be its mere contingencies: for instance, its agreements, its evaluations, its publicness and its persistent privacies. Cavell goes on to characterize the philosophical power of Wittgenstein's *Philosophical Investigations* as resting on written recollections and achievements of the human voice in its most ordinary settings. He thus isolates a dimension of Wittgenstein – and perhaps of philosophizing as such – that is potentially of special interest to students of aesthetics.

Cavell characterizes scepticism as embodying a wish to repudiate the 'givenness' of language and the apparent arbitrariness in the fact that human beings must express themselves in order to be understood. Accordingly, he characterizes as sceptical the various efforts to reconstruct human language and communication on a more 'rational' or more 'justified' foundation, one which would avoid the need for the less tidy and more disruptive aspects of ordinary speech. The overcoming of scepticism will occur not as a single theoretical event but as the repeated, practical efforts to recover human expressiveness from its suppression in philosophical and anti-philosophical theorizing. Some philosophers have found Cavell's responses to scepticism to constitute a merely literary solution to an intellectual problem. Students of aesthetics might follow Cavell and Wittgenstein in exploring a less reductive sense of human expression and hence a more interesting access to the literary conditions of philosophical questioning.

Cavell persistently tracks something like an aesthetic dimension of judgement and expression throughout the fields of epistemology, morality and the philosophy of language. It is therefore not surprising that his work does not leave much room for a set of intrinsically aesthetic problems, which might be treated in isolation from the rest of philosophy. Furthermore, it is of the essence of his approach to aesthetic questions that his work attempts to take on the issues of the critics that matter the most to him. Cavell's primary concern is to address the insights and mystifications of those critics, readers and viewers (himself included) who have already felt the pull of the particular work or experience in question. His investigations often move directly from the individual work (for instance, of Shakespeare or of film) to the issues of philosophy. Those who have felt the power and the exactness of his readings are unlikely to see the pertinence of the more generalized issues of academic aesthetics. Nevertheless, it is possible to specify some lines of investigation in Cavell's work that either belong explicitly to aesthetics or else can be seen to bear on the wider issues of literature and interpretation that increasingly occupy the attention of philosophers concerned with the arts. These aesthetic investigations can be divided into six major segments.

(1) The essays collected as his first book (Cavell, 1976a) include his most explicit treatments of specific aesthetic questions about intentions, pleasure, metaphor, musical form and 'significance', literary or dramatic genres and artistic media, and the relationship of aesthetics to criticism. This first book also includes extended instances of his critical activities (climactically, his essays on Samuel Beckett and *King Lear*), as well as a sort of Wittgensteinian proposal for the centrality of aesthetics within a newly self-critical practice of philosophy.

(2) Cavell's investigations of Shakespeare (Cavell, 1987) have secured him a place as one of the leading literary critics of the day. He continues to delineate his sense of the isomorphism between the convulsions of philosophy inaugurated in Descartes' methodologies of representative self-doubt and Shakespeare's preoccupation with the catastrophes in human knowing and with the traumatic constructions of the modern world.

Perhaps because of their resistance to regarding a work of literature as harbouring anything like the propensity for rigorous thought, Anglo-American philosophers have found this side of Cavell's project to be essentially inaudible.

(3) His work on film begins with an exploration of the relations between the photographic basis of the movies and their specific incarnation of narrative possibilities (Cavell, 1971; 1981). He comes to focus on the possibilities contained within a single genre – what he calls 'the comedy of remarriage' – and his investigations continue with a more recent series of articles on what he has dubbed 'the melodrama of the unknown woman'.

(4) His work on the relation of literary Romanticism to the critique and transformation of Kant begins with a book on Thoreau (Cavell, 1981a) and becomes a central theme of his Beckman lectures (reprinted in Cavell, 1988). The issue of Kant's inheritance is at the centre of his continuing encounters with Emerson. His stress on an Emersonian, anti-metaphysical strand of moral perfectionism – stretching from certain regions of Kant to Wittgenstein and Heidegger – leads him to his most prolonged, recent confrontation with American philosophy, as represented by John Rawls and Saul Kripke (Cavell, 1990).

(5) Again beginning with Thoreau, Cavell has steadily intensified his excavation of a problematic of reading, with a consequent emphasis on the fact of writing as a source and emblem of human activity and originality (Cavell, 1979; 1988; 1990).

(6) Finally, there is an increasingly explicit involvement with psychoanalysis that needs to be distinguished from other contemporary approaches. Cavell treats Freud's work neither as a perfected methodology of interpretation nor as the enlargement of our narrative capacity for self-dramatization. In Cavell's account the goal of a psychoanalytic reading is, above all, a better understanding of our prior seduction or bewitchment by the work, an understanding which frees us for a still more unsheltered engagement with the work's significance and fascination.

Cavell's use of psychoanalysis to create the freedom for a further encounter with the work can thus stand as an expression of one of his earliest motives for thinking about the arts. Already in his concern with the inescapability of intentions in our experience of art and in his related struggles against false pictures of the 'inside' and 'outside' of the work, Cavell has sought to block the idea that the significance of art can be appreciated from some safely externalized distance. Here, as elsewhere, he sees philosophy as crystallizing the human inclination to imagine ourselves exempt from the seductions of experience on the grounds that we are capable of analysing it. But philosophy is also a name for the place in which we might learn that there is no such place of exemption. There is no place from which to learn the significance of human works and expressions, apart from submitting to the specific demands they make on our capacities for understanding and response.

In Cavell's account, the task of aesthetics is to maintain the still more basic and ineradicable demand that we submit ourselves to the experiences that we are drawn to learn from. (This is his version of Kant's demand that we submit the object to our own eyes, for our own judgement.) But this thought goes together with his insistence that we bear in mind those ordinary surfaces of words and concepts and events, without which the struggle with the depths of our experience of a work is bound to lose its sense.

See also CRITICISM; MORALITY AND ART; PSYCHOANALYSIS AND ART; WITTGENSTEIN.

WRITINGS

Must We Mean What We Say? (New York: 1969); 2nd edn (Cambridge: Cambridge University Press, 1976).

The World Viewed: Reflections on the Ontology of Film (New York: 1971); enlarged edn (Cambridge, Mass.: Harvard University Press, 1976b).

The Claim of Reason: Wittgenstein, Scepticism, Morality and Tragedy (Oxford: Oxford University Press, 1979).

The Senses of Walden: An Expanded Edition (New York, 1972); (San Francisco: North Point Press, 1981a).

Pursuits of Happiness: The Hollywood Comedy of Remarriage (Cambridge, Mass.: Harvard University Press, 1981b).

Disowning Knowledge: In Six Plays of Shakespeare (Cambridge: Cambridge University Press, 1987).

In Quest of the Ordinary: Lines of Skepticism and Romanticism (Chicago, Ill.: University of Chicago Press, 1988).

Conditions Handsome and Unhandsome: The Constitution of Emersonian Perfectionism, Carus Lectures, 1988 (Chicago, Ill.: University of Chicago Press, 1990).

BIBLIOGRAPHY

Cohen, Ted and Guyer, Paul, eds: *Pursuits of Reason: Essays in Honor of Stanley Cavell* (Lubbock: Texas Tech Press, 1992).

Fischer, Michael: *Stanley Cavell and Literary Skepticism* (Chicago, Ill.: University of Chicago Press, 1989).

Fleming, Richard and Payne, Michael, eds: *The Senses of Stanley Cavell* (Lewisburg: Bucknell University Press, 1989).

Smith, Joseph and Kerrigan, William, eds: *Images in Our Souls: Cavell, Psychoanalysis and Cinema* (Baltimore, Md.: Johns Hopkins University Press, 1987).

TIMOTHY GOULD

censorship   In its broadest sense, the term is applied to any kind of suppression or regulation, by government or other authority, of a writing or other means of expression, based on its content. The main concern with censorship applies to kinds of work intended for sale, display or other manner of publication, though the term has been applied to the official activity of removing sensitive information from private letters written home by troops serving in war. It seems that the activity has at least to be publicly recognized in order to count as censorship, and interference with the mails by the secret police, or covert intimidation of editors, would be examples of something else. Accordingly, any censorship implies a public claim of legitimacy for the type of control in question.

The most drastic methods of control involve *prior restraint*: a work is inspected before it is published, and publication may be forbidden, or permitted only after changes have been made. Traditional absolutist regimes sought to control book publication by these means, and legal procedures to the same general effect, for the control of material affecting national security, still exist in many states. Until 1968, theatrical performances in England were controlled in this way by a court official, the Lord Chamberlain, whose staff monitored scripts before production, would demand changes on a variety of grounds (including disrespect to the monarchy), and attended performances to see that their instructions were being observed. In many jurisdictions, cinema films are inspected by some official agency before release, and its powers may include that of suppressing some or all of a film. However, the emphasis of these inspections has increasingly moved from suppression to labelling, the agency not so much censoring films as classifying them by their suitability for young people. (In Britain the relevant body has recently changed its name to express this.)

Prior restraint is essential when censorship is motivated by official secrecy: once the information is out, the point of the censorship is lost (the British government attracted ridicule in the 1980s by trying to ban a book on security grounds which had already been published elsewhere). There are other aims of censorship, however, including those most relevant to aesthetics, which do not necessarily demand prior restraint. If a work is thought objectionable on grounds of indecency, evil moral character or its possible social effects, the suppression of it after publication may still have a point, in limiting people's exposure to it. Actions of this kind, and laws under which they can be carried out, are also regarded as examples of censorship. This form of censorship avoids some of the objections to prior restraint – notably, its secrecy – and it is in relation to this kind of censorship that questions of principle are now normally discussed. It is important that censorship in this form still aims at suppression. Schemes of restriction or zoning, which require, for instance, that pornographic materials be sold only in certain shops and only to adults, are analogous to film classification, and are to be distinguished from censorship, strictly understood.

In 1774 Lord Mansfield said 'Whatever is *contra bonos mores et decorum* the principles of our laws prohibit, and the King's Court as the general censor and guardian of the public morals is bound to restrain and punish.' Although this dictum was approvingly mentioned by another English law lord as recently as 1962, few now would offer quite such a broad justification for censorship. In part, this is because of doubts about what 'the public morals' are, and by whom they are to be interpreted: pluralism, scepticism, sexual toleration and doubts about the social and psychological insight of judges have played their part in weakening confidence in the notion. A more basic point is that, even where there is a high degree of moral consensus on a given matter, it remains a question of what that may mean for the law, and of what, if anything, can count as a good reason for using the law in an attempt to suppress deviant opinions or offensive utterances. Liberal theories claim that freedom of expression is a right, which can be curtailed only to prevent serious and identifiable harms. This is, in effect, the conclusion reached by John Stuart Mill in his very influential defence of freedom of expression, though he himself did not theoretically favour the notion of a right. Other liberals who are better disposed to that notion insist, further, that the harms which justify suppression must take the more particular form of a threatened violation of someone's rights.

A very strong version of such principles is embodied in United States law, which has interpreted the First Amendment to the Constitution ('Congress shall make no law . . . abridging the freedom of speech or of the press') in such a way as to make censorship on any grounds very difficult. Mr Justice Holmes in 1919 produced an influential formula. 'The question in every case is whether the words used are used in such circumstances and are of such a nature as to create a clear and present danger that they will bring about the substantive evils that Congress has a right to prevent'; and restrictions in such terms have been taken to protect even overtly racist demonstrations, let alone publications. The 'clear and present danger' test is not used with regard to pornography, but the effect of Supreme Court decisions in that area has been that, at most, hard-core pornography can be suppressed. In many parts of the USA, all that the law enforces are zoning restrictions.

English law allows greater powers of suppression than that of the USA: publications designed to arouse racial hatred, for instance, may be illegal, and the same is true in other jurisdictions. In the case of pornography, the main concept used in English law is *obscenity*; in a formula inherited from a judgement of Chief Justice Cockburn in 1868, the principal statute defines a publication as obscene if it has a 'tendency to deprave or corrupt' those exposed to it. This professedly causal concept of obscenity implies that the rationale of the law is to be found in the harmful consequences of permitting a particular publication. However, as the House of Lords has itself observed, the courts could not apply this formula in a literal sense, and do not really try to do so. No expert evidence is allowed on the matter of causation, and in practice the question is whether a jury or a magistrate finds the material sufficiently offensive. As critics have pointed out, this not only makes the application of the law arbitrary, but reopens the question of its justification. As opposed to the principle that rights to free speech may be curtailed by appealing to harms in the particular case – the principle which Holmes' 'clear and present danger' test expresses in a very strict form – the mere fact that a work is found deeply offensive is likely to justify its suppression only to those who think that it is the business of the law to express any correct, or at least shared, moral attitude.

There has been a great deal of controversy about the effects of pornographic and violent publications, and a variety of anecdotal, statistical and experimental evidence has been deployed in attempts to find out whether there is a causal link between such publications and some identifiable class of social harms, such as sexual crime. It is perhaps not surprising that such studies are inconclusive, and more recent advocates of censorship, such as some radical feminists, have moved away from thinking of censorship in this area on the model of a public health measure, and concentrate on the idea that certain publications unacceptably express a culture of sexual oppression. This approach tends to treat legal provisions against pornography as like those against publications that endorse racial discrimination. In some systems, of course, this would still not make such censorship constitutional, even if the problem can be solved of making the provisions determinate enough for them not to be void on account of uncertainty.

Censorship laws typically encounter problems about artistic merit. The English law is not alone in allowing a 'public good defence', which permits acquittal of a work that possesses serious aesthetic, scientific or other such merits. (In English law a jury who acquit in a case where this defence has been made are not required to say whether they found the work not obscene, or found it meritorious although it was obscene.) Provisions of this kind have certainly helped to permit the publication of serious works such as *Ulysses* and *Lady Chatterley's Lover*, which were previously banned; but there are difficulties of principle, which have been clearly illustrated in the English practice of allowing expert testimony on the merits of the works under prosecution. Besides the inherent obscurity of weighing artistic merit against obscenity, and the fact that evidence bearing on this has to be offered under the conditions of legal examination, the process makes the deeply scholastic assumption that the merit of a given work must be recognizable to experts at the time of its publication. Moreover, the works that can be defended under such a provision must presumably be meritorious, which implies that they are to some considerable degree successful; but if a law is to protect creative activity from censorship, it needs to protect the right to make experiments, some of which will be very unsuccessful.

The idea of making *exceptions* to a censorship law for works with artistic merit seems, in fact, essentially confused. If one believes that censorship on certain grounds is legitimate, then if a work of artistic merit does fall under the terms of the law, it is open to censorship: its merits, indeed, may make it more dangerous, on the grounds in question, than other works. If one believes in freedom for artistic merit, then one believes in freedom, and accepts censorship only on the narrowest of grounds.

See also MORALITY AND ART; PORNOGRAPHY.

BIBLIOGRAPHY

Devlin, Lord: *The Enforcement of Morals* (Oxford: Oxford University Press, 1959).
Dworkin, Ronald: *A Matter of Principle* (Cambridge, Mass.: Harvard University Press, 1985), pt 6.
Hart, H.L.A.: *Law, Liberty and Morality* (Oxford: Oxford University Press, 1963).
Mill, John Stuart: *On Liberty* (1859) in *Three Essays* (Oxford: Oxford University Press, 1975).

BERNARD WILLIAMS

Chinese and Japanese aesthetics   The arts of China and Japan share with each other many features and in many respects are rooted in common philosophical traditions, but any particular example will be distinctly Chinese or Japanese, making it difficult to speak definitively of East Asian aesthetics. Here is described what can fairly be regarded as the common ground, and major monuments of Chinese and Japanese critical writing are introduced in order to refine the understanding of each culture's unique aesthetic.

THE FOUNDATIONS OF EAST ASIAN AESTHETICS

In East Asia, graphic arts, letters and music

have been nurtured by millennia of practice and description within relatively compact and continuous educated elites. Poetry, painting and music have attained high levels of refinement, and artists pursue their work with a profound consciousness of the traditions in which they function. Yet in the finest arts the highest ideal is a seemingly artless spontaneity that achieves a direct and untutored expression of beauty and emotion and appropriateness. These in their aggregate are called the Tao, or 'Way', a construct that is often the ultimate referent of art and art criticism, not to mention the well led life itself.

Broadly speaking, aesthetic sensibilities incline towards the understated, the evocative, the lyrical, with an interest in negative capability and quiet surface. The ideal in painting is the hidden and obscure, in music the inaudible, in acting the motionless, in poetry the unstated. Painting is best in monochrome, music best in song for one or two, poetry best in the fleeting sigh of the brief lyric. The aesthete refines the human capability to live artfully, to create art and to perceive the true and beautiful in art and nature – something always there, but rarely perceived.

East Asian traditions are rich in the achievements of artistic geniuses, yet there is little premium put on individuality and the expression of individual, personal feeling. In contrast to post-Romantic interests in the West, there is little mention of originality in the traditional discourse. Excellence resides in perfection of skills, mastery of the principles of an art genre, and submission to the inner order of the world. Artistic geniuses are praised for 'attaining the spiritual', 'being adept in all elements of the Six Laws', 'being perfect in the subtleties of form', 'achieving resonance and grace', and the like. Yet eccentricity is an ideal in life and art, and praiseworthy departures from the authority of past masters are related to expressions of eccentricity.

That is to say, the concept of innovation resides more in the personality and life of the artist than in his art. This reflects a general sense that the artists and their efforts are a more crucial locus of the aesthetic than the outcome – that is, the performance or objects themselves. Hence, the focus of much writing on aesthetics is on innate endowments, inner self-cultivation, reclusive lifestyles and the interactions between the artist and his media and between the artist and the outside world.

The major religious and philosophical traditions of Confucianism, Buddhism, Taoism, and Shintoism have all contributed to definitions of the Way and to the aesthetics of East Asia. In China, Taoism was often identified by poets and painters as their guiding doctrine, although Confucianism defined the role of art and culture in society. By the middle dynasties in China, a fusion of Taoist and Buddhist sensibilities emerged in the form of Chan Buddhism, which was transported to Japan as Zen Buddhism. Zen in Japan is most often cited as the source of ideas and expressions in aesthetic practice and discourse, although Shintoism is intimately implicated in the appreciation of nature.

There are no extended statements on aesthetics *per se* in the traditional literatures. It is from three types of writings that critical aesthetic theory is gleaned. Critics and philosophers have focused on particular arts and have written tracts that are evaluating, taxonomic, descriptive and prescriptive. Typically, one finds a discussion of twenty-four types of poetry, three grades of poets, nine grades of drama, eight faults of calligraphy, five defects of writing or six laws of painting. Historians and philosophers have written anecdotal sketches of artists, real and imagined, and touched upon questions of genius, perception and meaning. Artists themselves have contributed treatises and jottings that present metaphoric and provocative visions of the creative process and the constituents of value and quality in art.

Concern with aesthetic issues permeates much of the huge canon of Chinese and Japanese literature, in genres as diverse as medical guides, calendric treatises, historical biographies and novels of manners. In the written traditions of the major Asian cultures, a basic terminology and conceptual framework interconnects the discourses of moral and natural philosophy, statecraft, medicine, literature, painting, calligraphy and drama.

THE CHINESE ON ART AND LITERATURE

Chinese philosophy of art emerges before the first dynasty (third century BC) from an embroidery of early Confucian and Taoist writings that focused primarily on music and ritual. Confucianism addressed the arts in the context of governance and society, self-cultivation and public morality. Taoism, in contrast, focused on life in nature, life span, and the mysterious principles of the cosmos. In Confucianism, music, which included poetry and dance, was not only a force shaping individuals and society, but also a measure of their virtue. Many thinkers contributed to a debate on the connections between outside influences and feelings or perceptions. In Taoism, a central metaphor for an artless and wholly natural aesthetic was the musical pipings of heaven and earth, the excitation of tree hollows, caves, clouds and the like that constructed primal nature as a great organ, a system revealing the measure of its own processes and opening channels for communication with powers far greater than humankind. In both there were discussions of art, of self-cultivation and of the Way. The philosophical writings of major and minor schools and the bits and pieces of early mythology show an intense interest in the nature of representation, the relationship between linguistic and graphic signs and their referents, and systems or analogies that linked the diverse phenomena of life in a common dynamic process.

Until the third century AD, the discussion of art in China concentrated on the public and didactic. A positivist concept of the mind and the phenomenal world supported a belief that arts and their impact were objectifiable and generalizable across society and across time. In the early dynasties, musical activity was analysed and classified in phases of the vast scheme of correlates that occupied early court thinkers. Court ritualists specified pitches and performances according to a matrix of ritual calendrics, pitch names and scale names, directions and other correlates.

In the third century, beginning with the *Wenfu* ('Rhymeprose on Literature') by Lu Ji (261–303), a more mystical argument turned attention, on the one hand, to aesthetic processes, individual mental processes and their interaction with the outside world and on the other, to aesthetic traditions and learning. Creation of art was related to the Way of the Taoists, the ever-changing and infinitely subtle Way that became thereafter an inseparable element in art and art criticism in traditional China.

In his preface, Lu Ji talks about using an axe to make an axe handle–having the model always close at hand. Only poetry has the descriptive power to talk about poetry, so it is in verse that he explores his dozen topics – from motive, to meditation, to the working process, the poet views the expanse of the world, takes nurture from the wisdom of the past, attunes himself to the processes of nature and passing time, savours the perfection of beauty, and then sets brush to paper.

Lu Ji is concerned with excellence, and he explores the means of expression and the value of art. He likens artistic work to that of the carpenter, whose tape must fit precisely. To define five defects of poetry, he borrows a set of terms from earlier discussions of music and constructs a framework to judge poetry. These terms include 'correspondence' (or 'response', 'resonance'), 'harmony', 'gravity of feeling', 'restraint' and 'artful appeal'. These five function in dynamic balance, the strength of one constraining the excesses of the others, and thus they contribute to a prescription for the maintenance of aesthetic tension among competing demands in the making of art. Inspiration Lu Ji describes as 'moments when the mind and the outside world hold perfect communion'. Likened to lightning, these moments engender a powerful order that encompasses all things and overcomes chaos.

The *Wenxin diaolong* (*The Literary Mind and the Carving of Dragons*) by Liu Xie (465–523) is highly evocative exploration, in fifty essays, of literature and the literary artist. It is considered by some to be the greatest Chinese work on aesthetics. The first half begins systematically with a discussion of the 'original

Way' and the nature of sagehood and textual traditions, then delineates major genres of writing. The second half considers questions of imagination, emotion, content, ornamentation, devices, craft, media, composition, beauty, defects, cultivation, timeliness, objectivity and audience response. The vast scope of Liu Xie's work is realized with a vision and language that are sweeping and inclusive, highly refined and charged with ambiguity. There is no significant piece of criticism in any field of art subsequently that has not been profoundly indebted to Liu Xie; very few do not allude to him explicitly.

Liu Xie's essay on imagination and the arts is one of the most powerful and definitive in the *Wenxin diaolong*. He names imagination 'spiritual thought' or 'spirited thought', and begins with the couplet;

> The ancients said, 'One's form may be at sea, while one's mind resides under the towers of Wei.' This is speaking about 'spirited thought'. Literary thought is of far-ranging spirit.

He proceeds to recount in exquisite detail the first stirrings in the creative act, a process of congealing, concentration, tapping back into the deep springs of the past and ranging across the vast space of the world. In Liu Xie's vision, creation is an interaction among external stimuli that bear on the senses, a highly configured and cultivated mind, and a complex legacy of inherited languages and forms, all pivoting on the linchpin of artistic intent. Liu Xie's work proceeds with intricate and interlocked workings of inner and outer, mind and matter, objects and images, stillness and motion, and a host of other dialectic or dyadic pairs that place the artist and his work within the commodious space of a dynamic and organic cosmos.

Miscellaneous anecdotes and observations about painting are found in the classical philosophers and scattered about Han dynasty texts, but it is in the fourth–sixth centuries AD that key figures like Gu Kaizhi (345–406), Zong Bing (375–443) and Xie He (active c.500–35?) write descriptively about particular painters and their art, technique, and the relationship between painting and the Way. As was the case with literary criticism, these writers simultaneously have, on the one hand, an interest in a rather mechanical classification of their predecessors and on the other, a highly evocative and near-mystic discourse about the creative process and the relationship between mind and external reality. Xie He assigns previous painters to six classes of excellence, characterizing each with a pithy description of strengths and weaknesses. He lays out six laws of painting that are recited again and again in subsequent criticism. Zong Bing, a recluse and lay member of a Buddhist community, explores more abstractly the nature of representation, noting that at a distance the massive Kunlun Mountains could be encompassed by inch-small pupils, and the massive central peak could be captured on a square inch of silk.

These early works lay the conceptual and terminological foundation for a robust and voluminous canon of writing on arts and letters in China that continued uninterrupted until the twentieth century. In this complex tradition, which reached a peak of achievement in the Song dynasty (960–1279), a wide range of interests and issues were developed. Many writers continued to explore the dialectics of opposing concepts – substance versus ornament, outer beauty versus inner reality, formal likeness versus inner resonance. Others continued the tradition of ranking and critiquing individual painters and writers, comparing the best artists to the ancient sages, past masters, spirits and ghosts, or to the Way itself. Literati–artists, who themselves were involved in at least the three arts of poetry, painting and calligraphy, wrote of the relationship of the three and established themselves as arbiters of culture and of taste. Still others returned to the early practice of delineating systems of correspondence, symbolism and analogy, providing keys to interpreting the arts and a corresponding reality.

THE JAPANESE ON DRAMA, LITERATURE, AND CULTURE

The history of Japanese aesthetics in texts is

considerably shorter than that of China. The founding classics of Japanese literary art date back as early as the sixth century AD. By the Heian period (794–1185), poetry anthologies, diaries, collections of tales and lengthy narratives of court life provide a record of a highly aestheticized culture among Japan's aristocracy. Refined taste was demonstrated in food and drink, fragrances and dress, and daily engagements with poetry, word games, rituals and contents. Art was an inseparable part of daily life, and daily activities were shaped by a considerable range of aesthetic contraints, in effect shading the line between art and life. In some important collections of poetry, particularly poetry written in Chinese, the Heian saw the appearance of aesthetic notions that echo Liu Xie.

Centuries later, Zeami Motokiyo (1363–1443) emerged to become the most celebrated theorist of Japanese aesthetics. Zeami was a *nō* theatre performer and playwright who also wrote several key treatises in which he discussed the foundation of the art. The *nō* theatre itself was taken by Zeami and his father from a folk tradition to a highly literate, refined, aesthetic form that remains alive today. In many respects, the *nō* theatre through its ambiguous and polysemous poetry realizes in an aesthetic vein the subtle and mysterious doctrine of Zen Buddhism. Zeami's treatises are written in a highly evocative and poetic style, illustrated with metaphor and literary figures rather than the precise expository style of, for instance, Aristotle's *Poetics*.

Zeami's statements on aesthetics return frequently to a description of process or sequence in an aesthetic event. He divides the *nō* performance into three stages, *jo, ha* and *kyū*, and emphasizes the patterning, timing and rhythm of these, arguing that they are processes of nature as well as processes of art. He stresses that the audience and its response are as integral to art as the playwright, actor or painter. He calls attention to the moments of 'non-action' and silence, a concept derived from philosophical Taoism, that exist between the audible and visible songs and dances of the *nō* performer. In one celebrated *nō* play, the protagonist sits motionless at the front of the stage for the first hour of the performance.

The central concept in Zeami's treatises is *yūgen*, a grace or elegance that encompasses a sense of refinement, idealization and contrast. It is borrowed from Chinese philosophical texts where it pointed to the abstruse and mysterious aspects of nature and life. *Yūgen* embraced the dynamics of contrast. The central metaphor was a flower blooming on a rock or a dead tree. Much of the discussion of performance in the *nō*, including issues like training, imitation, verisimilitude and balance, is related to a metaphor of the flower. Various levels of attainment in the arts are named after flowers. The ultimate of the nine levels of the 'art of the flower of tranquillity', described as 'packing snow in a silver bowl', yielding a pure, white, frosted image, reflective but diffused, eternal yet fleeting.

Zeami draws a contrast between substance and function, compared to a flower and its scent or the moon and its light. This is subsequently related to an artist's skill, which Zeami relates to a state of self-understanding. The emphasis is always on function, giving rise throughout Japanese arts to a taste for the minimal. The actor is not to imitate real life in an obvious way, but rather to capture the essential spirit of the role played. Poetry forms are generally short, as are play scripts. The temperament is lyrical rather than epic. The highest examples of graphic art are understated in composition; suggestive rather than explicit; evocative and subtle. The most elegant calligraphy is a few bold strokes in the abbreviated 'grass' style that, in their severely compact expression, convey a formidable strength.

The highest art gives rise to feelings of *aware*, or melancholy elegance. Beneath a courtly exterior, a gentle humour and a gentle melancholy fill the pages of traditional Japanese literature. Artists focus on the moment the cherry blossom falls from the tree, the moment of passing of love and beauty, the touching of love by death. The great heros are those who show nobility at the moment of grand failure.

Among the most influential contemporary

statements on aesthetics in Japan is the concise work of the great novelist Jun'ichirō Tanizaki (1886–1965), *In Praise of Shadows*. It is ostensibly a conversational commentary on Japanese architecture. The initial discussion of the difficulties in stringing electrical wires and water pipes through a 'house in pure Japanese style' expands to encompass a provocative sketch of Japanese aesthetics and its encounter with the outside. Tanizaki applauds the sensitive use of shadow, the darkness in which the *nō* is shrouded, the beauty of things that gleam and glow in the darkness, the evils of excessive illumination, and the blackening of the courtesan's teeth and her green-black lipstick. They are all part of what he calls the oriental 'propensity to seek beauty in darkness' (Tanizaki, 1977, p. 30). His conversation turns as well to the luxurious palates of poor country people, Albert Einstein in Kyoto, the alluring hands of the Kabuki actor, the sheen of antiquity and the glow of grime on an ancient sculpture, and the notion of cleanliness in a Japanese toilet. The book is a realization of its own aesthetic ideals – brief, evocative avoiding definition and declaration, lurking in the shadows of philosophical discourse.

Considering East Asian arts as a whole, we can say that the most refined arts operate in the context of a well integrated, holistic view of nature and humankind. In contrast to major traditions in the West, society itself is a part of nature, a piece of a large and organic whole. The creation of art and the appreciation of art are not artificial and unnatural. In Chinese and Japanese, the terms used to discuss literature, painting, calligraphy, drama and music are unlike the English term 'art' with its relation to the matrix of terms 'artificial', 'artifice', 'artful', 'artefact' and 'artificer'. On the contrary, aesthetic undertaking itself is a natural and organic activity for humankind, a part of self-realization and self-refinement, practices that resonate with things in nature, proper adaptations to the physical and social landscape; in short, an orientation, a commitment and a process that brings both the creator and audience close to the Way.

BIBLIOGRAPHY

Birch, Cyril, ed.: *Anthology of Chinese Literature* (New York: Grove Press, 1965).

Bush, Susan and Hsio-yen Shih, eds: *Early Chinese Texts on Painting* (Cambridge, Mass.: Harvard University Press, 1985).

Bush, Susan and Murck, Christian, eds: *Theories of the Arts in China* (Princeton, NJ: Princeton University Press, 1983).

DeWoskin, Kenneth J.: *A Song for One or Two: Music and the Concept of Art in Early China* (Ann Arbor, Mich.: Centre for Chinese Studies, 1984).

Keene, Donald, ed.: *Anthology of Japanese Literature* (New York: Grove Press, 1960).

Keene, Donald: *The Pleasures of Japanese Literature* (New York: Columbia University Press, 1988).

Li Tse-hou: *The Path of Beauty: A Study of Chinese Aesthetics* (Beijing: Morning Glory Press, 1988).

Liu Xie: trans. Vincent Yu-chang Shih, *The Literary Mind and the Carving of Dragons: A Study of Thought and Pattern in Chinese Literature* (New York: Columbia University Press, 1959).

Sullivan, Michael: *The Birth of Landscape Painting in China* (London: Routledge & Kegan Paul, 1962).

Tanizaki, Jun'ichirō: trans. Thomas Harper and Edward G. Seidensticker, *In Praise of Shadows* (New Haven, Conn.: Leet's Island Books, 1977).

Uedo, Makoto: *Literary and Art Theories in Japan* (Cleveland, Ohio: Case Western Reserve University, 1967).

Zeami Motokiyo: trans. J. Thomas Rimer and Yamazaki Masakazu, *On the Art of the Nō Drama: The Major Treatises of Zeami* (Princeton, NJ: Princeton University Press, 1984).

KENNETH J. DEWOSKIN

Coleridge, Samuel Taylor (1772–1834)

English poet, philosopher, and critic; a leading figure in the Romantic movement. Coleridge's most significant writings on aesthetics are the three *Essays on the Principles of Genial Criticism* (1814), the paper *On Poesy or Art* (probably 1818), other fragments collected in J. Shawcross's edition of *Biographia Literaria* (1817), and scattered discussions in the

73

Shakespearean criticism and literary lectures of 1808–19. His concern is always practical, working out his thoughts in the business of literary criticism, the plays of Shakespeare in particular providing material, in their very diversity and dissonance, for exploration of the principle of 'multeity in unity', or 'that in which the *many*, still seen as many, becomes one' (Shawcross, vol. 2, 1907, p. 232).

By 1810, Coleridge had read widely in German aesthetic and literary criticism, although his key ideas in aesthetics were already established from Plotinus (to whom he continually refers), the Cambridge Platonists, Giordano Bruno and others. By far the greatest influence on him, however, was Kant's *Critique of Judgement* (1790), though important, too, were Schelling (especially in Coleridge's *On Poesy or Art*), Friedrich Schlegel and Schiller. Directly from Kant, Coleridge insisted upon the principle of 'the disinterestedness of all taste' and rejected the connection of beauty with utility. The aesthetic is concerned neither with appetite nor desire, for the perception of the beautiful is always intuitive and consonant with 'the inborn and constitutive rules of the judgement and imagination' (Shawcross, 1907, p. 243).

On Poesy or Art is Coleridge's most important discussion of the nature of artistic imitation and mimesis. It is heavily dependent on Schelling. Art is understood as the reconciler of nature and man, or the power of humanizing nature. Again, Coleridge insists that the sense of beauty is intuitive, art not simply copying 'the mere nature' (*natura naturata*), but perceiving its essence (*natura naturans*) in the reconcilement of external and internal, the union of sameness and difference.

The principle of beauty, defined as 'multeity in unity', refers back, in Coleridge's words, to the Pythagorean definition, 'the reduction of many to one' (Shawcross, vol. 2, 1907, p. 238). In the posthumously published *Theory of Life* (1848), he develops his aesthetic speculation from Schelling and Henrik Steffens, art unifying the diversity and complexity of nature, not merely pleasurably but ethically also. For him, aesthetics can never be separated from the moral consciousness and his task of establishing right and proper principles of thought and action. Far from being a suspension of moral and intellectual activity, aesthetic perception is a training of the intuitive judgement under universal principles.

Art and poetry bring 'the whole soul of man into activity', the imagination being stimulated in the first instance 'by the *will* and understanding, and retained under their irremissive, though gentle and unnoticed, control' (Shawcross, vol. 2, 1907, p. 12). In other words, in its imitation of the *Naturgeist*, or spirit of nature, art is not merely the slave of a universal law, even though Coleridge is at pains to assert the existence of a 'regulative principle' in the human soul, a universal sense for the beautiful, following Kant's notice of *Gemeinsinn*. But he is far from holding the view attributed to him by Walter Pater, in the essay in *Appreciations* (1889), that the artist is simply a mechanical agent at the mercy of the natural law of organic growth. Art, far from being a blind 'organic process of assimilation', is profoundly moral – indeed, its very disinterestedness confirms, in M.H. Abrams' words, a 'belief in the complete autonomy and the unique originality of the individual work . . . [which goes] hand in hand with a confidence in universal principles of value' (Abrams, 1958, p. 225).

For Coleridge, aesthetic speculation was a central element in his life of thought, a deeply moral activity that is 'mind in its essence' (Shawcross, vol. 2, 1907, p. 258). In the artistic reconcilement of the external with the internal, between a thought and a thing, he wove a reflective net which linked his concerns for poetry, theology, philosophy, criticism and religion. He was certainly not a particularly sensitive critic of painting or music, and admitted it, though across the spectrum of the fine arts he maintained what he somewhat curiously described as a 'ladylike *wholeness* with creative delight in *particular* forms' (Coleridge, 1815).

Although undoubtedly immensely influenced by his German contemporaries, who often provided him with a language for his speculation, Coleridge had already established the essence of his aesthetics long before he had read Kant. Like Schiller and Goethe, he developed his thinking in the practice of poetry, and also, in his case, in practical criticism of Shakespeare and discussions on literature. M.H. Abrams has compared his 'aesthetics of organism' with Cleanth Brooks' suggestion that 'the parts of a poem are related as are the parts of a growing plant.' Writing in 1948, Brooks described this recognition as 'the best hope that we have for reviving the study of poetry and of the humanities generally' (quoted in Abrams, 1958, p. 222).

See also KANT.

WRITINGS

Essays on the Principles of Genial Criticism. Felix Farley's Bristol Journal (1814).
On Poesy or Art (1818), first published in *Literary Remains*, vol. 1, ed. H.N. Coleridge (1836).
'Aesthetical essays', reprinted in S.T. Coleridge, *Biographia Literaria* (1817); 2 vols, ed. J. Shawcross (Oxford: Oxford University Press, 1907).
Shakespearean Criticism, 2 vols, 2nd edn, ed. T.M. Raysor (London: Dent, 1960).
Lectures 1808–1819 on Literature, ed. R.A. Foakes (Princeton, NJ: Princeton University Press, 1987).

BIBLIOGRAPHY

Abrams, M.H.: *The Mirror and the Lamp: Romantic Theory and the Critical Tradition* (New York: Norton Library, 1958).
Happel, Stephen: *Coleridge's Religious Imagination*, 3 vols (Salzburg: University of Salzburg, 1983).

DAVID JASPER

Collingwood, R(obin) G(eorge) (1889–1943) British philosopher and historian; Wayneflete Professor of Metaphysics at Oxford. An Oxford philosopher and historian of Roman Britain, Collingwood disassociated himself from the ordinary language philosophy and positivism of his colleages, and in aesthetics pursued a course which drew upon the work of Vico, Croce and others. Besides his contributions to aesthetics, Collingwood is known especially for his work on philosophy of history, and he wrote extensively as well in metaphysics, philosophy of mind, philosophy of language, philosophy of religion, ethics and politics. There is some controversy as to whether there is an essential continuity or discontinuity in the course of his philosophical career, which spans ten published books and one still unpublished. This question colours one's reading of his contributions to specific philosophical topics (see Bibliography).

Regarding mind as an activity rather than an entity, Collingwood's works may be viewed as an extended account of different types of mental activities or forms of experience. In his *Speculum Mentis*, he argues against the view that knowledge should be pursued in terms of delineable domains of inquiry, and emphasizes the essential unity of mind by charting the relations between its forms of experience: art, religion, science, history and philosophy. These forms are not exhaustive, for Collingwood allows the possibility that others might yet develop and that some subforms within this outline might be filled in. The question of the nature of the specific relations between these forms of experience concerned him for most of his philosophical career. In this 'map of knowledge' art plays an important role, for the aesthetic infuses all other forms of experience. Collingwood is primarily concerned with the connection between art and mental activity, and not with the defining features of works of art, nor with the criteria of 'good' works of art.

Generally, he identifies art with the movement from unreflective to reflective thought. Consequently, while there is a history of artistic achievements, there can be no history of artistic problems. Problems are understood in terms of questions and answers, and unreflective thought does not allow for the formulation of questions to start with.

Collingwood identifies 'art proper' as an imaginative experience. He holds (1938,

p. 305) that it is not an artefact or a perceptible thing fabricated by the artist. Rather, it is something that exists solely in the artist's mind. It is a 'creation of his imagination.' Thus, a physical painted picture is not a work of art proper. Yet it is a necessary accessory for a work of art proper. Correspondingly, he does not restrict art proper to objects ordinarily associated with the artworld. He holds that 'every utterance and every gesture that each one of us makes is a work of art' (Collingwood, 1938, p. 285).

He distinguishes between artistic making or creating, and fabricating. His distinction between creating and fabricating appears to be coextensive with his distinction between imaginary and real. He suggests (1938, p. 125) that while a work of art is made by the artist, it is not made by 'transforming a given raw material, nor by carrying out a preconceived plan, nor by way of realizing the means to a preconceived end.' His examples include an artist making a poem, or a play, or a painting, or a piece of music. He was not especially concerned to discriminate between art forms in this regard. By Collingwood's account, for a tune to exist it is not necessary for a composer to hum, sing or play it, nor is it necessary for him to write it down. While these are accessories of the real work and make the tune 'public property', they are not necessary for it to exist in the composer's mind. There it exists as an imaginary tune. The actual making of the tune is something that goes on in the composer's head, and nowhere else.

Creating involves making a plan, while fabricating involves imposing that plan on certain matter. A plan can exist only in a person's mind. An engineer's notes and sketches on paper, for example, may serve as an accessory in order for others to share (and retrieve, when necessary) the plan which is in his head. Finally, when the bridge (for instance) is built, the plan is 'embodied' in the bridge. The plan or the form was in the engineer's mind. Further, a plan or a work of art need not be made as means to an end, for a person can make these with no intention of executing them. Generally, works of art proper are not made as means to an end.

Generally, then, Collingwood draws the contrast in this way:

The relation between making the tune in his head and putting it down on paper is thus quite different from the relation, in the case of the engineer, between making a plan for a bridge and executing that plan. The engineer's plan is embodied in the bridge: it is essentially a form that can be imposed on certain matter, and when the bridge is built the form is there, in the bridge, as the way in which the matter composing it is arranged. But the musician's tune is not there on the paper at all. What is on the paper is not music, it is only musical notation. The relation of the tune to the notation is not like the relation of the plan to the bridge; it is like the relation of the plan to the specifications and drawings; for these, too, do not embody the plan as the bridge embodies it, they are only a notation from which the abstract or as yet unembodied plan can be reconstructed in the mind of a person who studies them (Collingwood, 1938, p. 135).

As already noted, his theory of art is an integral part of his larger 'map of knowledge'. We can see this in his philosophies of mind and language which serve as a context for his philosophy of art: 'The aesthetic experience, or artistic activity, is the experience of expressing one's emotions; and that which expresses them is the total imaginative activity called indifferently language or art' (Collingwood, 1938, p. 275). For him artistic creation does not answer to his so-called logic of question and answer, which he articulates, for instance, in his *Essay on Metaphysics*. In *The Principles of Art* he is concerned to show that art is not assertion; art predates assertion, and assertion presupposes art. That is, in the creative moment the product cannot be understood as an answer to a question (as such later thinkers as Karl Popper and Ernst Gombrich suggested it can), because creative activity is one in which the unconscious becomes conscious. It is in such moments that no putative questions can be formulated.

Consequently, although a critic or art historian may offer a 'rational reconstruction' of the creative moment in terms of questions and answers, such reconstructions cannot claim to be *historically* true. This thought undercuts any intentionalist programme in so far as the latter seeks to reconstruct the conscious problem situations of creators. Collingwood holds that intentions can exist only in their expression; they do not predate expression.

Further, he holds that there can be no unexpressed emotion. Expression and emotion are dilectically co-dependent. It is in the expression of emotion that one becomes conscious of it; consciousness of emotion follows its expression. Thus emotions are not objects that are possessed before one's consciousness of them. In this sense, emotion and its expression are one:

> What the artist is trying to do is to express a given emotion. To express it and to express it well, are the same thing. To express it badly is not one way of expressing it . . . it is failing to express it. A bad work of art is an activity in which the agent tries to express a given emotion, but fails. This is the difference between bad art and art falsely so called . . . In art falsely so called there is no failure to express, because there is no attempt at expression; there is only an attempt (whether successful or not) to do something else. (Collingwood, 1938, p. 282)

Yet, while there is no emotion without expression, there may be crude feeling at the level of the 'purely psychical'. which may reveal 'involuntary changes in [one's] organism' (Collingwood, 1938, p. 274).

Now, one may disown or repress feelings. That is, one may refuse to bring them to expression. Collingwood (1938, pp. 216–21) calls this the 'corruption of consciousness'. This happens when 'the conscious self disclaims responsibility for [feelings], and thus tries to escape being dominated by them without the trouble of dominating them. This is the "corrupt consciousness", which is the

source of what psychologists call repression' (1938, p. 224).

In the case of artistic creation, a corrupt consciousness gives rise to bad art. In order to actually apply this notion of corrupt consciousness in specific cases of works of art one would expect that rules or guidelines of application would be provided. But Collingwood does not offer any. His intention may not be to provide criteria for distinguishing between particular good or bad artworks, but rather to provide an account of the meaning of good and bad artworks – perhaps rather like Plato's offering an account of the meaning of a good person without thereby committing himself to criteria for identifying particular good individuals.

One might object to Collingwood's distinction between creating a tune and publishing it by suggesting that music may be created through improvisation – that is, through the interaction of a sometimes inchoate musical idea and the materials of music-making. It seems that he assumes that there is a sharp distinction between what is initially in the artist's mind and what is not. Not only do works of art characteristically not present themselves as plans independently of their embodying materials and forms, but such materials and forms characteristically help formulate the plan to start with. Put otherwise, it is in the interaction between the plan and the materials that the work of art comes to emerge.

But such an objection would be misplaced, for Collingwood's distinction allows that the activities of creating (or imagining) and making can go on simultaneously. The latter may be an accessory for the former. Put negatively, he is not committed to the view that creating precludes fabricating. There need be no instance of creating without fabricating: 'There is no question of "externalizing" an inward experience which is complete in itself. There are two experiences, an inward or imaginative one called seeing and an outward or bodily one called painting, which in the painter's life are inseparable, and form one single indivisible experience, an experience which may be described as painting imaginatively' (Collingwood, 1938,

77

pp. 304–5). But one might press the point by suggesting that while imagining and making may be understood as interacting simultaneously, they are also *emergent* in a sense that is not captured by the idea that they interact. That is, the work of art may well embody properties that are attachable to none of its contributing parts, be they imagining or making. This emergentist view would undermine Collingwood's idea that works of art are essentially expressive of what goes on in the mind of the artist. Correspondingly, it would pose difficulties for the view that the audience recreates what is putatively in the mind of the artist.

Collingwood believes that art is something that should have no further end. He seems not to have considered a now common observation that such a position in fact constitutes a politically liberal view, and turns out to have consequences quite beyond the specific aims to which a work of art is supposedly not put.

He tells us that the purpose of making sketches is to inform or remind others or oneself of the plan in one's head. The sketches are not the product of imaginative creation, and this holds for all *works* of art or art *objects*. Thus, works of art or art objects are not art proper. While consistent, this view must be rather odd for a realist. It is an open question whether Collingwood's talk of art proper being private or 'in the head' can survive the Wittgensteinian attack on the traditional private/public distinction. But here he could demur that art proper is not even formulable before its expression, and so art should not be understood to be private in a traditional (that is, Cartesian) sense.

This could forestall the criticism that has often been made of Collingwood's view—namely, that it is 'idealist'. Since 1970 debate between realists and idealists has shifted somewhat. 'Language' has replaced 'mind' as opposing external reality. Correspondingly, the question 'What sort of mind is capable, if any, of representing non-mental objects?' has been replaced by the question 'What sorts of statements, if any, can represent non-linguistic entities?' In the former case, the realist/idealist controversy arises; in the latter case it

does not. In his repeated rejection of the idealist label, Collingwood anticipates this shift.

See also CROCE; EMOTION; EXPRESSION; INEFFABILITY; ONTOLOGY OF ARTWORKS; THEORIES OF ART.

WRITINGS

Speculum Mentis: Or The Map of Knowledge (Oxford: Clarendon Press, 1924).

Outlines of a Philosophy of Art (1925), reprinted in his *Essays in the Philosophy of Art*, ed. Alan Donagan (Bloomington, Ill.: Indiana University Press, 1964).

Unpublished MS on folklore and magic (1936–7), Bodleian Library, Oxford. See Van Der Dussen's (1981) discussion of this material.

The Principles of Art (Oxford: Oxford University Press, 1938).

BIBLIOGRAPHY

Donagan, Alan: *The Later Philosophy of R.G. Collingwood* (Oxford: Oxford University Press, 1952).

Jones, Peter: 'A critical outline of R.G. Collingwood's philosophy of art', *Critical Essays on the Philosophy of R.G. Collingwood*, ed. Michael Krausz (Oxford: Clarendon Press, 1972).

Knox, T.M.: editor's intro. to *The Idea of History*, R.G. Collingwood (Oxford: Oxford University Press, 1946).

Mink, Lois O.: *Mind, History and Dialectic: The Philosophy of R.G. Collingwood* (Bloomington, Ill., Indiana University Press, 1969).

Rubinoff, Lionel: *Collingwood and the Reform of Metaphysics: A Study in the Philosophy of Mind* (Toronto: University of Toronto Press, 1970).

Van Der Dussen, W.J.: *History as a Science: The Philosophy of R.G. Collingwood* (The Hague: Martinus Nijhoff, 1981).

MICHAEL KRAUSZ

commitment and engagement Artistic projects are, it seems, frequently undermined by an overbearing ideological motif, and theorists have sometimes made the general claim that artists – used here generically to include writers, directors, composers, and so on – should keep their religious, moral or political convictions apart from their art. Similarly, influential doctrines have held that it is improper for critics to assess art by moral, political or religious criteria. Such concerns in the artist, it is suggested, will be detrimental to the art and are irrelevant to criticism. But others have argued that the success of certain kinds of art *depends* on the artist's commitment to a cause, and it seems true, at least, that much that goes under the name 'art' appears to have been inspired by moral, political or religious conviction.

Can its implicit ideological claims enhance the artistic quality of a piece of art? When, if ever, are political motives detrimental to artistic success? We can approach such questions via the familiar claim that art exists for its own sake and should be regarded as an end in itself, not a means to an end. One interpretation of the claim invites us to conclude that any value that art has in virtue of its contribution to a cause or ideology – for instance, in clarifying a political idea or inspiring a desire to act against injustice – is incidental to its character as art, adding nothing to its artistic value and having no relevance to the enjoyment it provides as a piece of art. On this interpretation the thesis of art for its own sake is a general claim about art as an institution, a claim that asserts that art is an autonomous category of culture with its own kind of value.

Just as philosophy, or political science, might be said to have distinctive kinds of value associated with the kinds of discipline they are, this interpretation takes the value of art to be distinct from that of objects belonging to other cultural categories, and sees the kind of attention it merits as having a focus that is separate from the concerns of philosophy, biography, history, science, politics, morals, religion, and so forth. And just as we would not expect a philosophical essay on social justice to be *philosophically* strengthened if rewritten in technically accomplished verse, it is here being suggested that, similarly, it adds nothing to the artistic value of a poem when it makes claims, however valid in themselves, about a subject like social justice. Thus I.A. Richards maintains that truth claims and claims about right and wrong do not contribute to the poetic value of poetry and should be ignored when poetry is read as poetry; otherwise, 'we have for the moment ceased to be reading poetry and have become astronomers, or theologians, or moralists, persons engaged in a quite different activity' (Richards, 1964, p. 277). Richards' view implies that the artistic value of a work of art is necessarily distinct from any contribution it makes to a public debate or cause.

If art, by nature, can only be enjoyed by our ignoring the kind of value it might share with activities or objects that are not art, this would explain our uneasiness about some ways in which art can be put to ideological use. For instance, if we feel that a work of art is a thinly disguised piece of propaganda, we usually lose some respect for it as art (even if we agree with its cause, or value its political usefulness), while in general we tend to be wary of the artistic seriousness of art that strives primarily to be informative or to inspire enthusiasm for a cause. However, these are tendencies and not hard and fast rules, and it is difficult to see how the conception of art as autonomous in the described sense could account for the full variety of aims that have inspired serious art, and for the way we respond to it.

Art that supports a cause does not always fail as art. Many great poets and painters have used their art to glorify their gods or to advertise the prestige of their patrons or the greatness of their nation. Goya's paintings express his horror at the world; Brecht's plays are aimed at changing it. And the bearing of art upon the world can be quite specific. Athol Fugard's plays would lose some of their *dramatic* hold on us if we failed to see their relevance to the condition of apartheid South Africa. There are clearly many counterexamples to the thesis that art has a specific function or domain which is exclusive to art and the sole source of its artistic value. These cases urge us to look for an account which accommodates the fact that, while a social or practical function may diminish some works

79

of art as art, it may add to the artistic value of others.

There is a second interpretation of the 'art for its own sake' claim, which takes seriously the idea that a work of art should be viewed as an end and not a means but gives a better account of the relation between art and a commitment to a cause or ideology. This second interpretation takes the claim to be about how we should approach particular works, given their individuality or uniqueness. It interprets the claim as saying that whatever features you value in a work of art, you value them in a way appropriate to art only if you view them in relation to how they fit with and contribute to an assessment of the work's overall character. In other words, you should respond to properties of the work primarily for the sake of understanding and assessing *it*, on its own terms, and never appropriate these for a preconceived purpose of your own.

This reading of the 'art for its own sake' claim, with its insistence on treating artworks as ends and its acknowledgement of the uniqueness of each work, invites us to see our responses to art as analogous to personal judgements of character. In judging a valued academic colleague or political ally *as* a person, you would not measure his or her value simply according to academic ability or political usefulness, but nor would you ignore these if you thought, as you probably would, that they told you something about the person's character. You would naturally take them into account as relevant factors among others. Similarly, in responding to a piece of art as art, you *need* to be alert to its politically significant features and effects, since these are likely to have a bearing on its character.

The injunction that you should attend to a work of art for its own sake is therefore best interpreted as saying simply that if you are interested in art as art, then your critical judgements will be based on an attempt to understand the particular character of each work. It does not enjoin you (as it may at first appear to do) to ignore the ideological, social or practical dimension of art. Such considerations do not push criticism aside, provided the end or purpose remains that of understand-ing and assessing the work, and political considerations are treated as a means to this end.

The analogy with ordinary judgements of character suggests that any virtue or vice that can be expressed in a piece of art can correspondingly affect its quality as art, and also that an artist's commitment to questions of politics may have a variety of effects, negative *or* positive, upon the artistic success of his work. Taking the case of literature, though the writing of Brecht and Fugard is typically perceptive and original it is an unfortunate matter of fact that highly prioritized political motives often result in the sacrifice of these and other virtues which in one or another combination, give a piece of writing an overall quality of a kind we associate with good literature. Writing that is primarily meant to advertise a popular cause will often show a disregard for truth, ambiguity and subtlety of observation, especially if it is aimed at a public without great intellectual sophistication. Such writing will probably not show much originality, being concerned to advance established doctrines rather than to examine the prejudices that underlie our everyday assumptions and the established ways in which we represent the world to ourselves. It will often be condescending to its public, consciously exploiting widely held stereotypes and easily assessible clichés. Art that is produced under the regimented conditions of a revolutionary political movement is often, for these reasons, boringly predictable. As socialist realism under Stalin illustrates, the same applies, for the same reasons, to art produced under the influence of an established regime that dictates to the artist.

On the present reading of the 'art for its own sake' claim, any ideological dimension of a work of art can contribute to or detract from its success as art. But that reading does place some limits on the way ideological motives and attitudes can enter into our dealings with art. It prescribes, first, that the work, viewed as art, should never be valued solely as a means to ideological or political ends. Second, it rules out, by implication, that artists be made to serve an ideology or public cause – as was required, for instance, by the

Stalinist Zhdanov (1975), who quite wrongly claimed he had the support of Lenin.

Take the first point. We can imagine a political climate in which suitable works are used as pedagogical devices or advertisements for a cause, while the rest are ignored or suppressed because of their failure to conform to the prevailing ideology. The result, presumably, would be the neglect of most works of art, and of all those varieties of non-political value that art can have, as well as a diminished grasp of the character of even those 'suitable' works that remained in circulation, since this approach to art would mean setting aside any concentrated effort to understand the unique set of concerns underlying each work. Turning to the second point, consider a society which prescribed suitable styles, themes and ideological content to its artists. In such a society we would have reason to expect art that was homogenized; particular works would have a common and familiar purpose that would provide the key to understanding them as a group. In such a society, what went under the name 'art' would be quite different in character from art as we usually conceive it, and from the way it is represented in the 'art for its own sake' claim as I have been interpreting it.

On this interpretation we treat individual works as unique, not even acknowledging a general function or purpose that works can be expected to have in virtue of being art. This fits with our association of art with a kind of inventiveness which refuses to recognize a preordained purpose among composers or writers or painters, and which can be expected to result in objects that reveal novel combinations of thought, experience and attitude, each to be assessed in its own right and not easily assimilated into the conventional wisdom of any established viewpoint, sympathetic or otherwise. Dictating goals to artists would, on this view, not so much subvert art to a cause but, rather, threaten to replace it with a different kind of institution–one which did constitute a category of culture devoted to a set purpose or end. Whatever virtues this substitute might have, it would largely lack the characteristic features that make our concern with art rewarding in that distinctive way that we associate with the enjoyment of art. Advertising and propaganda can doubtless be justified in themselves, but the question raised for the society that dictates to the artist is whether its loyalists and propagandists are enough, or whether it stands to benefit also from the efforts of its less orderly members, including its creative artists.

Finally, let us consider the view that, while a society may have no right to dictate to artists, they have a duty to ally themselves to just social causes and that this is essential to the value of their work as art. Jean-Paul Sartre (1950) – probably the best-known defender of *littérature engagée* – has argued that the properly 'engaged' writer consciously acknowledges his political commitments and expresses them in his writing, aware that silence on urgent political questions of his place and time amounts not to neutrality but to an act of evasion (Sartre, 1950). The force of this can be seen when we consider societies in the grip of political turpitude on a grand scale. Imagine a novelist producing an 'apolitical' novel of rivalry in love among the officers and staff of a concentration camp established by a racist regime for the liquidation of innocent people. The apolitical pretensions of the novelist–his refusal to address questions about the political and moral circumstances of his setting–would lay him open to surely justifiable charges of callousness or blindness.

Sartre has claimed that the expression of politically reprehensible values in literary works reflects on those works *as* literature, and hence that a racist novel cannot succeed as literature. What if someone replied that though creative writing is a public activity and may therefore, like any other such activity, reflect the moral character of the writer and work, immoral features do not reflect on the resulting work specifically as *literature*? The preceding discussion of artistic value suggests qualified support for Sartre's position against this response. The upshot of that discussion was that political ideas and attitudes will be relevant to the assessment of art *as art* when they tell us something about a work's general character. Furthermore, just as wit or verbal skill are virtues as such, whether we encounter them within art or elsewhere, so we should expect that, in general, the evaluation of art will accord with values that we embrace outside art. Hence Fugard's concern for the dispossessed people of South Africa reflects well on his art, and the romantic novelist's obliviousness to the bizarre concentration camp setting of his novel reflects badly on his novel. Sartre is therefore right to say that racism in a novel will corrupt it as art.

The qualification we ought to add is that, just as in ordinary moral contexts where a certain kind of evil may in a particular individual be mitigated by virtues, so too in art we might acknowledge much of value in a work despite the presence of undesirable features. This would account for the ambivalence we feel towards a writer like Ezra Pound, whose highly prized talents have given his writing a recognized place in literature despite the presence in that writing of repugnant political attitudes.

See also AESTHETICISM; FUNCTION OF ART; MARXISM AND ART; MORALITY AND ART; SARTRE.

BIBLIOGRAPHY

Beardsley, M.C.: *Aesthetics* (New York: 1958); 2nd edn (Indianapolis: Hackett, 1981), pp. 419–32, 558–71.
Budd, M.: 'Belief and sincerity in poetry', *Pleasure, Preference and Value*, ed. E. Schaper (Cambridge: Cambridge University Press, 1983), pp. 137–57.
Eagleton, T.: *Marxism and Literary Criticism* (London: Methuen, 1976), ch. 3.
Lenin, V.I.: 'Articles on Tolstoy', *Marxists on Literature: an Anthology*, ed. D. Craig (Harmondsworth: Penguin Books, 1975), pp. 346–62.
Richards, I.A.: *Practical Criticism* (London: Routledge, 1964), ch. 7.
Sartre, J.-P.: *Qu'est-ce que la littérature?* (Paris: 1948); trans. B. Frechtman, *What is Literature?* (London: Methuen, 1950).
Zhdanov, A.A.: 'Report on the journals *Zvesda* and *Leningrad*, 1947' (extract), *Marxists on Literature: an Anthology*, ed. D. Craig (Harmondsworth: Penguin Books, 1975), pp. 514–26.

PAUL TAYLOR

composition, musical   We can distinguish at the outset three sorts of questions about the composition of music. The first is essentially conceptual: what does musical composition *consist in* – that is, what are logically adequate *criteria* for its occurrence and, relatedly, what is the nature and status of the resulting product? The second is basically psychological: what typically characterizes the *process* of composition, on the plane of thought and action, from inception to completion? The third may be called technical: what are some of the salient *means and methods* involved in successful composing in a given style or tradition, and what are some common hurdles to be overcome or problems to be solved? In this article attention is devoted to the first and second of these questions, which have, unlike the third, a significant philosophical dimension.

One thing worth remarking at once is that we should allow that different answers may need to be supplied for different musical traditions, where the first, conceptual, question is concerned; and for different types of composer and different species of composition, where the second, psychological, question is concerned. What it is to compose may vary from one tradition to another – for instance, European symphonic music, improvised jazz or Javanese gamelan music – and what standardly goes on during compositional activity may have a different profile if, for instance, it is a matter of Mozart composing a contredanse rather than Brahms a violin concerto or Milton Babbitt a totally serialized string quartet.

The central act of composing may be, and has been, seen in different ways, even if we restrict our view to familiar notated classical music in the Western tradition. This action has been characterized variously as selection, discovery, invention, arrangement, construction and, finally, creation. There is probably some truth to each of these characterizations, though maximally so in respect of different objects. Thus, it may be that composers typically select certain instruments and forms, discover specific ways to modulate from one key to another, invent sound combinations, arrange sections and passages, and construct themes from intervals, motives and chords. Do composers, however, actually create anything in composing music, or do they, at most, perform these other actions creatively (Kivy, 1983; Cox, 1985; Levinson, 1990; Fisher, 1991a)?

Certainly, traditional description has it that a composer creates, if not the elements that he employs, then precisely the work or composition as a whole. This intuition seems worth preserving, if possible, especially as it links musical composition to artistic production in other spheres – for example, those of painting, sculpture and film. There is a problem, though, in that the most obvious candidate for the finished work – the total musical (tonal/instrumental) structure or pattern finally indicated by the composer, the upshot of his various acts of selecting, discovering and arranging – usually already exists within the well defined musical system in which composition standardly operates, and thus cannot strictly be created by the composer. However elaborate the sequence of performed sounds indicated may be, such a sequence pre-exists the activity of arriving at and electing it. If it be objected that that is just existence 'in the abstract', it may be replied that that is, after all, the mode of existence proper to structures and patterns *per se*.

One solution here is to recognize the musical work as ontologically more complicated than the musical structure at its core, as being something like *the structure qualified by the composer's historically situated indicating of it*. Acknowledging the work as this sort of complex entity gives us something that can, albeit in a rarefied sense, be brought into being by the composer. In addition, it allows us to individuate musical works, easily imaginable, which are sound-structurally identical but aesthetically or artistically distinct (Levinson, 1990).

So in the prevailing tradition of Western classical music, what composing essentially involves is the composer (X) indicating, or making normative for performance, a musical structure in a specific compositional context (C), and, in so doing, creating the work which is the structure-as-indicated-by-X-in-C. This is usually done by means of a score and various unstated conventions for its interpretation, but it might also be done by performative exemplification or, inefficiently, by verbal description.

A broader conception of what composing necessarily involves, applying more easily to musical traditions without notation, and possibly even to those without works as such, construes composing as ordaining, in some fashion or other, conditions for the correctness of future performings – that is, for what will count as making or sounding the 'same' music on other occasions (Wolterstorff, 1980; 1987). A related conception, one illuminating for avant-garde music employing aleatory methods and/or strongly visual scores (for instance, works of Cage, Stockhausen and George Crumb), is that composing is not so much the defining of a musical structure for future instancing as the giving of rules and prescriptions, or even just suggestions or promptings, for making sounds or doing things audibly with objects of various sorts (Tormey, 1974).

At any rate, composing clearly does not necessarily involve indicating a musical structure for performance by means of a score, even if we restrict our attention to music in the West. For in addition to notated compositions for standard instruments or voice we can cite *musique concrète*, computer-generated music, player-piano music and totally improvised music, most notably jazz (Alperson, 1984). These are composed, respectively, by arranging segments of recorded sound, by writing computer code, by hand-punching piano rolls, and by spontaneously playing an instrument. What they have in common is that they all entail ways of defining or fixing an identifiable unit or item of music – a piece, minimally speaking – something which can be, if not performed, then successfully re-sounded, or, in the last case, at least reproduced and emulated. Finally, it is worth noting that in certain folk traditions there may be recognizable pieces of music which have not been composed at all; that is, criteria for their correct sounding exist, but have not been laid down explicitly by any individual or individuals.

There are a number of different influential models of the creative process in musical composition. One, the *expressionist* model, is exemplified in the writings of the musicologist Deryck Cooke (Cooke, 1959). According to Cooke, there is at the root of every real act of composition a deep, inchoate emotion in the composer needing outward expression in musical terms. It finds this expression by gravitating towards key areas, harmonies, and melodic and rhythmic figures with which it has a natural correspondence. The process of composition is, then, the full externalization and exhaustion, in the musical domain, of this pre-existing emotional charge. A second, the *architectonic* model, has been propounded by the composer Paul Hindemith (Hindemith, 1952). According to Hindemith, every real act of composition presupposes a vision, as of a landscape illuminated by lightning, of a work as a whole, with all structural landmarks in place. This vision must occur early on, and be sustained throughout, the process of composition being a matter of progressively filling out, with suitable small-scale musical material, the basic framework grasped earlier. What distinguishes a true composer is not the quantity or quality of musical bits inhabiting consciousness (*Einfälle*), nor any special emotional condition or insight, but only the structural vision of a work in prospect.

A third model, which we can label *organicist*, has been usefully formulated by Roger Sessions (1950). According to this composer, musical composition characteristically involves an original musical germ or idea – for instance, a rhythm, motive, chord, key relationship – which provides an impetus for the creative process and a guiding force on the evolution of the piece throughout, serving as a touchstone for gauging the rightness or fruitfulness of what is essayed at any point. The process of composition is thus a matter of working out the full implications of the original musical germ in such a way as to always preserve its essential character, a thesis that Sessions illustrates through the familiar example of Beethoven and his sketchbooks. (The music theorist Heinrich Schenker can be seen as advancing what might be dubbed a *non-observable* version of the organicist model: the evolution of a piece of tonal music as invariably the progressive unfolding of an underlying *Ursatz* – or large-scale cadence – not perceived as such.)

Clearly the expressionist, architectonic and organicist models of how a composition comes to be will each have a limited validity, giving more or less accurate pictures of the creative process in different sorts of composers. However, if we are looking for a more invariant characterization of the creative process, we can probably find no better than that offered by Beardsley, in a Deweyan spirit, to the effect that whatever the specific creative psychology of a composer, and whatever the nature and style of the music he is engaged in writing, the only inevitable guiding factor in composition will be the state of the incomplete work as it exists at each point, and the possibilities – for expansion, retraction, modification, elaboration – that it presents (Beardsley, 1982). This we may call a *processive* model of composition. Creation in music, as in other realms, is a matter of phases of inspiration and invention alternating with phases of assessment and evaluation, and of a regular shifting of concern from level to level – for instance, local to global, emotional to architectural – as well (Cook, 1990). The only constant may be that one gauges where one has been and where one is going in relation to where one is at any point – that is, the torso of the music thus far composed. One's original impetus, whatever it was and however much it initially promised to shape the whole, may give out before the end, and one's overall plan, if any there was, may be blurred or shelved halfway through; but there is no alternative, in composing music as in living, to carrying on from wherever one is.

We may mention, finally, two obvious variables in the way composition of traditional music will be carried out. One is the degree to which the composer makes use of instruments in the course of composition – for example, trying things out on the piano, or blowing on a horn intermittently for inspiration. Obviously, some composers forgo this entirely, while others rely on it heavily; composers differ in the extent to which their musical imaginations need stoking by actual sound and movement. Another dimension of variation is the extent to which a composer will compose through external action of any sort, whether that of making inscriptions on music paper or searching for chords on a piano keyboard – as opposed to doing the essential work of devising and deciding on musical gestures and shapes in his head, as Mozart is supposed often to have done.

See also CREATIVITY; NOTATION; ONTOLOGY OF ARTWORKS; PERFORMANCE.

BIBLIOGRAPHY

Alperson, P.: 'Musical improvisation', *Journal of Aesthetics and Art Criticism*, 43 (1984), 17–30.
Beardsley, M.: 'The creation of art', *The Aesthetic Point of View*, ed. M. Wreen and D. Callen (Ithaca, NY: Cornell University Press, 1982), 239–62.
Cook, N.: *Music, Imagination, and Culture* (Oxford: Oxford University Press, 1990).
Cooke, D.: *The Language of Music* (Oxford: Oxford University Press, 1959).
Cox, R.: 'Are musical works discovered?' *Journal of Aesthetics and Art Criticism*, 43 (1985), 367–74.
Davies, S.: 'The ontology of musical works and the authenticity of their performances', *Noûs*, 25 (1991), 21–41.
Fisher, J.: 'Discovery, creation, and musical works', *Journal of Aesthetics and Art Criticism*, 49 (1991), 129–36.
Hindemith, P.: *A Composer's World* (Cambridge, Mass.: Harvard University Press, 1952).
Kivy, P.: 'Platonism in music: a kind of defence'. *Grazer Philosophische Studien*, 19 (1983), 109–29.
Levinson, J.: *Music, Art, and Metaphysics* (Ithaca, NY: Cornell University Press, 1990), chs. 4, 5 and 10.
Levinson, J.: 'Music, ontology of', in *Handbook of Metaphysics and Ontology* (Munich: Philosophia Verlag, 1991), 582–4.
Sessions, R.: *The Musical Experience of Composer, Performer, Listener* (Princeton, NJ: Princeton University Press, 1950).
Tormey, A.: 'Indeterminacy and identity in art', *Monist*, 58 (1974), 203–15.
Wolterstorff, N.: *Works and Worlds of Art* (Oxford: Oxford University Press, 1980).
Wolterstorff, N.: 'The work of making a work of music', *What Is Music?*, ed. P. Alperson (New York: Haven, 1987), 103–29.

JERROLD LEVINSON

conservation and restoration The act of preserving the artwork as the artist intended it to be seen, conserving what he made by restoring losses caused by ageing or the effects of time.

Since art history is based upon the assumption that what the historian views in the museum is what the artist made, a theory of restoration is a necessary starting point for art history. Unless the artwork we see has been successfully conserved, how can we accurately interpret it? Although restoration and conservation are concerns in every art, they are of special importance in visual art. Jane Austen wrote texts, which we interpret; Haydn created scores which the modern orchestra performs. So long as her text or his score has been accurately copied, the artwork is preserved. But in the visual arts the artist traditionally creates a physical thing. Unless the restorer can preserve that object, the artwork does not survive.

The goal of restoration is easy to state. The restorer aims to preserve what the artist made. The difficulties arise when we ask how to achieve that goal (Carrier, 1985). An artist makes an *artefact* with a certain *appearance*. With time, the picture may darken unless the restorer intervenes. But is the aim to preserve the *original artefact*, which will darken with time? Or should the restorer seek to preserve the *original appearance* of the artefact? In 1644–5 Pieter Saenredam made two paintings of the nave of the Buurkerk, Utrecht. One is now in the Kimbell Art Museum, Fort Worth, Texas, the other in the National Gallery in London (Schwartz and

Bok, 1990, pp. 198–9). When they were made, the panels were almost certainly similar in appearance. But now the first depicts stark white walls while the second shows a mellow brown interior. Treating these pictures differently, the restorers 'have performed . . . a series of changes . . . which have amounted to complete transformations of the aesthetic effect of the two panels'. Both paintings have survived, but until we can determine which of them provides an accurate record of Saenredam's activity, we cannot understand his art.

Often attempts are made to solve this problem by appeal to the artist's intention. Perhaps he wanted his picture to darken, showing its age. Or maybe he would have preferred the original appearance of his artefact to be preserved. On reflection, however, it becomes clear that appeal to intentions cannot solve this problem. In practice, usually the artist must first be concerned with how the work will appear to contemporaries. He is unlikely to be concerned with future viewers and may be unable to predict how his work will appear at a later time. But even if he says explicitly how he desires the work to appear in the future, we need not necessarily accept his viewpoint. Just as the artist is not necessarily the best interpreter of his work, so he may not be the final authority on how it should be conserved.

An analysis of restoration is unavoidably bound up with more general philosophical problems. Some thing, a substance, remains the same entity, though its properties change. We need some way to identify what has changed as the same thing; for, otherwise, speaking of change would be impossible. If we think of change as continuous, then we can describe how a thing gradually changes. That requires some way of identifying the self-same thing, that enduring entity which has changed. Four kinds of different substances have been considered by metaphysicians (Wiggins, 1980): artefacts, organisms, persons, artificial entities.

Artefacts can have their parts replaced and remain the same thing so long as that process procedes slowly. A car is the same car, the same functioning artefact, when its original components are replaced as they wear out. Organisms are substances which change as they mature. The same tree is first tiny, then large and then decays. These changes involve a natural process of growth in accordance with a built-in plan of development. Human beings also are organisms. But identity of persons may be different from identity of organisms. On some theories, a person can survive the destruction of his body. Artificial entities like states survive if there is enough continuity. Modern France is the same country as ruled by Louis XIII, though it is now a democracy and its borders have changed somewhat. But the Venetian Republic ceased to exist when it was incorporated into Italy and the last doge was deposed. The United States is the same country as that republic created in the late eighteenth century, although now slavery has been abolished, women have the vote and there are fifty states. There is enough continuity to identify it through these radical changes.

None of these substances are exactly like artworks. If artworks were artefacts, then they could survive the gradual replacement of all of their original parts. But if a fresco is gradually repainted, when none of the original paint survives the artwork has not survived, although the original design has been preserved. Organisms are born, grow to maturity, and die. But since normally artworks do not contain a built-in plan of development, they cannot be organisms. Usually the restorer seeks to arrest natural processes, intervening as the artwork decays. A person can continue to exist through radical changes in his physical qualities, because one test of continuity is memory or continuity of consciousness. An artwork is not that sort of thing.

Perhaps, then, the most promising approach to conservation involves treating artworks like artificial entities. Emphasizing the role of convention in restoration, that way of thinking focuses attention on the function of artworks. Most art in our museums was not made for the museum. If what the African tribal artisan made was a magical artefact, the object cannot be preserved when it is treated as an artwork and carefully presented in a temperature-controlled museum environment. Similar problems arise when sacred Christian works are taken from a church to a museum. We conserve in the museum the artwork made by the artist, secularizing what originally was a sacred work. We preserve the artwork by changing its function (Riegl, 1903). Like a country, the object treated as an artwork in the museum can survive such radical changes.

Some art historians deny that it is possible for the artwork to survive such changes (Wind, 1969). How we see Romanesque carvings is influenced by our experience of early modernist sculpture; the colours in old master art now look subdued because our eyes are accustomed to garish twentieth-century paintings. This implies that to preserve the original artwork we must preserve its effect, which is not the same thing as preserving the object itself. How we see that object depends upon our experience of other art which the artist did not know. Even if the artefact is preserved perfectly, yet now it will look different.

Were this argument correct, then it would be impossible to conserve artworks. But it is hard to state this sceptical argument in a consistent way. When an altarpiece is placed in a museum, and set near modern secular art, it looks different from how it looked in a church. But if every such change in context changes how we see the work, then how can we know that? Unless we were able to successfully imagine the original appearance of the work, we could not know that now its appearance has changed.

The settings of the African artefact and the Italian altarpiece are dramatically changed when they are put in the museum. If the identity of these objects depends upon their function, then they have not been preserved when they are placed in the museum. The object has survived, but, set in a new context, it has lost its original function. Some aestheticians solve this problem by claiming that artworks possess universally recognizable qualities. On this Kantian view, artworks are not artefacts because they 'do not normally, *qua* works of art, have any *function*' (Wiggins, 1980, p. 138). As artworks, the African artefact and Italian altarpiece do not have a function.

This is an ahistorical way of thinking. Until relatively recently, most art had a function. Still, in many (though not all) cases there is some overlap between how artworks were thought of in their original culture and how they are perceived in the museum. There is some connection between the function of these objects in their original culture and their aesthetic qualities which we appreciate in our museum. These artefacts had one function in their original context, and have another in the museum where they are treated as artworks. These changes of function involve enough continuity for us to say that they have survived.

We preserve the artefacts in our museums at the cost of changing rather drastically their function. Something is preserved even whilst these things are drastically changed. It is important to recognize that the problems of preservation of artworks involve understanding the function of the museum. Although our art museum is a creation of the late eighteenth century, there is enough continuity between the beliefs of that period and ours to permit us to speak of the same institution. A succession of gradual changes in the museum may add up to the effect of a revolution. But those successive changes are changes in the same institution, whereas by definition a revolution involves a break with tradition. Museums have changed radically, but there is enough continuity to permit us to identify them as the same institutions. The function of a museum is to give us knowledge of the past and aesthetic experience of artworks.

These philosophical arguments can seem of tangential importance to the conservator. He must act while philosophers go on talking. But how he proceeds in his important practical activity is ultimately determined by the broader culture's highly elusive ideas about how we should think of the identity of artworks.

See also ART HISTORY; MUSEUMS.

BIBLIOGRAPHY

Carrier, David: 'Art and its preservation', *Journal of Aesthetics and Art Criticism*, XLIII 3 (1985), 291–300.
Riegl, Aloïs: *Der Denkmalkultus, sein Wesen und seine Entstehung* (Vienna: 1903); trans. D. Wieczorek, intro. by F. Choay, *Le culte moderne des monuments. Son essence et sa genèse* (Paris: Éditions du Seuil, 1984).
Schwartz, Gary and Bok, Marten Jan: *Pieter Saenredam. The Painter and His Time* (New York: Abbeville Press, 1990).
Wiggins, David: *Sameness and Substance* (Oxford: Basil Blackwell, 1980).
Wind, Edgar: *Art and Anarchy* (London: 1963); 2nd edn (New York: Random House, 1969).

DAVID CARRIER

creativity It is impossible to give a simple definition of 'creativity'. The word and its cognates ('to create', 'creative', 'creator') are used in a number of different ways. Keeping these in mind can help one to find one's bearings in the often bewildering claims and debates in this area. Among the major distinctions to be made are the following.

1. To create is to *make* something. Creating in this sense goes beyond the arts: into politics, for instance, where we might speak of Peter the Great as the creator of modern Russia; or into ethics, with the notion of the autonomous individual as engaged in self-creation. But at the same time it is particularly associated with the arts. The artist has traditionally been seen as a maker, often by analogy with the creation myth of God's having made the world out of nothing. Elliott (1971) has argued that, while all artists may be said to make objects for our contemplation and to approach the divine paradigm to that extent, of some of them – for example, Dostoevsky, Beethoven, Shakespeare – we may say that they are closer still, in having created their own distinctive *worlds*.

2. One might, following Elliott, distinguish the 'traditional' concept of creativeness in sense 1 from a 'new' concept, where being creative has to do with the generation of new ideas. These cannot be just *any* kind of new idea, for a deranged person may make all sorts of novel connections yet not be a creative thinker. We have to add that the unconventional thinking remain within the bounds of appropriateness: a person asked to think of different possible uses for a brick could hardly be labelled 'creative' in this sense if he said – without further explanation – that it could be used as a trumpet. Being creative in sense 2 is thus equivalent to being imaginative. It is not – unlike sense 1 – associated especially with the arts, since one may think creatively in science, mathematics and other theoretical pursuits, as well as in practical problem-solving. Neither is creativeness in this sense found in all forms of art. It is absent from much of the art of ancient Egypt, for instance, as well as from tribal art. It is chiefly in sense 2 that creativity and its measurement are studied in psychology.

Senses 1 and 2 are connected, in that each brings with it the notion of bringing something new into the world, in the very broad sense of something which did not exist in it before. (In sense 1 this could cover making cars as well as making poems.) Sense 2 treats of a subdivision of this which has to do with the production of new ideas. Sense 2 also drops the logical link with making: thinking up hypotheses in science or brainstorming on a practical problem is not to be engaged in making an object (where 'object' includes an aesthetic object like a piece of music).

3. An artist could be creative in either of the first two senses without producing work of merit. But as the term is commonly used, it carries with it a positive value-judgement. Different criteria of value may be at work here, as the word can be used in a very wide sense and be virtually equivalent to 'good'. But sometimes these criteria are closer to senses 1 or 2. An artist or a work may be judged more creative than another because of the quality of the making that has been involved. For instance, success in integrating complex elements within a unified whole is widely recognized as one criterion of aesthetic excellence: greater creativity may be

ascribed because of greater achievements in this dimension. As for sense 2, in recent times originality – in the sense of breaking with current traditions – has come to be seen in many quarters as an important constituent of artistic excellence. Some feel things have gone too far in this direction and would challenge the value often accorded in our age to the merely unusual. They would put more stress on the role that working within traditions plays in the artistic life: Joyce is not necessarily a greater novelist than Pasternak, even though the former broke with traditional forms while the latter worked within them.

Kant writes of 'genius' rather than 'creativity', but his concept has close logical connections with all three senses above. For him genius 'is a talent for producing that for which no definite rule can be given' hence, 'originality must be its first property.' But since it is possible to produce original nonsense, its products 'must be models, ie exemplary', and must serve as a standard for others. In this latter remark Kant ties genius not only to producing work of merit, but also to having a place within a tradition: a genius provides an example 'to be followed by another genius, whom it wakens to a feeling of his own originality' (Kant, 1951 [1790], para 49). Tradition also enters Kant's account because, although there are no rules by which work of genius can be generated, in every art there is 'a mechanical element that can be comprehended by rules' (Kant, 1951 [1790], para 47). 'Shallow heads,' he tells us, 'believe that they cannot better show themselves to be geniuses than by throwing off the constraint of all rules' (para 47).

Related to this last point, one way in which Kant's account of genius moves away from some contemporary views of creativity in the arts has to do with how commonly these phenomena are said to occur. For Kant a genius is a rare phenomenon, a 'favourite of nature' who is blessed with a natural gift or talent (Kant, 1951 [1790], para 49). Not all works of art which are accounted beautiful are created by geniuses. Poems may be 'very neat and elegant, but without spirit' (para 49). 'Spirit', a defining property of the genius, is 'the faculty of presenting aesthetical ideas'.

These are products of the imagination which strive to transcend the bounds of experience, 'occasioning much thought' yet incapable of being fully encompassed in concepts. In this way Kant's account of genius is tied in his writings to his general metaphysics. On the other hand, those who would question his metaphysics might still agree with him about the rarity of genius.

As for the recent views of creativity just mentioned, these hold it to be a power which all or most of us possess, or which can be developed in us by suitable forms of education, and to different degrees. This 'democratic' concept is a staple of child-centred educational theory, where, following Herbert Read's (1943) idea of 'education through art', encouraging children's free expression in drawing and painting has been seen as a key to unlocking their creative abilities in every field. While there can be no doubt that virtually everybody can be creative in some sense (for instance, we can all make things after a fashion), putting us all on a continuum with Mozart and Pushkin and thus stressing our similarities with them may make some of us less appreciative than we otherwise would be of the wondrousness of their achievements.

Most of the various senses and accounts of creativity given so far make it dependent on a certain kind of product. Persons are called creative, or geniuses, in so far as they make things, generate novel thoughts, produce works of merit, express aesthetic ideas. Opposed to what might be labelled this 'objective' perspective is the 'subjective' view, which locates creativity in 'the creative process(es)' taking place in artists, scientists and other thinkers. This has been influential in the educational circles mentioned above, as well as among psychologists of different persuasions. Some of them have sought to explain how creativity in the objective sense comes about in terms of the creative process or processes. While psychoanalytic accounts emphasize the operations of the unconscious mind, a recent computational approach claims that creative processes in the arts are fundamentally similar to processes embodied in computer programmes (Boden, 1990). A central purpose in this and other similar works is to demystify artistic creativeness, to explain it in other terms.

Opposed to these endeavours are those philosophers who see creativeness as in its essence inexplicable. Kant claims that one cannot describe scientifically how genius brings about its products. A genius does not know how he has come by his ideas and cannot formulate precepts which will enable others to produce similar works. Plato sees poets as composing their work under the influence of divine inspiration: in doing so, they are 'bereft of their senses' (*Ion* 534c), producing them 'without knowing in the least what they mean' (*Apology* 22c); it is not they who speak, but the god who speaks to us through them (*Ion* 534d). In one way one can interpret Plato here as saying that creativeness is, after all, explicable: its origins lie in the desires of the gods. To that extent he can be classified with those who locate these desires in natural processes at the level of the unconscious mind or the physiology of the brain. In another way he can be read as saying, along with Kant, that artistic creation is a mystery that no amount of explanatory investigation will dispel.

What should be our verdicts on the related issues of objective versus subjective accounts of creativity and of its explicability? On the objective account, so-called creative processes are identified only as processes leading to creative products in some objective sense, and hence the subjective approach is parasitic on the objective; and we know from their works that Mozart and Shakespeare were highly creative persons without knowing anything about the psychological or physiological processes which they underwent, so in this way the objective view is not dependent on the subjective. As for the issue of explicability, Jarvie has argued that if one *could* explain in general terms how objectively creative works come about, this would be tantamount to explaining their creativeness away: 'Usually an explanation of something does not explain it away. When it does, something is wrong' (Jarvie, 1981, p. 123). On his view, like Kant's and Plato's, creation is and cannot but be a mystery.

Plato's view of creation, unlike Kant's (as we have seen above), puts all the weight on arational inspiration and none on the rational, including technical, procedures which artists follow in shaping, improving and correcting their works (see also Jarvie, 1981, § 6). Creativeness and critical thinking in the arts are often contrasted with each other, but on the non-Platonic view the former embraces something of the latter (Tomas, 1964, p. 99). This approach to artistic creation contrasts with that of Collingwood (1938, pp. 125–35). For him the making of a tune, a poem or a picture is something that goes on in the artist's head, and nowhere else, its embodiment on paper or on canvas lying outside creation as such. One weakness of Collingwood's theory is that there is no evidence that artists generally work in this two-stage way, their final vision of their work as a whole typically appearing only after much trial-and-error labouring with the materials specific to their art.

Creators of works of art are usually identified with *artists*, but on some views the consumers of arts can have a role in co-creating the work. Ingarden (1972) has claimed that works of art have 'areas of indeterminateness' which are filled out by those who appreciate them. In this way a work of art is 'the common product of artist and observer' (Ingarden, 1972, p. 40). Whether it is helpful to speak of observers as creating – rather than, say, interpreting, or seeing aesthetically interesting features in a work – is doubtful. Once again, our initial distinctions may be helpful. However much I add to a Beethoven piece in listening to it, I do not, as Beethoven did, literally engage in making something out of musical materials. On the other hand, in setting my imagination to work, so that I reach behind the formal qualities of the music and come to hear it, as it were, from within as expressing feelings of the artist, I may be engaged in creative thinking in Elliott's 'new' sense. To take this line would be – as with the rejection of the 'democratic' conception of creativity – to pay proper homage to the unique achievement of the artist as maker.

See also EDUCATION, AESTHETIC; KANT; ORIGINALITY; PLATO.

BIBLIOGRAPHY

Boden, M.A.: *The Creative Mind: Myths and Mechanisms* (London: Weidenfeld & Nicolson, 1990).

Collingwood, R.G.: *The Principles of Art* (Oxford: Clarendon Press, 1938).

Elliott, R.K.: 'Versions of creativity', *Proceedings of the Philosophy of Education Society of Great Britain*, 5: 2 (1971), 139–52.

Ingarden, R.: 'Artistic and aesthetic values', *Aesthetics*, ed. H. Osborne (Oxford: Oxford University Press, 1972).

Jarvie, I.C.: 'The rationality of creativity', *The Concept of Creativity in Science and Art*, ed. D. Dutton and M. Krausz (The Hague: Martinus Nijhoff, 1981).

Kant, I.: *Kritik der Urteilskraft* (Berlin: 1790); trans. J. H. Bernard, *Critique of Judgment* (New York: Hafner, 1951).

Osborne, H.: 'The concept of creativity in art', *British Journal of Aesthetics*, 3 (1979), 224–31.

Plato: *Collected Dialogues*, ed. E. Hamilton, trans. H. Cairns (New York: Pantheon Books, 1961).

Read, H.: *Education through Art* (London: Faber, 1943).

Tomas, V., ed.: *Creativity in the Arts* (Englewood Cliffs, NJ: Prentice-Hall, 1964).

JOHN WHITE

criticism Introducing a collection of papers entitled *Contemporary Criticism* in 1970, Malcolm Bradbury, whilst noting an increase in what he termed 'speculative theory', recorded nevertheless that 'today, literary criticism has become *the* method of literary study – its primary methodology, or "discipline", the self-conscious tactic of the subject' (Bradbury, 1970, p. 19). Almost twenty years later, however, we find Frank Kermode declaring that 'criticism seems to be in rapid decline, and is by many thought moribund, and all the better for that' (Kermode, 1989, p. 5). Not, of course, that this marks a decline in the productivity of teachers in literature departments, but rather

the replacement of 'criticism' by 'theory'. The latter, Kermode thinks, 'is often the work of writers who seem largely to have lost interest in literature as such' and to be hostile to criticism, desiring 'to destroy the end [it] had in view, which . . . was to deepen understanding of literature, and to transmit to others (including non-professors) interpretations and valuations which could and would be transformed or accommodated to new conditions as time went by' (Kermode, 1989, p. 5). For both Bradbury and Kermode, 'criticism' is to be contrasted with 'theory', and whilst the former is concerned with 'literature as such' and is directed towards the interpretation and evaluation of individual works, the latter, at least in its contemporary and dominant mode, intends the destruction of criticism and its goals.

This understanding of the object and goals of criticism is at one with that of the so-called 'New Criticism' developed in the writings of John Crowe Ransome, Allen Tate and especially Cleanth Brooks in the United States during the 1930s and 1940s, and which, through the textbooks *Understanding Poetry* (1938) and *Understanding Fiction* (1941) (both by Brooks and Robert Penn Warren), became the dominant force in the teaching of literature in American universities after the Second World War. Although the term 'New Criticism' was taken from the title of a book by Ransome which did not discuss any of the critics now associated with it, it nevertheless aptly marks the sense of a break with the previous practice of literary study. At the heart of this lay the question of the sense and role of history for literary study. Tate characterized the new criticism as opposed to the 'historical method', the research into the historical influence on and of a work of literature, which treated the literary as an historical object about which facts could be gleaned. This approach, however, presupposed a quite different relation to the work, through which its reputation could be established in the first place so that it could become a worthy object for the study of 'influences'. Such an engagement is essentially interpretative and evaluative.

In *The Well-Wrought Urn* (1947), Brooks

went on to argue against the tendency to reduce this evaluative and interpretative activity itself to a species of factual inquiry. 'The temper of our times is strongly relativistic,' he wrote, for 'we tend to say that every poem is an expression of its age . . . that we must judge it only by the canons of its age' (Brooks, 1947, preface). But such a position both conceals its own evaluative character, in determining which authors are to be taken as showing us the relevant canons, and makes impossible an engagement with contemporary work, which must first be evaluated before there can be any conception of a 'canon' at all. We can only evaluate current work in terms of standards appropriate for literature *as such*, and it is in terms of these too that we engage with the works of the past in so far as we are evaluatively engaged with them. Great poems, Brooks claims, bear a close relation to each other, in the qualities which make them poems and which determine whether they are good or bad. Poetry, as a distinct form of discourse, embodies general criteria against which poems may be measured. Such judgements, then, will not be relative to their age, nor to our own, but are made in terms of the nature of poetry *as such* (Brooks, 1947, p. 197). I shall return to what this involves shortly.

Now this is, Brooks claims, a new understanding of poetry and the critic's role. There have indeed been critical revolutions in the past, but if now we are to consider literature *as* literature, then these must have shared an essentially non-literary understanding of the literary work. These revolutions, the neo-classical at the end of the seventeenth century and the Romantic at the turn of the nineteenth, although opposed in many ways in their understanding of poetry, had their differences constituted within a unity. A poem was understood by both as essentially a statement, the test of which is its truth; the poetical aspect of the work lies in the decoration of this information with imagery and appropriate metre and sound. There was thus a distinctive poetry language, although what was taken as poetic changed.

One might justify this in relation to writing inspired by the importation of French neo-classical critics such as Boileau, René Rapin and Dominique Bouhours at the end of the seventeenth century, by referring to John Dennis's *Grounds of Criticism in Poetry* (1704, in Elledge, 1961). Here Dennis claims that poetry is an art, and 'if it is an art it follows that it must propose an end to itself and afterwards lay down proper means for the attaining that end . . . those proper means in poetry we call rules.' The end of poetry is twofold: 'the subordinate one is pleasure, and the final one is instruction . . . in reforming the manners.' Poetry is essentially the conveying of moral instruction in a pleasing form which will incline the reader towards virtue and against vice.

The particular kinds of poetry are concerned with different spheres of human life and the virtues and vices relevant to them. The epic thus concerns the highest forms of conduct concerned with the well-being of the state or of mankind itself; tragedy, the punishment of great vice or the endurance of great misfortune on the part of the virtuous; comedy, the common foibles and small vices of ordinary people, and so forth. Each kind of poetry has its own rules, determined by the end of pleasing by instruction through the imitation of the appropriate manners, which concern the various parts of the poem: plot, character, speeches, sentiments, imagery, diction and versification. Criticism brings to bear the appropriate end and rule for the kind of poem at issue, and exercises taste which Addison called 'that faculty of the soul which discerns the beauties of an author with pleasure and the imperfections with dislike'. Such criticism not only notes conformity with the rules, which Pope said resulted in 'exact disposition, just thoughts, correct elocution, polished numbers', but also that 'poetical fire' which marks the great from the commonplace in the production of daring and striking imagery, and so forth. The end of moral instruction requires reference to a universal morality and the depiction of individuals with reference to their general humanity, so that Dr Johnson tells us in *Rasselas* that 'the business of the poet is to examine, not the individual but the species; to remark general properties and large appearances'; and, in the preface to his edition of Shakespeare's plays, that 'it is always a writer's duty to make the world better, and justice is a virtue independent on time and place.'

If the Romantics objected to the production of imagery through fancy – which elaborates, as Wordsworth put it, 'the lurking affinities' in dissimilars – in favour of the imagination, and rejected the neo-classical 'kinds' of poetry, for Brooks they do so still in the name of a non-literary purpose. Imagination, Coleridge said, acts 'by impressing the stamp of humanity, of human feeling over inanimate objects' so that objects are not merely imitated, but 'a human and intellectual life is transferred to them from the poet's own spirit' (Coleridge, 1960, ch. 11). This is not merely a matter of seeing nature through an emotional colouring, as when in *Lear* 'the deep anguish of a father spreads the feeling of ingratitude and cruelty over the very elements of heaven', but a bringing of 'the whole soul of man into activity' (Coleridge, 1960, ch. 12). Imagination, which 'struggles to idealize and to unify', has the essential task of revealing the unity of the human with the universe at large and so, as Wordsworth put it, 'to incite and support the eternal'. Hence the appropriateness of the Romantic lyric form and the autobiographical poem – Wordsworth's *Prelude* being the greatest exemplar – in which the individual characteristically is shown moving from an instinctive unity with nature to an alienation revealed by man's capacity for freedom, which is in turn remedied through the revelation of a new and higher unity within which the individual achieves, as the *Prelude* (bk 14, lines 113–14) says, 'the highest bliss . . . the consciousness/Of whom they are'.

Thus, for Brooks, the aim of such poetry is to convey truths about 'the eternal', which may equally be transmitted argumentatively in philosophy, in a language and form calculated to incite the appropriate feelings. The critic's task is to enable the reader to participate in such feelings, a project which leads to an 'appreciative' criticism which itself conveys the feelings of the critic and which,

therefore, itself participates to an extent in the character of literature itself.

The previous critical revolutions, then, understood the poem instrumentally, as directed towards a non-literary end and to be judged accordingly. Whether it is 'to instruct by pleasing' or 'to incite and support the eternal', the poem's quality depends on the truth of its teaching and on the effectiveness of its poetic language in achieving the desired end. The poem has not been judged *as* literature but as a means to a non-literary end. To approach the poem *as* poetry and so noninstrumentally means rejecting the form–content distinction between the truth conveyed and the way it is presented. A poem, Brooks says, is not about whatever ideas it may contain. The imagery, rhythm and sound are not merely instruments by which a content is conveyed, but rather constitute the *meaning* of the poem itself. Poetry is a particular kind of discourse – figurative discourse – and the poem as poem is a dramatic unity of patterns of figuration. The unity of the poem lies in the ways in which tensions are set up by propositions, tropes, rhythm and sound and are ultimately resolved, again figuratively. The poem is thus to be understood in close proximity to a musical composition, as when in sonata form tonal tensions are set up, argumentatively developed, and resolved.

The significance of this figurative use of language lies for Brooks in literature's concern not with ideas but with the way a human being may relate to them, which requires figurative expression, as can be seen in our everyday lives when we have resort to simile and metaphor in order to express how we feel. Because the structure of the poem is to be understood in this dramatic way, the central terms of critical discourse are those of 'ambiguity', 'paradox', 'complex of attitudes', 'irony' and 'wit'. The poem is an *enactment* of attitudes and of their conflict and resolution, and the critic's task is to interpret, in the sense of bringing out the nature of the 'meaning', figuratively understood, as opposed to the mere paraphrasable content, and to evaluate the poem's success or failure as such enactment.

Brooks considers two critical revolutions prior to the advent of the New Criticism, and one might wonder why not more, given that literature and its discussion have a far longer history. George Watson (1973, p. 3) notes that it was Dryden who first used the term 'criticism' in relation to literature, at least in print, in the preface to *The State of Innocence* (1677), where he explains it as 'a standard of judging well' and claims it was instituted first by Aristotle. But evaluative interpretation of individual works is singularly lacking in ancient and mediaeval texts. Plato, concerned to dispute the educative value of poetry, and Aristotle, to defend it as a form of knowledge about human life, both take for granted the evaluation of the works they mention but provide little insight into its formation. The same is largely true of the tradition of so-called rhetorical criticism in the Hellenistic period, concerned as it was to preserve a culture of the past by making its accepted masterworks into unquestionable models for imitation, although there are hints of a critical practice at work in the descriptions of the appropriateness of particular rhythms, diction and sounds to the different 'styles' of poetry (see, for example, Demetrius in Russell and Winterbottom, 1972). The allegorical interpretation of the Middle Ages, deriving from neo-Platonic models utilized for Christian exegesis, consists in the application of a method to texts already selected on other grounds. One could get no indication from Dante's allegorical account of *The Divine Comedy* of how one could distinguish his work from the mediocre or incompetent, as his contemporaries and successors clearly did.

Let us, however, return to the question of the contemporary confrontation between criticism and theory. What is proposed by this in its various forms is that the practice of criticism involves presuppositions 'about language and about meaning, about the relationships between meaning and the world, meaning and people, and . . . about people themselves and their place in the world' (Belsey, 1980) which are never explicitly stated and defended. When these presuppositions are revealed by reflective thought, they are shown to be inadequate, and the practice which may then ensue, properly grounded in the appropriate theory, is no longer recognizably criticism. Theory takes a variety of contemporary forms depending on the sort of presuppositions identified and criticized, but perhaps the dominant modes have been deconstruction in the United States, and in Britain a form of poststructuralism centrally concerned with political history.

According to poststructuralist critics of both camps, literary criticism has sought to interpret works of literature and so provide us with access to their meaning. Such a meaning is assumed to be unitary, whether this is taken as a paraphrasable message or as the figurative unity sought by the New Critics, and only on the basis of this assumption are the interpretative practice and its characteristic forms of dispute and agreement intelligible. But this assumption is untenable, it is claimed. The meaning of any sign is produced only through its differing from others, and this process can have no given terminus as such an end would have to be a sign whose meaning was not the result of difference. Any particular determinant meaning is only possible because we have terminated this play of differentiation for practical purposes, and yet that meaning is only possible because the signs concerned can always be incorporated in another nexus of differences, another context, and so come to mean differently, in a way which cannot, in principle, be limited.

Deconstruction thus characteristically tries to show how a text, in trying to limit its meaning, at the same time undoes this work and shows its impossibility. Certain kinds of literary work are sometimes privileged within deconstructive approaches, as showing a reflective awareness of the differential nature of meaning, inviting interpretations which they at the same time resist. Thus, Barbara Johnson in a discussion of Melville's *Billy Budd* tries to show how the different readings of the text produced in literary criticism are replicated in the text itself, in the way Budd, Claggart, Dansker and Vere read the events of the story and each other. At crucial moments of the text, central to *deciding* a meaning, however, there is only the 'empty, mechanical functioning' of language, as when, for example, Vere dies simply repeating Budd's name. It is, Johnson suggests, 'these very gaps in understanding', which both provoke interpretation and prevent its success, that 'Melville is asking us to understand' (Johnson, 1980, p. 94).

British theorists have tended to regard American deconstruction as a continuation of the New Critical project by other means, within which one can restrict oneself to the formal aspects of a text. 'In the constant and repeated assertion of the evaporation of meaning there is no place to analyse the contest of meaning, and therefore no politics, and there is no possibility of tracing changes of meaning, the sliding of the signified, in history' (Belsey in Lodge, 1988, p. 403). For such theorists, the differential nature of meaning shows it as unfixed, 'sliding', and so a matter for political debate. The differential structures of meaning available at any time determine the limits of what it is possible to say and understand, and since the destination of meaning is the subject, 'subjectivity is discursively produced and is constrained by the range of subject positions defined by the discourses in which the individual participates' (Belsey, 1985, p. 6). This determines, therefore, what it is possible to *be* at any time. But since the play of meaning cannot be halted, all such determinations of subjectivity are unstable and embattled.

The discourse of literary criticism, in its various forms, assumes a particular form of subjectivity – the unified, autonomous individual for whom there is a unified, determinate and graspable meaning – the subjectivity of 'liberal humanism', which emerges out of conflict with mediaeval conceptions in the sixteenth century and achieves dominance in the seventeenth. Literature is one of the scenes within which such fundamental determinations of meaning are contested and reinforced. The aim of the work on literature is to undermine the hold of 'liberal humanism', through a demonstration of the way its fundamental conceptions have emerged through conflict and have maintained themselves through the suppression of alternative subjectivities. In this way, a contemporary space is to be formed within which radical change becomes possible. This reading practice is directed towards a 'political history from the raw material of literary texts' for which 'literary value becomes irrelevant: political assassination is problematized in Pickering's play *Horestes* (1567) as well as in *Hamlet*'; fiction is thus 'put to work for substantial political ends' (Belsey in Lodge, 1988, p. 409).

The plausibility of 'theory' obviously initially depends on that of the theoretical discourses it invokes, and especially here the differential account of meaning. If, for example, through a reading of the later Wittgenstein, one finds this incoherent, then theory's claims on one's allegiance will be radically diminished, and it is remarkable for a movement which emphasizes its reflective credentials how little such fundamental reflection is in evidence. Yet it is probably on the notion of literary value that one can expect future argument to centre, since, for both deconstruction and the political history of subjectivity, texts privileged by literary tradition become mere cases of a general textuality within which they have no preferential status. Not only does this remove the *raison d'être* for literature departments, but it divorces the study of literature from the non-academic concern with it in ways criticism never did, and reduces the non-professional to a prisoner chained within the cave of ideology or language.

I suspect we need to remind ourselves of a deeper sense of subjectivity, indicated in Kierkegaard's reminders to readers inclined towards an Hegelianism which is the historical forebear of theory, that 'if a man occupies himself all his life through with logic, he would nevertheless not become logic: he must therefore himself exist in different categories' – categories which cannot be recouped by a theory to which the individual would again have to relate. It might then be possible, once more, to connect literature to the relation that the existing individual has to her or his own life, which precludes the objectifications of theory but finds perhaps an appropriate form of appearance in the arts, which require, themselves, a passionate and interested response.

See also CANON; DECONSTRUCTION; FEMINIST CRITICISM; INTERPRETATION; JUDGEMENT, AESTHETIC; STRUCTURALISM AND POSTSTRUCTURALISM; TASTE.

BIBLIOGRAPHY

Belsey, C.: *Critical Practice* (London: Methuen, 1980).

Belsey, C.: *The Subject of Tragedy* (London: Methuen, 1985).

Bradbury, M., ed.: *Contemporary Criticism* (London: Arnold, 1970).

Brooks, C.: *The Well-Wrought Urn* (New York: Harcourt & Brace, 1947).

Coleridge, S.: *Biographia Literaria*, ed. G. Watson (London: Dent, 1960 [1817]).

Elledge, S., ed.: *Eighteenth-Century Critical Essays* (Ithaca, NY: Cornell University Press, 1961).

Johnson, B.: *The Critical Difference* (Baltimore, Md: Johns Hopkins University Press, 1980).

Kermode, F.: *An Appetite for Poetry* (London: Collins, 1989).

Lodge, D., ed.: *Modern Criticism and Theory* (London: Longman, 1988).

Russell, D. and Winterbottom, M.: *Ancient Literary Criticism* (Oxford: Oxford University Press, 1972).

Watson, G.: *The Literary Critics* (Harmondsworth: Penguin Books, 1973).

MICHAEL WESTON

Croce, Benedetto (1866–1952) Italian idealist philosopher, historian and critic; a dominant figure in his country's intellectual life in the first part of the twentieth century. Born in the Abruzzo region of Italy, Croce developed in his youth a taste for old books and the life of a self-styled scholar in literature and history. Gradually a passion for the free thinking that philosophy allowed drew him into writing in a philosophical vein. In 1883 he suffered a tragedy that reorientated his domestic life. He was on holiday with his family when an earthquake struck; his parents and sister were killed and he himself was buried for several hours before being rescued. He went to live in Rome with his uncle and when he finally emerged from the depression brought on by the tragedy and the subsequent displacement, he embarked on his philosophical career.

Croce's thinking drew from a variety of sources. Early on under the influence of Antonio Labriola, he was led to explore the work of J.F. Herbart and Marx. A more direct influence on his aesthetics, however, was Francesco de Sanctis, whose work he had begun reading as a schoolboy. His continuing attention to de Sanctis led, after the turn of the century, to study of Hegel and Vico and to the refining of his own brand of idealist aesthetics. In tracing the history of Croce's central notion of intuition it is of interest to note his assertion that he learned from de Sanctis 'in a very crude shape this central idea: that art is not a work of reflection and logic, nor yet a product of skill, but pure and spontaneous imaginative form' (Croce, 1928, pp. 78–9).

Croce's first work in aesthetics, an outline of his initial thoughts, appeared in 1900 as *Thesis of Aesthetics*. This was followed in 1902 by the publication of his central work on the subject, *Aesthetic: As Science of Expression and General Linguistic*. It is in the *Aesthetic* that he first fully describes his account of art as intuition. Intuition, as he understood it, is not a mystical acquisition of transcendent truths, but the immediate knowing, and thereby transforming, of impressions. Since intuitive knowing is active, Croce maintains, it can also be understood as expression. Thus, intuition is expression in so far as expression is the act of transforming impressions by active imagination (*fantasia*) into individual unified images or organic wholes: 'Intuition is the undifferentiated unity of the perception of the real and of the simple image of the possible' (Croce, 1964, p. 4). The result was that, for Croce, intuition–expression in itself is neither divisible into parts nor subsumable under intellectual genera or categories.

In identifying art as intuition–expression, Croce seemed to champion art for art's sake. The presence or absence of intuition marked off that which was art from non-art. Although he insisted that aesthetic activity is not restricted to artists in the professional sense, he believed it possible to identify them by their 'greater aptitude' and 'more frequent inclination fully to express certain complex states of the soul' (Croce, 1964, p. 13). However, he was also adamant in dismissing two extreme readings of art's autonomy. First, the aesthetic is not the only fundamental realm of the human spirit; rather, it has its place alongside logic, the practical (economics and ethics), and history. Second, despite its autonomy, art as intuition–expression cannot occur without the richness of human spirit in all its manifestations. Thus, aesthetics, although it is foundational, is not the monarch of all sciences, and artistic expression does not occur unfunded by other human activities.

On this foundation in the *Aesthetic* Croce built his fuller account of art as intuition. Scholars, however, disagree as to how to read the development of his ideas. Some argue that his views changed so drastically that it is best to understand his work as a series of distinct and inconsistent moments. However, he himself held that the development of his ideas was evolutionary, that his later thinking was an extension, not a refutation, of his earlier thinking. This was consistent with his adoption of a kind of historicism that acknowledged the growth of ideas. The evolutionary interpretation seems not only the most fruitful, but, at least in the first instance, the one that, given Croce's own endorsement of it, provides the likeliest avenue to understanding him.

Not only the nature of this development, but its method, is significant. In 1903, shortly after publication of the *Aesthetic*, Croce and Giovanni Gentile began publication of their journal *La Critica*. Croce's task was that of criticizing recent Italian literature. Thus, his philosophical development came to be deeply influenced by his work as a practical critic. Indeed, his life's work as a whole exhibits a dialectic of the practical and the theoretical. In his aesthetics, this dialectic resulted in the breaking down of his initial description of art as intuition into three stages: (a) the attribution of a lyrical character to intuition; (2) the defence of cosmic

totality in art; and (3) the distinction between poetry and literature.

The first development, begun in 1908 and summed up in *Guide to Aesthetics* in 1913, is perhaps the least problematic. The question that Croce faced was the efficacy of intuition: if intuition is not formed by intellectual concepts, how does it occur? His answer, which he attributed to ideas developed in his role as critic, was that intuition is 'lyrical'. That is, it is the expression of emotion or feeling. By this, however, he intended neither a 'letting-off of steam' nor a simply imitative theory of expression. Rather, the intuition–expression is idealized or transformed emotion. As Orsini puts it: 'The lyrical function of art is to express the personality of the artist – not, be it carefully noted, his "practical personality" as evidenced in his biography, but what Croce calls here the "soul" of the man' (Orsini, 1961, p. 48). The lyrical conception of intuition, in pointing to idealized emotion and personality, sets the stage for the second development of Croce's notion of art.

In a 1918 essay entitled 'The character of totality in artistic expression', Croce argued that intuition involves a kind of universality or cosmic totality (*totalità*). To many critics this move appeared problematic, in view of his earlier assertions that logical concepts are universal and expressive intuitions are individual. However, Croce wanted to argue for a special kind of universality in art. In assessing the work of Ariosto, Shakespeare, Corneille and others, he found himself searching for that which distinguishes their work from confessional, subjective articulations of emotion. What he suggested was that the best works of these artists express, in their individuality, something common to all humanity; they express or reflect a cosmic totality. This does not, as Croce saw it, imply an act of intellectualizing or philosophizing in art. An intuition–expression in itself is still not a general type governing a set of tokens. Rather, the universality or totality of art occurs together with art's individuality in an undifferentiated form, as is not the case in conceptual renderings of universality.

An interesting upshot of Croce's defence of

cosmic totality occurred when he began to search for its phenomenological attributes. From the mid-1920s, he began to argue that moral conscience is a condition of intuition–expression. If taken to mean that art depends on morality, this clearly and flatly contradicts one of his fundamental theses: the separation of the realms of the spirit. Moreover, critics saw in this suggestion the possibility of the very kind of moralism that Croce had always sought to reject. It is possible, however, that he had something more expansive in mind: 'It is impossible', he said, 'to be a poet or an artist without being in the first place a man nourished by thought and by experience of moral ideals and conflicts' (Croce, 1949, p. 133). He may have been searching not for a narrow moralism but for the kind of experience, even if imaginative experience, that can engender cosmic totality.

In the final turn in his aesthetics, Croce published in 1936 his *Poetry and Literature: An Introduction to Its Criticism and History*. Here he distinguishes poetry from literature. On the surface such a distinction may appear to contradict his earlier insistence against understanding art through types or genres. However, his project was to return to his distinction between art and non-art. The problem was to locate those items that appear to be poetry inasmuch as they appropriate artistic expressions, but are not themselves intuition–expressions. He had in mind particular items such as entertainment and prose that are practical or intellectual in nature. To these items he gave the name 'literature' to distinguish them from poetry or art. Thus, instead of establishing fixed genres within art, Croce was simply refining a distinction he had made in the *Aesthetic*.

His notion of art as intuition–expression in its various stages of development produced several interesting corollaries. First, it excised external production or the making of artefacts from art proper. For Croce, 'externalization' of intuition–expression was a practical affair, not an aesthetic one. This was, and is, anathema for aestheticians for whom the physical making is integral to art. Yet Croce's position is not as strange as it might seem at first glance.

On the one hand, even in his earliest work he recognized that externalization can be used to assist expression. On the other, he never discarded from intuition qualities such as tempo, rhythm, line and colour. The mistake, as he saw it, was an ontological one of assuming that these qualities are merely external, physical items or events. For him they *are* the intuition–expression in their unique unity; and they occur in the intuition prior to any physical recording of them.

This in turn led to Croce's assertion that the role that physical artefacts have to play is that of vehicle for communicating art. Thus, as Dewey independently suggested, critics and observers must use artefacts to re-create the intuition of the artist. As did Dewey, Croce faced opposition here from those who argued that such strict re-creation is impossible. However, it is doubtful that he had in mind anything like a technical isomorphism; rather, the *genius* of the producer and the *taste* of the critic achieve the same intuition of cosmic totality. It is in this way 'that our little souls can echo great souls, and grow great with them in the universality of the spirit' (Croce, 1964, p. 121).

The adoption of this method of criticism also meant that he rejected the efficacy of criticisms that rest entirely on intellectual categorizations of technique or content. For Croce, such categories, by virtue of their practical or intellectual natures, were incidental to art. Nevertheless, he did come to maintain that critics can use intellectual categories in their practice of criticizing, but only after a re-creation of intuition–expression has occurred.

Much of Croce's work remains underexplored in contemporary Anglo-American aesthetics, perhaps because much of it remains untranslated. Nevertheless, through the work of R.G. Collingwood his aesthetics has been indirectly influential beyond continental Europe. Moreover, Croce's discussions of the similarities between his ideas and those of John Dewey deserve further investigation. While Dewey attempted to disavow any debt to Croce, the similarities that exist are too compelling to be dismissed. If the flux of Croce's aesthetics makes it difficult to unify, the experiential soundness of its insights ensures it future importance.

See also COLLINGWOOD; DEWEY; EXPRESSION; ONTOLOGY OF ARTWORKS.

WRITINGS

Contributo alla Critica di Me Stesso (Naples; 1918); trans. R.G. Collingwood, Benedetto Croce: An Autobiography (Oxford: Clarendon Press, 1928).
Trans. E.F. Carrit, My Philosophy and Other Essays on the Moral and Political Problems of Our Time (London: George Allen & Unwin, 1949).
Estetica come Scienza dell'Espressione e Linguistica Generale (Bari: 1902); 10th edn (Bari: Laterza, 1958); trans. Douglas Ainslie, Aesthetic: As Science of Expression and General Linguistic (New York: Noonday Press, 1964).
Brevario di Estetica: Quattro Lezioni (Bari: 1913); trans. Patrick Romanell, Guide to Aesthetics (Indianapolis: Bobbs-Merrill, 1965).
La Poesia: Introduzione alla Critica e Storia della Poesia (Bari: 1936); 6th edn (Bari: Laterza, 1963); trans. Giovanni Gullace, Benedetto Croce's Poetry and Literature: An Introduction to Its Criticism and History (Carbondale, Ill.: Southern Illinois University Press, 1981).

BIBLIOGRAPHY

Brown, Merle E.: Neo-Idealistic Aesthetics: Croce–Gentile–Collingwood (Detroit: Wayne State University Press, 1966).
Moss, M.E.: Benedetto Croce Reconsidered: Truth and Error in Theories of Art, Literature, and History (Hanover, NH: University Press of New England, 1987).
Orsini, Gian N.G.: Benedetto Croce: Philosopher of Art and Literary Critic (Carbondale, Ill.: Southern Illinois University Press, 1961).

DOUGLAS R. ANDERSON

culture In the contents relevant here, the term has at least six distinct, though related, meanings:

1. Culture, generically speaking, is the distinctive feature of human as opposed to animal life, and the subject-matter of so-called philosophical anthropology. It denotes the whole realm of thought and behaviour whose patterns are not genetically, but socially, transmitted. Thus while the social animals interact (even when their behaviour is learnt) in more or less rigid, species-determined ways, human societies, over and above whatever 'natural' endowment their common characteristics may indicate, show almost infinite variability. Animal behaviour is explicable directly in terms of its biological function; but, while human behaviour may have a biological *foundation* (humanity being an animal species), it is not clear that it invariably has a biological *explanation* (as, for example, sociobiology postulates).

Several reasons may be advanced for scepticism in this regard:

(a) Much, perhaps most, human behaviour seems surplus to immediate biological requirements – for instance, in the matter of food, whose consumption is circumscribed by all kinds of non-alimentary considerations (religious, aesthetic, social, and so on).

(b) Unlike animal behaviour, human behaviour possesses a dimension of self-conscious *meaning* which itself constitutes an important source of motivation, and furnishes the agent with articulate reasons for his actions; barring the very simplest ('I am hungry', and the like), most of those are not easily reducible to 'biological' imperatives; the latter, moreover, when allegedly 'unconscious', could never constitute a reason for the agent himself.

(c) Animal behaviour may reasonably be treated as a pattern of biologically adaptive responses to a relatively constant natural environment; human beings, however, continuously modify, in ways whose consequences are unpredictable, both their natural and their social environments, so that, although their *ability* to respond to a changing environment is innate, their actual specific responses cannot be, in the sense that no genetic programme incorporating them could ever have had time to evolve.

'Culture' in this sense (or 'nurture') is conventionally contrasted with biological 'nature'. But this is not to say it is not 'natural'. In Aristotle's view, for example, the essence of culture is reason (in that it consists of things done for reasons, however misguided), and reason is to man what instinct is to the animals, a natural endowment. Culture is similarly opposed, in the sense of not being usefully reducible, to *physical* 'nature', even though, as in the case of biology, it is presumably grounded in it. For this reason Wilhelm Dilthey proposed two different kinds of study for cultural and natural phenomena, the *Geisteswissenschaften* and the *Naturwissenschaften* respectively (see also para. 3 below).

2. Cultures specifically, as defined by their differences, not from 'nature' or animal societies, but from each other; the province of sociology and social anthropology. A 'culture' denotes a distinct, historic group of people – a society – together with all its tools, artefacts, possessions, and characteristic ways and conceptions of life; indeed, 'culture' in this sense is often used interchangeably with 'society'. Built into it are various presuppositions:

(a) A culture is not a heap of unrelated phenomena, but an organic whole, so that each feature of it, however obvious its biological explanation, also has meaning in relation to the others.
(b) So far as its features are unique, or, if shared with other cultures, so transformed by their context as to 'mean' something substantially different, it too is unique.
(c) It is extended in time, as it must be to be transmissible between generations (even an emergent culture has emerged from something).
(d) It is also conscious of the fact, so that it conceives itself (in varying degrees) in terms of the past, present and future.
(e) In all the foregoing respects a culture resembles an individual, and thus possesses a quasi-personal identity, even though its self-consciousness may be located nowhere but in the minds of its individual members, and though it may lack any unitary 'will'.
(f) Though a response to circumstances (some of them of its own creation), a culture is a spontaneous growth (cf. (a)), and (unlike a purely sociopolitical order) cannot be invented, planned or imposed.

Without positively entailing it, (a) and (b) tend to favour 'cultural relativism', the idea (which stands in the way of any genuinely comparative social science), that cultures are to be judged not by any external standard, but only in relation to their own avowed or implicit aims. In one of its senses, so-called 'functionalism' ministers to this idea, in that every feature of a culture is seen (by E.E. Evans-Pritchard, for example) as conducing to the maintenance of the whole as a self-conscious and self-contained system. Functionalism in another sense (typified, say, by A.R. Radcliffe-Brown or Malinowski) runs counter to cultural relativism, in that it judges cultural features, and cultures as a whole, by their success or failure in meeting certain ulterior, universal or independently conceived goals (happiness, utility, biological survival, and so forth).

3. A culture's 'consciousness', or purely ideational component; a society's ideas, beliefs and values considered as a whole, and as distinct from its political, economic and technological structures. In this sense one can speak of the culture *of* a given society, of its being (under certain circumstances) at odds with society, or even (as with, say, French culture in Canada) of its being dislocated from its society of origin and subsisting independently. Confusingly, in this usage also 'society' is often substituted for 'culture', so that some other word than 'society' has to be found for a society's material or non-ideational components – or, as Marxism (which regards them as the ultimate determinants of 'consciousness') would call them, its 'base'. 'Culture' in this sense is often used to signify 'common culture' – that is, whatever ideas, beliefs and values are generally shared by all

members of a society (or culture) and are thus regarded as definitive of it.

A culture as a distinct, coherent and self-supporting system of beliefs is peculiarly difficult to 'explain', since it seems to its subscribers to need no explanation, being self-evidently 'natural' and 'true'. For this reason, epiphenomenal interpretations (such as those of Marx, Nietzsche and Freud), which see culture in the Platonic manner, as a shadow thrown by something of which the subscribers are unaware but which is supposedly more fundamental, seem questionable, since in substituting the observer's perspective for the believer's, they remove from the thing to be explained its most essential feature. On the other hand, to claim that a belief can be 'understood' only by its believers is to use the term 'understanding' somewhat oddly, since understanding is normally thought to follow upon explanation, rather than to be precluded or destroyed by it. Maybe what is required is Dilthey's *Verstehen*, the imaginative empathy generally associated more with art and history than with science, whereby the observer projects himself into beliefs he does not or cannot share (in the sense of not literally believing in or acting on them).

4. The word 'culture' is frequently used to mean 'subculture': for instance, 'youth culture', 'religious culture', 'working-class culture'. Such a culture is not fully autonomous, since it is defined, and defines itself, by reference to the wider culture surrounding it. Only from the global perspectives of anthropology, science, international sport and high culture does it seem plausible to see an otherwise autonomous culture and its products as subcultural: Polynesian society, German chemistry, Australian rugby, English painting. (The noun signifies the wider culture, and the epithet the subculture.)

5. The cultures (such as 'high', 'popular') pertaining exclusively to leisure (Aristotle's *scholē*); those elements of a culture in sense 2 which transcend all its explicitly practical, utilitarian or survival-related concerns (and, to the extent that they bear on those

concerns, its morality and religion too); the realm of purely spontaneous or 'useless' activities, and the ideas, objects and institutions associated with them. 'Useless', however, does not mean 'worthless', since an end in itself is both useless (by definition) and the underlying source of value in all those 'useful' things (work, for example) necessary to its realization.

Culture in this sense comprises:

(a) sport, entertainment and recreation ('popular culture', roughly speaking);
(b) the world of liberal intellect (that is, the cultivation, at an advanced level, of knowledge for its own sake);
(c) 'the arts' and the 'higher' aesthetic realm generally ('high culture', a category which perhaps also embraces (b), at least so far as to include the humanities; see para. 6 below).

It may be noted further that (a) remains essentially utilitarian, if thought of merely as a rehearsal for, or relief from, work; that, notwithstanding their 'uselessness', such pursuits (especially sport and high culture) may demand a high degree of effort and dedication; and that although, in token of their 'private' and superficially unserious character, their purely domestic conduct (except in totalitarian societies) is seldom thought to need political supervision, it is frequently subject to severe indigenous constraints.

Many social critics (notably Ruskin and William Morris) have acknowledged the importance of leisure, in recommending that work, or the labour necessary for physical sustenance, should also so far as possible seem worth performing for its own sake (as in crafts, the applied arts and the liberal professions). The intuition is that a man's personality, fulfilment and self-respect are most deeply bound up with his voluntary pursuits. This is perhaps why, in gregarious activities of the kind (as in the professions), the chief penalty for 'unethical' behaviour is disgrace.

6. 'High' culture specifically; 'culture' in this sense, in addition to its characteristic ideas, values, institutions, objects and artefacts, is, or signifies:

(a) an important subdivision of culture in sense 5;

(b) a personal accomplishment, often accompanied by a certain social grace;

(c) a quality more of taste and sensibility than of intellect, though it presupposes a fairly high degree of intelligence (as of aptitude and motivation);

(d) the product of an appropriate education, formal or otherwise, over and above that necessary for ordinary unreflective membership of society; the education itself;

(e) an unending process of development, both in the individuals undergoing it and in the collective product, possessing an identifiable tendency and certain immediate aims, but no final goal other than participation;

(f) the possession of a minority or elite, yet not of a subculture proper, since it implicitly offers to speak for culture as a whole;

(g) accordingly, an object of esteem or, more rarely, of resentment among those who do not share it, when they are not simply indifferent;

(h) a thing unavoidably local in its immediate origin, and perhaps in its ultimate loyalties, but generally outward-looking and open to cosmopolitan influence (though it has often, particularly in the arts, shown a nationalist or self-consciously 'ethnic' tendency, marked by an interest in 'roots' and by borrowings from 'folk' culture).

Large claims have been made for high culture, particularly since the Romantic period and the rise, during the eighteenth century, of aesthetics. High culture, or more particularly art (its central concern), has been thought to provide the intimations of unity, value and meaning in experience which were once provided by religion and are now threatened by the triumphantly 'disenchanted' world outlook of science. (The term 'disenchantment' was first used in this connection by Schiller, and has entered sociological discourse through Weber, who thought disenchantment the essence of modernity.) Aesthetic experience, indeed, whether of art or of nature, may actually be superior to religion. For its immediacy secures it against doubt, while (in the case of art) the purely imaginative 'belief' it demands is inexpugnable by argument, since nothing is literally being asserted.

In short, aesthetic experience is not a belief as to fact (and hence fallible), but a fact itself (and thence not). It reveals not the world's physical structure, but its human significance. Its 'truths' are not enunciated, but simply enacted and confirmed in the subject's consciousness. In this respect it resembles not religious doctrine, but religious practice. In other words, and like many other cultural practices, it seems to carry its meaning within it; and, not being dependent on substantive belief, it is also much less easily eroded by 'explanation' (see para. 3 above). In Matthew Arnold's view, moreover, the 'cultured' outlook to which it conduces – sensitive, tentative, catholic, scrupulous, empirical, at once pious and sceptical – not only issues in 'gentlemanly' behaviour (that is, minimizes social friction), but is of the greatest value in other fields, especially morals and politics, where unchallenged dogmatism and self-confident ignorance otherwise run riot.

In short, and despite (or even because of) having no such aim, 'culture' turns out to be positively functional. Arnold, in fact, makes much the same claim for it as Mill had made ten years earlier, and as Hayek was to make over a century later for liberalism (its chief enemy, in Arnold's eyes).

This conception of high culture, of course, lacks neither its difficulties nor its critics. For example, how do we persuade someone that his tastes are low or perverted, when their very 'immediacy' seems to justify them? And what if he accepts our judgement, yet persists in his preference? How far can we count on support from the 'common culture' (even supposing it would settle matters if we could)? And how could we expect any, given that high culture is almost by definition the preserve of a minority?

Only the last two questions admit of a short answer. High culture is opposed only to 'low' culture; that is, to (complacent) ignorance, crudity and bad taste. It is not opposed to popular culture *per se*, since its purpose is essentially different; the two, moreover, have something in common (see para. 5). But, except at its 'aestheticist' extreme (where it is largely a recreation for culture snobs, and, as has often been pointed out, is also compatible with the greatest cruelty and unscrupulousness), high culture may be thought of as a rediscovery, reworking and justification at the aesthetic level, of the common culture's deepest, most 'serious' and most definitively 'human' purposes, where they are void of any contingent (and irrelevant) instrumental value. Where a culture lacks those things, therefore, it is likely also to be 'Philistine' – that is, deficient in high culture, or hostile to it.

If further proof be required that common and high culture are interdependent, the following reflections may suffice. High culture's most prized artefacts are frequently popular in origin, in subject-matter, in perennial appeal, or in all those things together. Again, high culture is exclusive, but it is not the property of any particular socio-economic class. Whatever their origins and remaining ties, its representatives are quite literally 'in a class of their own', one which is open to anybody appropriately qualified, and which confers no *ex officio* membership upon the rich, the powerful or the well born (who are not, in any case, universally concerned to seek it). Finally, the suppression of high culture (usually in favour of an ersatz 'official' version) by the former communist regimes of the Soviet bloc merely underlined the natural continuity between high and common culture (which was also suppressed). Never has high culture been held in greater popular esteem, nor spoken, to the educated and uneducated alike, of their common concerns and with a voice that seemed more like their own, than when, as then, it was the voice of the oppressed.

This last example, moreover, should finally lay to rest the Marxist (and especially neo-Marxist or New Left) idea that culture generally, but particularly high culture, is merely and always the ideological servant of 'power', the heavily disguised utterance of a dominant

class intent on remaining so. No doubt ruling aristocracies have always commissioned (and, so far from disguising them, publicly displayed) flattering artistic representations of themselves; but so, on account of their collective purchasing power, have humbler classes such as the eighteenth-century novel-reading public, or (humbler still) Elizabethan theatre audiences and the readers of popular ballads. Which of these, especially in view of the comparative audience sizes involved, constitutes 'dominance'? And where, among these products taken as a whole, is the unanimity in moral values and (particularly) political outlook which the theory would lead one to expect?

It is true that among those few products (of any provenance) which have come to enjoy serious high-cultural esteem, an incipient community of outlook may be detected. And it is plausible to assume that the core values concerned, whether or not they form the 'real' principle behind this ostensibly 'aesthetic' selectivity, are at any rate not disagreeable to the sympathies of the high-cultural elite, or even to their interests (though those amount to no more than the will to protect what is most valued and to secure the best means of doing so). But it is implausible to attribute this vague consensus to the insidious workings of 'power', whether political or economic. As has just been pointed out, high culture is often intensely critical of rules, is by definition indifferent to utilitarian (that is, to economic) considerations (see para. 5), and, under communism, was in the custody of people who not only had no property, but, in many cases, no jobs either. That many 'ruling class' artefacts (and people) have nevertheless secured high-cultural approval points only to their consonance (explicit or implicit) with the aims of the common culture for which high culture professes to speak.

Recast in political form, that consonance is actually the test of any government's legitimacy. Thus if rulers seek acceptance – a thing they have every incentive to do, since, both psychically and materially, rule by mere force is highly diseconomical – they will do well to adopt their subjects' perspective. The process is the reverse of that diagnosed by Marxists. So far from being an instrument of legitimation (or of anything: see para. 2 (f)), culture is itself the source of legitimacy, as democratic governments make yet more obvious by explicitly suing, as they must, for its approval (for instance, by professing support for 'the arts', or for these or those commonly held 'values'). Both this example and the earlier, of totalitarian governments' suppressing what they can neither enlist nor control, illustrate in different ways what Václav Havel, a distinguished champion of both high and common culture, has called 'the power of the powerless'.

It might nevertheless be argued that, though autonomous, and no matter how broad-based, cultural values are still 'power' of a kind, and thus, at least from an anarchist or extreme individualist standpoint, objectionable.

See also AESTHETICISM; FUNCTION OF ART; MARXISM AND ART; POPULAR ART; RELATIVISM; RELIGION AND ART.

BIBLIOGRAPHY

Arnold, Matthew: *Culture and Anarchy* (London: 1869); ed. J. Dover Wilson (Cambridge: Cambridge University Press, 1963).

Dilthey, Wilhelm: *Dilthey: Selected Writings*, ed. H.P. Rickman (Cambridge: Cambridge University Press, 1976).

Eliot, T.S.: *Notes Towards the Definition of Culture* (London: Faber & Faber, 1948).

Hatch, Elvin: *Theories of Man and Culture* (New York: Columbia University Press, 1973).

Kroeber, A.L.: *The Nature of Culture*, esp. section 1, 'Theory of culture' (Chicago: University of Chicago Press, 1952).

Marx, Karl: *Selected Writings*, ed. David McLellan, esp. sub-sections 14, from *The German Ideology*, and 30, preface to *A Critique of Political Economy* (Oxford: Oxford University Press, 1977).

Scruton, Roger: 'Emotion and culture', *The Aesthetic Understanding* (London: Methuen, 1983).

Scruton, Roger: *Thinkers of the New Left* (London: Longman, 1985).

Scruton, Roger: 'Aesthetic experience and culture', *The Philosopher on Dover Beach* (Manchester: Carcanet Press, 1990).

Williams, Raymond: *Culture and Society 1780–1950* (Harmondsworth: Penguin Books, 1966).

R.A.D. GRANT

D

Danto, Arthur C(oleman) (1924–) American philosopher and art critic; for many years at Columbia University. Past president of the American Society of Aesthetics (1989–90) and of the American Philosophical Association (1983), Danto became art critic of *The Nation* in 1984, in whose service he produced a prize-winning array of articles that marry philosophical acumen with a rich knowledge of, and feeling for, the fine arts.

His entry into the philosophy of art was marked by his article 'The artworld' (1964), which brought the term 'artworld' from the vernacular into mainstream aesthetics. The term was appropriated and used by George Dickie and others in the development of institutional theories of art. Ironically, it was not used as Danto had recommended. For him, the artworld is constituted by 'a certain history, an atmosphere of theory' (Danto, 1964, p. 580), and is inhabited not by officers of a social institution, but by works of art. It is in terms of theory and history, not the decrees of a social institution, that Danto hopes to explain what it is that makes an object art.

This theme is taken up and developed in his most important work in aesthetics (Danto, 1981). Deeply influenced by Wittgenstein's concern with questions about the difference between indiscernibles – between my arm rising and my raising my arm – Danto posed a related question about art. What, he wanted to know, is the difference between two indiscernible objects – two identical urinals, for instance – one of which is a work of art, the other not (Danto, 1981, pp. 5–6)?

The difference resides in the fact that works of art are *about* the world in the way that ordinary objects are not (Danto, 1981, p. 52). Both art and philosophy are said to be about reality in much the way that language is when it is employed descriptively (Danto, 1981, pp. 82–3). Hence art is always representational – not merely (if at all) in the sense that it refers to something, but also in the the sense that it conveys the artist's way of seeing, viewing, understanding. Art is often about what has gone before it, and attains what sense it has because of this. Danto asks us to suppose that Picasso, in a moment of inspiration, painted one of his old neckties a bright blue. 'The paint was applied smoothly and carefully, and every trace of brushstroke was purged: it was a repudiation of painterliness . . .' (Danto, 1981, p. 40). This work, were it to exist, would be *about* the history and theory of painting itself. This is why the child who does similar damage to his father's tie will not have produced a work of art: the damaged tie is not about anything, and despite the wishes of his parents, the child is not a budding artistic genius.

The fact that Picasso's tie is a work of art, affords it properties which 'its untransfigured counterpart lacks' (Danto, 1981, p. 99). The distinction, then, between the child's and Picasso's imagined tie is an ontological, not an institutional, distinction. It is the historical and theoretical identity of the work – furnished in an interpretation – that gives it the aesthetic properties that it has. Interpretation, Danto argues, is essential to the *existence* of a work of art, and its interpretation is always informed by 'an atmosphere of artistic theory, a knowledge of the history of art' (1981, p. 135).

Artworks, in Danto's view, are representations that require interpretation. They differ, however, from newspaper reports (which are also representations that require interpretation), since an artwork is self-referential in the sense that it 'expresses something about its content'. There remains the obvious objec-

105

tion, though, that some self-referential reports and descriptions are not works of art. How is Danto to distinguish them from artworks? An artwork, he replies, is 'a transfigurative representation rather than a representation *tout court*' (Danto, 1981, p. 172). It comments on itself, in so doing transfigures itself, and thereby acquires properties which a mere physical object cannot itself possess.

These themes are deeply suggestive, but are not always well worked out. Could not a philosophical text comment on, and so transfigure, itself in just this way? And does this mean that philosophy is art; art, philosophy? Some of these issues are picked up and developed in a later work (Danto, 1986), although the main concern here is to show that philosophy has traditionally attempted to undermine and so disenfranchise art. It is not just the work of Plato and Kant, and hence traditional aesthetics itself, that 'ephemeralize' art. Hegel does so as well, for it turns out that what Duchamp did, most famously through his 'urinal' (Fountain), was to give Hegel's 'stupendous philosophical vision of history . . . an astounding confirmation.' Just as the world in its historical dimension is 'the revelation of consciousness to itself', so Duchamp's art 'raises the question of the philosophical nature of art from *within* art' (Danto, 1986, p. 16). In an Hegelian way, art has marginalized and disenfranchised itself. It has done precisely what Plato had hoped to do: art has turned itself into philosophy.

Part of Danto's attempt to re-enfranchise art involves returning to the relation between art and interpretation in order to show that works of art are not to be attended to merely for the disinterested pleasure they afford. Since it is possible to have two snow shovels both exactly alike, only one of which is a work of art, it cannot be the aesthetic appearance of the snow shovel that makes it a work of art. Rather, indiscernible objects become 'quite different and distinct works of art by dint of distinct and different interpretations' (Danto, 1986, p. 39).

Danto's treatment of interpretation is puzzling. Recognition that the snow shovel is a work of art depends not on interpretations

in any ordinary sense of this word, but on one's knowledge of certain theories and cultural conventions. If one has the requisite knowledge, then one recognizes that the snow shovel is a work of art, and one recognizes this quite independently of whether one understands the work. If puzzled by the work, one may venture to explain and in this sense interpret it. This, of course, is an altogether different process, but Danto seems to run the two together.

He never explains what would constitute a re-enfranchising philosophy of art. Must art be defended as *sui generis*? As ineliminable? As non-redundant? As distinct from life? If art is made to depend on interpretation in the way that Danto suggests, why is this not itself a kind of disenfranchisement? Although his writings range interestingly over many topics in the philosophy of art, he does not seem to answer these questions.

See also: DEFINITION OF 'ART'; 'END OF ART'; THEORIES OF ART.

WRITINGS

'The artworld', *Journal of Philosophy*, 61 (1964), 571–84.
The Transfiguration of the Commonplace: A Philosophy of Art (Cambridge, Mass.: Harvard University Press, 1981).
The Philosophical Disenfranchisement of the Commonplace (New York: Columbia University Press, 1986).
The State of the Art (New York: Prentice-Hall, 1987).
The Politics of Imagination (Lawrence: University of Kansas Press, 1988).

DAVID NOVITZ

deconstruction A form of textual analysis largely derived from the work of the French philosopher Jacques Derrida, one of the leading figures of the poststructuralist movement. It bases itself on the following assumptions: texts, like language, are marked by instability and indeterminacy of meaning; given such instability and indeterminacy, neither philosophy nor criticism can have any special claim to authority as regards textual interpretation; textual interpretation is a free-ranging activity more akin to game-playing than to traditional analysis.

The point of deconstructive reading is to destroy the illusion of stable meaning in texts. It does this by means of what Derrida calls 'active interpretation', an anarchic form of writing which makes extensive use of wit and word-play. Derrida speaks of the reader engaging in 'the joyous affirmation of the play of the world and of the innocence of becoming, the affirmation of a world of signs without fault, without truth, and without origin which is offered to an active interpretation' (Derrida, 1978, p. 292). Signs that are without fault, truth or origin are signs whose meaning has not been fixed in advance, as would be the case under a structuralist scheme of analysis. Their meaning at any given point will depend on the ingenuity of the reader's 'active interpretation'. Reading becomes a creative activity rather than an exercise in the recovery of meaning.

Deconstruction begins as a form of philosophy concerned to challenge the Western metaphysical tradition in general and its theories of meaning in particular, but it is probably best known in the English-speaking world as a style of literary criticism. Its popularity is largely due to the efforts of the Derrida-influenced 'Yale School': Geoffrey Hartman, Harold Bloom, Paul de Man and J. Hillis Miller. In the hands of critics such as these, deconstruction becomes a licence for a display of linguistic virtuosity that steers well clear of interpretation in the traditional sense: *explication de texte* is an activity to be avoided. For Hartman, 'interpretation no longer aims at the reconciliation or unification of warring truths' (Hartman, 1981, p. 51). Active interpretation takes as its goal the proliferation, rather than the reduction to schemes and codes, of meaning. It is questionable whether 'interpretation' is an appropriate word to use in this context, since it is normally taken to mean interpretation in terms of a scheme of some kind, having pretensions to truth of some kind. But such pretensions are precisely what Derrida is arguing are unsustainable.

Derrida sees meaning as being endlessly deferred by the action of *différance*, and the linguistic sign as having an odd sort of half-life; as Gayatri Spivak has described it, 'Such is the strange "being" of the sign: half of it always "not there" and the other half always "not that"' (Derrida, 1976, p. xvii). Deconstructionist critics plunder texts for evidence of *différance* and the indeterminacy of the sign, and playing with language is one of their primary strategies for drawing such phenomena to our attention. Pun and word-play are used to open up texts because they widen the field of meaning of words, thus suggesting that the sign is indeed always half 'not there' and half 'not that'. A word's sound quality can always bring to mind like-sounding, although not necessarily like-meaning, words, thereby breaking the notion of a one-to-one relationship between signifier and signified (word and concept). The pun, in effect, defers the union of signifier and signified.

Once we set off on a sequence of punning our frame of reference keeps shifting, thus preventing stable meaning from ever forming. It is an example of paradigmatic relation (or 'association of ideas') in operation, and deconstructionists consider that by undermining a text's linearity of argument they are undermining its pretensions to rationality (which is felt to depend on linear thought process). A typical sequence in Geoffrey Hartman moves by means of punning and association of ideas from the German word *Ecke* (corner) to the French word *coin* (corner), to the English 'coin', to the German word *Kante* (board) and then to the name of the philosopher Kant (Hartman, 1981, p. 85). This takes place in the context of a supposed commentary on Derrida's *Glas*, and can only serve to disorientate an audience habituated to expect logical argument and carefully ordered critique. Only the failure of the critic's ingenuity, or the reader's patience, can end such a sequence.

Hartman is here putting into practice Spivak's plan of operations for the aspiring deconstructionist:

If in the process of deciphering a text in

the traditional way we come across a word that seems to harbor an unresolvable contradiction, and by virtue of being one word is made sometimes to work in one way and sometimes in another and thus is made to point away from the absence of a unified meaning, we shall catch at that word . . . We shall follow its adventures through the text and see the text coming undone. (Derrida, 1976, p. lxxv)

The text comes undone because the critic's linguistic ingenuity – punning, word-play, allusion, association of ideas – demonstrates just how diffuse and unpredictable meaning is at any given moment. 'We are tempted to become associative and metaphorical,' Hartman argues, because 'the slippage [of meaning] is all around us, and the principle of stabilization not very conspicuous' (Hartman, 1981, pp. 149, 64). The point of deconstructive reading is persistently to reveal that slippage, the sheer undecidability of textual meaning.

Deconstructionists believe that such slippage is inevitably present in all texts, including philosophical ones. In one of the more provocative developments of deconstruction, literary critics have turned the techniques of their own discipline back on philosophy in what Christopher Norris has called 'the revenge of literary theory on that old tradition of philosophical disdain or condescension stretching back at least to Plato's *Republic*' (Norris, 1983, p. 3). The objective of such an exercise is to undermine philosophy's claims to be an arbiter of truth and knowledge, by exploring 'the various ways in which philosophy reveals, negotiates or represses its own inescapable predicament as written language' (Norris, 1983, p. 12). This 'inescapable predicament' means that philosophical texts are no more able to stabilize meaning than any others are.

Derrida's own aesthetic criticism uses various tricks to defer meaning and textual explication, such as a footnote running the whole length of the text in 'Living on: border lines', and a dwelling on marginal details such as frames, borders and signatures when discussing painting (Derrida, 1987). In a very real sense the act of criticism is never allowed to get under way in Derrida, and he argues that, when confronted with a text, the deconstructionist critic should resist the temptation to interpret it: 'We should neither comment, nor underscore a single word, nor extract anything, nor draw a lesson from it' (Derrida, 1979, p. 152). The entire strategy is to frustrate the normal expectations of the reader. Style becomes a battleground for the deconstructionist, who deliberately cultivates an anarchic way of writing for polemical purposes. It has been claimed that it is in the area of style that deconstruction's most important achievements lie.

Deconstruction has had a powerful impact on the American academic scene, where, it has been argued, it 'effectively displaced other intellectual programs in the minds and much of the work of the literary avant-garde' (Bove, 1983, p. 6). American deconstruction has, however, come under attack from several quarters as being a debased version of the philosophical original. Several commentators regard it as merely an updated form of New Criticism, and just as open to charges of ahistoricism (neither New Critics nor deconstructionists feel any need to go outside the text in their readings).

Derrida himself has expressed misgivings about what has been done in his name: 'This word [deconstruction] which I had only written one or twice . . . all of a sudden jumped out of the text and was seized by others who have since determined its fate in the manner you well know . . . But for me "deconstruction" was not at all the first or the last word, and certainly not a password or slogan for everything that was to follow' (Derrida, 1988, p. 86). This raises the interesting spectre of a misreading of Derrida by his American followers, which in a theory celebrating the inescapable instability of the sign and the perpetual presence of *différance* within language is somewhat ironic, to say the least; but it does suggest the need to discriminate carefully between deconstruction as philosophy and deconstruction as literary criticism. The former is a serious, if iconoclastic, contributor to the debate on the nature of meaning, the latter arguably more of a licence for a display of linguistic virtuosity for its own sake.

A more damaging indictment of the deconstructive enterprise is that it trades on notions of decidability while arguing its case for undecidability within meaning and language. Most philosophers and critics would be quite willing to admit that slippage of meaning occurs (poetry works on just such a principle), but would draw the line at saying that *nothing but* slippage occurs: it is hard to see how, if that were the case, we could even communicate such a state of affairs.

See also: CRITICISM; DERRIDA; INTERPRETATION; STRUCTURALISM AND POSTSTRUCTURALISM; TEXT.

BIBLIOGRAPHY

Bove, Paul: 'Variations on authority: some deconstructive transformations of the new criticism', *The Yale Critics: Deconstruction in America*, ed. Jonathan Arac, Wlad Godzich and Wallace Martin (Minneapolis: University of Minnesota Press, 1983).
Derrida, Jacques: *De la grammatologie* (Paris: 1967); trans. Gayatri Chakravorty Spivak, *Of Grammatology* (Baltimore, Md. and London: Johns Hopkins University Press, 1976).
Derrida, Jacques: *L'écriture et la différence* (Paris: 1967); trans. Alan Bass, *Writing and Difference* (London: Routledge & Kegan Paul, 1978).
Derrida, Jacques: trans. James Hulbert, 'Living on: border lines', *Deconstruction and Criticism*, Harold Bloom (London: Routledge & Kegan Paul, 1979).
Derrida, Jacques: *La vérité en peinture* (Paris: 1978); trans. Geoff Bennington and Ian McLeod, *The Truth in Painting* (Chicago and London: University of Chicago Press, 1987).
Derrida, Jacques: *The Ear of the Other: Otobiography, Transference, Translation*; ed. Christie McDonald, trans. Peggy Kamuf (Lincoln, Nebr. and London: University of Nebraska Press, 1988).
Hartman, Geoffrey: *Saving the Text* (Baltimore, Md. and London: Johns Hopkins University Press, 1981).
Norris, Christopher: *The Deconstructive Turn* (London and New York: Methuen, 1983).

STUART SIM

definition of 'art'   Can 'art' or 'work of art' be defined? Traditionally, this kind of question has meant 'Are there necessary and sufficient conditions for being a thing of a certain kind?' This kind of question has also traditionally meant 'Are there *two* conditions, each of which is *necessary* and both of which are jointly *sufficient* for being a thing of a certain kind?' Furthermore, the jointly sufficient conditions are supposed to pick out all and only things of the kind being defined.

For example, the ancient Greek definition – 'Man is a rational animal' – specifies *two* conditions: rationality and animality that jointly pick out the class of humans and only the class of humans. Such beings as angels are ruled out because, although they were conceived of as rational, they were not conceived of as animals. On the other hand, chimpanzees are ruled out because although they are animals, they are not thought of as rational, and so on. This definition may not be entirely adequate, but it does unambiguously locate the referents of the term it defines in the overlap of two distinct classes – the class of rational beings and the class of animals.

The two earliest definitions of art – the imitation and expression definitions – do not heed the guidelines of the traditional approach to definition. In the earlier case, Plato, in saying that art is imitation, was not so much interested in defining art as in setting it up to be attacked as metaphysically defective. He saw art as twice removed from reality – an imitation of an imitation of reality. Nevertheless, for over two thousand years thereafter, the view that art is imitation was around in a thoughtless kind of way as a slogan definition. The persistence of this implausible theory was due to a lack of interest in the philosophy of art; philosophers just never bothered to examine the view. In any event, the attempt to define art as imitation flouts the traditional approach by specifying only *one* condition rather than *two*, with the result that it claims art is imitation without any qualification. The definition asserts that all works of art are imitations. The definition, however, leaves unclear whether the class of works of art and the class of imitations are coextensive, or whether the class of works of art is just included within the class of imitations with there being imitations that are not works of art. The definition is defective in not unambiguously locating the referents of the term it defines.

In addition, the imitation definition is easy prey to counter-example. On the one hand, there are works of art that are not imitations in any way – many pieces of instrumental music and non-objective paintings. And, on the other hand, there are many imitations that are not works of art. (This second kind of case is a counter-example only if the definition is taken to assert that the class of works of art and the class of imitations are coextensive.)

The definition 'art is the expression of emotion', first promulgated in the nineteenth century, has the same sorts of difficulties as the imitation definition. Because this definition also specifies only one condition – the expression of emotion – it is inherently ambiguous and incomplete, and it is also easy prey to counter-example. On the one hand, many works of art are clearly not expressions of emotion. On the other hand, many expressions of emotion (father to son; 'you will do as I say, young man') are not works of art. In this instance also, the second kind of case is a counter-example only if the definition is taken to assert that the class of works of art and the class of expressions of emotion are coextensive.

The expression definition has an additional kind of problem that the imitation definition does not. Even when a work of art is an expression of emotion, it may not be possible to determine that it is – that is determine whether the work's creator was in the emotional state of which the work is expressive when the work was created. Knowledge of the actual emotional states of artists is just not attainable in the great bulk of cases. Thus, in the cases of some things that *obviously* are works of art, it would not be possible to determine that they are works of art, if 'art is the expression of emotion' is the correct definition of 'art'.

There is another kind of difficulty that occurs with some frequency in attempts to define 'art'. For example, Clive Bell's discussion of art implies the definition 'a work of art is an artefact that possesses *significant form.*' Since Bell claims that many things that we ordinarily think of as works of art lack significant form, his account has the unfortunate result of excluding obvious works of art. However, this kind of difficulty, which has already been encountered, will not be focused on here. According to Bell, significant form is the only characteristic that is relevant to the *goodness* of art; all other characteristics (for example, being a representation) are either neutral or destructive of art's goodness. Under the guise of defining 'art', Bell is really setting out a theory for the *evaluation* of art. Consequently, even if this project were to succeed, he would actually have characterized 'good art', and this leaves the question of what *art is* unresolved. That is, Bell's remarks leave unaddressed what may be taken to be the *basic* task of the philosophy of art – namely, the task of giving a value-neutral, *classificatory* definition that will cover not only good art but mediocre art, poor art, bad art and worthless art.

A theory of art must allow us to conceive of and talk about all art, not just good art. Some philosophers insist, however, that to *be* a work of art is to be valuable in some way or in some degree. Of course, the expression 'work of art' can be used in an evaluative way. When, for example, someone says (with indicated emphasis and pausing), '*This* [pause] is a *work* [pause] of *art*', that person is making an evaluative remark. There is, however, a *basic*, classifactory sense of 'work of art' that is the primary target of the philosophy of art. It should perhaps also be noted that, while the activity of making art is a valuable kind of activity, not every product of a valuable kind of activity needs to be valuable.

It has been shown that being an imitation or being an expression of emotion is not acceptable as a defining property of art because neither is even a *universal* characteristic of art. There is another kind of problem that arises in connection with the universal properties that members of classes actually have, when one attempts to specify a definition. How can one tell whether a universal characteristic of a class of objects is in fact a defining property or not? Earlier, in making use of the definition 'Man is a rational animal' as an illustration, I noted that rationality and animality jointly pick out the class of humans and only that class. However, featherlessness and bipedalism also jointly pick out the class of humans, and only that class. So, which of these two pairs of notions, or some other pair, is the necessary and sufficient defining pair? If one could rationally intuit the Platonic form of humanness and discover the forms that constitute the essence of humanness, then one would know what the defining properties of 'humanness' are. The Platonic option, however, is not obviously available to us, so we have to decide which of the universal properties are the most important from some point of view.

The difficulty of determining which universal properties are defining properties and the easy susceptibility to counter-example of the traditional definitions of art perhaps played a role, but it was a particular development in the philosophy of language that led many philosophers of art in the 1950s to despair of the possibility of defining 'art'. This development was Ludwig Wittgenstein's view that many concepts are 'family-resemblance' concepts. The members of the classes picked out by such concepts do not, Wittgenstein claimed, share any common defining features; they are members of the class only in virtue of overlapping resemblances among the members. Thus, member A of a particular family-resemblance class will share a property with member B and B with C, and so on, but members A and Z need not share any property. Many philosophers came to believe that *art* is a family-resemblance concept and that, consequently, 'art' cannot be defined in terms of necessary and sufficient conditions because works of art do not share any common or universal property. They even denied that all works of art are artefacts.

From the early 1950s until the middle of the 1960s, the influence of Wittgenstein's philosophy seems to have caused almost all philosophers of art to abandon as impossible the attempt to define 'art'. Then Arthur Danto (1964) and Maurice Mandelbaum (1965), arguing in different ways, concluded that 'art' might be successfully defined or at least generally characterized if philosophers would stop trying to rely on easy-to-notice characteristics, such as being a representation, and focus on the *context* in which works of art are embedded. Neither Danto nor Mandelbaum attempted a definition of 'art' in his article, but others were encouraged to do so.

The various definitions that have resulted since the middle 1960s are classified by Stephen Davies in his book, *Definitions of Art* (1991), as being either functional or procedural. Functional definitions define 'art' in terms of what is taken to be the point of art. Thus, functional definitions see works of art as things created to realize a particular end. Procedural definitions, on the other hand, define 'art' in terms of the procedures by which it is created.

Monroe Beardsley's is an example of a functional definition of 'art': 'An artwork is *either* an arrangement of conditions intended to be capable of affording an experience with marked aesthetic character *or* (incidentally) an arrangement belonging to a class or type of arrangement that is typically intended to have this capacity' (Beardsley, 1982). This particular functional definition clearly depends on the notion of aesthetic experience, but the existence and character of such a kind of experience has been called into question by a number of philosophers.

All functional definitions are faced with the problems of dealing with works that are explicitly created in defiance of what their makers take to be *the point* of art. For example, Duchamp's *Fountain* (a work made out of a urinal) and other Dadaist works are clearly not created to afford aesthetic experience. Beardsley tries to allow such objects to be works of art by claiming that, although *Fountain* and its ilk do not and are not intended to afford aesthetic experience, they are members of a class that is typically intended to afford aesthetic experience. On this view, the class of works of art divides into two distinct subclasses: the subclass of works intended to afford aesthetic experience, and the subclass of works not intended to afford aesthetic experience. The function of 'intended to afford aesthetic experience' seems to evaporate as a defining condition. In fact, the second disjunct of Beardsley's definition seems to imply that it is a procedure that is defining rather than a function.

Danto, in his later work, draws some definition-like conclusions of a functional sort about art. He appears to make two claims: (1) that artworks are always *about* something, and (2) that artworks are always *subject to interpretation*. These two necessary conditions clearly do not jointly pick out only works of art – statute laws are about something and subject to interpretation – and Danto does not present them as doing so. His functional remarks are thus not intended as a definition, but are his claims about the two necessary conditions of being art accurate? An interpretation of a work of art is a declaration of its meaning. For example, a critic might give a Freudian interpretation of a certain novel or painting. Certainly, many works of art are subject to interpretations of various kinds – they have 'handles' on to which interpretations can be fitted. But it is not clear that *all* works have such 'handles'; for example, a typical piece of instrumental music. Of course, we speak of a musician's particular way of playing a piece as an interpretation, but this is something entirely different and not a declaration of meaning.

What of the other alleged necessary condition of being art? Many works of art are *about* something – portraits are about their sitters, abstract paintings are about whatever they are abstractions from, and so on. What, however, are non-objective paintings about? Danto appears to think that such paintings are about *art*. For example, he speaks of a blank canvas entitled *Untitled* as being about art. It is at least debatable that such a painting could be about art. Even if it turns out that such *modern* non-objective paintings are about art, a typical piece of instrumental music composed by Mozart *in the eighteenth*

century does not seem to be about art, or anything else.

A number of what Davies calls procedural definitions of 'art' have been put forth since the late 1960s. I shall use my own institutional definition as an example of such a theory and shall examine it with an eye to seeing what kind of definitional problems are raised by procedural theories.

I give the following value-neutral, classificatory definition of 'work of art': 'A work of art is an artefact of a kind created to be presented to an artworld public' (Dickie, 1984, p. 80). Notice that the definition says nothing about what *the point* of artworks is – nothing is said about aesthetic experience, representation, expression, or the like.

Notice also that, like the imitation and expression definitions, this definition defines 'art' in terms of *one*, albeit very complex, property, and that it clearly asserts that the class of works of art and the class of artefacts of a kind created to be presented to an artworld public are coextensive. Does this mean that the institutional definition will capture things that are not works of art, as the imitation and the expression definitions do when they are read as saying that the class of works of art and the class of imitations or expressions are coextensive? No, because the specifying that it is an *artworld* public for which the artefact is created ensures that the property cannot occur outside the domain of art, and, hence, cannot capture objects outside the artworld.

There is, however, an apparent difficulty. Such artworld items as playbills and museum catalogues are artefacts of a kind created to be presented to an artworld public, but they are clearly not works of art. A distinction must be made within the artworld between primary and secondary objects: the former are works of art and the latter are objects such as playbills that are derivative from the primary objects. The definition is intended to apply to the primary objects of the artworld, and it could be so specified within the definition.

I define not only 'work of art' but also four other key related terms:

An artist is a person who participates with understanding in the making of a work of art.

A public is a set of persons the members of which are prepared in some degree to understand an object which is presented to them.

The artworld is the totality of all artworld systems.

An artworld system is a framework for the presentation of a work of art by an artist to an artworld public. (Dickie, 1984, pp. 80, 81, 82)

The five definitions provide the leanest possible description of the institution or practice of art.

The definitions are clearly circular. Circularity is generally regarded as a logical flaw in definitions, and sometimes it is. It is not a problem here because a definition of 'work of art' does not have to inform us about something of which we are ignorant. By the time one comes to ponder the meaning of 'work of art' one will already have had a great deal of experience with art and its cultural matrix. The task of defining 'work of art' is a matter of organizing and systematizing what we already know and have known from early childhood. Many other cultural concepts will involve the same kind of circularity: for example, the concepts of *statute law* and *legislature*.

Many are bothered by the fact that procedural definitions of 'art' do not incorporate the kinds of characteristics of art in which we are typically most interested – aesthetic, expressive and representational features, for example. These are important features of art, but they are not universal features, and, hence, cannot be used as defining properties. Art, it turns out, is an aspect of our culture that we have invented to do a lot of very different, important things, but no one of these things is *the* point of art. Nothing about procedural definitions, however, prevents any particular work of art from having these valuable, non-universal features.

If 'art' can be defined, it seems most likely that it can be done procedurally rather than functionally.

See also ARTEFACT, ART AS; 'ARTWORLD'; DANTO; DICKIE; FUNCTION OF ART; THEORIES OF ART.

BIBLIOGRAPHY

Beardsley, M.: 'Redefining art', *The Aesthetic Point of View*, ed. M.J. Wreen and D.M. Callan (Ithaca, NY: Cornell University Press, 1982), pp. 298–315.
Binkley, T.: 'Deciding about art', *Culture and Art*, ed. L. Aagaard-Mogensen (Atlantic Highlands, NJ: Humanities Press, 1976), pp. 90–109.
Danto, A.: 'The artworld', *Journal of Philosophy*, 61 (1964), 571–84.
Danto, A.: *The Transfiguration of the Commonplace* (Cambridge, Mass.: Harvard University Press, 1981).
Davies, S.: *Definitions of Art* (Ithaca, NY: Cornell University Press, 1991).
Dickie, G.: 'Defining art', *American Philosophical Quarterly*, 6 (1969), 253–6.
Dickie, G.: *The Art Circle* (New York: Haven, 1984).
Mandelbaum, M.: 'Family resemblances and generalization concerning the arts', *American Philosophical Quarterly*, 2 (1965), 219–28.
Weitz, M.: 'The role of theory in aesthetics', *Journal of Aesthetics and Art Criticism*, 15 (1956), 27–35.
Ziff, P.: 'The task of defining a work of art', *Philosophical Review*, 62 (1953), 58–78.

GEORGE DICKIE

depiction That pictures depict through resembling their subjects has been a commonplace at least since C.S. Peirce. For all its popularity, the view is, for a variety of reasons, untenable. Every object resembles every other. But not every object depicts every other. To depict something requires referring to it. And an object can resemble another without referring to it. Might depiction then consist of resemblance plus reference? This will not do, either. Since every object resembles every other, it would follow from this proposal that every referring symbol depicts its referent. Such is plainly not the case. Despite the resemblance to 'team', 'term' is no picture of 'team'. 'Term' denotes 'team' linguistically, not pictorially.

Perhaps what is required is that resemblance be the vehicle of reference. Then similarity between picture and referent would effect the referential connection between them. The difficulty here is that we often know what a picture depicts without knowing or caring whether it resembles its subject. We have no trouble recognizing pictures as, for example, St Jerome pictures, although we have no idea what St Jerome looked like. And we would be unlikely to alter our pictorial classification should we discover that the historical St Jerome looked nothing like the figure his pictures present. Moreover, fictive pictures cannot resemble their referents, for they have none. Whatever qualifies a Christmas card as a Santa Claus picture, resemblance to Santa Claus does not. For Santa Claus simply is not there to resemble.

Let us temporarily bracket the issue of fictive pictures and focus on works that depict something real. To be a picture *of* something evidently requires being a symbol that refers to that thing. This raises two questions: What kind of reference does depiction require? And what kind of symbol depicts?

REFERENCE

Pictures refer in a variety of ways. Some denote. A portrait, for example, denotes its subject; a landscape, its scene. Some exemplify. These refer to properties they possess – for instance, to their patterns, colours, shapes and styles. Some express: that is, exemplify properties they metaphorically possess – emotions, feelings, kinaesthetic forms and the like. Some allude, or indirectly refer – perhaps to other works or styles or treatments or subjects. Some refer via intricate referential chains composed of denotational and exemplificational links.

Not every picture refers in every way. Abstract works are non-denotational. They refer via literal and/or metaphorical exemplification, and in some cases via allusion and

other complex modes of reference. Representational pictures do not always literally exemplify or express. A schematic drawing in stick figures, for example, might denote the positions of its subjects without exemplifying any features of its own. The more indirect and complex modes of reference are rarer still.

Should we say that a picture depicts whatever it refers to? In that case, Van Gogh's *Vincent's Room* depicts not just the bedroom it denotes, but also the feverish agitation it expresses. And Pollock's *Number One* depicts the viscosity it exemplifies. Such a policy seems inadvisable. It does not conform to our pre-theoretical use of 'depiction'. And it threatens to conflate distinct modes of reference. We do better to construe depiction in terms of denotation. We cannot, however, identify depiction with pictorial denotation. That would mean denying that depictions ever have fictive subjects. But a work like Botticelli's *Birth of Venus* can hardly be treated as abstract art!

Fictive pictures lack denotata. They differ from abstract works in purporting to denote. Like vacuous terms, fictive terms are denoting symbols. They are of the same syntactic sort as symbols with real, non-null denotations. 'Venus' and 'Virginia Woolf' are alike proper names; Venus pictures and Virgina Woolf pictures, alike particular person pictures. Since fictive pictures are pictorial denoting symbols, it is reasonable to count them depictions. Since they fail to denote, it is reasonable to say they fail to depict. A Venus picture is a depiction that does not depict, just as 'Venus' is a denoting term that does not denote. A work need not denote, then, to qualify as a depiction. But it must be a denoting symbol. *The Birth of Venus*, like *Vincent's Room*, is a depiction. *Number One*, not being a denoting symbol, is not.

SYMBOLS

A portrait portrays Virginia Woolf, her head jauntily cocked. It can capture the exact tilt of her head, the exact line of her brow, for pictorial precision admits of no limit. Pictures are semantically dense. They belong to symbol systems with the resources to reflect the finest differences in their referential fields. Does our portrait simply depict Woolf? Or does it depict her looking relieved but slightly perplexed, or happy but mildly surprised, or bewildered but on the whole content, or what? There may be no way to tell, since the referents of these and kindred characterizations may differ beyond the threshold of discrimination. To determine firmly and finally just what a given work depicts may be impossible. For pictures are semantically non-disjoint. We are not always in a position to distinguish divergent referents.

Words, like pictures, are semantically dense and non-disjoint. Language has the resources to describe an item with any degree of precision, and linguistic descriptions are so related that it is sometimes impossible to tell their referents apart. Even so, descriptions are not depictions. The difference between verbal and pictorial symbols is syntactic, not semantic. Languages have alphabets – distinct and discriminable characters that compose their symbols. As a result, language admits of a criterion of syntactic equivalence – sameness of spelling. Inscriptions in a language that are spelled the same are interchangeable without syntactic effect.

Pictorial systems lack alphabets. They are syntactically dense. The exact colour, thickness, position and shading of each line in a drawing is critical to its identity as a pictorial symbol. No two lines are syntactically equivalent. For there will always be some difference in colour, thickness, shading, or other relevant respect. Any such difference, no matter how minute, qualifies as a difference between symbols. None can replace any other without altering the symbol's identity.

Not all syntactically dense symbols are pictorial. Maps, charts, graphs and diagrams are often syntactically dense as well. A stock-market chart, for example, plots fluctuations in prices as a continuous function. A map of Virginia plots the Blue Ridge Parkway as an unbroken line. Still, we would hardly call either a picture of its object. Why not?

Pictures are relatively replete. Comparatively many of their features function symbol-ically. Diagrams, maps, charts and the like are more attenuated. They symbolize along fewer dimensions. If the curve that denotes stock-market activity occurred in a picture, not only its position, but also its colour, texture, thickness and luminosity at every point would figure in its symbolic functioning. As a graph of market activity, only position matters. A symbol is syntactically dense if and only if every difference along the dimension(s) where it functions symbolically constitutes a difference in the identity of the symbol itself. A relatively replete symbol, such as a picture, functions symbolically along comparatively many dimensions (Goodman, 1976).

MOSAICS

Do mosaics, computer graphics, television images and the like supply counter-examples to the thesis that pictures are syntactically dense? Television images and computer graphics are generated by arrays of digitally encoded dots. Although the dots are close together, it is not the case that between any two there is a third. A mosaic consists of discrete tiles in a limited number of colours, sizes and shapes. These, like the computer's dots, seem to serve as an 'alphabet' – a system of repeatable basic units that make up the picture. That computer pictures, television images and mosaics are genuine pictures is beyond dispute. That they consist of discrete, discriminable syntactic elements is not.

Syntax is not determined by physical constitution, but by what constitutes an item as a symbol. To construe an item as a particular symbol is to classify it against a background of (perhaps implicit) alternatives. The symbol together with its alternatives constitutes a symbol scheme. Each element obtains its syntactic character from its place in the scheme. The same mark may be embeddable in several schemes, hence constitute several symbols. A mosaic pattern or a dot matrix design easily fits into a digital scheme – one whose characters are discrete and discriminable. But to construe them as pictures is to read them differently.

When we read a computer print-out as a

picture of the Albert Memorial, we treat the array of greys that compose it as drawn from the full range of possibilities. Any shade of grey, it seems, could have been used. When we read a mosaic as a nativity picture, we treat its colours, sizes and shapes as elements of a dense field of alternatives. Even if the artist was in fact limited in the choices available to him, we read the work as part of a scheme that provides unlimited options. Evidence for this can be found in our critical appraisals. When, for example, we recognize the mosaics at Ravenna as masterpieces, when we say that the mosaicist got them exactly right, we mean that no conceivable alternative would be better – not just that they are as good as can be expected, given the limited options available.

The schemes that constitute symbols as pictures thus provide for alternatives that discrete, discriminable characters cannot comprise. So when computer print-outs, television images or mosaic designs are construed as pictures, their material atoms – individual dots or tiles – do not function as their syntactic primitives. As much as paintings and drawings, such pictures are syntactically dense symbols.

The density, non-disjointness and repleteness of pictorial symbols explain why pictures reward repeated study. Interpretation is never fixed and final. There may be something more or different to be seen in a picture than anything we have yet discerned.

Any visible object looks many ways. Depictions of routine objects in familiar styles may simply convey the way those objects already look. More ambitious, challenging pictures create new looks. We come to see such pictures, their objects, and other aspects of the world differently, as a result of the approach they take. And our new ways of seeing amount to new ways of knowing. Pictures may be sources of delight or despair. They are primarily sources and repositories of understanding.

See also FICTIONAL ENTITIES; GOODMAN; RESEMBLANCE; SYMBOL.

BIBLIOGRAPHY

Elgin, Catherine Z.: *With Reference to Reference* (Indianapolis: Hackett, 1983).
Gombrich, Ernst: *Art and Illusion* (New York: Pantheon, 1960).
Goodman, Nelson: *Languages of Art* (Indianapolis: 1968); 2nd edn (Indianapolis: Hackett, 1976).
Goodman, Nelson and Elgin, Catherine Z.: *Reconceptions in Philosophy and Other Arts and Sciences* (Indianapolis: Hackett, 1988).
Schwartz, Robert: 'The power of pictures', *Journal of Philosophy*, 82 (1985), 711–20.

CATHERINE Z. ELGIN

Derrida, Jacques (1930–) French-Algerian philosopher whose 'deconstructionist' analyses of texts have had a great impact among literary critics. Derrida is part of the grand tradition of French *scepticism* that includes Montaigne, Descartes, Mersenne, Pascal, Bayle, Voltaire and Camus. Born in Algeria, Derrida began to study philosophy in 1950 in a Paris dominated by Camus and Sartre, and received a doctorate in literature in 1980 with his essay, *The Inscription of Philosophy: Research on the Interpretation of Writing*, having already received one in philosophy in 1967 with the essay *Of Grammatology*, 'on the enduring of the Platonic, Aristotelian, and Scholastic conceptions of the written sign'.

This last information comes from a three-page typewritten curriculum vitae, current up to 1984, that nicely dramatizes a problem to which Derrida has given much attention – namely, that of sources and origins, authorizations and legitimating laws. For I do not know how I came to have the curriculum vitae, and neither have I seen any other reference to the essay submitted for the degree in literature, nor does the curriculum vitae name the granting institutions. In a presentation made at the Sorbonne on 2 June 1980 to the thesis examining committee, Derrida drew a map of his career up to the time of the thesis.

Husserl and Hegel were his first interlocutors. The 1967 defence of grammatology had been preceded in 1954 by a master's thesis on the problem of genesis in the phenomenology of Husserl, and in 1957 by the registration of a first thesis topic, 'The ideality of the literary object', to be written under the direction of the Hegel scholar, Jean Hyppolite. The task was to fashion a new theory of the literary object with the techniques of transcendental phenomenology. Derrida has said that his most constant interest has been in the writing that is called literary and in questions like 'How is it that the fact of writing can disturb the very question "what is?" and even "what does it mean?" . . . Why am I so fascinated with the *literary ruse of the inscription* and the whole *ungraspable paradox of a trace* which manages only to carry itself away, to erase itself in marking itself out afresh' (Derrida, 1983, pp. 37–8); (italics added).

The trace is for Derrida that whose existence is proved by a Kantian transcendental deduction, an *a priori* argument to conditions necessary for the possibility of something or other's being the case. Its invisibility as well as its existence is assured by the occurrence of that of which it is a necessary condition. The trace 'carries its other within itself'. and here are opened up the fields on which play blindness and insight, presence and absence, death and life. The paradox of the trace is, Derrida would say, not only ungraspable but also unsolvable, with the result that there always is what cannot be grasped – there always is paradox. The effort to uncover the paradoxes that haunt writing, 'the literary ruse of inscription', has occupied Derrida from the start, where the ruse is that only in literature is writing opaque, intransitive, whereas in its other uses it is a more or less adequate record of speech, transparent (as speech is thought to be) to its object or to the mind of the writer.

His claim is that not only has all writing density and a life and destiny of its own, but also it is a precondition of speech. There is an arche-writing, an articulation, an engraving, a cutting out, a spacing, a carving out of what Ferdinand de Saussure refers to as the continuous ribbons of thought and of sound that precede speech and make it possible. This is no simple reversal, however, for the crucial step in this deconstruction of the opposition is the shift in the conceptual scheme that follows upon the reinscription of speech and writing within arche-writing. The change this discovery rings on familiar conceptual schemes amounts to their deformation, which is difficult in the extreme to make out unless one performs an experiment in imagination that consists in supposing the standard contract between reader and text to be null, and language to have power to resist the intentions of its users. These suppositions made, the experimenter can try out various of Derrida's strategies of reading, and she can try them out as Derrida later does on texts other than those of Plato, Condillac, Kant, Rousseau, Hegel, Husserl, Heidegger, Nietzsche, and Freud.

Having written a lengthy introduction to Husserl's *The Origin of Geometry* (1962), Derrida looked no longer for a theory of the literary object in phenomenology, because he found Husserl to have located writing *within* mathematical objects without noting how the logic of the inscription menaces from the outside the whole phenomenological project, with its presumption of the same presence to mind of ideal objects (meanings) to which speech lays claim. This thesis is worked out in the close readings in the three works published in 1967 (*Writing and Difference, Of Grammatology, Voice and Phenomenon*), where Derrida shows writing to have a logic of its own that relentlessly governs texts, despite their avowals that writing is necessary only because of the limits nature imposes upon the range of the voice, and dangerous because it ever tries to usurp the power of speech, whose handmaiden it is. This notion is akin to that of *pragmatic contradiction*, which occurs when what someone does contravenes what he says, when the performance of a speech act undercuts either what is said or a necessary condition thereof, as when someone says that he is silent or does not exist, with the difference that Derrida locates contradiction between what a text does and what it says.

This identification of a *textual unconscious*, to which dangerous writing is relegated in order to preserve the hegemony of the voice and speech fully present to conscious mind, and of the various manoeuvres performed by this unconscious, has been the subject of his work through the present, with the verbal text giving way to works of plastic art, institutions, lives and their stories. From 1963 to 1968 Derrida worked in solitude, for what he was doing was essentially different from the structuralism that prevailed in Paris. In 1967 he had so little inclination to question the necessity of the university and its general principle that he thought to divide his labour between a thesis on Hegel's semiology, to be done with Hyppolite, and the continuation of the work that 'decidedly did not conform to such university requirements' and was to 'displace, deform them in all their rhetorical or political bearing' (Derrida, 1983, p. 43). He registered this second thesis topic in 1967, but after the May uprising and the death of Hyppolite in 1968 he neglected the thesis, publishing three books in 1972 (*Dissemination, Margins of Philosophy, Positions*) and writing texts that became more and more playful. The play, however, was in the deadly serious service of breaking the habits of reading that refuse to search out the places in a text where what it does undermines what it says.

In 1974 he decided not to write the thesis, because doing so would be inconsistent with a political struggle over the place of philosophy in the French curriculum in which he was engaged as a founder (and activist until 1979) of the Groupe de Recherches sur l'Enseignement Philosophique. During this time, he notes, his work focused on questions of rights, on the proper, the signature, the name, 'on destination and restitution, on all the institutional borders and structures of discourses' (Derrida, 1983, p. 49). Philosophers' texts had given way to their institutional contexts, and the borders between them were shown to be highly pervious. After the final thesis of 1980, these texts are reinscribed in the philosophers' lives, as the issue of Nazism besets them and forces the question of the boundaries between professional, political and private, between the productions of and by institutions and individuals. In 1989 two books appeared in English: *Memoires for Paul de Man* and *Of Spirit: Heidegger and the Question*, about which last David Farrell Krell, a scholar translator of Heidegger, has asked, 'Will a more important book on Heidegger appear in our time?' – and he answered, 'No, unless Derrida continues to think and write in this spirit.'

See also DECONSTRUCTION; MODERNISM AND POSTMODERNISM; STRUCTURALISM AND POSTSTRUCTURALISM.

WRITINGS

De la grammatologie (Paris: 1967): trans. G. Spivak, *Of Grammatology* (Baltimore, Md: Johns Hopkins University Press, 1976).
L'écriture et la différence (Paris: 1967); trans. A. Bass, *Writing and Differences* (Chicago: University of Chicago Press, 1978).
Marges de la philosophie (Paris: 1972); trans. A. Bass, *Margins of Philosophy* (Chicago: University of Chicago Press, 1982).
'The time of the thesis: punctuations', *Philosophy in France Today*, ed. A. Montefiore (Cambridge: Cambridge University Press, 1983).

BIBLIOGRAPHY

Llewelyn, John: *Derrida on the Threshold of Sense* (London: Macmillan, 1986).
Norris, Christopher: *Derrida* (London: Fontana, 1987).

MARY BITTNER WISEMAN

Dewey, John (1859–1952) American Pragmatist philosopher, educator, and reformer; contributed significantly to every major field of philosophy. Considered one of the most prominent members of the school in American philosophy called the 'pragmatist movement'. While some have perversely dismissed this school as somehow bound up with the short-sighted materialism and unrefined egoism of the business civilization of the United States, those who have read even moderately in the literature recognize that aesthetics and its affiliated subject-matters play a central role in the work of C.S. Peirce and William James as well as – and pre-eminently – in Dewey's.

Though Dewey wrote only one book explicitly devoted to aesthetics, *Art as Experience* (1934), it remains one of the most significant and original treatments of the topic. It also offers an insight into the nature of Dewey's general philosophy, illuminating his abiding concern with the aesthetic dimension of experience. Some, however, like Croce, have regarded this book as radically inconsistent with Dewey's pragmatism (because of that prejudice towards pragmatism already mentioned), while others have thought that it carries within it two inconsistent strands – one idealist, the other naturalist. But it is important to note that the views expressed in this work lead directly to the underlying themes of Dewey's major philosophical *opus*, *Experience and Nature* (1925), and indicate not only the theoretical context of his aesthetics but also the ramifications for a radically novel metaphysical theory that takes aesthetic experience as central.

By the early years of the twentieth century, Dewey had aligned himself with the naturalistic side of the pragmatist movement. In his essay 'The reflex arc concept in psychology', he provided a successful model of learning activity which takes as primary the idea of an organism constantly acting and responding to its environment in a continuous and developing pattern of experience. By 1925, with *Experience and Nature*, the model had been expanded to account for how members of a community, rather than a single isolated organism, pursue through the use of symbol, expression and communication the ongoing project of directing experience towards intrinsically fulfilling ends which give human existence its depth of value and meaning. Thus, by Dewey's mature period, the term 'experience' had come to mean for him *not* what it connotes to the tradition of British empiricism (the subjective, discrete, static mental image somehow 'representing' an 'external world'). Rather, it signifies the *shared social activity* of *symbolically mediated behaviour* which seeks to discover the *possibilities* of our *objective situa-tions* in the *natural world* for meaningful, intelligent and fulfilling *ends*. And the skill at doing this Dewey calls 'art'.

Experience is a process in nature; it embraces potentialities as well as immediate actualities; it can be 'civilized' or 'cultivated' through education, whereby one becomes a participant in a social world; it can become 'intelligent' in so far as it can be directed by recognition of its possibilities, both desirable and undesirable. The idea that experience is such a process, capable of control, so that it can develop continuously rather than be suffered from moment to moment, is the *idea* of art, which Dewey describes as the 'greatest intellectual achievement in the history of humanity' (Dewey, 1984, p. 25; 1987, p. 31).

It is important, Dewey thinks, to understand the origin of art and the quest for aesthetic experience in the natural world of human action, especially since the cultural climate of the 'artworld' and its institutions, like the museum or the market value of 'great art', have been so uncritically taken as the starting point for aesthetic theory. He sees any theory like Clive Bell's, which treats art as an isolated, 'high' or 'pure' phenomenon standing unrelated to any other mode of human concern or experience, as a victim of a particular historically mediated cultural situation – one of which Dewey himself was highly critical. By separating the *idea* of art from life, we not only mystify art, but we thereby fail to recognize the pervasive *aesthetic* possibilities of human experience in general.

Dewey has been much misunderstood on this point. He is not rejecting the social function of public museums. (He was a member of the board of directors for the art collection of the Barnes Foundation.) Nor is he arguing that 'ordinary' human experience, left unrefined in all its massive crudities, *is* art in exactly the same way in which 'fine art' is art. What he does say is that the origin of art lies in the capacity to develop our ordinary experiences towards fulfilling ends. The traditional fine arts have done this exceptionally well, and thus can serve as a model for any activity that is fraught with the possibilities for truly fulfilling the human desire to exist with a vivid, complex awareness of the meaning and value of life. By putting the *idea* of art on a pedestal, as it were, we lose sight of its continuity as a development from the ordinary world (Dewey, 1987, p. 8).

Thus Dewey seeks to remind us of the constant involvement of 'the live creature' with its world. Our senses are extensions of our need for continuous, organized activity which maintains and develops our equilibrium. There is an underlying vital rhythm to any living being's existence, and these rhythms form an organic matrix out of which our sense of dynamic order arises. Our embodiment as organisms shapes the conditions of the aesthetic. This rhythm of 'doing and undergoing', of anticipating, acting and responding, builds up our overall framework of what a 'meaningful world' is. We come to experience in the light of remembered events and foreseen consequences, and cease thereby to be prisoners of the momentary sensation. The objects of our world arise from the temporality of human action constructing interpretations out of immediate events (Dewey, 1987, p. 13).

This leads to the most significant idea of Dewey's aesthetics: consummatory experience or '*an* experience', as he often referred to it. When the rhythmic interaction of individual and world comes to be consciously experienced as a developmental process culminating in the kind of organic integrity and wholeness which makes the event sensed as deeply meaningful, pervaded by a qualitative continuity which uniquely distinguishes the experience as such, then one has had '*an* experience'. Works of art are pre-eminent examples: the experience of a Bach fugue, the Medici chapel, Dante's *Commedia*. But, of course, many experiences also have this consummatory character – even experiences that are not particularly happy or uplifting. There is '*an* experience' of a special day spent with a child, a gourmet meal enjoyed with friends, and of heart-rending grief. What is common to these experiences is that, through their internal qualitative integrity, they have revealed the capacity of experience to be

meaningful on a profound level. The enemies of the aesthetic, says Dewey, are mindless habitual repetition at one extreme and random chaos at the other (Dewey, 1987, p. 40).

It is also extremely important to grasp that '*an* experience' is a process having developmental temporality as an intrinsic recognized feature. Aesthetic experience is not instantaneous or timeless. Its 'consummatory' nature lies not in the fact that the experience comes to an end – for all experiences do – but that it is marked off *from the start* by the element of 'closure'. This is what gives dynamic, growing *continuity* to the experience beyond the mere succession of anticipations and responses. The experience has a sensed movement about it which holds forth the promise of consummation or, in some cases, fails its promise, and so is sensed as a 'disappointment' (Dewey, 1987, p. 41).

Some of the most novel aspects of Dewey's theory lie in his discussions of expression and form. His is often misclassified, along with other 'expression theories' which simply regard expression as an aspect of the creative act. But Dewey treats expression as the ongoing relationship between the work of art and the public. He distinguishes the 'work of art' from the physical 'art product', such as the canvas and paint, ink and paper, or sound vibrations; the *work* of art is the result of the interaction of the art product and an appreciator; the 'work' becomes the meaningful integration of an art product and a life.

Like Collingwood, Dewey did not believe that 'emotions' or 'aesthetic intuitions' pre-existed their physical embodiment; as the work became objectified, so did they take on definition. Mere emotional outpouring is not 'expressing'. Expression is governed by the idea of *communication*, whether the art product is meant to be encountered by anyone else or not. Even while creating, the artist takes on the role of the appreciator in every act of critical assessment and response to what he or she has done. One is engaged in a dialogue with the self; as the product engages others, it becomes a dynamic dialogue within the experience of the human community – that is, culture. The *work* of art is to be found in the *life* it has within the culture. Thus there is not *one* 'real' *Hamlet*. Neither is *Hamlet* a meaningless name for a haphazard variety of subjective reactions. The work of art which is *Hamlet* lies in the continued life of its reception in the culture, which gives rise to many divergent interpretations and readings (Dewey, 1987, p. 81).

Likewise, Dewey takes form in a very dynamic sense. The work of art is temporal, historical, cultural, developmental. Its 'form' cannot refer to some static underlying skeleton. Rather, its form is the way the work gives organization to experience: it is the pattern of the 'working of the work', to use Heidegger's phrase. In Dewey's language, it is the 'operation of forces that carry the experience . . . to its own integral fulfilment'. Form is the process of accumulative richness or, to use another of Dewey's terms, 'funding' in *an* experience. Because the work of art is temporally experienced, not only is each moment of the process a 'summing up and a carrying forward', but it is *felt* and *perceived* as such (Dewey, 1987, p. 137).

Dewey also distinguishes the 'subject-matter' of a work of art from its 'substance'. The subject is what may be discursively and topically isolated or shared by many different works. *Paradise Lost* and the Sistine Chapel, for example, share the common subject-matter of the story of the creation and fall according to Genesis. But each work has disclosed its rendition in an entirely distinct way which can only be encountered through the work itself: this is what each work is really *about*; this is its *substance*. The substance is what is disclosed through the work, and it is this which give sense to the saying that a work of art is ultimately about itself (Dewey, 1987, p. 111).

Any philosophy of experience, Dewey states, is ultimately tested by its treatment of aesthetic experience (Dewey, 1987, p. 274). Because aesthetic experience signifies for him the most integrated and complete mode of experience in which the human quest for meaning directly imbues the events of life

with value, any short-sightedness here or lack of attention to vital factors, such as emotion, feeling and imagination, will be most evident in an aesthetic theory (or lack of one). It is remarkable how many philosophies stand condemned by this requirement. Dewey does not make this comment idly, and surely intends his own philosophy to be judged by it. It is perhaps one of the starker ironies of the history of philosophy that Dewey's philosophy has largely been judged on other, lesser merits. There are, obviously, weaknesses and problems in Dewey's theory, not least of which are the vagueness and rambling discursiveness of his prose. His heavy reliance on organic metaphors is often excessive or, at least, in need of clarification. He is not the connoisseur of fine art that Bell, Langer, Goodman or Cavell are. One wishes he dealt more forthrightly with the genuine problem of cross-cultural responsiveness to art, instead of naively believing that art communicates directly where language often fails.

But these are all minor points in the light of the fact that Dewey has given in his discussion of art and aesthetic experience one of the most powerful, original and challenging theories in the literature. Carried to its conclusion, his theory would have revolutionary effects not only upon the conclusions but upon the conduct of most Anglo-American philosophy.

See also EXPRESSION; FORM.

WRITINGS

Art as Experience (New York: 1934); reprinted in Jo Ann Boydston, ed., *John Dewey: The Later Works*, vol. 10 (Carbondale, Ill.: Southern Illinois University Press, 1987).

Experience and Nature (Chicago: 1925; 2nd edn, 1927); reprinted in Jo Ann Boydston, ed., *John Dewey: The Later Works*, vol. 1 (Carbondale, Ill.: Southern Illinois University Press, 1981).

BIBLIOGRAPHY

Alexander, Thomas M.: *John Dewey's Theory of Art, Experience, and Nature: The Horizons of*

Feeling (Albany, NY: State University of New York Press, 1987).

THOMAS M. ALEXANDER

Dickie, George (1926–) American philosopher of art, born in Palmetto, Florida; received his doctorate in philosophy from the University of California in 1959 – his thesis concerned Francis Hutcheson's ethical theory. He became one of the co-editors of the influential *Aesthetics: A Critical Anthology* (1977), and he is Professor of Philosophy at the University of Illinois, Chicago. His current research involves eighteenth-century theories of taste, notably those of Hutcheson, Alexander Gerard, Archibald Alison and Kant. He was appointed vice-president of the American Society of Aesthetics in 1990.

Dickie has made contributions to a number of important topics in analytic aesthetics, such as evaluation and intentionalism. However, the two areas of discussion where his work has sparked the most controversy and had the most impact are aesthetic theory and art theory.

Traditionally, aesthetic theory has been concerned with our responses to such things as natural beauties and artworks. The task of aesthetic theory – at least since the eighteenth century – has been to characterize the spectator's share in our commerce with nature and art in such a way that it can be seen as comprising a distinctive or unique mode of experience or perception, or as requiring or activating a distinctive attitude or faculty. Broadly put, aesthetic theory attempts to define a realm or dimension of the spectator's commerce with art and nature which is specifically or peculiarly aesthetic – that is, essentially distinguishable from any other mode of experience or activity such as the religious, the practical, the moral.

In the history of aesthetic theory, the aesthetic realm has been located in different places – experiences, faculties, attitudes and perceptions (to name a few) – which are connected to different qualities of affect, including pleasureableness, detachment and disinterest. Dickie's contribution to this debate has been to argue that the notion of a distinct realm of the aesthetic, such as aesthetic experience, is a myth. No principled distinction can be drawn between so-called aesthetic perception and ordinary perception. And the postulation of special faculties, like taste, or the aesthetic attitude is ill-advised.

Dickie has attacked many diverse attempts to formulate aesthetic theories. One of his central objections has been to the role that the notion of disinterestedness plays in so many aesthetic theories. For example, Jerome Stolnitz (1960, pp. 34ff.) defines an aesthetic attitude as 'disinterested and sympathetic attention to any object of awareness whatever for its own sake alone'. Here, the idea of the aesthetic is a matter of attending to something in a specifiable way – that is, disinterestedly. 'Disinterest', in turn, involves a lack of any ulterior purpose. But, Dickie notes, disinterest tells us something about a spectator's motives; it does not really point to any feature of the spectator's act of attention. If two people listen to a recording of a symphony – one in preparation for a music exam and the other for enjoyment – presumably the former has an interest and the latter is disinterested. But in attending to the music closely, both may attend to it in exactly the same way: both may attend to the same exact features of the music and appreciate their structures for the same musicological reasons. There is only one way to attend (albeit with different grades of sophistication) to the music, though there may be different motives for our attention. Thus, notions like interest and disinterest do not specify different modes of attention. Furthermore, there is no reason to invoke these ideas in order to explain why the theatrical producer who watches his production with an eye to the box-office is not responding appropriately. The problem is not that he is not attending disinterestedly. Rather, he is not paying attention to the play at all.

Along with his celebrated attacks on theories of disinterested attention. Dickie's attempts to construct a real or essential definition of art are his most noteworthy contribution to analytic aesthetics. It can be said that he reinvigorated the project of art theory in the name of what he initially called an 'institutional theory of art'. Prior to Dickie's intervention in the debate, aestheticians of the 1950s and 1960s were generally persuaded by the arguments of neo-Wittgensteinian philosophers, like Morris Weitz, who maintained (1) that art cannot be defined because it is an open concept; and (2) that the lack of a real definition of art should raise no philosophical anxieties, for there is an alternative way of identifying art – namely, the family-resemblance method.

Dickie rejected the notion of family resemblance as a serviceable means for telling art from non-art, on a number of grounds. One decisive objection was that the notion of family resemblance is ultimately only the idea of a resemblance, and, since everything resembles everything else in some respect, noting so-called family resemblances will finally force us to count everything as art. Moreover, since the family-resemblance approach is an obviously inoperable method for identifying art, one is compelled to take a second look at the rival method – that of identifying art by means of a definition comprising necessary conditions that are jointly sufficient. Weitz said that such definitions were inadmissable because art is an open concept. A real definition would somehow – in a way that was never made perfectly clear – preclude the possibility of originality and creativity in art. Dickie showed that this worry was groundless by producing a definition of art that placed no limits on artistic creativity with respect to artefacts. This definition, the 'institutional theory of art', states in one of its elaborations: 'A work of art in the classificatory sense is (1) an artefact (2) a set of the aspects of which has had conferred upon it the status of candidate for appreciation by some person or persons acting on behalf of a certain social institution (the artworld)' (Dickie, 1974, p. 34). Thus, *contra* Weitz, we have a definition that allows that an artwork could, for instance, look like anything – even a snow shovel – so long as the artefact is introduced by means of the right procedure: that is to say, by having status conferred upon it by the right persons.

The institutional theory of art was subjected to intense criticism. One such was that the definition is circular in so far as art (the artworld) is an ineliminable element of the definiens. Dickie concedes this point, but argues that the circularity is not vicious. Another line of objection to this theory is that the underlying analogy with formal institutions such as the law and religion is strained beyond breaking-point. Formal institutions of this kind have specifiable criteria governing what can be a candidate for a certain position (for instance, a potato cannot be a candidate for President of the United States) as well as specifiable criteria for who may officiate over certain procedures (for instance, only a bishop can confer Holy Orders). The artworld lacks criteria of this sort. Therefore, the artworld is not an institution in any rigorous sense. In other words, the second condition in Dickie's theory relies upon the putative existence of altogether bogus roles and procedures.

Feeling the pressure of this line of argument, Dickie has jettisoned talk of institutions in favour of talking about the art circle, a practice involving structured relations between artists and their audiences. In this context, he identifies a necessary condition for what it is to be an artwork: 'A work of art is of a kind created to be presented to an artworld public.' This, in turn, is elucidated by the following four propositions: 'A public is a set of persons the members of which are prepared in some degree to understand an object which is presented to them'; 'An artworld system is a framework for the presentation of a work of art by an artist to an artworld public'; 'An artist is a person who participates with understanding in the making of an artwork'; and 'The artworld is the totality of artworld systems' (Dickie, 1984, pp. 80–2). Dickie waves aside anticipated charges of circularity here, on the grounds that it is not vicious, while also conjecturing that it is a feature of cultural concepts that they will be circular – or, as he prefers to say 'inflected' – in this way.

Nevertheless, even if the theory of the art circle successfully deflects some of the objections levelled at the institutional theory of art, it would appear to provoke some problems of its own. There is the genuine question, for instance, of whether this theory is indeed a theory of art. For though Dickie's set of inflected definitions mentions 'art' at crucial junctures, the overall framework could be filled in just as readily with the names of other complex, coordinated, communicative practices, such as philosophy. For example, we might say that 'a work of philosophy is a discourse of a kind created to be presented to a philosophy world public', and go on to adjust the related, inflected propositions, systematically replacing the word 'art' with the word 'philosophy', the word 'artist' with the word 'philosopher', and the word 'artworld' with the words 'philosophy world'.

But then the question arises as to whether Dickie has really said anything specific about art, as opposed to producing something like the necessary framework of coordinated, communicative practices of a certain level of complexity, where such practices cannot be identified in terms of their content. Art is one example of this kind of practice. But in illuminating the necessary structural features of such practices, Dickie has not told us anything about art *qua* art; rather, he has implied that art belongs to the genus of complex, coordinated, communicative practices, along with showing, by example, some of the interrelated structures of these practices. This analysis is not without interest. But it does not seem to qualify as a definition of *art* – the very thing that he believes is the point of art theory.

Though Dickie's contributions to aesthetic theory and art theory may appear to be independent, they are not. For in dismissing the viability of the notion of the aesthetic, he undermines the possibility of aesthetic theories of art – theories such as Clive Bell's, that maintain that artworks are artefacts designed to cause aesthetic experiences. In so far as aesthetic theories of art are rivals to institutional theories, Dickie's rejection of the aesthetic can be seen as a dialectical thrust against a major competing view. The other major competitor to the institutional approach was the neo-Wittgensteinian notion that art might be identified in virtue of family resemblances. One major theme that underpins his theoretical choices, in contradistinction to the tendencies of aesthetic theories of art and neo-Wittgensteinian family resemblances is the importance he places on social context for art theory. Dickie's leading competitors – aesthetic theories of art and neo-Wittgensteinianism *à la* Weitz ignore the relevance of social context for identifying art. Whether the details of Dickie's theories are finally correct, it is nevertheless the case that he, along with Arthur Danto, has put the significance of social context on the agenda of contemporary philosophy of art.

See also ARTEFACT, ART AS; 'ARTWORLD'; ATTITUDE, AESTHETIC; DEFINITION OF 'ART'; THEORIES OF ART.

WRITINGS

'The myth of the aesthetic attitude', *American Philosophical Quarterly* 1 (1964), 56–65.
'Defining art', *American Philosophical Quarterly*, 6 (1969), 253–66.
Aesthetics: An Introduction (Indianapolis: Pegasus Books, 1971).
Art and the Aesthetic: An Institutional Analysis (Ithaca, NY: Cornell University Press, 1974).
The Art Circle: A Theory of Art (New York: Havens, 1984).
Evaluating Art (Philadelphia: Temple University Press, 1988).
Aesthetics: A Critical Anthology, ed. with R. Sclafani and R. Roblin (New York: St. Martin's, 1977, 1989).

BIBLIOGRAPHY

Davies, Stephen: *Definitions of Art* (Ithaca, NY: Cornell University Press, 1991).
Stolnitz, Jerome: *Aesthetics and Philosophy of Art Criticism* (Boston, Mass.: Riverside, 1960).
Weitz, Morris: 'The role of theory in aesthetics', *Journal of Aesthetics and Art Criticism*, 15 (1956), 27–35.

NOËL CARROLL

Dufrenne, Mikel (1910–) French philosopher, best known for applying Phenomenology in the study of visual art. Dufrenne studied under Alain and Souriau, and has taught at the universities of Poitiers and Paris-Nanterre, and of Buffalo, Michigan and Delaware. He was the chief editor of

10/18, the well known French aesthetic and art journal transformed in 1974 from the *Revue d'esthétique*, which he had co-edited.

His principal Sorbonne thesis, published in 1953 as *Phénoménologie de l'expérience esthétique*, is his largest and most comprehensive work of aesthetics, and focuses mostly on the study of aesthetic experience, aesthetic objects and aesthetic values. Like Ingarden, he rejects the traditional 'objectivist' and 'subjectivist' aesthetics, and accepts the phenomenological point of departure: the analysis and description of the acts of consciousness and their intentional correlates at the moment of encounter of the subject with a work of art.

Dufrenne follows Husserl in his critique of psychologism, physicalism and relativism, and in the phenomenological method of description, though he rejects the notion of *pure transcendental ego*, claiming that the consciousness is always individualized and concrete, as is its correlate, the aesthetic object. Like Merleau-Ponty, he emphasizes the concrete, lived, corporeal and sensuous (*sensible*) experience of art. Like Ingarden, he distinguishes between the work of art and the aesthetic object – which is the only true form in which the work of art can be appreciated. Nevertheless, he criticizes Ingarden's thesis of works of art as *purely intentional*, and Sartre's thesis of *irreality*, though it seems that his critique of Ingarden is based more on terminological than on conceptual differences between them.

The most interesting aspect of Dufrenne's aesthetics seems to be his theory of the categories *affective a priori*, arising out of his interest in 'the possibility of a pure aesthetics'. Kant's notion of *a priori* is extended to affective categories *a priori* as the 'conditions under which a world can be felt' (Dufrenne, 1973, p. 437). Specifically, Dufrenne distinguishes between the cosmological and existential *a priori*, the former residing in the object (making it perceivable), and the latter in the subject (making him capable of perceiving aesthetically). We are capable of having an aesthetic experience because we have the existential categories *affective a priori* which allow us to emotionally penetrate a work of art, to decipher its sense and value, and to feel its unique climate: the pathos of Beethoven's music, the tragic in the works of Sophocles, or the comic in Molière.

The work of art expresses emotions; the cypresses in Van Gogh's painting are not just trees, but the expression of passion. The *affective a priori* in a work of art constitutes its value, its 'soul', which is always associated with truth, for art grasps the elements of reality that cannot be expressed otherwise. To discover values is to discover the truth of nature. 'The artist exists in the service of Nature which seeks to be incarnated in the work through his agency' (Dufrenne, 1973, p. 454), for he has a special sensitivity (categories *existential a priori*) for discovering its true sense, which the perceiver will be able to feel, thanks to his categories. 'Aesthetic experience can thus become the basis for the reflection between man and the real' (Dufrenne, 1973, p. 456). Thus, the cosmological and the existential are united in the aesthetic experience in which we learn truths about art, nature and ourselves.

Dufrenne comes back to this theme in his subsequent *Poétique*, where he insists that the aesthetic experience does not stop with the aesthetic object but transcends it to contemplate the truth of nature, accessible in no other way than through the archetypes expressed in art. In this sense nature needs art as much as art needs a spectator for 'the glory of appearing'. Art can express truths, and man can perceive them sensually because the categories *affective a priori* are antecedent to both – like human beings, and art, they belong to being itself.

It seems that the project of pure aesthetics has been frustrated in favour of Heideggerian ontology, which actually leads Dufrenne to anthropology (see his *Pour l'homme* [For man]), ultimately denying the possibility of transcendental philosophy. His statement that the *a priori* is revealed only in the *a posteriori* is an ambiguous attempt at combining the empirical and the transcendental, as well as absolutism and relativism, especially when he addresses Max Scheler's antinomy between the absoluteness of values transcending the relativity of history and the 'historicity of the feeling of values' (Dufrenne, 1973, p. 494).

Dufrenne's works from 1980 provide analyses of those contemporary works of art which, programmatically, go against all traditional schemata, genres, styles and methods. The work ceases to be the ultimate goal of artistic creativity, and Dufrenne's attention shifts now to illuminate the process of creation as an end in itself. The contemporary work of art, with its elements of improvisation and participation of the perceiver, defies finality and the traditional subject–object structure. It disrupts the limits artificially imposed on art by institutions, and opens up new possibilities for freedom and creativity, whose end is the liberation of humankind from oppressive practices – such as violence, ideology, commercialization, fashion and power structures – that negate human values.

Artistic practices may actually be only marginal to the whole commercialized and institutionalized industry called 'the artworld', but for aesthetics they should be of central interest, since spontaneous creation and aesthetic perception are two most important experiences in life. For in creation 'man reveals himself as capable of escaping the realm of necessity', and in aesthetic experience 'man reveals himself capable of wonder' (Dufrenne, 1987, p. vii). Thus, what really remains as the end in itself for Dufrenne is man and his values, which are revealed in artistic and aesthetic experience, the only 'innocent and free praxis' left in 'the world sinking into barbarism' (Dufrenne, 1987, p. xii). The joy and spontaneity of such experiences, based on love and not domination, are subversive – they go against the established orders, show the possibility of change, and promise liberation.

Dufrenne remains the defender of humanism in his numerous polemics with its critics – namely, Heidegger, Althusser, Lévi-Strauss and Lacan. His dialogue with French postmodernism is of particular value, and not only to students of aesthetics. Some of his discussion of Barthes, Bachelard, Derrida and Lyotard can be found in *In the Presence of the Sensuous*. This anthology, the first English collection of Dufrenne's writings, spanning almost the whole of his career, exhibits the unusual versatility of his philosophical interests – imagination, artistic creativity, aesthetic values, the death of art, nature and aesthetic experience, language and reality, literary criticism, humanism amd postmodernism. All of these phenomena are analysed with his usual depth and honesty and he takes care to reveal what should never be lost: the irreducibility and value of being.

See also 'ARTWORLD'; TRUTH IN ART.

WRITINGS

La Poétique (Paris: Presses Universitaires de France, 1963).
La notion de l'apriori (Paris: 1953); trans. E.S. Casey, The Notion of the A Priori (Evanston, Ill.: Northwestern University Press, 1966).
Pour l'homme (Paris: 1968).
Phénoménologie de l'expérience esthétique (Paris: 1953); trans. E.S. Casey, The Phenomenology of Aesthetic Experience (Evanston, Ill.: Northwestern University Press, 1973).
Esthétique et philosophie, 3 vols (Paris: Klincksieck, 1967, 1976, 1981).
Trans. and ed. M.S. Roberts and D. Gallagher, In the Presence of the Sensuous (Atlantic Highlands: Humanities Press, 1987).

WOJCIECH CHOJNA
IRENA KOCOL

E

education, aesthetic   The idea that education should attend carefully to the development of aesthetic capacities and experience has a long and distinguished history. Different accounts of the nature of the aesthetic, and in particular of its relationship to the arts, has, however, resulted in radically different notions of the significance of aesthetic concerns within education.

In the past, the term 'aesthetic' has at times been used to distinguish a particular aspect of all experience or thought resulting from the exercise of some general capacity such as the imagination, the ability to discern unities, or even, following Dewey, the ability to resolve discrepancies in thought. On such a view, aesthetic education is understood as covering activities that promote the development of the relevant general capacity, perhaps particularly through attention to the arts as exemplifying its paradigmatic use. Such a wide interpretation of the aesthetic within experience, however, has relatively little support in modern educational theory, where the term has instead come to be used much more specifically for a particular, distinctive category or domain of experience particularly associated with experience of the arts.

Two major approaches to aesthetic education can be readily distinguished in modern accounts, though elements of both can be seen in numerous much earlier writings, perhaps notably in Schiller's influential *Letters on the Aesthetic Education of Man*. There the thesis is developed that genuine works of art are free creations in which physical desires and feelings and the demands of reason are harmonized. In such works matter is shaped by form, but in a way that both appeals to our senses and can educate by ordering our emotions. In this work aesthetic education is still understood very widely, as a preparation for a balanced life dominated by neither reason nor desires and leading to the development of a harmonious society. But the account is specific enough to show that Schiller saw links, on the one hand, between the arts and the formal ordering of given material, and on the other between the arts and human feelings. These two concerns have resulted in the two sharply contrasted positions that characterize modern debates on aesthetic education.

What can, for convenience, be labelled the *formalist* view sees aesthetic experience as centrally the perception of certain qualities of a formal, structural or relational nature that can be discerned not only in the various fields of sense perception but also in patterns of abstract ideas, in symbolic expressions and in social and political relations. On this view the aesthetic qualities in, say, a natural situation or a work of art are not its immediate physical properties or its representational or expressive character, but the qualities of, say, elegance, balance or unity to be found in the movement of sounds, the structure of shapes or colours, or the pattern of personal relationships. Awareness of such formal features abstracted from their substantive content or base is further seen as the ground of distinctive appraisals of value which generate peculiarly aesthetic emotions of delight.

In its most extreme version, formalism sees aesthetic concerns as constituting a unique, autonomous domain of experience, sometimes considered to provide a distinctive type of understanding and knowledge – as fundamental a characteristic of what it is to be human as, say, our understanding of the physical world or our moral understanding. Others see the prime significance of aesthetic experience to be the distinctive kind of delight it provides. On the former view the arts are, above all, concerned with the intentional production and presentation of objects or events that reveal aesthetic form. On the latter view, the arts exist above all for the enrichment of life through the enjoyment they engender.

On a formalist approach, aesthetic education is above all directed at developing aesthetic experience for the understanding and enrichment that results. Such experience is generally pursued by encountering a broad range of artistic works and activities that are commonly considered to embody aesthetic qualities of a high order. In this way, concepts necessary for ever more sophisticated sensitivity to aesthetic form can be developed.

In the process it is important that a clear distinction be made between an awareness and understanding of the basic content employed in each work of art and a recognition of its formal features. If those features are to be appreciated, however, the content that embodies them must first be recognized or understood in its own right. Detachment from direct attention to this is then imperative. To this end education must begin with detailed attention to the content of works of art. But it then requires the contemplation of each work for its peculiar internal properties, so that these come to be valued and enjoyed for their own sake. All other considerations, such as those of the history of art, the intentions of the artist or the work's moral or social significance may be helpful in grasping the work's basic content. But when it comes to an awareness of aesthetic qualities, these matters must be transcended.

Such disinterested aesthetic focusing is usually considered to be best fostered by those who can direct attention to the features of works that might otherwise be missed and where aesthetic qualities are to be found. Artistic activity that attempts to create and present works of art also has its educational place in encouraging an understanding of the way the content of any object or event provides opportunities and constraints for the occurrence of aesthetic qualities. But for most, the considerable demands in time and skill that the controlled manipulation of any content makes set severe restrictions on the value and range of what can be achieved through such practical activities.

To formalists, the use of the arts for purposes of moral, social, historical or any other form of non-aesthetic education is to direct attention away from the unique educational value of the arts to a role that can be fulfilled by other and more direct means. That is not to deny the value of aesthetic delight as leading to education through the content of works of art. Nor is it to forget that aesthetic qualities are to be found outside the arts and that teachers in other areas can contribute significantly to aesthetic education. What is crucial, however, is that works of art be recognized as above all else essentially aesthetic in their significance, and that they therefore have the central role in aesthetic education.

Attractive and persuasive though the formalist approach is in many respects, it is widely rejected as, to say the least, mistaken in its strict limitation of aesthetic experience to a concern for formal features of objects and events. This is considered by many to be distorting in its account of the significance of the arts in life and in education. It is argued that the particularly sharp distinction made between the formal and other qualities of experience cannot be drawn, and that what we enjoy as aesthetic qualities – in, say, delight in textures, colours and movements – is not confined to formal matters. To thus limit aesthetic concern is held to be falsely dissociating it from all the main areas of human experience and reducing it to something trivial. Aesthetic education is thereby being given a unique role, but at the expense of its being made irrelevant. What is more, if the arts are understood as merely concerned with formal qualities, their highly important contribution to life and education is simply being dismissed.

What is lost by formalists, argue many, is recognition of the fundamental expressive power that is the hallmark of all works of art and aesthetically appealing natural occurrences. It is their capacity to express emotions or feelings that is central to their character.

Aesthetic education in these terms is not concerned with the appreciation of a self-contained, autonomous realm of experience, but with the education of feelings.

Expressionist theories, however, differ considerably in how this is to be understood. In unsophisticated accounts works of art are simply the products of feelings publicly expressed, and are capable of evoking the same feelings in others. Educationally the development of creative capacities in artistic activities is seen as learning to articulate one's feelings, in the process clarifying precisely what one feels and making it possible for others to share this. Through appreciation of the arts, one's whole experience of feelings can be both extended in range and refined in sensitivity. Any view of this sort, however, is not only difficult to justify as a coherent account of the communication of emotion, it also blatantly ignores the very real differences in character between the experiences we have of emotions and feelings in daily life in general, often referred to as 'real life', and our experiences of these feelings in attending to works of art. Careful consideration of the value of the arts in education therefore requires a more complex account of the expression of emotion in the arts. Just what it is of real-life feelings that works of art can express, and how they do this, are thus considerations that have coloured much work on the nature of aesthetic education.

Under the influence of Susanne Langer, it has not infrequently been maintained that the value of the arts educationally lies in their capacity to symbolize the life of feeling and thereby to convey the form of feeling. Art is regarded as objectifying for our contemplation and understanding the subjective reality of sentience, emotions and moods – an aspect of experience which, it is asserted, discursive thought and language cannot express. In this the arts do not, like a natural language, point to feeling as something beyond itself; rather, they present the form of feeling, its movement and tone, for something like direct vision.

The distinctive role of the arts in education is in these terms the education of the subjective life, a task seen as significantly complementing the education provided in all other areas. Such a claim for education in the arts seems important and persuasive, but on close examination proves far from clear. Just what is meant by the 'form of feeling' is elusive, and how this educates our feelings is not convincingly set out. In response, L.A. Reid and others have maintained that, whilst works of art can in some senses express or embody real-life feelings, they necessarily do that in a distinctively aesthetic way. But that is to insist on a unique aesthetic element which Langer explicitly sought to deny, seeing the distinctiveness of the arts, rather, in capturing the form that real-life feelings have. If Reid is right, then the role of the arts in education is not as directly concerned with the subjectivity of real life as Langer wished to assert.

In seeking to maintain the role of the arts in the direct education of real-life feelings, Best has endeavoured to map further the way in which feeling is expressed in art, using a Wittgensteinian approach to mental states. The arts he sees as forms of social practice in which individual works provide the public criteria for the feelings that they, of their very nature, express as products of that practice. What is more, the practice is characteristically – again, of its nature – concerned with contemporary moral, social and political issues. In so far as a work is a portrayal of some aspect of a real-life situation, it is constructed in terms of concepts and conventions that are themselves, in part, those of real life. It can therefore be the vehicle for an emotional response which is an analogue of one's response in real life.

By means of this tight link with life, works of art can indeed be a means for the education of feelings directly related to those of real life. In the construction of a work of art, the artist may well be clarifying his own conceptual grasp of a situation and thus clarifying his own feelings in setting out their public criteria. Educationally, then, the attempt to create works of art within the conventions of an existing social practice can be a powerful vehicle for emotional development, development that can have significant impact in real-life experience. In the appreciation of existing works of art, one's response depends on the concepts used, and by change in these concepts one's response can be significantly extended and even more finely discriminating, with consequent impact on one's responses in real life. In his concentration on expression in the arts and its relationship to real-life experience, consideration of the properties that formalists label 'aesthetic' is of minor concern to Best. He recognizes their presence in both created works and natural objects and events, but regards focusing on these as important to the role of the arts in education as a high danger. What can be lost by such 'aesthetic' attention to the arts is sight of their crucial task in educating feeling.

Best's particular form of expressionism gives important leads for a clearer understanding of how the arts can serve to educate real-life emotions and thereby contribute to the individual's personal, moral and social education. The form of learning involved in this is also clarified and shown to have distinctive force, in that it is of itself an emotional experience. Seeing the arts as essentially social practices is also a helpful key to clarifying their relationship to the moral and social values in the wider society, a relationship that many thinkers, from Plato to Marx, have rightly recognized as educationally significant. But Best largely ignores other forms of educating the emotions in which direct attention is paid to personal, moral and social practices and issues. He thereby tends to exaggerate the place of the arts in the education of emotions.

In his disregard for formalism he is, however, himself seriously diminishing the importance of the arts in education. For even if the validity of his form of expressionism is accepted, there is no contradiction between its educational aspirations and those of formalists who see great value in the enrichment of life through increased appreciation and enhancement of life's uniquely aesthetic properties. It is not difficult to see in such discussions of aesthetic education the beginnings of an approach that avoids the extremes of an exclusive self-contained formalism and an exclusive exaggerated expressionism. It is perhaps time that we recognized the need for a more eclectic view, if in both personal and social terms we are to reap the benefits of the full range of aesthetic and artistic experience now readily available to all.

See also FORM; SCHILLER.

BIBLIOGRAPHY

Best, D.: *Feeling and Reason in the Arts* (London: Allen & Unwin, 1985).
Collinson, D.: 'Aesthetic education', *New Essays in the Philosophy of Education*, ed. G. Longford and D.J. O'Connor (London: Routledge & Kegan Paul, 1973).
Hirst, P.H.: *Knowledge and the Curriculum* (London: Routledge & Kegan Paul, 1974).
Langer, S.: *Feeling and Form* (New York: Scribner, 1953).
Phenix, P.H.: *Realms of Meaning* (New York: McGraw-Hill, 1964).
Reid, L.A.: *Ways of Understanding and Education* (London: Heinemann Educational, 1986).
Ross, M., ed.: *The Claims of Feeling* (London: Falmer, 1989).
Schiller, F.: *Letters on the Aesthetic Education of Man* (1794); trans. E.M. Wilkinson and L.A. Willoughby (Oxford: Clarendon Press, 1967).
Smith, R.A., ed.: *Aesthetics and Problems of Education* (Urbana: University of Illinois Press, 1971).
Smith, R.A., ed.: *Aesthetic Concepts and Education* (Urbana: University of Illinois Press, 1973).

PAUL H. HIRST

Eliot, T(homas) S(tearns) (1888–1965) Poet, critic and dramatist, Eliot was born in St Louis, Missouri, and educated at Harvard University and Oxford. He settled in England from 1914. His earliest interest was in philosophy, mainly in the Idealist tradition of Josiah Royce, R.G. Collingwood and Joachim, but was also taught by Russell. His 1917 dissertation on Bradley was published in 1964, encouraging views of a significant Bradleyan influence on his criticism. Bradley probably reinforced a native scepticism, and infected his literary manner, but any influence on his aesthetics would seem to have been lost in absorption.

Arriving in London equipped with Laforguesque poems and an enthusiasm for French poetry derived from A.J. Symons's *The Symbolist Movement in Literature* (1899), he was quickly absorbed into Ezra Pound's milieu. Poetry was finding its way out of its post-Paterian aestheticism, seeking alternative sources of influence, sharing Pound's determination to 'Make it New'. 'Symbol', passed from Blake and his precursors to Yeats, tested to destruction by Mallarmé and his contemporaries, carried a dubious freight of transcendentalism, magic, elusive suggestiveness, which the new objectivism was intent on scouring away in the interests of 'honest registration'. For Symons, poetry had to rid itself of 'descriptiveness', had 'to *be*, rather than to express'. 'Image' replaces 'symbol' in current usage without, however, completely severing its deepest symbolist concerns. To stop at the object, at the natural object, did not fulfil Pound's desire to 'present an intellectual and emotional complex in an instant of time'. The aesthetic 'shot' here prescribed is symbolist. Shown Eliot's *Prufrock*, Pound identified a poetry moving in the right direction.

Eliot's seminal essays in *The Sacred Wood* (1920) declare no allegiances, but nevertheless 'write their time'. Setting out with Arnoldian confidence to define 'the critical intelligence', they legislate for a 'pure motive' in criticism consonant with the nature of the 'object as in itself it really is'. That object is 'poetry and not another thing'. Morals, politics, religion, psychology, irrelevant personal concerns, are firmly excluded from the 'pure contemplation' within which the critic will elucidate, compare, and analyse.

'Tradition and the individual talent' applies the same clinical rigour to the poet. The topic of tradition is preceded by what will become a familiar warning against the meretricious value given to 'individuality'. The poet writes from within a 'tradition' comprising all the literature of Europe from Homer onwards. This is described as an 'ideal order', a 'simultaneous existence' of past and present, requiring for its comprehension the 'historical sense' not only of the pastness of the past, but of its presence. To this 'order the

new work will 'conform', 'cohere', not by slavish imitation, but by what may presumably be described as 'traditional novelty'. The difficulty in prescribing for originality is compounded by the crucial condition that the process involves for the poet 'a surrender of himself . . . to something which is more valuable. The progress of the artist is a continual self-surrender, a continual extinction of personality.' (Eliot, 1928, pp. 52–3.)

The self-immolating tone here, seeming to detach itself from aesthetic discourse, is not inadvertent, although the motives behind it will not declare themselves until later in his career. It does for the moment lead conformably enough to the issue of 'impersonality'. The analogy of the mind of the poet as a platinum catalyst in a chemical mixture is perhaps more modish than felicitous (Gourmont perhaps, or Baudelaire's 'chemist' poet). But the implied image of the catalytic mind as 'inert, neutral, and unchanged' seems a reversion to the mechanical views of 18th-century empiricism which Coleridge had rejected for the vital creativity of perception. But even if the creative process is not the immediate issue for Eliot here, the analogy illustrates the separation 'between the man who suffers and the mind which creates' only in the bleakest sense, giving little substance to the assertion that the poet is 'only a medium and not a personality'. That 'poetry is not a turning loose of emotion, but an escape from emotion . . . not the expression of personality but an escape from personality' returns the argument more recognisably to the terms of the anti-Romantic debate. (Eliot, 1928, pp. 56, 58.)

Yet this is a line which can be traced from Coleridge's 'Spinozistic Deity', Keats's 'camelion poet' to Flaubert and the Joycean creator preoccupied with his manicure. But Eliot's formulation, one may suspect, suggestive of the ionic poet re-radiating to the thermionic reader, is simply a device for frightening the horses of Romanticism. And he has, as it transpires, set the scene for what comes to be called the 'New Criticism' – giving the critic a severe professionalism, a nucleus of aesthetic doctrine, and exemplary models. The products of this 'common pursuit' are the autonomy of the poem, a contextualist methodology, and a critical orthodoxy proscribing intention, belief, biography, affectivity as heresies. Yet, unsurprisingly suspended – as indeed Eliot was – between coherence and correspondence views of truth, they wanted somehow to say that 'poetry will save us'. By 1927 a declared Anglo-Catholic, Eliot was dismissive of poetry's redemptive efficacy and was already placing literature under the scrutiny of religion and ethics. To the New Critics he was a lost leader.

In *The Sacred Wood*, however, the supporting essays on individual authors show Eliot diverting attention from the Romantics back toward the 16th and 17th centuries – back indeed, ultimately, to Dante and Virgil. Although the earlier formulation of 'tradition' was non-prescriptive, he is here, in effect indicating where the tradition might run. The historical locale chosen has particular doctrinal interests rooted in Irving Babbitt's 'classical humanism'. In *Rousseau and Romanticism* (1919) Babbitt advocated 'the need to restore to human nature . . . the "old Adam" that the idealists have been so busy eliminating.' Contemporaneously, T.E. Hulme, the Imagist proponent, was also proclaiming, in his *Speculations* (1924), the importance of the concept of original sin as a reminder of man's limitations, linking his argument likewise to the Romantic/classical opposition (man, for the Romantic, 'a well'; for the classicist 'a bucket'). Eliot's use of both terms carries similar connotations, although his 'classicism' acquires distinctively Christian associations. Looking for the point in time where things went wrong he chose the 17th century.

In defining the crisis at this point in history he derives a double advantage. It marks an end to the kind of poetry whose qualities he values, and a crisis in politics and religion. Metaphysical poetry, exhibiting a 'direct sensuous apprehension of thought, or a re-creation of thought into feeling' and providing 'a mechanism of sensibility which could devour any kind of experience' ('Spinoza . . . and the noise of the typewriter') offered a model to the modern poet (Eliot, 1951, p. 287). The conceit, especially in its 'far-fetchedness', made an attractive amending model for the symbol. The historical scene itself retained many of the traditional valencies of the medieval church, a sense of order and discipline he associated with classicism. In describing the consequences of that crisis as a 'dissociation of sensibility' whereby subsequent writers think and feel only 'by fits' he is making a generalization as untenable as that of locating his 'second fall' in that particular century. Yet this is not anything so simple as poor scholarship or unscrupulous theorizing. From the days of his Harvard seminars he had been aware that interpretation becomes part of its object, that hypothesis is a sceptical instrument. The case that he makes here, as in many of his heuristic conceits, is credible as a 'convincing possibility' within the *mythos* of the time, not the truth, but like the truth.

The mechanism for expressing in art these equivalences for emotions he terms the 'objective correlative' (Eliot, 1928, p. 100). However, the impressive packaging contains the easily acceptable advice that objects or situations have to be found which will carry the appropriate emotion to the reader. More significant in the 'Hamlet' essay where this occurs are the remarks subsequent to his allegation that Hamlet's emotions are 'in excess of the facts as they appear'. He refers to 'emotions ecstatic or terrible, without an object or exceeding their objects' which he claims are normally suppressed but which 'the artist keeps alive by intensifying the world to his emotions' (Eliot, 1928, p. 102). Read back into the 'objective correlative', and recalling the central character in *Family Reunion* who speaks of 'The glow upon the world that never found its object' and is forced to 'give you comparisons in a more familiar medium', we are returned to the realm of an almost unamended symbolist aesthetics. The self with its emotions and visions has lost a world where these would have been embodied. Travelling, Wordsworth, in his emotional encounters, found guarantees of the exquisite fit of mind and nature. That concord broken, nature as *Geist* is, for Eliot and the Modern, simply 'available'. The objective correlative is a strategy, not for 'understanding' the world, but for using it.

Such an aesthetic of 'contraptions', 'halcyon structures' would seem to explain Eliot's downgrading of 'meaning' as 'a bit of nice meat for the house-dog' while the poem does its real work in bringing us its 'serenity, stillness and reconciliation' (Eliot, 1933, pp. 51–2). But then, he says, it is to leave us 'as Virgil left Dante, to proceed toward a region where that guide can avail us no further' (Eliot, 1957, pp. 86–7). The context is that of symbolist aesthetics; the promised destination belongs to another order or reality, to interests and needs which find no place in the function of criticism.

These interests increasingly alter his earlier views on all those value systems he had pronounced as extraneous to poetry. They appear in the arrogant judgments of the moralist in *After Strange Gods*, and with more amenity in 'Religion and Literature'. Here the poet's beliefs are no longer a matter of 'suspension of disbelief', no longer seen as addressed to a special 'aesthetic sense', but as addressing us wholly as human beings. This might be taken as a defensible and welcome relaxation of the strict conditions of isolation in which the poem was seen to exist. But our 'reality' as whole human beings is to depend on knowing what we are by knowing what we ought to be. And that knowledge is religious before it is ethical. Literary criticism has therefore 'to be completed from a definite ethical and religious standpoint' (Eliot, 1951, p. 388). The audience he is addressing are the elect, the world in which they live is 'corrupted by Secularism', 'wormeaten with Liberalism'.

His editorship of *Criterion* from 1922 draws him increasingly towards politics, society, religion, where he is strongly attracted by the 'monarchism, Catholicism, classicism' of Charles Maurras. Eliot absorbs the less extreme elements of Maurras into his 'classicism' and his Anglo-Catholicism, which, in the turmoil of the 1930s, he translated into terms of political and social discipline, stewardship of traditional values, 'orthodoxy'. There is an air in the later lectures and writings of one defending a minority position,

addressing an unregenerate majority. The essays on Culture, usefully expanding the early 'Tradition' into a whole 'way of life' of a nation, are thoughtful, but lack zest, seeming to speak in their 'non-Tory' Conservatism, to and of a society which had disappeared, and perhaps never existed.

Eliot's substantial and enduring contribution is the definitive direction he gave to a literature in crisis in the early decades of the century. He offers no systematic aesthetic. He endeavours instead to remain close to the practice he admires in Aristotle, of providing for the needs of his time an example 'not of laws, or even of method, for there is no method except to be very intelligent, but of intelligence itself swiftly operating the analysis of sensation to the point of principle and definition' (Eliot, 1928, p. 11). We must, however, remind ourselves that it is the poem which is the best critic of poetry. The 'deep disquietudes' of Eliot's own poetry force us to confront the 'deep disquietudes' of our ways of living, of knowing, of saying.

See also CULTURE; RELIGION AND ART; SYMBOL; TRADITION.

WRITINGS

The Sacred Wood (London: Methuen, 1920; 2nd edn, 1928).
Selected Essays (London: Faber and Faber, 1932; 3rd edn, 1951).
The Use of Poetry and the Use of Criticism (London: Faber and Faber, 1933).
Notes Towards the Definition of Culture (London: Faber, 1948).
On Poetry and Poets (London: Faber, 1957).
Knowledge and Experience in the Philosophy of F.M. Bradley (London: Faber, 1964).

BIBLIOGRAPHY

Kenner, Hugh: *The Invisible Poet: T.S. Eliot* (London: Methuen, 1965).
Kojecky, Roger: *T.S. Eliot's Social Criticism* (London: Faber, 1971).
Shusterman, Richard: *T.S. Eliot and the Philo-*

sophy of Criticism (London: Duckworth, 1988).

J.A.M. RILLIE

emotion Emotion figures in art and in the aesthetic experience of the natural word in many different ways. Some of these are unproblematic, but others are less easy to understand and to grasp their full aesthetic significance.

Perhaps the most difficult issues about art and emotion are these. First, there is the problem of the artistic expression of emotion. Works of art can not only describe emotion or depict or otherwise represent its manifestation in the body, but also express it. What is the relation between a work and a certain emotion, when the work expresses that emotion? This question arises in its purest form when the expressive work lacks any representational content, as is usually the case with music. Remarkable claims have often been made about the great superiority of music to language as a vehicle for the expression of emotion, especially in its capacity to express nuances of emotion that elude the net of language.

Whatever the truth of these claims, it is clear that some musical works are valued partly in virtue of their being heard as expressive of emotion; and yet it is by no means clear what this experience is and how, if at all, the emotionally expressive aspect of a work endows it with musical value. Does the experience consist in the recognition of some property of the music (the music's resemblance to one of the ways in which the emotion can be expressed in the human body or voice, for example), or the recognition of some symbolic relation in which it stands to the emotion it expresses; or does it involve responding to the music with emotion of some kind, or is it some combination of these? Whatever the correct answer to this question may be, there is a further issue about artistic expression: is there a unitary sense in which works of art are experienced as being expressive of emotion, or does the sense change from one art form to another?

Second, there are various problems about the emotions aroused by works of art. One of these concerns the nature of the mental state of someone who reacts with emotion to a fictional state of affairs represented in a work of art. It seems often to be the case – in the cinema, at the theatre, in an art gallery, or when reading fiction – that we are moved by what we know not to be real, but only fictional. But how is it possible for a fictional person or state of affairs to be the object of our emotion, when we are fully aware of their unreality? And if we do feel emotions about people or states of affairs that we are conscious of as merely fictional is it rational for us to do so?

Another problem about the artistic arousal of emotion concerns the so-called negative emotions, emotions like fear and horror that involve a negative attitude towards what they are about and are distressing to experience. Aristotle located fear and pity at the heart of the experience of tragic art, identified the tragic *pleasure* with that of fear and pity, and maintained that the arousal of fear and pity by a tragedy effects 'catharsis'.

There is a long-standing problem about the correct interpretation of Aristotle's conception of catharsis. But there is a further problem, for Aristotle defined both fear and pity as forms of pain, which would appear to preclude their constituting the distinctive pleasure of tragedy. Hume inherited this problem, and tried to resolve it by means of a doctrine about the conditions under which one emotion will be transformed by another, so that a normally painful emotion will lose its painful aspect and increase the strength of the pleasurable emotion that dominates it. But there is a more general issue about the occurrence of negative emotion in the experience of a work of art that is found valuable, which does not presuppose that this experience must be pleasurable: namely why is it ever reasonable to value a work of art for its ability to arouse negative emotions?

Finally, there is a problem about the education of emotion through art. A common justification of art is that it has a beneficial effect on the emotions of both the artist and the public: its successful practice requires the control and development of the artist's emotional life, and its products are unrivalled in their ability to introduce those who appreciate them to unfamiliar and superior forms of feeling, and to encourage in them more adequate or more rewarding feelings about many aspects of the world in which they live. Yet the variety of ways in which art can accomplish these desirable ends, and the sense or senses in which emotion can be refined and educated through artistic practice and appreciation, are not well understood. This is especially true of non-representational works of art.

It is possible to make some progress with aesthetic problems concerning emotion, whilst remaining unclear about the nature of emotion in general and the various natures of the different emotions. But proposed solutions of these problems are often rendered null by a defective understanding of the emotions, and definitive solutions must be founded upon a sound understanding. However, the field of the emotions is highly contentious, within both philosophy and pyschology, and it is by no means easy to achieve a firm grasp of the topic.

What are the emotions? As a first approximation: the emotions are attitudes or reactions to how the world is represented as being, and they are distinguished from one another by the different representations or responses they involve. Each emotion requires the world to be represented to its subject in a certain way, as fear requires the representation of a threat, jealousy a rival, and sorrow the death of a loved one, for instance. Such a representation can be realized in many different forms, such as perception, experiential memory, imagination or thought.

But an emotion requires more than the right kind of representation, for unless the representation induces the response distinctive of the emotion, the subject is not in that emotional condition. Both pity and Schadenfreude include the representation of someone's misfortune; but it is possible to be emotionally unaffected by someone's misfortune; and pity and Schadenfreude are different emotions because they involve opposite responses to the represented misfortune that is common to them. This encourages the thought that the emotions can be defined in terms of the representations and responses that jointly constitute them. But what kind of response to a representation is an emotional response? What needs to be added to a representation to make it an instance of an emotion?

Now, an emotion can exist in either a dispositional or an experiential form. If you have a general fear (of dogs, for example), or you are afraid of a particular person or that a certain state of affairs will come about, you need not be undergoing any experience of fear – you might even be dreamlessly asleep, experiencing nothing at all. Your fear is a dispositional state, which is manifested not only in a tendency to avoid the feared object or to reduce the likelihood of the threatening state of affairs or to reduce your vulnerability to the threat it poses, but also in experiences of fear targeted on particular objects or concerned with possible states of affairs. When you experience an emotion, typically you *feel* the emotion – you feel afraid, ashamed, embarrassed, proud, or whatever. This suggests that the specifically emotional ingredient in a mental state is a feeling: an emotion requires the right representation plus the right feeling. Whether or not this is so, the idea of experiencing an emotion is of crucial significance for aesthetics, for the central problems about emotion turn on it. So what is it to feel a certain emotion? What kind of feeling is the feeling of jealousy, admiration, remorse or amusement, and what makes a feeling a feeling of one of these emotions rather than another?

The best-known account of the nature of emotional feelings identifies the feeling of an emotion with the experience of bodily sensations. A bodily sensation is a feeling of an occurrence in or a state of the body. When you feel a pain in your back or when you feel hot, it feels to you as if something is going on in some part of your body or that your body is in a certain condition; and what is felt to occur or how your body feels to you determines the nature of the sensation you experience. Now, it is true that when you experience an emotion it will often be the case that you experience bodily sensations. But it is mistaken to represent the feeling of sadness, envy, pride or regret as being composed of bodily sensations.

This suggestion exists in two forms. The stronger claim maintains that for each emotion there is a set of distinctive bodily sensations such that whenever the emotion is felt this set of bodily sensations is experienced: it identifies a type of emotional feeling with a collection of types of bodily sensation. Perhaps the best way for this suggestion to be developed is to maintain that a set of bodily sensations constitutes an emotional feeling, not simply in virtue of the intrinsic character of the set of sensations, but because it has been caused by the right kind of representation of the world. The weaker form of the suggestion maintains only that for each episode of emotion what is felt is a set of bodily sensations: it identifies each instance of an emotional feeling with whatever bodily sensations are caused on that occasion by the representation integral to the emotion. Whereas the stronger version requires that each instance of an emotional feeling of the same kind (admiration, say) consists of bodily sensations of the same kind, the weaker allows bodily sensations to vary across different instances of the same emotional feeling. But neither form is correct.

It is sometimes thought to be sufficient, to refute the identification, to point to the intentionality or directedness of emotions and the lack of intentionality of bodily sensations: whereas emotions are about something or other, bodily sensations are not. But this objection presupposes that bodily sensations are not representations of the body's condition: if they are, they possess intentionality. Perhaps it will be thought that, nevertheless, they would not possess the right intentionality. For, unless the object of an emotion is the subject's own body, as it might be in a case of pride or shame, emotions are directed towards the world outside one's body, whereas bodily sensations indicate the current state of one's body. But this consideration is inconclusive, since it would be possible for an adherent of the identification to reply that an emotional feeling is inherently only body-directed, its world-directed intentionality being derivative from the mental representation intrinsic to the emotion.

It is unnecessary to pursue this issue, however, for there is a more decisive objection. When you feel admiration, amusement, disgust, gratitude, sadness, shame or shyness, it is unnecessary for you to be aware of any bodily sensations, so that the feeling you are aware of cannot be composed of bodily sensations either in the stronger or the weaker sense. Furthermore, it is never sufficient in order to experience a certain emotion that you should feel various bodily sensations as a result of the representation of the world integral to the emotion: if the perception of danger causes you to feel the pounding of your heart and the bristling of your hair, you might feel afraid of the threat, but you might instead feel excited at the challenge it poses. An emotion is not a causal compound of a mental representation and bodily sensations.

If an emotional feeling is not a set of bodily sensations, what else might it be? A more plausible suggestion emerges if we are guided by the account of the emotions in Aristotle's *Rhetorica*. Aristotle defines the emotions as 'all those feelings that so change men as to affect their judgements, and that are also attended by pain or pleasure'; a good illustration is his definition of anger as 'an impulse, accompanied by pain, to a conspicuous revenge for a conspicuous slight directed without justification towards what concerns oneself or towards what concerns one's friends' (*Rhetorica* II, 182). The great advantage of Aristotle's account is that it exploits and articulates a crucial feature of the emotions – namely, their power to initiate action and to affect thought. For many emotions involve not only mental representations but forms of desire or aversion, pleasure or pain, or other kinds of pro or con attitudes; as amusement and pride involve pleasure, hope a wish that something is or will be so and regret a wish that things had turned out differently, shame the desire to conceal and anger the desire to oppose or overcome, grief and fear distress, envy an eversion to a perceived inequality and pity the impulse to help. So the suggestion is that what we must feel if we are to experience an emotion is the pleasure or pain or the (apparent) frustration or satisfaction of the desire or wish integral to the emotion.

Note that this allows that when we experience an emotion we may often feel various processes take place in our body; but it denies that this is what the feeling of amusement, anger, envy, fear, grief, hope, pity, pride, regret or shame amounts to. Rather, it is an experience of satisfaction or frustration, pleasure or pain. It is important to distinguish between what we *must* feel if we are to feel shame, say, and what in fact we feel on some occasion (or even all occasions) when we feel shame. The feeling of shame is the first of these, not the second. Note also that this theory does not rest on the common doctrine that a desire lies at the heart of each emotion: the truth is that some emotions lack constitutive desires. Nor does it presuppose that we always derive satisfaction from the known satisfaction of a desire, and experience displeasure if a desire is thought to be unfulfilled. What it maintains is that we experience an emotion that contains a desire that appears to us to be frustrated or threatened, only if we experience displeasure at that prospect or certainty: to feel the emotion is to experience the displeasure.

Note, finally, that this suggestion does not identify any emotion with a feeling. What it offers is an account of what is felt when an emotion is experienced; but there is more to any emotion than the feeling that partly constitutes it. There is a difference between what is felt when an emotion is experienced and what it is to feel that emotion. Although what it is to feel one emotion is not the same as what it is to feel a different emotion, there is a sense in which what is felt (pleasure, for example) may be the same in the two cases. The nature of the feeling does not determine the nature of the emotion felt. For an emotion is a causal structure: unless the feeling intrinsic to an emotion is caused by the representation intrinsic to the emotion and is directed at what the representation is about, the emotion is not experienced.

This suggestion maintains that the experience of an emotion is a product of a mental representation, typically a belief, and a positive or negative attitude towards the content of the representation, which attitude either is an affect or combines with the representation to produce one. If this is a true account of what it is to feel the emotions mentioned, does it hold for all emotions? Certainly, it applies to a number of other emotions (embarrassment, for example). Not only, though, do the emotions form a heterogeneous class, which militates against a unitary account of the kinds of feeling intrinsic to them; but the boundaries of the class are uncertain, so that it is unclear whether certain kinds of reaction fall within the boundaries and therefore are emotions.

For instance, if surprise and amazement are correctly thought of as emotions, what we experience when we undergo them does not conform to the account, since the experience of surprise or amazement is not one of being frustrated by or distressed about something, or in which pleasure or satisfaction is derived from some state of affairs. Even so, these experiences are not bodily sensations. (They are the confounding of expectations – as the experience of wonder is the surpassing of expectations.) So there may well be counter-examples to the suggestion. It may also be necessary to qualify the suggestion by introducing additional kinds of feeling into the analysis of certain of the emotions for which the suggestion holds – felt impulses to action, the feeling of being invigorated or the feeling of lassitude, for example.

I believe that the best strategy is not to attempt to design a theory that captures every member of the accepted class of emotions, since this class may be both ill conceived and indeterminate. It is better to try to accommodate the great majority of the members within a single theory, and to place the exceptions outside the newly drawn boundaries of the class. This is how the suggestion outlined above should be understood. But even if this suggestion captures most emotional feelings, it does not follow that it is better than any other, for another account might capture equally many, if not more. Furthermore, without an exhaustive list of the emotions, it is unclear whether the suggestion is in fact true of most, or only a minority, of emotional feelings. If it holds only for a minority, a different strategy recommends itself: recognize the diversity of emotional feelings and abandon any attempt to redraw the boundaries of the class in order to impose uniformity upon its members. This strategy appears to be especially appropriate within aesthetics, where problems about emotion benefit from a case-by-case approach.

See also ARISTOTLE; CATHARSIS; EDUCATION, AESTHETIC; EXPRESSION; PLEASURE, AESTHETIC.

BIBLIOGRAPHY

Aristotle: *Rhetorica*, trans. W.R. Roberts (Oxford: Clarendon Press, 1924).

Budd, M.: *Music and the Emotions* (London: Routledge & Kegan Paul, 1985), ch. 1.

Gordon, R.M.: *The Structure of Emotions* (Cambridge: Cambridge University Press, 1987).

Hepburn, R.W.: 'The arts and the education of feeling and emotion', *'Wonder' and Other Essays* (Edinburgh: Edinburgh University Press, 1984).

James, W.: *The Principles of Psychology* (London: Dover, 1950), vol. 2, ch. 25.

Lyons, W.: *Emotion* (Cambridge: Cambridge University Press, 1980).

Sachs, D.: 'Wittgenstein on emotion', *Acta Philosophica Fennica*, 28 (1976), 250–85.

MALCOLM BUDD

'end of art' Inspired by views presented by Hegel, Arthur C. Danto has offered the idea that the history of art is the record of its progress towards self-realization through self-understanding. He suggests that, in the twentieth century, art has fulfilled this, its destiny, so that now the history of art is at an end. Art has entered its 'post-historical' stage. The relevant arguments are most conveniently to be found in Danto's *Philosophical Disenfranchisement of Art* (1986).

Danto has argued that artworks are embedded in socio-historical contexts, in that their artistically significant properties depend upon their location within socially-rooted traditions of art-making. Artworks do not possess their properties independently of their historical and cultural locations, as do 'mere real things'. Artworks are constituted as such by the interpretations placed upon them – they are objects conjoined with 'an atmosphere of theory'. This atmosphere of theory varies from time to time and place to place.

Danto is fond of making his point by comparing objects which, as mere real things, would be perceptually indiscriminable. Raindrops falling on tin cans might produce a sound-structure identical to that of a performance of a Mozart symphony, but, as an artwork, Mozart's symphony has properties which the sound of rain could not possess. Mozart's symphony exploits and extends the possibilities of sonata form; it employs a style which Mozart played a role in developing; it draws on the work of Haydn; and so on. Even where an artwork imitates a mere real thing, it has an intensional character which prevents it from collapsing on to ahistorical, acultural reality. In a similar fashion, the work of a modern composer must possess properties which distinguish it from Mozart's even were the two works to share the same sound-structure. In this case, the modern work is archaic, whereas Mozart's piece is in the contemporary style; the avoidance of extreme chromaticism, of the use of saxophones, and so on, is a significant feature of the contemporary work, but not of Mozart's; the contemporary work contains quotations, allusions and influences which Mozart's does not.

Artists cannot bridge the temporal gap which separates them from their predecessors and, in that sense, cannot achieve with the same means what was achieved by their artistic forebears. Neither, though, can artists break free from the art of the past. Even where they set out to reject the styles and techniques of earlier artists, their works take part of their significance from the act of repudiation. The styles and techniques eschewed retain their relevance for their having been rejected. Artworks can be identified and appreciated only through their proper location within art-making traditions which generate the atmospheres of theory which make them what they are.

Because artworks derive their identity and significance from their place within a temporal context, artistic change is directional and irreversible. (The point is consistent with spirals of change in which, for example, Romantic and Classical tendencies ebb and flow in turn.) The possibilities for the route of artistic change are shaped not only by technical innovations which impinge on the 'artworld' from the wider culture, but also by the direction in which earlier artists have led the artworld. What is possible at any time depends on what has been achieved in the art of the past. The artworld has to be 'ready' for the new movements, because they build on or challenge the possibilities of the art of the past. Duchamp, had he lived in the fifteenth century, could not have succeeded in making a urinal into an artwork, for such a work could have found no place within the tradition which made the artistic developments of the fifteenth century possible. Duchamp's innovations were made possible by the art context of his time.

The course of art is directional, but is there some goal towards which this process of change aims? Is there artistic progress? In dialectical mode, Danto rejects two models of art history in favour of a third in which aspects of the first two models are synthesized.

The first model sees art as aiming at perceptual fidelity, as motivated wherever possibly by an imperative to replace inference to perceptual reality with something equivalent to what perceptual reality itself would present. On this view, the history of painting is to be characterized in terms of the development of pictorial conventions the purpose of which is to render space and perspective faithfully. (Danto accepts, as many who would challenge this view would not, that the conventions for realism in pictorial representation cannot be entirely arbitrary.)

Danto rejects this model on several grounds. There is no sense to the idea that there could be progress towards accuracy in description through changes in natural languages, so the theory fails to accommodate

narrational art forms. Anyway, it fails to account for the history of those arts to which it most naturally applies – painting and sculpture. Around the turn of the twentieth century, painters departed from mimetic accuracy. These departures could not be explained as resulting from failures in technique or limitations inherent in the media they employed. The invention and development of 'moving pictures' in the cinema had made clear that optical fidelity might be achieved there more successfully than could be hoped for in painting. This led those committed to painting to question the nature of their art and, ultimately, to abandon the goal of representational accuracy in favour of other concerns.

The second model of art history arose from the ashes of the first. Attention shifted to the expressive achievements of the new art movements and, with the realization that expression need not rely on representation at all, came the rejection of definitions of art according a central place to the goal of mimetic faithfulness. An advantage of this second model, according to which art is expression, is that it encompasses literature and music, as the first model did not. But the universality of the theory is purchased at a price – the notion of progress must be abandoned. The art movements (many being the province of a single artist) which developed after Fauvism each could claim to establish their own distinctive, incommensurable 'vocabularies' of expression. Expression was not a goal of which one could fall short for lack of artistic technique or technological development. The history of art, as conceived by this model, reduces to a list of individual acts which are not unified by shared progress towards a common ideal.

According to Danto, the poverty of this second model was soon revealed by the burgeoning number of art movements many of which obviously involved much more than expression. From Fauvism onward, the important common element seemed to be not expression, but reliance on a quite complex theory in order that the often very minimal objects could be 'transacted on to the plane of art'. In abandoning the view that the goal of art was mimetic faithfulness, artists had been forced to examine the fundamental character of their art. Art became self-conscious and, from that point on, any distinction between what art is and a philosophical consideration of its nature was undermined; for, once the goal of mimetic faithfulness had been called into doubt, it was only through conscious attention to its own philosophical character that art could continue to develop. Every work and movement became a kind of theory in action. Nowhere was this more obvious than in Duchamp's presentation of his ready-mades as art, for in those pieces the artistic 'work' is done not by the 'naked' aesthetic properties of the object appropriated, but by the idea married to the object through the act of presentation. Duchamp's works, says Danto, raise the question of the philosophical nature of art from within art, implying that art is already philosophy in a vivid form.

In later versions of the argument, Danto has conceived the second model more as a type, of which the argument given above is only one instance. The type in question sees the history of art not in terms of progression, but, instead, as the succession of one dominant paradigm by another. On this view, there can be no trans-historical perspective from which one might judge and compare these various paradigms. It is this denial which Danto is concerned to reject in his dismissal of the second model of art history.

This leads to the third model of art history and the restoration of the idea of historical progress in art-making. The goal of art is its self-realization through self-comprehension. The aim is not the attainment of knowledge of some ahistorical, acultural reality, but a cognitive process towards self-realization in which the quest itself transforms the character of the object. To the extent that artworks are surrounded by an atmosphere of theory, they are constituted as much by theory as by anything else. And to the extent that self-conscious philosophizing about art affects this atmosphere of theory, understanding what artworks are is inescapably reflexive – 'so that virtually all there is at the end is theory; art becoming vaporised in a dazzle of

pure thought about itself'. The density of art is its 'transmutation into philosophy'. The history of art is the measure of art's progress towards this condition.

This third model is inspired by remarks in Hegel's *Phenomenology of Spirit* and *Philosophy of the Fine Arts*. Hegel suggests that art, through its own development, reaches a stage at which it contributes to the goal of human thought, which is an understanding of its own historical essence. The stage is transitional – a step on the path to self-knowledge which encompasses art as one important aspect of human culture. When the phase in which the energies of art mesh with those of history is passed, the history of art has ended. Art's philosophical history consists in its being absorbed ultimately into its own philosophy.

Danto comments: if this view is plausible, it is reasonable to ask how far art has progressed towards its goal. He maintains that, with pop art, the goal has been attained, so that the history of art has reached its end. The artwork has become 'irradiated by theoretical consciousness', so that the division between object and subject is all but overcome. Art, above all, has achieved the condition which Hegel calls 'absolute knowledge'. The liberation of art from its history, on this view, will not lead to its re-invigoration for, in having achieved its destiny, it has fulfilled its purpose, so that art-making continues only by habit, deprived of that which formerly gave it point. (Note, however, the optimistic suggestion in 'Approaching the end of art' that art, having achieved self-comprehension, could return to the serving of largely human needs.)

The hallmarks of the post-historical phase, said to be apparent in the art of the late twentieth century, are identified by Danto as follows. Anything can become an artwork, he maintains – where all directions are available there no longer can be progress. What art is and what it means already have been revealed, so it is not possible that art should continue to astonish us. As the atmosphere of art theory thickens, so the objects of art become thinner, more minimal, even dispensable. Traditional boundaries between the art forms tend to become radically unstable. The institutions of the artworld, the existence of which is predicated on ideas of artistic history and progress, begin to wither and die.

Now, one might question the accuracy of Danto's account of Hegel, but it should be remembered that he does not offer his argument in the name of exegetical scholarship. One might note that the works which carry the burden of the argument, such as Duchamp's ready-mades, sometimes are regarded as not having established their credentials as artworks. One could observe that Danto's argument concentrates on the 'high' arts and seems far less plausible when a more liberal notion of 'art' is adopted. And, if one were to follow the modern intellectual fashion according to which all values and truths (save this one) are relative to conceptual paradigms which themselves are historically and culturally relative, one would reject the possibility of a transcendental perspective such as that which Danto purports to assume. But let us put such issues aside.

If Danto is right, modern art confronts a condition not faced before. Is the claim reasonable? Art always has been self-conscious in that it involves concern with style and technique, with the features and limitations of media, and with historical precedent. This, though, is consistent with Danto's thesis – that art did not become fully reflexive until such concerns turned from goals such as the pursuit of optical fidelity to that of the exploration of its own nature. Still, the thesis that full reflexivity is a modern phenomenon is questionable in the case of music, for it is not clear that the disintegration of the tonal system in the first decades of the twentieth century was any less radical or traumatic than the gradual collapse of the system of church modes four centuries earlier. Music, at least from the advent of purely instrumental forms, has concerned itself with 'self-realization' and has done so without emptying itself of interest or significance.

Undeniably, though, high art of the late twentieth century, including music, is more thoroughly alienated from the general public than ever it was before, and the spread of artistic activities seems directionless and often pointless in its variety. This is predicted by Danto's hypothesis. But the tendency for each generation to see itself as coming at the apocalyptic culmination of history, a general suspicion of grandiose theories about the meaning of life and of destiny, and the availability of alternative diagnoses, provide grounds for scepticism. In many respects, the 'crisis' of modern art seems to mirror the general state of social and political life. In that case, an explanation of the condition of high art might be sought more appropriately in a wider context than the one considered by Danto. While he regards art as rooted in its cultural context, his approach is unconvincingly narrow in treating the condition of art as generated by forces uniquely internal to the artworld.

The universality of art from the earliest times suggests that art answers to some deep human needs, and that art might serve those needs for so long as the fundamental character of human nature remains unchanged. Given that we remain all too human, there is reason to doubt that art no longer could have anything 'new to say'. If much modern art seems to be empty, this is not because we now understand what art is and what it means. That philosophical knot is no easier to unravel than ever it was.

See also ART HISTORY; 'ARTWORLD'; DANTO; HEGEL.

BIBLIOGRAPHY

Belting, Hans: *The End of the History of Art?* (München: 1983); trans. Christopher S. Wood (Chicago: Chicago University Press, 1987).
Brown, Lee B.: 'Resurrecting Hegel to bury art'. *British Journal of Aesthetics*, 29 (1989), 303–15.
Cebik, L.B.: 'Knowledge or control as the end of art', *British Journal of Aesthetics*, 30 (1990), 244–55.
Danto, Arthur C.: *The Philosophical Disenfranchisement of Art* (New York: Columbia University Press, 1986).
Danto, Arthur C.: 'Approaching the end of art', *The State of the Art* (New York: Prentice-Hall, 1987), pp. 202–18.

Danto, Arthur C.: 'Narratives of the end of art', *Encounters and Reflections: Art in the Historical Present* (New York: Farrar, Straus & Giroux, 1990).

Lang, Berel, ed.: *The Death of Art* (New York: Haven, 1984).

Ross, Stephanie: 'Philosophy, literature, and the death of art', *Philosophical Papers*, 18 (1989), 95–115.

STEPHEN DAVIES

engagement *see* COMMITMENT AND EN-GAGEMENT.

environmental aesthetics Much of our aesthetic appreciation is not confined to art, but, rather, directed towards the world at large. Moreover, we appreciate not only pristine nature – scenes of sunsets and mountains – but also our more mundane surroundings: the solitude of a neighbourhood park on a rainy evening, the chaos of a bustling morning market-place, the view from the road. Thus, there is a place for the notion of environmental aesthetics, for in such cases – in our appreciation of the world at large – our aesthetic appreciation often encompasses our total surroundings: our environment. Environments may be large or small, more or less natural, mundane or exotic, but in every case it is central that it is an environment that we appreciate. This fact signals several important dimensions of such appreciation, which in turn contribute to the key issues of environmental aesthetics.

The first of these dimensions follows from the delineation of the subject. The 'object' of appreciation, the 'aesthetic object', is our environment, our own surroundings, and thus we are in a sense immersed in the object of appreciation. This fact has the following ramifications. We are in that which we appreciate, and that which we appreciate is also that from which we appreciate. If we move, we move within the object of our appreciation and thereby change our relationship to it and at the same time change the object itself. Moreover, as our surroundings, the object impinges upon all our senses. As we reside in it or move through it, we can see it, hear it, feel it, smell it and perhaps even taste it. In brief, the experience of the environmental object of appreciation from which aesthetic appreciation must be fashioned is initially intimate, total and somewhat engulfing.

These dimensions are intensified by the unruly nature of the object itself. The object of appreciation is not the more or less discrete, stable and self-contained object of traditional art. It is, rather, an environment; consequently, not only does it change as we move within it, it also changes of its own accord. Environments are constantly in motion, in both the short and the long term. Even if we remain motionless, the wind brushes our face and the clouds pass before our eyes; and, with time, changes continue seemingly without limit: night falls, days pass, seasons come and go. Moreover, environments not only move through time, they extend through space, and again seemingly without limit. There are no predetermined boundaries for our environment; as we move, it moves with us and changes, but it does not end; indeed, it continues unending in every direction. In other words, the environmental object of appreciation does not come to us 'framed' as do traditional artistic objects, neither in time as a drama or a musical composition, nor in space as a painting or a sculpture.

Much of what has been noted relates to a deeper difference between environments and traditional artistic objects. The latter, works of art, are the products of artists. The artist is quintessentially a designer who creates a work by embodying a design in an object. Works of art are thus tied to their designers not only causally but conceptually; what a work is and what it means has much to do with its designer and its design. However, environments are paradigmatically not the products of designers. In the typical case, both designer and design are lacking. Rather, environments come about 'naturally'; they change, they grow, they develop either by means of natural processes or by means of human agency, but even in the latter case only rarely are they the result of a designer embodying a design. Thus, the typical environmental object of appreciation is unruly in yet another way: neither its nature nor its meaning are determined by a designer and a design.

The upshot is that in our aesthetic appreciation of the world at large we are initially confronted by – indeed, intimately and totally engulfed in – something which forces itself upon all our senses, is limited neither in time nor in space, and is constrained concerning neither its nature nor its meaning. We are immersed in a potential object of appreciation, and our task is to achieve some aesthetic appreciation of that object. Moreover, the appreciation must be fashioned anew, without the aid of frames, the guidance of designs, or the direction of designers. Thus, in our aesthetic appreciation of the world at large we must begin with the most basic of questions, those of exactly what and how to aesthetically appreciate. These questions raise the key issues of environmental aesthetics, essentially issues concerning what resources, if any, are available for answering them.

Concerning the questions of what and how to aesthetically appreciate in an environment, there are two main lines of thought. One, which may be characterized as subjectivist or perhaps as sceptical, holds that, since in the appreciation of environments we seemingly lack the resources normally involved in aesthetic appreciation, these questions cannot be properly answered. That is to say that since we lack resources such as frames, designs and designers and the guidance they provide, then either there is not appropriate or correct aesthetic appreciation of environments or else such appreciation as there is is not real aesthetic appreciation. Concerning the world at large, as opposed to works of art, the closest we can come to appropriate aesthetic appreciation is simply to open ourselves to being immersed, respond as we will, and enjoy what we can. And whether or not the resultant experience is appropriate in some sense or aesthetic in any sense is not of much consequence.

A second line of thought, which may be characterized as objectivist, points out that there are in fact two resources to draw upon – the appreciator and the object of appreciation. Thus, roles that are played in the aesthetic appreciation of traditional art by the designer and the design can be played in the aesthetic appreciation of an environment by either or both of these. In such appreciation the role of designer is typically taken by the appreciator and that of design by the object. That is to say that in our aesthetic appreciation of the world at large we typically play the role of artist and let the world provide us with a design. Thus, when confronted by an environment, we ourselves select the senses that are relevant to its appreciation and set the frames that limit it in time and space. Moreover, as a designer creatively interacts with his design, so too in our selecting and setting we creatively interact with the nature of the environment we confront. In this way the environment itself, by its own nature, provides its own design. And thus it offers the necessary guidance in the light of which we, by our selecting and setting, can appropriately answer the questions of what and how to appreciate – and thereby fashion our initial and somewhat chaotic experience of an environment into genuine aesthetic appreciation.

As is typical in disputes between subjectivist or sceptical positions and more objectivist ones, the burden of proof falls on the latter. The objectivist account may be elaborated and supported by consideration of some examples. The basic idea of the objectivist position is that our appreciation is guided by the nature of the object of appreciation. Thus, knowledge of the object's nature, of its genesis, type and properties, is essential to appropriate aesthetic appreciation. In appropriately appreciating, say, a natural environment such as an alpine meadow it is useful to know, for instance, that it has developed under constraints imposed by the climate of high altitude, and that diminutive size in flora is an adaptation to such constraints. This knowledge can guide our framing of the environment so that, for example, we avoid imposing inappropriately large frames, which may cause us to simply overlook miniature wild flowers. In such a case we will neither appreciatively note their wonderful adjustment to their situation nor even attune our senses to their subtle fragrance, texture and hue. Similarly, in appropriately appreciating man-altered environments such as those of modern agriculture, it is helpful to know about the functional utility of cultivating huge fields devoted to single crops. Such knowledge encourages us to enlarge and adjust our frames, our senses and even our attitudes, so as to more appreciatively accommodate the expansive uniform landscapes that are the inevitable result of such farming practices.

The basic assumption of environmental aesthetics is that every environment – natural, rural or urban, large or small, ordinary or extraordinary – offers much to see, to hear, to feel, much to aesthetically appreciate. The different environments of the world at large are as aesthetically rich and rewarding as are works of art. However, it also must be recognized that special problems are posed for aesthetic appreciation by the very nature of environments, by the fact that they are our own surroundings, that they are unruly and chaotic objects of appreciation, and that we are plunged into them without aesthetic guidelines. Both the subjectivist and the objectivist approaches recognize the potential and the problems. The main difference is that while the latter attempts to ground an appropriate aesthetic appreciation for different environments in our knowledge of their specific natures, the former simply invites us to enjoy them all as fully as we can and will. Perhaps in the last analysis both alternatives should be pursued.

See also ARTEFACT, ART AS; ATTITUDE, AESTHETIC.

BIBLIOGRAPHY

Carlson, Allen: 'Appreciation and the natural environment', *Journal of Aesthetics and Art Criticism*, 37 (1979), 267–75.
Carlson, Allen: 'Nature, aesthetic judgment, and objectivity', *Journal of Aesthetics and Art Criticism*, 40 (1981), 15–27.
Carlson, Allen: 'On appreciating agricultural landscapes', *Journal of Aesthetics and Art Criticism*, 43 (1985), 301–12.
Hepburn, Ronald W.: 'Aesthetic appreciation of nature', *Aesthetics in the Modern World*, ed. Harold Osborne (London: Thames & Hudson, 1968), pp. 49–66.
Kemal, Salim and Gaskell, Ivan, eds: *Landscape, Natural Beauty, and the Arts* (Cambridge: Cambridge University Press, 1993).
Sadler, Barry and Carlson, Allen, eds: *Environmental Aesthetics: Essays in Interpretation* (Victoria: University of Victoria, 1982).

ALLEN CARLSON

expression   The idea that the concept of 'expression' might be central to a philosophical understanding of the nature of art derives much of its contemporary force from the influence of an expression theory of art which was developed at the beginning of the twentieth century, to which the names of Croce and Collingwood are jointly yoked. This article summarizes the essence of that theory, outlines the major criticisms that have been levelled at it, and addresses the question of whether such criticisms entail that the concept of 'expression' can find no legitimate home in this area.

According to the expression theory, an artist is someone who gives articulate expression to emotions or feelings in the various artistic media. He begins in an emotional state whose chaotic indeterminacy perturbs him, and leads him to search for a clearer conception of it; and his search ends when he has succeeded in giving concrete expression to that state in a work of art. Artistic creation is thus a process of self-exploration, and the enhanced self-understanding which results is embodied in the work of art itself. Its creation confers clarity because the artist finds in its concrete specificity the precise lineaments of the feelings which originally perturbed him; attaining this reflexive clarity is thus inseparable from the process of creating the work of art, and the specific nature of the work itself makes manifest the specific nature of the feeling to which it gives expression. In short, the artwork does not so much *describe* the feeling as encapsulate it: it resembles natural symptoms of emotional states (for instance, a blush) in that it is the direct manifestation of an emotion, but it differs from them in that it is articulate. Any work of art is thus the articulate embodiment of the originally inchoate feeling which drove the artist to create it.

From this central claim, Croce and Collingwood developed many more specific doctrines. First, they concluded that there is no place for technique in artistic endeavour. For it seems to follow from their central claim that creating a work of art is a process whose product or end is neither foreseen nor preconceived (since if the nature of the artwork *could* have been specified prior to the process of creating it, the artist would not have needed to embark upon that process). But any activity lacking a preconceived end is one which must do without technique: for (the theorists tell us) the existence of any body of general rules or precepts which serve to guide a practitioner presupposes a conception of what the practitioner is aiming to achieve – just as a recipe presupposes a certain conception of the finished dish. The expression theory thus incorporated a sharp distinction between the artist, struggling to body forth a specific emotion in all its inchoate uniqueness and so unable to rely upon blueprints or received wisdom, and the craftsman, methodically working towards an independently specifiable product according to tried and tested principles.

Second, Collingwood and Croce had a very particular idea of what an audience's understanding of a work of art might consist in. According to Collingwood, if we understand the emotion expressed in a given artwork, then we will have that emotion in our minds, and so will in some sense experience emotions of our own in terms furnished by the artist. This blurring of the distinction between apprehending an emotion and experiencing it is not only confusing, and seemingly contrary to his official view that artists give expression to their own emotions rather than arousing them in others; it also implies that the physical work of art is a species of transmission mechanism, a means of conveying to the minds of others the clarified expression of feeling that the artist has achieved in his own mind.

This picture entails that the real artwork is mental, and the concrete artefact is of secondary importance – useful for communicative purposes but entirely inessential to the artist's primary task of achieving reflexive clarity through the articulate embodiment of feeling. It will, of course, be vital to this mental articulation (to what Croce calls the 'intuition') that it be couched in terms of one *conceived* medium or another – whether the intuition is given expression in musical as opposed to sculptural terms is integral to its specific identity; but the externalization of that intuition (whether in a performance or in a lump of marble) is seen as entirely dispensable. So, when Croce asserts that the development of intuitions is the development of their expression – that intuition and expression are one – the expression to which he refers is mental rather than physical.

It is not difficult to see that many elements of the Croce–Collingwood theory are open to potentially devastating criticism – criticism which goes far beyond querying the theory's seemingly arbitrary refusal to countenance the idea that works of art might be expressive of ideas or religious doctrines as well as feelings and emotions. First, the terms in which the distinction between intuition–expression and externalization is drawn presuppose an idealist philosophy of mind deriving from Hegel, and so are vulnerable to any criticisms that might be made of that baroque metaphysical structure. Moreover, any attempt to draw such a distinction in less bizarre terms will still have the consequence of banishing the physical work of art to the status of a dispensable vehicle for the communication of the real, mental artwork. This disparages the artefact in a way that entirely ignores the respect for its concrete particularity which is manifest in our practices of evaluating, displaying and preserving artworks; it dignifies the contents of the artist's mind in a way that goes equally against the grain of those practices; and it entails such counter-intuitive conclusions as that the real work of art fades away as the artist's original conception of it dims, and ceases to exist when the artist dies. Paradoxically enough, by downgrading the physical artefact the expression theorist undercuts the aspect of his theory which has most intuitive appeal – namely, the idea that the concrete work of art is the immediate and uniquely apt manifestation, the very embodiment, of that which the artist wishes to express.

However, other expression theorists have downplayed this expression/externalization distinction (Dewey, for example, stresses that the artist's physical struggle with pigment and stone is integral to the clarificatory process; see Dewey, 1934). So it may be that these criticisms do not place pressure on the nerve of the theory. What, then, of the claim that artistic creation is not a matter of technique? It seems clear enough that the process of externalizing one's intuitions in a physical medium will require the use of certain techniques; and even accepting for a moment that the true artistic labour is that of producing an articulate mental intuition, then, given that this intuition must necessarily be articulated in one conceived medium or another, it must respect the rules and principles appropriate to that medium (for instance, principles of harmony and composition in music). It seems that the expression theory inflates a humble truth (that an artist might not be fully aware of what he wants to create until he has created it) into a dogma that is primarily designed to denigrate the workmanlike activities of the craftsman in favour of the isolated but elevated mental agonies of the Romantic genius.

A defender of the theory might accept these points, but argue that the claim that artistic endeavour is not a matter of technique is a dispensable part of the theory; for it has no essential connection with the truly central assertion of that theory – namely, that all works of art are the result of an artist's endeavour to achieve an articulate embodiment of his emotions or feelings. Unfortunately, this claim too has little to be said in its favour. If it is understood as an empirical generalization, the evidence which supports it is extremely weak: indeed, in the vast majority of cases, we simply have no idea whether an artwork was in fact the final stage of such a process. And if it is understood as a definition of art, the condition it specifies

is neither a necessary nor a sufficient one: not every work of art is necessarily produced in such a manner (what about Greek temples or Ming vases?), and not every artefact produced with such an aim in mind is necessarily a work of art (my adolescent diaries certainly are not). This expressive claim exemplifies a genetic fallacy: the question of whether a given artefact is a good work of art, or even a work of art at all, is not settled by unearthing facts about the psychological processes involved in its production. Aesthetic judgements about works of art are not judgements about the artist or his creative agonies.

It does not, however, follow from the demise of the classical expression theory that the concept of expression does not have a central role in art and aesthetics. For we can rephrase the expression theorist's central claim in a way which avoids the genetic fallacy. Perhaps what he really wants to maintain is not that artworks give expression to the *artist's* feelings, but rather that they are expressive; and that what people understand when they understand a work of art is the feeling (or complex of feelings) of which it is an articulate embodiment. Here, the intuition which drives proponents of expression theories of art is closer to the surface; but as it stands, even this revised claim remains too dogmatic. For once again, the condition specified is neither necessary nor sufficient for an artefact to be considered a work of art: not all artefacts which satisfy the condition are works of art, and not all works of art satisfy the condition. The Romantic genius is still lurking in the background; a substantive aesthetic judgement – 'only that art which is expressive of emotion is truly great' – is being introduced in the guise of a partial elucidation of the very concept of a 'work of art'.

Moreover, some philosophers have harboured more fundamental doubts about this reformulated expressive doctrine; they have queried the very intelligibility of the idea that *any* work of art can be said to be expressive of an emotion which is neither that of the artist nor that of his audience. How can anything other than a human being (or at least an animal) give expression to a feeling? Such puzzlement seems very natural; but remarks such as 'The music is unbearably sad' or 'The monument is expressive of deep grief' are by no means uncommon in aesthetic discussions, and seem perfectly intelligible in the contexts in which they emerge. So the real question here is: why should such otherwise acceptable remarks seem unintelligible when we come to reflect upon them philosophically?

We do not have to look far for an answer. Philosophers are naturally led to compare the use of psychological terms in aesthetic contexts with their central use in characterizing the psychological states of human beings; and such a comparison brings out a wide range of differences. Sadness is expressed in human behaviour through weeping, a glum face, a dull tone of voice, general low spirits and so on; it emerges as a response to certain sorts of events or experiences, and it can be alleviated or overcome in certain ways – by the sympathy of others, the irruption of distracting or joyful events, and so on. Such concepts thus have a place in a complex and tightly woven web of behaviour and circumstance; and none of this weave is evident when that concept is applied to a piece of music. We describe the music as sad, even when we cannot say *how* it manifests this sadness, when it doesn't make us *feel* sad (although of course it may sometimes have that effect), and when we don't necessarily believe that the sadness it manifests is a sadness that the composer experienced when creating the piece. With this comparison in mind, it is hardly surprising that we begin to doubt the intelligibility of such descriptions.

However, a different object of comparison may make things seem less puzzling. I want to use terminology developed in Wittgenstein (1953), and suggest that words such as 'sad' are used in aesthetic contexts in a *secondary* sense. An example of secondary uses of words that Wittgenstein himself employs is 'Wednesday is fat.' Given the ordinary meaning of the words 'fat' and 'thin', I might be asked whether I would be inclined to say that Wednesday was fat and Tuesday thin, or vice versa; and I would have a strong inclination to choose the former alternative. In saying

that Wednesday is fat, I am clearly using the word 'fat' in a way very different from its usual or primary mode of employment; but I could not have expressed what I want to say here about Wednesday by using any other word. Furthermore, if asked what I really meant by 'fat' in this context, I could only explain the meaning of the word in the usual way, in a manner consonant with its primary sense. It is only because 'fat' has the primary meaning that it does that I want to use it in a very different, secondary sense here.

A secondary sense is thus non-metaphorical (in that, unlike most metaphors, it is not amenable to paraphrase), logically dependent upon the word's primary sense and yet significantly different from it. It will be inaccessible to anyone ignorant of the term's primary meaning, but knowledge of that primary meaning will not *guarantee* comprehension of the inclination upon which the secondary use rests. In other words, the assimilation of a word's primary sense makes possible a new realm of spontaneous linguistic reactions which transcend what has been assimilated but which are none the less shaped by what they transcend; and these reactions can form the basis of new language-games. If this ultimate reliance upon a shared (linguistic) reaction makes the accessibility of the new language-game seem fragile, it is worth remembering that even primary language-games are accessible only to those whose (non-linguistic) reactions to training permit them to absorb what counts as going on in the same way.

Talk of the girth of weekdays is an instance of a secondary sense which is of little intrinsic importance; but characterizing music in terms of the emotions or feelings it expresses is fundamental to musical appreciation, and it too seems to manifest all the features distinctive of secondary language-games. This mode of employing 'sad' is unlike its primary employment in relation to human beings, but parasitic upon it – accounts of its meaning in this context would necessarily invoke explanations and paradigms of its primary sense. It is not a metaphorical use – no paraphrase is available, no other word would do – and those who share this linguistic reaction or inclination can go on to engage in complex language-games devoted to the characterization and appreciation of music.

The fact that most people *do* share this inclination may be an essential part of any attempt to account for the centrality of music in human culture (since it means that music is characterized in the very terms which inform our understanding of – and relationships with – ourselves and other people); and what might *explain* this fact may be studied by anthropologists, psychologists and the like. But if they are to be genuinely explanatory, such investigations must build upon a clear understanding of the nature and status of that shared reaction; and this means seeing it as the *bedrock* of *new* language-games – as a response which is attributable only to those who have mastered certain linguistic techniques, but which is not merely a further *application* of those old techniques. The desire to go on in this new way can perhaps be *elicited* from those initially unable to share it, by invoking striking examples of music which seems obviously to call forth the use of psychological terms, but it cannot be *justified*: either it exists, or it does not.

Of course, we can also attempt to dissolve the puzzlement of those who find instances of this linguistic phenomenon in musical appreciation bizarre. We might point out that musical appreciation which does not involve psychological terms seems to exemplify the same phenomenon (for instance, talk of high and low notes, of falling and rising cadences), and ask whether they seem equally bizarre. We might highlight examples of primary and secondary meanings in non-musical contexts. Or we might find intermediate cases between that of a weeping man and that of a sad piece of music – cases such as a sad face (which need not be a manifestation of sadness) or a sad book (which need not have been written in tears, and need not elicit tears from its readers). In the end, however, we must simply recognize that this language-game is played.

Even if we recognize that psychological terms of this kind can perfectly legitimately be applied to artworks, it is vital to note that their role is more one of characterization than evaluation. Only someone capable of distinguishing sad music from joyful music will be capable of distinguishing self-indulgently sad music from music expressive of the most profound melancholy; but in coming to perceive that a piece of music is sad, I have settled nothing about its aesthetic value. Moreover, this particular notion of aesthetic expressiveness must be distinguished from another, equally significant, one; we must distinguish 'This music is expressive of sadness' from 'This music is very expressive.' The latter use of the term 'expressive' has been called its intransitive use by Roger Scruton (see Scruton, 1983); unlike the transitive use upon which I have been concentrating, in the latter case no sense attaches to the question 'Expressive of what?' Here, 'expressiveness' intimates impact, power; it implies that the work makes a striking impression, but one which may not be specifiable in any way other than by referring back to the work as a whole. And once again, to recognize the expressiveness of a work of art in this sense is not to offer an evaluation of its aesthetic worth.

To summarize: the grain of truth behind the Romantic dogma which is the expression theory of art is the fact that certain types of artwork can legitimately be characterized in terms of what they express (transitive use) and in terms of their expressiveness (intransitive use). This conclusion does not confer a role of absolutely central importance upon the concept of 'expression'; but it has the merit of capturing a significant and interesting strand in the complex of practices which go to make up what we call aesthetic judgement.

See also COLLINGWOOD; CROCE; EMOTION; ONTOLOGY OF ARTWORKS; THEORIES OF ART; WITTGENSTEIN.

BIBLIOGRAPHY

Beardsley, M.: *Aesthetics from Classical Greece to the Present* (Montgomery, Ala.: University of Alabama Press, 1966).
Bouwsma, O.K.: 'The expression theory of art',

Aesthetics and Language, ed. W. Elton (Oxford: Basil Blackwell, 1954).

Collingwood, R.G.: *The Principles of Art* (Oxford: Oxford University Press, 1938).

Croce, B.: *Estetica come scienza dell'espressione e linguistica generale* (Bari: 1902); *Aesthetic as Science of Expression and General Linguistic* (London: Macmillan, 1922).

Dewey, J.: *Art as Experience* (New York: Putnam, 1934).

Hospers, J.: 'The concept of artistic expression', *Proceedings of the Aristotelian Society*, 55 (1956), 313–34.

Hospers, J.: 'The Croce–Collingwood theory of art', *Philosophy*, 31 (1956), 291–308.

Scruton, R.: *The Aesthetic Understanding* (Manchester: Carcanet Press, 1983).

Wittgenstein, L.: *Philosophical Investigations*; trans. G.E.M. Anscombe (Oxford: Basil Blackwell, 1953).

STEPHEN MULHALL

F

---

feminist criticism In 'A criticism of our own: autonomy and assimilation in Afro-American and feminist literary theory', Elaine Showalter discerns five ideologies that have been influential in feminist literary criticism and theory (Showalter, 1986). The first, 'androgynist poetics', denies that there is any specifically male or female way of writing or approaching texts, maintaining that the human imagination is essentially genderless. With the rise of the women's movement, feminists initiated a critique of male culture and advanced a 'female aesthetic' celebrating women's culture. Believing that our sexual identities cannot be separated from our expressions and creations, advocates of the female aesthetic maintain that women's writing expresses a distinct female consciousness, is more discursive and conjunctive than classifying and linear.

By the mid-1970s the emphasis had shifted to 'gynocriticism', or the study of literature by women. Arguing that the female aesthetic is problematic in its presupposition of an eternal, universal feminine 'essence' shared by all women, gynocritics preferred to focus on locating and examining texts by women, and undertook a historical analysis of the problems of talented women attempting to create in a male tradition. In the early 1980s, proponents of 'gynesis' charged that gynocritics were confining themselves to a women's literature ghetto, and advocated a confrontation with the patriarchal canon. Following the lead of French writers such as Hélène Cixous and Luce Irigaray, these feminists explore representations and expressions of the feminine in Western thought. The French feminists in particular also suggest that women should discover, explore and 'write their bodies', and that this writing of the body will lead to a style of 'openness, fragmentation, non-linearity and disruption'.

Although gynocriticism and gynesis continue to be strong, the late 1980s were characterized by the rise of 'gender theory', concerned with integrating the study of gender differences into the various disciplines. Rather than concentrating on women and 'reifying feminine marginalization', gender theorists seek to produce comparative studies of men and women and their works, and to focus on social constructs of gender rather than on biology (see Showalter, 1985).

A feminist approach has also been taken to art, architecture, theatre, film, and dance. Joanna Frueh has offered a history of feminist art criticism in three stages that echo the categories of feminist literary criticism presented above (Frueh, 1988, pp. 155–7). The first stage, comparable to gynocriticism, was and is a resurrection of lost or ignored women artists. In highlighting 'minor artists', this stage has led to new perspectives of art history and new bodies of knowledge. Traditionally, portraits, still-lifes, miniatures and crafts have been prominent among women artists, and the presentation of craft or craft-like art in 'high' art contexts by contemporary women artists has served to blur the distinction between 'high' and 'low' art. The second phase, comparable to the female aesthetic and equally controversial, posits a women's art distinct from the tradition of patriarchal culture, an art based on a 'female imagination' or 'female sensitivity'. Active in the mid-1970s, advocates of a female artistic sensibility maintained that women's art is characterized by central core imagery or apertures, rifts and cracks (thought to symbolize female genitalia), circular or repeated patterns, open, fluid forms, soft colours, repetitive patterning, the decorative, and subjective or personal subject-matter. The third phase of feminist art criticism is more theoretical, and centres on gender analysis of the art of both women and men, and interconnections between an artwork and its historical and cultural context.

These phases in literature and art can be instructive for the development of a feminist criticism in music. There have been calls for a feminist musical criticism within and outside the discipline, and suggestions on the directions that such a criticism could take. Researchers in music have become serious about identifying, analysing and recording musical works by women throughout history, considering the contexts in which women in music have been active, and assessing the status of women in various musical disciplines (Bowers and Tick, 1987). I have considered the possibility of a music analogous to *l'écriture féminine*, the writing claimed to arise out of women's bodies and sexual experience (Cox, 1992). While 'phallocentric' culture is based on the singularity, identity and specificity of male genitalia and sexual experience, female genitalia are multiple and contiguous, and the sexual experience of women tends to be indefinite, cyclic, without set beginnings and endings. Correspondingly, *l'écriture féminine* is said to be heterogeneous, process-orientated and fluid. Growth and development are continuous, and boundaries are unclear. There are frequent repetitions, and phrases are rephrased or conjoined. There is a resistance to the definitive, the highly structured, to closure, hierarchies, and the dialectical process. (It is interesting to note that descriptions of *l'écriture féminine* echo some of the most important tenets of Romanticism.)

A music comparable to *l'écriture féminine* would have a flexible, cyclical form, and would involve continuous repetition with variation, the cumulative growth and development of an idea. It would serve to deconstruct musical hierarchies and the dialectical juxtaposition and resolution of opposites, disrupt linearity, and avoid definitive closures. Such music would not be reflective of the experience of all women, and could be and has been composed by both men and women. Yet discerning this style in the music of women would provide an opportunity for interested feminists to celebrate what has been identified or culturally conditioned as feminine or womanly.

There have been a few works written on musical expressions of the feminine and the masculine in canonical masterworks. Susan McClary has suggested that in Bizet's *Carmen* chromaticism is associated with a seductive, deadly feminine sexuality. The music of the slithery, slippery Carmen is predominantly chromatic, while Don José and the pure, chaste Micaëla sing diatonically. Because Carmen makes us so aware of her body and her sexuality when she sings, we come to associate her sexuality with the chromaticism; we likewise associate Don José's and Micaëla's diatonicism with the abstract ideals of society, Church and state that they strive to uphold. These associations become significant when we look at how chromaticism is handled within the opera and the tonal system in general. Although Carmen and her music are interesting and attractive, there is something in us that seeks resolution of the instability of the chromaticism, that seeks the clarity and closure of diatonicism and the tonic triad. In seeking this resolution, we may on some level – probably an unconscious one – be expecting or even wanting Carmen to be somehow overcome, to be appropriated into the system both musically and socially. In the opera and literature of the time, women who do not conform to the social order may eventually submit to marriage, enter a convent or be committed to an asylum. But those who will not be tamed usually wind up dead; and when Carmen dies, her unstable music resolves into diatonicism. The stability and order of the tonic is 'violently imposed' (McClary, 1991, pp. 53–69).

Dramatic music, song and programmatic music from all eras are ripe for gender analysis of this kind. Discerning the masculine and feminine in instrumental music (like abstract art) will be more difficult, yet it should lend itself to gender analysis once trends in the texted and programmatic works are established. Romantic conceptions of the masculine and feminine in music are already fairly well known. The so-called 'masculine' music or theme of the Romantic era is characterized by a dramatic quality, large intervals, volume, sforzandos, full orchestral scoring and predominant wind and brass instruments, while feminine music is more likely to be lyrical and legato, with delicate instrumentation, small intervals and regular rhythms (Rieger, 1985, pp. 139–40). The 'masculine cadence' is definitive and achieves closure, while the 'feminine cadence' is inconclusive or implicative. All of this helps to explain why the work of certain composers is easily 'gendered': the forceful and definitive music of Beethoven, for example, seems masculine relative to the lyrical, inconclusive and disruptive music of Chopin or Debussy. Most contemporary music scholars have avoided using the terms 'masculine' and 'feminine' in their discussions of music or musical themes. But because some composers, analysts and listeners of the past were thinking in these terms, and because these associations may be reinforcing stereotypes, it seems most desirable to make such associations as explicit as possible.

It seems clear that conceptions of women's writing, art or music can be quite similar to expressions of the feminine in traditional works by men. Yet there is an important difference between the types of expression, in that the traditional works often present the feminine as trivial, weak or dangerous, while women's art may reconstruct this subject-matter and cast it in a positive light. However similar the aesthetic content of the works, radically different perspectives will be brought to this content. Feminist critics, whatever their opinions of traditional notions of the feminine or of women's art, can identify, consider and critique these perspectives.

See also CANON; CRITICISM; KRISTEVA.

BIBLIOGRAPHY

Bowers, Jane and Tick, Judith, eds: *Women Making Music: The Western Art Tradition* *1150–1950* (Urbana and Chicago: University of Illinois Press, 1987).

Cox, Renée: 'Recovering *jouissance*: feminist aesthetics and music', *Women and Music: A History*, ed. Karin Pendle (Bloomington, Ill.: Indiana University Press, 1992).

Frueh, Joanna: 'Towards a feminist theory of art criticism', in Arlene Raven, Cassandra Langer and Joanna Frueh, *Feminist Art Criticism: An Anthology*, ed. Donald Kuspit (Ann Arbor, Mich.: UNI Research Press, 1988), 153–66.

McClary, Susan: 'Sexual politics in music', *Feminine Endings: Music, Gender and Sexuality* (Minnesota: University of Minnesota Press, 1991), 53–79.

Rieger, Eva: ' "*Dolce semplice*"? On the changing role of women in music', *Feminist Aesthetics*, ed. Gisela Ecker, trans. Harriet Anderson (Boston, Mass.: Beacon Press, 1985), 135–49.

Showalter, Elaine, ed.: *The New Feminist Criticism: Essays of Women, Literature and Theory* (New York: Pantheon, 1985).

Showalter, Elaine: 'A criticism of our own: autonomy and assimilation in Afro-American and feminist literary theory', paper read at the School of Criticism and Theory, Dartmouth College, 1986.

RENÉE LORRAINE

fictional entities Amongst artworks there are stories told by story-tellers in words or in pictures, or acted out on stage. We call some of these stories 'fiction', some 'history'. What distinguishes fiction from history? One common answer is that the teller of a fictional story brings into existence fictional or imaginary characters, events and places, whereas the historian merely describes real people, events and places. This response implies that fictional characters, events and places belong, along with real people, events and places, in an inventory of reality (an *ontology*). We use the expression 'entity' as a label for anything included in an ontology. The expression 'fictional entities' is a label for those entities – for instance, fictional characters, created by the teller of a fictional story.

An ontology classifies reality; it is an inventory of the sorts of things that make up the world, not of the innumerable particular things in the world. What sort of thing is a fictional entity? Here we have two options. Either fictional entities are a subset of a more general sort, or they are *sui generis* – that is, they require their own place in the ontology. Beginning with the first option, we examine the sorts of entity already proposed by philosophers for inclusion in the ontology, in order to find those which most resemble fictional entities. Four candidates emerge.

We say that it is true of Ophelia that she loved and suffered. Since real people have the properties of loving and of suffering, we may choose to regard Ophelia as much like a person, but with a vital metaphysical difference – namely, that Ophelia does not exist. Thus, we need to find a sort of entity which embodies this idea. There are two contenders: *unreal* (or *non-existent) objects* and *possible* (or *non-actual) objects*. These are different sorts of entity. An unreal object is an object of which it is true that, although it does not exist, it has some other ontological property which is like existence. On this view, Ophelia 'subsists' or 'fictionally exists'. A possible object has no existence-like property: it is an object which might have existed but does not exist. On this view, the sister I might have had, had my parents had another child, is a possible object.

We also say of Ophelia that she is a brilliant creation. To do so is, it appears, to regard Ophelia as much like the other literary devices – for example, the plot or denouement – out of which Shakespeare builds his story. This suggests two further sorts of entity that fictional entities may be. The first is a *type*. A type is that of which different particular things are instances (tokens). For example, two people who have their own copies of *The Blackwell Companion to Aesthetics* have different tokens of the same book type. On this view, a fictional character will be a person type, a fictional event an event type and a fictional place a place type. So I may say of a friend, 'She's a real Mrs Malaprop', meaning that my friend is a token of the Mrs Malaprop type. The second is a *theoretical entity*. These are entities the existence of which is implied by our theories. For example, physical theory implies the existence of forces and fields, political theory the existence of social classes, and history implies nation states. On this view, critical aesthetic discussion constitutes a theory which commits us to the various theoretical entities of aesthetic criticism, including fictional characters, events and places.

Many philosophers dislike these four sorts of entity – that is, unreal objects, possible objects, types and theoretical entities. Why? First, it is argued that none is necessary to the classification of reality and that, since the most economical ontology is best, we should leave these sorts out. For example, we can explain talk about social classes without bringing in theoretical entities, in terms of the behaviour and beliefs of particular people. Second, it is argued that the inclusion of any of these four sorts of entity, unlike the inclusion of other sorts of entity, leads to an astronomical increase in the number of things in the world. For example, once we admit unreal objects, we find them everywhere; anything imaginable – such as a mauve parrot sitting on your shoulder as you read this – subsists. Third, it is argued that the inclusion of any of these four sorts of entity raises more questions than it answers. For example, if Sherlock Holmes in *The Hound of the Baskervilles* and in *A Study of Scarlet* is described slightly differently, then are these stories about the same possible object or different possible objects? These are objections based on principles of parsimony. How much notice we need take of them here is inversely proportional to how useful we find the introduction of any of these sorts of entity in explaining fiction.

What about fiction needs explanation? We require an account of all the highly diverse claims we make of, say, Ophelia – that she loved and suffered, that she is a brilliant creation, and that she never existed – that responds to the intuition that in each case we are talking about the same thing and that in each case we speak truly. The four versions of the claim that fictional characters are fictional entities do badly at putting the disparate pieces of this jigsaw together. Each fails to account for some of what we say about fictional characters. If fictional characters are unreal objects, then, since unreal objects do not exist, the sentence 'Jimmy Porter existed in the time of Elizabeth II, not of Elizabeth I' is not true. If fictional characters are possible objects, then the Cheshire Cat is not a fictional entity, since it could never actually have existed. If fictional characters are types or theoretical entities, then since on each view the entity Santa Claus exists, 'Santa Claus doesn't really exist' is false. Also, on both views Raskolnikov is a highly abstract entity. Since the property of being a murderer is one strictly applicable only to concrete objects, we cannot mean what we say when we say, 'Raskolnikov was a murderer'. All these results run counter to our intuitions.

Proponents of fictional entities evade these objections in one or more of three ways. The 'definition' strategy enables an account to manoeuvre around the difficulty: for example, a proponent of unreal objects may stipulate two senses, a weaker and a stronger, of the expression 'exist', and claim that in the weaker sense unreal objects do exist. The 'limitation' strategy permits a retreat from the phenomenon which causes the particular problem: for example, a proponent of possible objects might admit that her theory applies only to certain fictions (namely, those which, unlike the stories of Lewis Carroll, contain no contradictions), but insist that these are the central cases. The 'translation' strategy allows the account to translate statements about fictional characters into statements with which the account can deal: for example, we might translate the sentence 'Raskolnikov was a murderer' into the sentence 'The Raskolnikov type includes or exemplifies the property of being a murderer.' Each strategy has advantages, but each also has costs.

Perhaps we should turn to our second option: namely, that fictional entities are *sui generis*? There is no reason in advance to think that *sui generis* fictional entities will be vulnerable to the objections outlined above. However, until we are given some account of these entities – they are mentioned only fleetingly in the literature – there is also no reason to think that they will not. In the light

of the objections to fictional entities, many simply deny that the teller of a fictional story creates entities. In the view of these philosophers, the story-teller creates only the illusion or appearance of entities – that is, the semblance of people, events and places. 'Fictional entities' are illusory entities, and illusory entities are no more entities than toy animals are animals.

It would be a mistake, however, to abandon fictional entities quite so hastily. We make another demand of a philosophical account of fiction: namely, that it explain certain logical features of fiction. Fictions – also dreams, illusions, myths, 'let's pretend' games, and so on – appear to be cut off in three respects from the rest of our experience and from the actual world. First, fictions are semantically cut off or contained. For example, my nephew Fred has an invisible mechanical friend, R3D4. Had Fred not invented his imaginary friend, the expression 'R3D4' would have no meaning. *Outside the make-believe, the names of fictional or imaginary characters do not refer to anything.* Second, fictions are inferentially cut off. If in Fred's make-believe he has fifteen invisible friends, this enables me to conclude that in Fred's make-believe he has more than five invisible friends, but it does not enable me to conclude that, outside the make-believe, in reality, Fred has even one invisible friend. *From the fact that a proposition is true in a fiction we cannot infer that the proposition is true.* Third, fictions are cut off from normal appraisal. If Fred tells me that I am unwittingly sitting on R3D4, it would be a conceptual error if I were to accuse Fred of lying, or even merely of saying something false. *Outside the make-believe, tellers of fictional tales do not make truth claims (assertions).* What cuts fiction off in these ways?

For the proponent of fictional entities there is nothing puzzling here. The names of fictional characters do not refer to real entities, but they do refer, namely, to fictional entities. Propositions true in fiction are propositions true of fictional entities. Consequently, we cannot infer from the fact that a proposition is true in fiction that it is true in fact – that is, true of real entities. Propositions uttered in the course of fiction or make-believe are asserted, but they are asserted only of fictional entities and so are to be appraised only in terms of the fiction in which they figure.

The opponents of fictional entities have a much harder task. It is difficult to explain the cut-off-ness of fiction without invoking entities. The various explanations on offer in the literature frequently introduce technical ideas which are poorly explained, such as a 'make-believe operator' which qualifies all propositions in a fiction, cutting them off from propositions in fact. Some of these technical ideas generate apparent paradoxes. For example, it is claimed that by the device of 'mock-assertion' I can say such-and-such is the case without committing myself to the truth of what I say. Some of these explanations offer implausible paraphrases of our talk about fictional characters: for example, by saying that all talk about R3D4 is really talk only about Fred or Fred's utterances. So, although by denying fictional entities we eliminate the ontological mysteries, we introduce other mysteries.

Where does this leave us? By postulating fictional entities we get a simple account of the 'cut off' quality of fiction. Nevertheless, the cost of this account is our acceptance of curious objects. Moreover, allowing these objects has not helped us to make sense of the disparate things we say about fictional characters. On the other hand, the difficulties of finding a satisfactory alternative explanation should not be underestimated.

See also GOODMAN; IMAGINATION; TRUTH IN ART.

BIBLIOGRAPHY

Evans, G.: The Varieties of Reference, ed. J.H. McDowell (Oxford: Clarendon Press, 1982).
Hintikka, J.: 'Are there nonexistent objects? Why not? But where are they?', Synthèse, 60 (1984), 451–8.
Parsons, T.: 'A Meinongian analysis of fictional objects', Grazer Philosophische Studien, 1 (1975), 73–86.
Ryle, G., Braithwaite, R.B. and Moore, G.F.: 'Symposium: imaginary objects', Proceedings of the Aristotelian Society, suppl. vol. 12 (1933), 18–70.
Van Inwagen, P.: 'Creatures of fiction', American Philosophical Quarterly, 14 (1977), 299–308.

DIANE PROUDFOOT

forgery Within the arts, a work can be classified as a fake if it is deliberately misrepresented as something authored by a specific artist, or something of a particular style, or something from a particular art-historical period. A fake is a forgery when it was created to be fraudulently presented as a specific artwork by a specific artist. This article is concerned with forgery, though in the literature the terms 'fake' and 'forgery' (and even 'copy') sometimes are used interchangeably.

No existing art form is exempt, in principle, from possible contamination by forgeries. Something's being a forgery does not require its being a copy, does not require that the artwork that the forgery claims to be exists (or existed), and does not require the forgery's being created by someone other than the person it is attributed to (for example, artists can create new works and misrepresent them as their earlier works). Where a forgery is of an existing work, there is no requirement deriving from the concept of forgery that the forgery bear any resemblance whatsoever to the original. What suffices to deceive a specific audience is contingent upon the audience's historical beliefs. Initially successful forgeries seldom remain so, both because the intended audience's beliefs change over time, and because the audience's membership cannot be limited to the intended audience indefinitely.

As Francis Sparshott observes, what people generally find wrong with forgery is that it involves lying. Fraudulently misrepresenting a work's identity, and especially creating a work specifically designed for this purpose, violates the trust essential to the artworld's conduct of its affairs. For the most part, however, the immorality of deceit is not, in itself, the aspect of forgery that most seems to interest philosophers. What interests philosophers is forgery's presumed relevance to questions of ontology and value. Discussions of these questions in the literature usually reach quite general conclusions, yet too often derive these conclusions by focusing upon a small subclass of forgeries (the many discussions of Hans Van Meegeren's work, for example). Almost all discussions of forgery unavoidably require the reader to accept specific ontological assumptions – specific assumptions about what constitutes artistic (or aesthetic) value, specific assumptions about the nature of human perception, specific assumptions about art history, and (sometimes) specific assumptions about semantics. A brief yet fair treatment of forgery is difficult, because many of the familiar disagreements about forgery ultimately turn on their author's undefended beliefs in the areas just cited, the conclusions about forgery that are expressed being merely the implications of such beliefs.

I distinguish questions of moral value from questions of artistic value. Sparshott's observation deals with moral value. Two general questions of artistic value are (1) must a forgery be of no artistic value? And (2), where there is an original, must a forgery be of less artistic value than the original? Discussions of both questions usually assume, mistakenly, that all forgeries will attempt to replicate the artistically relevant properties of the original (or the artistically relevant properties of other known works where there is no original) by attempting to reproduce slavishly the perceptual properties of the original (or of other relevant works). Treating forgeries generally as slavish copies of works or styles (and assuming, mistakenly, that slavish copying is the best route to perceptual indistinguishability) immediately raises ontological questions. Discussions of a forgery's possible artistic value cannot proceed until such questions are resolved.

The possibility always exists that a work thought by everyone (including its maker) to be a forgery is instead an instance of the original. A very naïve audience might refuse to accept anything other than Greene's original manuscript as the authentic *Our Man in Havana* by Graham Greene. A very sophisticated audience might refuse to accept a painting as another instance of the *Portrait of Madame Cézanne* by Roy Lichtenstein, even were they to grant that they will never be able to tell the two paintings apart. Nelson Goodman's arguments often are taken to show that the sophisticated audience, unlike the naïve one, cannot be mistaken in its insistence that, even if perpetual indistinguishability is guaranteed, the case in question cannot possibly be one in which we have two instances of the same artwork. This position overlooks the work of Joseph Margolis and others, who have shown us that neither perceptual indistinguishability nor, for that matter, sameness of artistic (or aesthetic) properties is required for two things to be instances of the same work. If artistic (or aesthetic) predicates sometimes ascribe properties, it even seems possible that two distinct artworks, each in its own way, coincidentally instantiate all the same artistic properties and so possess the same value (including art-historical value, for the kinds of art-historical roles each plays may be the same – being a turning point in the genera, and so on – even though the events themselves are not).

Philosophers have yet to decide these issues satisfactorily. Until they do, discussions that assume that forgery essentially involves attempts to produce objects that are indiscernible from originals (or indiscernible from, for instance, works in a given style) run the risk of being beside the point, since even with fraud as a motive successful reproduction may result not in a forgery but in another instance of the original. Romanticized notions of oil painting aside, perhaps one reason why the possibility just suggested is not taken more seriously is that the examples of famous forgeries that fill the literature fall far short of being works that are indiscernible from the originals they copy (or fall short of successfully copying the appropriate style, and so on).

On questions of a forgery's potential artistic value, philosophers quickly part company several times over. Those who are concerned exclusively with aesthetic value (in the narrow, non-Hegelian sense) part company with those concerned with artistic value in general (a value that may include a work's historical value). Those philosophers interested in aesthetic value, who understand an object's aesthetic value to be accessible only when the object is perceived yet is not experienced as being any kind of thing in particular, part company with those who believe that experiencing an object's aesthetic or artistic properties requires experiencing it as of some kind or the other (usually the art-historical kind it really is, such as an original 1964 Andy Warhol silk-screen). Aestheticians such as Monroe Beardsley fall into the first group. They believe that if any forgeries ever are indiscernible from originals these forgeries will be identical in aesthetic value with the originals (though for various psychological reasons, presumably having to do with mistaken beliefs about forgery, this value may be accessible only to audiences unaware that the works experienced do not have the histories attributed to them).

If some form of the view of artistic value held by aestheticians like Beardsley is correct, then while forgery remains morally wrong, and despite the difficulty some people report in negating their tendency to be affected by the belief that what they are experiencing is a forgery, a particular forgery's aesthetic value may be as great as that of any other aesthetic object. Disputes about any object's value, forgery or not, can be decided only by appropriately experiencing the object.

The majority view at present among philosophers who discuss forgery assumes that discerning the properties which give artworks aesthetic or, more generally, artistic value requires, as a matter of psychological fact, seeing a work as of some kind or the other. The majority view also assumes, again as a matter of psychological fact, that seeing a work as of the kind 'forgery' results in experiencing it as devoid of aesthetic or artistic value. But here, in opposition to philosophers like Beardsley, the majority conclude that this result is exactly as it should be, since, after all, forgeries cannot have aesthetic or artistic value. The reasons supporting this position all involve claims about roles which known forgeries cannot be

seen as fulfilling. For example, since forgeries are not causally linked with the relevant psychological states of the relevant artists, they cannot be seen as expressions of the specific feelings they purport to express. Or, since forgeries are not appropriately linked with the 'linguistic' acts of the relevant artists, they cannot be seen as saying what they purport to say. Or, more generally, since forgeries are not appropriately linked with any other genuine artistic activities, such as discovering a solution to an artistic problem, they cannot be seen as marking the artist's success in such endeavours. Finally, since an artwork's having aesthetic or artistic value is tied to its playing and being experienced as playing roles of the above sort, forgeries cannot have aesthetic or artistic value.

What arguments of the sort outlined above ignore is that in each case the function of an artwork is to give the audience access to certain information, and that any information derivable from a given object is derivable from any relevantly similar object by anyone possessing the relevant contextual knowledge, regardless of the latter object's etiology. Maintaining that information which it will benefit us to possess is information that we must refrain from deriving from some object merely because the object is not the prototypical bearer of the information is pointless if not perverse, if in fact we can get the information from the object (for more on prototypes, see Joseph Margolis, 1980; Sparshott, 1982).

Arthur Danto likes to cite examples of cases where like forms embody different meanings as proof that like forms sometimes cannot carry the same information. What he fails to see is that from a sophisticated audience's perspective, indistinguishable material objects that embody artworks carry all of the meanings instantiated by each of the separate but perceptually identical artworks they embody. (For example, for an artwork to be a type-identical semiotic token of an artistic accomplishment, it need not be the same material object with which the success was achieved.) If many real-life forgeries fail as semiotic equivalents of originals it is because, as often is emphasized, in real life forgeries seldom are like originals in the required respects.

The second thing that arguments of the sort outlined above overlook is that, in principle, any given information can be instantiated in more than one way. Two works may present audiences with the same information (expression, statement, or whatever), though they are entirely unlike one another perceptually (tokens need not be of the same semiotic type to be bearers of the same information). Semiotic art theories like those described above make it very difficult to draw the line between some forgery and some replication. Supporters of these theories insist that when we experience forgeries we keep in mind that forgeries are, after all, only forgeries – lest we forget ourselves and enjoy them either for what also can be discovered elsewhere, in the 'original', or for what they give us in their own right (the forger's expression of contempt, statement about gullibility, or solution to the problem of how to create forgeries that will be recognized as such, but not before the forger's death).

For simplicity, I write as if works that some philosophers classify as forgeries could turn out to be instances of originals. But what is more likely is that a replica is to some degree an instance of the work, depending upon, as the philosopher Rudolf Arnheim expresses it, how much 'aesthetic substance' is shared. Knowing an artwork's prototype, or at least the prototype's historical setting, is essential, because it is in terms of the prototype's historical context that the success of a replica is judged.

In one obvious respect forgery is morally wrong, but on views like Beardsley's this has no bearing on a forgery's aesthetic value. The alternative is to agree that perceiving always involves perceiving *as*, but to recognize that the essentially semantic nature of 'perceiving as' ultimately undermines the distinction that adherents of this alternative want to draw between forgeries and replicas. But this alternative still leaves us unable to explain why the best forgeries (those that are not mere slavish copies) are not expressive or otherwise artistic accomplishments in their own right. Either way, then, the fact that a

work was created to be fraudulently presented as a specific artwork by a specific artist leaves open the question, once the work's etiology is known, of the work's aesthetic or artistic value, either as a replica of an existing work or the prototype of a new one.

See also CONSERVATION AND PRESERVATION; ONTOLOGY OF ARTWORKS; ORIGINALITY; PROPERTIES, AESTHETIC.

BIBLIOGRAPHY

Beardsley, Monroe C.: 'An aesthetic definition of art', *What is Art?*, ed. Hugh Curtler (New York: Haven, 1983), pp. 26–7.

Clark, Roger: 'Historical context and the aesthetic evaluation of forgeries', *Southern Journal of Philosophy*, 22 (Fall, 1984), 317–22.

Currie, Gregory: *An Ontology of Art* (New York: St Martin's Press, 1989).

Danto, Arthur C.: *The Transfiguration of the Commonplace* (Cambridge, Mass.: Harvard University Press, 1981).

Dutton, Denis, ed.: *The Forger's Art* (Berkeley, Calif.: University of California Press, 1983); includes essays on forgery by Arnheim, Beardsley, Dutton, Goodman, Lessing, Margolis, Meiland, Meyer, Sagoff, Sparshott, Werness and Michael Wreen.

Goodman, Nelson: *Languages of Art* (Indianapolis: Bobbs-Merrill, 1968), ch. 3.

Kennick, W.E.: 'Art and inauthenticity', *Journal of Aesthetics and Art Criticism*, 44 (1985), 3–12.

Margolis, Joseph: *Art and Philosophy* (Atlantic Highlands: Humanities Press, 1980), ch. 4.

Sparshott, Francis: *The Theory of the Arts* (Princeton, NJ: Princeton University Press, 1982).

Wreen, Michael: 'Counterfeit coins and forged paintings: caveat emptor', *Analysis*, 40 (1980), 146–51.

GEORGE BAILEY

form It is possible to regard the production of art as involving the arrangement of some stuff – stone or paint or words or sounds or bodily motions or images, as may be – by a maker into a form, so that a certain end or effect may be achieved. But a central ambiguity has continuously haunted discussions of the nature of artistic form.

When a work resembles other works in its arrangement of materials and more or less shares an effect with them, then we are tempted to say that artistic form is a kind of arrangement that different members of the same genre may share. When, however, we are struck by the distinctiveness of a particular work and by how any alteration in it would ruin its particular sense and effect, then we are tempted to say that an artistic form is just what is proper to any particular work. It may be helpful, then, to distinguish *genre* form from *individual* form. Artists are, however, typically concerned with both individual and genre form simultaneously. 'How,' they ask themselves in practice, 'may I arrange material so as to make a striking, successful, and distinctively individual work that is a lyric or still-life or trio or movie [and so on]?'

Aristotle, concentrating on tragic drama, was the first to attend carefully to the distinctions and interrelations among matter, maker, effect, and form in bringing about the work, but some distinctions and relations among these things had already been noted in informal practice for some centuries. Plato, in the *Republic* (3.398c–400c) discusses various musical modes or restricted sets of notes for arrangement, such as the Lydian, Dorian, mixed Lydian, and Phrygian, as each having specific emotional effects. Two different works thus might have similar effects in virtue of being in the same mode – in virtue, that is, of having a common form or being arranged out of a common restricted stock of notes. Such discussions of common genre structures and their specific effects are presented as commonplace. Plato's treatment of poetry is similar. He is concerned to mark out the formally characterized kind of plot that, by his lights, poets ought to produce: for example, the proportion of dramatized speech to authorial narration should be small (*Republic*, 3.396e). Organizations of words – literary forms – that have the favoured features will be artistically successful; forms that lack them will not.

At the same time, however, Plato is aware of the transgressive character of some apparently successful art. In the *Ion*, he observes that 'all the good epic poets utter all those fine poems not from art [*technē*], but as inspired and possessed, and the good lyric poets likewise' (*Ion* 533e). Here what is at least striking is an individual form, produced through inspiration, not in accordance with rules for form-making. Aristotle likewise acknowledges this point, as he observes that 'poetry implies either a happy gift of nature or a strain of madness' (*Poetics* 1455a), and that in certain cases 'error [in the form] may be justified, if . . . the effect of this or any other part of the poem is thus rendered more striking' (*Poetics* 1460b). This awareness of the interest of rule-transgressive individual form is memorably continued by Longinus in *On the Sublime*, where he praises the poet's vehement emotion that 'inspires the words as it were with a fine frenzy' (*Sublime* 8.4). More modern construals of successful art as a product of genius or as expressing its maker's individual emotions likewise echo this awareness of our interest in singular arrangements of material.

The history of the theory of the arts is marked, then, by alternation between perhaps mutually correcting concentrations on striking individual arrangements of material and on arrangements of material that are common within a genre of art. These historically persistent senses of the distinct importances of individual form and genre form are variously expressed within efforts to *explain* what makes any artistic form, individual or generic, successful. These efforts at explanation may be roughly divided into three or four kinds, although most interesting efforts transcend tidy classification.

Plato, who notoriously makes substantial philosophical use of the notion of form (*eidos*), argues that a successful artistic form must mirror the ideal organization – itself something fully real, something more real than its sensible instances – of a good thing of its kind. Since he construes a good thing as the most highly stable, unified and integrated thing of its kind, he construes the most successful works of art as themselves the most fully integrated ones. Unruly, inspired, passionate and transgressive works, although striking to many people, are to be condemned. This critical stance on Plato's part follows from his construal of properly successful artistic forms as responsible to their natural subject-matters, the forms or organizations of good things.

Aristotle, suspicious of Plato's metaphysics of forms of things as more self-subsistent than their sensible instances, focuses instead principally on the relations of artistic forms to their audiences. The function or aim of tragedy, for example, is to 'excite pity and fear' in the audience, thence 'to effect the catharsis of these emotions' (*Poetics* 1499b27–8), in order thereby distinctively to please and instruct the audience. Characteristics of the forms or plots required for successful tragedies are then deduced as means for fulfilling tragedy's end. Successful artistic forms are responsive to the interests and tendencies of response of their audiences as they stand.

A third line of explanation of success in the arts, perhaps best expressed by R.G. Collingwood, suggests that successful artistic forms are, in contrast, responsive to the psychic needs of their makers. In *The Principles of Art* (1938), Collingwood claims that all psychic experiences, including all simple sensations, all conscious recognitions of things and all thinkings of theoretical thoughts, are charged with specific emotions. These emotions must be discharged; otherwise, an intolerable psychic burdening will result. This discharge happens immediately through bodily motion for emotions attendant upon unconceptualized sense experience. But the discharge of emotions attendant upon recognition and of emotions attendant upon thought requires a difficult and specific work, the work of art. A successful artistic form, then, is a singular organization of a matter, through the generation of which burdensome emotions attendant upon recognitions and thoughts are clarified and discharged.

Collingwood then argues that contemporary audiences apprehending a work will likewise have their own emotions clarified and discharged, for, since contemporary artists and audiences within a common

culture are likely to recognize the same things and think similar thoughts, they are also likely to have the same emotions to be discharged. Recognitions and thoughts are, moreover, possible for us only in so far as we share with some others a language through the terms of which our consciousness may be focused on things at all. Yet the emphasis remains in Collingwood, in the first instance, on the needs of the maker of the work. This carries the interesting consequence that his views are more directed towards individual form than towards genre form. The traditional genres of art, for him, are at best persistent but still accidental vehicles for satisfying our psychic needs through the making and apprehension of individual expressive forms; and he attacks traditional Aristotelian craft-orientated aesthetics, arguing that the notion of form as a means to an end simply does not apply to art.

Perhaps a fourth view, bearing some affinities with Plato's concern with ideal unities and evident, for example, in the writings of Francis Hutcheson and in the New Critical doctrine of the heresy of paraphrase formulated by Cleanth Brooks, holds that successful artistic forms, in having all their complex parts fully integrated, are irreplicably individual instances of perfection. According to Hutcheson, the criterial feature of all successful art is its uniformity amidst variety. Successful poems, Brooks holds, involve a kind of integrated, controlled play of rich ambivalences, a kind of unity despite paradox. The suggestion is that this kind of unity despite paradox is worth appreciating in itself, rather than for either its embodiment of truth about a subject-matter, or its satisfaction of the needs and interests of audiences or makers. Although it is possible to distinguish the central attention to organizations of complexities in themselves, as it were, from the other lines of explanation, this view nonetheless tends, as do most formalisms, to collapse into one of the three other views, as the realization dawns that some explanation is required of why human beings either do or ought to take an interest in unique organizations of complexities.

The history of the aesthetic theory of successful artistic forms is the history of various mixtures of one or more of these explanatory tendencies with varying degrees of attention either to individual or to genre form. The general tendency – a function, perhaps, of the seventeenth-century simultaneous atomistic rejection of forms in nature and assertion of the self-shaping character of human subjectivity – is away from concentration on successful genre forms and on either forms in themselves or their subject-matters, and instead towards concentration on individual forms and individual audience members. That is, the general tendency is towards the subjectivization and individualization of the conditions of success of artistic forms.

At its extreme, this tendency culminates in a now common aesthetic subjectivism: a successful artistic form is an organization of matter that any individual whatsoever happens to like, where this individual liking carries no implications either about what other individuals either do or ought to like, or about whether even that individual will or ought to like a work with a similar form. Post-structuralism tends towards this stance, in so far as it sees any individual work as less a formed unity of elements than an arbitrarily delimited and functionally insignificant (except for the perpetuation of political power) heap or amalgam of ill-fitting parts. The interest of extreme subjectivist positions may well, however, be parasitic on the fact – which remains in need of construal and explanation – that human beings do take an interest in some specific individual and genre forms and do seem to be capable, in criticism, of offering reasons for their interests.

The most interesting Marxist cultural theory of the twentieth century centres on an effort to resist modern aesthetic subjectivism. Attempting to avoid both the vulgar Stalinist aesthetics that favours such things as posters of happy industrial workers and boy-meets-tractor novels, and the subjectivism of a consumer society, Adorno and Marcuse have argued that successful artistic form is embodied in works that negate existing society and its intersubstitutable commodities and offer us instead a glimpse of a freely organized social world in and through a freely created, non-commodity-like but still organized, artistic work. In so far as Marxist theory moves in this direction, however, distinguishing successful artistic works from commodities as original and irreplicable, and in so far as it comes up against works with little readily obvious social content such as lyric poems, abstract paintings and works of music, it finds itself beginning to replicate the positions of Aristotle or Collingwood, or some mixture of them, as it begins to assign to human beings an interest in artistic form that is independent of their interest in a socialist society.

The most promising construal of the nature of successful artistic form would be one which focused on the needs and interests principally of audiences – since artists themselves are among the audience for their own works, and since they continually modify the work throughout its creation in the light of their own evolving receptions of it – and which elucidated our interests both in the transgressive singularity of works and in their likenesses to other members of their genre. Kant develops an aesthetic theory of this kind in his *Critique of Judgement*. According to him, the successful work of art is required to be both *original* – that is, transgressive and not generatable in accordance only with any known or knowable rules of form, in ways that awaken members of the audience to a sense of their own human autonomy in shaping their lives – and *exemplary* – that is, disciplined against the academic demands of taste (unlike 'original nonsense') and admitting of useful, elucidatory comparisons with other works in its genre, in ways that suggest that our individuality and autonomy may be consistently and intelligibly housed in the sorts of things that we do along with others. The key to fulfilling these two requirements is that the artist must, through practice, aim at 'making the form adequate to [the] thought without prejudice to the freedom in the play of those powers' (Kant, 1928 [1790], p. 174). Our self-shaping subjectivity is here to be creatively, originally and yet intelligibly housed in the successful work, as artists singularly, unpredictably, yet intelligibly and within a genre find the forms that uniquely fit their self-shaping subjectivities.

It may be objected against this view that it posits a general human interest, rooted in individuals and in individual artistic productions, that is typical of the (decadent) moral stances of modern bourgeois life. Or it may be objected that it is impossible to distinguish form from content. If, for example, a painting represents Hendrijke Stoeffels, then it has Hendrijke Stoeffels as part of its thought or content (what it is about), while this content significantly determines its form, the way it looks as a Hendrijke Stoeffels portrait. So how can form and content be pulled apart so as to be related in the work?

These objections will be hollow, however, as long as we find ourselves taking an interest in works both as having singularly effective organizations and consequent specific powers, and as having organizations and powers that they share with other works within a genre. It seems likely that we will continue to be interested in works in this way, as aesthetic theory variously indicates that we have been for millennia. We are, it seems, concerned to find forms that appropriately house not, or not only, things in the world, but our senses of things in the world – the content of our art – as these senses are developed within a tradition by a self-conscious and free subjectivity. We have, it seems, an interest in appreciating original yet intelligible housings of subjectivities in the works of others. We seem to find ourselves concerned as members of an audience with this novel or this portrait or this sonata not, or not only, as a Hendrijke Stoeffels representation but as a representation of Hendrijke Stoeffels as she is apprehended, with specific casts of love or regard or hope, by an artist at a particular time and place, who has been concerned to express in a form or organization of matter a distinctive self-shaping subjectivity and its specific contents.

See also ARISTOTLE; COLLINGWOOD; GENRE; KANT; MARXISM AND ART; PLATO; STRUCTURALISM AND POSTSTRUCTURALISM.

BIBLIOGRAPHY

Adorno, Theodor: *Philosophie der neuen Musik* (Frankfurt: 1948); trans. A.G. Mitchell and W.V. Blomster, *Philosophy of Modern Music* (New York: Seabury, 1974).

Aristotle: *The Poetics of Aristotle*, ed. and trans. S.H. Butcher (London: Macmillan, 1911).

Brooks, Cleanth: *The Well-Wrought Urn* (New York: Viking, 1947).

Collingwood, R.G.: *The Principles of Art* (Oxford: Clarendon Press, 1938).

Danto, Arthur C.: *The Transfiguration of the Commonplace* (Cambridge, Mass.: Harvard University Press, 1981).

Hutcheson, Francis: *An Inquiry into the Original of Our Ideas of Beauty and Virtue* (London: 1725); part I, *An Inquiry Concerning Beauty, Order, Harmony, Design*, ed. Peter Kivy (The Hague: Martinus Nijhoff, 1973).

Kant, Immanuel: *Kritik der Urteilskraft* (Berlin: 1790); trans. J.C. Meredith, *Critique of Judgement* (Oxford: Oxford University Press, 1928).

Longinus: *On the Sublime*, trans. W.H. Fyfe (London: Loeb Classical Library, 1953).

Marcuse, Herbert: *The Aesthetic Dimension* (Munich: 1977); trans. E. Sherover (Boston, Mass.: Beacon Press, 1978).

Plato: *Ion*, trans. W. Lamb (London: Loeb Classical Library, 1925).

Plato: *Republic*, trans. D. Lee (Harmondsworth: Penguin Books, 1955).

RICHARD ELDRIDGE

function of art The belief that works of art are functional and serve certain important ends has a very long and distinguished history – one that begins with Plato and has persisted in a variety of forms to the present day. The opposing idea that genuine art is non-functional, that it is always autonomous and is produced merely for its own sake, is a comparatively recent invention.

The distinction between the useful arts (or crafts) and arts that serve no purpose and are attended to solely as ends in themselves is not to be found in Plato or Aristotle; nor is it to be found in medieval theories of art. It was only at the time of the Renaissance that the notion of fine art began to take root as a way of distinguishing the functional from the non-functional arts. Up until then, all of what we now call fine art was considered to have a purpose – although in the case of some art forms like music and decoration the precise nature of its function was specified only with difficulty.

Functional views of art take at least two distinct forms. Some are normative, and insist that art *ought* always to serve a specified function. To the extent that a work of art performs its designated function, it is considered meritorious; reciprocally, when a work fails to serve its function it is considered inadequate or bad. In this article, this is referred to as normative functionalism. Descriptive functionalism, by contrast, contends that by their very nature works of art serve certain metaphysical, psychological, or cultural functions, and do so whether or not the artist knows or intends it. Descriptive functionalism treats a particular function as a *necessary* feature of all art, although it is true that both descriptive and normative functionalists are generally quite happy to allow that particular works of art may contingently serve a function on a certain occasion – where this function is entirely unrelated to its status as art.

Those functional views of art that are normative in character tend often to view that art ought to act as a medium of instruction. Thus, for instance, Plato tells us that art ought not to deceive, and ought instead to imitate the 'Forms' and thereby convey intellectual insights into reality. In bk 10 of the *Republic* Socrates is said to have advocated the banishment of those poets who either could not or would not abide by his injunction. Their art imitated appearances rather than the eternal forms, and was, for that reason, irredeemably bad. Aristotle in the *Poetics* also believed that art should imitate the real nature of things, but his account of real essences differed from Plato's, and he believed that the proper function of art was both the imitation of the functions of things and the achievement of certain pleasurable and cathartic effects. The medieval Church, long after, wanted an art that would illustrate the gospels and so convey the glory of God. One can continue in this way: Leonardo thought that art should imitate physical

reality, while John Constable believed that painting should convey appearances scientifically, and would be especially good if it did so. Leo Tolstoy thought that good literature ought to convey truths about human nature and morality; while realist painters of the nineteenth century, and twentieth-century socialist realists, argued that serious art should convey the realities of social and political life.

Descriptive functionalism, by contrast, while clearly concerned with the functions served by works of art, is not concerned to isolate those functions that are thought to make art worthwhile or good. Indeed, descriptive functionalists seem often to be of the opinion that the functions served by a work of art need have very little, if anything at all, to do with artistic merit. They are more concerned with social and psychological theory, and with the role that art plays in our lives, than with the critical assessment of works of art. Sigmund Freud, for example, sees all art as the imaginative expression and fulfillment of certain deep-seated desires that cannot be fulfilled in the artist's everyday life. On his view, thwarted desires in the real world lead most people to daydream or fantasize. However, the artist learns to control these fantasies, and to mould them into works of art. Of course, good artists will do this more effectively than poor artists; but irrespective of whether they do it well or badly, on Freud's view all works of art perform this function, and they do so whether or not the artist knows it.

In much the same way, Karl Marx, as a descriptive functionalist, sees art as a phenomenon that arises out of the economic interests of groups of individuals within the economy, and which in some way helps reinforce or else advance these interests. Although he qualifies this in important respects by allowing that certain periods of art are not directly connected to the growth and development of society and its economy, he does nonetheless believe that art somehow expresses and, in this way, helps reinforce, various economic interests within the economic 'base' of the society.

In an altogether different vein, Ortega y

Gasset (1925) sees art as a social safety valve: an early-warning system that can, if properly attended to, inform us of social directions and so promote an understanding of our society. There is no shortage of such theories. Using *Gestalt* theory, Rudolf Arnheim (1974) has argued that the function of art is to symbolize the entire pattern of feelings and meanings (what he calls 'expressiveness') that is embodied in the perception of the artist. In a similar, but more philosophical, way Susanne Langer argues that art always captures and symbolizes non-verbal human feelings.

Freud, Marx, Ortega, Arnheim, and Langer are each in their own way descriptive functionalists. All hold that art serves certain psychological and social ends, and that it must do so whether or not an artist intends it to. It is however, no part of the descriptive functionalist's view that the performance of these functions is sufficient for something's being a work of art; the same functions can be, and often are, performed by non-art. Freud and Marx treat their chosen functions only as a necessary feature of art, although Freudians are not entirely consistent in this matter, and are inclined at times to treat the functions that they isolate as a contingent feature of art. It is arguable, for instance, that while Freudian critics believe that representational painting necessarily performs a specific psychological function, this need not be the case, say, with minimalist or conceptual art. They veer between being descriptive functionalists for specific genres, and contingent functionalists for others.

Of course, if the performance of a particular function is a necessary feature of an artwork, it cannot be a mark of its merit. This notwithstanding, it is entirely consistent for a descriptive functionalist to approve of the way in which a function is performed. Thus, for instance, a work that exposes the corrupt structure of bourgeois society may be praised on that account by Marxists and socialist realists, while one that lends strength to a free market ideology may be criticized. In much the same way, Freudian critics are often inclined to praise a work on the basis of how subtly and efficiently it fulfils its psychological function.

Quite often one and the same thinker turns out to embrace both normative and descriptive functionalism. We find, for instance, that Tolstoy believes that a work of art must always express the emotions of its artist and infect its audience with similar emotions. To this extent Tolstoy is clearly a descriptive functionalist. However, he also argues that in order for a work to be good, the emotions it expresses must be moral: it must encourage progress towards the well-being both of individuals and of humanity. To this extent, he is also a normative functionalist. This suggests that the distinction I have drawn between descriptive and normative functionalism marks ideal positions that often merge in subtle and quite complex ways. In part, this is why traditional aesthetics has tended to criticize functionalism as if it were a single, homogeneous position. Edward Bullough's (1912) arguments, for instance, against the normative functionalist account of evaluation, leads him to the undefended conclusion that art is always non-functional. In a similar way, Stuart Hampshire (1959) tries to show that aesthetic judgements are not informed by practical interests, but from this concludes that descriptive functionalism is false: that art is necessarily gratuitous and so always non-functional.

This tendency to ignore the distinction between normative and descriptive functionalism can further be explained by the fact that as High Renaissance art shaded into mannerism, baroque and eventually neoclassicism, the emphasis came to be placed not just on the functions of the artwork, but also, and increasingly, on the formal properties of the work. As a result, the status of objects as art, as well as their critical assessment, gradually became detached from their function. In this climate of increasing hostility to functionalist views of art, subtle distinctions between types of functionalism were not of interest, and were never drawn.

The antagonism to functionalist views of art was brought to a head in the second half of the nineteenth century. The demise of feudalism and, with it, the disappearance of an aristocratic class that was willing to act as patron of the arts, threw all practising artists on the mercy of the market-place. Many artists refused absolutely to pander to what the market demanded: they refused to produce art that would serve some or other fashionable end, and instead insisted on producing art for its own sake. The aesthetic movement, and with it the cry of art for art's sake, had come of age.

The pursuit of purely artistic values, and the production of art for the sake of art alone, meant that many artists were no longer concerned with what ordinary people wanted from art. Their attention was wholly absorbed by the demands of the medium, and it was largely because of this that artists grew increasingly out of touch with what their audiences expected and could understand. The result was that the rank and file of society grew disillusioned with much fine art, and began to attend instead to what they found interesting and entertaining. In this way, painters, poets, musicians and sculptors gradually began to lose their audience, and in the process they lost whatever impact they had once had on the broader society.

On one functionalist view, this series of historical accidents meant that the fine arts had effectively neutered themselves, had chosen the path of silence, and could no longer challenge the hegemony of the ruling classes (Novitz, 1989). Partly because of this, those in positions of power found art for art's sake congenial and helped entrench its position in the broader society. Quite soon, the 'proper' appreciation of art as an end in itself came to signal one's inclusion in the upper classes, and was taken as a sign of refinement and high culture. Those who looked for a message in art, and who, worse still, attempted to evaluate art in terms of that message, were considered vulgar and uninitiated: they failed in the round to understand what art and culture were all about.

If this is right, it helps explain the strong allegiance that some people have to the view of art as an end in itself. It is arguably a political allegiance, since commitment to it is thought to assure one of a place in an intellectual, cultural and class elite. One result of all of this was that in the middle years of the twentieth century aesthetics became little more than an apologetic for a specific and very restricted view of the fine arts. Its concern, for the most part, was to defend the view that art was properly an end in itself, that it existed for its own sake, and that our understanding and evaluation of it should not concern itself with matters extraneous to the work such as its intended function.

One standard argument against functionalist views of art and in favour of autonomist views maintains that if a work of art serves a particular function – say, the function of informing you about the workings of American or British society – then anything which performs the same function – say, a sociology text – ought to be capable of serving as a substitute for a work of art. But this conclusion, it has been argued, is counter-intuitive. For if I cannot locate a copy of *Bleak House*, I do not refer you instead to a report on the practice of law in nineteenth-century London, even if it turns out to be the case that both texts are equally instructive in this respect. Autonomists infer from this that what is important about a work is not its function but its formal properties. However, functionalists have generally contended that the function of a work of art, while artistically important, is not all-important. The *way* in which the function is performed is what is of singular importance about a work of art (Beardsmore, 1971).

In arguing for the possibility of artistic values that are not tied to practical interests, traditional aestheticians have failed to acknowledge the extent to which the values that attach to art are dependent on the roles that works of art play in our lives: that is, on their functions. It is wrong, of course, to think that there is a single function that art invariably performs. Rather, there are many different functions, which vary from genre to genre and from period to period.

Traditionally an art was conceived of as a practice consisting of an organized package of more or less integrated, but invariably useful, skills (Sparshott, 1982, pp. 25–6). In this sense, medicine and shoe-making are arts, as are plumbing and sheep-shearing. All consist of sets of skills, often housed within institutional frameworks that perpetuate and regulate them. It is precisely because doctors, shearers and cobblers have an interest in doing their job well that they think about, and try to improve, their skills. Consequently, the skills themselves, and not merely the ends that they serve, become objects of attention. It is, according to Sparshott, when an art (an organized body of skills) comes to be treated as an end rather than as a means that the fine arts begin to emerge.

This, I think, is why we should not allow the work of art to occlude our awareness of the useful skills that are exercised in its execution, and of the value that we attach to these skills. It is all but impossible to look at a painting, a drama, a sculpture or a dance without being aware, however remotely, of the practical skills exercised in these works of art. The skills of pictorial representation, for instance, have an obvious practical value, for they not only facilitate the communication of attitudes and information, but enable us to negotiate situations of which we have no first-hand experience. Again, we find that poets and novelists are normally skilled not just in the use of language (which is itself highly prized), but also in inventing a world of people and in telling a story about them. The capacity to invent, to be innovative and original, has obvious utility in a world that requires people to respond in new and useful ways to the problems that confront them. And, of course, skills of invention are praised everywhere in the fine arts of the twentieth century.

One can continue in this way to outline the many practical interests and concerns that mediate our appreciation of all art forms. We can learn about our world from works of art; they may sharpen our moral sensitivities, and in so doing either unsettle or entrench certain of our commitments, enlist loyalties, and thereby foment or resolve social conflicts of one sort or another. Although these are not the only functions that works can serve, they greatly influence our assessment of, and hence the values that we attach to, particular works of art. It is simply a fact, then, that our religious, economic, moral, ecological and intellectual values can, and often do, intrude on our response to a work of art. The remote-

ness and concern of Titian's madonna in his *Madonna with Saints*, for instance, is valued not just because of the formal correctness of the painting, but also because of the religious and gender-related values that we bring to it.

The assumption that art is wholly non-functional, and that our evaluation of it has nothing at all to do with our practical interests and concerns, is simply misleading. This, of course, is not to deny that works of art are sometimes appreciated for their textures, colours, timbre, and other formal properties. But such appreciation is not determined by the nature of art itself. On the contrary, people learn to appreciate art in this way, and they do so because they are the beneficiaries of a particular art education. The threat of being considered incompetent, insensitive or ignorant about art gives them an interest in attending textures and grains rather than messages or themes. In such a case, the viewer's artistic (or aesthetic) values are clearly mediated by social considerations. And at least part of their reason for subscribing to formal artistic values is that they want to be accepted and acknowledged within a certain social network. In this case, art and its appreciation can fairly be said to serve a specific social function: the function, that is, of assuring oneself of a place in a specific social group.

See also AESTHETICISM; ARISTOTLE; MARXISM AND ART; PLATO; PSYCHO-ANALYSIS AND ART; REALISM; TOLSTOY.

BIBLIOGRAPHY

Arnheim, R.: *Art and Visual Perception* (Berkeley, Calif.: University of California Press, 1974).
Beardsmore, R.W.: *Art and Morality* (London: Macmillan, 1971).
Bullough, E.: '"Psychical distance" as a factor in art and as an aesthetic principle', *British Journal of Psychology*, 5 (1912), 87–98.
Hampshire, S.: 'The logic of appreciation', *Aesthetics and Language*, ed. William Elton, (Oxford: Basil Blackwell, 1959).
Novitz, D.: 'Ways of artmaking: the high and the popular in art', *British Journal of Aesthetics*, 29 (1989), 213–29.
Ortega y Gasset, J.: *The Dehumanization of Art*

and Other Writings on Art and Culture (Madrid: 1925); trans. Helen Weyl (Princeton: Princeton University Press, 1972).

Sparshott, F.: *The Theory of the Arts* (Princeton, NJ: Princeton University Press, 1982).

Wolff, J.: *The Social Production of Art* (London: Macmillan, 1981).

DAVID NOVITZ

G

Gadamer, Hans-Georg (1900–) German philosopher; a pupil of Heidegger, and the leading 'hermeneutical' theorist in the late twentieth century. Gadamer once described his approach to art as an attempt to transform the systematic problem of aesthetics into the question of the experience of art (Gadamer, 1976, p. 97). Broadly speaking, his concerns might be described as phenomenological: the question of our access to the artwork and the need to guard against misdescribing our experience of it under the influence of unwarranted philosophical prejudices. The approach Gadamer adopts to these concerns in his numerous short essays on art and poetry is hermeneutical. Indeed, in the first part of *Truth and Method* (1960), where he gives his most sustained consideration of art, the presentation is supposed to legitimate, as well as to exemplify, hermeneutics.

Gadamer legitimates the hermeneutical idea of truth by showing how, once one has dropped the restriction of truth to its scientific conception, the artwork can also be understood as making a claim to truth. The same discussion exemplifies hermeneutics by showing that, although written as a critique of aesthetic consciousness, the historical tradition of reflection on art itself makes a claim to truth. Gadamer rehabilitates the tradition by recalling the legitimate experiences which underlie traditional terminology – as, for example, when he finds the much maligned concept of *mimesis* appropriate even to 'pure poetry' and to non-objective painting (Gadamer, 1986, pp. 36, 103, 117). One does not find in him a wholesale rejection of the conceptual language which has mediated the experience of art in the West. In this he differs from his former teacher, Martin Heidegger, to whom he nevertheless remains deeply indebted.

Gadamer employs the term 'aesthetics' in a technical sense to refer to a specific consciousness of art which, though prepared for earlier, only became clearly apparent towards the end of the eighteenth century. *Truth and Method*, his major work, records in its first part the rise of aesthetic consciousness in the passage from Kant's *Critique of Judgement* to the writings of Schiller. In the course of that transition, the concept of genius is said to take the place of judgements of taste, and at the same time the artwork loses its connection with the world. Gadamer's challenge to aesthetic consciousness does not take the form of denying that its experience of art is genuine. The point is, rather, that aesthetic consciousness misunderstands its experience; it is more than it knows itself to be.

Gadamer, typically, does not ask his readers to open themselves up to new experiences so much as to awaken themselves to familiar experiences. So, even the term 'consciousness' in the phrase 'aesthetic consciousness' is ultimately found inadequate in so far as the artwork is the underlying subject of the experience of art, rather than the human subject. His frequent appeals to the model of play are in large measure introduced to render this idea more acceptable. What draws and holds the player is the game, which thus itself becomes the *subjectum* of the playing (Gadamer, 1989, pp. 106, 490).

It is striking to find that Gadamer's first scholarly essay, 'Plato and the poets', anticipates, and even illuminates, his subsequent writings on art. Plato's critique of mimetic art in bk 10 of the *Republic* is read by Gadamer as a critique of the moral consequences of aesthetic consciousness. Plato banished the poets from the ideal state, on Gadamer's interpretation, because the joy taken in their imitations led to a kind of self-alienation in which one forgets oneself. Losing oneself in a poem or a piece of music in this way was precisely the frame of mind that aesthetics cultivated. In other words, Gadamer understood Plato to have attacked the attitude that would subsequently become known as 'aesthetic'. What aesthetic consciousness tended to forget, but which was well known to Plato, was that there are forms of art which clearly escape these limitations and thus serve as a corrective to the interpretation. Hymns of praise sung to a god or some outstanding individual bind those who hear it to each other. They prepare their audience to meet its obligations.

Although Gadamer would most probably now find anachronistic his early attempt to read Plato as exposing the limitations of an aesthetic consciousness that, at least according to the later writings, had not yet arisen, the essay illuminates Gadamer's practice. In his early essay, he appears to accept Plato's distinction between different kinds of poetry, and simply follows Plato's displacement of the question of poetry into philosophical dialogue. Philosophical dialogue has its own poetry, which makes it the song of praise most appropriate for those politics that are 'almost incurable' (Gadamer, 1980, p. 66). In the later texts, Gadamer would be more likely to conclude that all works of art, and not just hymns of praise, make a claim on their audience. That is to say, self-alienation is only one moment of the experience of art which, properly described, also includes a return to self.

Nevertheless, the self to which one returns following the experience of art is not the self with which one began. 'The experience of art . . . does not leave him who has it unchanged' (Gadamer, 1989, p. 100). Art does not represent a realm into which one can escape, only to return subsequently to the life one had temporarily bracketed. The artwork issues a challenge to everybody who experiences it. By its dissolution of the familiar the artwork says not only, 'You are this', but, with Rilke, 'You must change your life [Du musst dein Leben ändern]' (Archaïscher Torso Apollos, cited in Gadamer, 1976, p. 104). In German, one would say that the experience of art is an *Erfahrung*, in the Hegelian sense of a transformative experience that one undergoes, and not an *Erlebnis*, the lived experience described by Dilthey.

Aesthetics is not only a frame of mind. It has an institutional reality, for example, in the museum. Just as aesthetic consciousness attempts to take up the aesthetic quality of the work independently of its moral or religious content, thereby abstracting from the conditions of the work's accessibility, its purpose and its function, so the isolation of works from their contexts by placing them in 'collections' can seem to disregard everything in which a work is rooted. Gadamer calls this abstraction 'aesthetic differentiation' (Gadamer, 1989, p. 85). Whereas cultural historians respond to aesthetic differentiation by attempting to reconstruct the conditions of the original construction, as if one could thereby reproduce an understanding of the original purpose of the work, Gadamerian hermeneutics takes a somewhat different approach. The point at which aesthetics becomes reabsorbed in hermeneutics, beyond anything that simply historiological investigations can accomplish, is when one attains a living relationship with the work, such that it still has something to say to us as people in history (Gadamer, 1989, pp. 164–9).

See also ATTITUDE, AESTHETIC; AUTONOMY, AESTHETIC; HEIDEGGER; HERMENEUTICS; MUSEUMS.

WRITINGS

Kleine Schriften II. Interpretation (Tübingen: 1967). (Some of the essays in this volume may be found in translation in *The Relevance of the Beautiful and Other Essays* (see below).)
'Ästhetik und Hermeneutik' (1964); trans. D.E. Linge, *Philosophical Hermeneutics* (Berkeley, Calif.: University of California Press, 1976), pp. 95–104.
Plato und die Dichter (Frankfurt: 1934); trans. P. Christopher Smith, 'Plato and the poets', *Dialogue and Dialectic* (New Haven, Conn. Yale University Press, 1980), pp. 39–72.
Die Aktualität des Schönen (Stuttgart: 1977); trans. N. Walker, *The Relevance of the Beautiful*

and Other Essays (Cambridge: Cambridge University Press, 1986).

Wahrheit und Methode (Tübingen: 1960); trans. J. Weinsheimer and D.G. Marshall, Truth and Method, 2nd rev. edn (New York: Crossroad, 1989).

ROBERT BERNASCONI

genre A type or kind (of art); the term is frequently used as a substitute for a general concept of stylistic kind.

There is a slightly special sense of the word that applies to a certain sort of painting – namely, to paintings of low life or 'real' or 'ordinary' life – behind which, it is tempting to suppose, lies the somewhat snobbish idea that people and scenes of that sort are 'types' or 'characters' rather than individuals of the sorts that one might know personally as sitters for portraits, or know of as fictional or mythical personages. Elsewhere, the idea of genre has come to mean a kind of art in a rather specific sense, which has far more to do with subject-matter than with style, so that style may indicate genre but not define it.

In the case of literature and the narrative arts generally – perhaps the easiest route to understanding the concept of genre – recognizing genre is a precondition for any sort of fair critical judgement. To read Macbeth as a detective story, as James Thurber suggested, or the first two books of Paradise Lost as if they were an early form of science fiction, would clearly be absurd. Similar mistakes may be more subtle, hence more misleading. Some people object to the sort of fairy-story that ends with the princess and the woodcutter getting married and 'living happily ever after', insisting that such tales are grossly unrealistic; or that the stories of P.G. Wodehouse lack deep sexual motivation. But, with stories of that sort, that genre, such objections are not to the point. 'Living happily ever after' is how it is in fairy-stories, and indeed, that style of ending itself indicates the genre to which the tale one has been told belongs, just as Wodehouse's style indicates the sort of tale he is telling. It seems as absurd to object to the lack of psychological depth in a 'standard' detective story or science fiction fantasy as to object of Genesis or of Gilgamesh that it is hard to identify with the main character.

The tacit principles here are roughly this. We are invited by fictional narratives to assume certain events or situations, so that what we may be told happens next will be against a background of the non-fictional expectations that we, as readers, will have. Our capacity to be surprised, reassured, unconvinced or astonished by the outcome we are in fact given constitutes our intelligently understanding the narrative. In the case of a purely factual narrative, we bring to bear on this all that we know or believe about the 'real' world, whether in terms of general principles of inference, laws of nature or, more loosely, how we suppose facts and situations to 'hang together'. Thus, if a factual report has it that someone called Pickwick or Holmes did such and such at such a place and time, any further information – birth certificates, meteorological records, the latest discoveries in medical science, and so on – will be relevant to assessing the truth or plausibility of the story we are told. But, if a story about Holmes or Pickwick is a fiction, clearly no failure to find the birth certificates, no check on the weather at the time of the events, will be relevant. Yet, for all that, plausibility must be in question at some point. Snow in London in August would, in a Sherlock Holmes story, clearly count against its plausibility and thus be relevant first to our understanding of the narrative, and then to our critical judgement. For a narrative, however fictional, to be intelligible at all there must be a minimal, normally very rich, reference to what both reader and author take to be the way the real world actually is. Narrative genre essentially has to do with how this may play a part in our understanding of the work.

It can be useful to distinguish between the fictional elements in a story (fictional characters, places, events) and the quite differently fictional assumptions that we, the readers, will have to make in order to follow the kind of story we are being told. These latter have to do with genre. L.C. Knights, in his 'How many children had Lady Macbeth?' (1946), rightly objected to those who, reading the line of Lady Macbeth's, 'I have given suck, and know/How tender 'tis to love the babe that milks me', deemed it appropriate to ask how many children, then, we should suppose her to have had. (It is clearly not an appropriate question, even though it is a logical truth that if anyone has had some children she must have had some number of children – and it would, moreover, even here, be out of place to entertain the thought that such a lady might have been a wet nurse in previous employment.) A then fashionable stricture to limit the reader's interpretative attention to the 'words on the page' is misleading: questions about tacit psychological motivation are, clearly and especially for Shakespeare, of central relevance, yet plainly involve questions that go well beyond the merely verbal text.

In a detective story, precisely the sort of question that Knights ruled out for *Macbeth* would be relevant, though other questions might not be. Again, when Rapunzel lets down her hair for her lover to climb up, questions about the subsequent state of her scalp are no more relevant than are questions about the likelihood of giants exceeding escape velocity when they put on seven-league boots: though such questions might well matter for some science fiction.

In that central genre of narrative fiction which F.R. Leavis identified by the canon of the 'great tradition', concerns with the plausibility of motivation are all-important, since questions for the reader about what it would have been like to be a protagonist in such a story are central to that genre: the 'trade off' may be that doubts about how we might trust that the writer could possibly know the relevant inner thoughts of the characters do not arise – as they must do, should a similar story be told as a piece of straightforward history. Yet the assumption that such characters have a peculiar psychological transparency (or that the author has a peculiar omniscience) is no more part of the fictional narrative than it is part of the plot of a play staged 'naturalistically' before an audience that one of the walls of the room is transparent; or part of the narrative that when Hamlet speaks in soliloquy the other fictional characters at Elsinore go strangely deaf. Such devices control those judgements of plausibility that we need to make in order to construe the narrative. They define fictional genre.

Fictional genres such as fairy-stories, the heroic epic, fantasy, nonsense fantasy that makes fiction out of the logically absurd (such as the stories of Lewis Carroll), science fiction, detective fiction, the novel of psychological insight and so on are, if loose classifications, fairly familiar ones. Often stylistic devices in the manner of telling the tale, or in the ways in which the reader is addressed, can be relied upon to indicate to him or her what sort of assumptions he or she should make when construing the tale – what to expect, what to take for granted. But there have always been deliberately ambiguous fictional genres. Tragicomedy was for the seventeenth century something of this sort, and so two hundred years later is so-called 'magic realism': in such cases the point is to specifically challenge the reader, via a self-conscious awareness that it is with fiction that he or she has to deal, into a direct confrontation with the very idea of plausibility, or verisimilitude itself. For what might be termed 'genre unease' can be one of the most effective ways of enforcing a reader's reflection, via those devices of art that exploit these very capacities, on the nature of imagination and belief.

In the case of non-literary, non-narrative, art these issues press in on us in slightly different ways. Various forms of figurative and non-figurative painting, and sorts of music that can be hard to classify, raise similar embarrassments: all have to do with the propriety of critical presuppositions. What, for instance, does one have the right to expect of, say, popular music, rock music with a political content, popular as opposed to pop art, graffiti art, amateur art with pretensions towards something else, highly professional painting with the superficial appearance of amateur art, various forms of minimalist and conceptual art . . . and so on? To present the list, even at random, is to indicate a further twist to the puzzle – namely, that it is very much integral to the subject-matter of modernist and postmodernist art to make such embarrassments a central theme of the process of art itself (compare Danto, 1981). From Dada onwards, what might be called deliberate 'genre shock' can seem to be what the arts are about. In effect, this is to incorporate within the content of art 'philosophical' anxieties about the status of the works, and hence philosophical questions valid in their own right.

See also FICTIONAL ENTITIES; NARRATIVE; STYLE.

BIBLIOGRAPHY

Danto, Arthur: *The Transfiguration of the Commonplace* (Cambridge, Mass.: Harvard University Press, 1981).
Dodsworth, Martin: 'Genre and the experience of literature', *Royal Institute of Philosophy Lectures*, vol. 6, *Philosophy and the Arts*, ed. Godfrey Vesey (London: Macmillan, 1973), pp. 211–27.
Fowler, Alastaire: *Kinds of Literature* (Oxford: Clarendon Press, 1982).
Frye, Northrop: *Anatomy of Criticism* (Princeton, NJ: Princeton University Press, 1957).
Knights, L.C.: 'How many children had Lady Macbeth? An essay in the theory and practice of Shakespeare criticism', *Scrutiny*, 10.3 (1946); reprinted in *Explorations* (London: Chatto & Windus, 1958).
Warren, Austin: *Theory of Literature*, 2nd edn (New York: Harcourt Brace, 1956), p. 216.

ANDREW HARRISON

Gombrich, Sir **Ernst (Hans Josef)** (1909–) Austrian-born historian and theorist of the visual arts; Director of the Warburg Institute until 1976.

'There really is no such thing as Art. There are only artists', are the opening words of Gombrich's immensely popular *The Story of Art* (1950, p. 5). Still, until the twentieth century at least, and despite some deviations, painters and sculptors have, since the very

earliest times, been inspired by a predominant endeavour – to provide 'convincing representations' of the visible world (or 'illusions' as Gombrich, perhaps misleadingly, calls them). That is why a story of art is possible. And not just a story, for Gombrich's starting point is the fact – one which we should find surprising – that painting and sculpture have a *history*. Despite its sub-title, the 'central problem' of his most influential work, *Art and Illusion: A Study in the Psychology of Pictorial Representation*, is 'why representation should have a history; why it should have taken mankind so long to arrive at a plausible rendering of visual effects that create the illusion of life-likeness' (1980, p. 246).

That painting has a history, and not simply a chronology, is evident from the existence of styles and traditions which enable us, usually without much trouble, correctly to allocate anonymous paintings to their periods. More than that, we should recognize with Heinrich Wölfflin that 'not everything is possible in every period' (Wölfflin, 1932: quoted in Gombrich, 1980, p. 4). A thirteenth century work that looked very like a Monet would not be an Impressionist painting, since Impressionism is intelligible only as a response to the canons of the Academy. Gombrich has hailed Hegel as 'the father of art history' precisely because of the latter's acute awareness that painting not only develops, but that in crucial respects the stages of this development could not have occurred in a different order. (Gombrich, 1984).

That certain fashionable views, old and new, about the nature of artistic activity make it impossible to understand how art could have a history is sufficient reason for rejecting them. If painting were simply a matter of an individual's 'copying what he sees' or 'only . . . an expression of personal vision, there could be no history of art' (1980, p. 3). But these views are anyway inadequate on psychological and philosophical grounds. According to Gombrich, as we will see, no clear sense can be attached to the notion of 'copying what one sees'; and even the 'abstract expressionist' must rely on tradition, not only to furnish an inherited vocabulary of 'affects', but as something which gives a point – albeit a rebellious or nihilistic one – to his work.

Granted that art has a history, we require an adequate psychology if this history is to be properly characterized. It is implausible, for example – and despite the favoured rhetoric of many contemporary art teachers – to suppose that in any serious sense of 'see', Egyptian artists, Giotto, Constable and Monet 'saw' the world differently from one another. Perception may have altered in marginal ways, but not in the massive ways we should have to suppose if we took all these artists as accurately recording what they perceived. This may encourage us to jump to an opposite extreme and argue that their paintings merely manifest a number of different 'conventions' for representing the world, barely constrained by – and not to be judged by – any ideal of fidelity to how that world actually looks. But not only is this contradicted by the stated aim of many such artists to provide 'convincing representations', it also denies the obvious. One should indeed 'stress the conventional element in many modes of representation', but carried to an extreme this is 'also nonsense'. For while Constable's *Wivenhoe Park* 'is not a mere transcript of nature . . . it still remains true that it is a closer rendering of the motif than is that of the child' (1980, p. 252). *Pace* Herbert Read, perspective is no mere convention, but enables a genuine and objective similarity between a painting and a scene viewed through a window to be achieved (Gombrich, 1980, ch. 8; Gombrich, 1982).

But it is to the ideal of the 'innocent eye' that Gombrich devotes most critical attention. On this view (Ruskin's, for example), painting has progressed through artists' gradually setting aside the assumptions and knowledge which intrude between their recognition or interpretation of the scenes before them and what they actually and directly *see* – coloured specks, shimmers, etc. Only with Turner and the Impressionists have painters achieved this disengagement and succeeded in recording the deliverances of 'innocent' perception. Gombrich is not entirely unsympathetic to this view, for he

too wants to stress the role that knowledge of the real world, or 'expectations' based on experience of it, play in our recognition of what is there to see. Indeed, his objection is that these 'expectations' play such a crucial role in perception that there can be no complete 'disengagement' from them. '[W]e cannot disentangle seeing from knowing, or rather, from expecting' so as to 'see' anything free from all interpretation and thereby proceed to paint what we 'innocently' 'see' (1980, p. 187). There is another obstacle to 'innocence': for our perception of the world has been indelibly shaped by the traditions of painting itself. Even if we could 'bracket' the world of material objects so as to focus on shapes, colours etc., how we focus on these and how we would record them in our own paintings will have been irredeemably influenced by the Claudes, Constables or Monets that belong to our cultural inheritance.

Debates about the roles of convention and tradition, and about the possibility of 'pure' observation, are familiar of course in the history and philosophy of science. Gombrich, inspired by Constable's rhetorical question 'Why . . . may not landscape painting be considered as a branch of natural philosophy, of which pictures are but the experiments?', takes this parallel very seriously. Indeed, it is Sir Karl Popper's 'logic of scientific discovery' which, Gombrich believes, provides a key to the understanding of artistic discovery as well. According to Popper, scientific theories cannot result from unaided observation and induction since, except against the background provided by some hypothesis, one would have no idea what observations were relevant, nor what they could possibly show. Science proceeds, rather, through a process of 'conjecture and refutation', with scientists *creating* hypotheses which indicate observable data which would, if obtained, serve to falsify the hypotheses. Science, therefore, is *essentially* historical, for without a context of earlier theories succumbing to refutation, there would be nothing to motivate the conjecturing of new hypotheses. While science progresses, through refutations of earlier theories, no theory can pretend to truth since, if it has real empirical content, it too must stand open to falsification.

Analogously, for Gombrich, painting proceeds, not through artists copying unguided observations of nature, but through 'schemas and corrections'. ' "Making comes before matching" . . . the matching process itself proceeds through the stages of "schema and correction". Every artist has to know and construct a schema before he can adjust it to the needs of portrayal' (1980, p. 99). At a more macro-level, the 'schemas' which characterize the style of an age are 'corrected' when the paintings they generate fail to 'match' aspects of experience that have become important to people to capture. So art, like science, is essentially historical. And just as no scientific theory can pretend to truth, nor can any genre of painting: for we can never exclude new dimensions of experience which only an artist of genius is able both to reveal and to record. It takes a Van Gogh, for example, to discover that 'you can see the visible world as a vortex of lines' (1980, p. 203).

Gombrich's account of the activity and history of art is certainly persuasive, but critical questions can nevertheless be raised – especially concerning his rejection of the 'innocent eye' approach. It is unclear, for a start, that we should compare too seriously the artist's 'problem' of representing the scene before him with that of the scientist erecting a theory on the basis of the data he observes. Does the former really have to 'interpret' in the same sense as the latter?

Secondly, one wonders whether, without the 'innocent eye', it is possible, as Gombrich insists it is, to speak of paintings having an 'objective likeness' or 'fidelity' to our experience of the world. He defines 'objective likeness' in terms of the accurate information about the world which a painting may afford us. But this seems to elide the difference between a 'convincing representation' and a correct verbal description. It is difficult not to suspect that the analysis is the wrong way round: a painting gives accurate information, typically, because it really is like its motif.

Finally, Gombrich's confidence in experimental psychology's having established

that seeing is always a matter of interpreting may be misplaced. Doubtless, there is a sense of 'see' in which a person can only be said to see X if that is what he takes it to be. But it is a philosophical issue whether there is not a different, and possibly more basic, sense in which one can be said to see X without conceptualizing it as such (Dretske, 1988). At the very least, it sounds exaggerated to hold that 'To "see" *means* to guess at something "out there" ' (1980, p. 254; my italics), or that 'it is *always* hard to distinguish what is given to us from what we supplement in the process of projection' (1980, p. 203; my italics). Is it really that hard to distinguish the bare lines of the famous duck/rabbit drawing from my 'projection' on to them of a rabbit (or a duck, as may be)?

Despite these queries, there is no doubt that Gombrich's work – and I have focused almost entirely on just one book – has served to set the agenda for subsequent reflections on the history and perceptual psychology of art.

See also ART HISTORY; ILLUSION; PERCEPTION; PERSPECTIVE; REPRESENTATION; RESEMBLANCE; TRADITION.

WRITINGS

The Story of Art (London: Phaidon, 1950).
'Illusion in art', *Illusion in Nature and Art*, ed. E. Gombrich and R. Gregory (London: Duckworth, 1973).
Art and Illusion: A Study in the Psychology of Pictorial Representation (1960); (Oxford: Phaidon, 1980).
The Image and the Eye (Oxford: Phaidon, 1982).
'The father of art history: A reading of the *Lectures on Aesthetics* of G.W.F. Hegel', in E. Gombrich, *Tributes: Interpreters of Our Cultural Tradition* (Ithaca, NY: Cornell University Press, 1984).

BIBLIOGRAPHY

Dretske, Fred: 'Sensation and perception', *Perceptual Knowledge*, ed. J. Dancy (Oxford: Oxford University Press, 1988).
Wölfflin, Heinrich: *Kunstgeschichtliche Grundbe-*

griffe (Munich, 1915); trans. P. and L. Hottinger, *Principles of Art History* (New York and London, 1932).

DAVID E. COOPER

Goodman, Nelson (1906–) American philosopher who has made major contributions to epistemology, metaphysics, and philosophy of science, as well as to aesthetics. In his youth he ran an art gallery, and throughout his life he has been an avid collector of art. He is Professor Emeritus of Philosophy at Harvard University.

The arts enhance understanding, Goodman contends, and aesthetics explains how they do so. Aesthetics, then, is a branch of epistemology (Goodman, 1976). He maintains that understanding a work of art is not a matter of appreciating it, or finding beauty in it, or having an 'aesthetic experience' of it. Like understanding an utterance or inscription, understanding a work of art consists in interpreting it correctly. This involves recognizing how and what it symbolizes, and how what it symbolizes bears on other visions and versions of our worlds. Works of art, then, belong to symbol systems with determinate syntactic and semantic structures. Much of *Languages of Art* (first published in 1968) is devoted to delineating the structures of the systems that the various arts employ, detailing their powers and limitations.

Goodman recognizes two basic modes of reference: denotation and exemplification. A symbol denotes whatever it applies to. A name denotes its bearer; a portrait, its subject; a predicate, the members of its extension; and so on. Fictive symbols fail to denote. Their significance, he believes, depends on what symbols denote them. Because the term 'Ophelia description' denotes a range of names and descriptions in Shakespeare's play, those names and descriptions collectively fix Ophelia's fictive identity (Goodman, 1972, pp. 221–38).

Some symbols – including abstract art, most instrumental music, much dance – do not even purport to denote. They deploy other modes of reference exclusively. Prominent among these is exemplification, whereby a symbol refers to some of its own properties. A Mondrian painting, for example, exemplifies squareness. It not only consists of squares, but points up this fact about itself. That is, it refers to the squareness of the shapes it contains. No more than denotation is exemplification peculiar to the arts. It is critical in commerce and science as well. A commercial paint sample exemplifies its colour and sheen; a blood sample, the presence of antibodies. In art and elsewhere, exemplifying symbols afford epistemic access to properties that they sample.

Exemplification and denotation are not mutually exclusive. Works of art that denote typically exemplify as well. *Wivenhoe Park* exemplifies Constable's style while denoting the park. Tolstoy's description of the Battle of Borodino describes the battle and exemplifies his attitude towards war. Critical to Goodman's aesthetics is the recognition that symbols can, and often do, simultaneously perform a variety of referential functions.

Denotation and exemplification need not be literal. A distinctive feature of Goodman's theory is that metaphorical symbols genuinely refer to their figurative subjects. 'Bulldog' genuinely denotes Churchill; the *Pietà* genuinely exemplifies sorrow. Reference, then, is not restricted to literal reference, nor truth to literal truth.

Symbols typically belong to schemes – systems of signs that collectively classify the objects in a realm. 'Bulldog' belongs to a scheme that, in its literal application, sorts the realm of dogs. In metaphor, Goodman maintains, the scheme transfers to a new realm. The organization of dogs into breeds is reapplied to classify people. Because under that transfer Churchill falls within the extension of 'bulldog', Churchill is metaphorically a bulldog. New patterns and distinctions in the human population emerge; for the metaphor sorts people into classes that no literal predicate exactly captures. This is one reason why metaphors resist literal paraphrase.

In referring to a property that it metaphorically possesses, an object metaphorically exemplifies that property. Thus, Churchill metaphorically exemplifies bulldoggishness when serving as an example of that trait. Expression, Goodman contends, is a form of metaphorical exemplification. A work of art, functioning as such, expresses the properties that it metaphorically exemplifies. Being inanimate, the *Pietà* cannot literally exemplify sorrow. But it can and does exemplify that property metaphorically. It therefore expresses sorrow. Expression, as Goodman construes it, is not restricted to feelings. For aesthetic symbols metaphorically exemplify other features as well. Music may express colour; sculpture, motion; painting, depth. There is evidently no *a priori* limit on the features that works of art can express (Goodman, 1976, pp. 45–95).

Reference need not be exclusively denotational or exclusively exemplificational. Sometimes, Goodman maintains, reference is transmitted via chains consisting of denotational and exemplificational links. Allusion is a case in point. The simplest allusions involve three-link chains. A symbol alludes to its referent by exemplifying a feature that it shares with its referent, or by denoting an object that exemplifies its referent. Thus, passages in *Ulysses* allude to Roman Catholic prayers by exemplifying the cadences of those prayers. And the figure of a dog in a Dürer print alludes to loyalty by denoting dogs, which exemplify loyalty. Longer and more complex chains also occur. And multiple routes of reference may secure an allusion. Regardless of length or configuration, so long as reference is transmitted across such a chain, indirect reference occurs (Goodman, 1984, pp. 55–71).

A variation must be like its theme in some respects and different from it in others. But merely having shared and contrasting features is not enough. Otherwise, every passage would be a variation on every other. A passage does not qualify as a variation, Goodman contends, unless it refers to the theme via the exemplification of both sorts of features. Variation, then, is a form of indirect reference (Goodman and Elgin, 1988, pp. 66–82).

Scientific symbols, Goodman urges, are relatively attenuated. They symbolize along comparatively few dimensions. Aesthetic symbols, by contrast, are relatively replete. Comparatively many of their aspects function symbolically. The same configuration of ink on paper might be an electrocardiogram or a drawing. If the former, only the shape is significant. If the latter, the precise colour and thickness of the line at each point, the exact shade of the background, the exact size and shape of the paper and of the line on the paper, even the quality of the paper itself, may be significant. Moreover, the electrocardiogram is referentially austere. It denotes a heartbeat and perhaps exemplifies certain symptomatology. The drawing is apt to perform myriad complex and interanimating referential functions. Via denotation, exemplification, expression and allusion, it refers to a multiplicity of referents through a variety of routes (Goodman, 1976, pp. 229–30).

The status of a line as an electrocardiogram or a drawing depends on its function. It counts as a work of art so long as it functions as an aesthetic symbol. And it may function aesthetically at some times and not at others. The crucial question, then, is not 'What is art?', but 'When is art?' Although Goodman supplies no criterion of aesthetic functioning, he identifies its symptoms: exemplification, relative repleteness, complex and indirect reference, syntactic and semantic density. A symbol system is syntactically dense if the finest differences among signs make for different symbols. It is semantically dense if it has the resources to mark the finest differences among objects in its domain. As symptoms, these features are neither necessary nor sufficient, but they are indications that an object is functioning as a work of art (Goodman, 1978, pp. 71–89).

Interpreting a work involves discovering what symbols constitute it, how they symbolize, what they refer to, and to what effect. Because of the richness and complexity of aesthetic symbols, the task may be endless. And multiple, divergent interpretations may be correct. But it is not the case, Goodman maintains, that every interpretation is correct. Only such interpretations as make maximally good sense of the work's symbolic functions are acceptable. His pluralism consists in his recognition that more than one interpretation may do so (Goodman and Elgin, 1988, p. 222).

To construe works of art as symbols and the aesthetic attitude as a quest for understanding might seem to anaesthetize art. It does not. For the feelings that a work evokes are sources of understanding. Emotional sensitivity, like perceptual sensitivity, enables us to discern subtle but significant features. In the arts, Goodman maintains, emotions function cognitively (Goodman, 1976, pp. 245–52).

Merit, too, transforms from an end to a means. Rather than seeking to understand a work in order to evaluate it, we use evaluations as sources of understanding. An unexpected assessment kindles curiosity, prompting us to attend more carefully to the work – to search for features that previously eluded. The knowledge that a given work has (or lacks) aesthetic merit may then help us to understand it better (Goodman, 1972, pp. 120–1).

See also DEPICTION; EXPRESSION; LANGUAGE, ART AS; METAPHOR.

WRITINGS

Problems and Projects (Indianapolis: Hackett, 1972).
Languages of Art (Indianapolis: 1968); 2nd edn (Indianapolis: Hackett, 1976).
Ways of Worldmaking (Indianapolis: Hackett, 1978).
Of Mind and Other Matters (Cambridge, Mass.: Harvard University Press, 1984).
(With Elgin, Catherine Z.), *Reconceptions* (Indianapolis: Hackett, 1988).

BIBLIOGRAPHY

Elgin, Catherine Z.: *With Reference to Reference* (Indianapolis: Hackett, 1983).
Mitchell, W.J.T.: 'Pictures and paragraphs: Nelson Goodman and the grammar of difference', *Iconology* (Chicago, Ill.: University of Chicago Press, 1986), pp. 53–74.
Schwartz, Robert: 'The power of pictures', *Journal of Philosophy*, 82 (1985), 711–20.

CATHERINE Z. ELGIN

H

Hanslick, Eduard (1825–1904) Austrian music critic, the most famous critic of his day, and an acerbic enemy of excessive romantic tendencies in nineteenth-century music. His verdicts on contemporary compositions greatly affected their reception, especially in Vienna, where he lived for most of his career. His first important publication, *The Beautiful in Music* (1854), is deservedly the most famous work of musical aesthetics.

Hanslick's aim in writing the book was to establish the thesis that, in his own terms, 'the beauty of a composition is *specifically musical.*' In other words, he attempted to show that musical value is autonomous, in the sense that the value of music as an art, or the value of any piece of music *as music*, is independent of its relation to anything extra-musical. Instrumental music has no subject-matter extraneous to its combinations of musical sounds, and its artistic value is determined only by the intrinsic beauty of the audible forms that compose it, so that its aesthetic appeal resembles that of an ever-changing kaleidoscope or a mobile arabesque, which pleases in itself, rather than sub-serving a further function. The illustrative power of music is minimal, consisting only in the imitation of sounds (bird calls, for example); and the introduction of reproductions of sounds of the natural world into a musical work always serves a poetic, not a musical, purpose.

The principal target of the book is the doctrine that the aim of music as an art is the representation of feelings or emotions. This doctrine maintains that the proper subject-matter of music is the emotional life and that the musical value of a work is determined by how successful it is in representing emotional feelings and, perhaps, by the nature of the feelings it represents. This doctrine, Hanslick believed, is buttressed by the thesis that the aesthetic function of music is to arouse feelings. This is his subsidiary target.

He brings three main considerations against the supporting thesis. First, there is no invariable causal nexus between a musical work and the feelings, if any, it arouses: the feelings excited by a particular work vary both from person to person and within a single life. But a composition's musical merit is unvarying. Second, the power to awaken feelings is not confined to music, and the feelings excited by any musical work could be aroused by another, non-musical, stimulus. So music does not possess an aesthetic monopoly of the function of evoking feelings. Third, emotional feelings are states either of satisfaction or of discomfort. But a musical work that arouses a discomforting feeling is not valued for doing so, and its capacity to arouse such a feeling is not a musical merit.

To establish his principal negative thesis, Hanslick uses three main arguments. The first and most important of these is designed to restrict the scope of the musical representation of feeling. A definite feeling, such as a feeling of love, anger, sorrow or fear, is not only a state of pleasure or dissatisfaction, but a state that possesses 'intentionality': the felt pleasure or dissatisfaction is not free-floating but has an object – namely, the state of affairs represented by the thought that is partly constitutive of the feeling. For example, the feeling of hope involves the thought of a desired outcome and the feeling of grief the thought of someone's death. Hanslick argues that music cannot represent definite feelings, since it cannot represent the thoughts in which such feelings partly consist: music can represent only the 'dynamic' properties of definite feelings, the ways in which feelings vary in intensity and the changing aspects of the movements in or of the body that are felt in an episode of emotion.

But the argument is not yet finished. For music cannot represent these dynamic properties *as* being properties of feelings, and feelings are not the only phenomena that can change in strength and kind of movement. So Hanslick reaches the conclusion not only that music cannot represent definite feelings, but also that it can neither represent indefinite feelings nor indefinitely represent feelings.

He brings two additional arguments against his prime target. The first asserts that it cannot be necessary for music, considered from the point of view of its being an art, to represent definite feelings, since at least some musical works are admitted by all listeners not to do so. The second claims that even if music could represent definite feelings, its doing so would not be a requirement of musical value. Hanslick offers two reasons why this requirement would not apply. The first is the existence of valuable music that does not have feelings as its subject-matter. The second is that, if there were any music that represented feelings, it would not be valuable to the degree that it represented feelings accurately; for, so Hanslick argues, musical value would always be inversely proportional to representational accuracy.

Despite its clarity and boldness, Hanslick's philosophy of music is not entirely successful. It places a salutary emphasis on the fact that music as an art must be appreciated for its own sake, rather than merely for the feelings it may awaken. It certainly demolishes the unvarnished thesis that music has no other aesthetic function than the arousal of feelings. It follows that, if there is an aesthetically significant role for the musical excitation of feelings, music must possess other aesthetic functions in virtue of which it elicits definite feelings. It is also clear that, if representation is understood as a relation which involves a noticeable resemblance between the related items, instrumental music cannot represent the thought that forms the core of a definite feeling, so that the musical arousal of feelings cannot be an aesthetic response to

music's representation of the emotional life. But this is not sufficient to show that the appreciation of musical value cannot require hearing music in a manner that relates it to a definite emotion. If there is such a mode of perception, an aesthetics of music that does not recognize and explicate it is incomplete.

See also COMPOSITION, MUSICAL; EMOTION; EXPRESSION; FUNCTION OF ART; REPRESENTATION.

WRITINGS

Vom Musikalisch-Schönen (Leipzig: 1854); 7th edn (Leipzig: 1885); trans. G. Cohen, *The Beautiful in Music* (London and New York: Novello, Ewer, 1891).

Aus meinem Leben [From my life] (Berlin: Allgemeiner Verein für Deutsche Litteratur, 1894).

Hanslick's Music Criticisms, trans. and ed. H. Pleasants (New York: Dover, 1988).

BIBLIOGRAPHY

Budd, M.: 'The repudiation of emotion: Hanslick on music', *British Journal of Aesthetics*, 20 (1980), 29–43.

MALCOLM BUDD

harmony and symmetry 'Harmony' is an important term in music theory, with a well defined range of application. The aesthetic use of harmony is undoubtedly based on musical analogies; within philosophical aesthetics, 'harmony' has an extended range of uses which are important in their own right. There are at least three senses of 'harmony' which need to be examined.

The first use can be traced back to Pythagoras and extends through much of the classical and mediaeval use of the term in aesthetic contexts. The specific root is in the small-number ratios of a vibrating string, which relate frequency of vibration to the length of the string. This elementary physical discovery is projected on to a cosmological scale, so that harmony is understood as a relation between what there is in the world and the spheres that form the universe. 'The music of the spheres' can be taken as a literal phenomenon, and harmony as the relation that holds between the spheres and the earth. Extended to aesthetics, then, harmony in works of art and of nature is a fundamental cosmological relation. A harmonious statue reflects not the actual forms of the body but the ideal forms of the body in their relation to purely intelligible forms which remain unseen.

The leading advocate of this view of harmony is Plotinus. Tractate 6 of bk 1 of the *Enneads* incorporates all of the essential elements of metaphysical harmony which are subsequenty exploited by aesthetics. Plotinus bases his identification of beauty upon likeness and communion: 'We hold that all the loveliness of this world comes by communion in Ideal-Form.' Its opposite is shapelessness. Its perfection is unity. 'Where the Ideal-Form has entered, it has grouped and coordinated what from a diversity of parts was to become a unity: it has rallied confusion into cooperation: it has made the sum one harmonious coherence: for the Idea is a unity and what it moulds must come to unity as far as multiplicity may' (*Enneads* 1. 6. 2). On the other hand, Plotinus rejects symmetry as a criterion for beauty. The counter-examples cited range over the field of possibilities, but the underlying argument is that symmetry would make beauty impossible in cases of identity and unity, while introducing it in cases which have merely repetitious iteration.

In the classical and mediaeval uses of harmony, the harmonious relation and the beauty it produces are objective. A harmony in the object reflects a harmony in the cosmos. The famous definition of beauty by Aquinas in the *Summa Theologiae* sums up this use: 'For beauty includes three conditions: *integrity* or *perfection*, since those things which are impaired are by that very fact ugly; due *proportion* or *harmony*; and lastly, *brightness*, or *clarity*, whence things are called beautiful which have a bright colour'. Beauty itself, as Aquinas describes it here, bears a likeness to a property of the second person of the Trinity, whose mediating function is theologically central, so the

harmony or proportion which makes up beauty is essential to the relation between the divine and the human.

The second use of 'harmony' shifts the relation from cosmology to the response of the spectator. In itself, this is not contrary to the more objective use, since a harmony of response implies a teleology and final cause in a transcendent reality. In the seventeenth- and eighteenth-century reformulations of aesthetic principles along empiricist lines, harmony remains a prominent term. However, harmony is within the senses. Francis Hutcheson, for example, claims: 'There are vastly greater pleasures in those complex ideas of objects, which obtain the names of beautiful, regular, harmonious' (Hutcheson, 1725, p. 8). Shaftesbury, whom Hutcheson acknowledges, had already provided a link by shifting the neo-Platonic concepts of beauty and virtue into more experiential contexts. Hutcheson and the eighteenth-century theorists who follow him all agree not only that beauty is fundamentally a feeling experienced uniquely by the subject, but also that a harmonious feeling which is pleasurable in itself produces that beauty. All of the attempts to systematically identify this aesthetic feeling focus on a pleasure which is immediately felt and suggest criteria for producing this feeling which in one way or another include harmony. Hutcheson's 'uniformity amidst variety' is only one among many such attempts.

A third use of 'harmony' emerges from this subjective turn. For Shaftesbury and Hutcheson and for the major practitioners in both the visual and the literary arts, harmony is achieved through the arrangement of the object. If they refer that arrangement to the experience of the audience, still they believe that a correlation can be worked out according to rules and empirical generalizations about responses. But such rules and generalizations prove impossible to establish in the face of counter-examples. The alternative is to find harmony not in the arrangement of the object at all but in the play of the faculties themselves. This move begins to be worked out in writers such as Joseph Priestley and Edmund Burke, who suggest that aesthetic pleasure arises from the way the faculties are stimulated and employed. To be found aesthetically pleasurable, works must employ the faculties of the mind in moderate ways – neither over-stimulating nor boring it. This faculty psychology emerges into a full-fledged aesthetic theory in Kant's *Critique of Judgement*.

Kant bases the universality of aesthetic judgements not on some cosmic harmony but on a common operation of the faculties of judging themselves: 'Now this merely subjective (aesthetic) judging of the object, or of the presentation by which it is given, precedes the pleasure in the object and is the basis of this pleasure, [a pleasure] in the harmony of the cognitive powers' (Kant, 1987 [1790], p. 62). Harmony in this usage is not a harmony of parts of the object at all. It is a harmony which exists in the faculties and the way that they construe the sensory input available to them. Benedetto Croce makes this Kantian project the foundation for his claim that it is the activity of the cognitive imagination itself which constitutes beauty, by the very act of giving organization and coherence to cognitive activity.

This Kantian sense of harmony and its neo-Kantian and idealist extensions to imagination are difficult to apply. Harmony becomes psychological, but other terms such as Kant's 'disinterestedness' and Edward Bullough's 'psychical distance' do a better job of evoking the psychological states of the audience, without binding aesthetic theory to a faculty psychology. Harmony suffers something of the same fate as beauty, with which it is so closely identified. Both tend to drop out of the modern aesthetic vocabulary because they imply metaphysical commitments for which empiricist, subjectivized aesthetics has little need.

The theme common to all of the uses described thus far is order. Beauty is identified with order. Harmony describes the ordering principles of art and aesthetic response, whatever they may be. As aesthetic theory shifts in a subjective direction, so the source of order shifts. It is found by later writers not in the cosmos but in the ordering mind itself. But it remains the case throughout that the presence of order is a final cause of aesthetic qualities. The mythological move from chaos into order first appears as a harmony in the universe and subsequently makes its way into the subjective harmony of the faculties.

In twentieth-century aesthetics, 'harmony' and 'symmetry' are important terms in formal analysis, but their priority is reversed. They still have their roots in a quest for order and proportion. But symmetry, not harmony, most effectively describes formal properties. The kind of counter-examples used by Plotinus to show that 'symmetry' could not be a necessary or sufficient condition for beauty no longer work if one gives up the requirement that the term be used as a part of a definition of beauty.

Moreover, symmetry in particular seems to permit conditions of applicability. It differs in this respect from terms such as 'graceful' and 'garish'. Frank Sibley has argued that the aesthetic use of those terms and others like them is not condition-governed at all. But one can establish conditions for formal symmetry in most arts. One can say of a Mondrian painting that it is symmetrical, while a Barnett Newman is asymmetrical, and point to precisely the conditions which establish the symmetry of the one and the asymmetry of the other. However, it is not clear what one has accomplished aesthetically with such descriptions. Disharmony and asymmetry do not seem to be conditions which prevent aesthetic response. Seeing the symmetry in a poem or painting is obviously aesthetically important, but neither the presence nor absence of symmetry determines what one's response will be.

As technical terms, symmetry and harmony have a clear sense; they function in the same way as terms such as 'saturated' (of colour) and 'first person' (of narrative). Thus, as descriptors in formal analysis, they continue to be useful. But if they are to retain any significant aesthetic function, they must be reintegrated into a theory, and in a period when aesthetic theory is itself in rather bad repute, it is not clear how that is to be done. Arthur Danto might suggest that the use of such terms is itself constitutive of theory – that they in effect carry their theory with them. But that ignores the well worked out role that harmony has played in earlier theories of beauty.

If one could first say what it is for something to be an aesthetic object, then it might be possible to say whether harmony and symmetry play a significant theoretical role in the way that they did within the aesthetics of beauty. But there is no guarantee that they would. The importance of dissonance and randomness in modern art may limit the role that harmony and symmetry will play in aesthetic theory.

See also BEAUTY; FORM; HUTCHESON; KANT; PLOTINUS.

BIBLIOGRAPHY

Danto, Arthur: 'The artworld', *Journal of Philosophy*, 61 (1964), 571–84.
Hutcheson, Francis: *An Inquiry Into the Original of Our Ideas of Beauty and Virtue* (London, J. Danby, 1725).
Kant, Immanuel: *Kritik der Urteilskraft* (Berlin: 1790); trans. Werner S. Pluhar, *Critique of Judgement* (Indianapolis: Hackett, 1987).
Plotinus: *Enneads*, trans. Stephen MacKenna (London: Faber & Faber, 1966).
Sibley, Frank: 'Aesthetic concepts', *Philosophical Review*, 67 (1959), 421–50.

DABNEY TOWNSEND

Hegel, Georg Wilhelm Friedrich (1770–1831) The most important German philosopher of the early nineteenth century; his all-embracing Absolute Idealism was an immense influence on later thinkers, including such critics as Kierkegaard and Marx. Hegel's writings provide what is arguably the most systematic and comprehensive aesthetic theory of the modern world (and *a fortiori* for all time, since aesthetics, in the strict sense, is a discourse that begins only in the eighteenth century).

It has become customary to describe as 'Hegelian' all of those approaches to the arts which understand them in terms of a meaningful succession of styles, or as expressions of the world views of cultures or historical periods. While this is a rather loose designa-

tion, it is indeed the case that Hegel's aesthetics played a fundamental role in the formation of literary history and the history of art in the nineteenth century. It would be only a slight exaggeration to say that every philosophical aesthetician in the nineteenth and twentieth centuries has been either a Kantian or a Hegelian. Kantian aesthetics focuses on those characteristics of aesthetic experience that differentiate it from others (knowledge and action) and insists, in one way or another, on the contemplation of form as the defining characteristic of the aesthetic. Hegelian aesthetics emphasizes the meaning and the content of works of art and takes those works to be superior, everything else being equal, which have as their content the most concrete and fully articulated idea.

Despite this contrast, Hegel's aesthetics (like his entire philosophical project) would not have been possible except for Kant's thought and for post-Kantian romanticism, which regarded art and beauty as providing our most profound access to the real. Hegel's early writings show him to be first a participant in and then an early critic of this romantic aestheticism. In 'The earliest system-programme of German idealism' (which apparently emerged out of youthful exchanges between Hegel, Hölderlin and Schelling), Hegel writes that 'the highest act of reason, the one through which it encompasses all ideas, is an aesthetic act and . . . truth and goodness only become sisters in beauty'; and he speaks of the need for philosophy to become poetic and poetry to become philosophical, in order that a new aesthetically appealing religion of reason may arise.

By the time of his first major work, *The Phenomenology of Spirit* (1807), Hegel had become a critic of aestheticism and spoke now of the absolute priority to be accorded to *Wissenschaft* (science, wisdom or knowledge) over the representational, intuitive and figurative knowing that mark the limits of art and religion. Nevertheless, the *Phenomenology* contains some of the most significant philosophical writings on the arts, including a speculative analysis of tragedy, a theory of the development and dissolution of Greek art and a commentary on Diderot's comic and satiric masterpiece, *Rameau's Nephew*. The *Phenomenology* can be read as a contest between the claims of art and those of philosophical science, and while it is clear where Hegel's final allegiance lies, recent philosophers (notably Jacques Derrida in *Glas*) have pointed out that, despite his assurances, Hegel's text is less scientific and more artistic than he would have us believe.

Beginning after his arrival at his final teaching position in Berlin, Hegel began to lecture periodically on the philosophy of fine arts, or aesthetics. The text that is called Hegel's *Aesthetics* is a collation of various student transcripts and some of Hegel's own manuscript notes for these lectures, over a number of years (the publication and editing of such materials is still going on, and while the main outlines of Hegel's mature aesthetics are clear, we ought to expect some new emphases and analyses to emerge). Hegel – in a way that is documented of no earlier philosopher – took a comprehensive and many-sided interest in the arts, travelling to picture galleries and reading extensively in the literatures of the world; this artistic concern reached a peak in Berlin, where he took a passionate interest in opera and the theatre and befriended a number of actors. Nevertheless, by the time of the lectures Hegel is announcing what is (somewhat misleadingly) called his 'death of art' thesis, opening his lectures with the claim that art has exhausted its potential and that 'it is now, on its highest side, a thing of the past.' Art, he argues, has not merely been displaced by science (a science of dialectical wisdom, we should recall), but is now a subject-matter for science; in other words, this is the era of institutions such as the museum and the formation of such intellectual constructions as 'world literature' (a notion apparently invented by Hegel's contemporary, Goethe), in which it is possible to know peoples and cultures by a comparative study of their literary expressions.

HEGEL'S DIALECTICAL THEORY OF ART: THE *PHENOMENOLOGY OF SPIRIT*

Most accounts of Hegel's aesthetics are based almost exclusively on the lecture course. This is unfortunate, because the lectures tend to focus on the meaning of art independently of the role of the artist and the audience. In the *Phenomenology*, in the sections entitled 'Natural religion' and 'The religion of art', Hegel develops a complex account of the dialectic of the production and reception of artworks, or of intention and interpretation, in which the meaning of the work is a triadic relation between the artist, the artefact and the audience. Although Hegel's concrete material for this analysis is taken only from the ancient world (Egypt, the Near East and Greece), the lines of analysis are arguably applicable to all artistic production and reception; this is not surprising if we recall that he thinks of the Greeks as the supremely artistic culture. Hegel provides a narrative account of how art first emerges from a more mechanical, crafts-like endeavour; he then proceeds to explain the development of Greek art as the increasingly conscious and articulate attempt to overcome the gaps of sympathy and understanding that arise when an artefact must mediate between producer and consumer; the story ends, like so many Hegelian narratives, with a moment of attained recognition or identity in difference among all the parties to the artistic transaction.

In the inital form of the religion of art, which Hegel calls 'abstract', a created work such as a sculpture stands as something of an obstacle between artist and audience. Those who admire the finished piece do not really comprehend it if they focus only on its surface beauty and fail to grasp the thought, activity and labour that the artist put into his work. The artist, too, will reflect on the discrepancy between the static form (of the god or hero) and the life or vitality it was meant to embody. By implication Hegel is critical of a major tradition in German thought (represented by Wickelmann and Kant, among others) according to which Greek sculpture is an unsurpassable model; for Hegel it is a failure, despite its beauty. Faced with this failure or impasse artists turn, on Hegel's analysis, to forms that aim at collapsing the distinction between artist and audience;

these are works of 'living art' such as hymns, Dionysiac revels or Olympic games (twentieth-century analogies would be participatory theatre or 'happenings', just as Hegel's 'abstract art' would find its parallel in such movements as minimalist art).

The problem that Hegel finds with the living work of art is that it fails to achieve a fully conscious wholeness, or totality, because it must be either completely transient (in active forms like the revel) or static and detached (as in more disciplined, choreographed displays of human bodies). What is needed, he says, is a medium that is both internal and external, exhibiting characteristics of both motion and rest. This he finds in language, which offers the possibility of an identity of meaning for artist, work and audience. Even within this 'spiritual' art, however, Hegel sees a series of approximations to this identity in the forms of epic, tragedy and comedy. The content of these genres has to do with the relations of men and gods, and for Hegel that relation is a figurative way of talking about the relation between finite and infinite mind.

The epic presents an ultimately confused picture of all action in which the ostensible agents, the gods, sink to trivial and all too human behaviour, while men can obtain a heroic stature apparently not accessible to immortals. The same situation is reflected in the communicative structure of the epic itself, in which the singer claims to be nothing but a mouthpiece for the muse and the audience is alienated from the poem's content by the realization that the latter tells of human beings of a long-lost heroic era beside which they appear insignificant. Hegel takes the presence of fate in the epic to be the sign that there is something seriously flawed in the way that this artwork understands itself and the task of art. The development of art requires a more daring and less qualified form of consciousness that will expel fate, depopulate the heavens, and leave all the participants with the deep sense that they have learned about their own humanity.

Tragedy takes a significant step in this direction because its characters are themselves poets who are artists in so far as their speeches 'make the very inner being external'. However, the chorus and the spectators are still relatively passive and removed from the life of the poet–actors. While the gods tend to be reduced to the single figure of Zeus or to an impersonal fate, either of these still leaves tragedy subject to an uncomprehended necessity.

Comedy, the ultimate form of the religion of art, demonstrates the identity of artist-actors and their audience. While Zeus is dethroned and the vortex reigns in his place, all recognize that 'there's no one here but us human beings.' The mask which stood between artist and audience in tragedy now becomes dispensable, and a mutual recognition is achieved which coincides with an unparalleled 'state of spiritual well-being' – that is, a celebration of human self-consciousness. Hegel marks this achieved identity with a profound pun: 'The actual self of the actor [*Schauspieler*] coincides with his persona or mask [*Person*], just as the spectator [*Zuschauer*] is completely at home in the drama performed before him and sees himself playing in it.' Production and consumption or intention and interpretation are not, on this dialectical view, always and necessarily distinct; it is in fact the task of art to bring them together.

HEGEL'S SYSTEM OF AESTHETICS

For Hegel, aesthetics is concerned essentially with the beauty of art rather than with natural beauty or some free-floating aesthetic experience. This is because art is one of the modes, along with religion and philosophy, or absolute spirit, in which mind comes to know itself and its activities. Hegel defines the beauty of art as the manifestation of the idea in sensuous form. The idea is not any random thought or concept, but the idea of the whole, or totality, the self-expression and self-understanding which is the aim of all human thought. Art is a way in which the mind comes home to itself, displaying and reflecting on its truth. Much of the content of art is religious, but it must be remembered that for Hegel religion is not intrinsically mysterious; it is, rather, a revelation of what mind is.

In the lectures, Hegel distinguishes three main forms of art that are differentiated in terms of the relation that holds in each between idea and sensuous form. In *symbolic art* there is a discrepancy between the idea grasped in a relatively crude and minimal way and a profusion of specific forms that attempt to embody the idea. The paradigm of such art for Hegel is the religious art of India and Egypt in which, as he sees it, there is a restless search for the appropriate form for the gods, or a series of hints and approximations that are never fully adequate to their object. Symbolic art is typically sublime in so far as it testifies to a failure of adequation and to the insufficiency of artistic means. Hegel manages thus to demote the sublime from the position it occupied in eighteenth-century aesthetics (for instance, in Burke and Kant) as coordinate with or even more significant than the beautiful; for him, the sublime is a lower or preparatory stage of beauty itself, and its relative inadequacy is a function of just that indeterminacy and formlessness which impressed earlier thinkers.

The most sophisticated form of symbolic art are works like the sphinxes of Egypt, which on the one hand embody a sense of mystery and on the other hint at its solution as the human form begins to emerge from animal and geometrical shapes. While Hegel's account of non-Western art may sound naïvely chauvinistic, it is based on a rather extraordinary range of knowledge for a thinker of his time; and the lectures on aesthetics themselves were a major impetus in the Western movement, gathering momentum in the nineteenth century, to accord a significant status to non-Western art.

The middle term of the three great art forms is *classical art*, and here Hegel's material is drawn mainly from ancient Greece. Here the form 'is the free and adequate embodiment of the idea in the shape peculiarly appropriate to the idea itself in its essential nature' (Hegel, 1975, p. 77). Although Hegel is still regarded by some as an extreme idealist and rationalist, he argues that the anthropomorphism of this form of art is absolutely necessary, 'since spirit appears sensuously in a satisfying way only in [a human] body' (Hegel, 1975, p. 78). The beautiful bodies of Greek sculpture are echoed in Greek poetry, where word and action are perfectly adequate to conception and all residues of mystery have been eliminated. The price that must be paid for the supreme beauty of classical art, however, is a certain limitation in the depth and intensity of its spiritual world.

In *romantic art*, spirit is known as 'infinite subjectivity' and 'absolute inwardness', such that its riches could never be presented in any sensuous form. This romantic art (which Hegel sometimes identifies as Christian art) often takes as its theme the very inadequacy and insufficiency of bodily beauty; representations of the crucifixion, for example, can be seen as negations of the perfect, unblemished bodies of Greek sculpture. If classical art is supremely beautiful, romantic art is more spiritual. Hegel traces the development of romantic art from its explicit concern with Christian themes, through their gradual secularization in the literature of chivalry, which deals with the deeply internal themes of honour, love and fidelity, to the formation of modern characters (like those of Shakespearean drama) that have an independence and freedom not known in art's earlier phases. It is here that he begins to speculate about the dissolution (*Auflösung*) of art, sometimes referred to (a bit simplistically) as 'the death of art'. His claim is that the romantic concentration on inwardness and subjectivity has led to a condition in which art is no longer determined by any specific content; rather, the artists themselves have been liberated through criticism and reflection, and now they are radically free in their choice of styles and themes. Interest in art has shifted to the artist's persona, and the artist of the late romantic phase may exploit this interest in a humorous or ironic mode (here we might think of Picasso's career of many styles, or the profound irony of Marcel Duchamp, in order to suggest the plausibility of Hegel's projection of art's new vocation). Hegel, of course, never claimed that the production and appreciation of art would simply cease; in that sense he held no 'death of art' thesis. He did argue that a certain essential history of art had come to an end, and that once this history had become an object of knowledge (for aesthetics, the history of art, the museum and so on) artists themselves would become inspired and cheerful players in an inexhaustible game of the imagination.

Coordinate with Hegel's distinction between the general symbolic, classic and romantic forms of art is his theory of the individual arts and their system. It should come as no surprise that he thinks of the individual arts as forming a hierarchy, rising from those most tied to the constraints of the material world (for instance, architecture) to those that are first, or most ideal, in this respect (for instance, poetry). Art becomes actual only in particular works in specific media, and every concrete work must be understood in terms of the specific potentials and limits of the individual art of which it is an instance. Architecture is the attempt to master and subordinate an external inorganic medium to make it an appropriate vehicle for spirit. Because of the obstinacy of its medium, it is typically a symbolic art; however, it is not exclusively so, and Hegel comments penetratingly on architecture's development from such enclosed symbolic forms as the Egyptian pyramids to structures of a more human scale like Greek temples, and then to Gothic architecture which dematerializes matter in soaring cathedrals where light transforms the resistant stone. Similarly, sculpture is paradigmatically but not exclusively a classical form of art. In the first instance it presents the image of a god, or of a human being conceived on the model of the gods' tranquillity and self-sufficiency. Sculpture no longer processes its material externally as architecture did, simply in order to bear and distribute weight or provide shelter from the elements, but constructs its works under the aspect of the bodily form.

The individual arts are further dematerialized in painting, which is a relatively ideal medium because it is limited to two dimensions and is concerned with appearance as such, where appearance is understood as something that must be subjectively enter-

tained. This play with appearance allows painting a far greater range of subjects, styles and treatments than the preceding more material arts. Painting portrays not only the many forms of human consciousness by capturing expression and nuances of mood; it also conveys the subjective act of perception as such, when (as in Dutch painting of the seventeenth century which seems to be, for Hegel, the highest variety of painting) it exhibits human vision as such in manifesting evanescent qualities of light, atmosphere and texture. Music moves further into the inner world by abandoning spatial form altogether; sound has no obvious material embodiment and it must be heard sequentially – that is, perceived only in time, which is, of course, the form of the inner life. Even more specifically, the musician's ability to repeat a theme with variations and the listener's capacity to grasp and recall it are forms of what Hegel calls *Erinnerung*, reinternalization or a making inward again, at a higher level. (For Hegel, *Erinnerung* is the very form of spirit's activity in realizing and becoming aware of itself; the English 'recollection' is at best a pale translation of this fundamental concept.)

Poetry, by which Hegel designates what we would call imaginative literature, is the supremely inward art. He claims that its external embodiments are relatively accidental and that it exists completely in the imagination, so that it is fully translatable from one language to another: 'Poetry is the universal art of the spirit which has become free in itself and which is not tied down for its realization to external sensuous material; instead, it launches out exclusively in the inner space and the inner time of ideas and feelings' (Hegel, 1975, p. 89). Poetry is the most philosophical art, exhibiting dialectical relations and structures in the imaginative worlds it creates; Hegel devotes about as much space to it as to all of the other arts together. Where much philosophical aesthetics claims that the meaning of poetry is ambiguous, implicit, metaphorical or suggestive, Hegel holds that its meaning is explicit – although we must grasp this explicit meaning in a dialectical way, rather than in terms of the propositional logic of the understanding. He analyses these dialectical structures in considering the three genres of epic, lyric and drama with respect to their various transformations of the subject–object relation.

The *epic* poet might seem to be a subject passively recording a world external to him. Yet the content of the epic (he is thinking of Homer in particular) yields a different view. The hero of the epic is neither simply a product of his world nor its cause; epic society cannot be understood either as a collection of human atoms nor as a holistic unit whose properties determine all its members. The hero emerges from his world and is of it, yet he transcends it in his individuality, as Achilles does with his towering wrath and his demand for honour from Zeus. The epic world is a poetic one, prior to the fixed ordinances of law and based on more flexible forms of individual allegiance. Even the items or objects of this world are understood in terms of their makers and their histories, rather than as neutral objects. The *lyric* stance is that of the individual poetic voice who has reflectively withdrawn from a regularized world in which he or she had been engaged. The lyric is not a merely solipsistic meditation or retreat, however, but the site of a conflict between the independent freedom of the poet and its infinitely variable subject-matter.

The *drama* is the most dialectical of poetic forms because it exhibits both subjects becoming objective (the character's action constituting the dramatic world) and the objective becoming subjective (the world giving rise to individual expression). Drama is concerned specifically with conflict and its (possible) resolution. Hegel's analysis of ancient tragedy is that it is an art demonstrating the inevitable conflict of two forces, each having its own legitimacy; in *Antigone*, which he calls the supreme tragedy, it is the clash between the male, explicit law of the public world (or state) and the female, implicit law of the private world or family. Such clashes are necessary in the ancient world because human beings there are split between their public and private dimensions; poetry is the way in which that world becomes conscious of itself. In modern drama dialectical developments are more complex and are not tied to the social structures of the ancient world; modern drama deals with individuals who are no longer types of the different social spheres into which the ancient world was divided. At the height of modern drama (Shakespeare, for example), these individuals become poets themselves, showing by their beautiful speeches that they have risen beyond their terrible circumstances to a poetic vision of their own careers (cf. the last soliloquies of Macbeth and Cleopatra). It is this rise to self-consciousness that is typical of Hegel's understanding of art, and which forms the guiding theme of his metanarrative of art's history.

See also ART HISTORY; AUTONOMY, AESTHETIC; BEAUTY; 'END OF ART'; FUNCTION OF ART; RELIGION AND ART.

WRITINGS

Hegel on Tragedy, ed. Anne and Henry Paolucci (New York: 1962).
'The earliest system-programme of German idealism', *Hegel's Development: Toward the Sunlight*, H.S. Harris (Oxford: Oxford University Press, 1972), pp. 510–12.
Hegel's Aesthetics: Lectures on Fine Art, 2 vols (Berlin: 1835–8); trans. T.M. Knox (Oxford: Oxford University Press, 1975).
Hegel's Phenomenology of Spirit, trans. A.V. Miller (Oxford: Oxford University Press, 1979).

BIBLIOGRAPHY

Bungay, Stephen: *Beauty and Truth: A Study of Hegel's Aesthetics* (New York: 1984).
Derrida, Jacques: *Glas* (Paris: 1974); trans. John P. Leavey, Jr, and Richard Rand (Lincoln, Nebr.: University of Nebraska Press, 1986).
Desmond, William: *Art and the Absolute: A Study of Hegel's Aesthetics* (Albany, NY: State University of New York Press, 1986).
Pöggeler, Otto, ed.: *Hegel in Berlin* (Berlin: 1981).
Shapiro, Gary: 'An ancient quarrel in Hegel's *Phenomenology*', *Owl of Minerva*, 17: 2 (1986), 165–80.

Shapiro, Gary, ed. 'Hegel on art and literature', *Clio*, 11, 4 (1982).
Steinkraus, Warren and Schmitz, Kenneth, eds *Art and Logic in Hegel's Philosophy* (New York: Humanities Press, 1980).

GARY SHAPIRO

Heidegger, Martin (1889–1976) German philosopher; a pupil of Husserl, and a main inspiration for several twentieth-century developments, including existentialism, hermeneutics, and postmodernism.

Poetry, and the arts more generally, became central to Heidegger's thought during the years 1934–7. The first part of *Being and Time* had been published in 1927 and was left unfinished. Then, shortly after the disastrous rectoral address of 1933 in which he aligned himself with National Socialism, Heidegger turned his attention to art, and to Hölderlin and Nietzsche. He devoted one term to a lecture course on Hölderlin's poetry, *Hölderlins Hymnen 'Germanien' und 'Der Rhein'* [Hölderlin's hymns 'Germanien' and 'The Rhein'], from which the essay 'Hölderlin and the essence of poetry' was largely drawn; he gave the lecture course *An Introduction to Metaphysics*, which included a reading of the chorus on man from Sophocles' *Antigone*; he wrote the lectures 'The origin of the work of art', first published in 1950; and he delivered, under the title 'The will to power as art', the first of four lecture courses on Nietzsche.

Heidegger locates the origin of the work of art not in the genius of the artist or the taste of the observer, but in art itself. The claim of 'The origin of the work of art', that art is an origin, translates into philosophical language Hölderlin's line, 'But what remains the poets establish'. But with Hölderlin (1770–1843) as his guide to poetry and the arts in general, Heidegger seems more often to be concerned with translating philosophical language into poetic language than vice versa. According to Heidegger, poetic language has a unique capacity to introduce and preserve novelty, which is why he refers all the arts, and language itself, to poetry (Heidegger, 1971b, p. 74). He attaches an importance to poetry

virtually unparalleled in the philosophical tradition. It might not be too much to say that he resolves the 'old quarrel between philosophy and poetry' by placing philosophy at the service of poetry (Heidegger, 1979, p. 190).

The brief history of aesthetics and art to be found in the 1936–7 course on Nietzsche establishes the proper context for reading Heidegger's writings on art (Heidegger, 1979, pp. 77–91). He claims that aesthetics, in the sense of reflection on feelings inspired by the beautiful, did not begin until Plato and Aristotle, who came after the great period of Greek art. If aesthetics began when art started to decline, it is fitting that aesthetics attained its highest point with Hegel and the claim that great art had come to an end. Far from questioning Hegel's declaration that art is 'in its highest vocation . . . a thing of the past' (Hegel, 1975, p. 11), Heidegger suggests that the greatness of Hegel's achievement derives from this recognition of the end of great art. But Heidegger ends his history of aesthetics with Nietzsche and not Hegel. Whereas Hegel turned to religion and philosophy as the place where the absolute was to be established following the sublation of art, Nietzsche thought that religion and philosophy had lost their creative force and that art was to be pursued as the counter-movement of nihilism. Heidegger shares Nietzsche's conviction that turning to art is the thinker's best recourse in this crisis, and he assigns to the thinker the task of overcoming aesthetics and so preparing for the possible return of great art.

In 'The origin of the work of art' Heidegger takes up that task by addressing aesthetics, and especially Hegel's *Aesthetics*, in at least two different ways. First, 'The origin of the work of art' confronts the Greek interpretation of art in terms of *technē*. According to Heidegger, *technē* does not mean 'art' or 'craft' so much as 'know-how', the mode of knowing appropriate to *poiēsis*, which itself is to be understood not just as 'production' but as 'bringing forth' (Heidegger, 1971b, p. 59). The breadth of the Greek conception determines not only subsequent philosophical reflection on art, but also the basic categories in terms of which all things are understood, and not just things produced by human beings for their own use. So, according to Heidegger, the form–matter distinction derives from the experience of making and is properly applied only to equipment or use-objects. That this distinction provides one of the most pervasive frameworks in terms of which art and poetry are analysed within aesthetics lends some of the impact to Heidegger's suggestion that the artwork would be better approached in terms of world and earth. The work of art does not use up its materials as a piece of equipment does. It opens up a world and sets the world back on the earth, the ground on which and in which human beings dwell.

The culmination of Heidegger's reflections on *technē* can be found in 'The question concerning technology'. In this 1953 essay, he refers the dominance of technology within the West to the dominance within Greek thought of the experience of *poiēsis* and *technē*. Whereas he was earlier somewhat ambiguous on this point, in this context he regards it as something positive that the Greeks lacked a special word for art and employed the pair of terms, *poiēsis* and *technē*, to cover all man-made products. Heidegger reminds his readers that in a technological world one has the impression of living in an environment in which human beings seem to encounter only themselves and their products. This description recalls the basis that Hegel gave for establishing the place of art within his system: art is 'born of the spirit and born again' (Hegel, 1975, p. 2), and so constitutes a site where spirit recognizes itself in its own products.

However, according to Heidegger, this widespread impression, and the Hegelian philosophy that appeals to it, are misleading. Human beings do not everywhere encounter themselves in such a world, because they nowhere encounter human essence as such. More precisely, they do not see themselves as addressed by what Heidegger refers to as 'the historical determinations of Being'. And yet the very proximity of making, on the one hand, and poetry and the arts, on the other – as suggested by the fact that they were both understood by the Greeks in terms of *poiēsis*,

or revealing – comes to suggest to Heidegger that poetry may possibly rescue us from this impasse by reawakening our sense of being as that which grants to things their appearance (Heidegger, 1977, p. 35). Although the language is obscure at this point, it would seem to correspond closely to what he understands by the 'excess' of the origin at the earlier essay on art (Heidegger, 1971b, p. 75). To put it another way, essences do not endure permanently so as to underwrite timelessly valid concepts. Essences, including the essence of poetry, are historical and belong to a specific time (Heidegger, 1968, p. 313).

A second way in which 'The origin of the work of art' can be said to contribute to the overcoming of aesthetics is in its approach to the question of the so-called death of art. Hegel may not be mentioned explicitly by Heidegger in the 1935 lecture version of 'The origin of the work of art' until the epilogue, but the question of the end of art, reformulated as the question of whether great art is still possible, dominates the text and is left open at its conclusion. For Heidegger, the vocation of art is to be an origin, a distinctive way in which truth, in the Heideggerian sense of 'unconcealment', becomes historical. Two of his examples have since become famous. Van Gogh's painting of peasant shoes reveals more about such shoes than any direct examination of them would show: Heidegger says that the painting reveals their truth and that of the world to which they belong. More telling still is the example of the Greek temple. That the temple gave 'to things their look and to men their outlook on themselves' exemplifies what it means to write of the truth of the artwork, because it seems clearer in this case in what sense art might be an origin. The example also suggests that an artwork ceases to be a work when it no longer opens up a world – which happens, in this case, when the gods have fled from it (Heidegger, 1971b, p. 43).

Hegel's question of the death of art, therefore, becomes the question of whether art is to serve simply as a way of cultivating our feelings and of maintaining contact with the past, or whether it may still open up or found a world. This is an open question for Heidegger, and neither his reference to Van Gogh nor his subsequent discussions of Stravinsky, Klee, Gottfried Benn, Rilke, Stefan George or Georg Trakl provides an answer. It was far from clear to Heidegger that these contemporary examples were great art in the operative sense of announcing and enshrining the truths of an epoch. For him, the fate of Hölderlin would decide the issue.

In Heidegger's essays and lectures on Hölderlin, Hegel's question of the past character of art finds itself transposed into the question of the time between the gods who have fled and the coming gods. Because Heidegger came to prefer Hölderlin's language to a more traditionally philosophical language, he has been accused of retreating into occultism. And because the turn to poetizing came so soon after his resignation as rector at Freiburg University it has been understood as a result of his disillusionment with politics, following disillusionment with the Nazi party. However, the publication of his lectures, and two early versions of 'The origin of the work of art', tell a different story (Bernasconi, 1992). Heidegger describes his first writings on Hölderlin as politics 'in its highest and most authentic sense' (Heidegger, 1980, p. 214). He makes it clear that he has turned to Hölderlin not simply because he is 'the poet of poets' (Heidegger, 1968, p. 295); but because he is also 'the poet of the Germans' (Heidegger, 1980, p. 214). Art is not to be considered something given. The case for reading Hölderlin is not made on the grounds that his status as a great poet has already been established. That remains to be decided, and it will be decided only by the German people – or rather, on the basis of whether the German public becomes a people, a *Volk*, in listening to Hölderlin's poetry. In opening up a world, the aspect of the artwork emphasized almost exclusively by 'The origin of the work of art' until its final page, the poet also founds a people.

The nationalistic language in which Heidegger approached Hölderlin casts a shadow over his lectures from the 1930s, made all the more disturbing by his failure after the Second World War to address the context in which they were written. It goes almost unnoticed that, by referring art to the people, Heidegger did at least expose the isolating tendency characteristic of so much of modern aesthetics, where the aesthetic experience has often been largely a matter of subjective feeling.

In his devotion to Hölderlin, Heidegger places the thinker at the service of the poet: 'The historical determination of philosophy reaches its summit in acknowledging the necessity of creating a hearing for Hölderlin's word' (Heidegger, 1989, p. 422). The thinker's task is to prepare the space for art to create its own space. Nevertheless, the thinker does not submit to the poet. This is apparent in the transformation which Hölderlin's poetry undergoes in the course of the dialogue between poetizing and thinking – a transformation which, as scholars have emphasized, amounts at times to pure distortion. One can even construe such errors in interpretation as being partly responsible for more far-reaching errors (Gethmann-Siefert, 1989, p. 79), thereby giving the debate a seriousness that threatens Heidegger's attempt to distance himself from the scholarship of literary history (Heidegger, 1971a, p. 7).

There is also the question of whether the transformation undergone by thinking in the course of its dialogue with poetizing does not also tempt it to abrogate its responsibilities. But before such charges can be substantiated, more must be done to appreciate the far from trivial concerns that led Heidegger down this path. In the 1950s, especially in the essays inspired by George and Trakl, he sought an experience with language that would be not just a matter of the feelings of a human subject, but transformative of historical existence. These essays represent one further step in a long-standing attempt to break the grip of the so-called rational or calculative thinking of modern philosophy, and return to the 'poetic thinking' characteristic of early Greek thinkers. For Heidegger, the poetic is the basic capacity for what he calls dwelling, which is why his thought has proved inspirational in some of the more academic corners of the ecology movement.

Heidegger's adoption of Hölderlin's language throughout his later work has mys-

tified the uninitiated and frustrated traditionally minded philosophers. Most frustrating to
aestheticians is that Heidegger does not offer
a philosophy of art in the familiar sense, so
that it is far from easy to assess where he
stands in relation to the standard debates.
Heidegger was engaged in the overcoming of
aesthetics. He showed how certain characteristics of Western metaphysics have
governed the philosophical approach to art:
such characteristics as its conceptions of
truth as correctness, and of space as something to be occupied; its reliance on the distinction between form and matter; and its
appeal to the lived experience of the isolated
individual.

Above all, art, for Heidegger, was not one
sphere of philosophical investigation among
many. Art, which had been isolated from the
truth, was now said to have a unique relation
to it. Previous generations of Heidegger's
readers have asked whether his reflections on
art succeed in twisting art free of aesthetics.
Late-twentieth-century readers find themselves obliged to ask, in addition, whether it
is only accidental that, to the extent that his
writings on art succeed in surpassing the
confines of aesthetics and enter the political
arena, those writings are found to be conta-
minated by the disastrous politics of national
socialism. Heidegger's thought has already
had such a massive impact on the theory and
practice of literary criticism that it is unlikely
that any consensus will emerge on these
questions in the foreseeable future.

See also 'END OF ART'; HEGEL; TRUTH
AND ART.

WRITINGS

Einführung in die Metaphysik (Tübingen: 1953);
trans. Ralph Manheim, *An Introduction to
Metaphysics* (New Haven, Conn.: Yale Uni-
versity Press, 1959).
'Hölderlin und das Wesen der Dichtung', *Das
Innere Reich* (Munich: 1936); trans. D. Scott,
'Hölderlin and the essence of poetry', *Exist-
ence and Being* (London: Vision, 1968), pp.
293–315.
Erläuterungen zu Hölderlins Dichtung (Frankfurt:
Klostermann, 1971a).

'Der Ursprung des Kunstwerkes', *Holzwege*
(Frankfurt: 1950); trans. A. Hofstadter, 'The
origin of the work of art', *Poetry, Language,
Thought* (New York: Harper & Row, 1971b),
pp. 17–87.
'Die Frage nach der Technik', *Vorträge und
Aufsätze* (Pfullingen: 1954); trans. W. Lovitt,
'The question concerning technology', *The
Question concerning Technology and Other
Essays* (New York: Harper & Row, 1977), pp.
3–35.
Nietzsche, vol. 1 (Pfullingen: 1960); trans. D.F.
Krell, *Nietzsche. The Will to Power as Art* (New
York: Harper & Row, 1979).
Hölderlins Hymnen 'Germanien' und 'Der Rhein',
in *Gesamtausgabe* [Collected Works], vol. 39
(Frankfurt: Klostermann, 1980).

BIBLIOGRAPHY

Bernasconi, R.: *Heidegger in Question* (Atlantic
Highlands, NJ: Humanities Press, 1992),
chs 6, 7, 8.
Gadamer, H.-G.: 'Zur Einführung', *Der
Ursprung des Kunstwerkes* (Stuttgart:
1960); trans. D.E. Linge, 'Heidegger's later
philosophy', *Philosophical Hermeneutics*
(Berkeley, Calif.: University of California
Press, 1976), pp. 213–28.
Gethmann-Siefert, A.: 'Heidegger und Höl-
derlin. Die Überforderung des "Dichters in
dürftiger Zeit" ', *Heidegger und die praktische
Philosophie* (Frankfurt: 1988); trans. R.
Taft, 'Heidegger and Hölderlin: the over-
usage of "Poets in an impoverished time" ',
Research in Phenomenology, 19 (1989), 59–
88.
Hegel, G.W.F.: *Vorlesungen über die Ästhetik*, 3
vols (Berlin: 1835); trans. T.M. Knox, *Aes-
thetics*, 2 vols (Oxford: Oxford University
Press, 1975).
Pöggeler, O.: *Der Denkweg Martin Heideggers*
(Pfullingen: 1963); trans. D. Magurshak
and S. Barber, *Martin Heidegger's Path of
Thinking* (Atlantic Highlands, NJ: Humani-
ties Press, 1987), pp. 167–90.
Taminiaux, J.: 'Le dépassement Heideggérien
de l'esthétique et l'héritage de Hegel' [The
Heideggerian overcoming of the aesthetics
and heritage of Hegel], *Recoupements*
(Brussels: Ousia, 1982), pp. 175–208.

ROBERT BERNASCONI

hermeneutics Construed as *that* theory of interpretation that begins more or less with the work of Friedrich Ast (1778–1841) and Friedrich D.E. Schleiermacher (1768–1834), and includes among its principal lights Wilhelm Dilthey (1833–1911), Hans-Georg Gadamer and Paul Ricoeur (1913–   ), hermeneutics appears to be the unique philosophical tradition spanning two continuous centuries down to the late twentieth that has always centred on the analysis of human understanding as a phenomenon inseparable from a grasp of cultural context, intention and historical change.

Philosophically, these are much more important themes than its ideological roots in the Lutheran Reformation and its initial concern with developing various technical instrumentalities for ensuring the recovery of the original meaning of sacred, legal and classical texts. As a distinct movement, hermeneutics begins very nearly at the turn of the nineteenth century, in the interval just starting to reflect on the significance of the French Revolution for the metaphysics and methodology of history and human culture, for the understanding of history, and for the historical nature of understanding and interpretation. It begins in the interval between the completion of Kant's systematic work and the radical attempt by Hegel to understand thinking as a historically formed competence. It has, in this respect, preserved through its disputatious career a unified sense of a distinct constellation of conceptual themes that, until very recently, has been effectively marginalized, at times even pronounced pernicious, in the strong Anglo-American literature focused on extensional logic, physicalism and the philosophy of the physical sciences.

All that has now changed – quite radically – with the late-twentieth-century doubts about the supposed canons of genuine science, about reductionism, about the elimination of intentionally complex phenomena and about the adequacy of extensionalism, together with the dawning realization of the global importance of two master themes: the Kantian, regarding the symbiosis of the structure of the intelligible world and the structure of thinking; and the Hegelian, regarding thinking's being inherently historicized. For the second has been seen to entail the indefensibility of positing strict necessary invariances regarding the first (*contra* Kant, and possibly also *contra* Hegel), although it has taken the better part of two centuries to appreciate this radical consequence. Since at least the early hermeneutic efforts of Heidegger in *Being and Time* (1927), the theme has come to dominate the hermeneutic tradition and to infect nearly all contemporary philosophical movements, no matter how distant from the original sources of that tradition.

The principal figure of post-Heideggerian hermeneutics, Gadamer, particularly in *Truth and Method* (1960), has effectively installed the notion of the flux of history, the transcience and contingency (and primacy) of cultural tradition, the social emergence and constructive nature of human selves, and the impossibility of giving priority to logical and methodological analysis over the metaphysics of human existence. One finds cognate developments in any number of distinct philosophical programmes that have no particularly close connection with hermeneutics – and which affect the theory of artworks and the theory of their interpretation – for instance, Deweyan pragmatism, Marxian and early Frankfurt critical philosophy, Kuhnian-like philosophies of science, and poststructuralism (notably, in the work of Michel Foucault (1926–89). Late phenomenology shows similar tendencies, as in the work of Merleau-Ponty, but phenomenology and hermeneutics have been inextricably linked ever since the work of Dilthey and Heidegger.

In any case, hermeneutics has developed almost ineluctably along the following lines:

(1) the replacement of a psychologistic interpretation of speakers' linguistic intentions by an interpretation that is more directly centred on the collective *Geist* of particular cultures (within which the psychological has its rightful place);

(2) the replacement of a model of universal human rationality by a more constructivist view of the self, partly adjusted to the divergent traditions of different his-

torical cultures (the theme of so-called classical historicism, as in the work of Leopold von Ranke (1795–1886), and partly adjusted (particularly towards the end of the twentieth century, though admittedly quarrelsomely) to the radical historicity of human existence;

(3) the subordination of logical, methodological and epistemological questions to questions concerning the metaphysics of the historicity of thinking (Heidegger's and Gadamer's essential theme);

(4) the attempt to recover, under radical history, some more perspicuous sense of the discipline of interpretative judgement itself, particularly in the work of Ricoeur and Jürgen Habermas (1929–   ) – also, more reactively (against Gadamer), in the work of Emilio Betti (1890–1969) and E.D. Hirsch, Jr (1928–   ).

Hermeneutics is becoming increasingly difficult to distinguish from theories of interpretation that have quite different pedigrees. This is largely because, first, the historicity of the human world has come to dominate late-twentieth-century thought; and, second, hermeneutics has so far failed to recover in a compelling way a theory of interpretative judgement or, indeed, a theory of the clear connection between interpretation as an actual discipline and (self-)understanding (*Verstehen*) and the description and explanation (*Erklären*) of physical nature, or of the connection between competent judgement and the metaphysics of human existence.

Dilthey has exerted an immense influence on the late development of hermeneutics by entrenching an overstrong disjunction between *Verstehen* and *Erklären* with regard to the human and natural sciences: the unfortunate consequences of this are clear enough in Gadamer, despite his seeming resistance to methodological questions and his explicit opposition to Dilthey's concessions to the admirable rigour of the independent physical sciences. But more recent efforts (notably by Ricoeur and Habermas) to integrate understanding and explanation have foundered in skirmishes that have postponed a recovery of the methodological side of her-

meneutics – without falling back, that is, to necessities *de re* or *de dicto* (a fault in Habermas and Ricoeur). All such efforts have failed to claim the notion of radical history that is endorsed in views as disparate as those of Marx, Nietzsche, Heidegger and Gadamer, and Foucault. There is simply a failure of nerve here. The problem is still very much with us; but it is difficult to suppose that late contributions to the matter can be expected to continue to single out hermeneutics as a distinct, privileged, relatively homogeneous stream of philosophical analysis. Hermeneutics has given way to historicized semiosis (for instance, through a critique of structuralism) and hybrid theories of interpretation at large.

Technically, what is now needed is a systematic reconceptualization of the central notions that were originally called into play (at least implicitly) in the distinct methodologically minded early phases of hermeneutics, and that have proved to be much the same as those still central to the largely ahistorical orientation of Anglo-American philosophy: namely, reference, predication, numerical identity, re-identification, truth and the assignment of truth values and the like. That is, the seemingly restricted question of the methodology of 'hermeneutic' treatments of interpretative judgement is really a special case of the more general question ('hermeneutic' in this new sense) of the possibility and structure of objective judgement *under conditions of radical history*.

By 'radical history' is meant:

(1) that thinking has a history, is an artefact of history, hence is not realiably invariant in terms of rationality, norms, values, rules of coherence and the like;

(2) that human existence is distinguished by the nature of thinking;

(3) that the real structures we impute to physical nature are inseparable from the conditions of reflexive (self-)understanding;

(4) that, however embedded in physical nature, the human world is understood only in terms of the understanding, mutual and self-directed, of the members

of a common cultural tradition or society;

(5) that human beings and the things of their world are interpretatively altered and affected, historically, by their ongoing efforts at understanding themselves and their world;

(6) that the intelligible world, as historicized, has no necessary fixity, supports no strict *de re* or *de dicto* necessities.

Put this way, 'the' hermeneutic question is the essential philosophical puzzle of the late nineteenth century: addressed as much to logic and the physical sciences as to the human sciences, history, and the interpretation of art. But it certainly is one of the principal foci for grasping the radical change in late-twentieth-century views of the rigour of interpreting artworks.

Hermeneutics in the narrow sense may be divided, very roughly, into two phases: one, spanning the tradition from Schleiermacher to Dilthey and, somewhat reactively, even retrogressively (following the appearance of Gadamer's *Truth and Method*), to Betti, Hirsch, Ricoeur and Habermas; the other, spanning the tradition from Heidegger and Gadamer, reaching back to Nietzsche and pressing forward to non-hermeneuts also interested in interpretation under the flux of history, such as Foucaut. The first is methodologically and epistemologically centred, intent on identifying a clear sense of the objectivity with which the real meaning of a text, linguistic utterance, action, pattern of social life, artefact or artwork is uniquely and reliably determined.

Originally, in Ast and other early figures, hermeneutics was compartmentalized in terms of specific procedures for determining original intent within a given historical *Geist*, with respect, disjunctively, to the law or to religion or the like. In Schleiermacher, a common discipline is generalized for written texts, still strongly cast in terms of personal intention, though with some appreciation of the tacit influence of an encompassing culture. In Dilthey, it is enlarged still further to range over more than literary remains, and is more and more centred on the

recovery of historical rather than biographical intention, though with the same emphasis on a rigorous recovery of meanings. These conceptions somewhat justify Gadamer's well known charge against romantic hermeneutics: that the pertinent theorists (Dilthey as well as Ranke) failed to grasp satisfactorily that their interpretation of historical materials was itself historical – historicized, preformed (in Heideggerian terms) by the historical 'fore-structuring' of their consciousness (*wirkungsgeschichtliches Bewusstsein*: 'effective-historical consciousness').

The second phase, then, is distinctly *not* methodological but metaphysical, focused on the inherent conditions of human existence – that is, on the fact that man is and becomes what, under preformative 'prejudice', he comes to understand his own 'being' to be. In place of methodological issues, validity gives way to authenticity. Human beings live, are formed by, and change as a result of living in, the historical tradition to which they belong. They *are* histories in a sense, whose 'present' is already preformed by the historical 'past' that they claim to recover and understand. Hence, the interpretation of the 'texts' (or artworks) produced in the past ('text' now signifying, for Gadamer particularly, any suitably interpretable historicized referent: persons, artworks, literary texts, events of history) already implicates a present 'horizon' (a tacit, conceptual as well as affective and practical, orientation in life) – that is, a 'fusion of horizons' (*Horizontverschmelzung*), a fusion of recovered past and active present, operative in and only in the present ongoing life of actual societies. In this sense, Gadamer sets certain strenuous conditions on any would-be theory of interpretation, but he himself does not meet the question: he is not really interested in it. His own contribution to the theory of interpreting artwork holds that the interpretation of art (or texts) and self-interpretation are inseparable and affect one another (*subtilitas applicandi*).

There is, therefore, no standard form that can be ascribed to hermeneutics. It ranges from a methodologically focused account of interpretation committed to the recovery of original authorial intent or original *geistig* meanings by way of a rational discipline suited in principle to any historical period, to a metaphysically focused account of interpretation that holds that man and his world are constituted and continually reconstituted by his reflexive efforts at interpretative understanding. These efforts are tacitly skewed in a perspectival or horizonal way by the conditions of historical formation and ongoing life, incapable of supporting any invariant methodology or of yielding true and false propositions in the sense favoured by the first phase of hermeneutics, or by the explanatory work of the physical sciences.

The decisive mark of these large changes in the hermeneutic tradition, particularly bearing on the interpretation of artworks, rests with the nature of all the changes in the conception of the *hermeneutic circle* that the tradition has favoured at one time or another. For Ast, for example, there is apparently one supreme ('infinite') *Geist*, relative to which all the diverse cultures of the world are alternative manifestations. Understanding, therefore, is simply the human capacity to find in particular texts 'the spirit of the whole': proximately, through the various 'spirits' of particular cultures, ultimately in terms of an all-encompassing *Geist*. We are, apparently, able to discern the 'universal spirit'. So the hermeneutic circle is a relatively straightforward matter for Ast. Schleiermacher is more doubtful about the likelihood of recovering a truly 'general hermeneutics' or of grasping the 'infinite' that is language, which appears to be required in order to resolve the problem of the hermeneutic circle adequately. But within these troubling limits, Schleiermacher emphasizes an author's 'thought' and the formation of his thought through the genres of the language in which he expresses himself – which capture the 'whole' of his historical language and culture.

An institution of this sort is fundamental to all versions of romantic hermeneutics, if we understand by that term the extension of the appropriate methodology, beyond narrowly biographically focused thought, to what is historically *geistig* at large, as in Dilthey and Betti and, possibly most accessibly, in Hirsch.

But even in Schleiermacher, as with the interpretation of the New Testament, 'a minimum of psychological interpretation is needed', he says, 'with a predominantly objective subject.' Interpretation begins, then, with a guess that probably does not recover at once either pertinent genres of discourse (which effectively fix the whole of a text's meaning) or the thought that produces a particular text; hermeneutic skills rework such commentaries in order to bring them into congruity with these criterial constraints.

One sees, here, the incipient structure of a relatively late romantic hermeneutic position such as Hirsch's, which is characteristically sanguine about the benign form of the hermeneutic circle. The tell-tale difficulty in Hirsch (1967) is a dual one – that adversely affects all more or less essentialist conceptions of the circle and its would-be resolution: (1) there is no satisfactory way of demonstrating that there *are* relatively fixed constitutive genres of discourse, in accord with which every properly formed 'thought' (author's or artist's original intent) is formed and then interpretatively recovered by suitably informed respondents; and (2) there is no satisfactory way of fixing constitutive genres so that new poetic or other artistic acts or utterings, presumably formed within them, are truly governed by them.

Such genres function only heuristically, then: only on the assumption that human nature and understanding were essentially fixed through the whole of history could the contemporary solution of the hermeneutic circle possibly be sustained. Hirsch probabilizes the treatment of genres, but he fails to resolve the question just raised. The hermeneutic circle ceases to enjoy any disciplined criterial function, begins to mean only that human understanding proceeds by constructing part/whole constellations of meaning, without relying on methodological rules of any fixed sort. But that is just Gadamer's position – the point of his objection to Betti's attack on his having relied on the historically changing role of the interpreting subject. It was in fact Betti's 'first canon' of interpretation that held that, since 'meaningful forms' (texts, say, read in a large sense) are 'objectifications of mind', they must be interpreted by way of reference to 'that other mind' and not in accord with the intrusion of one's own intentional life or thought. The irony is that this itself forms a remarkable (but unintended) analogue of the New Critical theory of interpretation. But Betti was unable to explain just how the distinction could be reliably confirmed.

Once the insolubility of the puzzle is acknowledged, it cannot but be difficult (or impossible) to resist Gadamer's twin doctrines of *wirkungsgeschichtliches Bewusstsein* and *Horizontverschmelzung*. The hermeneutic circle becomes a characterization of the metaphysics of human existence, rather than a criterial principle for canonical interpretation. One might almost say that, trivially, human understanding proceeds by way of generating open-ended part/whole relations of meaning, since meaning and rationality are inherently holistic notions. There would then be no sense in speaking of the right closure of interpretation: closure merely becomes practical or heuristic. There would then also be no need for closure, since every change in experience would invite the construction of a new circle. The admission, in this new sense, of the hermeneutic circle confirms the irreducibility of what is interpretable (in the human world) to the non-intensional (or, non-intentional) features of physical nature. But to put matters thus still leaves unresolved the methodologically insistent question of the rigour of interpretation (whether in the spirit of the hermeneutic tradition or not) under the conditions of radical history.

We may risk, here, one last finding that the hermeneutic tradition would be willing to support: that is, it would be impossible to recover *any* viable sense of the objectivity of an interpretation of a text or artwork without supposing that such objectivity lies within the competence of the consensual practices of an actual historical society – lies within its *Lebenswelten* or *Lebensformen*, or modes of production or *Geist* or *epistemes* or the like. Would-be norms would then be constructed rather than discovered, would be provisional rather than fixed, pluralistic and relativistic rather than universalized, and would be unable to claim legitimate priority for 'rules' in actual use as opposed to what ongoing practices might yield.

This means that all presumptions of canonical objectivity, which assume that the interpreted 'world' is independent of the 'world' of the interpreter, utterly fail. The interesting fact remains that the devices of truth-claiming discourse – reference, predication, individuation, identity, the ascription of truth values – are *all* (must be) inherently dependent on the processes of historical self-understanding. The matter has been neglected in the tradition of the unity of science, as well as in the tradition that distinguishes the *Naturwissenschaften* from the *Geisteswissenschaften*. Grant this much: then, of course, the physical and formal sciences *are* human sciences, abstracted for certain purposes; then hermeneutic problems obtain ubiquitously (as Gadamer supposed); but then, too, there are no privileged cognitive universalities by which to recover any interpretative canon. The idea that interpretation may be disciplined in a public way remains entirely coherent – even ruggedly attractive.

See also GADAMER; HEIDEGGER; INTERPRETATION; TEXT.

BIBLIOGRAPHY

Ast, Friedrich: *Grundlinien der Grammatik, Hermeneutik und Kritik* (Landshut: Thomann, 1808).

Dilthey, Wilhelm: 'The development of hermeneutics' (1900); in *Dilthey: Selected Writings*, trans. and ed. H.P. Rickman (Cambridge: Cambridge University Press, 1976).

Gadamer, Hans-Georg: *Truth and Method* (1960); trans. Garrett Barden and John Cumming (New York: Seabury Press, 1975).

Heidegger, Martin: *Being and Time* (1983); trans. John Macquarrie and Edward Robinson (New York: Harper & Row, 1962).

Hirsch, Jr, E.D.: *Validity in Interpretation* (New Haven, Conn.: Yale University Press, 1967).

Ricoeur, Paul: *Hermeneutics and the Human Sciences* (1981); trans. and ed. John B. Thompson (Cambridge: Cambridge University Press, 1981).

Schleiermacher, Friedrich D.E.: *Hermeneutics: The Handwritten Manuscripts*, ed. Heinz Kimmerle (1838); trans. James Duke and Jack Fortman (Missoula, Mont.: Scholars Press, 1977).

JOSEPH MARGOLIS

Hume, David (1711–76) Scottish philosopher, historian, economist, and critic of religion; arguably the greatest of the British empiricists, and a leading figure of the Scottish Enlightenment. 'Of the standard of taste' (1757) is Hume's main writing on aesthetics. Here he examines attributions of beauty and deformity and says that such judgements are not 'matters of fact' or 'opinion', but arise from 'sentiment'. Despite some mentions of architecture and the beauty of the human form, his specific examples are drawn almost exclusively from literature; and this holds for his other essays in aesthetics, as is evident from their titles – 'Of tragedy', 'Of essay writing', 'Of eloquence', 'Of simplicity and refinement in writing'.

Hume characterizes two apparently antithetical positions that must be rendered consistent. First, the deliverances of taste vary enormously, not only across the centuries and between distant nations, but amongst critics sharing a culture and language. Second, there are judgements of taste that have something approaching universal acceptance – 'common sense' treats as ridiculous an equation of the merits of Ogilby with Milton, or Bunyan (*sic*) with Addison: 'No one pays attention to such a taste.' Can an account of taste be given that allows for variety, but also provides 'a rule by which the various sentiments of men may be reconciled, or at least a decision afforded confirming one sentiment and condemning another?'

Judgements of opinion refer to matters of fact, but 'sentiment has a reference to nothing beyond itself.' This allows the argument that 'beauty is no quality in things themselves; it exists merely in the mind which contemplates them; and each mind perceives a different beauty.' To seek real beauty or deformity, it may be thought, is as

fruitless as to seek real bitterness or sweetness, for those qualities depend on 'the disposition of the organs'. Curiously, Hume rejects Locke's distinction of primary and secondary qualities and elaborates Berkeley's arguments against it (see Hume, 1978, pp. 226–31), but is nevertheless repeatedly tempted to assimilate beauty to the secondary qualities.

Can a standard of taste be given by rules of composition? There are such rules and they are discovered through experience. They are 'general observations concerning what has been universally found to please in all countries and ages'. But there is no answer here, for these rules do not bind. They can be transgressed, and a work of art enhanced by the transgression. It is not application of rules but *delicacy of taste* that detects merit. Hume illustrates this notion with an anecdote from *Don Quixote*. Two accomplished judges of wine praised a fine wine but one judged it slightly metallic and the other thought he tasted leather in it. The judgements were ridiculed as affectations, but vindicated when a key with a leather thong was found at the bottom of the vat. 'Where the organs are so fine as to allow nothing to escape them, and at the same time so exact as to perceive every ingredient in the composition, this we call delicacy of taste, whether we employ these terms in the literal or the metaphorical sense.'

But delicate taste alone is not sufficient for congruence of judgements. Practice is needed to cultivate taste, comparisons must be made, prejudice must be expelled and I must 'forget, if possible, my individual being and my peculiar circumstances'. Most particularly, acuteness of understanding is required to judge whether a work of art attains the ends it aims at, and to see whether, in poetry or narrative, there is justness of reasoning and verisimilitude of character, purposes and plot. These conditions fulfilled, the standard of taste is set by the judgements of critics of delicate taste. 'The just verdict of such, wherever they are to be found, is the true standard of taste and beauty.'

Note that Hume is locked into the idea of judgements of taste as expressions of 'sentiment', and although he remarks that 'it seldom or never happens, that a man of sense, who has experience in any art, cannot judge of its beauty', and that 'it is no less rare to meet with a man who has a just taste without a sound understanding', he cannot incorporate understanding as essential to taste, but must represent it as something external, facilitating the proper operation of a faculty.

By what marks is the true critic to be known? It is a matter of fact, says Hume, whether a man is endowed with good sense, free from prejudice, and of delicate imagination. As with other matters of fact, disputes may arise, but they can be resolved to the extent that such matters can.

There can be true and false judgements about secondary qualities because 'the appearance of objects in daylight, to the eye of a man in health, is denominated their true and real colour, even while colour is allowed to be merely a phantasm of the senses.' Most men can judge of colours, but why can only a minority judge effectively of artistic worth? Just as defect in organs prevents some people judging colour correctly, lack of practice, failure of comparisons and limitations of understanding disqualify many from judging art. But still the case is not the same as with the secondary qualities, for in addition to the above factors there are two 'natural' barriers that make unanimity unattainable. These are 'the different humours of particular men' and the particular manners and opinions of an age or country. Cultural influence and individual predilections give a particular turn to someone's taste. One man values simplicity over ornament, one prefers harmony, another energy. A young man with amorous passions will allegedly prefer Ovid to Tacitus, and these matters 'can never reasonably be the object of dispute, because there is no standard by which they can be decided'.

There are sound and unsound judgements on works of art. There is a level of agreement amongst those fitted to judge, and their discernment informs and alters that of a community. Nevertheless, beauty remains a phantasm of the senses, and to a greater degree than with the secondary qualities, for there are natural obstacles that cannot be discounted so as to achieve a total agreement in matters of taste. But this lack of total agreement is not the defect it might seem. It is in matters of speculative opinion that real instability is to be found. Philosophies and theologies that prevail in one age are exploded in another, and 'nothing has been experienced more liable to the revolutions of chance and fashion than these pretended decisions of science.' By constrast, the beauties of eloquence and poetry prevail over time, and though Cicero's philosophy is disregarded, his oratory is still admired.

Hume sets in fine tension major themes of the philosophy of art – the nature of qualities, the relativity of standards, the authority of the discerning critic, the defeasibility of rules. Labels such as 'subjectivist' and 'emotivist' travesty his position, for in his discussion of aesthetics he is as complex and slippery as in all the rest of his philosophy.

See also BEAUTY; CRITICISM; JUDGEMENT, AESTHETIC; TASTE.

WRITINGS

'Of the Standard of Taste' and Other Essays, ed. J.W. Lenz (New York: Bobbs-Merrill, 1965). This volume also includes 'Of the delicacy of taste and passion', 'Of tragedy', 'Of essay writing', 'Of simplicity and refinement in writing', 'Of refinement in the arts', 'Of eloquence', and 'The sceptic' (which has some passages of relevance to aesthetics).
'Of beauty and deformity', A Treatise of Human Nature, ed. L.A. Selby-Bigge (Oxford: Oxford University Press, 1978), bk 2, pt 1, §8, pp. 298–303.

BIBLIOGRAPHY

Jones, Peter: 'Hume's aesthetics reassessed', Philosophical Quarterly, 26 (1976), 48–62.
Kivy, Peter: 'Hume's neighbour's wife: an essay on the evolution of Hume's aesthetics', British Journal of Aesthetics, 23 (1983), 195–208.
Lenz, J.W.: Introduction to Hume, 'Of the

Standard of Taste' and Other Essays (New York: Bobbs-Merrill, 1965).

Mothersill, Mary: *Beauty Restored*, (Oxford: Clarendon Press, 1984), pp. 177–209.

MICHAEL SMITHURST

humour Few would deny that humour is an important quality in much literature and drama, but the question of what, exactly, makes something funny, is a notoriously problematic one. Various theories of humour have been advanced but, before discussing them, two warnings should be sounded.

Firstly, some theorists write about laughter rather than humour. This can lead to confusion, since laughter, of course, can arise as a result of experiences and sensations other than reading humour or witnessing humorous effects: joy, hysteria, or exposure to nitrous oxide, for instance. Many theorists write without reference to the humour–laughter distinction, making it unclear whether they are talking about humorous laughter, or *all* laughter. Others, though conscious of a distinction, still attempt to explain all laughter, humorous and non-humorous, in terms of a single theoretical formula. However, most theories, whether or not offering an explanation intended to be as all-encompassing as in this latter case, normally at least *include* an attempt to explain humour (and laughter thereat), so in what follows, such theories will be judged according to their success, or otherwise, in this enterprise.

The second warning is that until very recently there has been no terminological consensus in theoretical writing on humour: different theorists use different terms to mean the same thing, and the same word to mean different things. For instance, some use 'the comic' for what others mean by 'the ludicrous', whereas in other writings 'the comic' is a subdivision of 'the ludicrous', along with such other subdivisions as wit and satire. (This problem of terminology is exacerbated by the difficulties of translation.) In contemporary cross-disciplinary research, however, 'humour' is used as a general umbrella term for what is perceived, thought of, or experienced, as funny or amusing. Following this usage, humour should be understood in what follows as the general term of which wit, satire, jokes, stage comedy, etc., may be viewed as sub-categories.

That said, we can go on to identify the three main humour-theoretical traditions. These attempt to explain the phenomenon in terms of incongruity, superiority and the release of energy respectively.

THE INCONGRUITY TRADITION

The most regularly subscribed to of the three theoretical traditions amongst contemporary humour researchers, the incongruity tradition is usually viewed as having its origin in a comment by Kant. For Kant, 'laughter is an affection arising from a strained expectation being suddenly reduced to nothing' (Kant, 1952 [1790], p. 199). If taken literally, this is an adequate explanation of only a very tiny field of humour. However, 'reduction to nothing' could be interpreted in a way more favourable to Kant. Many jokes set up the mind to follow a particular path, but the outcome suddenly makes us realise that we have followed completely the *wrong* path: the one we have followed turns out to lead nowhere; or at least not to the same place as the punchline of the joke. If understood in this way, Kant can be seen as having given birth to the kind of incongruity theory more explicitly outlined by Schopenhauer. The core of Schopenhauer's formulation is that: 'The cause of laughter in every case is simply the sudden perception of the incongruity between a concept and the real objects thought through it in some relation, and laughter itself is just the expression of this incongruity' (Schopenhauer, 1883 [1818], vol. 1, p. 76).

Some recent writers in this tradition have argued that what is amusing is not the perception of an incongruity itself, but rather the *resolution* of that incongruity: amusement results from fitting what appears to be an anomaly into some conceptual schema. (For instance, John Sparkes's story about his grandmother's strange phobia: fear of the floor. When asked by a psychiatrist why she isn't afraid of 'something sensible, like heights', she replies that it isn't heights that kill you; it's the floor.) However, though some humour is well-explained by incongruity-resolution, in other cases (such as the opening lines of Lewis Carroll's *Jabberwocky* or nonsensical riddles such as 'What's the difference between a duck?' 'One of its legs is both the same'), our amusement stems precisely from our inability to find a conceptual schema which will allow us to make sense of the material.

Humour theorists have used the word 'incongruity' to describe a very wide range of humorous phenomena. It has been used to explain humour involving:

(1) logical impossibility ('Lincoln was a great Kentuckian. He was born in a log cabin, which he built with his own hands.')

(2) ambiguity (including *double entendres* and the literal interpretations of figures of speech, such as: 'I woke up one morning and my girlfriend asked me if I slept good. I said, "No, I made a few mistakes"' (Steven Wright))

(3) irrelevance ('How is it possible to find meaning in a finite world given my waist and shirt size?' (Woody Allen)), and

(4) general 'inappropriateness': 'the linking of disparates . . . the collision of different mental spheres . . . the obtrusion into one context of what belongs in another' (Monro, 1951, p. 235).

Many examples of humour can be subsumed under one or other of these headings, and to illustrate examples of humour based on different types of incongruity in the above way is a valuable enterprise (see Swabey, 1961). Yet there remain doubts as to whether all of the above may be said to be genuinely interchangeable with the term 'incongruity'. Just as we cannot explain all humour in terms of incongruity–resolution, neither can we do so in terms of incongruity without stretching the meaning of the term so far that it ceases to be very informative.

Arguably the most important objection to incongruity theories is that even if, in any given example of humour, it is possible to identify an element of incongruity, it is not necessarily this incongruity itself which is the predominant reason for amusement. To put all the emphasis upon a factor such as incongruity is to stress form or structure at the expense of content. Yet clearly content is often vitally important in humour appreciation: two jokes, structurally identical, will often be rated as of greatly differing funniness if their content or subject-matter is different, since some subjects – sex, for instance – lend themselves to 'getting a laugh' far more easily than others. Moreover, the incongruity theorist must explain why some incongruities are perceived as funny while others are not, and why a particular incongruity will amuse some people but not others. This highlights the need for any adequate theory of humour to take into account factors such as: the content of humour; the context within which it is set; and the attitude of the hearer or reader, as well as the structure of jokes and the cognitive side of humour on which the incongruity tradition concentrates.

THE SUPERIORITY TRADITION

Though Plato and Aristotle's brief comments on laughter justify placing them in this tradition, the most commonly quoted superiority theorist is Thomas Hobbes. For Hobbes, 'laughter is nothing else but sudden glory arising from some sudden conception of some eminency in ourselves, by comparison with the infirmity of others, or with our own formerly' (Hobbes, 1840, p. 46). We laugh when we realize we are, or perceive ourselves as being, superior in some way to the object of our laughter.

Clearly, important areas of humour can be explained in this way: much humour has a 'victim' and involves, in one way or another, laughing at the perceived 'infirmities of others'. (Racist and sexist jokes are two obvious humour categories thus explicable; stock comic characters, too, tend to have some defect or 'infirmity'.) But a similar objection can be raised as was raised against incongruity theorists above: why do some feelings of superiority, or 'sudden glory', result in laughter, while others do not? Hobbes fails to pay due attention to the fact that the feelings of the laugher must be sparked off by something: there must be an object of amusement. (Hobbes is thereby like those aesthetic theorists who put all the emphasis on the audience's response to a work of art, completely ignoring the work of art itself.) Furthermore, it is perfectly possible to be amused by a joke or a piece of humour for its own sake; in other words, it can often be the object of amusement itself, rather than the hearer's feelings, which cause laughter. Just as the incongruity tradition puts all the emphasis upon the structure of humour at the expense of the attitude or feelings of the laugher, Hobbes, by paying all his attention to the feelings of the amused party, and none to the qualities of the humour itself, can be seen as making precisely the opposite mistake.

A further criticism of Hobbes is that the feelings of the laugher are by no means always those of superiority. This will seem obvious if we consider the superiority tradition to be claiming that the pleasure afforded by humour is essentially *Schadenfreude*, which is how it has often been read. In fact, disciples of Hobbes have attempted to offer superiority-based explanations of humour which are more subtle than this. For Ludovici (1932), all laughter – humorous and non-humorous – is explicable in terms of 'superior adaptation'. A major problem with this is that Ludovici attempts to subsume under this 'ambiguous verbal formula' (Monro, 1951, p. 106) experiences so diverse as both *Schadenfreude* and the pleasure taken, when amused at nonsense and absurdity, for instance, in a momentary escape from having to obey the rules of reason and logic. Though Ludovici's formula is able to account for more humour than Hobbes, he succeeds in linking *all* humorous experience only by stretching his use of terminology to an almost ridiculous degree: the reservations we expressed concerning the range over which the term 'incongruity' was used apply all the more strongly to Ludovici's use of 'superior adaptation'.

Clearly, then, for 'superiority' to have any real meaning, it must be used in a stronger sense than this. And yet such a use will be unable to account for the feelings or attitude appropriate to much humour. Hobbes and his followers tend to overlook the attitude of childlike playfulness which is so important to the enjoyment of much humour based upon nonsense and absurdity, for instance.

Finally, superiority theorists have great difficulty in adequately explaining the phenomenon of laughing at oneself. Hobbes claims that the self at which we laugh is a former self to whom we are now superior; Ludovici that, finding ourselves in a position of inferior adaptation, we feign the sign of superior adaptation. Both explanations ignore the fact that it is perfectly possible to find one's current self genuinely amusing. This is relevant not only to being able to 'take a joke' in everyday life; much humour in literature involves recognizing in a character something of one's own characteristics and defects.

One other theorist who should be mentioned in this section is Henri Bergson. Central to Bergson's theory is the idea that laughter's function is to act as a social corrective. The key elements in the comic are mechanism and inelasticity: what is funny is 'something mechanical encrusted on the living' (Bergson, 1956 [1900], p. 84). Each member of society must pay constant attention to his social surroundings, and those who fail to do so thereby demonstrate unsociability, a kind of inelasticity, which renders a character comical. Nobody likes being thought of as comical and being laughed at. Having this experience, or seeing a comic character treated thus, therefore coerces the individual, by humiliation, into acting as a social being, as society demands.

Bergson, too, can be accused of excessive reductionism; of attempting to reduce humour and laughter to one kind. Like other superiority theorists, he overlooks the importance of innocent childlike playfulness, which is so far removed from his laughter of social correction. It is also difficult to see, on Bergson's view, why each individual values a sense of humour so strongly as people do: from the individual's point of view, all that can be said in favour of comedy and laughter, on Bergson's account of them, is that they allow society to pursue 'a utilitarian aim of general improvement' (Bergson, 1956 [1900], p. 73).

THE RELEASE TRADITION

The central idea in this third main tradition is that laughter provides a release of tension: nervous or psychical energy built up in the nervous system can be discharged through laughter. Though a relatively simple version of this theory was propounded by Herbert Spencer, the most important and elaborately worked-out theory in the tradition is that of Freud. Freud divides jokes into two main categories: innocent and tendentious. The pleasure derived from the former is normally less than that from the latter. This is because the pleasure attainable from innocent jokes comes from their 'technique' alone – the jokes are indulged in for their own sake – whereas tendentious jokes have 'purpose' (*Tendenz*) as well as technique. There are basically two kinds of purpose which a tendentious joke can serve: 'It is either a *hostile* joke (serving the purpose of aggressiveness, satire, or defence) or an *obscene* joke (serving the purpose of exposure)' (Freud, 1976 [1905], p. 140). Civilization forces us to repress both our aggressive and our sexual desires. Tendentious jokes allow us to enjoy these pleasures, by circumventing the obstacle that stands in the way of the hostile or lustful instinct. Such obstacles are of two kinds: external (the difficulty of venting our aggression on someone who stands in a position of power in relation to ourselves, for instance) and internal (our inner, civilization-induced aversions to smut and hostility). A tendentious joke either saves us from having to create the inhibition necessary for self-restraint, or allows an already existing inner obstacle to be overcome and the inhibition lifted. This works as follows: the technique of the joke provides a small amount of pleasure, the 'fore-pleasure' (Freud, 1976 [1905], p. 188), which acts as an 'incentive bonus' (ibid.) by means of which the suppressed purpose gains sufficient strength to overcome the inhibition and allows the enjoyment of the much greater amount of pleasure which

can be released from the purpose. Since in creating or maintaining an inhibition we expend psychical energy, Freud claims, it is plausible to conclude that the yield of pleasure derived from a tendentious joke corresponds to the psychical expenditure that is saved, and the psychical energy saved can be discharged in laughter. (A similar explanation is given of the pleasure derived from innocent jokes: in the enjoyment of nonsense and absurdity, for instance, the psychical energy saved is that which one would normally expend on obeying the rules of coherence, reason and logic.)

Just as tendentious jokes involve a saving of the energy of inhibition, so what Freud calls 'the comic' involves a saving of the energy of ideation: a character who expends, in comparison to ourselves, more on the physical and less on the mental, is comic. Similarly, what Freud calls humour involves a saving on feeling: in gallows humour, for instance, an emotion – pity – is generated, seen as irrelevant, and the energy thus built up is then free for discharge in laughter.

The central idea of laughter's serving as a release of tension is a plausible one in much humour; the very phrase 'comic relief' lends some support to such a view, and it does seem reasonable to say that we operate under a number of constraints, and that laughter can act as a 'safety-valve'. While these constraints are not, *pace* Freud, limited to the pressure to restrain sexual and hostile urges – indeed, the pressures to live up to the ideals of sexual potency and 'macho' aggressiveness can themselves be felt as constraints – it is true that we are under pressure to conform to social norms and moral codes; to obey the laws of reason and logic; and that even the need to be serious for most of the time can be felt as a constraint. We can see that it makes sense to claim that humour which breaks these rules can afford us a release, albeit transitory, from these constraints.

However, Freud's claims are stronger than this, and his key error is to offer his theory as a scientific one; his view that all phenomena are determined by physical and chemical laws leads him to take the notion of 'psychical energy' literally, and thereby to attempt to quantify it. Aspects of the details of the theory remain highly dubious too. For example, Freud maintains that those who expend most psychical energy in repressing their sexual and hostile urges will laugh most at humour which affords relief from these inhibitions. Yet experimental research has suggested the opposite: that it is those who readily express sexual and aggressive feelings who laugh most at sexual and aggressive humour. It is also difficult to see why the fore-pleasure, which on Freud's own admission is a small amount of pleasure, is enough to overcome deep-rooted inhibitions. Freud's distinctions between jokes, the comic and humour can be questioned, too. Finally, the objection can be raised that any explanation of humour in terms of energetics merely attempts to explain what happens *when* I find something funny; it does not explain *why* I find it so.

Some philosophers view as unjustified the assumption popular in aesthetics that there is some feature common to all examples of art. We have seen that humour theorists working from similar essentialist presuppositions have failed to provide an adequate general theory of humour. Furthermore, a synthesis of these theories would still not make for an adequate general theory, since their inadequacies are not merely those of omission, whereby a combination with another theory or set of theories which looked at the phenomena from a different perspective would solve the problem. Rather, some of the most important defects are *intrinsic* to the theories, such as the stretching of terminology observed in both the incongruity and superiority traditions. In the light of this, it becomes very tempting to take a sceptical view of the likelihood of achieving an adequate general theory, of humour as of art; to suspect that no comprehensive theory of humour can be found because there is no one factor which all humour has in common. This is essentially to side with the common-sense view that the variety of humour is too vast adequately to be explained in terms of a single formula. To suggest this is not to deny, however, that existing theories of humour do shed consider-able light upon the complex phenomenon with which they deal.

See also IRONY; PSYCHOANALYSIS AND ART.

BIBLIOGRAPHY

Bergson, H.: *Le Rire* (1900); trans. C. Brereton and F. Rothwell, *Laughter* (London and New York: Macmillan, 1911); also in Sypher, W., ed., *Comedy* (Baltimore: Johns Hopkins University Press, 1956), pp. 61–190.

Freud, S.: *Der Witz und seine Beziehung zum Unbewussten* (1905); trans. J. Strachey, *Jokes and their Relation to the Unconscious* (Harmondsworth: Penguin, 1976).

Hobbes, T.: *Human Nature*, in W. Molesworth, ed., *The English Works of Thomas Hobbes*, vol. 4 (London: John Bohn, 1840), pp. 1–76.

Kant, I.: *Kritik der Urteilskraft* (1790); trans. J.C. Meredith, *The Critique of Judgement* (Oxford: Clarendon Press, 1952).

Lauter, P., ed.: *Theories of Comedy* (New York: Doubleday, 1964).

Ludovici, A.M.: *The Secret of Laughter* (London: Constable, 1932).

Monro, D.H.: *Argument of Laughter* (Carlton: Melbourne University Press, 1951).

Morreall, J.: *Taking Laughter Seriously* (Albany: State University of New York Press, 1983).

Morreall, J., ed.: *The Philosophy of Laughter and Humor* (Albany: State University of New York Press, 1987).

Nelson, T.G.A.: *Comedy: the Theory of Comedy in Literature, Drama, and Cinema* (Oxford: Oxford University Press, 1990).

Schopenhauer, A.: *Die Welt als Wille und Vorstellung* (1818), trans. R.B. Haldane and J. Kemp, *The World as Will and Idea* (London: Routledge, 1883).

Swabey, M.C.: *Comic Laughter: a Philosophical Essay* (New Haven and London: Yale University Press, 1961).

JOHN LIPPITT

Hutcheson, Francis (1694–1746) Scottish moral and aesthetic philosopher; Professor at Glasgow University, and a leading representative of the 'moral sense' school.

Three important and substantial treatises,

published in the first quarter of the eighteenth century, inaugurated the modern discipline of aesthetics and, at the same time, by no means coincidentally, established what Paul O. Kristeller has called the 'modern system of the arts'. They are J.P. de Crousaz' *Traité du beau* (1714), the Abbé Dubos' *Réflexions critiques sur la poësie et sur la peinture* (1719), and Francis Hutcheson's *Inquiry Concerning Beauty, Order, Harmony, Design* (1725), the first of two works published together under the title, *An Inquiry into the Original of our Ideas of Beauty and Virtue.* These must be considered the first book-length studies in the field of aesthetics and the philosophy of art, at least in the way we now conceive of them – which is to say, as a fully autonomous intellectual enterprise within the general confines of philosophy. And although Hutcheson's work is neither the first of the three nor the most expansive, it is unique in the clear philosophical direction that he was able to give to the subject as he understood it, in his brief but concentrated monograph.

The model of aesthetic perception that Hutcheson chose derived from the Lockean account of how we perceive secondary qualities. Take, for example, my perception of a red barn. As Hutcheson would have understood Locke, here is what is happening. The microstructure of the material object – the 'primary qualities' – causally interacts with my sense of sight, to produce in me the sensation of redness. Strictly speaking, the term 'red' refers to the sensation or 'idea' that is experienced, because if there were no such idea, there would be no occasion for me to call the object 'red'. It is customary, nevertheless, also to call the object itself 'red' and the 'power' it possesses of causing the idea of sensation in us, 'redness'. Redness is a simple quality – which is to say, the sensation or idea is a simple idea, not a complex one. And the perception of it is non-epistemic in the sense that we need know nothing about the causal apparatus, or what it is in the red object that possesses the appropriate powers, to perceive redness. This basic outline is followed, point for point, by Hutcheson in his account of how we perceive what he calls

'absolute beauty', although some of the points are in the nature of analogies rather than literal.

On his view, 'the word *beauty* is taken for *the idea raised in us*, and a *sense* of beauty for *our power of receiving this idea*' (Hutcheson, 1973 [1725], p. 34). The 'property' in 'objects' that causes this idea of beauty to be raised in us is a relation among the parts of the object that Hutcheson called (the French had already used the phrase) *uniformity amidst variety*; and so 'where the uniformity of bodies is equal, the beauty is as the variety; and where the variety is equal, the beauty is as the uniformity' (Hutcheson, 1973 [1725], p. 40). This we know, presumably, by inductive inference.

Analogous to the physical object, the red barn, that raises in us the idea of redness, is not a physical object that raises the idea of beauty, but rather a different kind of 'object' – namely, a complex of ideas of primary and secondary qualities, perceived not by an outer but by an 'inner' sense: what Hutcheson tended to call, in his later writings, '*reflex* or subsequent, by which certain new forms or perceptions are received, in consequence of others previously observed' (Hutcheson, 1747, pp. 12–13). Thus the property in 'objects' that raises the idea of beauty, although it plays the same kind of causal role that the primary qualities of external objects do in arousing ideas of secondary qualities, is not a congeries of primary qualities, not a property of the external world at all, but the relational property of the internal world of ideas.

There are, then, three different 'ideas', properly so called by the Lockean, that are involved in Hutcheson's account of aesthetic perception. There is the complex idea, consisting of ideas of primary and secondary qualities, that possesses the relational property of *uniformity amidst variety*. There is the simple idea of beauty, aroused by that property, which Hutcheson sometimes describes as something like a secondary quality but more often as a 'pleasant idea' – by which, clearly, he means 'pleasure'. And there is, finally, the complex idea of uniformity amidst variety that one forms when one comes to know that uniformity amidst variety is the cause of the idea of beauty.

Now each of these ideas can, on the Lockean scheme with which Hutcheson is working, be called with some propriety the 'idea of beauty'; and this has led some to falsely assert that Hutcheson believed the idea of beauty to be complex. But, speaking with the learned, only the simple idea of beauty, the pleasure raised by the sense of beauty, is 'beauty' properly so called. That is the genuine doctrine. And we know that the idea is simple by virtue merely of the fact that a special 'sense' is required for its perception. (Locke required no such 'sense' of beauty because for him beauty *was* a complex idea.)

Another mistake to guard against is that of concluding that Hutcheson is really maintaining an epistemic account of aesthetic perception because, on his account, we can consciously perceive that certain objects possess uniformity amidst variety, the cause of the idea of beauty, whereas we cannot consciously perceive the micro-structure of matter that causes the ideas of secondary qualities. However, Hutcheson does *explicitly* say that uniformity amidst variety functions in a way exactly analogous to the way the micro-structure of matter functions in causing the ideas of secondary qualities; and he does say *explicitly* that uniformity amidst variety causes us to have the idea of beauty without our necessarily being aware that the object possesses uniformity amidst variety, or that uniformity amidst variety has anything to do with beauty, just as people were seeing red long before they knew anything of Locke's account of perception. Indeed, in one place Hutcheson says both in the same breath.

But in all these instances of beauty let it be observed that the pleasure is communicated to those who never reflected on this general foundation, and that all here alleged is this, that the pleasant sensation arises only from objects in which there is *uniformity amidst variety*. We have the sensation without knowing what is the cause of it, as a man's taste may suggest ideas of sweets, acids, bitters, though he be ignorant of the forms of the small bodies, or their motions, which excite these perceptions in him. (Hutcheson, 1973 [1725], p. 47)

I have explicated at length Hutcheson's account of what he calls 'absolute beauty' because that is the part that was most influential in the eighteenth century. But, in fact, the larger portion of the *Inquiry Concerning Beauty* is taken up with what he calls 'relative beauty', which is to say, the beauty of 'imitation'. Naturally, what he has uppermost in his mind in this regard is representation in the fine arts.

One might have expected that tackling the beauty of imitation would force Hutcheson to abandon, for that very different-seeming kind of beauty, the causal, non-epistemic account which served for absolute beauty. For, after all, it would seem palpably obvious that seeing something as a representation or 'imitation' of something else is a clear case of 'perceiving that . . .'. Such, however, is not how he saw things. The foundation, for him, is still the same: *uniformity amidst variety* – 'this beauty [of imitation] is founded on a conformity, or a kind of unity between the original and the copy' (Hutcheson 1973 [1725], p. 54), with the variety, it must be supposed, being supplied by the fact that the original and the copy are *different* sorts of things altogether, although unified by the similarity of their appearances.

On the assumption, then, that uniformity amidst variety must be functioning in the same way in the case of relative beauty as in the case of absolute – or it would not have been introduced in the former at all – Hutcheson must be maintaining, it is clear, that although the complex idea we have of X imitating Y is composed of various 'knowings' as well as 'perceivings that . . .' the uniformity amidst variety that these conscious 'knowings' and 'perceivings that . . .' possess we are not aware of at all. And it is this hidden property of our conscious 'knowings' and 'perceivings that . . .' that causes to arise in us, through our internal sense, the simple, pleasurable idea of relative beauty. Whatever may be said of the plausibility of Hutcheson's position here, its consistency is undoubted.

See also BEAUTY; PERCEPTION.

WRITINGS

An Inquiry into the Original of our Ideas of Beauty and Virtue (London: 1725); 4th edn (London: 1738).
A Short Introduction to Moral Philosophy (Glasgow: 1747).
Inquiry Concerning Beauty, Order, Harmony, Design (1725); 4th edn (London: 1738). ed. P. Kivy (The Hague: Martinus Nijhoff, 1973).

BIBLIOGRAPHY

Kivy, P.: *The Seventh Sense: A Study of Francis Hutcheson's Aesthetics and its Influence in Eighteenth-Century Britain* (New York: Burt Franklin, 1976).
Michael, E.: 'Francis Hutcheson on aesthetic perception and aesthetic pleasure', *British Journal of Aesthetics*, 34 (1984).

PETER KIVY

I

iconoclasm and idolatry

ICONOCLASM

Assaults against images occur in all cultures. In analysing the various forms of aggression against images, one may want to distinguish between acts of vandalism (including acts of war), pathological or psychotic violence, and destruction or mutilation for reasons of principle (political or religious); but in practice the motives are much less clear and much more difficult to unravel. There is also more of a continuum than may first be apparent between spontaneous acts of individual violence and concerted and organized group hostility. In situations where public or theological motives are adduced for the iconoclastic deed or event, individual psychological motives may well appear to receive a kind of legitimation in the social, legal, theological or philosophical domain.

The term 'iconoclasm' is popularly used in a metaphorical sense; it will not be so discussed here. At issue are physical acts against physical images, whether two- or three-dimensional, and sometimes buildings.

The more clearly definable motivations for iconoclasm include the following:

the desire for publicity (as in the *locus classicus* of this motivation, the destruction of the temple of Diana at Ephesus by Eratostratos, and in any number of psychopathic assaults on images in the twentieth century, where the targets have been exceptionally well known works of art);
the fear of the life inherent in an image (whether because of the imagined conflation of sign and signified, or in the case, as often in the Reformation, of images operated by deceptive mechanical means);
the desire to demonstrate that an image is not a live thing, in the end, but merely dead material;
the belief that an image is pornographic or may be sexually arousing;
the view that too much wealth is invested in a material object, relative to perceived social need;
the sense that an image is too beautiful or too stylish to convey the message it is meant to convey (as in those cases where art and artistry are believed to be too distracting, such as the sixteenth-century polemics against Michelangelo's style);
the desire to draw attention to a felt social or personal injustice;
the need to avenge such an injustice by attacking or destroying a work that is known to be popularly venerated – or one which has become a particularly important local or national symbol (as with the attacks on Rembrandt's *Nightwatch* in Amsterdam, or those on paintings by Dürer in Munich).

Finally, there is the whole gamut of cases where the image or building is taken to be a symbol of an oppressive, hated or overthrown order or individual. This includes those occasions when all images that might recall a deposed regime are removed (as in that of the persistent removal of images in Old Kingdom Egypt and in the great Soviet iconoclasm of 1989), or where images that stand in one way or another for a suppressed religion are destroyed. It is in such contexts that one can understand those many instances where the pictures and statues of a hated authority have one or another form of violence visited upon them, or on parts of them. In almost all such cases it is not hard to see the plausibility of the rationale. Only in those instances where the assailant believes that he or she has been instructed by God or some other supernatural being or force to attack a work is it difficult to see the possible continuity with normal rational behaviour.

The range of iconoclastic acts is great: they vary from surface defilement to total destruction. Amongst the commonest examples are partial mutilation, as in the removal of sexual organs (in attempts to reduce the putative sexual affectiveness of the image) or of the limbs of unjust judges; or in the removal of those parts of the body – generally the face (the eyes, but often the mouth or nose), or a limb or two – which most betoken the imagined life of the image. The passage from censorship to iconoclasm – and vice versa – is a common one.

IDOLATRY

Perhaps the commonest basis for iconoclasm is the belief that the image must be destroyed, or have its putative power reduced, because it is something other than it ought to be; or that is has powers that it ought not to have; or that it is testimony to skills which are regarded as supernatural. The aim in all such cases is to deny the power of the image.

Amongst the more characteristic of the iconoclastic injunctions is one to be found in Exodus 20: 3–5 (the first or the first and second of the commandments, depending on one's Church), where the injunction, 'thou shalt have no other gods before me . . . [nor] bow down thyself to them, nor serve them', is followed by the firm prohibition (sometimes regarded simply as part of the first commandment and sometimes – more rigorously – as the second), 'thou shalt not make unto thee any graven image, or any likeness of anything that is in heaven above, or that is in the earth beneath, or that is in the water under the earth.' Equally typical is the passage in the Islamic ḥadith, where the artist who has the temerity to create figurative images is summoned, in the next world, before God, and is instructed to breathe life into his creations. Failing to do so (since that ability is reserved only to God), he is cast into outer hell for his effrontery in attempting to enter, by imitation, what is God's province alone – namely, the creation of living beings.

In both cases the crime is one that falls under the rubric of idolatry.

One of the more persistent allegations against images, especially in Christian cultures, is that pictures and statues, being essentially material, are by their very nature incapable of adequately circumscribing the divine, the spiritual and the essentially immaterial. To attempt to do so is also to make false gods, which have to be cast down in order to preserve the purity of religion or the state.

The notion that images are idolatrous forms an important element in the motivation for many iconoclastic acts and attitudes. Images are taken to be idols when they do not represent the true god; when they are identified with the god or divinity itself (rather than simply as mediators); and when they are wrongly or abusively worshipped or venerated (the German *Abgott* and Dutch *Afgod*, for example, convey more closely the sense of a deceptive deviation from the genuine god). They are seductive because they give the illusion of the godly or divine (as in the original sense of *eidolon*, ghost, phantom). With idolatry there is always a sense of devotion to a substitute for what ought to be the real object of devotion: hence idolatry can occur in the case of real, physical images, and in the more metaphorical sense in which we speak of 'false gods', usually something that is the subject of moral disapprobation. For the sixteenth-century Protestant reformers, avarice was regarded as an idol just as much as any image. Indeed, one consistent element in all allegations of idolatry is the moral dimension. There are no cases in which idolatry is taken to be something good or morally acceptable.

In iconoclastic movements, as well as in some individual cases, the iconoclasts may allege that the images of god (or the approved images of a particular society, whether god, ruler, or symbol of the regime) are not godly, but rather idolatrous. As if to demonstrate that they do not in fact have the powers attributed to them, or which true gods are supposed to have, they are mutilated, overthrown or destroyed. At the end of the sixth century, Gregory the Great threw the pagan idols – that is, the statues of classical antiquity – into the Tiber. They were idols not only because they were beautiful and therefore seductive, but because they were the replete symbols of a corrupt religion, only recently hostile to the true one.

One of the most consistent bases of all those reservations about images that terminate in their mutilation, removal or total elimination is the association between material images and sensuality. Precisely because of their materiality they cannot mediate with the world of the spirit. Both their materiality and their form engage and provoke our senses, through the channel of sight. Excessive engagement with the aesthetic pleasures of art leads only to luxury and seduction (as is frequently alleged in the case of the history of the Roman republic); the purity and primitive virility of the people are better preserved if images are not allowed to corrupt such virtues. Exotic images – and excessive interest in art – make people soft. Images – especially artistic ones – are thus proscribed, in the interests of the commonweal, of moral purity, and of a spirituality untrammelled by sensuality or materiality.

The same fears concerning images surface in modern societies, not simply in relation to the varieties of pornography, but also, in general, in relation to television. And just as in the old arguments, words and texts are assigned a truth value and a spiritual and cultural status that images, by their very nature, are not believed to have. They cannot attain this status, because they are material and sensual, and are perceived by the eyes, the most direct channel of all to the senses. Hearing now takes the place of seeing, not only as a more reliable form of perception, but also as a less potentially dangerous one. Words replace images in societies that are purified of idolatry: written texts in literate societies, the spoken word in illiterate ones. The way is prepared first by censorship, and then, increasingly, by one or more of the varieties of iconoclasm

See also CENSORSHIP; PORNOGRAPHY.

BIBLIOGRAPHY

Freedberg, David: *Iconoclasts and Their Motives* (Maarssen: Schwartz, 1985).
Freedberg, David: *The Power of Images: Studies in the History and Theory of Response* (Chicago, Ill.: Chicago University Press, 1989).
Warnke, Martin, ed.: *Bildersturm: Die Zerstörung des Kunstwerks* (Munich: Hanser, 1973).

DAVID FREEDBERG

idolatry   *See* ICONOCLASM AND IDOLATRY.

illusion   A false or mistaken belief about something actually present to the senses; to be distinguished from delusion, in which the perceiver does not merely make a mistake in what he sees but suffers from a whole range of grossly disordered beliefs – such as in hallucination, when, for example he or she might be seeing pink elephants when there are no elephants in the visual field to be seen.

Illusion has given rise, throughout the ages, to several blanket theories of art – to the effect that all art is illusory – from Xenophon and Plato to, in the twentieth century, Samuel Alexander and Ernst Gombrich. Illusion in art is often described as 'illusionism', whereby the artist attempts such a degree of verisimilitude in representation – holding up the mirror to nature – that the spectator is, to a lesser or greater degree, inclined to believe that the pictured object is the real object, while, at the same time, continuing to be aware that he or she is confronted by a picture and not the real object. In a narrower sense, illusionism is used to describe modes of representation such as perspective to achieve *trompe l'oeil* effects, designed to deceive the spectator utterly into taking what is represented for real. For example, a painted curtain, obscuring part of a picture, is rendered with such verisimilitude that the spectator attempts to pull it aside.

A powerful illusion theory of art is that of Alexander, who contrasts seeing real objects with seeing pictured ones in a representation. In both cases part of what the spectator sees is supplied by the imagination, and part by what he or she directly perceives. But in the case of the real object, the qualities imputed to it by the spectator really do belong to it, while in the case of the pictured object, these qualities are illusory. Further, in ordinary perceptual illusion, the illusion disappears on closer examination, but in picture illusion, illusion is of the very essence in rendering the picture's object significant.

Another powerful and extremely influential illusion theory of art is that of Gombrich who, in his book *Art and Illusion* (introduction and ch. 7), and in a somewhat modified way in his later essay 'Illusion in art', emphasizes the role of the imagination in creating conditions of illusion in the context, for example, of action. The hobby-horse, a mere stick, turns imaginatively into a horse when ridden by a child; similarly, bison cave drawings are punctured by spears, and cult images are carried in religious processions. But when action is removed, Gombrich argues, 'art has to cast around for means to strengthen the illusion and to create the twilight realm of suspended disbelief, which the Greeks first explored. But here, and ever since, illusion could turn into deception only when the context of action set up an expectation which reinforced the artist's handiwork.'

In the case of paintings, illusion turning into deception is achieved by projection, the application of what Gombrich calls the 'ETC. principle'. By this he means the assumption that the spectator tends to make that to see a few members of a series is to see them all. No painting, however realistically complete, is ever absolutely so. The artist simply cannot represent all that is there to be represented, but is forced to employ visual clues by means of which the spectator projects on to the painting what is simply not represented there, by using the ETC. principle. For example, the heavenly host trailing off into the sky will be represented by carefully delineated angels in the foreground, which gradually become mere dots as the depicted host nears the picture's upper frame. So, even at this level, representation entails illusion. But even more radically than this, is there not illusion involved when what are, inspect-

ed close up, the dabs of paint in a picture, turn themselves miraculously into a view of a landscape as one steps back?

Quoting Kenneth Clark, Gombrich in his introduction labels the attempt, always in vain, to fix the turning point as the attempt to 'stalk an illusion'. As one steps back from the canvas, at what point do the patches of paint on the canvas transform themselves into what is represented? The impossibility of capturing that turning point, Gombrich argues, is illustrated by Jastrow's famous duck/rabbit picture (as deployed also by Wittgenstein in part 2, § 11, of his *Philosophical Investigations*. The drawing of the duck can, by turning it through 90 degrees, be transformed into a drawing of a rabbit. But it is impossible, argues Wittgenstein, to see the drawing as *both* a duck and a rabbit simultaneously. By analogy, argues Gombrich, we cannot simultaneously see both the canvas and its configurations of paint *and* what these items represent.

However, as Wollheim, Scruton and Wilkerson have subsequently argued, the latter anology does not hold. For the duck and the rabbit are both representations, whereas what Gombrich uses that analogy to explain is the relationship between the patches of paint on the canvas and what these represent. The dichotomy of duck and rabbit is one of representations, whereas what Gombrich needs to explain is the dichotomy between canvas and what is represented on it. Wollheim goes on to say that an artist, in painting a scene before him, must surely be able, *pace* Gombrich, to attend to *both* the configurations of his paint on canvas *and* what these configurations are used by him to represent. So Gombrich's impossibility resolves itself into an unproblematical case of bidimensional seeing.

Unlike Alexander, Gombrich stresses the similarities, not the differences, between seeing real objects and seeing pictured objects. But, as Wollheim, Wilkerson and others have argued, we need to concentrate on the great differences between them. Seeing an object X under the description Y (say, 'ash-tray') entails *in normal circumstances* that there is indeed a Y (ash-tray) in our visual field. This is how we acquire true beliefs about the world (or false ones if the description Y does not apply), and the acquisition of such beliefs is not voluntary. But picture-seeing, by way of contrast, is akin to 'the dawning of an aspect' type of seeing. That is, we choose to see the appropriately shaped object X (say, a cloud) under the description Y (for instance, 'elephant') if it is sufficiently elephant-shaped. But, of course, we need not choose to see the cloud like that. 'Dawning of an aspect' seeing is not a case of belief acquisition, and is to a greater or lesser degree voluntary; looking at such a cloud does not make us believe that there is an elephant in the sky.

Gombrich's theory has been seminal, since it has spawned a host of other theories of pictorial representation by way of rebuttal, such as those of Nicholas Wolterstorff and Flint Schier. An interesting defence of Gombrich's theory has been offered by Alastair Hannay (1970) in his criticism of Wollheim's essay 'On drawing an object'. Wollheim had considered, in his own essay, a minimal case of representation (a black dot on a white canvas) in his pamphlet 'On Drawing an Object' (1964). It is possible either to represent such a dot as being as it actually is on the white canvas, or, with suitable shading, it can be made to appear either that the dot is being seen through a hole in the white canvas and is therefore behind it, or that it protrudes in front of the canvas. Because of these cases, Wollheim finds it necessary to distinguish the pictorial dimension of the representation from the physical dimension of it. In the second and third cases the relations between dot and canvas of 'behind' and 'in front' are not really

visible, but only as they appear, or are pictured, to be. Hence illusion must be involved – or so argues Hannay in reply.

Further, he draws a distinction between two types of resemblance: normal or symmetrical resemblance and asymmetrical resemblance. Picture-seeing, unlike looking at a model of an object, involves asymmetrical resemblance. This is akin to the case of a psychotic person who sees the legs of the Eiffel Tower as threatening soldiers' legs. It is clearly asymmetrical, because, conversely, the same person cowering in front of actual advancing and threatening soldiers' legs does not thereby conjure up the Eiffel Tower's legs. In this kind of case, unlike that of looking at a model, a description of what an object is seen as must accompany the seeing. Since there are only the legs of the Eiffel Tower to be seen, and no soldiers' legs, this means, according to Hannay, that illusion must be involved. He illegitimately concludes, however, that illusion must be involved in pictorial representation. He is correct in arguing that asymmetrical resemblance characterizes picture-seeing, but unwarranted in supposing that illusion is required to explain the difference between seeing a real object and seeing an object in the picture.

It is worth noting, finally, that some philosophers have argued that theories of pictorial representation have little to do with aesthetics, since theories of pictorial representation explicate pictures both with and without aesthetic merit. But there have been others, notably Kant and Harold Osborne, who have stressed the importance of the distinction in trying to explicate what it is for a picture to be a picture.

See also GOMBRICH; REPRESENTATION; RESEMBLANCE.

BIBLIOGRAPHY

Alexander, Samuel: *Philosophical and Literary Pieces* (London: Macmillan, 1939).

Gombrich, Ernst: *Art and Illusion* (Oxford: Phaidon, 1960).

Gombrich, Ernst and Gregory, R.L., eds: *Illusion*

in Nature and Art (London: Duckworth, 1973).

Hannay, Alastair: 'Wollheim and seeing black on white as a picture', *British Journal of Aesthetics*, 10 (1970), 107–18.

Peetz, Dieter: 'Some current philosophical theories of pictorial representation', *British Journal of Aesthetics*, 27 (1987), 227–37.

Schier, Flint: *Deeper into Pictures* (Cambridge: Cambridge University Press, 1986).

Scruton, Roger: *Art and Imagination* (London: Routledge & Kegan Paul, 1974).

Wilkerson, T.E.: 'Representation, illusion and aspects', *British Journal of Aesthetics*, 8 (1978), 45–58.

Wollheim, Richard: 'On drawing an object', *Aesthetics*, ed. H. Osborne (Oxford: Oxford University Press, 1972).

DIETER PEETZ

imagination A word used in a variety of ways, usually to denote a mental capacity. As a technical term of philosophy it has at least two senses: First, the capacity to experience 'mental images', and, second, the capacity to engage in creative thought. The connection between these two senses is obscure, partly because each is obscure in itself, and very much dependent upon the theory with which it is associated.

THE CAPACITY TO EXPERIENCE 'MENTAL IMAGES'

Mental images occur in thinking, in dreaming, in perceiving and in remembering. They also occur when we are trying to imagine something (in the second sense of the term). Because they occur in so many different contexts, it would be quite misleading to suppose that a theory of mental images is the same as a theory of imagination, in the second sense, or even a necessary *part* of such a theory. For one thing, there seems to be nothing wrong in the suggestion that animals have mental images: for certainly they perceive, dream and remember (after a fashion). But it strains credibility to say that they have imagination in the second sense – if we mean by this that they can engage in the thought-processes involved in story-telling, painting or creative science.

IMAGES AND THOUGHTS

A mental image is like a thought in the following ways:

(1) It is 'of' or 'about' something. This feature – sometimes referred to as 'intentionality' – implies that a creature's capacity for mental imagery strictly depends upon its cognitive powers. If it cannot, for example, have *thoughts* about the past, then it cannot have 'memory images' either.

(2) It may be true or false: a true image of your friend's face is one that *shows him as he is* – that is, which corresponds to the reality.

(3) It stands to thoughts in relations of implication and contradiction. My image of Venice may contradict your thoughts about the town; it may also imply them.

However, a mental image is not *merely* a thought. I can think about Venice, even produce an accurate mental description, and yet fail to be visited by any Venetian imagery. I can remember a text without having an image of it on the page; I can think my way through a musical score, without 'hearing it in my head'; and so on. Images are like perceptions: they have a component that we are inclined to call 'sensory', and which relates them to the experiences that we obtain through our senses.

IMAGES AND SENSORY EXPERIENCES

It is not easy to say, in precise terms, what the 'sensory' character of imagery consists in, partly because it is not easy to say what we mean in general by a 'sensory' character. The following features of images are, however, shared with various other 'sensory' experiences, and could be assumed to provide a pre-philosophical definition of the idea:

(1) Images can be precisely dated in time: they begin at a certain moment, last for a while, and then cease.

(2) They may be more or less intense (like a pain, or a visual experience). This is not a matter of being more or less *detailed*, but is something *sui generis*.

(3) They can be fully described only by reference to a corresponding *perceptual* experience: my image of Venice can be conveyed only by describing what it would be like to *see* such and such a vista; my image of a piece of music must, likewise, be described in terms of how the music is *heard*, and so on.

(4) There is a 'subjective' aspect to every image, which we may express by saying that there is a 'what it's like' to have the image. It is doubtful that there is a 'what it's like' in the case of a *thought*.

CREATIVE IMAGINATION AND MENTAL IMAGERY

Mental images occur when we dream, when we remember, and also when we *imagine* things. Sometimes we describe a person as imagining what he thinks is there but isn't. In this sense 'imagining' means something like 'suffering an illusion', and to 'imagine things' is to acquire *false beliefs* about the real world. Creative imagination, however, is not a matter of illusion. The person with a strong imagination does not suffer more false *beliefs* than his less imaginative neighbour: rather, he thinks more widely, more creatively, less literally. His thought roams among possibilities and is more ready to 'suspend' both belief and disbelief. Imaginative thoughts in this sense are not illusions about the real world, but undeceived depictions of a world that is not only unreal but also known to be so. (To be *taken in* by this world – for example, by the world of a play – is to exhibit a deficiency of imagination rather than a superabundance of it.)

Imagery has a part to play in creative imagination, although it is neither a necessary nor a sufficient ingredient. When I imagine, for example, a dialogue between Socrates and Xanthippe, I may also envisage it, in the sense of imagining what it would be like to *see* and *hear* the encounter between them. In such a case, my imaginative thoughts are partly embodied in images. (Imagery is, indeed, an essential ingredient in 'imagining what it's like'.) Such images differ from dream images and perceptual images, in that they lie within the province of the will. It

makes no sense to command a person to dream something, or to see something. But we can certainly command him to imagine something, and he may 'summon' or 'construct' the image without further ado, and using no method other then the direct application of his will.

It is one of Wittgenstein's most interesting observations in this area, that mental states can be classified according to whether they are or are not 'subject to the will', and that the distinction cuts across the traditional divisions between the sensory and the intellectual, between the animal and the rational, between the affective and the cognitive, and even the 'passive' and the 'active' (as these were described, for example, by Spinoza). There are perceptions which are subject to the will (seeing an aspect) and also cognitive states (supposing, hypothesizing); but wherever belief or sensation is involved, the will, as it were, withdraws. I can command you to suppose that the moon is made of rock (rather than cheese), but not to believe it; I can command you to injure your finger, but not to have a pain in your finger; and so on.

One reason for thinking that memory and creative imagination are closely related is that both involve imagery, and in both cases the imaging process remains at least partly within the domain of the will. When I 'summon up remembrance of things past' I am *doing* something which I might have refrained from doing. I deliberately call to mind the appearance and character of past events and objects, so as to undergo again, in some faint and helpless version, the experiences which were once imprinted on my senses. There is an art in this, which is not unlike the art employed in fiction, and while not everyone is able to achieve what Proust achieved in reworking the past as though it were entirely the *product* of creative imagination, there is no doubt that 'powers of recall' and 'powers of creation' have, in this area, much in common and speak to a single emotional need.

CREATIVE IMAGINATION

The voluntary nature of imaginative acts

gives a clue to creative imagination. For, whether or not it involves imagery, imagination always involves the summoning or creating of mental contents which are *not otherwise given* (as they are given, for example, in perception and judgement). When I stand before a horse it involves no act of creative imagination to entertain the image of a horse – for this image is implanted in me by my experience, and is *no doing of mine*. Likewise, if I listen to a story of some battle, or read an account of it in the newspaper, my thoughts are not my own doing, and I play no creative role in the unfolding of them. In general, things perceived and things believed, in the normal course of our cognitive activity, are imprinted upon us, and are both passive and independent of our own creative powers.

When, however, I summon the image of a horse in the absence of a real horse, or invent the description of a battle which I have heard about from no other source, my image and my thought go *beyond* what is given to me, and lie within the province of my will. Such inventive acts are paradigm cases of imagination. And, in so far as they involve thoughts, these thoughts are of a distinctive kind – they are not beliefs about the actual world, but suppositions about an imaginary world.

How should we understand such thought processes? A useful device is suggested by Frege's theory of assertion. In the inference from p and p implies q to q, it is clear that the proposition p occurs unasserted in the second premise, regardless of whether it is asserted in the first. Yet p is the *same* in both premises: otherwise the inference would be fallacious through equivocation. It follows that assertion is no part of the meaning of a sentence – that a proposition does not change merely because it is affirmed as true. This elementary result enables us to draw an important conclusion – namely, that the content of a belief may be exactly reproduced in a thought that is *not* a belief, in which the content is merely 'entertained'. This happens all the time in inference: it is also what primarily happens in imagination.

We may therefore venture an account, at least, of one central component of creative imagination: the capacity to 'imagine that p'. In imagining that p, a person entertains the thought that p, without affirming it as true; the thought that p goes beyond what is given to him by his ordinary cognitive and perceptual powers; and his summoning of p is either an act of will, or within the province of his will (so that he could, for example, choose at any moment to cancel it, and to summon not-p instead). When, as may happen, the thought that p contains a perceptual component, it may be embodied in or absorbed into an image; and this image too is an exercise of imagination.

Not all creative imagination fits easily into this model, since not all imagination is an 'imagining *that* . . .'. Some works of imagination are pure images, without subject-matter other than the sensory forms themselves. For example, composing a melody is a work of creation: it involves putting sounds together to form an interesting totality. This is a voluntary act, which goes beyond what is given in perception; but it is not an expression of a thought in Frege's sense. A melody is not a proposition; nevertheless, it is *like* a proposition, in having an intrinsic order, sense and communicative power. Such processes, which are like thoughts but which do not involve the creation of imaginary worlds, may lie, as it were, in the same domain as 'imagining that . . .': and this is what we instinctively feel to be true of music, abstract painting and architecture. Hence we freely use the word 'imagination' of all the creative arts. Nevertheless, it is a work of theory to show that we are entitled to suppose that these various exercises of imagination involve *one* mental capacity, rather than several.

IMAGINARY WORLDS

Fiction – whether in drama, poetry or prose, whether in figurative painting or mime – is a prime instance of creative imagination, and one which also shows the importance of imagery in the full elaboration and understanding of imaginative thoughts. It is tempting to argue that a fiction is something like a possible world: or at least a glimpse into such a world. The work of imagination involves the construction (or, for a realist, the discovery) of possibilities – the purpose being, perhaps, to set the actual world in the context of these possibilities. Since our everyday thought automatically involves us in assessing possibilities and probabilities, the capacity to envisage 'possible worlds' is already implied in our day-to-day psychology. For this reason we may wish to affirm the old theory (espoused for a variety of reasons by Hume, Kant and Hegel) that imagination is a part of ordinary thought and perception.

The suggestion is misleading in various ways. First, although we must invoke possible worlds in order to account for the meaning of modal sentences, and although modal thoughts (about possibilities, necessities and probabilities) are involved in all scientific thinking, we do not have to *envisage* these possibilities, or to spell them out in narrative terms, in order to make our everyday judgements that depend on them. Second, when we *do* spell out the narrative of an imaginary world, we are not bound by the constraints of possibility. In a tragedy, Aristotle remarked, impossibilities may be countenanced provided that they are – in the narrative context – probable. However possible, an *improbability* involves a failure of imaginative drive. What is meant by 'probability' here is 'truth to character'. Thus, when Fafner the giant, in Wagner's *Ring*, turns into Fafner the dragon, a profound spiritual and moral truth is enacted before us, even though such a transformation is metaphysically impossible (cf. Ovid's *Metamorphoses*).

The creation of an imaginary world is a distinct enterprise, with a purpose all of its own. Understanding fictions involves recognizing the 'fictional context', in which events, persons and objects occur, bracketed not only from the realm of actuality, but also at times from the realm of possibility. And yet, in the successful fiction everything proceeds with its own kind of necessity: notwithstanding its deliberate unreality, it aims always to be 'true to life'.

The emotional response to imaginary worlds is one of the most interesting of all mental phenomena. For it seems that we can feel towards these fictitious scenes a version of the emotions which animate us in our real existence. Yet – because the objects of these emotions are not only unreal but known to be so – we are not motivated to act as we should normally act. On the contrary, we relax into our emotions, and live for a while on a plane of pure untroubled sympathy, laughing and crying without the slightest moral or physical cost. This mental exercise is a strange one – for in what sense are we really moved by that which has, for us, no reality? And why should it be so precious to us, to exercise our sympathies in this seemingly futile way? These are among the most important questions in aesthetics.

FANTASY AND IMAGINATION

An imaginary world is, *ex hypothesi*, not a real world. Imagination does not aim at truth, as belief aims at truth. On the contrary, it aims, in a sense, to avoid truth. And yet it is governed by the attempt to *understand its own creations*, and to bring them into fruitful relation with the world that is. We expect the work of imagination to *cast light* on its subject-matter, and on the real originals from which its subject-matter is ultimately drawn. In short, imaginative thoughts are constrained by the need to be *appropriate* to reality. And though appropriateness is more nearly a moral than a logical ideal, it is undeniable that 'truth to life' is a normal part of it.

Coleridge's distinction between fancy and imagination may therefore still have a lively attraction: for we should distinguish the kind of disciplined story-telling which illuminates reality and enables us in a novel way to come to terms with it, from the undisciplined flight from reality into worlds of sentimentality and make-believe. Fantasy may seem to be a step further along the path taken by imagination; in fact it is a distinct exercise of the mind, involving the creation of substitute objects for old emotions, rather than new emotions towards the familiar human world. The nature of the fantasy object is *dictated* by the passion that seeks it. (Pornography, therefore, is a prime instance of fantasy.) By contrast, the truly imaginative object produces and controls our response to it, and thereby educates and renews our passions, so as to redirect them towards the actual world.

IMAGINATIVE PERCEPTION

There is a particular exercise of the imagination that is of vital concern to the student of aesthetics: the kind involved not in creating an imaginary object, but in perceiving it. My image of the horse that stands before me is a straightforward perception: the horse is 'given' by the experience that I cannot help but have. But my image of the horse presented in a picture is not like this at all. First, I neither believe, nor am tempted to believe, that the horse is real. Second, I perceive the horse only to the extent that I am prepared to 'go along with' the lines and impulse of the painting – I recreate in imagination a living creature, out of what is at best a two-dimensional outline. What I see goes beyond what is given, in just the way that a fictional thought outstrips reality. Third, my experience lies within the domain of the will – a fact that is conclusively proved by such ambiguous pictures as the duck–rabbit, in which I can decide at will to see now a duck, now a rabbit, in the shape before me. (It will be said that this is a special case; on the contrary, it is merely an emphatic version of the normal case. Even in the most realistic and unambiguous of Stubbs's horses I may choose to see the creature now as an eighteen-hand giant, now as a fifteen-hand ladies' horse, now as resting, now as poised for movement, and so on. It lies in the logic of the case that what I see is only partly determined by the physical picture in which I see it, and needs to be completed by an act of attention.)

This 'seeing in' provides a paradigm for many acts of aesthetic attention: as when I hear movement in music, hear the tone of voice in poetry, see the dignified posture in a building. It also provides us with an interesting contrast, between seeing X in Y, and noticing a resemblance or analogy between X and Y. (Clearly, I can notice the resemblance between the duck–rabbit and a rabbit even while seeing it as a duck, an experience which forbids me from seeing it as a rabbit.) This contrast runs parallel to that between metaphor and simile, in the first of which one object is (if the metaphor is successful) embodied in another, rather than merely likened to it. Since understanding metaphor is an integral part of, and paradigm case of, all the higher forms of literary experience, it is clear that we have a clue, here, to the work of the imagination in aesthetic understanding.

IMAGINATION AND NORMATIVITY

Images and metaphors may be more or less successful; stories more or less true to life; paintings more or less insightful; music more or less sincere. All the works of the imagination seem to invite our criticism; for imagination is involved too in understanding them, and once our thought has been released into imaginary worlds it is bound by the laws of this new-found freedom. Imagination is a rational capacity, one which not only is peculiar to rational beings but which also compels them to exercise their reason, to ask 'Why?' of every phrase, work and line, and to judge their appropriateness to the familiar world of reality. In the works of imagination, therefore, a peculiar form of judgement arises: we sense that, however freely the imagination may roam, there is a right way and a wrong way to go. And in making this judgement we endeavour to bring the imagination back to earth, to use it as an instrument of knowledge and understanding, rather than an instrument of flight. This is perhaps what Freud meant, when he described art as a passage from fantasy back to reality. It is perhaps, too, why Kant discerned an act of universalizable judgement – a kind of incipient legislation – behind every aesthetic experience. At any rate, it is the origin of criticism, and the foundation for our belief that imagination is not merely a fact, but also a value.

See also CREATIVITY; FICTIONAL ENTITIES; METAPHOR; PERCEPTION.

BIBLIOGRAPHY

Frege, Gottlob: *The Philosophical Writings of Gottlob Frege*, trans. P. Geach and M. Black (Oxford: Basil Blackwell, 1952).

Kant, Immanuel: *Critique of Judgement* (Berlin, 1790); trans. J. Bernard (New York: Hafner, 1966).

Sartre, Jean-Paul: *Psychology of the Imagination*, R. Wollheim, Seeing Painting, C. Wmyenthen, Philosphical investigations, 11 xi Kendall Walton, Mimesis as make believe R. Scruton, Art & Imagination (Paris, 1940); trans. B. Frechtman (New York: Philosophical Library, 1948).

Sartre, Jean-Paul: *Imagination: A Psychological Critique* (Paris, 1936); trans. F. Williams (Ann Arbor, Mich.: University of Michigan Press, 1962).

Scruton, Roger: *Art and Imagination: A Study in the Philosophy of Mind* (London: Routledge & Kegan Paul, 1982).

Walton, Kendall: *Mimesis or Make-believe*.

Warnock, Mary: *Imagination*, (Berkeley, Calif.: University of California Press, 1976).

Wittgenstein, Ludwig *Philosophical Investigations*, trans. G. Anscombe (Oxford: Basil Blackwell, 1953).

Wittgenstein, Ludwig: *Remarks on the Philosophy of Psychology*, trans. G. Anscombe; I, ed. G. Anscombe and G. von Wright; II, ed. G. von Wright and H. Nyman (Oxford: Basil Blackwell, 1980).

Wollheim, Richard: *Art and Its Objects*; 2nd edn with six supplementary essays (Cambridge: Cambridge University Press, 1980).

ROGER SCRUTON

Indian aesthetics

The life that flows through my veins, day and night,/Dances in wondrous rhyme in the heavens,/Courses through the pores of the earth,/Scattering joy to leaves, flowers and grains. (Rabindranath Tagore, *Vichitra*)

The music of the words jumps out of the pages and engulfs us. We admire a poem because of its melody and spontaneity, depth of imagination and (what Keats calls) 'fine excess', and because of the environment it creates. It draws us in, and we melt into it. But what are the conditions that contribute to the making of a poem? This is a question to which Indian rhetoricians have attended very carefully, and the outcome is an array of divergent views.

The word that enters the vocabulary of every view relating to the making of a poem is *pratibha*. There is uniform recognition of *pratibha* as an important requisite for poetic creation. This does not mean that *pratibha* is confined to discussions of *poetry* alone; on the contrary, it figures crucially in Indian deliberation on *every form of creative activity*, including visual art and music. So to discuss *pratibha* in connection with poetry is to discuss not just one particular issue about poetry, but the issue on which Indian thinking about art has focused. Since the concept plays a central role in Indian aesthetics, Indian philosphers have devoted much of their time and energy towards the delineation of it.

What is *pratibha*? How is it to be explained? As a universal (*jati*), or as an unanalysable, ultimate, concept? Is *pratibha* inborn or spontaneous (*sahaja* or *naisargiki*)? Or can it be acquired? Is it sufficient for any creative production?

First, *pratibha* means creative (poetic) disposition, or 'internal disposition' (*antargata bhava*), as Bharata (1894, 7.2) designates it; without it poetry is impossible or, if attempted, ridiculous. Or, it is a state in which, in the words of Stephen Spender, one writes one's best poetry, and which leads to the sudden germination of a line or phrase or something still vague, a dim cloud of an idea which the poet feels must be condensed into a shower of words; and thus a miraculous poem grows. Hence *pratibha* is also a power (*sakti*), a spark that triggers a poem conveying new, wonderful and charming combinations and relations of words and things.

The central question is about the fundamental identity of *pratibha*. Is it universal (*jati*)? The answer is, perhaps, no. The reasons may not be far to seek. *Jati* is *nitya*, eternal or atemporal, but *pratibha* may wane with the passage of time, on account of old age and infirmity. Again, *jati* is distinct from, but inheres in, many individuals. There is the same universal in all the individuals of a class. It is because all people have one common core, that they all come within the class of humanity and are considered as essentially the same. What we have said about *jati* is analogous to Bertrand Russell's enunciation of a universal as 'an eternal timeless entity which may be shared by many particulars'. But *pratibha* is not a universal, since it does not belong to many persons; the poetic flame is not lit in all souls.

Again, the relation between a *jati* and the members it embraces is intrinsic (*samavaya*); one cannot remain without the other; humanity and the particular individuals under it are united into an essential bond of correlation. *Jati* is manifested only in the context of this inseparable relation. But the bond between *pratibha* and the aesthetic form it creates is not one of *samavaya*. *Pratibha* remains, even in the absence of poetic production, just like the cloud before the shower it brings. Even if a poet ceases to write poems for the time being, his creative power is still with him. Hence *pratibha* is a specimen of *non-jati*. It is an unseen power capable of being inferred only from its effects. It is unanalysable and beyond the bounds of a precise and clear-cut definition. Therefore, Jagannatha (1913, chap. 1) rightly describes it as an ultimate concept (*akhanda upadhi*).

But what is the secret behind the blossoming of *pratibha*? Is it spontaneous, natural, like our breath? Or is it a matter of acquisition, a result of hard toil? The consensus of opinion among Indian philosophers is that the creative power is a native endowment blossoming without any reason, though a few like Rudrata (1906) also concede some role to training and learning, or knowledge and scholarship (*vyutpatti*), in the flare-up of creative (poetic) disposition. They stress the *spontaneity* of *pratibha*, but at the same time acknowledge that *pratibha* may be *acquired*. However, with Jagannatha, *pratibha* is not a natural propensity but an outcome of unimpeded cultivation (*utpadya*); and perhaps he is alone in this conviction.

The crucial issue is whether *pratibha* is sufficient. Different answers to this question may be categorized as follows:

(1) *Pratibha* is the only requisite for a poetic composition. It is alpha and omega. This is the view of Jagannatha.

(2) Inborn *pratibha* is the fundamental condition for propelling a poetic creation; but this does not remove the necessity for *vyutpatti* and *abhyasa* (practice), though they are lower in the hierarchy. This constitutes the view of Anandavardhana Vagbhata and others.

(3) Equal emphasis is placed upon inborn creative disposition, training and knowledge, and untiring practice as working conjointly towards the making of a poem. This is held by Dandin, Mammata, Vamana and others.

Jagannatha, as noted, regards *pratibha* as the sole factor for creating poetry; and he explains it as inaugurating the sudden flash of sound and sense tinged with emotion. But this *pratibha*, or creative disposition, is not inborn, or *sahaja*; in some it is the outcome of divine grace, while in others, the outcome of special proficiency and practice. This generation of *pratibha* through different causes is analogous to the generation of fire sometimes from grass and sometimes from a piece of wood.

Therefore, it would be wrong to assert that the creative power is the product of divine grace, proficiency and repeated practice taken together. We cannot argue that proficiency and repeated practice alone give birth to creative power, for this power is noticeable even to a child who is already enriched by it through divine grace prior to his *learning* the ways of the world or any *venture* with poetical compositions. Of course, one may argue that, in the case of such a child, learning and practice in previous incarnations contribute towards the production of *pratibha*. But the effect is explicable without indulging in the assumption of learning and practice in previous incarnations. If it is wrong to account for *pratibha* in terms of *vyutpatti* and *abhyasa* alone, it is equally wrong to account for it in terms of divine grace alone. For men who in earlier years could not compose poems may do so later, after prolonged training and practice. To hold that this is made possible by divine grace is to render inexplicable the non-manifestation of *pratibha* in their early years.

In some people, then, *pratibha* flowers from the grace of God and of great men, but in others it flowers from proficiency and practice, and it is through this creative propensity that poetry comes into being. But does this not entangle us in perplexity and the old fallacy of plurality of causes? If the effects emanate from two different sets of causes, how do they become the same *pratibha*? Jagannatha holds that the poetic disposition is of two types – one activated by divine merit, and the other by proficiency-cum-effort. These two kinds of *pratibha* do not coalesce, because their roots are different. But the same difficulty pops up again. How can two different *pratibhas* (causes) lead to one and the same effect or one and the same poetic composition (*kavya*)? Jagannatha escapes this difficulty by arguing that *pratibha* caused by merit leads to one kind of poetry, while that created by *vyutpatti* and *abhyasa* leads to poetry of a different kind.

But what is the reason for insisting that *pratibha* is of different kinds? Is it because it has different roots/causes? If so, the picture is not very convincing. I may earn £200 either by winning a lottery or by delivering lectures. But it is the same money that I have earned, not money of different kinds. Does *pratibha*, strictly speaking, admit of kinds? The difficulty is particularly increased by Jagannatha's contention that *pratibha* is an unanalysable concept. This means that we cannot devise any criterion to separate different kinds of poetic power. A related problem is how poetry produced by *pratibha* via divine grace can be of a different kind from that inaugurated by *pratibha* via *vyutpatti* and *abhyasa*.

Perhaps these difficulties are linked with Jagannatha's appraisal of poetic disposition, as being *acquired* or caused. For this poetic disposition, arguably, is unlearned; it gushes forth without any reason. Spender has told how a certain line, 'a language of flesh and rose', 'flashed into [his] head' during a train journey through the coalfields of the Black Country, when a stranger remarked, 'Everything there is man-made' (Spender, 1964, p.

41). His observation serves to highlight the fact that poetic disposition is the spontaneous awareness of a line or a phrase, of a 'rhythm, a dance, a fury', waiting to be realized in a poem. It is the inborn music which the poet condenses into a shower of words. If the poetic sense or disposition is not already there in its own right, with all its warmth and spontaneity, *vyutpatti* and *abhyasa* or any other kind of accomplishment cannot kindle it. It is not without reason that Dandin and others have looked upon *pratibha* as being primarily *naisargiki* (congenital or natural).

There is, however, another variation of Jagannatha's theme, dwelling equally on *pratibha* as the womb of poetry, though with a different accent on proficiency and practice. Vagbhata, Hemacandra and others agree with Abhinava Gupta (1928) that creativity is fundamentally an internal disposition, or a consciousness, or a sentience (*prajna*) capable of creating excellent objects, or giving birth to poems possessed of relishable feeling, clarity and beauty. At the same time they acknowledge some accessory role of *vyutpatti* and *abhyasa*. For them, *vyutpatti* means proficiency in the ways of the world, in the different branches of learning, such as grammar and history, along with intimate familiarity with masterpieces. *Abhyasa* is repeated practice, intensive, uninterrupted writing. But neither *vyutpatti* nor *abhyasa* can cause poetry: this is the privilege belonging to *pratibha* alone. To say that *kavya* (poetic composition) emerges in collaboration with *pratibha* and *vyutpatti* is incorrect. For, if *pratibha* is competent enough to create elegant poems with charming or beautiful images, sounds and ideas, *vyutpatti* loses its efficacy in this causal story. What, then, is the function of *vyutpatti* and *abhyasa*? They do not figure in the causal story; nonetheless, they contribute to poetry – each in its own benign way. Proficiency ornaments a poem, adds charm to it, while practice helps in prolific creations.

Yet the picture remains unclear. If *pratibha* is capable of producing charming poems, why the necessity for *vyutpatti* to make them charming? And it is perhaps disheartening to see knowledge and practice given such secondary roles. Anandavardhana does not give knowledge its proper due when he holds that it is possible to conceal lack of knowledge by the inborn poetic power, but not conversely; lack of poetic capability leaps to the eye at once (Anandavardhana, 1928). This places more confidence in *pratibha* than in knowledge, and denies that natural poetic sense, refined intellect and unflagging effort have equal mandates in the making of poems.

But this is not a correct way of looking at the modalities of poetic creation. A poem is deprived of its effect not only by lack of *pratibha*, but also by lack of proficiency. Absence of proficiency can be as conspicuous as that of *pratibha*. Poetic sense cannot bloom into the flower of poetry without the aid of knowledge and practice. All of them work together and need each other, as when a seed shoots up into a plant only when it comes in contact with earth and water. Creativity unfolds within the horizon of the concert of *pratibha*, *vyutpatti* and *abhyasa*. And this is the story told by Dandin, Bhamaha, Mammata, Rudrata and Vamana. I shall elaborate and defend this position.

Nothing mysterious is claimed when we emphasize *pratibha* for poetic art. Just as one cannot be a musician without musical sense, one cannot write poems without having a poetic disposition. A poem rises up only when there appears in consciousness a glimmer of an idea waiting for appropriate words. Unless there is this poetic spark, there are no poems. That is why Vamana, Rudrata and others have described *pratibha* as an impression that serves as the very seed of poetry. Without this seed, knowledge or practice leads only to prodigal expenditure of pen and ink.

But, equally, *pratibha* alone is not enough for poetic creations. *Vyutpatti*, as already noted, is knowledge of or proficiency in metre, lexicon, grammar, fine arts and ways of the world. Let us now explore why this knowledge is essential for a poetic composition.

Poetry has a melodious form of its own which distinguishes it from the formal aridity of philosophical discourse. In the words of Rabindranath, it is invigorated with the music of rhyme, the harmony of sounds, the glamour and sonority of words, and their clever but graceful concatenation (Tagore, 1943, p. 8). This propels Vamana to find the soul of a poem in diction. This diction relates to the density of words, their particular arrangements which give a poem a special tonality, a special charm, and a distinctive flavour. Hence writing poems demands command over metre, grammar, 'significant form', lexicon and language.

At the same time poetry is not merely, nor a kind of, musical elocution alone, as Mallarmé, Valéry and Sartre are wont to think. Sartre, in particular, expresses this conviction when he holds that poetry is opaque in the sense in which we think of things as opaque, as existing in themselves and without ulterior references. Poetry, according to him, does not say or communicate anything: it only captures the inner depth and music of words. In the realm of poems we are concerned with words as words, with their sonority and length, with their masculine or feminine endings and not with what they are about. In a poem 'the poet has chosen the poetic attitude which considers words as things and not as signs' (Sartre, 1969, p. 497).

Mallarmé, Valéry and Sartre wanted to make poetry as abstract as music, which is identified primarily in terms of its inner harmony. They thought that the artistic creation of a poet reveals its glory when divested of content or meaning. But poetry is not analogous to music. The signification of a melody, provided we can speak of signification at all, is nothing outside of its inner pattern. Even if music does not say anything about the world, its beauty and vitality are yet manifested in the graceful combination of notes. Its beauty lies in its significant form. But this is not the case with poetry. It is anchored in language, and language is so enmeshed in meaning that a poem reaches us not only through the melody of its form, its tonality: we want to know what it says. We are affected by a poem only when it is infused with a richer meaning, a profound way of looking at the world which is woven by intellect and deep feeling. This is exactly the point that Rabindranath has emphasized – this union of form with content. That is why his poems are always tied up with intimate perception of the world. Now, if this is not trivial, if a poem conveys a deeper realization of life and the world, if it is not an escape *from* but *into* the world, the necessity of having knowledge or experience of the ways of the world cannot be overestimated in the story of making poems

Last but not least, *pratibha* should be united not only with *vyutpatti* but also with the pain of devoted undertaking, serious effort (*abhyasa*). Spender reminds us how, after writing a poem, he tries several revisions of it before he feels his way towards the clarification, the music and the inner feeling (Spender, 1964, p. 39). The lesson is obvious: the need for several versions, for sweat and toil, before a poem emerges in its complete grandeur.

Along with *pratibha*, *vyutpatti* and *abhyasa*, brief mention should be made of another important factor contributing to the making of a poem. This is what Vamana calls concentration (*cittaikagryamavadhanam*). Concentration for the purposes of writing poetry is, to invoke Spender again, 'different from the kind of concentration required for working out a sum. It is a focusing of the attention in a special way, so that the poet is aware of all the implications and possible developments of his idea' (Spender, 1964, p. 35). This expresses the kernel of what Vamana would like to say about concentration. But he also wants to drive home how concentration requires a right time and place: the place should be secluded, and the time is the fourth quarter of the night (Vamana, 1977, pp. 92–3). This seclusion and this silence constitute the conditions within which a poem comes to life.

BIBLIOGRAPHY

Abhinava Gupta: *Dhvanyalokalocana*, (Bombay: Nirnaya Sagara Press, 1928).
Anandavardhana: *Dhvanyaloka* (Bombay: Nirnaya Sagara Press, 1928).
Bharata: *Natya Sastra*, Kavyamala series, vol. 42, (Bombay: Nirnaya Sagara Press, 1894).
Dandin: *Kavyadarsa*, ed. Hemchandra Bhattacharya (Calcutta: Sanskrit Book Depot, 1965).
Jagannatha: *Rasagangadhara* (Bombay: Nirnaya Sagara Press, 1913).
Mammata: *Kavyaprakasa*, Anandasrama series (Poona: Anandasrama, 1991).
Rudrata: *Kavyalamkara*, Kavyamala series (Bombay: Nirnaya Sagara Press, 1906).
Sartre, Jean-Paul: 'What is literature?', *Philosophy of Art and Aesthetics*, ed. F.A. Tillman and S.M. Cohen (New York: Harper & Row, 1969).
Spender, Stephen: 'The making of a poem', *Creativity in the Arts*, ed. V. Thomas (Englewood Cliffs, NJ: Prentice-Hall, 1964).
Tagore, Rabindranath: *Sahityer Svarupa* (Calcutta: Visva Bharati, 1943).
Vamana, *Kavyalamkarasutravrtti*, ed. A.C. Basu (Calcutta: Sanskrit Pustak Bhandar, 1977).

KALYAN SEN GUPTA

ineffability That which cannot be communicated, nor even expressed perhaps, by words (in their literal uses, at least). Reviewing a performance of Beethoven's Fifth Symphony in 1810, E.T.A. Hoffmann wrote that 'music opens up an unknown realm to man . . . in which he leaves behind all the feelings which are determinable by concepts in order to devote himself to the unsayable' (quoted in Bowie, 1990, p. 184). The date is of some significance in that one does not find, much before the beginning of the nineteenth century, many similar claims for the power of art, especially music, to 'open up' the ineffable – meaning that which cannot be represented or communicated through (literal) language, and deriving from a Latin verb meaning 'to speak'.

Ancient thinkers, indeed, tended to regard art as an obstacle to insight into the ineffable realm – whether because, as in Plato's *Republic*, it anchors us in the world of mere appearance, or because, as for Chuang-Tzu, its artificiality is inimical to the 'natural' attitude which responds to the intimations of the Tao, which is 'beyond words'. It is important, here, not to confuse the rather modern claim that art can communicate what is ineffable, with an older one to the effect that it can and should remind us that there exists such a realm. Zen artists apparently aimed at 'the evocation . . . of an atmosphere of mystery (*yūgen*)', but insisted that this mystery 'remained inexpressible' in *any* medium (Hrdlička and Hrdlička, 1989, p. 56).

Over the last two centuries claims like Hoffmann's have multiplied to the point of becoming clichés in some circles. Developments in both art and philosophy help to explain this. Within the growth of art forms which were neither representational in aim nor, as with Beethoven's music, designed merely to amuse or entertain, the question of the function and justification of art assumed some urgency. A tempting answer has been that the artist's role is to communicate what cannot be communicated through ordinary, literal language – a view encapsulated, a little hysterically perhaps, in Dewey's remark that 'if all meanings could be adequately expressed by words, the arts of painting and music would not exist' (quoted in Kennick, 1961, p. 309). The doughtiest opponents of 'realism' and 'representationalism' seem to find it difficult, after all, to renounce a signifying role for art. 'Even in the most extreme experiments in abstraction . . . *something* is being represented . . . even if the something is not identifiable' (Dufrenne, 1973, p. 119).

The urge to carve out an autonomous role for art was aided and abetted by various philosophical developments. These include the Romantics' elevation of the emotions to crucial cognitive functions, and the German idealists' view of consciousness and reality as a seamless unity, with its corollary that 'to attempt to objectify our relationship to nature' through the categorizing apparatus of language 'must be a failure. The turn to art became the attempt to say the unsayable' (Bowie, 1990, p. 80). Later there emerged theories of meaning, like the verificationism of the Vienna Circle, which so restricted the range of what is literally signifiable by words that, if meanings outside this range can be conveyed at all, it must be through the medium of poetic language or other arts.

As these remarks suggest, there is no single thesis of art and the ineffable, and the true complexity of the discussion becomes apparent from the plethora of answers to the following questions – What kinds of item are ineffable? Why are they ineffable? How does art nevertheless succeed in acquainting us with them? Answers to the 'What . . . ?' question range from 'subjective' items like feelings, to 'objective' ones like a thing's true essence; from 'intentional' items, such as meanings, to minute perceptual features of an artwork. Reasons why items may be ineffable range from the uncanniness of certain feelings evoked by a painting or poem, to the unarticulated 'oneness' of the reality revealed in such a work.

As to how a work might convey the ineffable, schematic suggestions include mimicry (as Schopenhauer seemed to think, in the case of music's depiction of the unconceptualizable will), showing or presenting, incorporating or embodying, and evoking or evincing. There is no unanimity, moreover, as to the meaning of the term 'ineffable'. For some, 'that is ineffable for which there . . . can be no suitable words' (Kennick, 1967, p. 181); for others, there may be suitable words, but ineffability remains if we possess no procedure for correctly applying them; and for yet others, more moderately, something is ineffable when no description, however correctly applied, serves to communicate its nature to people lacking direct acquaintance with it. (It is in this last sense, of course, that several philosophers, such as Rudolf Carnap, have regarded colours and other 'simple' qualities as ineffable.)

To lend some order to the motley of claims on behalf of art's capacity to 'eff' the ineffable, it is useful to distinguish two broad directions from which most such claims are reached. The first takes as a datum the experience that a person may often have when, trying to describe an encounter with an artwork, he finds that he is unable, to his satisfaction, to tell people just how it was (see Cavell, 1976, pp. 191ff.). The attempt is then made to diagnose this frustrating situation. Thus it might be concluded, in the manner of Schleiermacher, that what resists communication – words being general in their application – is the 'complete determinacy of the singular', unique work (quoted in Bowie, 1990, p. 169).

Proceeding from the second direction, one begins with a theory of language and its limits and then proposes how artworks sometimes manage to transcend those limits. For example, the young Wittgenstein held, roughly, that only contingent propositions stating empirical facts can strictly *say* anything, for they alone have informational content. Other kinds of utterance may nevertheless *show* what is unsayable (for instance, that the world is a totality). Wittgenstein is therefore able to write, apropos of a poem by Ludwig Uhland, that the unutterable is 'unutterably *contained* in what has been uttered', and that the poet succeeds in conveying it precisely through not trying to state it (and thereby producing nonsense) (quoted in McGuinness, 1988, p. 251).

Some authors take both directions. Susanne Langer, for instance, explains the difficulty in communicating an experience of an artwork by the fact that the knowledge of feeling and sentience it affords is too exact to be captured by the 'crude designations' – 'joy', 'sorrow' and so on – of our psychological vocabulary. Beyond this, however, literal language communicates by means of structured propositions which are 'incommensurable' with the unarticulated stream of our 'inner life'. Art manages to express the relevant knowledge of feeling and sentience because its devices – melodies, for example, or Joycean 'stream of consciousness' monologues – are commensurable with these 'inner' processes (Langer, 1957, pp. 91ff., 22ff.).

Critics, then, must reject both the diagnoses of our difficulties in telling of aesthetic encounters and the theories of meaning which make ineffabilism seem tempting or even inevitable. Thus a critic may concede to Schleiermacher that, in one sense, no description can do full justice to the 'complete determinacy' of an artwork, but argue that this is due not to its language-defying uniqueness, but to the unsurprising fact that there is always more that *can* be said about a work – or any individual object, for that matter – however long we go on describing it.

Again, if 'communicating a feeling' means producing that feeling in another person, then a description of a painting is unlikely to communicate what the painting does. But, a critic will point out, this is an attenuated sense of 'communicate', and one in which a painting is no more ineffable than a wasp sting, which also causes a feeling that a description of the sting fortunately does not. As for the theories of meaning which inspire aesthetic ineffabilism, these are typically guilty, it is charged, of a 'mimetic fallacy' in assuming that for a sentence to express or state X, it must somehow be *like* X – in terms of shared elements or structure, say. Langer is surely mistaken to hold that the natural resemblance between a melody and an emotion – both may rise and fall, and have climaxes – makes the melody a more adequate expression of the emotion than a description of it (unless, of course, she is stipulatively defining 'expression' as resemblance, in which case her point is trivial).

More sympathetic critics try to discern in the claims of ineffabilism expressions, exaggerated or misleading though they may be, of what are nevertheless important insights into art and our responses to it. Thus it is at once true and of significance for sensibility and taste that artistic performances (in music, dance, or whatever) possess features which are perceptually discriminable, but which could only be linguistically differentiated in a language too complex and cumbersome to be manageable by speakers. This is why sensitive listeners can hear, yet not describe, the differences between two violinists' renditions of a certain trill; and why, more generally, a performance may have its own 'evanescent corona of unreportable pitches, rhythms, timbres . . . and so on' (Raffman, 1988, p. 698). Note, though, that such ineffable features are not peculiar to artistic performances, since car engines may have them as much as violins; and that it would be wrong to speak, in connection with such features, of works 'expressing' or 'communicating' anything ineffable.

Again, it is of the first importance that some paintings, like Van Gogh's of a pair of old shoes, inspire a vivid sense of the sheer materiality, the 'mere thingness', of what they depict, so that in viewing them the usual categories in terms of which we categorize the things (for example, as shoes) are put in abeyance, as it were. But it will not follow, as Heidegger perhaps thinks, that we are thereby acquainted with 'a nameless, precon-ceptualizable . . . stuff'. For, as one critic puts it, 'to confront an entity simply as a material object in its own right rather than as a specific *kind* of thing, is not to strip away all conceptual structures' (Mulhall, 1990, p. 154). All that may be 'stripped away', rather in keeping with Kant's criterion for the 'disinterested' aesthetic attitude, are the everyday functional and pragmatic categories in which we usually characterize things.

Is it possible to be still more sympathetic and discern actual truth, and not simply mis-leadingly voiced insights, in some versions of ineffabilism? Two very different, though not incompatible, claims deserve, at any rate, close consideration. The first begins with the frequent observation that in giving expression to, say, a feeling, the artist does not always, nor even often, start with a clear, determinate experience which he only later translates into paint, stone or sounds. Rather, it is precisely *through* constructing his work that the feeling assumes a determinate shape and identity. If the artist is right to insist, as he may well do, that no other work would have been an expression of just that feeling, it will follow that the feeling cannot be iden-tified in isolation from its manifestation in that work. In the terminology of the later Wittgenstein, the work will be an *Äusserung* ('utterance', 'expression') of the feeling: something, that is, that is a *criterion* for the feeling, and not a symptom or causal product of some 'inner' state identifiable independent-ly from the work (see Mulhall, 1990). The feeling will then be ineffable in the sense, at least, that it could not be communicated to someone unacquainted with the work, since it is defined by means of ostensive reference to the latter – 'that *Grande Jatte* feeling', 'that *Appassionata* mood', or whatever (see Colling-wood (1938) for a somewhat similar view).

A second claim deserving serious attention extrapolates to works of art a point some-times made concerning certain metaphors – some of which, after all, merit Paul Ricoeur's label 'poems in miniature' (see Cooper, 1992). Literal descriptions of the world, it is argued, presuppose that things 'open' or manifest themselves to us in some ways (for example, as tools) and not others. The purpose or effect of some metaphors may be to open up new ways, so that they prime us to experience things under aspects less sedimented than the usual ones. In his sonnet, 'The world is too much with us', Wordsworth deploys a range of metaphors to induce in us a pantheistic perception of the natural world – for instance, the sea – as replete with purpose and significance. But why should this vision not be conveyable by literal statements of the poet's pantheistic beliefs? The reply will be that having such a vision is no more exhausted by assenting to such propositions than, say, the moral point of view is equivalent to subscribing to a set of ethical propositions. In both cases, the propositions are intelligible only to those who, as Heidegger puts it, 'comport' themselves towards the world in certains ways, who display a readiness to behave, respond, feel and speak in appropriate manners.

Propositions and the beliefs they state are then derivative, intellectualized registers of the 'comportments'. If some metaphors may be usefully regarded in the above light, there is no obvious reason why certain paintings and other artworks should not also be so regarded. Perhaps, indeed, it was a similar point, in connection with music, that Hoffmann was trying to make in the quote with which we began. Beethoven's music, like Wordsworth's metaphors, might 'open' us to, and give voice to, a 'comportment' towards things which, as the precondition for articulated statements of a view of the world, cannot be reduced to such state-ments.

See also AUTONOMY, AESTHETIC; EX-PRESSION; FUNCTION OF ART; LANGER; LANGUAGE, ART AS; METAPHOR; WITTGEN-STEIN.

BIBLIOGRAPHY

Bowie, Andrew: *Aesthetics and Subjectivity: From Kant to Nietzsche* (Manchester: Manchester University Press, 1990).

Cavell, Stanley: *Must We Mean What We Say?* (Cambridge: Cambridge University Press, 1976).

Collingwood, R.: *The Principles of Art* (Oxford: Oxford University Press, 1938).

Cooper, David E.: 'Truth and metaphor', *Knowledge and Language: Metaphor and Knowledge*, ed. H. Mooij and F. Ankersmit (Holland: Kluwer, 1992).

Dufrenne, M.: *The Phenomenology of Aesthetic Experience* (Evanston, Ill.: Northwestern University Press, 1973).

Hrdlička, Z. and Hrdlička, V.: *The Art of Japanese Gardening* (London: Hamlyn, 1989).

Kennick, W.E.: 'Art and the ineffable', *Journal of Philosophy*, 58 (1961).

Kennick, W.E.: 'The ineffable', *Encyclopedia of Philosophy*, ed. P. Edwards, vol. 4 (New York: Macmillan, 1967).

Langer, Susanne K.: *Problems of Art* (New York: Scribner, 1957).

McGuinness, B.F.: *Wittgenstein: A Life – Young Ludwig 1889–1921* (Berkeley, Calif.: University of California Press, 1988).

Mulhall, Stephen: *On Being in the World: Wittgenstein and Heidegger on Seeing Aspects* (London: Routledge & Kegan Paul, 1990).

Raffman, Diana: 'Towards a cognitive theory of musical ineffability', *Review of Metaphysics*, 41 (1988).

DAVID E. COOPER

Ingarden, Roman (1893–1970) Polish philosopher, best known for his application of phenomenology to the study of literature. He studied under Kazimierz Twardowski and Husserl and wrote voluminously in many areas of philosophy, most notably aesthetics. Here his work remains unrivalled in its scope and depth of analysis, especially in the philosophy of literature, mostly discussed in his *The Literary Work of Art* and *The Cognition of the Literary Work of Art*.

The main theses of the first book are as follows:

(1) The literary work of art is a multi-layered creation consisting of (a) the stratum of word sounds and higher sound formations, (b) the layer of meanings of words and sentences, (c) the layer of schematized aspects (*Ansichten*) through which the objects are presented, and (d) the layer of the presented objects themselves.

(2) The artistically valuable work of art contains the aesthetically valuable qualities in potentiality.

(3) Most of the sentences of the literary work of art are *quasi-judgements*: unlike the predicative statements of non-literary text, they have no referents outside the presented world.

(4) The literary work has also a *quasi-temporal* dimension in the succession of its sentences and larger units.

(5) The work itself should be distinguished from each of its *concretizations* constituted during the reading, or staging (filming) of it.

(6) Unlike the concretizations, the work itself is schematic – it contains 'places of indeterminacy', which in the course of reading are to a large extent eliminated.

(7) The literary work is a *purely intentional object*, which originated in the creative acts of the author and which is embodied in some form of material substratum. Yet it has an enduring identity which transcends the multiplicity of acts of consciousness and mundane reproductions. In principle, it can be shared by anyone, and always as identically the same despite the differences in interpretations and evaluations (Ingarden, 1973b, preface).

Phenomenologically speaking, *The Literary Work of Art* presents the content of the idea of any literary work of art whatsoever, arrived at through Husserl's famed method of *eidetic intuition*, which Ingarden favoured over any empirical studies. Similarly, in his subsequent books he presents the results of his phenomenological analyses of the various types of cognition of the literary work; of the ontological peculiarities of other types of art (Ingarden, 1989); of the nature of artistic creation; of the ontology and phenomenology of artistic and aesthetic values; of the nature of the aesthetic experience and the constitution of the aesthetic object; of problems of the cognition of the constituted aesthetic object; of the study of aesthetic and metaphysical qualities; and of the seven different notions of truth in art. All these analyses are supported not only by rigorous argumentation, but also, and most importantly, by intuitive evidence – that is, the description of the phenomena as they are directly experienced.

Ingarden's thesis of works of art as *purely intentional* bears close affinities with Husserl's treatment of 'objectivities of understanding' as *irreal* in his *Formal and Transcendental Logic* (see preface to *The Literary Work of Art* for Ingarden's discussion of similarities and differences between Husserl and himself). Ingarden's thesis entails the following claims. First, against physicalism: works of art are logically and essentially distinct from their material embodiment – musical works from the concrete physical sounds or material notation, pictures from the pigment on canvas, film from the ribbons of celuloid. Second, against psychologism: works of art cannot be identified with the mental processes of the artists and perceivers. Third, against Platonic idealism: works of art derive their existence from the acts of the artist's consciousness, and can only be appreciated through aesthetic concretizations – their 'life' comes to an end when they are forgotten. Fourth, against traditional realism: a work of art is schematic and two-sided. One side is the work itself, the history of its composition, its reception and its intentional stratification. The other side is its content, which is the proper object of our aesthetic appreciation.

It is the content that contains 'places of indeterminacy'. For example, some of the qualities of characters in a novel, of tones in music or of action in a film are simply not specified by the author. Since they cannot be appreciated as such, the performers of a musical work, for example, have to decide 'which tones in the totality of tonal material should be emphasized . . . and whether the tones should sound "soft" or "hard", and so on' (Ingarden, 1989, p. 106). Similarly, the reader is free to envision his favourite charac-

ters in the way he likes, within the limits delineated by the text. Each successful aesthetic concretization carries with it various aesthetic qualities synthetized into a coherent, valuable whole, which is its aesthetic value. Since perceivers differ in individual preferences, education, expectations, imagination, temperament and so forth, they complete the indeterminacies and constitute the aesthetic qualities in ways that also exhibit significant differences. Add to this the changes in the whole cultural atmosphere, in language, in musical instruments – and the puzzle of differences obtaining between various interpretations and evaluations of the same work of art is solved in a way precluding both essentialist and relativist conclusions. The aesthetic values differ, but so do the objects of which they are values. The artistic value of the work of art itself remains the same, and it is the function of the work's ability to inspire a multiplicity of valuable aesthetic experiences and concretizations.

Aesthetic qualities and values were the subject of Ingarden's many analyses, published in 1969 and in many collections of articles and lectures. He made lists of hundreds of words denoting such qualities in both German and Polish, and was aware of the necessity of creating new words capable of expressing further differentiations between them.

Over seventy years after the publication of *The Literary Work of Art*, Ingarden's contribution to the philosophy of art remains unmatched – and virtually unknown, especially amongst Anglo-American philosophers. His two main works on literature were translated only in 1973, and in such a way that his dazzling constructions and captivating style were lost in the complexity of the argument. In Europe, his influence has already been considerable: Nicolai Hartmann, Emil Steiger and Mikel Dufrenne have appropriated some of his findings, and others have used his methodology in their analyses of concrete texts, especially art critics in Poland and Germany. Many philosophers have taken an interest in the problems that Ingarden thematized – among others, Heidegger, Sartre, Langer, Wollheim and Margolis.

New translations should attract more interest in Ingarden's aesthetics, but appreciation of the complete system is hardly possible without knowledge of the ontological and phenomenological foundations for the grand ontologico-metaphysical edifice begun in the three-volume *Der Streit um die Existenz der Welt* [The controversy over the existence of the world]. The metaphysical part was not completed, but these volumes contain many significant distinctions important for a comprehensive view of Ingarden's philosophy of art: for instance, the distinction between existential, formal, and material ontology; the problem of the identity of real, ideal and purely intentional objects, and of states of affairs, processes and relations; nine conceptions of matter/form relations; and no less than sixty-four possible solutions of the realism/idealism controversy.

Like every great philosophical system, Ingarden's is both comprehensive and incomplete, which makes it all the more fascinating for students of aesthetics, not least because it invites us to continue where Ingarden left off.

See also DUFRENNE; ONTOLOGY OF ARTWORKS.

WRITINGS

Das literarische Kunstwerk (Halle: 1931); trans. G.G. Grabowicz, *The Literary Work of Art* (Evanston, Ill.: Northwestern University Press, 1973a).

The Cognition of the Literary Work of Art [in Polish] (1937); trans. [from 1968 German ed.] R.A. Crowley and K.R. Olsen (Evanston, Ill.: Northwestern University Press, 1973b).

Ontology of the Work of Art. The Musical Work. The Picture. The Architectural Work. The Film; trans. [from 1962 German ed.] R. Meyer and J.T. Goldthwait (Athens, OH: Ohio University Press, 1989).

Der Streit um die Existenz der Welt, vols 1–3 (Tübingen: Niemeyer, 1964, 1965, 1974).

Selected Papers in Aesthetics, ed. P.J. McCormick (Washington, DC: Catholic University of America Press, 1985).

WOJCIECH CHOJNA

intention It is commonplace for us to judge the things people do by reference to their purposes and intentions. It is equally commonplace to assume that what we understand when we understand an utterance is what its speaker intended to convey. Given these propensities, it is tempting to assume that since a work of art is something that someone has made, it is to be judged, at least in part, by reference to the purposes of its creator: and since, additionally, many works of art, notably literary works, have a meaning, it is equally tempting to assume that the meaning of a work is what its creator intended to say.

These two assumptions have, however, been under continuous attack in twentieth-century literary theory. Thus Eliot wrote in 1919 that 'honest criticism . . . is directed not upon the poet but the poetry.' At the same time the Russian formalists lay emphasis on the effect of the public words of the poem and excluded any interest in the private psychology of the poet, a view echoed by such New Critics as Cleanth Brooks (1968) and canonized in Beardsley and Wimsatt's 'The intentional fallacy' (1976). Again structuralists such as Barthes and Sartre and poststructuralists such as Derrida have directed attention to the words of the text, which may in their view yield infinitely more than the creator of the work could intentionally have conceived.

A battery of arguments has been offered against the relevance of reference to artists and their intentions. Thus it has been said that they are unreliable guides to their intentions; that knowledge of intention is not to be had in the case of such writers as Homer and Shakespeare (a lack of which does not hamstring criticism); and that too much attention to what artists say they intend may lead us to read things into works that are not actually there. These considerations are, however, secondary to three major lines of attack.

First there is what may be called the 'two-objects argument'. The first premise (Beardsley, 1981, p. 25) is that the work itself is one thing, and the creator of the work, including his or her intentions, quite another. To that is added the premise that the critic's task is solely to concentrate on the work itself. And from that it follows that any references to artists, including reference to such states of mind as intentions, is irrelevant.

Those, such as Beardsley, who deploy this argument do not deny that inferences can be made from facts about the work to facts about its creator, and from facts about its creator to facts about the work. But when these inferences are *from* facts about the work to facts about its creator, then, although the inferences may be relevant to biographical inquiries, they are irrelevant to criticism of the work. For they take us *away from* the proper object of criticism, the work, to an object, the creator, who is irrelevant to critical inquiries. And when the inference is from facts about the artist to facts about the work, the inference is dispensable. For to test the inference, we must eventually go to the work to check that it actually has the inferred properties. But, then, we could in that case have gone directly to the work without taking a detour through the artist. Thus, inferences from artist to work are dispensable and inferences from work to artist are irrelevant.

One objection to the two-objects argument (Lyas, 1973) is that it is not always possible to distinguish talking about works from talking about their creators. The distinction does work when terms such as 'graceful' are being used. Again, we can distinguish calling a requiem sad from saying of its creator that he or she was sad when composing it. But when a critic calls *Lady Chatterley's Lover*, say, 'pretentious', or Swift's *Modest Proposal* 'ironic', then a reference seems to be made to qualities that the creator displays *in* his or her work.

A second major argument is then deployed (see Beardsley and Wimsatt, 1976, p. 5; Beardsley, 1970, pp. 59–61; Beardsley, 1981, pp. 238–42). It is claimed that in every literary work we can distinguish a speaker from a situation with which that speaker is confronted. But this speaker is a *dramatic speaker* and should not be identified with the creator of the work. Indeed (Beardsley, 1970, p. 238), to create a literary work is to engage in an act of imitation or pretence to be a speaker of a certain sort. Hence the speaker and her or his intentions are to be distinguished from the writer and her or his intentions.

If this argument is intended to report on the facts of literary composition (let alone pictorial or musical composition), it is false. Many poets, painters and musicians do not *pretend* to the attitudes, beliefs and the like expressed in their works. Perhaps, though, the argument is meant to prescribe that when we treat something as a literary work of art, we should treat it as if it were a pretence. There are, then, two further difficulties.

Take, first, Beardsley's favoured example (1981, pp. 238–42) of the Sherlock Holmes stories, told in the persona of Doctor Watson. Here Conan Doyle professes to speak in the voice of Watson, so the work is in part a pretence, and there is that element of truth in Beardsley's view that a pretence is going on. But now consider: Watson is bluff, obtuse and often uncomprehending, whereas the stories are subtle, ironic and perceptive. Who, though, is being subtle, ironic and perceptive, if not the controlling intelligence of the work: and who is that if not the creator of the work? (It would, incidentally, be odd to suppose that the creator was pretending to a subtlety, irony and capacity for perceptivity that he did not possess. For one who successfully succeeded in that pretence would exhibit those very qualities.) Belsey (1980) argues that a work may reveal more about the authorial controlling intelligence of a work than that controlling intelligence may intend. That shows only that a controlling intelligence may not be the best judge of her or his performance: but that is not to show that the controlling intelligence is not present in the work for our judgement.

To that may be added the following consideration. We do indeed appreciate and enjoy imitation in the arts and elsewhere. But we do so only when the intention to imitate is clear to us. (Notice here how an enjoyment of Swift's *Modest Proposal* depends on the recognition of an imitative intention. A failure to spot the imitative intent might leave us revolted by this piece of writing.) But then to insist that imitation is central to art is to insist that the intention to imitate show itself; and thus an imitation account merely reinstates in a central place the need to know the intention of the work.

A third major argument against the relevance of references to intention attempts to establish the irrelevance of intention to the interpretation of *meaning*. It is common to Beardsley, Sartre, formalists, structuralists and poststructuralists. The claim is that the meanings of words, singly or in combinations, depend on the public rules of syntax and semantics and not on the private intentions of speakers. Hence, to interpret a poem we need only dictionaries and grammars. Here a powerful argument can be derived using the practices of Lewis Carroll's Humpty-Dumpty, who claimed to be able to make a word mean whatever he wanted by his mere act of will. This meant, of course, that he had to explain each of his words as he used them. Suppose, now, that Humpty-Dumpty decides that by 'glory' he will mean 'fine knock-down argument'. He explains this by saying, 'By "glory" I mean "fine knock-down argument".' But, on his own account, he now has to explain what he means by 'fine knock-down argument'. Suppose he says, 'By that phrase I meant "stickleback".' But now the question repeats itself: 'And what did you mean by "stickleback"?' Now, either there is an infinite regress of such explanations, in which case the speaker can never succeed in making his meaning clear, or eventually he will have to use words that have an agreed public meaning independently of his will. And then his claim that meaning can be given only by private acts of will refutes itself.

Meaning, then, is ultimately possessed because of public *structures* of rules and agreements (an insight that is a motive force of structuralism), and not because of private intentional acts of meaning designation. Since a literary work is nothing other than a set of words, it would seem that we can set

aside artists and their intentions and let the words speak for themselves.

Powerful though this argument is, it does not eliminate authors and their intentions. First – a point made by Derrida in breaking with structuralism – the set of structural rules of a language is not closed. I can extend the system, as when – and this is commonplace in poetry – I project a word into new contexts: for example, when I take the word 'vivid' from its original use to talk of colours and use it to characterize turns of phrase. This projection is not something done by the language itself, but something that speakers of the language must do. This is related to a point made by Merleau-Ponty (1960, p. 30): the language is inert until put into force by individual speakers. And to that I add that, although the words used by speakers must have, antecedently, a public meaning, it is in the complex activity of using them that the attitudes, intentions and beliefs that can give us so clear a sense of a controlling intelligence of a work are revealed. Even if that controlling intelligence may not be aware of what she or he reveals, it is none the less he or she that is revealed.

It is sometimes said that, all the same, the reader is allowed a complete liberty to play with the infinite possibilities of interpretation allowed by the words of a language. That suggestion invites two responses. First, it becomes unclear, if there is such a complete liberty, what the study of literature as a discipline is to become. How, if at all, will interpretations be assessed? Second, although a work may contain vastly more than its writer ever intended, it may still be the case that part of what the work contains will be traces of the controlling intelligence of its creator. To ignore this will be to ignore part of what is actually there in the work: and since critics are supposed to report what is there, to ignore this aspect is to fail one's critical duty.

Finally, there is an ambiguity in the claim that meaning and intention are related. This may mean (Hirsch, 1967) that the meaning of a text is given to it by a prior act of authorial will. That is merely to repeat Humpty-Dumpty's mistake. But an alternative would be to claim that the existence of the public words of a language allows us to see what an author meant (and even what he failed to mean). True, the reader has to understand the work, and can do so because it is written in a public language. But the public language is one that allows us to make our meanings clear, so that often we can see precisely what a writer wished to say, where that becomes one of the standards for the interpretation of the work. The alternative seems merely to replace authorial will with audience whim.

See also BEARDSLEY; 'INTENTIONAL FALLACY'; INTERPRETATION; STRUCTURALISM AND POSTSTRUCTURALISM.

BIBLIOGRAPHY

Barthes, R.: *Image, Music, Text* (London: Fontana, 1977).

Beardsley, M.C.: *The Possibility of Criticism* (Detroit: Wayne State University Press, 1970).

Beardsley, M.C.: *Aesthetics* (New York: 1958); 2nd edn (Indianapolis: Hackett, 1981).

Beardsley, M.C. and Wimsatt, W.K.: 'The intentional fallacy', *On Literary Intention*, ed. D. Newton de Molina (Edinburgh: Edinburgh University Press, 1976).

Belsey, C.: *Critical Practice* (London: Methuen, 1980).

Brooks, C.: *The Well Wrought Urn* (London: Methuen, 1968).

Derrida, J.: *Of Grammatology* (Baltimore, Md: Johns Hopkins University Press, 1974).

Eliot, T.S.: *Selected Prose* (Harmondsworth: Penguin Books, 1953).

Hirsch, E.D.: *Validity in Interpretation* (New Haven, Conn.: Yale University Press, 1967).

Lyas, C.: 'Personal qualities and the intentional fallacy', *Philosophy Looks at the Arts*, ed. G. Vesey (London: Macmillan, 1973).

Merleau-Ponty, M.: *Signes* (Paris: 1960); trans. R. McCleary, *Signs* (Evanston, Ill.: Northwestern University Press, 1964).

COLIN LYAS

'intentional fallacy'   Takes its name from a seminal article with that title published by Monroe C. Beardsley and William K. Wimsatt in 1946. The initial emphasis of the article is on a denial of the relevance of a reference to intention in literary evaluation: the denial that 'in order to judge a poet's performance we must know what he intended' (Beardsley and Wimsatt, 1954, p. 4), where 'intention' is understood as 'the design or plan in the author's mind'.

However, and somewhat confusingly, the article has a wider scope than this. In addition there is, first, the denial that reference to intention has any relevance to the *interpretation* of a literary work. Second, there is the claim that the true speaker of a poem is a 'dramatic speaker' *in* the poem who is not to be identified with its creator (who may be pretending to speak in that voice). Third, there is the much more general claim that 'personal studies' – that is, investigations into the biography and psychology of writers – can be distinguished from 'poetic studies'. The belief is that a work of art and its creator are two discrete entities, the critic's sole proper concern being the former.

Influential though 'The intentional fallacy' was, it is more a set of assertions than a clearly articulated body of argument, and the target of its attack is not always clear. Beardsley (1970, 1981) and Wimsatt (1976) later attempted to redress this unclarity. It is possible, however, to detect at least two suppositions upon which 'The intentional fallacy' is based. First, there is the supposition that a work of literature and an authorial mind are two discrete entities. This supposition is encouraged by the propensity of Beardsley and Wimsatt to speak as if an intention were a 'private' object *in* the writer's mind, and the work itself a 'public' object available for 'objective' scrutiny. Granted that the work is one thing and the author's intention another, and granted that the job of a critic of a work of literature is to talk about that work and nothing else, it follows that reference to the author is irrelevant. For the author just is a different object from the work itself. Hence the intentional fallacy is a fallacy of irrelevance: required to talk about the work itself, the critic who commits this fallacy digresses into talk about a different thing altogether – the author and her or his intentions.

This first supposition, that an intention is a private event in a mind and a work a public event in the world, seems committed to a view of mind that would occasion severe problems for an account of knowledge of other minds. Here there is a dilemma for Beardsley and Wimsatt. On the one hand, if intention is a private event in a mind, knowledge of it seems in jeopardy. At times this conclusion seems almost welcome (Wimsatt, 1976): intention really is unavailable and private, so we are left only with the public work of art. But that buys the irrelevance of intention only at the cost of making *any* knowledge of *any* mind impossible. The alternative is to adopt an account of intention according to which states of mind, such as intentions, can be seen *in* and known through their manifestations in action and behaviour. But then intention ceases to be locked up in a private mind and can display itself in action: and since a literary work may be the product of a complex set of actions, it is unclear why we should not see its creator's intentions made manifest in it (as they clearly are in, say, Milton's *Paradise Lost*). (It should be noted, as Beardsley and Wimsatt stress, that an author may not be the most reliable source of information about his or her intentions. But a demonstration that authorial assertions about intentions ought to be ignored is not a demonstration that we should ignore the evidence of their intentions that their works themselves provide. As Wimsatt himself (1976, p. 131) somewhat inconsistently says, a poet's denial of ironic intent may be belied by his or her performance.)

The second supposition made in 'The intentional fallacy' is about meaning. The claim is that the meaning of a word is a public matter, to be determined by dictionaries and not by references to the intentions of its users. A poet cannot make the word 'cup' mean 'saucer' just by declaring an intention so to use the term. *He* or *she* may mean that by it, but that is not what the word means. And what words, used in combinations such as sentences, mean is decided by equally public rules of syntax and semantics. From this it seems to follow that if we wish to know the

meaning of a poem, we can determine this by reference to dictionaries and grammars. We do not need to make reference to the intentions of authors. Beardsley and Wimsatt say (1976; Beardsley, 1981, p. 25), 'The poem belongs to the public. It is embodied in the language, the peculiar possession of the public.' Hence the distinction in 'The intentional fallacy' between 'internal' evidence of the meaning of the poem, discovered through 'syntax and semantics, grammar and dictionaries', and 'external' evidence, such as letters and diaries of the author, which are 'not part of the work as a linguistic fact'.

Critics (Cioffi, 1963–4) have queried this distinction between internal and external evidence, which is anyway muddied by Beardsley and Wimsatt, who introduce an intermediate category of 'semi-private' meaning (1976). Further, although at one level the meaning of a poem can be settled by dictionaries and grammars, this still leaves scope for references to authorial intentions. For there remains the question about what the author was doing *in* using those words: Was he being ironic? Did he wish to make allusions? Those questions seem *prima facie* to involve reference to intention. Attempts in 'The intentional fallacy' to show that allusion in poetry can be handled without reference to intention are not happily framed (see Wheeler, 1977).

See also BEARDSLEY; INTENTION; IRONY.

BIBLIOGRAPHY

Beardsley, M.C. and Wimsatt, W.K.: The intentional fallacy', *On Literary Intention*, ed. D. Newton de Molina (Edinburgh: Edinburgh University Press, 1976).

Beardsley, M.C.: *The Possibility of Criticism* (Detroit: Wayne State University Press, 1970).

Beardsley, M.C.: *Aesthetics* (New York: 1958); 2nd ed (Indianapolis: Hackett, 1981).

Cioffi, F.: 'Intention and interpretation in criticism', *Proceedings of the Aristotelian Society*, 64 (1963–4), 85–106.

Wheeler, M.: 'Biography, literary influence and

allusion as aspects of source studies', *British Journal of Aesthetics*, 2 (1977), 149–60.

Wimsatt, W.K.: 'Genesis: a fallacy revisited', *On Literary Intention*, ed. D. Newton de Molina (Edinburgh: Edinburgh University Press, 1976).

COLIN LYAS

interpretation Quite astonishingly, the theory of interpretation has changed so rapidly that one could not have anticipated the radical themes favoured in the 1990s from their rather well entrenched sources in the 1950s. This is not to suggest that the entire range of interesting theories of interpretation is somehow rightly confined to that very brief interval or, of course, that the theory of interpretation simply sprang full-blown at that late beginning. But the salient disputes about the nature of interpretation have indeed taken the most extreme forms in our time, and exhibit a certain dialectical boldness that justifies confining our attention to a handful of conceptual options. The suggestion here is that nearly everything of importance about interpretation can be recovered through the economies of a small number of alternative strategies.

A very good first pass at managing the unwieldy spread of contemporary theories follows the lead of organizing answers to cognate questions regarding the nature of the human sciences. Two opposing intuitions dominate our thinking there. On one, every would-be science preserves objectivity more or less in accord with the model central to the movement in the philosophy of science that came to treat physics as the paradigm of all science: from the period of the 1920s and 1930s, the heyday of the Vienna Circle and logical positivism, to the subtler and leaner movement that was in part its principal beneficiary, the so-called unity of science movement, that has dominated the discussion of the nature of science very nearly down to our own day.

The other intuition, drawn from the entirely different post-Kantian tradition of science that counts Wilhelm Dilthey as its most distinctive champion, emphasizes, rather, two oddities of the human sciences: first, that, paradigmatically, the human sciences are reflexive, so that observer and observed are one, or that objectivity may be preserved by an extension from reflexive studies through intermediary cultures somewhat within our ken; and, second, that the 'objects' of such study have distinctive properties (lacking in purely physical nature) such that:

(1) the human sciences are, methodologically, *sui generis*;
(2) objectivity cannot be construed in the same way as in the physical sciences;
(3) the human sciences are primarily centred on the meanings and the semiotic and interpretable features of the things of the human world; *and*
(4) the actual properties of the 'objects' of that world – those that are interpretable – may (the matter is disputed) be altered in a distinctive way as a direct result of their interpretation under the conditions of changing history.

On the first intuition, knowledge is essentially ahistorical, even in admitting historical progress among the sciences; on the second, particularly as we approach the viewpoint of the 1990s, the historicity of knowledge becomes deeper and more problematic.

We may fairly claim that the methodological treatment of interpretation in the arts within the Anglo-American literature (critical as well as philosophical) that dominated the 1950s through the 1960s and part of the 1970s noticeably favoured the New Criticism and romantic hermeneutics. In the philosophical literature, there can be little doubt that the influential views of Monroe C. Beardsley, occasionally developed in collaboration with the literary critic William K. Wimsatt, Jr, characteristically defined the task of interpretation in a strongly empirical (even empiricist) manner that deliberately approached the supposed rigour favoured by the unity of science programme without ever formally urging a specific connection.

What is striking, here, is the clear conviction Beardsley conveys that interpretable artworks – literature pre-eminently but not exclusively – may be treated, for the purpose of objectively testing interpretative claims, as 'objects' not significantly different in methodologically pertinent respects from the objects of any other bona fide science. Even the matter of determining their 'meanings', certainly a mark that differentiates poems from stones, could be treated, Beardsley held, as objectively 'there', 'in' the poem, rather as with the local properties of a stone discernible and therefore testable by a fair extension of empirical discrimination.

Beardsley did not actually practise as an interpretative critic, and the New Criticism with which he was associated produced much interpretative work that could not always be easily subsumed under the practice he recommended. But on the view he professed, the historical and biographical circumstances of an artist's life could only be causally – that is, extrinsically – connected with the production of particular artworks, and could not bear directly in any pertinent way at all on the empirical analysis of their actual properties or meanings. For similar reasons, the artist's or author's intention *in* producing particular poems or paintings proved quite irrelevant (as such) in determining or testing the specific meaning that an interpretative critic might correctly explicate. These are the essential themes of 'The intentional fallacy' – probably one of the most celebrated (and condemned) of contemporary philosophical essays on the arts.

As it happens, these themes also deliberately rule out as illicit the master thesis of the alternative interpretative methodology of romantic hermeneutics. In fact, Beardsley explicitly excoriates the views of E.D. Hirsch, Jr, a well known, comparatively late romantic hermeneut, an American literary critic and theorist who has sought to redeem a conservative sense of interpretative objectivity and rigour from the extravagances of so-called post-Heideggerian hermeneutics, as practised, for instance, by the *doyen* of contemporary Western hermeneutics, Hans-Georg Gadamer. For the moment, we may simply take note of the fact that Hirsch's methodology is utterly opposed to Beardsley's as well as to Gadamer's; Hirsch simply favours an entirely different model of the human sciences from that of the unity programme; and, within the German tradition of the *Geisteswissenschaften*, he opposes Gadamer's relatively radical historicizing of hermeneutics.

Beardsley advances three principles regarding art and its interpretation: first, the 'principle of independence' – that 'literary works exist as individuals and can be distinguished from other things'; second, the 'principle of autonomy' – that 'literary works are self-sufficient entities, whose properties are decisive in checking interpretations and judgements', and third, the 'principle of the intolerability of incompatibles' – that 'if two [interpretations] are logically incompatible, they cannot both be true (and they implicitly claim to be true [of the same work])'.' (What holds for literary works holds as well for artworks of other sorts.) Conjointly, the three principles are meant to support the complex thesis that:

(1) artworks are individual, differentiable, relatively free-standing, independent, stable, well boundaried 'objects', that

(2) clearly have or lack the properties predicated of them; so that

(3) interpretation is a rigorous probing of the actual properties of artworks by way of a certain expertise not logically different from that of description, but perhaps primarily concerned with meanings, significance, expressiveness, representation, symbolic or semiotic or rhetorical or metaphorical functions; so that

(4) interpretations are straighforwardly true or false (on a bivalent logic), and interpretations incompatible on a bivalent logic can never be jointly confirmed.

Beardsley's model, then, brings critical discourse into a congenial alliance with a relaxed empiricism (since meanings are not sensibilia) and a relaxed unity conception of science (since interpretation is not causal explanation). In this sense, it marks one extreme pole of interpretative theory. Romantic hermeneutics may be straightforwardly characterized as opposing Beardsley's first two principles, but not in the interest of opposing the third; and post-Heideggerian hermeneutics, particularly Gadamer's, opposes (at least implicitly) all three principles. The hermeneuts, of course, adhere one way or another to the post-Kantian bifurcation of the sciences. Also, one finds no discussion within any of these three models of the necessity of adhering to a bivalent logic – that is, of adhering to either or both excluded middle or *tertium non datur*.

Hirsch's model is probably the most ramified version of the romantic theory that may be found in English. Opposing Beardsley, Hirsch is extremely cautious about speaking of a poem or story as of an actual 'object' that is 'given' or encountered in experience. He speaks instead of 'manuscripts', 'holographs', written remains and the like – which, properly examined, permit us to construct or reconstruct a reasonable conception of a text or artwork open to interpretation. Both phases of this effort – the imaginative reconstruction of a text and the proper reading of the text thus constructed – involve interpretation, in the sense that they involve the recovery of original authorial intent. Evidence may be adduced, then, including biographical, historical and stylistic remains, that enables us to form a correct conception of the 'text' that some inscription imaginatively subtends.

The text is a representation (at once realist and idealist) of an author's creative intention; the author, as an apt member of a particular culture, intends, in uttering some inscription or other, to conform (whether he is aware of it or not) with the 'intrinsic genres' (the essential organizing literary structures) of his own cultural world; and apt readers, guided by an understanding of those genres, are able to recover an author's text from his inscription. The poem or text is reconstructed, then, in the shared space of common culture, through imagination. There must, therefore, already be 'in place', in a given culture, a variety of genres – meaning-constitutive types of linguistic practice – by employing which, authors produce what they produce, and by reference to which readers correctly interpret what they read.

Hirsch is committed to texts being rightly ascribed uniquely determinate meanings.

Still, he cannily admits that it may be impossible to recover with certainty those same genres. He retreats to 'probability' considerations. But the fact remains that, for Hirsch, probabilizing signifies our limited access to the *Geist* of a culture, rather than the arguable truth that the supposed constitutive genres are themselves no more than heuristic artefacts: (1) contingently posited within the changing course of history, (2) neither constitutively nor regulatively prior to or necessary for the intelligibility of any creative or interpretative act, and (3) themselves freely altered and affected by ongoing artistic and critical efforts. Hirsch opposes (1)–(3).

This bears directly on Gadamer's seemingly unanswerable challenge to the romantic hermeneutic view: Gadamer claims that the romantic fails to acknowledge that his own interpetation of a text (his aptitude for interpreting and the exercise of that aptitude) is itself historicized – structured, orientated, limited, biased by the process of enculturation. Gadamer explicitly holds that the events to be interpreted must be constructed and reconstructed from a changing present vantage point in history, and that the interpretation of that construction cannot fail to reflect the historically contingent 'prejudice' (in the etymological sense) from which any critic or historian makes his effort. So the historical past – *a fortiori*, 'original historical intent' – is itself an interpretative construction from the present (the 'fusion of horizons': *Horizontverschmelzung*); and the interpretation of what is thus constructed is organized by a consciousness itself shaped by ongoing history ('effective–historical consciousness': *wirkungsgeschichtliches Bewusstsein*).

On Gadamer's view, history and human culture are a flux, and artworks and persons are provisionally boundaried constructions responding to the salient processes of cultural influence. Gadamer therefore radicalizes the famous 'hermeneutic circle' that the romantic hermeneut would use criterially (that is, in accord with constituting genres). The circle – that is, the thesis that the meaning of an entire text depends on its parts and the meaning of its parts depends on the meaning of the whole text – now cannot be assigned more than a provisional or heuristic closure; whereas, for the romatic, closure is objectively and uniquely imposed on interpretation by reference jointly to original intent and constitutive genres. The upshot is that Gadamer construes hermeneutics in terms only of the metaphysics of culture and human existence, not in terms of the logic and methodology of interpretation as a cognitive discipline. He has next to nothing to say about methodology, although he himself takes a distinctly conservative line in reconciling the threatening relativistic spread of interpretation with the (now oddly) invariant values of the Hellenic world.

There is a tell-tale lacuna here that the hermeneutic tradition has never satisfactorily filled. It accounts in part for the perceived prominence of a large variety of so-called poststructuralist theories of interpretation – notably, in the work of Michel Foucault, Roland Barthes and Harold Bloom – which have seized a space left somewhat unattended by the effective defeat of the New Critical and romantic hermeneutic views, the failure of post-Heideggerian hermeneutics to work out its own methodology, the self-contradictory tendencies of phenomenology running from Roman Ingarden to Wolfgang Iser's 'reader response' theory, the occasional suggestiveness and over-large pretensions of structuralism, the constant need of Marxist and Althusserian theory to rectify its orthodoxy, and the sheer opportunism of late pragmatist conceptions that have somehow incorporated the spirit if not the letter of Jacques Derrida's deconstruction. Given the pressures of space, we shall have to rely on a very broadly sketched picture of what is central to the radical currents of the late twentieth century.

Certainly, Gadamer's theory precludes the fixity and determinacy of the natures of texts or other interpretable referents. There are no such 'objects'. Similarly, Gadamer's theory precludes the adequacy of a bivalent logic applied to interpretation. Interpretation is at best 'authentic' rather than true or accurate; depends as much on the interests and orientation of present respondents as on *their* (informed) reconstruction of a text produced in the past. Iser's theory betrays the impossibility of recovering any would-be standard form of objectivity within such terms – by way of an analogous theory that is, however, noticeably more formal than historical in its approach: for Iser cannot quite decide between assessing how a reader 'concretizes' the schematic structures of a text in terms of the putative fixities of that text, and constructing such concretizations as justifiably affecting the text interpreted (thereby imposing additional constraints on the relevance of subsequent interpretations). Iser's inclination is to favour the first, but what he concedes fails to disallow the second. (Iser's example is meant to suggest the constancy and ubiquity of the conceptual puzzles we have identified – by way of theories and practices as local as the phenomenological.)

It will pay us to collect, here, certain general philosophical doctrines regarding interpretation that may help to offset the impression (otherwise nearly ineluctable) that recent currents in theorizing are simply irresponsible, inadequately developed, even incoherent. The point is that it is impossible, now, to assess the viability and validity of theories of interpretation against a conceptual backdrop that is more or less canonically constant. There are no such canons. There certainly are none that are not seriously on the defensive at this late date. Recent theories of interpretation are conceptually inseparable from equally radical larger reconstructions of the very nature of science, philosophy, intellectual inquiry in general.

The master themes of the larger reconstruction may be roughly tallied as follows:

(1) The real world is cognitively untransparent in terms both of physical nature and human culture; there is no privileged access to what is true about the world.

(2) The intelligible world is symbiotized as such; there is no principled disjunction between the structures of human thinking and the structures of the encountered world; the very independence of the physical world is a dependent posit within a symbiotized space.

(3) Human thinking, reason, science, inquiry, logic have a history; they are horizoned effects or products of changing historical processes, hence not reliably invariant over the whole of history.

(4) There are no *de re* or *de dicto* necessities; or, whatever are taken to be such appear only under the preformative constraints of historicized thinking; they are therefore subject to historical change themselves.

(5) The reflexive critique of thinking and inquiry, as of norms of intelligibility, translation, coherence, truth, validity and the like, is itself subject to the same constraints of history that infect the thinking and judgement that it seeks to organize in a rationally systematic way.

It would not be unreasonable to affirm that these five doctrines dominate Western thinking at the end of the twentieth century. They are certainly not incontestable; but it would be extremely difficult to specify any thesis that directly contradicted them, that either had a stronger backing among the pertinent professions (the physical and formal sciences, philosophy, the human sciences, history and interpretation) than was true, say, in the first half of the twentieth century, or that could be shown to be impossible or unreasonable to reject on pain of incoherence or total absence of compelling methodological advantage. So (1)–(5) constitute a very distinct revolution of sorts: each doctrine has made its way against formidable opposition over the centuries. The result is that the remarkable flurry of recent radical theories of interpretation that converge with the general thrust or (1)–(5) also entrenches the expectation that the assessment of their advantage will accord with those same developments.

Once this much is in place, we may go on to add some further doctrines that cohere with (1)–(5) but are more narrowly pertinent to the radical claims of recent interpretative theories. These are bound to be more controversial – possibly, in part, because they are not often explicitly examined. But the argument may be made that if (1)–(5) were

conceded, it would be very difficult indeed to deny that these further claims could be discounted – at least on grounds of coherence, consistency, avoidance of paradox and the like. That alone would be something of a surprise, because objections to the family of claims that we must now consider normally take the form of insisting that their advocacy cannot be coherent. (If they are coherent, then there may also be good reason to favour them.) Here, then, is a compendium of the most important of these claims:

(6) The principal functions of discourse permitting the ascription of truth values – reference and predication – are inherently informal, logically incapable of being regularized algorithmically in natural languages; and inseparable from a society's ongoing memory of its historical practice of reference and predication.

(7) The individuation, numerical identity and re-identification of the referents of discourse do not presuppose or entail the fixed nature – *de re* or *de dicto* – of such referents; identity, under change, depends (once again) on a society's ongoing memory of its practice of individuation and identity.

(8) The referents of the human world – artworks, in particular – lack fixed natures, have only histories (predicatively) or are (referentially) only histories.

(9) Interpretation is primarily addressed to those features of given referents that are linguistic, semiotic, significative, symbolic, rhetorical, stylistic, historical, traditional or the like, however they are embedded or manifested in the physical world; but they are real features of the (human) world, irreducible to the physical, consensually confirmed within the collective practices of given societies, and subject to change through the processes of history and reinterpretation.

(10) Objectivity with respect to the description and interpretation of the human world, as well as its reality, is meth-

odologically distinct from that accorded physical nature: in the sense that, whatever stability it may be ascribed, the human world presupposes and entails no more than the reflexive capacity of the members of human societies to understand themselves as they understand others and to understand others as they understand themselves, and to understand the artefacts and products, effects and deeds, of their world in terms of their primary understanding of themselves; it makes no sense to suppose that the human world is in any regard independent of the actual process of human (reflexive) understanding, in contrast to what is often conjectured regarding physical nature.

(11) Whatever is interpretable is, in principle, open to infinitely many interpretations, both synchronically and diachronically; synchronically, interpretations that, on a bivalent logic, would yield contradictories, need not be judged to do so on the substitution of a many valued logic (as of reasonable, apt, plausible claims, graded as finely as we please); such interpretations will be no more than 'incongruent' – that is, such as would generate contradictories on a bivalent logic but not now; also, the selection of an appropriate logic or theory of truth depends essentially on the theory of the structure of the referents of the real world that we mean to speak about – such matters cannot be disjoined or hierarchically ordered.

The important point is that each member of the set of (1)–(11) is consistent and internally coherent, and the entire set is consistent and coherent. More than that, the entire thrust of the late twentieth century – in terms of the theory of interpretation, history, the human sciences, and the general relationship between the logic and methodology of the physical sciences and these other matters – very strongly favours, perhaps more strongly that ever before in the history of Western thought, large subsets of (1)–(11). Whatever

may be said about the seeming anarchy of recent theories of interpretation, their most extreme features depend on the viability of some subset or another of (6)–(11) in concert with (1)–(5).

This may be shown, for instance, in the critical practice and/or theories of Barthes, Foucault and Bloom, at least. For instance, Foucault (1973), in the interpretation of Velázquez's painting *Las Meninas*, applies his conception of the historically formed structure of human thought, both in the baroque period of Velázquez (in what he calls the 'classical' *episteme* of the seventeenth century) and in his own review of *Las Meninas* (in what we have called the post-structuralist *episteme* of the late twentieth century: a use of terms that Foucault does not support). On that reading, and pursuing a rigorous application of his (our) own conceptual orientation to that of the earlier period (reconstructed, of course, in a way not altogether different from the hermeneut's), the meaning of Velázquez's painting may be assigned in terms that, on the argument, would have been inaccessible to Velázquez himself and would have been incompatible with any canon rightly drawn from that *episteme*; and yet Foucault's interpretaton is strongly congruent with the details of the painting viewed in terms of the history of its reception as well as Foucault's own theory of the historicity of interpretation. (Our present purpose, remember is only to confirm the coherence and reasonableness of this change of view. We can hardly attempt a full-scale defence of it here.)

Foucault is nearly unique in pursuing his thesis both in interpretative practice and at the level of philosophical theory – in the radically historicized way in which he does. Both Bloom (1975) and Barthes offer what may be called formal analogues of Foucault's fully historicized notion of *epistemes*: in a sense not altogether unlike that in which Wittgenstein's notion of *Lebensformen* is a formal (that is, non-historicized) analogue of Foucault's *epistemes*. (Their theories are paler than Foucault's, but not their interpretative practice). Bloom easily confirms the energy and promise and distinctive rigour of an interpretative practice that deliberately works through the 'misprision' of a 'strong' poet or ancestral text. (Here, one might think of Euripides' *Iphigenia* as a misprision of Homer.) For Bloom, poetry is interpretative criticism ('verse-criticism'), and criticism is an attenuated poetry ('prose-poetry'). That is, both may be said to depend on the same logic, although interpretation makes explicit truth claims.

Barthes' *S/Z* (1970) may well be the most sustained, explicitly poststructuralist attempt at an interpretative practice that tests the limits of arbitrariness within the familiar boundaries of the whole of Western culture. In the process, Barthes explores the difference between what he (elsewhere) calls 'readerly' (*lisible*) reading (interpretation) and 'writerly' (*scriptible*) reading, which in effect demonstrates, by example, the compatibility of an interpretative practice more or less in accord with a large subset of (1)–(11) and a more conventional practice – one that converges, say, with something like the limiting models championed by Beardsley or Hirsch. That is, one can actually construe 'canonical' theories – those that insist on a determinate 'object' (of interpretation), or that insist on a strong bivalence for determinate authorial intentions or the like – as special cases falling within the terms of reference of a larger practice in accord with some pertinent subset of (1)–(11). Reading Barthes thus, a comprehensive overview of interpretative theories may be formed, admittedly prejudicial to the exclusionary pretensions of the 'canon', but coherent and hospitable enough in terms of the rising themes of the end of the twentieth century. There is every reason to believe that the larger vision has introduced relatively permanent changes in the theory of interpretation. In any case, its innovations cannot be discounted without recovering the older canons of general philosophy.

See also BARTHES; BEARDSLEY; CANON; CRITICISM; GADAMER; HERMENEUTICS; 'INTENTIONAL FALLACY'; STRUCTURALISM AND POSTSTRUCTURALISM.

BIBLIOGRAPHY

Barthes, Roland: *S/Z* (1970); trans. Richard Miller (New York: Hill & Wang, 1974).
Beardsley, Monroe C.: *The Possibility of Criticism* (Detroit: Wayne State University Press, 1970).
Bloom, Harold: *A Map of Misreading* (Oxford: Oxford University Press, 1975).
Foucault, Michel: *The Order of Things*, trans. anon. (New York: Vintage, 1973).
Gadamer, Hans-Georg: *Truth and Method* (Tübingen: 1960); trans. Garrett Barden and John Cumming (New York: Seabury Press, 1975).
Hirsch, Jr, E.D.: *Validity in Interpretation* (New Haven, Conn.: Yale University Press, 1967).
Ingarden, Roman: *The Cognition of the Literary Work of Art* (Tübingen: 1968); trans. Ruth Ann Crowley and Kenneth R. Olsen (Evanston, Ill.: Northwestern University Press, 1973).
Iser, Wolfgang: *The Act of Reading: A Theory of Aesthetic Response* (Baltimore, Md: Johns Hopkins University Press, 1978).
Margolis, Joseph: 'Reinterpreting interpretation', *Journal of Aesthetics and Art Criticism*, 47 (1989).
Wimsatt, Jr, William K.: *The Verbal Icon* (Lexington, Ky.: University of Kentucky Press, 1954). Contains both 'The intentional fallacy' and 'The affective fallacy', co-authored with Monroe C. Beardsley.

JOSEPH MARGOLIS

irony Irony is a topic of interest to philosophy, not least the philosophy of literature, for several reasons. To begin with, it is a many-sided concept within which distinctions need to be made and connections sought. Second, since irony involves a kind of simulation – the Greek *eironeia* means 'simulated ignorance' – we need to explain both why we indulge in it and how we manage to communicate through it. There is, third, a recurrent claim to the effect that the *world* or *existence* is inherently ironic which requires investigation. Finally, and of most relevance in the context of this *Companion*, we need to understand and assess the surprisingly frequent claims that irony is central to serious literature, that – in Roland Barthes' words – it is 'the essence of writing' (in Culler, 1983, p. 86).

TYPES OF IRONY

Whether or not it is actually ambiguous, 'irony' is certainly applied to several categorically different kinds of objects – single utterances, discursive styles, and events, for example. To begin with, there is irony as a particular trope or figure of speech, classically illustrated by a remark like 'What a fine friend!', said of someone who turned out to be treacherous. But it is wrong to generalize from this example and define irony, as many dictionaries do, as 'meaning the opposite of what is actually said'. Not only does that definition fit lying as much as irony, but the ironist by no means always intends to convey the *opposite* of what his words literally say. 'Ah, some Raphaels!', said at an exhibition of a new third-rate artist, is not meant to convey, pointlessly, that the paintings are *not* by Raphael. So the usual definition needs doubly amending. While an ironic trope must convey something that vividly contrasts with what is literally meant by the words, this need not be the 'opposite' of the latter. And the utterance is not intended to deceive generally, since some people, at least, are meant to 'catch on'.

Ironic speech and writing do not, typically, consist in the production of ironic tropes, and it is not for the production of these that writers such as Swift, Voltaire, Heine and Anthony Powell are celebrated as masters of irony. That there are other modes of ironic discourse is established by the existence of so-called 'Socratic irony'. In Plato's *Dialogues*, Socrates characteristically feigns modest ignorance of a topic and sympathy with his opponent's position, thereby leading him on until the absurdity of that position becomes clear. Another ironic device – employed, for example, by Voltaire, in *Candide* – is an *ingénu* character, the exaggerated naïvety of whose questions and observations throws into relief the pomposity and pretentiousness of the views expressed by other characters in the work.

Such devices of irony have at least two broad features in common with the trope of irony. The words used by a speaker or a character in a book are not intended to convey, to an alert audience at least, the attitude which they superficially convey. And the purpose of the devices, as with the 'Raphael' example, is a critical one – typically ridicule, mockery, and the like.

It is less easy to perceive connections between these forms of verbal irony and that which we often attribute to events or circumstances – such as those in the O. Henry story where a husband sells his watch to buy a comb for his wife who, in the meantime, has sold her hair to buy a chain for the husband's watch. But here too ridicule is effected through vivid contrast, for the wonderful incongruence between the actions of husband and wife serves to mock the sentimental optimism that pervades a certain romantic and literary tradition. So viewed, the irony belongs not to the events in themselves, but to the mute comment they pass on certain beliefs and sentiments. In so-called 'tragic irony', too, – though ridicule is no longer quite the point – the irony owes to the incongruence between the actual dispensation of Fate and the hero's own understanding of events.

EXPLAINING IRONY

The typical purposes of ironic devices are ridicule, mockery, and the like. But why should we achieve this by using words to convey something different from what they standardly convey? A plausible suggestion is that irony has the same kind of attraction as criticism through *mimicry*. The ironist 'echoes' the words that someone holding the opinions mocked actually or might well have used. (See Sperber and Wilson, 1981, and, for some reservations, Cooper, 1986.) Thus, Socrates ridicules his opponents through mimicking the speech of their obsequious disciples. But why should we so often prefer this roundabout tactic instead of coming 'straight out' with our criticisms? One possible explanation appeals to our fondness for belonging to 'in-groups'. It is a feature of much of the best irony that it is only recognized by people with the appropriate knowledge, acumen, and intimacy with the speaker or writer. *A Modest Proposal*, in which Swift 'advocated' eating Irish babies to solve the population problem, was taken by many readers as a serious recommendation. Why we should take an 'in-group' pleasure in having the right credentials for 'catching on' to 'coded' communications is a question that belongs, presumably, in the recesses of philosophical anthropology.

The problem of *how* an audience 'catches on' to the ironist's intentions is a vexed one. One proposal appeals to the recognition that *if* the writer intended his words literally he would be violating some 'maxim' of proper discourse, such as truth-telling. The reader then searches, by way of interpretation, for a proposition which, if intended by the writer, would save him from the charge of culpably having violated any 'maxims' (Grice, 1975). But while this may fit some cases, it suffers from the false assumption that the ironist must always intend to convey some particular propositional message. While Swift must certainly be understood as ridiculing the solutions to 'the Irish problem' offered by contemporary politicians, there is no reason to assume he was also trying to communicate some specific proposition(s) about Ireland. Generally speaking, irony aims more to express fairly unspecific attitudes than to communicate particular beliefs.

'WORLD-IRONY'

We saw that it is not only words, but events too, which get described as ironic, and some philosophers have even wanted to describe the world – or history, or existence – as ironic. Thus Hegel's reference to 'the universal irony of the world' was picked up by the young Kierkegaard, who took it to mean that 'each particular historical actuality . . . bears within itself the seeds of its own destruction'. (Kierkegaard, 1965 [1841], p. 278). But it is hard to see why something's containing the seeds of its own destruction should in itself, make us regard its existence as ironic. Time-bombs are not ironic. As with 'the irony of events', however, perhaps the point should

be, not that the world (history *etc.*) is *per se* ironic, but that there is an ironic contrast between how it really is and certain conceptions of it – as the arena of undisturbed progress, for example. To the naïve observer, the stages of world history have a meaning which the real processes of history, as discerned by Hegel or Kierkegaard, serve to mock.

IRONY AND 'THE ESSENCE OF WRITING'

While many writers are esteemed precisely because of their mastery of irony, there are many others who would not usually be thought of as ironists, but who are also admired – Tennyson, Dostoievsky, Zola and Hemingway, for example. So it comes as a surprise to be told that irony is of the essence of good literature. Yet, since the time of Friedrich Schlegel at least, this is the claim of several literary critics. The nineteenth-century Romantic Karl Solger called irony 'the most complete fruit of the artistic understanding' (in Schmitt, 1980, p. 115); for Thomas Mann 'irony . . . is the sense of art itself' (Mann, 1974, p. 353); while for Barthes, as we saw, it is 'the true test of writing as writing . . . the essence of writing'. On these views, irony is not, in Julian Barnes' words, simply 'a drinking companion of resonance and wit' (Barnes, 1985, p. 67), but central to the enterprise of literature.

One version of these large claims is inspired by the idea of world-, or historical, irony mentioned above, Kierkegaard, for example, argues that since 'actuality' is itself ironic, it is the writer's duty to take a 'negative', distanced stance towards it. And Lukács holds that since existence, in modernity at least, is one of intrinsic 'dissonance, breakdown or failure', the novel which is true to existence must be 'essentially ironigenic' (in Muecke, 1982, p. 96). Such views will not, of course, be especially appealing unless one shares these writers' visions of existence. And even if one does share them, one might think that there are other aspects of existence with which literature might respectably deal. Morever an unrelenting diet of novels about failed aspirations or the burgeoning of the seeds of self-destruction might soon become indigestible. One can only read *Tender is the Night* or *The Heart of Darkness* so many times.

More common, however, is an appeal not to the irony of the world which literature is about, but to something inherent in literature itself. The general thought is that paradox and irony necessarily infect authorship and literary texts, and can only be mitigated by writing in a self-consciously ironic manner which reveals to the reader the contradictions inherent in the craft.

The emphasis, in one development of this thought, is upon the ironic contrast or 'contradiction' between a text's status as an *artifice* and its effect upon the reader of immersing him in a world of events and characters that can seem as real and natural as the actual world. Related to this is the contrast between the apparent passion and commitment that may pervade a text and the comparatively cool detachment the author requires in order to craft it. Schlegel, who makes much of such 'contradictions', urges that the honest author who is properly aware of them should visibly 'hover' above his text, reminding readers of its artificial nature through such devices as 'authorial interference'. (Schlegel, 1971). (A classic example of this device is Thomas Mann's use, in *Doktor Faustus*, of a narrator who continually intrudes himself between the story and the reader).

In a different development, much favoured among Structuralists and Deconstructionists, the focus is on the ironic gap between the author's effort to convey a certain message and his inability to 'control' how his text will in fact be understood. This gap is due to a 'play of codes' which intervenes between the author's intentions and his readers and may severely refract the text's intended meaning. The honest author, once again, will admit to this 'contradiction' and, like Flaubert according to Roland Barthes, will write in a manner 'fraught with uncertainty' by way of confirming that 'the meaning of the work' is not governable by the author himself (quoted in Culler, 1983, p. 86).

It is not possible here to assess these claims about the nature of literature, but we can question the appropriateness of expressing them in the form of a thesis about literature's essential irony. At least four observations are pertinent.

(1) It is misleading to speak of the ironic nature of writing when what is apparently meant is that there is something ironic in the act of writing or the condition of being a writer. There is irony, no doubt, in a virgin writing a novel of torrid sexual passion, but it need not therefore be an ironic novel.

(2) We should note how much of our familiar concept of irony is being left out in the claim that all writing is ironic and in the recommendation that authors should therefore write in a self-consciously ironic manner. In particular, the typical purpose of irony – ridicule, and the like – is being ignored. It is unclear, for example, that the alleged contrast between the artificiality of the text and its 'realistic' effect on readers serves to mock or pass critical comment on anything. Nor is it clear that a device like 'authorial interference' has a purpose that deserves to be called 'ironic' in the way that, say, Socrates' 'simulated ignorance' does.

(3) Where connections between the 'ironies' discussed by the theorists mentioned and our familiar concept can be discerned, they are tenuous and superficial. It may be that the author is 'detached' from the story he tells, and that the ironic speaker is also 'detached' from the words he utters. But the two kinds of 'detachment' are quite different. The author is 'detached' from, say, the passions and commitments of his characters, whereas the speaker is 'detached' from his words in that he does not believe what they literally express. Again, there may be a 'gap' between what the author intends and the meaning of his text, and a 'gap' between the ironic speaker's intention and the meaning of his words. But, once more, the 'gaps' are quite different. In the one case, it is between what the author wants to convey and how his readers – because of a 'play of codes' or whatever – interpret his text. In the other case, the 'gap' is between what the speaker wants to convey and what is literally conveyed by the words uttered. It is certainly not part of our ordinary understanding that

an ironist must fail to communicate what he intends to.

(4) Even if the author's position is inherently ironic, it will not follow that he should write in a manner that makes this painfully visible to readers – through 'authorial interference', say, or a style 'fraught with uncertainty'. Only someone who would welcome 'the death of the novel' and other genres could want all authors to emulate Thomas Mann, Samuel Beckett, and others who parade their 'predicament' as writers. There are, after all, many important features of the writer's 'situation' – from his need to make a living to the influence upon him of certain literary traditions. But it is neither desirable, obligatory, nor even possible for the author to keep reminding his readers of all these aspects of the literary enterprise. And if he tries, he will soon find himself without readers to remind.

See also BARTHES; DECONSTRUCTION; HUMOUR; METAPHOR; SCHLEGEL (F); STRUCTURALISM AND POSTSTRUCTURALISM.

BIBLIOGRAPHY

Barnes, Julian: *Flaubert's Parrot* (London: Picador, 1985).
Booth, Wayne C.: *A Rhetoric of Irony* (Chicago: Chicago University Press, 1975).
Cooper, David E.: *Metaphor* (Oxford: Basil Blackwell, 1986)
Cooper, David E.: 'Irony and "the essence of writing"', *Philosophical Papers*, 18 (1989), 53–73.
Culler, Jonathan: *Barthes* (London: Fontana, 1983).
Grice, H.P.: 'Logic and conversation', *Syntax and Semantics*, ed. P. Cole and J. Morgan, vol. 3 (London: Academic Press, 1985).
Kierkegaard, Søren: *The Concept of Irony* (1841); (New York: Harper & Row, 1965).
Mann, Thomas: *Die Kunst des Romans* [The art of the novel], *Gesammelte Werke*, vol. 10 (Frankfurt: Fischer, 1974).
Muecke, D.C.: *Irony and the Ironic* (London: Methuen, 1982).
Schlegel, Friedrich: 'Lyceum-Fragmente', *Kritische Schriften* (Frankfurt: Hansel, 1971).
Schmitt, H.-J., ed.: *Romantik I* (Stuttgart: Reclam, 1980).
Sperber, Dan and Wilson, Deidre: 'Irony and the use-mention distinction', *Radical Pragmatics*, ed. P. Cole (London: Academic Press, 1981).
Wilde, Alan: *Horizons of Assent: Modernism, Post-Modernism, and the Ironic Imagination* (Baltimore: Johns Hopkins University Press, 1981).

DAVID E. COOPER

J

Japanese aesthetics *See* CHINESE AND JAPANESE AESTHETICS.

judgement, aesthetic There have been a huge number of attempts to understand the nature of the aesthetic judgement. This article is concerned only with what seem the most significant. These are placed in two broad categories, and called here – not altogether appropriately – objectivism and subjectivism.

SIMPLE OBJECTIVISM

According to a simple form of objectivism, the correct application of an aesthetic judgement, even one as general as 'This object is beautiful', is wholly determined by whether certain qualities or relations are perceived to exist in the object; the judgement makes no essential reference to the feelings of any spectator judging. Consequently, the rules governing our use of aesthetic judgements are here taken to apply only to the perception of features belonging to the object; and all that can ever be required, in order to make a justified judgement, is to establish the extent to which the object is possessed of qualities and relations that instantiate these rules.

An important corollary of this account is that when a spectator affirms that an object is, for instance, beautiful, his judgement must be implying that everyone without exception, who judges the object aesthetically, ought to find it beautiful. This implication is carried because what he is claiming is only that the object is composed of certain qualities arranged in a given way. So, provided his judgement has been correctly made, it follows that anyone else judging the object aesthetically ought equally to affirm that it is beautiful.

Simple objectivism has been subjected to several related criticisms. Many have found counter-intuitive the idea that one can, in theory, decisively settle the beauty of an object by reference to rules of composition alone. This or, at any rate, a closely connected criticism is often put in the following way: whatever aesthetic rule of composition is proposed, it is never self-contradictory to accept that the object unequivocally falls under the rule, yet deny that it is beautiful (whereas, on the analysis proposed, this must sometimes be self-contradictory).

Again, the analysis leaves no intrinsic role for a spectator's feelings in the determination of beauty. Admittedly, a defender of the analysis can, and very probably will, allow that the judgement is normally *accompanied* by a feeling of pleasure or displeasure (for example, on the ground that we obtain satisfaction from perceiving that the parts of an object are in accord with an aesthetic rule); but, as we have seen, the question of an object's beauty must always be in principle resolvable quite independently of any spectator's feelings. Finally, the evaluative force of the judgement is not adequately accounted for: in judging an object to be beautiful, more is being claimed than that it possesses certain properties disposed in a given way; one is claiming that it *merits* attention. And it would not be enough to argue, as some defenders have, that an object is judged aesthetically valuable when it is seen to reflect valuable capacities in the artist or creator. For, even assuming that such an argument could convincingly be made, it would merely leave us with the original difficulty in an amended form – namely, that of understanding how, on the simple objectivist analysis, we can recognize these capacities as valuable.

SIMPLE AND SOPHISTICATED SUBJECTIVISM

But, if the above analysis is rejected, what should replace it? According to simple subjectivism, we conceive of the aesthetic judgement as determined only by the pleasure or displeasure that perception of the object happens to arouse in any given spectator. This position has had few tenacious defenders. It implies that if, under the same circumstances, one individual, A, judges that an object is beautiful and another, B, judges that it is not, they could never be contradicting each other. Yet it seems evident that, at least for some pairs of individuals on some occasions, they could be. Moreover, an aesthetic judgement is made (clearly or confusedly) on the basis of our perception of features in the object; and, when challenged, we are normally expected to try to show that the judgement rests upon features which render our response a *justifiable* one. This is not consistent with holding that we think of the judgement as depending only on whatever feelings of pleasure or displeasure the perception of the object may occasion in any spectator.

In the light of these and other criticisms, subjectivists have usually accepted that the aesthetic judgement cannot be conceived as, in intention, a bare statement or expression of personal liking or disliking. At the same time, they have wished to preserve a central tenet of simple subjectivism – namely, that the judgement is ultimately determined by the feelings of (at least some) spectators and not by the mere perception of features in the object.

A sophisticated subjectivist account was skilfully defended by Hume in the eighteenth century; and most subsequent subjectivist theories have remained greatly indebted to it. The basic idea is often introduced by seeking to draw an analogy between colour judgements and aesthetic judgements. Even those who construe an object's perceived colour as, in fact, nothing more than an occurrence in the observer's mind, allow that there are standards for assessing both the appropriateness of particular colour judgements and the capacity of individual observers to make such judgements. These standards depend on (1) similar general principles governing most people's colour perception (as testified by, for instance, the substantial consensus in colour judgements, anyway in broad outline), and our accepting that those within the consensus who can make maximum discriminations between colours have the best colour vision; (2) widespread agreement among the maximum discriminators about the precise colours of given objects. Similarly, the sophisticated subjectivist urges, we should think of standards in art criticism as resting on (1) the same, or nearly the same, general principles governing most people's aesthetic taste, and our acknowledging that those within this majority who are capable of experiencing the fullest and most discriminating range of contemplative feelings have the most perfect taste; (2) a large measure of agreement among the maximum discriminators about the precise feelings that are produced by given objects.

Clearly, if the subjectivist is to make good this analogy, he will need to defend his belief that the majority of people *are* governed by similar principles of taste (the consensus on colours is uncontentious). This he attempts to do by pointing to the long-running survival of certain admired works among diverse nations; and by arguing that most of the grosser disagreements can be put down to factors like prejudice or lack of education (of course, these factors themselves will need to be explicated in a non-question-begging way). Additionally, he will need to produce a decision procedure for establishing which spectators are the most discriminating. Here he may refer to certain of those admired works that have survived through the centuries; and try to show that principles, now generally accepted to be operating in these, can also be shown to be operating in a more recent work where only a few people, independently, have felt their effect. By tests of this kind, the sophisticated subjectivist hopes to show that, within a given area of the arts, some people are possessed of a high degree of discrimination and that there is an acceptable measure of agreement among them. (In fairness, it should be said that *any* theorist, who believes in aesthetic rules, needs to tackle the issue of disagreement: this is not a problem for the sophisticated subjectivist alone.)

Even allowing that the analogy with colours can survive the existence of aesthetic disagreement, it still fails to explain why we should talk of the beauties or blemishes of *objects* (the feelings of pleasure/displeasure manifestly belong to the subjects judging), or why in backing up our judgements, especially within the finer arts, we typically engage in careful *analysis* of the object, often including detailed comparison with other objects (nothing like this occurs with colour judgements). To meet these objections, the sophisticated subjectivist refers to those features of objects, the awareness of which causes the majority's contemplative feelings of pleasure or displeasure. He insists, in particular, that the capacity to notice intricate relationships between the parts of a complex work of art or natural object is, as a matter of fact, a causally necessary condition for the fullest experience of the appropriate feelings. Accordingly, we are educated in the appreciation of the finer arts by being shown (what are believed to be) these causally responsible features in established works; and we learn that in order to *justify* our responses as aesthetic ones, they need to be grounded in the awareness of such features – which, frequently, can be most sharply highlighted by comparing one object with another. They become denominated the 'beauties' or 'blemishes' or whatever of objects, despite their existence, so named, being dependent on the sensibilities of discriminating spectators within the majority. On this account, any aesthetic rules of composition that may exist will simply be empirical generalizations, based on the discovery that features of a recognizably similar kind have been found to please discriminating spectators in a variety of different objects.

Sophisticated subjectivism incorporates many of the properties that have been widely seen as central to aesthetic appreciation. It permits a prominent, indeed a necessary, role to reasoning and the comparison of cases in the justification of aesthetic judgements, at least in the finer arts; yet it gives to contemplative feelings of pleasure or displeasure the ultimate determining ground of the judgement. And since any acknowledged general rules of art are only contingently connected with this determining ground, it can explain why it is never self-contradictory to admit that certain features fall under an accepted rule, while also denying that they are beautiful. Furthermore, it can offer an account of why we place such a value on aesthetic appreciation: not only are the discriminating feelings, upon which judgements in the finer arts depend, of an intrinsically satisfying nature, but they also have a strong tendency (together with the analytical skill required for their experience) to civilize a person's attitude towards moral and intellectual matters. Since both these consequences are almost universally regarded as highly desirable, it is not surprising that aesthetic discrimination should be considered an admirable quality and its objects worthy of appreciation.

On the other hand, a subjectivist cannot allow that the aesthetic judgement claims the agreement of everyone without exception. For, according to him, it is possible for some spectators to be entirely unmoved or, even, displeased by their awareness of the very features whose perception pleases the majority (though many in the majority may only feel their effect in an undiscriminating way); and these spectators need be guilty of no fault in denying their beauty. Unlike the objectivist, a defender of subjectivism, including the sophisticated variety, cannot maintain that a judgement, if correctly made, *must* hold for everyone without exception who judges aesthetically. At best, the aesthetic judgement can only lay claim to a contingent universality, or near-universality, based on an *empirical* generalization concerning the sensibilities of human beings. To those of us whose sensibilities may happen to be governed by totally different principles from the majority's – always a possibility for a subjectivist – the judgements of discriminating spectators within that majority can have no logical force.

SOPHISTICATED OBJECTIVISM

This position, which was originally developed by Kant, shares with simple objectivism the view that the judgement of taste lays claim to the agreement of everyone without exception; but it shares with sophisticated subjectivism the view that, for us, its determining ground must always be the feeling of contemplative pleasure or displeasure. Even if this is, so far as it goes, a correct analysis of the aesthetic judgement, its appearance of having one's cake and eating it raises very acutely the question of whether application of the judgement can ever be justified.

In Kant's own case, the justification is intimately linked with his metaphysics. Two people can only be perceiving the same object in so far as they possess the same faculties of understanding and imagination, operating identically in both of them. The feeling of contemplative pleasure or displeasure, by which we determine the aesthetic judgement, also has to arise from the interlocking of these two faculties in an act of perception. More especially, we correctly pronounce an object to be beautiful if, in an act of purely reflective perception upon the relations holding among its formal features, we find – by means of the ensuing feeling – that the imagination is permitted maximum freedom from the rule-governed constraints of the understanding (the latter faculty supplies the framework of all our ascertainable general rules). On this account, it is *impossible* for two people to be perceiving the same object, while making different, equally well grounded, aesthetic judgements. It is impossible because we are each said to make a well grounded aesthetic judgement on the basis of a feeling which has to depend for its existence only upon an identical, formal, use of those perceptual faculties that are necessarily shared, and shared to the same extent, by everyone with a capacity for experiencing the object at all. (Differences in judgement are held to arise because people seldom reach a decision solely by means of the feeling that arises from a purely reflective perception upon the formal features of the object and, hence, from simply allowing the imagination its free play.)

So although we decide upon an object's beauty on the basis of feeling, Kant thinks that what we are thereby estimating is the extent to which the object's mere form or design gives scope to the imagination's free play. But there can be no discoverable general rules for establishing when this free play is at its greatest, precisely because the imagination is here maximally *un*constrained by the faculty of rules, as this operates within our experience. Only if we had access to the ground of all experience – the supersensible world – would it be possible to comprehend the principles governing the free play; and, hence, to determine directly from a purely reflective perception of the object (thus prior to and independently of feeling) the extent of its beauty. Failing, as we do, to achieve this insight into the supersensible, each of us can only estimate beauty by means of his own individual feeling – though with the assurance that, provided the feeling has arisen only from allowing the imagination free play, the ensuing judgement can rightly claim the agreement of everyone without exception.

I have located Kant's theory in the objectivist camp because of his insistence that a well founded aesthetic judgement must, in reality, ultimately rest upon principles (albeit unknowable to us) that obtain independently of any spectator's feelings and that apply identically to everyone's purely reflective perception of features in the object. Arguably, his position rests on an unjustified, or even meaningless, metaphysical structure; relatedly, it relies on an extremely narrow formalist conception of art and natural beauty. Still, even if these criticisms are accepted, Kant's analysis does raise a serious problem for the subjectivist, which is to account for the persisting contention that the aesthetic judgement claims what he called 'strict universality' – that is, the agreement of everyone *without exception*. (This problem is the analogue of one facing the subjectivist in ethics – namely, to explain the seeming *categorical* force of moral ought-judgements.)

A common subjectivist line has been to argue that because the exercise of aesthetic judgement, notably in the finer arts, requires extensive experience and reflection, many have erroneously supposed that *all* differences in unprejudiced verdicts must stem from differences in knowledge or analytical skill. And this explanation is reinforced with the observation that the feelings resulting from careful aesthetic reflection are often so comparatively gentle, especially when one has become well informed and practised in any art, as to pass unremarked as the crucial determining factor in the verdict. For the subjectivist, then, any inclination to claim strict universality for the aesthetic judgement arises from explicable delusion: in the appreciation of the finer arts, it is easy to be misled into thinking that the judgement depends wholly on factors belonging to the mere perception of the object; and, under such a misapprehension, one will naturally take it that the verdict claims strict universality. In fact, however, the most that can be claimed is a universality covering all who *happen* to possess a similar sensibility. Agreed, we are able to talk of aesthetic standards or rules, but their application is wholly relative to the majority community. It cannot reasonably be maintained that *anyone*, who is to respond to an object aesthetically, must judge in accordance with them.

FURTHER DEVELOPMENTS

How convincing is the sophisticated subjectivist's account? Fundamental to it is the belief that the aesthetic judgement is ultimately determined by a merely contingent connection – more particularly, a causal connection – between object and spectator's response: that is, his feeling of pleasure or displeasure. On two counts, this belief has been strenuously disputed in the twentieth century.

First, it has been held that the spectator must be the final authority on what aspects of an object ground his response. Others, no doubt, may help him to identify the precise reasons for his satisfaction or dissatisfaction, and this may include leading him to alter an earlier identification. But it is always the spectator himself, on the basis of his own experience of the aesthetic object, who must authorize any suggestions from others before they can be considered correct. Yet – the argument runs – on the supposition that the connection between object and response is a causal one, no authorization by the person concerned would be required. (If someone has toothache, his agreement is not required before any claim to have located its cause can be accepted as correct; whereas the same cannot be said about any claim to have identified what someone is dissatisfied about in, for instance, the closing scenes of *King Lear*.)

Second, it has been held that although the spectator is the final authority on the ground of his response, that response can only be justified as an *aesthetic* one if the reasons for it appropriately fall under aesthetic rules. Perhaps the rules themselves were first laid down because the features which answered to them were believed to satisfy the sensibilities of influential people. Still, whatever their origins, the fact is that, now, only judgements in accord with these given rules can be considered well founded. In short, they have become a constitutive element in manifesting aesthetic appreciation: *anyone*, who is to justify his judgement as aesthetic, must be able to show that what satisfied him about the object are features that suitably relate to these rules. Consequently, the connection between response and object, in so far as the response is to be thought of as genuinely aesthetic, cannot be merely contingent, since if it were, one could identify that response *independently* of knowing whether its grounds were in accord with aesthetic rules. This is not to say that the rules must be capable of being formulated as packaged generalizations: for their elucidation may require direct comparison and contrast between different objects, in order to bring out the family-resemblance features that typically characterize the nature of aesthetic rules. Nor need a person's awareness of rules be displayed through critical discussion: appreciation of them may be manifested in several other ways, most obviously by means of artistic performance. What is crucial is that there exists a fundamental framework of given rules, within which alone it is possible to talk of the making, defending and so on of particular aesthetic judgements.

This dual attack on subjectivism, which derives from the work of Wittgenstein, evidently has strong affinities with Kant's position. It defends the strict universality of the aesthetic judgement; it admits that aesthetic rules may be incapable of formulation as generalizations; it affirms an internal, and not a merely contingent, relation between the spectator's perception of the object and his making an aesthetic judgement; and it insists that no reference to discoverable principles can ever, by itself, establish the reason for the spectator's pleasure or displeasure with an aesthetic object – his own individual experience must always be the final court of appeal.

Despite its ingenuity, it is doubtful whether the attack's central claim – that the connection between object and spectator's response is essentially non-contingent – should be conceded. Admittedly, it does seem right to say that the spectator must authorize any suggestion as to the precise reason for his satisfaction or dissatisfaction, before that suggestion can be considered correct (as the first criticism of subjectivism contended); and this does differentiate an aesthetic explanation from many overtly causal ones. At the same time, it also seems right to say not only that the spectator's feeling of pleasure or displeasure can be expressed separately from his identification of its precise ground (thus explaining how he can feel satisfied or dissatisfied with an object while still wondering precisely why), but also that we think of any identification by him as subject to a familiar form of causal falsification: namely, where we point to a parallel instance where the alleged reason (cause) is absent while the response (effect) is still present, or vice versa.

For example, we question whether certain features can be the real reason for a spectator's pleasure at an object (even though he identified them as the precise ground of his response) if, on another, similar, occasion, their absence did not alter the degree of his pleasure. In such a case, we say things like, 'Those features cannot really be why he was moved'; just as, with an indisputably causal claim – for example, in the physical sciences – the production of a parallel falsifying instance leads us to say that the alleged cause cannot really have been why a given event took place. So whereas the spectator may be able to *rule out* suggestions as to the reason for his satisfaction (and is, in that way, the final authority), he cannot justifiably continue to *affirm* that such-and-such features are the real reason for that response, if it can be shown that his awareness of them formed an insignificant part of its cause.

Once it is admitted that the features which figure as the real reason for a spectator's pleasure or displeasure at an aesthetic object do, after all, carry a causal implication, it would be implausible to hold that given aesthetic rules form an immovable framework that serves to define the possible content of aesthetic judgements (as the second criticism of subjectivism contended). For suppose it is discovered that certain features of an object, although fully in accord with an accepted aesthetic rule, are not the cause of the discriminating spectator's response, despite being picked out by him as its ground; and suppose, further, that other features which he also perceived were acting as the cause. Since it is implied that the spectator's awareness of the properties named in an aesthetic explanation cause his response, this discovery would force a change in the rules, so that they did pick out the object's causally efficacious features. Henceforth, people would be educated to an awareness of these features: they would be taught to see them (and not those features falling under the original rule) as mainly responsible for the object's value – and, thereby, as what should form the ground of a response, if it is to count as genuinely aesthetic.

According to this argument, it follows that aesthetic rules are ultimately dependent on the sensibilities of human beings, in the very manner that the sophisticated subjectivist maintains. Of course, since this dependence can only generate rules that apply *contingently* to (at best) all or most spectators, the subjectivist must still regard any claims to a strict universality for the aesthetic judgement as delusory (brought about in the ways already indicated). On the other hand, he can counter that it would be ridiculous to stick with a given rule, once it is established that the features falling under it do not cause the discriminating spectator's response. How can any arrangement of qualities be conceived as aesthetically valuable, if it is known not to produce those feelings towards the object which we prize? As the subjectivist sees it, we can readily understand how objects, composed of features that are taken to produce both delicate emotions and a civilizing effect upon the moral sensibility, should be acknowledged as meriting appreciation. But, he insists, unless this causal implication holds, we shall simply be unable to conceive of any occasion on which to make a justified ascription of aesthetic value.

Earlier, a distinction was drawn between the analysis of the aesthetic judgement and its justified application. It has transpired that this distinction is not clear-cut. The subjectivist has argued forcefully that, without a causal implication to aesthetic reason-giving, there can be no conceivable case where the assignment of aesthetic value would be justified. But if no case can be so much as conceived of, all talk of 'aesthetic value' must be devoid of sense. For we cannot give a meaning to words or signs, unless we know what would count as their correct use. It turns out, therefore, that if the objectivist tries to analyse the aesthetic judgement without the causal implication, he will be in grave danger of having to deny that its application ever entails an evaluation; or, rather, of having to deny that he can even understand what is purportedly being entailed. This is an absurd consequence. It raises, again, a difficulty that we encountered in connection with the views both of Kant and of the simple objectivists: namely, of whether objectivism can provide a comprehensible account of aesthetic value. Unless such an account is forthcoming – or, at the very least, an explanation is given of why it is not required – no persuasive alternative to sophisticated subjectivism appears to be available; and we shall just have to confess that there is an element of delusion, a tendency to affirm a stricter universality than

can be warranted, in our application of the aesthetic judgement.

See also BEAUTY; KANT; PLEASURE, AESTHETIC; RELATIVISM; TASTE; THEORIES OF ART; WITTGENSTEIN.

BIBLIOGRAPHY

Berkeley, George: Third Dialogue, §§8 and 9, *Alciphron or the Minute Philosopher*, 3rd edn (London: 1752); reprinted as vol. 3 of *The Works of George Berkeley, Bishop of Cloyne*, ed. T.E. Jessop and A.A. Luce (London: Thomas Nelson, 1950 [1732]).

Hume, David: 'The sceptic' (1742), 'Of the delicacy of taste and passion' (1742), and 'Of the standard of taste' (1757); reprinted in *Essays Moral, Political and Literary* (Oxford: Oxford University Press, 1963).

Kant, Immanuel: 'Introduction' and 'Critique of aesthetic judgement', *Critique of Judgement* (Berlin, 1790); trans. J.C. Meredith (Oxford: Clarendon Press, 1952).

McDowell, John: 'Aesthetic value, objectivity, and the fabric of the world', *Pleasure, Preference and Value*, ed. Eva Schaper (Cambridge: Cambridge University Press, 1983).

Mackie, John L.: 'The subjectivity of value', *Ethics: Inventing Right and Wrong* (Harmondsworth: Penguin Books, 1977).

Moore, George E.: 'Wittgenstein's lectures in 1930–33', *Philosophical Papers* (London: Allen & Unwin, 1959).

Pears, David F.: 'Causes and objects of some feelings and psychological reactions', *Questions in the Philosophy of Mind* (London: Duckworth, 1975).

Reid, Thomas: 'Of taste', in *Essays on the Intellectual Powers of Man* (Edinburgh, 1785); (Cambridge, Mass.: MIT Press, 1969).

Wittgenstein, Ludwig: 'Lectures on aesthetics', *Lectures and Conversations on Aesthetics, Psychology and Religious Belief*, ed. C. Barrett (Oxford: Basil Blackwell, 1966).

Wittgenstein, Ludwig: *Zettel*; trans. G.E.M. Anscombe, ed. Anscombe and G.H. von Wright (Oxford: Basil Blackwell, 1967), §§155–75.

ANDREW WARD

K

Kant, Immanuel (1724–1804) The greatest eighteenth-century German philosopher, and one of the subject's most influential figures, in epistemology, ethics, and metaphysics as well as aesthetics; a leading champion of European Enlightenment.

Kant's analysis of the nature of aesthetic judgement forms the first part of his third *Critique*, the *Critique of Judgement* (1790), the second part of which is an investigation into the role of teleological judgements in our descriptions of the natural world. This division corresponds to the ways in which the apparent purposiveness of natural forms may be viewed: either subjectively – the aesthetic standpoint; or objectively – the teleological standpoint. The most influential part of Kant's theory of aesthetic value concerns the notion of beauty, which he treats as applying primarily to natural objects and only secondarily to works of art. However, he considers the value of a work of fine art to depend not only on its beauty, but also on its being the vehicle for aesthetic ideas.

An aesthetic idea is an intuition of the creative imagination for which an adequate concept can never be found. It is the counterpart of an idea of reason for which no intuition is adequate. The latter include such non-empirical notions as God, eternity, virtue. Aesthetic ideas may go some way towards giving sensory embodiment to such ideas, but without imparting knowledge of any kind. Their other role is to 'body forth to sense' empirical notions such as love, death and fame, but 'with a completeness of which nature affords no parallel' (Kant, 1928 [1790], p. 177). They provide the imagination with a powerful incentive 'to spread its flight over a whole host of kindred representations that provoke more thought than admits of expression in a concept determined by words'. Their expression is typically symbolic, but as no truth is being asserted, there would be no point in trying to paraphrase them. This free flight of the imagination is an activity that is worth while for its own sake, giving to works of art an intellectual as well as a purely aesthetic appeal, without which, says Kant, they would lack 'soul'. The invention of aesthetic ideas is ascribed to genius, whilst their expression in beautiful forms, upon which their communicability depends, is ascribed to the faculty of taste.

The 'Critique of aesthetic judgement' (part I of the third *Critique*) is chiefly concerned with the question of how aesthetic judgements can be subjective and yet universally valid. Kant distinguishes two main types of aesthetic judgement: judgements about the beautiful, or pure judgements of taste; and judgements about the sublime. The most obvious difference between them is that, whereas the beautiful is grounded in the spatial and temporal form of objects (figure and play), and thus on that which is limited in space and time, the sublime depends on that sense of limitlessness which is evoked by the unimaginably vast (the mathematically sublime) and the overwhelmingly powerful (the dynamically sublime).

Strictly speaking, our experience of the sublime is only partly aesthetic because, unlike the beautiful, it needs to be mediated by ideas of reason and morality. In the case of the mathematically sublime, such as the starry heavens, reason is exalted by enabling us to think of what lies outside the reach of the imagination as a totality; and in the case of the dynamically sublime, such as a storm at sea, we are reminded of our worth as moral beings in contrast to the weakness of our empirical selves. In both cases, an otherwise unpleasing experience is tempered by feelings of admiration and respect. It would be fair to say, however, that although Kant's account of the sublime contains many points of interest, it lacks both the plausibility and the overall importance of his account of the beautiful.

To find a thing beautiful, whether it be natural or man-made, is to take pleasure in it simply on account of how it looks or sounds. This means, says Kant, that judgements of beauty – or judgements of taste, as he calls them – are based on the feelings of pleasure or displeasure which denote nothing in the object and so cannot be other than subjective. Such judgements can be neither true nor false, since to discriminate on the basis of feeling alone is to contribute nothing to knowledge. The most they can aspire to is a kind of intersubjective validity.

In the four sections, or 'moments', of his 'Analytic of the beautiful', Kant attempts to define beauty in terms of the type of pleasure it affords. From this it emerges that beauty is a perceptual form whose subjective finality is *felt* as a disinterested, universally communicable and necessary pleasure. Its finality assures us that it is worth contemplating for its own sake, although it is only through feeling that this feature can be apprehended. Thus, to understand the nature of beauty, we need to understand the nature of aesthetic pleasure.

Kant distinguishes three types of pleasure: pleasure in the agreeable, or gratification; pleasure in the good, or approval; and pleasure in the beautiful, or free liking. Only the last is disinterested. To reflect on a thing in a disinterested way is to adopt a non-moral, non-practical, non-egoistic attitude towards it. Hence any value that we attach to it belongs to it alone and is not dependent on considerations of morality, utility, personal advantage, or sensory gratification. If aesthetic merit is conferred on things as a result of such a contemplative attitude, then it follows that aesthetic values are non-derivative and so autonomous – as Kant claimed moral values also to be. Few ideas in the history of aesthetics have been more pervasive than that of the disinterestedness of the

aesthetic attitude. It has figured prominently, in various guises, in the writings of eighteenth-century English empiricists and of nineteenth-century German idealists, and in much twentieth-century writing. The idea can be traced back to Lord Shaftesbury (1671–1713), but Kant was the first to incorporate it into a theory about the logical character of aesthetic judgement.

Kant's own criterion of disinterestedness is stricter than the one given above, for he defines 'interest' as 'the delight which we connect with the representation of the real existence of the object. Such a delight, therefore, always involves a reference to the faculty of desire, either as its determining ground, or else as necessarily implicated with its determining ground' (Kant, 1928 [1790], p. 42). Further, 'one must not be in the least prepossessed in favour of the real existence of the thing, but must preserve complete indifference in this respect in order to play the part of judge in matters of taste' (p. 43).

Part of what is being claimed here is that aesthetic delight is delight in what *appears* to the subject regardless of its ontological status. Compare, for example, the indifference of the traveller in a desert who admires the beauty of what he takes to be a lake, on learning that it is only a mirage, with the disappointment of the traveller who is dying of thirst. Since aesthetic value resides in the pleasure taken in the intentional object, the real nature of the object is irrelevant. On the other hand, the same might be said of the reflective pleasure we sometimes take in smells, tastes and colours, which Kant regards as being merely sensory and so 'interested'.

This shows that disinterestedness on its own is not a sufficient condition for pleasure to count as aesthetic, despite some suggestions to the contrary (for instance, Kant, 1928 [1790], p. 49), although it might still be a necessary condition. However, if Kant's other three conditions – universal communicability, necessity, and the subjective finality of the intentional object – are taken into account, then a more adequate criterion emerges.

Clearly, Kant is mistaken in supposing that disinterested pleasure can only be taken in the perceptual form of the object and never in what he terms 'the matter of sensation'. If smells and tastes are to be excluded from the realm of the aesthetic, it should be on grounds other than interest; for example, their incapacity for formal organization or the more personal and idiosyncratic nature of our response to them, which would breach the universality condition. Again, Kant's insistence on treating our delight in colour as merely sensory seems to be a mistake, since it is no more dependent on our antecedent needs or desires than is our delight in perceptual form. Moreover, colours are capable of formal arrangement, although it must be admitted that one's response to colour is likely to be more personal than one's response to shape, say; people have their favourite colours but not their favourite shapes.

A more general objection might be raised against Kant's insistence that we 'must preserve complete indifference' as to the real existence of the thing in order to judge it aesthetically on the grounds that most aesthetically sensitive people would in fact regard an object's beauty as a very good reason for wanting to preserve it. This objection is perhaps unfair to Kant, since nothing he says rules out the possibility of treating one's disinterested pleasure in beautiful things as a first-order attitude, and one's approval of their existence as a logically independent second-order attitude. Thus one might, for example, feel, as Aristotle did, that one had a duty to develop one's perceptual and cognitive powers to their fullest extent, and to see this as a practical benefit of, albeit not the purpose of, aesthetic reflection. One would then have a moral reason for preserving beauty. Kant, too, might have a further motive for doing so in that he sees the beautiful as a *symbol* of the moral. Nevertheless, the first-order attitude in no way determines the second-order attitude, and may even be in conflict with it. For example, it is quite possible to disapprove of beautiful things and want to destroy them, as some Puritans have done, whilst being fully sensible of the their beauty. This might be a way, albeit an extreme one, of asserting the supremacy of moral or religious values over aesthetic ones.

According to Kant, the disinterestedness of pure judgements of taste helps to explain the possibility of their universal validity, which is what chiefly distinguishes them from judgements upon the merely agreeable. Both are *singular* judgements in which the subject makes his judgement on the basis of an immediate, and therefore subjective, response to a particular object; for instance, 'This is delicious', 'This is beautiful.' In each case, the proof of the pudding is in the eating, as it were. The crucial difference is that, whereas in the case of the agreeable the subject only judges for himself – for instance, 'This Canary wine is agreeable to me' – in the case of the beautiful the subject judges 'not merely for himself, but for all men, and then speaks of beauty as if it were a property of all things' (Kant, 1928 [1790], p. 52); for example, 'This rose is beautiful.'

To call something beautiful is to put it 'on a pedestal' and *demand* the same delight from others. The disinterestedness helps to explain why we feel entitled to do this. 'For where any one is conscious that his delight in an object is with him independent of interest, it is inevitable that he should look on the object as one containing a ground of delight for all men' (Kant, 1928 [1790], p. 50). In other words, if one is aware that one's delight in the beautiful is not dependent on any fact about oneself that might be peculiar to oneself, as with needs, desires and appetites, then one is entitled to assume – or at least one has no reason for not assuming – that it is grounded on something which one shares with all human beings: that is, with beings who are both animal and rational and who share one's perceptual and cognitive faculties.

This does not, of course, prove that our aesthetic feelings must in principle be universally communicable, but it does help to explain why we should feel them to be so. It helps to explain, for instance, in a very general way, why we would be extremely puzzled by someone who genuinely considered a typical multi-storey car park to be more beautiful than the Taj Mahal, but not surprised by an Eskimo who genuinely preferred the taste of raw whale blubber to lobster soufflé. It is true that one can often predict with a fair degree of accuracy what others will find agreeable or disagreeable, and thus make judgements with which most, if not all, people would concur: for example, that the smell of freshly roasted coffee is delicious. However, to demand universal assent to a pure judgement or taste is not to predict a similar reaction in others, but to require it. In other words, others *ought* to agree, even if they do not. Judgements upon the agreeable, on the other hand, can, at best aspire only to a general validity and contain no hidden 'ought'.

The aesthetic 'ought' differs from the 'ought' of practical judgement in not resting on the concept of an end. This is because when an object pleases aesthetically in the Kantian sense, it does so apart from any concept. To judge a thing purely beautiful is to judge it on the basis of perceptual form alone without reference to how it might be described or what purpose, if any, it might serve. The case is otherwise with the good, whether morally good or only usefully good, for a thing can be good or bad, right or wrong, only under a description which must include reference to an end: in the case of an object, its purpose; in the case of an action, the intention behind it. All such judgements are 'interested' in Kant's sense, for 'the good is the object of will' and 'to will something, and to take a delight in its existence, i.e. to take an interest in it, are identical' (Kant, 1928 [1790], p. 48).

For this reason, an object cannot be judged beautiful or ugly on the basis of a general description of it, as can the rightness or wrongness of an action. Thus aesthetic disagreements cannot be settled by rational argument in the way that moral and practical disagreements can; that is to say, 'there can be no rule according to which any one is to be compelled to recognize anything as beautiful.' For where there are no concepts there can be no rules, or at least no rules capable of formulation. Thus holds good the dictum that there can be no disputing about tastes.

The only procedure for settling aesthetic disagreements is for the parties concerned to attend to the object with greater care, in case the perceptual form has not been properly apprehended. But even when those features of the object which contribute to its beauty can be named, no rule can be formulated which says that any object possessing such features must be beautiful. One can, of course, improve one's taste by exercising one's perpetual and imaginative faculties in the right way on objects which are considered exemplary in respect of their beauty, but one cannot be forced to abandon a judgement simply because others disagree with it (Kant, 1928 [1790], pp. 137–9).

A pure judgement of taste is, then, one which expresses a disinterested and universally communicable pleasure in the perceptual form of an object, considered apart from any concept. The subjective principle which determines what it is about the perceptual form which pleases or displeases by feeling alone, Kant calls the 'Form of Finality'. Since the form of finality can only be felt and not known, there is very little that can be said about it apart from its effect on the subject, which is to induce an harmonious interaction between the faculties of imagination and understanding. We know *a priori*, Kant says, that such harmonious interaction is possible because it is a necessary condition of the possibility of all empirical knowledge. In other words, the mere possibility of the universal communicability of empirical truth, which is objective, assures us of the possibility of the universal communicability of aesthetic feeling, which is subjective.

There are two types of form: figure, which is the product of design; and play, which is the product of composition. Painting is an example of the first, and music of the second. Dance combines the two. Subjective finality can be ascribed to the form when it is so well adapted to our powers of cognition that it is found pleasing for its own sake. When this happens, the imagination, whose normal role is to supply data for the understanding to synthesize, enters into a free, self-sustaining and harmonious interaction with understanding, whose normal role is to bring the data under concepts with a view either to knowledge or to action. The interaction is free, because unconstrained by determinate concepts. Thus, the form of finality has the appearance of purposiveness or design, but without purpose. It is that for the sake of which we exercise our perceptual powers, when we have no practical or theoretical interest in the object.

See also ATTITUDE, AESTHETIC; BEAUTY; JUDGEMENT, AESTHETIC; PLEASURE, AESTHETIC; SUBLIME; SHAFTESBURY; TASTE.

WRITINGS

Kritik der Urteilskraft (Berlin and Libau: 1790); trans. J.C. Meredith, *The Critique of Judgement* (Oxford: Clarendon Press, 1928).

BIBLIOGRAPHY

Cohen, T. and Guyer, P.: *Essays in Kant's Aesthetics* (Chicago, Ill.: University of Chicago Press, 1982).

Coleman, F.X.J.: *The Harmony of Reason: A Study in Kant's Aesthetics* (Pittsburgh, Pa.: University of Pittsburgh Press, 1974).

Crawford, D.W.: *Kant's Aesthetic Theory* (Madison, Wis.: University of Wisconsin Press, 1974).

Guyer, P.: *Kant and the Claims of Taste* (Cambridge, Mass.: Harvard University Press, 1979).

Kemal, S.: *Kant and Fine Art* (Oxford: Clarendon Press, 1986).

McCloskey, M.A.: *Kant's Aesthetic* (London: Macmillan, 1987).

Osborne, H.: *Aesthetics and Art Criticism* (London: Longman, 1968).

Schaper, E.: *Studies in Kant's Aesthetics* (Edinburgh: Edinburgh University Press, 1979).

Scruton, R.: *Kant* (Oxford: Oxford University Press, 1982).

Warnock, M.: *Imagination* (Berkeley, Calif.: University of California Press, 1976).

DAVID WHEWELL

Kierkegaard, Søren (1813–55) Danish philosopher and theologian; an inspiration, in the twentieth century for both existentialism and Protestant thought.

In *Either/Or* (1843) Kierkegaard writes pseudonymously to his *symparanekrōmenoi* ('fellow-moribunds') of his own sense of the nihilism of his age (Hong and Hong, vol. 1, 1987, p. 168). Describing the 'music of the storm', he comments: 'People do say that the voice of the divine is not in the driving wind but in the soft breeze, but our ears, after all, are constructed not to pick up the soft breeze but to swallow the uproar of the elements.' The vortex is the world's core principle, and he wishes that 'it might erupt with deep-seated resentment and shake off the mountains and the nations and the cultural works and man's clever inventions.'

Whether or not he was right to find the sources of nihilism in the work of Fichte, in the Romantics or in Hegelianism, he searched for an understanding of 'the aesthetic' (an existential category) in relation to this vortex, loving poetry and art and all the works of the imagination (aesthetics as artistic practice) while setting limits to them (Hong and Hong, 1987, vol. 2, p. 273). For, as he says (under one of his pseudonyms), 'they provide only an imperfect reconciliation with life . . . when you fix your eye upon poetry and art you are not looking at actuality.'

Kierkegaard's manner of presenting his views on aesthetics was possible only for a writer capable of the range of experiments in style and thought exhibited in his private papers as well as in his published work, and it is this which gives his writing special distinction (the modern editions (Hong and Hong, 1983; 1987) collate material from the private papers into the published work). His pseudonymous writing has to do, he says, with deliberately created 'author-personalities' (Hong and Hong, 1987, vol. 2, p. 451) by means of which he enables his readers to explore aesthetics, and themselves, and to discover what finally matters to them.

There are three main aesthetic 'ideas', which represent the lyric (Don Juan – sensuous immediacy), the epic (the wandering Jew – despair), and the dramatic (Faust – doubt). Don Juan belongs to the Middle Ages, while Faust is a parody of the Reformation, abandoned to himself and needing completion in the wandering Jew. The latter is the unhappiest of men because he cannot die; he stands for the aesthetic, without meaning or purpose, and powerless against the boredom of the modern age. In 'The Seducer's Diary' (a story within *Either/Or*), he entertains himself by creating in a young girl, 'the motions of infinity' (Hong and Hong, 1987, vol. 1, p. 392), in which she learns 'to swing herself, to rock herself in moods, to confuse poetry and actuality, truth and fiction, to frolic in infinity'.

There are, then, those like the Seducer for whom life becomes a stage, and those who perform, for example, 'The Immediate Erotic Stages or The Musical Erotic', of which the supreme example is Mozart's *Don Giovanni*. In this work is to be found the 'thoroughgoing mutual permeation' of form and subject-matter, like-for-like (Hong and Hong, 1987, vol. 1, pp. 52–3). The Don's sensuous immediacy has its absolute medium in music, in its power, life, movement, continual unrest, continual succession (Hong and Hong, 1987, vol. 1, p. 71). We lose ourselves in the music in which the Don unfurls himself. But a different form, and therefore a different response, is appropriate for different subject-matter. So in a comedy like *The First Love*, a play he saw, what is important is that:

In it there must not be a single character, not a single situation, that could claim to survive the downfall that irony from the outset prepared for each and all in it. When the curtain falls, everything is forgotten, nothing but nothing remains, and that is the only thing one sees; and the only thing one hears is a laughter, like a sound of nature, that does not issue from any one person but is the language of a world force, and this force is irony. (Hong and Hong, 1987, vol. 1, p. 273)

It is a reflection on Emmeline (a character in *The First Love*) and her illusions, disclosed by the comedy, remaining afterwards for contemplation, and fostered by repeatedly seeing the comedy, which distinguishes watching it from losing ourselves in the Don's music.

Kierkegaard also explores the relation between the ancient and the modern in tragedy. The crucial difference is that modern tragedy has no 'epic foreground', for the hero or heroine stands or falls entirely on his or her own deeds. 'The wrath of the gods is terrible, but still the pain is not as great as in modern tragedy, where the hero suffers his total guilt, is transparent to himself in the suffering of his guilt' (Hong and Hong, 1987, vol. 1, p. 148). And in a remarkable piece of necromantic fantasy he sketches out how he would re-characterize *Antigone* (in marked contrast to Hegel, in his *Aesthetics*). It is precisely that capacity for reflection associated with comedy, but now, as it were, attributable to a character in tragedy itself, which robs tragedy of something essential to it: for 'the power which is the source of the suffering has lost its meaning' and the spectator has lost the compassion which is tragedy's authentic expression.

Reflection can still leave one with illusion, or drive one from aesthetics to ethics, from the masks of the self's shadow-play as in *Repetition* (Hong and Hong, 1983, p. 156), which have their place in a life, to feel oneself present as a character in a drama that the deity is writing, in which poet, prompter and actor are at one (Hong and Hong, 1987, vol. 2, p. 137). And some things, such as daily dying, or the patience that contends against time (pp. 135–6), cannot be portrayed in poetry or art – there is no form for them.

Finally, it is an image taken from the theatre that provides Kierkegaard with the form for the content of his own authorship.

In a theater, it happened that a fire started offstage. The clown came out to tell the audience. They thought it was a joke and applauded. He told them again, and they became still more hilarious. This is the way, I suppose, that the world will be destroyed – amid the universal hilarity of wits and wags who think it is all a joke. (Hong and Hong, 1987, vol. 1, p. 30).

He is to be ridiculed if there is only the endless

shadow-play to see, rather than the need to give birth to the self (Hong and Hong, 1987, vol. 2, p. 206). 'Therefore it is quite all right that in modern drama the bad is always represented by the most brilliantly gifted characters, whereas the good, the upright, is represented by the grocer's apprentice. The spectators find this entirely appropriate and learn from the play what they already knew, that it is far beneath their dignity to be classed with a grocer's apprentice' (Hong and Hong, 1987, vol. 2, p. 228).

See also IRONY; MORALITY AND ART.

WRITINGS

Gjentagelsen by Constantin Constantius [one of Kierkegaard's pseudonyms] (Copenhagen: 1843); trans. and ed. H.V. Hong and E.H. Hong, *Fear and Trembling, Repetition* (Princeton, NJ; Princeton University Press, 1983).
Enten/Eller, ed. Victor Eremita [one of Kierkegaard's pseudonyms] (Copenhagen: 1843); trans. and ed. H.V. Hong and E.H. Hong, *Either/Or*, 2 vols (Princeton, NJ: Princeton University Press, 1987).

BIBLIOGRAPHY

Pattison, G.: *Kierkegaard: The Aesthetic and the Religious* (London: Macmillan, 1991).
Walsh, S.I.: 'The subjective thinker as an artist', *History of European Ideas*, 1 (1990), 19–29.

ANN LOADES

Kristeva, Julia (1941–) Naturalized French theorist of language, literature, and psychoanalysis; an important influence on several late twentieth-century intellectual developments, including Feminist Criticism.

Born in Bulgaria, Kristeva studied linguistics and literature at the University of Sofia, while working as a journalist on a newspaper for communist youth. She went to Paris in 1966 on a French government doctoral research fellowship, and worked as research assistant at Claude Lévi-Strauss's Laboratory of Social Anthropology. Lucien Goldmann directed her doctoral thesis, a study of the emergence of the novel in the late mediaeval period as exemplified by the writings of Antoine de la Sale. Published in 1970 as *Le Texte du roman* [The text of the novel], this study draws upon the 'postformalism' of Mikhail Bakhtin, in particular his account of the heterogeneity of the textual and cultural materials making up the novel form, and analyses the shift in the concept of the 'sign', from meaning as closure to open-ended processes of signification.

In *Séméiotiké: Recherches pour une sémanalyse* (1969), the neologism 'semanalysis', stemming from the conjunction of semiotics and psychoanalysis, is defined as a 'critique of meaning, of its elements and laws', 'conceiv[ing] of meaning not as a sign-system but as a *signifying process*'. Rejecting the static model of language upheld in much semiotic and linguistic theory, Kristeva focuses attention on the conditions of meaning-production. Psychoanalytic theories of language and signification, particularly Jacques Lacan's reformulations of Freudian thought, become increasingly central to this project. Kristeva's intention is to bring issues of subjectivity and the role of the 'speaking subject' into play; questions largely excluded from semiotic and linguistic theory – social and psychic processes, the pre- or extra-linguistic, and the dynamic and 'wild' language of literary texts – thus become central.

These concerns are developed in one of her most important works, originally her doctoral thesis, published as *Revolution in Poetic Language* (1974). This ambitious study is both an account of avant-garde literary and linguistic practices at the end of the nineteenth century, making particular reference to works by Lautréamont and Mallarmé, and an attempt to produce a comprehensive theory of poetic language, drawing upon a variety of theoretical traditions and modes of analysis – philosophical, linguistic and psychoanalytic. Of its many theoretical strands, two of the most important are Kristeva's use of psychoanalysis and of Hegelian dialectics, particularly her reformulation of Hegelian negativity as motion and process, expulsion or 'rejection' (*rejet*). In articulating an account of the 'semiotic' and the 'symbolic' as the two modalities of all processes of signification, she draws upon Freud's distinction between pre-oedipal and oedipal sexual drives and Lacan's concepts of 'imaginary' and 'symbolic'. Following Plato's *Timaeus* she defines the place of the pre-symbolic or 'semiotic' (where the symbolic is understood as the condition of ordered, 'rational' signification) as the space of the maternal *chora*, (enclosed space, womb, receptacle), which in turn corresponds to the 'poetic' function of language. 'The *chora*,' Kristeva writes, 'as rupture and articulations (rhythm), precedes evidence, verisimilitude, spatiality and temporality.' It is also seen as the space of instinctual drives and of a 'bodily' relationship to the rhythmic–intonational aspects of language.

The 'semiotic', then, is represented as the transgressive, 'feminine' materiality of signification, which becomes evident in 'madness, holiness and poetry' and surfaces in literary texts, particularly those of the avant-garde, as musicality and linguistic play. It should be noted, however, that Kristeva's concept of the relationship between 'semiotic' and 'symbolic' is a dialectical one; the order of the 'symbolic' and the 'thetic' allows the 'semiotic' entrance into social and psychic relations, allowing negativity a mode of articulation. The 'semiotic' has to work through the very order of logical and syntactic functioning that it subverts, in order to enter into representation at all; the 'symbolic', which is the realm of the speaking subject, makes positionality (psychic, social and political) possible.

Kristeva's relationship to the contemporary avant-garde should be understood in the context of her involvement with the journal *Tel Quel*, her primary intellectual forum from the late 1960s until 1983, when it was reformulated under the title *L'Infini*. Philippe Sollers, avant-garde novelist and essayist, has edited it in both its manifestations, and Kristeva has been closely involved with his work. In her collection of essays, *Polylogue*, the title essay is a review of Sollers' novel *H*, which she describes as 'external polylogue' rather than 'internal monologue'; the collection also contains essays on Antonin Artaud

and Georges Bataille. The dominant theme of these essays is, in accord with the *Tel Quel* project, the articulation of the links between language, subjectivity and transgression in the avant-garde text. The influence of Roland Barthes' work was of paramount importance to this project, not least in the correspondences he claimed between the challenge to literary conventions and subversion at a social and political level.

The more overtly 'political' involvements of the *Tel Quel* group were at their height at the beginning of the 1970s, when it broke off relations with the French Communist Party and declared its support for the Chinese Cultural Revolution. Kristeva's account of her visit to China was published as *About Chinese Women* (1974). The *Tel Quel* group's Maoist affiliations did not survive long after this visit, and Kristeva has ascribed her own more pronounced withdrawal from direct political involvement to her disillusionment with aspects of Chinese society. Similarly, despite the centrality of her work to feminist theory, she has expressed ambivalence towards feminism as a social and political movement, though repeatedly emphasizing the importance of addressing women's psychic and social condition.

The consolidation of Kristeva's theoretical concerns with 'the individual life' may be linked to her increased professional and intellectual engagement with psychoanalysis. During the mid-1970s she trained as an analyst, starting her own psychoanalytic practice in 1979. Since 1980, her theoretical work has demonstrated a very close engagement with psychoanalytic theory, and art and literature are used extensively to explore psychoanalytic concepts and psychic processes. In *Powers of Horror* (1980), she analyses the concept of 'abjection' and 'horror', incorporating in these terms her earlier focus on 'negativity' and 'rejet'. 'Abjection' is described as 'what disturbs identity, system, order'; the 'abject' can be exemplified by those 'unclean' and 'improper' aspects of corporeality and instinctual life which are disavowed in order for the subject to enter into the 'symbolic order'. Drawing on Freud's cultural criticism, particularly *Totem and*

Taboo and *Civilization and its Discontents*, and Mary Douglas's *Purity and Danger*, Kristeva's 'anthropological' focus is also on the ways in which societies and religions have erected taboos against the 'abjects' (food, waste and the bodily signs of sexual difference). What is expelled, however, is never wholly destroyed, but remains as an ambiguous, liminal area of instability threatening the individual's assumption of unity and cohesion.

In the last part of *Powers of Horror*, Kristeva turns to the work of Céline, whose writing 'speaks' horror and whose political vision, including a violent anti-semitism, is to be understood as a symptom, which both enacts and exposes the horror and fascination of psychic violence. More generally, in her later work she emphasizes that 'the problem of art in the twentieth century is a continual confrontation with psychosis . . . a crisis of subjectivity which is the basis for all creation.' In *Black Sun: Depression and Melancholy* (1987), she discusses the work of Holbein, Dostoevsky, Nerval and Duras, writers and artists for whom 'the experience of art was lived as a salvation' or, as in Nerval's case, where art failed to save.

Other works include *Tales of Love* (1983), in which images of Western love are analysed in myth and religion and through figures such as Don Juan and Romeo and Juliet, which 'have woven our amorous imaginary'. The concept of maternal love also plays a crucial role in this text, as elsewhere in Kristeva's work. Very recently she has turned to the themes of foreignness, exile and nationalism in her *Étrangers à nous-mêmes* [*Strangers to ourselves*] (1988) and *Lettre ouverte à Harlem Désir* [An open letter to Harlem Désir] (1990). Her first novel, *Les Samouraïs* [*The samurai*] (1990), a *roman-à-clef* about Parisian intellectuals, marks a turn in her intellectual career towards fiction writing.

See also BARTHES; FEMINIST CRITICISM; PSYCHOANALYSIS AND ART.

WRITINGS

Séméiotiké: Recherches pour une sémanalyse, (Paris: Éditions du Seuil, 1969).

Le Texte du roman. Approche sémiologique d'une structure discursive transformationnelle (The Hague: Mouton, 1970).

Pouvoirs de l'horreur. Essai sur l'abjection (Paris: 1980); trans. L. Roudiez, *Powers of Horror* (New York: Columbia University Press, 1982).

La Révolution du langage poétique (Paris: Éditions du Seuil, 1974); pt 1 trans. M. Waller, *Revolution in Poetic Language* (New York: Columbia University Press, 1984).

Polylogue (Paris: Éditions du Seuil, 1977); part trans. Thomas Gora, A. Jardine and L. Roudiez, *Desire in Language* (Oxford: Basil Blackwell, 1984).

Histoires d'amour (Paris: 1983); trans. L. Roudiez, *Tales of Love* (New York: Columbia University Press, 1987).

Étrangers à nous-mêmes (Paris: Fayard, 1988); trans. L. Roudiez, *Strangers to Ourselves* (Brighton: Harvester Press, 1991).

Soleil noir, dépression et mélancolie (Paris: 1987); trans., *Black Sun* (New York: Columbia University Press, 1989).

Lettre ouverte à Harlem Désir (Paris, Rivages, 1990).

Les Samouraïs (Paris: Fayard, 1990).

BIBLIOGRAPHY

Fletcher, John and Benjamin, Andrew, eds: *Abjection, Melancholia and Love*, (London: Routledge & Kegan Paul, 1990).

Kolocotroni, Vassiliki: interview with Julia Kristeva, *Textual Practice*, 5: 2 (Summer 1991), 157–70.

Lechte, John: *Julia Kristeva* (London: Routledge & Kegan Paul, 1990).

Moi, Toril, ed.: *The Kristeva Reader* (Oxford: Basil Blackwell, 1986).

LAURA MARCUS

L

Langer, Susanne (1895–1985) American philosopher, best known for her contributions to philosophical anthropology and aesthetics. One of the most important aestheticians of the century, her views on art are integrated with a general philosophical position of some intricacy. Her aesthetic theory had its genesis in her book on the nature of symbolism and meaning, *Philosophy in a New Key* (1942), became the focus in its sequel, *Feeling and Form* (1953), her best known work, and was expanded and deepened in her three-volume masterpiece, *Mind: An Essay on Human Feeling* (1967, 1972, 1982). In all these works, Langer lucidly wove together an astounding variety of influences with a sensitive understanding of art. The writings of A.N. Whitehead, Ernst Cassirer, Wittgenstein, C.S. Peirce and Rudolf Carnap feature strongly in her work, not to mention those of biologists, psychologists, anthropologists and numerous writers on art. Only the portion of her work directly concerned with the aesthetic is considered here.

Langer began by accepting the great division made by positivism between cognitive and emotive expression, but it was her intention to rescue the emotive from being dismissed as meaningless by describing how it exhibits an alternative *form* of meaning best illustrated by art. Human beings are essentially *symbolic* animals; this capacity cannot be regarded as a mere extension of animal psychology. Her last work undertook to describe the 'great shift' from the rhythmic patterns of organisms, to symbolic meaning, to mind. By then, in her view, feeling mediated between the biological and the symbolic, lying as it does at the very basis of rationality (Langer, 1967, p. 23).

Symbolism is the capacity to think *about*

something without implying that object's existence, differing in this way from the denotative function of a sign (or 'signal'). Experience exhibits certain *forms* which provide the basis of abstractive rationality. With the early Wittgenstein, Langer agrees that our discursive thought, expressed in language, offers logical pictures of states of affairs in the world. Because of its complex syntactic nature and immense vocabulary, language must build up its picture from discrete units governed by logical laws. It cannot even begin to present the world *simul totum*. Langer believes that here a crucial error has been made: since discursive language has been the medium of philosophical reflection, philosophy has been willing to identify meaning with discursivity. Hence the question 'What is the meaning of art?' became an undesirable either/or: either a work had *no* meaning or its meaning could be *translated* into literal, propositional language. Her challenge is to offer a *non-discursive* mode of symbolism, a 'presentational' mode, which begins with the 'grammar of the eye and ear' in sensation, and then becomes highly articulated in art (Langer, 1957a, p. 89).

Through symbolism we gradually organize our world of meaning. The symbol, through its capacity for generality, liberates rationality from immediate stimuli and finite practical concerns. Even in perceiving ordinary objects, we are transforming a complex manifold of sensation into a 'virtual world' of general symbols (Langer, 1957a, p. 144). Beginning with dreams, our awareness of meaning grows through the use of metaphoric thinking. In tribal culture, the awareness of presentational meaning lies at the root of totemism. Myth constitutes a further development towards a symbolic understanding of the great forces governing human existence. But here, with Cassirer, Langer believes that a fork in the road is taken: discursive understanding must drop the metaphoric for the literal mode, aiming at metaphysical rigour and scientific description; the myth, further developed, becomes the epic – that is, art. Science, and art are the two ultimate refinements of meaning, the one consuming our practical concern with nature, the other our power of 'envisagement'.

In *Philosophy in a New Key*, Langer discusses music as the paradigm instance of presentational meaning because it best exhibits the distinctive concern with 'pure form' (Langer, 1957a, p. 208). All works of art aspire towards 'significant form', she claims, adopting Clive Bell's term while rejecting his psychologistic view that it expresses a distinct 'aesthetic' emotion. Music is not a psychological expression of emotions, but a logical, symbolic expression *about* feelings. Thus it reflects the composer's knowledge of human feeling, not his emotional constitution at the time. Music seems to resemble language; we speak of its syntax and vocabulary. But it has no literal meaning: it is an 'unconsummated symbol' expressing 'vital import'. It cannot achieve the denotational conditions of conventional linguistic reference. Music expresses the 'forms of human feeling' and is 'our myth of the inner life' (Langer, 1957a, pp. 235, 245; see also Langer, 1953, p. 27).

While the plastic arts, like painting, easily become 'model-bound' and so become confused with the goal of literal representation, music demonstrates that art is truly about significant form. The plastic arts can express significant form *through* depicting objects; music does not. It is the work as a *whole* which bears artistic or 'vital import', conveying 'knowledge by acquaintance' rather than indirect 'knowledge about'. The arts in the past have drawn on myth and religion, but no longer need to do so. Art, thus liberated, can freely serve human expressivity.

Feeling and Form continues these general themes, applying them to the entire range of the arts. One of the joys and strengths of this work lies in Langer's concrete applications. Her grander claim is to organize the whole of aesthetics by focusing on the question of creation. 'Once you answer the question "What does art create?", all the further questions of why and how, of personality, of talent and genius, etc., seem to emerge in a new light from this central thesis' (Langer, 1953, p. 10). The perennial paradoxes which have stymied aesthetics, most notably that between 'feeling and form' (feeling leading to subjectivist theories, form to objectivist ones), will disappear. Feeling and form are not opposed. Feelings may be objectively symbolized in certain forms, which then are capable of being abstracted in experience. Hence 'art works *contain* feelings, but do not feel them' (Langer, 1953, p. 22). Since 'significant form' is the essence of art, art is defined as 'the creation of forms symbolic of human feeling' (1953, p. 40). 'Creation' must refer, then, to the creation of such symbols, not to the ordinary production of artefacts. One can produce painted canvases, but one may or may not create significant forms in the process.

Langer's discussion of 'semblance' contains the cardinal points of her theory. Artworks are distinguished from ordinary objects above all by their sheer 'otherness', their 'unreality', giving a sense of illusion. The art image is not copied, but created, making a 'virtual object'. Unlike ordinary objects, the virtual object does not exist for all the senses, but focuses instead on one or two. Adopting Jung's term, Langer calls this character 'semblance', though it also has strong affinities to what Schiller called *Schein*. The semblance or *Schein* of a work disengages us entirely from the practical demands of belief, making it a 'strange guest' among 'the highly substantial realities of the natural world'. Like discursive meaning, the presentational symbol reveals 'a new dimension apart from the familiar world', the dimension of articulate but non-discursive feeling (Langer, 1953, p. 50). Works of art are not representations of objects in the natural world so much as explorations in this new dimension of meaning. And yet Langer insists that what art expresses are the forms *of life*, of vital feeling, 'forms of growth and of attenuation, flowing and stowing, conflict and resolution', and so on – 'the elusive yet familiar patterns of sentience', as she calls it elsewhere (Langer, 1953, pp. 27, 52). Art is 'essentially organic', creating the '*appearance* of life' (1953, p. 373). Her great *Essay* itself addresses the question, 'Why must artistic form, to be expressive of feeling, always be so-called "living form"?' (Langer, 1967, p. xv).

The artist abstracts the significant form from experience and uses it to create an object which directly expresses it. Thus there can be no real distinction between the form and its 'content'. The 'content' of a work is its import, and this accounts for its 'transparency', its alien presence which reveals immediately a dimension of meaning, the *idea* of feeling. In so far as a work of art confuses this significant form with other aims, such as utilitarian or representational ones, or simply fails to create a truly expressive form, it ceases to be art. There are no high or low arts, simply good and bad artworks. A great work, presumably, is one which powerfully expresses a highly significant feeling. This symbol of feeling is intuitively grasped. Even though a work may take time to unfold, from the beginning there is an 'intuition of the whole presented feeling' (Langer, 1953, p. 379).

All of these themes are developed in her last work, a work at once in the tradition of a philosophy of symbolic form, like Cassirer's, and a process metaphysics which, like that of her 'great mentor' Whitehead, makes feeling and creativity the basis of nature. It would be easy to question some of the sharp distinctions she sets forth (especially the fundamental one of presentational versus discursive meaning); her eclecticism; the repetition of such central terms as 'significant form' which remain none the less vague; the fact that, for all her stress on the 'logical' nature of presentational symbols, they are objects of intuition pure and simple; and her claim that language has an origin in an expressive rather than a communicative need. But this would be to miss the greatness of her vision. In a century dominated by rigid epistemologies, Langer saw the problem of mind also in terms of symbol, ritual, myth, expression and feeling, as well as factual description and logical justification. Against crude mechanistic theories of mind, meaning, and nature, she argued for a view of nature in which form and creativity are at work in the very heart of things.

See also EDUCATION, AESTHETIC; EMOTION; INEFFABILITY; SYMBOL.

WRITINGS

Feeling and Form (New York: Scribner, 1953).
Philosophy in a New Key (Cambridge, Mass.: 1942); 3rd edn (Cambridge, Mass.: Harvard University Press, 1957a).
Problems of Art (New York: Scribner, 1957b).
Mind: An Essay on Human Feeling, 3 vols (Baltimore, Md.: Johns Hopkins University Press, 1967, 1972, 1982).

BIBLIOGRAPHY

Bertocci, Peter: 'Susanne K. Langer's theory of feeling and mind', *Review of Metaphysics*, 23 (1970), 527–51.
Danto, Arthur: 'Mind as feeling, form as presence', *Journal of Philosophy*, 11 (1984), 641–6.

THOMAS M. ALEXANDER

language and pictorial art The nature of pictorial art has been a matter of philosophical debate at least since the iconoclastic controversy in the eighth and ninth centuries. In the twentieth century, this debate has focused on the analogies and disanalogies between the manufacture and enjoyment of pictures and the use of language. Here I examine the debate, and argue that the analogy between pictorial art and language has not provided philosophy with a cogent answer to the question which, by common consent, lies at the heart of the matter.

(1)

The question is this: How does a picture convey to the eye the appearance of a part of the visible world? How can it be possible to gaze at a canvas smeared with pigment and see a fairground thronging with men and women or a glass bowl laden with fruit?

The architect and humanist Leon Battista Alberti answered that the things depicted by a painter and their pictorial representations subtend a similar set of angles to the eye. Two hundred years later Descartes denied this, and maintained instead that a painting is apt to cause an affection of the soul similar to that which would be caused by seeing what it depicts. But if we study the various answers that have been proposed since the Renaissance, we can discern a clear pattern in their variation. They have, in fact, marched in step with the theory of vision. Alberti's answer is purely geometrical because the visual theory with which he was familiar was the medieval theory of perspective, and Descartes' remarks on the problem appear in, and are entirely subservient to, his *Dioptric*.

In short, a consensus underlies these different theories: depiction depends upon some sort of optical correspondence between a picture and its subject. And since the degree of this correspondence plainly varies, it has been generally supposed that the use of perspective, shading and other so-called 'naturalistic' techniques will tend to ensure an especially perfect correspondence between a painting and its subject.

This orthodoxy was not challenged by those American philosophers – Charles Morris, Susanne Langer, John Hospers and others – who aimed to bring aesthetics under the aegis of the semiotic, but it was couched in a new terminology. The semiotic theorists' principal claim was that a picture is a pictorial representation, a sign or symbol of its subject; and with this claim there was associated a definite body of theory. A sign was regarded as a kind of surrogate, something that causes a response similar to that which would ordinarily be caused by its referent; and the various modes of signification were distinguished in terms of the various kinds of sign, the various ways in which they could be combined, and the various kinds of thing signified.

Accordingly, the distinctive feature of a pictorial symbol was located in the first of these differentia: 'If a work of art [that is, a picture] has a given thing as its subject-matter,' Hospers wrote, 'it is said to imitate or represent that thing, and hence to symbolize it . . . and the symbolism is of the natural type because there is a close natural relationship, namely likeness or resemblance, between symbol and thing symbolized' (Hospers, 1946, p. 401). Drawing on C.S. Peirce's elaborate taxonomy of the various species of signification, a picture was described as an *iconic* sign, one which signifies by virtue of the natural relation of resemblance. It is a matter of convention that the words 'cat' and 'dog' denote the animals they do. But the significance of many other signs is more or less independent of custom and agreement. Shadows and footprints, paintings and photographs were thought to be such iconic signs, and an iconic sign was said to denote 'any object which has the properties (in practice, a selection from the properties) which it itself has' (Morris, 1939–40, p. 136).

The doctrine of the iconic sign is deeply flawed. Its principal defect, which it shares with any theory that seeks to explain depiction in terms of resemblance, is that it misidentifies the things which can normally be said to resemble each other.

Suppose that I am struck by a resemblance between Renoir's *Girl with a Falcon* and the postman's daughter. The resemblance which strikes me is not between the postman's daughter and a canvas smeared with pigment, but between the postman's daughter and the girl in the picture. This is obvious as soon as I say how they resemble each other. For I may have been struck by the fact that the postman's daughter and Renoir's girl have the same red hair and small nostrils and the same pretty smile; but it would be sheer nonsense to say that the canvas or a part of it has, or even looks as if it has, small nostrils and a pretty smile. Furthermore, this evident absurdity cannot be avoided by saying that, when I look at the canvas, just as when I look at the postman's daughter, I see a reddish patch at the top and a darker curve a little below, for that is certainly not what I normally see in either case. And, as a matter of fact, the colour of pigment used to depict the girl's hair will probably be somewhat different from the colour of the postman's daughter's hair, and rather less uniform, if their hair is the same colour.

Just the same considerations apply in the case of a portrait. For example, Raphael painted a portrait of Tommaso Inghirami, which now hangs in the Isabella Stewart Gardner Museum. The canvas hanging in Boston does not resemble the Vatican's librarian, but the man in the picture does, or so we believe. It may be tempting to object that the man in the picture cannot be said to resemble Count Inghirami, since he *is* the count. But this objection betrays an important confusion. For the phrase 'the man in the picture' can be used in two different ways, corresponding to an object-accusative and an intentional accusative.

The distinction between an object-accusative and an intentional accusative is familiar from the case of verbs such as 'to believe' and 'to suspect' (see White, 1972). If we answer the question 'What does A believe?' by saying 'The story that B told' or 'The report in *The Times*', we are giving an object-accusative, signifying something which must exist for A to believe it. If on the other hand, we answer the question by saying, 'A believes that p', we are giving an intentional accusative. 'A suspects B' gives an object-accusative; 'A suspects foul play' gives an intentional accusative. (There does not need to have been foul play for A to suspect it.) The same distinction applies in the case of the verb 'to depict'. If we say 'Raphael's portrait depicts the Vatican's librarian' we are giving an object-accusative, and the verb 'depicts' expresses a genuine relation between two independently existing things; whereas if we say 'Raphael's portrait depicts a man with a pen in his hand' we are giving an intentional accusative.

Let us call the use of the phrase 'the man in the picture', which corresponds to the object-accusative, 'external'; and the use of the same phrase which corresponds to the intentional accusative, 'internal'. We can now say that, in the case of a portrait, it is not the canvas, but the man in the picture (internal use) that resembles the man in the picture (external use); or, purely for convenience, we can say that the *internal subject* of the picture resembles its *external subject*.

There are exceptional cases in which it is correct to say that the pattern of pigment on the surface of a canvas resembles what the painting depicts. For example, the parts of Gerard ter Borch's canvases which depict a lustrous satin dress or a shimmering satin bodice do in fact resemble satin, and in the right circumstances, might even be mistaken for satin. Moreover, it may be correct to say that in order to depict satin, one must be able to transform the appearance of a piece of canvas in this way. Be that as it may, the fatal error in any theory which seems to explain depiction in terms of resemblance is the confusion of the marks on the painted surface with the *internal subject* of the picture.

This confusion has a very distinguished history. When Plato complained that perspective and shading are deceitful techniques, he made just the same mistake. For example, if a painting depicts, in perspective, a receding colonnade, then the patches of pigment which serve to depict the nearest and the furthest columns manifestly differ in height but not in distance from the spectator, whereas the columns in the picture manifestly differ in distance from the spectator, but not in height. However, because Plato failed to distinguish between the marks on the painted surface and what they depict, he thought that such a painting leads us to make a false judgement about the relative heights of two painted columns. And he regarded the use of a technique which misleads us in this way as deceitful – indeed, as 'nothing short of witchcraft' (Plato, *Republic*, 602 c–d).

(11)

The most influential philosopher to have rejected the traditional ideas about depiction is Nelson Goodman. His book *Languages of Art* is at once the most refined and the most heretical product of the semiotic tradition in aesthetics, and the theory of depiction adumbrated in its first and last chapters has proved to be the most influential part of the book. The point of departure for Goodman's theory is his rejection of the doctrine of the iconic sign. As we have seen, artists and philosophers used to agree that a painter, however much he simplifies, idealizes, schematizes or embellishes, must produce at least an approximate visual simulation of his subject; and this traditional assumption was incorporated into the doctrine of the iconic sign. Goodman argues that it is thoroughly confused.

The appearance of an object is the sum of its visible properties, and so a painting will reproduce the appearance of an object if the predicates which denote these properties apply to the picture. According to Goodman, what we choose to call 'the appearance of an object' and what we are content to acknowledge as a significant measure of visible similarity will therefore depend upon what predicates we are accustomed to employ when describing our visible environment: and the visible properties that we shall require a painting to possess in order to qualify as reproducing the appearance of an object will vary correspondingly. Leonardo declared that 'painting is the most to be praised which agrees most exactly with the thing imitated'; but any measure of agreement will bear the stamp of our habitual methods of representation, pictorial and linguistic, or else of some equally conventional alternative. We cannot admire the sheer verisimilitude of Houdon's *Voltaire* or Van Eyck's self-portrait, but only their verisimilitude-in-a-traditional-European-style-of-representation (Goodman, 1981, p. 37).

Goodman's argument is intended to discredit the idea that pictorial verisimilitude can be explained in terms of the reproduction of the visible properties of depicted things, or the repetition of visual experience. Instead, *Languages of Art* defends an elaborate analogy between the manufacture and enjoyment of pictures and the use of language. This analogy has existed in one form or another since Plato. It was certainly implicit in the doctrine of the iconic sign. However, nobody before Goodman supposed that the analogy is

sufficiently close to disconnect depiction and resemblance.

Goodman begins with the case of a portrait. In this case, he argues, the relation between the picture and the man, like the relation between a name and its bearer, is a particular sort of denotation. The portrait of Tommaso Inghirami denotes Tommaso Inghirami, and a view of Westminster Abbey denotes the abbey. However, a painting of a satyr, although it may be said, with perfect propriety, to depict or represent a satyr, denotes nothing at all, for there exist no satyrs to be denoted. In this sort of case, the verb 'depict' does not signify a relation between two independently existing things, it is part of a complex one-place predicate. A painting of a satyr is not something, a painting, which stands in a certain relation, depiction, to another thing, a satyr. Rather, it is a certain kind of painting – as it were, a satyr-painting.

If the portrait of Tommaso Inghirami, like his name, denotes him, whereas a painting of a satyr, like the word 'satyr', denotes nothing, what is it that makes the two paintings, each of them an intricate disposition of pigments upon a canvas, examples of pictorial representation, whilst the two strings of letters 'T–O–M–M–A–S–O – I–N–G–H–I–R–A–M–I' and 'S–A–T–Y–R', are linguistic symbols? Not, as Hospers and the other semioticians supposed, a 'close natural relationship, namely likeness or resemblance', or, for that matter, any other sort of relationship between the pictures and what they depict: 'Descriptions are distinguished from depictions not through being more arbitrary but through belonging to articulate rather than to dense schemes; and words are [no] more conventional than pictures . . . if conventionality is construed in terms of . . . artificiality' (Goodman, 1981, pp. 230–1).

This is an extraordinary idea. It is not just the insipid thought that pictures are rather like descriptions. It is indisputable that in some cases pictures and linguistic signs are interchangeable. For example, the following figure is a perfectly intelligible inscription, in which a couple of pictures do duty, respectively, for a proper name and a sortal noun.

's father was a — maker'

Goodman's proposal is much more bizarre and radical than this. It is that the manufacture of pictures, like the use of language, is a symbolic activity governed by a complex array of semantic and syntactic rules. A scheme or system is representational only if it provides for infinitely many symbols, 'so ordered that between each two there is a third' (Goodman, 1981, p. 136), and if any modification of a symbol belonging to the scheme affects a change in what that symbol represents. Hence the distinctive character of a pictorial system of representation depends essentially upon the 'syntactic and semantic relationships among [its] symbols' (1981, pp. 227–8), and has nothing whatever to do with any putative resemblance between pictures and their subjects. If the English language were modified in such a way that every difference in intonation, volume and pitch corresponded to a difference in meaning, it would become a representational language; or rather, it would cease to be a language and become instead a means of making audible representations, distinguishable from pictures only by the fact that they would be constructed out of sounds rather than colours. The rules that govern a system of *pictorial* representation correlate pictorial properties with denotata; and a characterization of the pictorial properties of a painting is one that says 'what colors the picture has at what places' (1981, p. 42).

Different pictorial styles are different schemes, and we are inclined to say that some styles are more naturalistic than others. But if Goodman's argument is sound, then it would certainly be absurd to suggest that a style is naturalistic according to the degree to which paintings in that style resemble what they depict. Instead, he proposes, it is the familiarity of the style in which it is painted, rather than an especially perfect optical correspondence between a painting and its subject, that leads us to regard it as more naturalistic than another: 'Realism is relative, determined by the system of representation standard for a given culture or person at a given time. Newer or older or alien systems are accounted artificial or unskilled' (Goodman, 1981, p. 37).

(III)

Goodman's theory has attracted a great deal of attention, partly because it is elegant and ingenious and partly because it represents such a radical rejection of the view widely, and with some injustice, associated with the Academic tradition and the great writers of the Renaissance from whom that tradition stemmed. They had held, or so it was thought, that painters, unlike poets, really do hold a mirror up to nature. To many, this view has seemed both theoretically naïve and ideologically retrogressive, and *Languages of Art* has prospered accordingly.

The Cambridge philosopher Frank Ramsey once recommended that where philosophical debate has polarized, and it seems as if we are forced to choose between two diametrically opposed alternatives, we should discover what they agree about and challenge that. The theory of depiction adumbrated in *Languages of Art* has two things in common with the doctrine of the iconic sign. First, they both focus attention on the dichotomy between nature and convention; and second, they both assume that the question which a philosophical theory of depiction needs to address is the question of how, faced with a pattern of colours or pigments, we are able to identify what I have called its *external* subject.

Goodman's reaction against the tradition and against the doctrine of the iconic sign did not extend to challenging the ancient and simplistic dichotomy between nature and convention. On the contrary, this dichotomy is taken for granted by the question which is the point of departure for Goodman's theory – namely, is the relation between a picture and what it depicts a natural relation, like the relation between a man and his sister, or a conventional relation, like the relation between a man and his wife?

This question has many defects. For present purposes, two are especially significant. First, it ignores the distinction between the *internal* subject of a picture and its *external* subject. Second, it fails to distinguish between two kinds of rule or convention which play very different roles in the manufacture of pictures: (1) iconographic conventions, such as the symbolic attributes of saints and the colour of the Virgin's dress, and (2) technical rules or procedures, such as the rules of perspective adumbrated in Alberti's treatise on painting or the rules which govern Sumi-e, the traditional Japanese art of ink-painting. In fact these defects are closely related, because the difference between iconographic conventions and technical rules can only be stated clearly by employing the distinction between the *internal* and the *external* subject of a picture. Iconographic conventions are rules of inference. If, and only if, we know the relevant iconographic convention, we can replace a description of the *internal* subject of a painting – say, 'man with a lion at his feet', or 'woman nursing an ageing prisoner' – with an identification of its *external* subject or with a statement of its allegorical significance – 'St Jerome' or 'Charity'.

Technical conventions are quite different. They are technical procedures rather than rules of inference, and they mediate between the surface of a painting and its *internal* subject. For example, Greek vase-painters used various technical conventions (or conventional techniques) to depict the ankle bone; and Sumi-e includes highly specific techniques for painting bamboo and blossom. These are techniques for the application of slip or ink, which ensure that a man or woman's foot, a stem or a branch, will look as it should. Unlike iconographic conventions, there is normally no need for the spectator to know anything at all about them: our ability to identify bamboo in an ink-painting need not depend in the least on our knowledge of the techniques which guided its manufacture.

It should therefore come as no surprise that Goodman does not offer an example of the sort of rule which his theory postulates, for this sort of rule is supposed to mediate between the surface of a painting and its denotatum or denotata – that is, its *external* subject. Remember: the rules that make up a pictorial system of representation are 'rules correlating symbols with denotata' (1981, p. 228): this is why Goodman says (1981, p. 5) that 'denotation is the core of representation.' Rules of this kind deal with patterns of pigment, as technical rules do; however, like iconographic conventions, they are rules which we are supposed to depend upon when we identify what a picture depicts, even if familiarity makes us prone to overlook the fact.

Only in extremely unusual cases are 'rules correlating symbols and denotata' involved in making pictures. One example might be this: in order to make a picture of Hitler, sketch a closely packed series of diagonal lines in the form of a trapezium above a closely packed series of vertical lines in the form of a square, thus:

But even in a case of this sort, we do not need to use the rule to identify the man portrayed, so long as we know what he looked like. One of the fundamental errors in Goodman's theory of depiction is the idea that the manufacture of pictures depends directly (in the case of pictures which have an *external* subject) or indirectly (in the case of pictures which do not) on rules of this kind. Another is the idea that we could not identify the subject of a picture (in either case) if we did not know these rules.

(Gombrich also confuses technical rules

and iconographic rules. 'Whatever can be coded in symbols,' he writes, 'can also be retrieved and recalled with relative ease. The tricks of how to draw this or that – a cat, for instance – . . . can really be described as such simple methods of coding' (Gombrich, 1982, p. 16). But this is confused. The pictorial codes which make it relatively easy to identify a saint or decipher an allegorical picture are iconographic conventions, whereas 'the tricks of how to draw this or that' are technical rules.)

The second feature which Goodman's theory has in common with the doctrine of the iconic sign is that both assume that the question which a philosophical theory of depiction needs to address is the question of how, faced with a pattern of colours or pigments, we are able to identify what I have called its *external* subject.

This question is highly misleading. To see why, consider the case where we are able to identify the *external* subject of a portrait because the portrait is a good likeness. In order to see the likeness, we need to know both what the *internal* subject of the picture looks like and what its *external* subject looks like. So identifying the man portrayed – that is, the man in the picture in the *external* sense of the phrase – presupposes that the appearance of the man in the picture, in the internal sense of the phrase, has already been determined. Individualized portraiture presupposes, and therefore cannot explain, the depiction of a particular physiognomy. The first question we must ask is therefore the question that has traditionally been addressed only second – namely, how are we able to identify the *internal* subject of a picture? (See Wolterstorff, 1980, pp. 262–85.) The answer to this question is simple. It is not: by recognizing resemblances between the pigments smeared on its surface and its actual or potential *external* subject. Nor is it: by interpreting the pattern of colours by reference to a set of conventional rules which correlate these patterns with denotata. The answer is: by looking.

It is true, of course, that one of the great pleasures to be gained from certain sorts of painting is derived from the study of the intricate and often baffling relationship between the surface and the subject of a picture. But we could not enjoy the subtle correspondences between surface and subject – between the visible record of an artist's technique, and the end towards which it was directed – unless we could already see what a picture depicts. It is also true that some pictures need to be disambiguated, and we disambiguate by considering the intentions of the artist and other factors. However, disambiguating means choosing between alternatives, and we *see* what these alternatives are. The key to the difficulties that face us when we consider the phenomenon of depiction from a philosophical point of view is the fact that we do not interpret or recognize or construe or infer or read a picture until we are already aware of what it depicts; and we see what a picture depicts. That is, we see the *internal* subject of a picture.

This proposition combines a logical truth and an empirical truth. The logical truth is this: we do not need to be capable of describing the non-pictorial properties of a painted surface – that is, the disposition of the various pigments adhering to it – in order to be capable of describing what the painting depicts. The empirical truth is this: we generally find it easier to describe what a painting depicts than to describe its non-pictorial properties, and we are often quite unable to describe its non-pictorial properties except in the crudest terms.

What obstacle has prevented philosophers from accepting the thesis that we see what a picture depicts, and from appreciating that the question of how we are able to identify the *external* subject of a picture cannot be answered first? The obstacle is an argument which runs as follows: when we see a picture – say, Dürer's engraving of St Jerome – what do we actually see? Well, what we actually see is what is actually there, before our eyes. And that is certainly not a gourd, a lion, a dog, a skull, and so on. What is actually there is ink on paper. So we cannot see, directly and immediately, what the picture depicts. Perhaps we construe the inky marks. Perhaps we realize what they resemble. But for sure we do not *merely* look and see.

This argument is invalid. It is true that what is actually before our eyes when we look at Durer's engraving is not a gourd, a lion, a dog or a skull. But it does not follow that we do not see the *internal* subject of a picture immediately and directly. For what is before our eyes is not *merely* inky marks on paper, either, but inky marks which depict a gourd, a lion, and so on. If we imagine that we are immediately and directly aware of an abstract pattern of inky marks which needs interpreting, we are simply applying the so called myth of the given to pictures: it makes no more sense to deny that we see the *internal* subject of a picture immediately and directly that to deny that we see the visible objects in our environment immediately and directly, rather than mere patterns of light and colour.

(It should not come as a surprise to discover the myth of the given applied to pictures, for the mistaken notion that our perceptual awareness of visible things is mediated by mere patterns of light and colour was intimately associated with the idea that the concept of a picture has a key role to play in the theory of vision. These two expressions of what is fundamentally the same confusion are linked also in the minds of the theorists and historians of art who have subscribed to the myth of the given in respect of pictures. (See Wittkower, 1977, pp. 174–87, esp. 174; and Panofsky, 1970, pp. 51–81, esp. 51–3.))

In the twentieth century, the philosophical problems raised by the manufacture and enjoyment of pictures have been tackled – as so many other philosophical problems have – with tools drawn from the study of language. In general, philosophy has benefited immeasurably from our obsession with signs and symbols; and the study of art has also benefited, as the work of writers such as Panofsky and Wind shows. However, the philosophical study of depiction belongs more properly with the theory of perception than with semiotics. The analogy between pictorial art and language has enriched the study of iconography, but it has led philosophy astray.

See also DEPICTION; GOODMAN; PER-SPECTIVE; REPRESENTATION; RESEMBLANCE.

BIBLIOGRAPHY

Beardsley, M.C.: *Aesthetics: Problems in the Philosophy of Criticism*, 2nd edn (Indianapolis, IND: Hackett, 1981).

Gombrich, E.H.: *Art and Illusion*, 5th edn (Oxford: Phaidon, 1977).

Gombrich, E.H.: 'Visual discovery through art', *The Image and the Eye* (Oxford: Phaidon, 1982), 11–39.

Goodman, N.: *Languages of Art* (Brighton: Harvester, 1981).

Hospers, J.: *Meaning and Truth in the Arts* (Chapel Hill, NC: University of North Carolina Press, 1946).

Morris, C.: 'Aesthetics and the theory of signs', *Erkenntnis*, 8 (1939–40), 131–50.

Panofsky, E.: 'Iconography and iconology: an introduction to the study of Renaissance art', *Meaning in the Visual Arts* (Harmondsworth: Penguin Books, 1970), 51–81.

Plato: *Republic*, trans. H.D.P. Lee (Harmondsworth: Penguin Books, 1955).

White, A. R.: 'What we believe', *Studies in the Philosophy of Mind*, ed. N. Rescher, APQ monograph series no. 6 (Oxford: Basil Blackwell, 1972), 69–84.

Wittkower, R.: 'Interpretation of visual symbols', *Allegory and the Migration of Symbols* (London: Thames and Hudson, 1977), 173–87.

Wollheim, R.: *Art and its Objects*, 2nd edn (Cambridge: Cambridge University Press, 1980).

Wolterstorff, N.: *Works and Worlds of Art* (Oxford: Oxford University Press, 1980),

JOHN HYMAN

Lessing, Gotthold Ephraim (1729–81) German dramatist and literary critic; an important figure in the German Enlightenment. Lessing's *Laocoon, An Essay on the Limits of Painting and Poetry* (1766) is a major text in the continuing debate about the relationships between verbal and visual signs. The essay aims to explicate the laws governing the boundaries between the literary and the pictorial arts. Although the polemical intention is to establish a more aesthetically austere classical foundation for the arts in opposition to the refinements of French neo-classicism, the work has become one of the critical foundations of modern notions of the autonomy of art and the distinctiveness of genres.

The point of departure is a disagreement with Johann Winckelmann about the expressive qualities of a classical sculptural group depicting the death of Laocoon and his sons. Winckelmann claimed that the fact that the figure was not shown crying out in his agony was a sign of Greek stoicism and steadfastness of soul. Against this Lessing argues that the expressive restraint of the work is to do with the conditions and limits of the sculptural medium. Thus Lessing shifts critical attention away from what is represented in a work of art to the conditions of representation itself.

In arguing for the distinction between the figurative and the literary arts, Lessing challenges the *ut pictura poesis* doctrine in which painting and poetry are assimilated together as sister arts. Modern critics, says Lessing, in their rage for allegory in painting and description in poetry, draw the crudest conclusions from the correspondence between painting and poetry. The truth in the doctrine, he agrees, is that they are both mimetic arts. But painting and poetry are distinct, both in their subject and in the manner of their imitation.

Lessing's initial argument is dependent on explicit classical assumptions about the nature of painting. (He groups painting and sculpture together as plastic arts, with no regard for differences in spatial ontology.) The proper goal of painting, he says, is the depiction of physical beauty. If the artist had shown Laocoon crying out, as Virgil had done in his poem, then the figure would have been ugly and deformed. Thus, unlike modern artists, who debase art in order to show their skill in depicting nature, says Lessing, the artist of the Laocoon group is an example of the true artist who aims at the perfection of nature. In this argument, the equivocation between the qualitative and normative nature of the laws distinguishing the literary and the figurative arts, which

pervades Lessing's essay, already begins to be apparent.

His main arguments distinguishing the arts are based on his claim that painting is essentially an art of space and poetry an art of time. Painting is an art of the contiguous arrangements of bodies in a unified and coherent space, the perception of which is instantaneous, whereas poetry is about the narration of actions, which both in themselves and in their narration involve the succession of events in time. Several features characterizing the two art forms follow from this.

In that the painter can depict only one arrested moment, he must choose the most pregnant, from which what precedes and follows will be most easily apprehended, and around which the viewer's imagination will be most fully engaged. Poetry is not limited in this way. If a character submits to some extreme of feeling, the event is prepared for in what precedes it and is supplemented by what follows. Furthermore, a painter is restricted by the fact that all is made visible in a coherently staged space. Therefore he cannot depict such things as the superior status of the gods or their ability to make themselves invisible without resorting to ridiculous means, such as enlarging the figures or painting fogs. And yet further, painting, in its employment of 'natural' signs, is limited to the depiction of the particular. So in order to personify abstract or moral qualities, the visual artist has to resort to allegory and append various symbols. Thus, says Lessing, painting degenerates from its proper domain to an arbitrary form of writing, whereas poetry, through its use of arbitrary signs, is able easily to express abstract and general ideas and even indicate senses other than sight.

The distinction between time and space in the arts is not, as commentators point out, as clear and exclusive as Lessing claims. He does himself acknowledge that painting can indicate movement and that poetry can depict bodies, but only in a secondary sense, through suggestion. But this distinction between what is directly and indirectly represented is a distinction which cannot be made with the generality required by Lessing's arguments. His arguments clearly privilege poetry, which employs arbitrary signs, over painting, which is here presented as having some natural relationship with what it depicts. Lessing tells us that what pleases in art pleases not the eye, but the imagination through the eye. Thus, poetry, we infer from his essay, is a more comprehensive art than painting: it leaves wider scope for imagination, ideas and the delineation of moral character. W.J.T. Mitchell (1986, pp. 94–115) argues that although Lessing's application of the distinction between space and time is untenable, his insistence on it can be understood as a very particular articulation of the iconoclasm which pervades Western criticism and poetics, The *paragone*, or debate between poetry and painting, he says, is never just a contest between two kinds of signs, but a struggle between competing notions of body and soul, world and mind, and nature and culture.

Lessing's essay has been put to diverse uses in the furtherance of modernist criticism in painting and in literature. Both Clement Greenberg in his 1940 essay, *Toward a Newer Laocoon*, and W.K. Wimsatt in his *Laocoon: An Oracle Reconstructed* (1970), have put Lessing's name to the service of their views.

Lessing was also a distinguished dramatist and critic. While official critic to the National Theatre of Hamburg he wrote a series of papers, the *Hamburgische Dramaturgie* [The Hamburg dramaturgy], criticizing contemporary French theatre, promoting Shakespeare and the English tradition, and putting forward a radical interpretation of Aristotle. Although Lessing was a man of the German Enlightenment, his ideas on the role of feeling and imagination in the arts anticipate Romanticism.

See also GENRE; REPRESENTATION.

WRITINGS

Werke, 6 vols, ed. H.G. Gopfert (Munich: Carl Hanser Verlag, 1974).
Laocoon: oder über die Grenzen de Malerie und Poesie (Berlin: 1766); trans. E.A. McCormick,

Laocoon, An Essay on the Limits of Painting and Poetry (Baltimore, Md: Johns Hopkins University Press, 1984).

BIBLIOGRAPHY

Gombrich, E.H.: *Lessing. Proceedings of the British Academy*, 1957 (Oxford: Oxford University Press, 1958).
Mitchell, W.J.T.: *Iconology: Image, Text, Ideology* (Chicago and London: University of Chicago Press, 1986), §§ 1, 4.
Savile, A.: *Aesthetic Reconstructions* (Oxford: Basil Blackwell, 1987), chs 1–3.
Wellbery, D.: *Lessing's Laocoon: Semiotics and the Age of Reason* (Cambridge: Cambridge University Press, 1984).

CAROLYN WILDE

Lukács, Georg [György Szegedy von Lukács] (1885–1971) Hungarian Marxist philosopher and literary critic; a member of Nagy's short-lived Government in 1956. His work on aesthetics includes theory and its application in a wide range of literary studies. His career, and his study of aesthetics, falls into two main parts: his pre-Marxist period extending until the end of the First World War, and that following his conversion to Marxism. His interest in aesthetics is a main factor connecting his pre-Marxist and his Marxist writings. When he converted to Marxism, he had already written two books on aesthetics. Marx and Engels provided hints, but did not develop a systematic theory of the subject. Lukács's claim that his own contribution is the first attempt to work out a Marxist aesthetic theory in systematic form has gained acceptance.

His brilliant early Marxist work, *History and Class Consciousness* (1923), has profoundly influenced the Marxist discussion but has had little impact on non-Marxist philosophy. His contribution to aesthetic theory may ultimately turn out to be his most important contribution to philosophy in general. Although his views on aesthetics have attracted more attention than other aspects of his position, they have not been discussed as often as their intrinsic importance seems to

fixed, determinate core of descriptive properties of the work on which interpretations and evaluations had to be based, but during the 1980s he has abandoned this idea through increasing emphasis on the role of interpretation (Margolis, 1989b). For the distinction between what is a descriptive fact about an artwork and an interpretation of it is often itself a matter of interpretation.

(3) Margolis's theme of interpretation, long central to his aesthetics of relativism, latterly has been developed in wider ways which dovetail with his metaphysics of culture (including the ontology of artworks) and which reflect his shift from traditional analytic philosophy and aesthetics. This shift involves 'hermeneuticizing' naturalism, recognizing that interpretation not only functions to explain or elucidate the entities or texts that we encounter, but that it is already actively involved in constituting those entities as entities for interpretation. In other words, the cultural world – that is, not merely the artworld but the human *Lebenswelt* – is one whose objects are constructed through interpretative efforts, which means through language, and thus its objects are better understood as texts rather than as 'objects' in the traditional naturalistic sense. Margolis's most recent work focuses on the relations between constitutive and explanatory interpretation. He gives his own brief account of the development of his aesthetic theory in 'The eclipse and recovery of analytic aesthetics'.

See also HERMENEUTICS; ONTOLOGY OF ARTWORKS; RELATIVISM.

WRITINGS

The Language of Art and Art Criticism (Detroit: Wayne State University Press, 1965).
Persons and Minds (Dordrecht; Reidel, 1978).
Art and Philosophy (Atlantic Highlands, NJ: Humanities Press, 1980).

Culture and Cultural Entities (Dordrecht: Reidel, 1983).
Philosophy Looks at the Arts (New York: 1962); 3rd edn (Philadelphia: Temple University Press, 1988).
The Persistence of Reality, 3 vols (Oxford: Basil Blackwell, 1986, 1987, 1989a).
'Reinterpreting interpretation', *Journal of Aesthetics and Art Criticism*, 47 (1989b), 237–51.
'The eclipse and recovery of analytic aesthetics', *Analytic Aesthetics*, ed. Richard Shusterman (Oxford: Basil Blackwell, 1989c), pp. 161–89.
'Hermeneutics' and 'Interpretation' in the present *Companion*.

RICHARD SHUSTERMAN

Marxism and art Marxism has proved very fertile in the areas of aesthetic and literary criticism, though less so in the actual production of works of art in virtue of certain limitations associated with the rigid application of the Marxist point of view. The Marxist view of art follows from the Marxist theory of the relation of superstructure and base. In general terms, the basic principle is that art, like all higher activities, belongs to the cultural superstructure and is determined by socio-historical conditions, in particular economic ones. It is argued that a connection can always and must be traced between a work of art and its socio-historical matrix, since art is in some sense a reflection of social reality.

Marxist writers on aesthetics, particularly Georg Lukács, have gone to some lengths to construct a Marxist aesthetics on the basis of hints contained in the writings of Marx (1818–83) and Engels (1820–95). The list of Marxist and non-Marxist writers influenced by the Marxist approach to art in general is long and distinguished, including, apart from Lukács, Edmund Wilson, Peter Demetz, Theodor Adorno, Frederic Jameson, Ernst Bloch, Lucien Goldmann, Hans Mayer, Bertolt Brecht, Maurice Merleau-Ponty and Christopher Caudwell. There are a number of different, even incompatible, views of Marxist aesthetics, all of which claim to find support in the classical Marxist texts, above all in the writings of Marx and Engels.

The official Marxist insistence on social realism, prominent in Lukács's writings, has no clear anticipation in Marx's position but is based squarely on certain indications in the later Engels. The positions of Marx and Engels are demonstrably different (although this difference is not often observed by commentators). For political reasons, it was routinely denied by official Marxism for decades. The usual tendency to conflate the views of Marx and Engels is present as well in the Marxist approach to art. Although their writings have been seen as providing the basic principles of a Marxist theory of art and aesthetics, the precise relation of the resultant theory to the views of the founders is controversial.

Both Marx and Engels had early literary ambitions that largely evaporated when, still young and unknown left-wing radicals, they became acquainted in the early 1840s. Both retained a lifelong interest in literature, although their backgrounds and literary tastes differed widely. In the field of literature as elsewhere, Engels was largely self-taught. As a young man, he wrote poetry and literary criticism. He also translated Thomas Carlyle. Engels's literary taste was formed by nineteenth-century Romanticism, and included an appreciation of nationalist German poetry.

Marx had an excellent education in classical languages in the German high school (*Gymnasium*), that influenced his later appreciation of art and literature. His literary tastes remained within the framework of eighteenth-century classicism. He shared the widespread German intellectual graecophilia, illustrated by Winckelmann, Goethe and Hegel. His favourite authors were Aeschylus, Shakespeare and Goethe. When he began his university studies in Bonn, Marx spent most of his time studying Greek art and mythology as well as writing poetry. He also attempted a novel (uncompleted) and wrote the draft of a tragedy. After 1837 he did not return to the study of aesthetics, although there is an aesthetic cast to some of his writings, and on occasion he concerned himself with specific aesthetic questions.

An important example of the aesthetic bent to Marx's thought is his conception of human being. In the *Paris Manuscripts* (1844), he argues that alienation is the result of the institution of private property, characteristic of capitalism. As a result of the transition to communism, in which private property is abolished, Marx foresees the opportunity for what might be called the full development or fulfilment of human being. In the third of the *Paris Manuscripts*, full human development is described as the full development of the various senses. It is characterized from a slightly different perspective in *The German Ideology* (1845–6) – in a famous passage often criticized for its Romantic idealism – as the real possibility, following on from the abolition of the division of labour that prevails in capitalism, for each person to perform a full variety of tasks. The aesthetic view of human being as self-realizing in its free activity is indebted to Schiller's idea of the aesthetic as the basic harmonizing element of human life.

The fragmentary nature of Marx's comments on aesthetic themes does not represent a mature aesthetic theory. In his writings, the most considered passage on aesthetic themes occurs in the introduction to the *Grundrisse* [Rough draft] (1857). Here he advances the idea of the uneven development of material production in relation to artistic development. He refers to the well-known fact that artistic flowering is on occasion unrelated to the general development of society, to its material foundation. He maintains that Greek art specifically presupposes Greek mythology. The problem, as he remarks, is not that Greek artistic production is bound up with a certain social stage, but, rather, that Greek art has a universal value unrelated to its material conditions.

Here, Marx is more faithful to his aesthetic judgement than to his theoretical commitment. The result is a clear contradiction between his artistic sensitivity, honed by his classical education, and the theory he recommends. His evident appreciation of the permanent value of Greek art clearly contradicts his effort, in this and other texts, to comprehend all forms of culture as a function of the underlying economic organization of society.

The difference in literary background and taste is evident in the different reactions of Marx and Engels to specific literary works, particularly the Greek classics. Whereas Marx was deeply interested in the artistic merits of Greek literature, Engels more than once treated the world classics merely as illustrations of basic economic principles – for instance, he once remarked that Homer's *Iliad* represents the highest point of Greek barbarism.

None the less, Marx and Engels share a broad perspective. The common element that subtends their rather different approaches is their basic commitment to a contextualist approach to aesthetics. In aesthetics, contextualism of all kinds differs from isolationism in insisting on the importance of context to comprehend the work of art. Hegel is a contextualist in virtue of his insistence on the inseparability of the result from the process leading up to it. Typically, he is concerned with art less as a form of beauty than as offering a particular access to truth. In Marxism, art is typically held to offer insight into the nature of the society in which it emerges.

The central shared insight, that takes many different forms even in the works of Marx and Engels, is the approach to art and other forms of culture as a function of an underlying economic dimension of society. This is the famous relation of superstructure to base, or the effort to comprehend all spiritual or mental phenomena – everything that for Hegel would fall under the heading of spirit (*Geist*) – as directly or indirectly a function of material relations. In this approach, the meaning of the term 'material' is left undefined. Although Marxism is widely identified with historical materialism and even dialectical materialism, Marx's own position, unlike Marxism, is independent of any particular view of matter. Yet it is clear that Marx and Marxism share the idea that all cultural phenomena can be regarded against the background of the form of society in which they arise.

The central view that matter determines spirit, including art, underlies the specifically Marxist approach to aesthetics. It is possible to distinguish stages in the development of the superstructure–base relation. In *The German Ideology*, in opposition to the usual view of German philosophy, Marx and Engels assert:

> The production of ideas, of conceptions, of consciousness, is at first directly interwoven with the material activity and the material mental intercourse of men, the language of real life. Conceiving, thinking, the mental intercourse of men, appear at this stage as the direct efflux of their material behaviour. The same applies to mental production as expressed in the language of politics, laws, morality, religion, metaphysics, etc. of a people. (Marx and Engels, 1970, p. 47)

Another, different, form of this view is provided in the famous preface to *A Contribution to the Critique of Political Economy* (1859). In an influential passage, Marx writes:

> In the social production of their life, men enter into definite relations that are indispensable and independent of their will, relations of production which correspond to a definite stage of development of their material productive forces. The sum total of these relations of production constitutes the economic structure of society, the real foundation, on which rises a legal and political superstructure and to which correspond definite forms of social consciousness. The mode of production of material life conditions the social, political and intellectual life process in general. It is not the consciousness of men that determines their being, but, on the contrary, their social being that determines their consciousness. (Tucker, 1978, p. 4)

Instead of the more indeterminate relation, Marx here substitutes a causal determinism of the form of society on the cultural phenomena, including aesthetic phenomena, that occur within it.

With respect to the precise understanding of the relation of superstructure and base, the inconsistency of Marx's texts no doubt reflects his inability to resolve the problem in his own mind. It is notable that in a number of letters written after Marx's death, towards the end of his own life, Engels took a somewhat softer, interactionist line. Examples include the letter to J. Bloch (21 September 1890) in which Engels asserted that 'according to the materialist conception of history the determining element in history is *ultimately* the production and reproduction in real life', as well as the letter to H. Starkenburg (25 January 1894) in which, in a passage that weakens the concept of economic determination beyond all intelligibility, Engels writes: 'The further the particular sphere which we are investigating is removed from the economic sphere and approaches that of pure ideology, the more shall we find it exhibiting accidents in its development, the more will its curve run in a zig-zag (Marx and Engels, 1942, pp. 475–518).

The view of aesthetics, as well as all other cultural phenomena, as deriving from – in effect, as produced by – the economic structure of society is independent of the realist cast of most Marxist aesthetics. Marx's position is often regarded as realist, but there is absolutely nothing in his writings to indicate a view of aesthetic realism. On the other hand, this doctrine finds support in the later Engels, in the period following Marx's death. In letters to two aspiring novelists, Minna Kautsky and Margret Harkness, Engels made clear his rejection of so-called tendency literature that directly espoused the 'correct' political message in favour of a realist approach from which the 'correct' perspective could emerge. In his objection to Harkness, who regarded her novel as realist, Engels maintained that it was not realist enough. Realism, he argued, requires the faithful reproduction of detail as well as truthful representation of typical characters under typical circumstances.

Several examples will serve to illustrate the range of Marxist aesthetic theory. Before the Russian Revolution, Plekhanov, Lenin's teacher, attacked doctrines of art for art's sake and the separation of the artist, in either theory or practice, from society in *Art and Social Life* (1912). After the Revolution, there was a debate between Marxists and formalists. Trotsky argued in *Literature and Revolution* (1924) that art has its own peculiar laws and cannot be reduced to economic motifs. In line with his doctrine of 'partyness' ('*partiinost*'), Lenin maintained that the writer should put art at the service of the party. At the First All-Union Congress of Soviet Writers in 1934, the party established control over the topic in adopting the view expressed by Engels in his letter to Margret Harkness. According to this view, in order to forward the revolutionary developments himself, the artist is to reveal the moving social forces and portray his or her characters as expressions of these forces.

In the twentieth century Marxist aesthetics has developed in a series of different directions. One theme is the contemporary viability of the concept of realism that led to an important debate between Lukács, who represents the classical nineteenth-century literary perspective, and Brecht, who argues that this perspective is no longer appropriate for twentieth-century audiences. A second view is the theory of art as ideology, now prominently represented by Terry Eagleton (1990). A third topic is the link of aesthetics and politics that is developed, for instance, in Marcuse's (1978) view of aesthetics as pointing towards a better world. Fourth, there is the effort to relate forms of art to forms of society, as in Caudwell's (1937) discussion of poetry. A fifth theme is the notion of aesthetic value. Lukács (1964), for example, insists on realism, as exemplified by Balzac, since great literature is said to penetrate beneath the surface to reveal the social reality, with all its contradictions. Conversely, the same author dismisses the importance of such writers as Beckett and Kafka as mere reflections of a decadent capitalist society. Although Marxist aesthetics has traditionally been one of the most viable branches of Marxist theory, it remains to be seen if it will maintain its vigour after the political collapse of official Marxism in Eastern Europe.

See also ADORNO; AUTONOMY, AESTHETIC; LUKÁCS; REALISM.

BIBLIOGRAPHY

Cauldwell, Christopher: *Illusion and Reality: A Study of the Sources of Poetry* (London: Macmillan, 1937).

Eagleton, Terry: *The Ideology of the Aesthetic* (Oxford: Basil Blackwell, 1990).

Lukács, Georg: *Studies in European Realism* (New York: Grosset & Dunlap, 1964).

Marcuse, Herbert: *The Aesthetic Dimension: Towards a Critique of Marxist Aesthetics* (Boston, Mass.: Beacon Press, 1978).

Marx, Karl: *Grundrisse* (Moscow: 1939, 1941); trans. Martin Nicolaus (Harmondsworth: Penguin Books, 1973).

Marx, Karl and Engels, Friedrich: *Selected Correspondence* (New York: International Publishers, 1942).

Marx, Karl and Engels, Friedrich: *The German Ideology*, pt 1 (Zurich: 1884); (New York: International Publishers, 1970).

Tucker, Robert C., ed.: *The Marx–Engels Reader* (New York: Norton, 1978).

TOM ROCKMORE

Medieval and Renaissance aesthetics   There is no single correct answer to the question of when medieval philosophy began and ended, and the Renaissance period is similarly indeterminate in its chronological boundaries. For present purposes, however, it will be useful to regard the medieval era of art and thought as beginning between the births of Anselm of Canterbury (1033–1109) and of Abbot Suger of St-Denis (1081–1151), and to view the end of the Renaissance period as falling early within the lifetimes of Shakespeare (1564–1616) and Hobbes (1588–1679).

These vague boundaries contain over five hundred years of magnificent architecture, painting, sculpture, literature, philosophy and theology; and along with the centuries of classical antiquity they constitute the greatest eras of Western humanism. Thus no effort to understand the history of that tradition can succeed without taking something of the measure of the medieval and Renaissance contributions. In attempting to do so, one soon notices a striking structural feature of the cultural activities of these centuries. If one places on a timechart of the period 1100–1600 the names of the greatest figures in the various branches of art and learning, it becomes clear that there is a difference in the development of those branches. The era of greatest philosophical and theological achievement lies between 1200 and 1350, while the period of greatest artistic progress and accomplishment is 1400–1550.

AESTHETICS AND CHANGING
PHILOSOPHICAL CONTEXTS

In briefiest outline, one might characterize medieval aesthetics as an aspect of a tradition of theologically informed metaphysics and epistemology. In similarly broad terms one may represent Renaissance aesthetics, where it does not simply repeat medieval thinking (in largely secularized versions), as an emergent theory of the nature of artistic activities and of the value of their exercise.

The task of working these outlines into a comprehensive and comprehensible history faces two problems. First, the scale of the subject-matter; and second, the conceptual incongruity involved in using the contemporary idea of the *aesthetic* to capture the concerns of these earlier periods. As regards the problem of scale, the obvious difficulties are compounded by the fact that the histories of philosophy and of art have not yet reached a point of interconnection that allows the easy passage of information between them; in particular we remain, in general, fairly ignorant about the relationship between art and philosophy in the Renaissance period (though see Summers, 1987).

The problem of incongruity arises because thinking about art and beauty shifted importantly in the late modern period – that is, during the eighteenth century. Up to that point, the focus of philosophical attention was principally upon the unifying *objects* of certain kinds of experience – namely, *beauty*, and what it manifests or betokens, which is to say, reality. Thereafter, however, attention passed to the nature of the experience itself, and writers came to discuss what features and attitudes mark out an experience as *aesthetic*. This shift was itself a consequence of a movement in speculative inquiry away from the structure of the world, conceived of as something independent of the human mind, towards the structure of human psychology.

One reason for this movement was a change of view of how thought stands with respect to its objects. In antiquity, in the Middle Ages, and even in the time of Descartes (1596–1650) and Locke (1632–1704), philosophers were apt to regard *ideas*, the building blocks of thought, as being in one or another way identical with the structuring principles of reality itself. Whether these principles were taken to be received into the mind through experience (*abstractionism*) or to be placed there pre-natally (*innatism*), their presence in the intellect guaranteed that all thought is either directly about reality or traceable back to it. With Hume (1711–76) and Kant (1724–1804), however, a quite new picture was developed, within which concepts originate in the mind itself. Accordingly, the objects of thought and experience came to be regarded as in some sense mental constructions. Given this imagery, it becomes intelligible that Kantian and post-Kantian aesthetics should focus on the nature of aesthetic experience rather than on its objects. For if we think that what we encounter is what we have placed before ourselves, then speculative interest will attach to the modes of placement and the conditions of repossession. It is no accident, then, that Kant's three great *Critiques* replace the tradition of metaphysical descriptions of reality with interconnected logical analyses of the three different modes of thinking: the theoretic (*Pure Reason*), the practical (*Practical Reason*, and the imaginative (*Judgement*). Of course, it is possible to find anticipations of philosophical aesthetic-psychology in writings earlier than the eighteenth century; but this does not tell against the general point that in the medieval and Renaissance periods the primary focus of interest was on those aspects of an independent reality which induced experiences of beauty.

MEDIEVAL AESTHETICS

The royal portal at Chartres was built around 1150, and is one of the earliest surviving parts of the cathedral. On it are carved various figures. Some are recognizably religious: Christ, the virgin mother and various prophets and saints. Others are of regal bearing – Old Testament kings and queens, but not easily identifiable; and there are figures of yet other sorts. In the moulded framing above the left-hand door are representations of the signs of the zodiac, while the right-hand portal includes personifications of the seven liberal arts (the medieval *trivium* and *quadrivium*): Grammar, Dialectic and Rhetoric, Arithmetic, Music, Geometry and Astronomy. Along with these allegorical representations are depictions of ancient practitioners of each of the arts, and among them are set the figures of Euclid and Pythagoras, the former with geometer's compasses, the latter, oblivious to place and time, hunched over a musical instrument.

In the twelfth century, Chartres and the abbey of St-Denis were the sites of a number of architectural innovations associated with the emergence of what was first known as the 'French style' and later, in the Renaissance, as the 'Gothic'. These included the development of pointed arches, rose-windows, ribbed vaulting and representational (often narrative) decoration. At St-Denis, Abbot Suger had an inscription placed on the original brilliant gilded doors of the west front: 'Bright is the noble work; but being nobly bright, the work should brighten the minds so that they may travel, through the true lights, to the True Light where Christ is the true door ... The dull mind rises to truth, through that which is material and in seeing this light, is resurrected from its former submersion.'

This text reveals the influence of two ideas. According to the first, which has its philosophical origins in Plato and which was associated with Neoplatonism, sensible forms and images are symbols of an invisible transcendent reality and channels of communication with it. The Judaeo-Christian counterpart of this notion is found in scripture: 'From the greatness and beauty of created things comes a corresponding perception of their Creator' (Wisdom 13: 5); and 'Ever since the creation of the world his invisible nature ... has been clearly perceived in the things that have been made' (Romans I: 20). These scriptural passages also provide a source for the second idea, which is that, in creating forms embodying a transcendent meaning, the artist is showing one way in which he is himself an image of God (*imago dei*).

The design of St-Denis and the narrative scheme of the Chartres royal portal embody important aspects of the medieval world view at a critical stage of its development; thus they are apt and useful focal points for studying its ideas about art and beauty. Chartres was also the site of an influential cathedral school. This integrated the theology of the Church with the philosophy of antiquity and the earlier medieval period. The latter was Neoplatonic, but in the twelfth century Chartres was one of the significant points of reception of the more naturalistic philosophy of Aristotle. (The influence of Greek ideas is evident in the representations of Pythagoras as a practitioner of music.) In the scheme of liberal arts, music featured as a branch of mathematics – being concerned with the proportions and relations between fixed elements, the notes. The choice of Pythagoras derives from his association with the mathematical study of music, but more important is his authorship of the idea that all reality is ultimately mathematical in nature and that beauty is the manifestation of this perfect order. Here, then, the notion that the sensible symbolizes the transcendent becomes the thought that in making things according to due proportion, as in the work of the arts, one creates beauty and, *ipso facto*, establishes a link with the Divine.

THE RISE OF NATURALISM

These ways of thinking were pervasive throughout the medieval period, and find poetic expression in *The Divine Comedy* of Dante (1265–1321). By that point in the early fourteenth century, however, the reception of Aristotelian ideas encouraged by Albert the Great (1206–80) and their extensive development by Aquinas (1225–74), together with the elaboration of Gothic artistic innovations, had produced a more

naturalistic view. In Byzantine religious art the human figure was treated abstractly, without reference to its solidity or occupancy of a natural environment. Images of Christ and of the saints were mere icons located within the timeless, depthless plane of heaven, where natural light was replaced by celestial illumination – the point being to affirm the spiritual nature of reality. At Chartres, however, one can see stylized forms giving way to naturalistic representations. The volume of the human body, the disposition of its limbs, and even the facially expressed character of its emotions begin to be depicted; likewise, the shapes and details of flora and fauna.

So, by stages, Platonic dualism came to be replaced by a view of spirit as incarnate and of order as immanent within nature. This trend continued through the medieval period, and with William of Ockham (1290–1350) and the rise of nominalism (which, in insisting that every real thing is an individual entity, went even further from the Platonic belief in transcendent forms) led to a type of humanistic naturalism that ushered in the Renaissance. Indeed, so strong was the naturalizing trend, even within religious art, that it became common to affirm the humanity of Christ by emphasizing his sexual identity through depicting the naked infant or the loin-cloth-clad figure of the crucifixion.

RENAISSANCE AESTHETICS

The Vatican fresco now known as *The School of Athens* was painted by Raphael (1483–1520) in the years 1509–11, and is one of the very finest works of the High Renaissance. Like the Chartres portal, it includes a representation of Pythagoras, this time engaged in mathematical calculation involving the measure of musical intervals. Notwithstanding the quasi-ecclesiastical location of the fresco (the Vatican Palace), however, the realistically depicted setting is quite different from that of Chartres. It shows, as if seen through an aperture, various figures from antiquity gathered within a classical temple, and behind them a series of archways open to the sky. The central magisterial characters are Plato (modelled on the features of Leonardo da Vinci) and Aristotle; but around and below them are gathered several groups of metaphysicians, mathematicians and scientists, including Socrates, Heraclitus (modelled on Michelangelo), Empedocles, Euclid and Ptolemy (Raphael offers a self-portrait in the depiction of one of the figures standing with these last two). The architectural interior of the temple is itself dominated by two sculpted figures representing Apollo, god of the sun and divine patron of the arts, and Athena, goddess of wisdom and patroness of Athens.

That such a work should grace a papal study room is a striking measure of how the new humanism, inspired by the rediscovery of the art, literature and science of antiquity, had taken hold of educated minds. Fifty years before its completion Marsilio Ficino (1433–99) had founded the Neoplatonic Academy in Florence under the patronage of Cosimo de' Medici (1389–1464). There the identification of beauty with mathematical proportion, and of each with a transcendent reality, was formulated in neo-classical-cum-mystical vocabulary. In connection with this idealizing of compositional order, painting and sculpture began to be separated from practical crafts and treated as branches of higher learning.

It was in Florence, also, that Raphael came under the influence of the ideas, methods and sensibilities of the two senior figures of the High Renaissance trinity – namely Leonardo and Michelangelo – both of whom were native Florentines. While the subject-matter of Renaissance art owes much to the revival of classical mythology and mystical philosophy, the *manner* of depicting scenes was transformed, from what had been common in the medieval period, by technical advances in painting and design. In his *On Painting* of 1435, Alberti (1404–72) describes a system of linear perspective based on a single vanishing point; and the possibility of depicting spatial depth and solidity through geometrical composition and other devices (as effectively realized in *The School of Athens*) was a major preoccupation of the period. Similarly, Alberti and Leonardo urged upon their con-

temporaries the importance of studying the details of natural forms in order to be able to produce worthy images. According to Alberti: 'The function of the painter is to draw with lines and paint in colours on a surface, any given bodies in such a way that at a fixed distance and with a certain position what you see represented appears to be in relief and just like those bodies' (Alberti, vol. 3, p. 52).

Likewise, in his writings on art (later collected in what is known as the *Treatise on Painting*), Leonardo presses the case for precise empirical observation – 'The mirror, above all, should be your master' – and connects this with a belief in the mathematical order of reality. He also argues for the superiority of painting over other arts on the grounds that, through its wide range of representational resources, it is best able to reflect the forms of nature. The idea of painting as a reflective medium, and of other arts (including music) as similarly representational of an ordered world, suggests that art itself is an activity governed by rational and codifiable principles of operation. Leonardo voices this thought in the *Treatise*, and it became a dominant theme of later writings about the nature and status of painting. Interestingly, there is in this development a parallel with the sort of thinking about thinking which led in due course to Descartes's *Rules for the Direction of the Mind* (1628).

To some extent, my earlier claim that 1400–1550 was a period of greater artistic progress and achievement than 1200–1350, which saw more in the way of philosophical genius, disguises the fact that it was the innovations made at Chartres, St-Denis and elsewhere which made possible the profound representational realism achieved in the Renaissance. But to this it must be added that the later period was more concerned with developing the techniques of art than it was with questioning the nature of the reality it sought to represent. There would not be another period of innovative thought on these matters until the rise of rationalism in the seventeenth century, and it was over a hundred years after that that philosophical aesthetics, as we understand it, came into being.

See also AQUINAS; ART HISTORY; PLOTINUS; RELIGION AND ART.

BIBLIOGRAPHY

Alberti, L.B.: *Opuscoli morali di L.B. Alberti* (Venice: Francesco Franceschi, 1568); *De pictura* and *De statua* trans. and ed. C. Grayson, *On Painting and Sculpture* (London: Phaidon, 1972).

Baxandall, M.: *Painting and Experience in Fifteenth-Century Italy* (Oxford: Oxford University Press, 1984).

Beardsley, M.: *Aesthetics from Classical Greece to the Present: A Short History* (Montgomery, Ala.: University of Alabama Press, 1975).

Blunt, A.: *Artistic Theory in Italy: 1450–1600* (Oxford: Oxford University Press, 1973).

Eco, U.: *Sviluppo dell'esthetica medievale* (Milan: 1959); trans. H. Bredin, *Art and Beauty in the Middle Ages* (London: Yale University Press, 1986).

Fubini, E.: *Estetica musicale dall'settecento a oggi* and *Estetica musicale dall'antichità al settecento* (Turin: Einaudi, 1987); trans. M. Hartwell, *The History of Music Aesthetics* (London: Macmillan, 1991).

Leonardo: *Leonardo on Painting: An Anthology of Writings by Leonardo da Vinci*, trans. M. Kemp and M. Walker, ed. M. Kemp (London: Yale University Press, 1989).

Martindale, A.: *The Rise of the Artist in the Middle Ages and Early Renaissance* (London: Thames & Hudson, 1972).

Panofsky, E.: *Gothic Architecture and Scholasticism* (New York: Meridian/New American Library, 1976).

Suger: *De rebus administratione sua gestis*, and other writings (c. 1125–50); trans. and ed. E. Panofsky, *Abbot Suger on the Abbey Church of St-Denis and its Art Treasures* (Princeton, NJ: Princeton University Press, 1979).

Summers, D.: *The Judgement of Sense: Renaissance Naturalism and the Rise of Aesthetics* (Cambridge: Cambridge University Press, 1987).

Tatarkiewicz, W.: *History of Aesthetics*, 3 vols. Vols 2, 3 (The Hague: Mouton, 1970).

JOHN HALDANE

Merleau-Ponty, Maurice (1908–61) French philosopher of the period following the Second World War, best known for his analyses of human existence, perception and action in *Phenomenology of Perception* (1945). Merleau-Ponty was co-founder with Jean-Paul Sartre of the literary magazine *Les Temps Modernes*, and professor at the Universities of Lyons and Paris; he later (1952–61) held the chair of philosophy at the Collège de France. His writings cover a wide range, from philosophical psychology and philosophy of language to political philosophy, philosophy of history and the philosophy of art.

Like his friend (and sometimes friendly enemy) Sartre, with whom his thought had much in common, Merleau-Ponty had no fully developed aesthetics. Yet, again as with Sartre, he often wrote critical essays on the arts – chiefly on painting, but also on the novel and film (some are included in *Sense and Non-Sense* (Merleau-Ponty, 1964a)). Moreover, his entire approach to the human situation was aesthetic and has implications for aesthetics.

At the core of Merleau-Ponty's philosophy is an attempt to recapture in experience (and to analyse) what it is like to encounter the world in a 'primordial' way – that is, prior to describing and explaining it in objective, scientific terms. Drawing on the gestaltists, he proposes that one's primordial experience is to exist towards things through a living (perceiving, feeling, and acting) body. It is to struggle to achieve an equilibrium with things against the background posed by the global environment, on the one hand, and one's 'body schema', one's developed repertoire of perceptual–motor skills and habits, on the other. Through this reciprocal interplay, as he sees it, one's way of being in the world and the primary perceptual world itself become formed and instituted. Since the environment includes others, one becomes an embodied social being and one's perceived world becomes a social world as well. Each bodily movement, each object one sees and responds to, each performance one carries out, is thus, in a sense, an aesthetic achievement – an expression of the meaning of one's individual style within a concrete situation. The involved, living body is to be understood as an expressive medium, and every perception, feeling and action as a work of art.

From this starting point, it is quite natural for Merleau-Ponty to go on to say that a work of art is itself a kind of expressive body: like the body, 'a novel, a poem, a picture, a piece of music are individuals, that is to say beings in which it is impossible to distinguish the expressive vehicle from its meaning, whose meanings are accessible only in direct contact, and which radiate their significance without leaving their temporal and spatial position' (Merleau-Ponty, 1962, p. 151).

Works of art thus have a kind of gestural meaning. Of course, they exhibit a complex vocabulary and syntax. But we comprehend them, Merleau-Ponty suggests, in much the same way in which we grasp the meanings of bodily gestures – not, in the first instance, by thinking about them, by trying to decipher them, but rather by lending our bodies to them, by living through their words, lines, colours or sounds, and following out their tacit perceptual implications. The process of creating artworks is also best understood as a pre-reflective, bodily one. In this way it is much like creative speech: 'Like the functioning of the body, that of words and paintings remains mysterious to me: words, lines, colours which express my thoughts come from me like gestures; they are forced upon me by what I want to say as my gestures are by what I want to do' (Merleau-Ponty, 1964b, p. 75). Descartes was therefore wrong: neither in speaking nor in painting are there two actions, one of thinking and another of mobilizing the body – on the contrary, one thinks with one's words and with one's hand, brush and paints. Nor is there an idea 'behind' the word or the work, or somewhere 'beyond' them, but only 'in' them and inseparable from them. Merleau-Ponty's thesis throughout is that the possibility both of language and painting rests upon the primordial, expressive possibilities of the human body.

Merleau-Ponty was enamoured of Cézanne. He saw in Cézanne a philosopher – indeed, he saw himself – working with paint. In 'Cézanne's doubt' (1945), he shows how Cézanne struggled to define his own style in the face of academic painting, with its linear, 'objective' realism, on the one hand, and his

friends the impressionists on the other, who, like him, wished to reject that sort of realism, but who seemed to leave natural things behind entirely and focus solely on light, air and patches of colour. What Cézanne finally managed to do, Merleau-Ponty thinks, was to cut through the conceptual biases of these other styles and, like a faithful phenomenologist, let the solid, weighty, voluminous presence of perceived things appear. By attending to surfaces and the structures perceptible beneath them, by painting the modulations of colour at the edges of things and including perspectival distortions, he made canvases in which these elements 'are no longer visible in their own right, but rather contribute, as they do in natural vision, to the impression of an emerging order, of an object in the act of appearing, organizing itself before our eyes' (Merleau-Ponty, 1964a, p. 14).

In the last work that he saw published ('Eye and mind' (1960) in Merleau-Ponty, *The Primacy of Perception*, 1964c, pp. 159–90), written for the first issue of *Art de France*, he returns to Cézanne, as well as Klee, Matisse and others, to suggest that painting can have a distinctive ontological function. Precisely because painting does not 'copy' things, and because it does not offer things to thought as does science but presents them immediately and bodily, in their depth and movement, so that we seem to be 'present at the fission of Being from the inside' – for these reasons painting gives us a true sense of 'the internal animation' of the world and what it means 'to see' it (Merleau-Ponty, 1964c, p. 186).

See also EXPRESSION; LANGUAGE, ART AS; SARTRE.

WRITINGS

Phénoménologie de la Perception (Paris: 1945); trans. C. Smith, *Phenomenology of Perception* (New York: Humanities Press, 1962).

Sens et nonsens (Paris: 1948); trans. H.L. Dreyfus and P.A. Dreyfus, *Sense and Non-Sense* (Evanston, Ill.: Northwestern University Press, 1964a).

Signes (Paris: 1960); trans. R. McCleary, *Signs*

(Evanston, Ill.: Northwestern University Press, 1964b).

The Primacy of Perception, trans. and ed. J.M. Edie (Evanston, Ill.: Northwestern University Press, 1964c).

BIBLIOGRAPHY

Kaelin, E.F.: *An Existentialist Aesthetic* (Madison, Wis.: University of Wisconsin Press, 1966).

JOHN J. COMPTON

metaphor A verbal composition which, on the basis of novel semantic relations among its components, evokes a complex and productive set of mental responses. Ever since Aristotle's *Poetics*, there has been widespread agreement on the important role played by metaphor in literature, especially poetry. Metaphor has been seen – by, among others, Shelley, Valéry and I.A. Richards – as a main source of both the pleasure and the interest to be gained from poems. More recently, philosophers have become aware of the considerable difficulties surrounding this concept, and it is on these theoretical problems concerning the nature and scope of metaphor that this article concentrates.

Theories of metaphor may be divided into those that see metaphor as a secondary use of language, a departure from its basic function of describing our responses to the outside world, and those that see it as an essential characteristic, inherent in the nature of language itself. Put otherwise, the question is whether all language is metaphoric or whether there is a literal as well as a metaphoric use of it.

Implicit in this is the assumption that language is a means for transacting relations between the thoughts that a speaker has and conditions as they obtain in the world. One of the inferences from this assumption is, then, that a speaker, in carrying out such a transaction, can use the language in a manner which is factually objective and epistemically neutral – a use, thus, in which the function of language is purely descriptive and its use strictly literal. Metaphor on this view is some modification or extension of literal language,

and is to be explicated by the use of linguistic analysis or the theory of speech acts.

Alternatively, one may regard the role played by one or another of the components in the linguistic transaction as functioning not neutrally but with a characteristic predilection. Thus, one may regard the thought component as so indoctrinated by human experience that all such transactions are epistemically tendentious and the language consequently biased. It is a corollary of this position that language is congenitally and pervasively metaphoric, and that explication is to be achieved by examining the conceptual prepossessions of the speaker.

Another approach centres on language; it holds that, in routinely accommodating itself to broader and broader segments of human experience, a language acquires a metaphoric character as an autonomous function of its historical development. Explication here involves the study of linguistic change – in particular, an examination of how the words of a language widen their extensions in consequence of their use to comprehend new objects and ideas. A variant of this position makes an even stronger claim – that language is metaphoric *ab origine*, its metaphoric character deriving from the very fact that, as we might put it, words are not the things they refer to, or that language is representative of but is not the same as our experience of the world.

It might appear that the remaining component in our analysis is not capable of prejudicially asserting itself – that is, that the constitution of the world is simply what it is and cannot be made to function other than passively in the linguistic transaction – and thus that the role played by the world in that transaction cannot be exploited for metaphoric purposes. This is no doubt true; at the same time, however, nothing prevents someone from employing in the interpretation of metaphor a *conception* of the world that is at variance with empirical conditions. Thus, flowers may not laugh or feel happy in our world, but one can *conceive of* a world in which such states of affairs are possible. Conceptions of this sort, it should be noted, are not (conceptual) prepossessions; they come into being in the act of interpreting metaphors literally.

When regarded as the modified use of literal language, metaphor may take one of two basic forms: in one, the modification reflects itself in an incongruity between the literal sense of the expression and the (non-linguistic) environment in which it occurs; in the other, the incongruity is reflected in the expression itself. Thus, in responding to an opponent's argument, a speaker might say, 'That's a pile of garbage'; a poet, to describe the formation of dew at nightfall, might say, 'When the weak day weeps'. The latter expression – Shelley's – is syntactically well formed, but it is semantically deviant, in that the grammar of English does not 'sanction' predicating *weak* and *weep* of *day*. In the first type of metaphor, on the other hand, nothing in the expression is linguistically unorthodox; there is, however, a form of deviance in the *use* to which the expression is put; we might refer to metaphors of this type as pragmatically deviant.

As the example in the preceding paragraph indicates, the deviant character of metaphor is a consequence of collocations that comprise incompatible semantic valences. Beardsley (1962) remarks on this semantic opposition or 'tension' in metaphor, and argues that from this opposition a 'twist of meaning' is forced; in 'the spiteful sun', for instance, the predicate 'spiteful' acquires a new intension, 'perhaps one that it has in no other context'.

Black (1954–5) characterizes his approach to the analysis of metaphor as 'interactional'. Taking as his example 'Man is a wolf', he defines two subjects: principal ('man') and subsidiary ('wolf'). To each of these subjects there pertains a 'system of associated commonplaces', these being beliefs that the average person holds about the referents of the names. In the construal process these commonplaces interact, some being, as it were, transferred from one to the other subject and its import assimilated into the 'meaning' of that subject, others being filtered out as incompatible. Black does not explicitly invoke semantic deviance in his

discussion, but it figures implicitly in that his interactional process is a non-trivial function only if some sort of deviance is assumed.

In the face of semantic deviance, Searle (1979) refers, in his analysis of metaphor, to the difference between sentence meaning and speaker's meaning. This prising apart of the speech act into two separate components is a tactic used by Searle also in his analysis of irony and indirect speech acts. In all these cases, the speaker says one thing but intends another. Thus, in 'Sally is a block of ice', the rationalization of its metaphoric function does not take the form of operations performed upon the utterance itself; the metaphoric meaning devolves, rather, upon what the speaker had in mind when uttering the sentence – namely, that Sally is a cold, unresponsive person. It is a significant aspect of Searle's approach that the words in a metaphoric expression comprise or have conferred upon them no additional, special, *ad hoc* or 'metaphoric' meaning – in this respect differing from Beardsley and Black.

Davidson (1978) is in agreement with Searle that the words in a metaphoric utterance have only their literal meaning. However, the consequence for Davidson is not semantic deviance but patent or obvious falsity. Moreover, rationalization of the expression's metaphoric quality is not accomplished by adverting to speaker's meaning; instead, the interpretative activity is localized in the reader of the metaphor, who will be set to calibrating a series of novel and provocative juxtapositions of objects and ideas. It is in the prompting of these novel relationships, which the 'patently' false expression causes the reader to notice, that the metaphoric function consists.

That metaphor is a question primarily of thought and only secondarily of language is the argument of Lakoff and Johnson (1980). According to them, our experience of the world – its physical features and human activities – implicitly conditions our mental development in such a way that certain concepts become so impressed on our thought processes that we are predisposed to respond 'metaphorically' to the affairs of everyday life. Thus, such notions as

'Argument is war', 'Time is money', and 'Happy is up' are for Lakoff and Johnson conceptual metaphors, mental figures in which elements from one domain are mapped on to correlative elements of another. In a conceptual metaphor like 'Time is money', elements like concreteness, short supply and value are mapped from the source domain, money, on to the target domain, time – the mapping manifesting itself in such locutions as 'I spent a solid week on that problem', 'I can't spare the time', 'That cost me a night's sleep.'

As these examples make evident, conceptual metaphors (which need not be articulated as such) leave their traces in (and may be inferred from) the expressions that we use in everyday speech. Of the linguistic expressions themselves, Lakoff and Johnson claim that they too are metaphoric; in fact, vitally metaphoric, and this despite the fact that the senses of the words occurring in these expressions are 'conventionally fixed within the lexicon of English'.

In the treatment provided by Levin (1988) it is again the thought component that figures as the essential focus. Instead, however, of that focus bearing on preconceived experiential notions (the conceptual metaphors of Lakoff and Johnson), it bears, rather, on the responses that one might make to metaphors that one encounters in poetry. Consider again Shelley's 'When the weak day weeps'. However one approaches their analysis, it is clear that, if taken literally, the truth claims made by most metaphors (Shelley's example being paradigmatic in this regard) describe conditions that are ontologically and empirically bizarre. Levin proposes that instead of trying to rationalize the meaning of such metaphors – make their interpretation conform to conditions in the actual world – one takes them at face value and attempts, rather, to conceive of a 'world' in which what the metaphor purports to describe represents a possible state of affairs. This approach to metaphor might be called conceptional in nature.

It is a natural proclivity of language (an economy measure, actually) to widen the scope and applicability of its semantic units. Thus, in its normal use and development the meaning of a word will automatically gain new senses as the range and nature of its reference is extended. A large part of this process is routine, raising no theoretical problems and requiring no particular comment. When a word like 'leaf', say, is applied successively to different individual leaves, to various species of leaves, and further extends its range to designate the sections of a shutter or the pages of a book, the semantic consequences of the extension are comparatively unproblematic. This is because the referents, throughout the extension, are uniformly concrete. Something significant emerges, however, when the extension in question represents a move from the domain of physical to that of mental activities. For inasmuch as a good deal of the scientific and philosophical literature is conducted via words which have made just this semantic transfer, the question is raised as to whether language can still be used to describe reality straightforwardly; or whether language is not in fact fundamentally and ineluctably metaphoric.

Derrida (1974) adopts the latter of these alternatives, and educes from it the following argument: if it is the case that philosophical language is intrinsically metaphoric, then it follows that no non-circular account can be given of metaphor, since the language of that account would itself be metaphoric. As a temper to the drastic nature of this conclusion, one might raise the issue of dead metaphor, in the case of which the emergent sense gets registered in the lexicon of the language. Additionally, one might invoke the role played in these developments by catachresis, in which the range of a word is extended not to replace an already existing word but, rather, to fill a lexical gap.

Cooper (1986), Kittay (1987) and Ricoeur (1977) are three comprehensive and valuable treatments of metaphor, in each of which original observations are made about various aspects of the problem.

See also INEFFABILITY; IRONY.

BIBLIOGRAPHY

Beardsley, M.C.: 'The metaphorical twist', *Philosophy and Phenomenological Research*, 22 (1962), 293–307.

Black, M.: 'Metaphor', *Proceedings of the Aristotelian Society*, 55 (1954–5), 273–94.

Cooper, D.E.: *Metaphor* (Oxford: Basil Blackwell, 1986).

Davidson, D.: 'What metaphors mean', *Critical Inquiry*, 5 (1978), 31–47.

Derrida, J.: 'La mythologie blanche', *Poétique*, 5 (1971), 1–52; trans. F.C.T. Moore, 'White mythology: metaphor in the text of philosophy', *New Literary History*, 6 (1974), 5–74.

Kittay, E.F.: *Metaphor: Its Cognitive Force and Linguistic Structure* (Oxford: Clarendon Press, 1987).

Lakoff, G. and Johnson, M.: *Metaphors We Live By* (Chicago and London: University of Chicago Press, 1980).

Levin, S.R.: *Metaphoric Worlds: Conceptions of a Romantic Nature* (New Haven, Conn. and London: Yale University Press, 1988).

Ricoeur, P.: *La métaphore vive* (Paris: 1975); trans. R. Czerny, *The Rule of Metaphor: Multi-Disciplinary Studies in the Creation of Meaning in Language* (Toronto and Buffalo: University of Toronto Press, 1977).

Searle, J.R.: 'Metaphor', *Metaphor and Thought*, ed. A. Ortony (Cambridge and New York: Cambridge University Press, 1979), pp. 92–123.

SAMUEL R. LEVIN

mimesis *See* ARISTOTLE; REPRESENTATION; RESEMBLANCE.

modernism and postmodernism Modernist aesthetics is characterized by the attempt to define the nature of aesthetic experience *in itself*. In twentieth-century avant-garde modernism, this conception is joined with a revolutionary commitment to endless experiment and innovation in artistic form. Postmodernism may be defined as a simultaneous refusal and intensification of this innovatory force of modernism. Where modernism stresses the unity and autonomy of the work of art, with both radical and conservative consequences, postmodernism stresses the hybridity of the work of art and its complex relatedness to its context.

It can be argued that there is a close relationship between the idea of the aesthetic and the inauguration of the modern in philosophy and cultural life more generally. The great division effected by Kant between the autonomous spheres of science, morality and art established the notion of the aesthetic *as such*, the notion that the only appropriate judgement of a work of art was one that suspended all extrinsic and instrumental considerations, and responded to it in itself and on its own terms. Modern aesthetics may be said broadly to represent an unfolding of this Kantian intuition. There are two distinct but related aesthetic claims characteristic of modernism: the claim that works of art are *unified*, and the claim that they are *autonomous*.

The first claim – exemplified, for instance, in modernist architectural theory and throughout the literary criticism of I.A. Richards, F.R. Leavis and the American New Critics of the 1940s and 1950s – suggests that works of art are successful and valuable to the degree that they effect reconciliations or unifications of complex discontinuities, and bring unity out of discord. The second claim may be conveniently demonstrated in the work of the art critics Clement Greenberg and Michael Fried. For both of these writers, the task of the authentic work of art is to explore the conditions of its own medium in order not to represent the world, but in order to give expression to its own nature. The task of art and criticism, Greenberg wrote in 1965, 'became to eliminate from the effects of each art any and every effect that might conceivably be borrowed from or by the medium of any other art. Thereby each art would be rendered "pure", and in its "purity" find the guarantee of its standards of quality as well of its independence' (Greenberg, 1982, pp. 5–6).

The requirement of unity and the requirement of autonomy are brought together in the work of Fried, who rejects what he calls the tendency towards 'theatricality' in works of painting and sculpture, by which he means the attempt to imitate the effects of other arts or to call attention to any circumstances which distract attention from the work's integral absorption in itself. Examples of theatricality might be, for example, the imitation of narrative or drama in painting, the attempt to establish a relationship between the work of art and the contingent circumstances of its museum or display environment, or the attempt to build temporal process into the work of art – for example, in performance art. *'The success, even the survival, of the arts has come increasingly to depend on their ability to defeat theater,'* warns Fried. 'The concepts of quality and value – and to the extent that these are central to art, the concept of art itself – are meaningful, or wholly meaningful, only *within* the individual arts. What lies *between* the arts is theater' (Fried, 1968, pp. 139, 42).

For such modernist aesthetics, therefore, the single most important criterion of value in an aesthetic work is its purity, and the single most important purpose of criticism and aesthetic theory the hygienic differentiation of authentic aesthetic practice from the degraded forms of expression typical of modern mass culture. The assertion of aesthetic autonomy may have politically radical consequences, for, in freeing art from its traditional forms of social responsibility, it may make it possible to generate revolutionary new forms of expression and consciousness or to resist the systematizing and regularizing tendencies of modern life. But the very distance from social responsibility maintained by modernist aesthetics may also serve, paradoxically, to insulate society from these revolutionary effects.

Against the modernist doctrine of aesthetic autonomy, postmodernist aesthetics involves a project of despecialization. Postmodernist aesthetics proposes to go beyond what it perceives as the fictive and restrictive claims for unity, identity and purity of the aesthetic object, and embraces the opposite principles of heterogeneity, hybridity and impurity. Fredric Jameson has suggested correspondingly that the passage from modernist to postmodernist aesthetics can be seen as the movement away from a 'deep' aesthetic of unique personal style to a 'flat' aesthetic of

pastiche and the multiplication of styles (Jameson, 1985, pp. 114–23).

Similarly, where modernist aesthetics had proposed a clear distinction between authentic art and the forms characteristic of mass culture, postmodernist aesthetics willingly embraces the art forms of the popular and mass markets, intentionally mingling the 'high' and the 'low'. The purpose of such mingling, however, is not to effect a reconciliation of opposites, but rather to heighten the sense of ironic play between them. This tendency may be seen not only in the 'quoting' of familiar objects and everyday forms alongside classical forms in contemporary architecture, but also in the use of popular forms such as the Western, the romance and the detective story in much contemporary fiction. Also characteristic of postmodernist art and aesthetic theory are a deliberate tolerance and incitement of 'theatricality' as negatively defined by Fried. Examples of this might include those forms of contemporary sculpture which, instead of closing themselves off in introverted self-absorption from their contexts, require an acknowledgement and reflection upon those contexts. The minimalist sculpture of Carl André and the installation or environmental work of artists such as Robert Smithson and Richard Long, are validated by a postmodernist aesthetic theory which stresses the uncertain relationship between art and the non-artistic world, rather than attempting to maintain a strict distinction between these two realms. Where a modernist aesthetics would stress the *instance* of art, we may say, a postmodernist aesthetics stresses its *circumstance*.

The evidence of postmodernist 'theatricality' is also to be seen in the preference for various kinds of mixed media over the modernist absorption in the conditions and possibilities of a singular medium. Examples here might include the mixed-media performance art of Laurie Andersen, the overlayering of film and literary styles in Robert Coover's novel *A Night at the Movies* (1987), and the Ontological-Hysteric Theater of the American dramatist Richard Foreman, which concentrates together complex and incongruous experiences of sound, music, light and words. Such mixings of media are also characteristic of many works which one might wish to designate as modernist, of course; but it seems useful to distinguish between a modernist ideal of the blending or unification of different media (in the cubist practice of collage, or the Wagnerian *Gesamtkunstwerk* [Total artwork], for example) and a postmodernist ideal of a mingling without unification, in which the differentiated media are intended to remain in abrasive non-identity.

Another important marker of the distinction between modernism and postmodernism is the relative value attached to spatiality and temporality. In an influential article, Joseph Frank (1963) suggested that modernist literary works were characterized by 'spatial form': works such as T.S. Eliot's *The Waste Land* (1922) and James Joyce's *Ulysses* (1922) tended to substitute for a linear sense of the passage of time a spatial sense of the recurrence, persistence and parallelism of time – for example, in what Eliot, writing of Joyce's *Ulysses* in 1923, called the 'mythic method', whereby the artist maintains 'a continuous parallel between contemporaneity and antiquity' (Eliot, 1975, p. 177). The work and its reader are thereby lifted out of time and given the opportunity of tracking back and forth across past, present and future. This analysis may be confirmed by the dominance within modernist aesthetics of ideas such as Virginia Woolf's 'moments of vision', or James Joyce's 'epiphanies', which emphasize the work of art's distillation of privileged moments of insight or intense experience out of the flow of quotidian time. These characterizations of the work of art are accompanied and reinforced by interpretative practices such as those derived from structuralism in Europe – which emphasized the synchronic unity of the work of art and the literary system to which it belongs over the diachronic dimension of its development and reception through time – and from the New Criticism, which construed the patterns of tension and resolution in literary texts as blended into timeless unity, apprehensible to an ideal and totalizing critical gaze.

Against the modernist aesthetics of space, postmodernist aesthetics embraces the impermanence and contingency of temporal passage. William V. Spanos, and the influential postmodernist American journal *boundary 2* which he edits, were instrumental in the 1970s in promoting an ideal of literary value and interpretation based on the philosophy of Heidegger, which stresses dynamic and temporal 'being-in-the-world' over metaphysical abstractions and refusals of history. Spanos (1979) correspondingly sees the purpose of contemporary literature as being not to assert the ahistorical integrity of the work of art, but to open itself up to the contingencies of history, and promotes the ideal of a criticism which no longer pretends to occupy a spatializing position of command over the text or work of art, but frankly acknowledges its partiality and historicity.

Marjorie Perloff, similarly, has stressed the movement away from the dominance of the lyric in modernist poetry, with its associated effects of singularity, privileged insight and hermetic closure, towards various kinds of narrative poetry in postmodernism – for example, in works such as Ezra Pound's *Cantos* (1917–75) and Louis Zukovsky's *A* (1928–74), both of which present human experience as unfinished and transitional, and moving towards no point of final insight or timeless epiphany. Similarly, where modernist aesthetics proposes a 'closed' notion of the work of art as a finished and complete object, postmodernist aesthetics privileges an art in process, which opens on to change and the unexpected – as evidenced, for example, in the performance art of Joseph Beuys, John Cage and Alan Kaprow. This kind of performance art has been seen as dominated by an 'aesthetics of absence [which] subjects art to the wiles of history, embraces time', as opposed to a modernist 'aesthetics of presence [which] seeks to transcend history, to escape temporality' (Sayre, 1983, p. 174).

A renewed sense of historical contingency is also characteristic of other areas of postmodernist art and culture. If the imperative of modernism was, in Ezra Pound's words, to 'make it new', to effect an absolute break from history, then postmodernist art and culture return to history. This may take the conservative form of revivalism or traditionalism, as in some areas of contemporary architecture, or the more radical and ironic form of a questioning of the relations between present and past, tradition and newness. This latter approach is exemplified in Salman Rushdie's *Midnight's Children* (1981), which explores the complex intermingling of official and unofficial, real and fictional versions of history. Characteristic of such 'historiographic metafiction', as Linda Hutcheon (1988) has called it, is a sense of history not as the repository of truth or reality, but as itself produced out of the aesthetic activities of narrating and representing.

This shift in the conception of the artistic object or work relates closely to the question of art's ordering capacity. While it is true that both modernism and postmodernism are responses to a sense of the increasing complexity and indeterminacy of the social (and physical) world, the nature of the response is very different in each case. Where modernist aesthetics stresses that the work of art provides what T.S. Eliot (1975, p. 177) called 'a way of controlling, of ordering, of giving a shape and a significance to the immense panorama of futility and anarchy which is contemporary history', postmodernist aesthetics tends to accept and even to embrace the disorderliness and complexity of the world. In postmodernism, as Alan Wilde (1981, p. 131) has put it, 'a world in need of mending is superseded by one beyond repair.'

The work of Samuel Beckett offers a strikingly clear example of this distinction. In a joke told by a character in his play *Endgame*, Beckett offers a perfect summary of the modernist aesthetic of reparation, in which the artist makes up for the obstinately chaotic nature of the world by the perfection of his artifice; a tailor (= artist), confronted by a customer demanding angrily to know why he has taken three months to finish making a pair of trousers when God made the world in six days, replies, scandalized, 'But my dear Sir, my dear Sir, look – at the world – and look – at my TROUSERS' (Beckett, 1986, p. 103). But Beckett also spoke periodically of his own work as an attempt to find a form which would accommodate the mess of human life, rather than transfiguring it, and as an exploration of the conditions of impotence and failure rather than mastery and success (Schenker, 1956).

This distinction between orderliness and disorderliness underlies the influential characterization of postmodernism offered by Jean-François Lyotard. He draws on Kant's account of the sublime, recalling that, for Kant, the sublime consists not merely in the apprehension of vastness or grandeur as such, but also in the feeling of disproportion between that vastness and the capacity of the mind to conceive and present it to itself. Lyotard suggests that modernism 'calls forth' the unpresentable (here conceived as the inconceivable complexity and heterogeneity of the social–linguistic world rather than the awe-inspiring vastness of the natural world) and allows it to become perceptible through and within aesthetic form (Lyotard instances the work of Proust and Joyce). Where aesthetic form provides some kind of substitute for the unpresentable in modernism, postmodernism preserves the gulf between the unpresentable and the act of presentation, *within the act of representation itself.*

> The postmodern would be that which, in the modern, puts forward the unpresentable in presentation itself; that which denies itself the solace of good forms, the consensus of a taste which would make it possible to share collectively the nostalgia for the unattainable; that which searches for new presentations, not in order to enjoy them but in order to impart a stronger sense of the unpresentable. (Lyotard, 1984, pp. 80–1)

As with other accounts of the cultural and historical transition from modernism to postmodernism, Lyotard's distinction may also describe an ambivalence within a particular work or body of work. It is not entirely clear, for example, whether such a work as Eliot's *The Waste Land* ought to be thought of as a nostalgic attempt to make good the chaos and fragmentation it presents, or as an enactment of the inescapability of that fragmentation. It is for this reason that Lyotard resists making a clear and absolute distinction between modernism and postmodernism, arguing that the aesthetics of the sublime represents the inaugural moment of and within modernism (for example, in the aesthetics of Dada) rather than a simple surpassing or suppression of it.

In so far as such shifts in attitude constitute an assault on the ways in which the realm of the aesthetic has been defined since Kant, postmodernism may be said to be defined, at least in part, as a refusal of the aesthetic as such. Characteristic of much postmodernist art and theory is an impatience with the separation of art and its effects from the social and political world which is effected in modernism. An important critical influence here has been the work of the French sociologist Pierre Bourdieu, who proposes in his massive work *Distinction*:

> a transgression which is in no way aesthetic . . . [a] barbarous reintegration of aesthetic consumption into the world of ordinary consumption [which] abolishes the opposition, which has been the basis of high aesthetics since Kant, between the 'taste of sense' and the 'taste of reflection', and between facile pleasure, pleasure reduced to a pleasure of the senses, and pure pleasure, pleasure purified of pleasure. (Bourdieu, 1984, p. 6)

The point of this transgression is to show the ways in which the allegedly transcendent values of art and culture always in fact serve the interests of certain groups, such that the apparent distinction *between* art and society serves unjustly to maintain actual class distinctions *within* society. Many postmodernist artists have drawn such critical and theoretical speculation on the social effects and functions of art and cultural representation into their work, in an attempt not so much to undermine or dissolve the category of the aesthetic, as to make art the occasion for ironic reflection on its own inescapably social and historical nature.

See also ABSTRACTION; HEIDEGGER; IRONY; KANT; POPULAR ART; STRUCTURALISM AND POSTSTRUCTURALISM; SUBLIME.

BIBLIOGRAPHY

Beckett, Samuel: *The Complete Dramatic Works* (London: Faber & Faber, 1986).

Bourdieu, Pierre: *La distinction: Critique sociale du jugement* (Paris: 1979); trans. Richard Nice, *Distinction: A Social Critique of the Judgement of Taste* (London and New York: Routledge & Kegan Paul, 1984).

Connor, Steven: *Postmodernist Culture: An Introduction to Theories of the Contemporary* (Oxford: Basil Blackwell, 1989).

Eliot, T.S.: 'Ulysses, order and myth', *Selected Prose of T.S. Eliot*, ed. Frank Kermode (London: Faber & Faber, 1975), pp. 175–8.

Frank, Joseph: 'Spatial form in modern literature', *The Widening Gyre: Crisis and Mastery in Modern Literature* (Bloomington, Ill.: Indiana University Press, 1963), pp. 3–62.

Fried, Michael: 'Art and objecthood', *Minimalist Art*, ed. Geoffrey Battcock (New York: E.P. Dutton, 1968), pp. 116–47.

Greenberg, Clement: 'Modernist painting', *Modern Art and Modernism: A Critical Anthology*, ed. Frances Frascina and Charles Harrison (London: Harper & Row and Open University Press, 1982), pp. 5–10.

Hutcheon, Linda: *A Poetics of Postmodernism: History, Theory, Fiction* (New York and London: Routledge & Kegan Paul, 1988).

Jameson, Fredric: 'Postmodernism and consumer society', *Postmodern Culture*, ed. Hal Foster (London and Sydney: Pluto Press, 1985), pp. 114–23.

Lyotard, Jean-François: *La condition postmoderne: rapport sur le savoir* (Paris: 1979); trans. Geoffrey Bennington and Brian Massumi, *The Postmodern Condition: A Report on Knowledge* (Manchester: Manchester University Press, 1984).

Perloff, Marjorie: *The Poetics of Indeterminacy: Rimbaud to Cage* (Evanston, Ill.: Northwestern University Press, 1981).

Sayre, Henry: 'The object of performance: aesthetics in the seventies', *Georgia Review*, 37 (1983), 169–88.

Schenker, Israel, 'Moody man of letters' (interview with Samuel Beckett), *New York Times*, 6 May 1956, § 2, p. 3.

Spanos, William V.: *Martin Heidegger and the*

Question of Literature: Towards a Postmodern Literary Hermeneutics (Bloomington, Ill.: Indiana University Press, 1979).

Wilde, Alan: *Horizons of Assent: Postmodernism and the Ironic Imagination* (Baltimore, Md: Johns Hopkins University Press, 1981).

STEVEN CONNOR

morality and art   A complex topic – partly because 'morality' and 'art' may be used in wider or narrower senses. Morality may be seen as having to do with following codes of behaviour, living dutifully in accordance with principles, possessing virtues (especially of an altruistic kind), or, more broadly, living a flourishing life as a member of a community. If we do not insist on altruistic attachments but simply talk of personal flourishing or well-being, the term 'morality' may hardly seem appropriate. At the same time, there are important questions about the contribution of art to human flourishing, which are closely linked with questions about its relationships to morality in the other senses outlined. For that reason, although in what follows the emphasis will be on morality, we shall also be touching on the place of art in personal well-being.

To turn from 'morality' to 'art', we may be interested in relating any of the things just mentioned to the arts as human creations, or to aesthetic experience – itself a term which can be taken in various ways – more generally. A central question is: can art or aesthetic experience be understood without some reference to morality in one or more of its senses? On one view we are dealing with two logically autonomous domains – which is not to rule out various kinds of empirical connection; while other writers would claim a conceptual link.

Kant and Schiller both belong to the latter group. Kant writes that 'the beautiful is the symbol of the morally good.' In terms of the above distinctions, he wants to say that we cannot understand aesthetic experience except by relating it to our moral natures as followers of universal principles. How can this be? Kant bifurcates human nature. We exist partly in the world of sense experience, and partly in the supersensible world of reason and freedom. Aesthetic experience is rooted in the former, morality in the latter. Yet there are links between the two in all three areas of aesthetic experience that Kant distinguishes: contemplation of artistic beauty, of the sublime, and of natural beauty.

Artists of genius are capable of expressing in their works what Kant calls 'aesthetical ideas'. These are products of the creative imagination which are rich in thought but cannot be wholly expressed in concepts. They strive beyond the bounds of experience to present rational (that is, supersensible, moral) ideas for our contemplation (Kant, 1951 [1790], 49). These include particular moral ideas like love and honesty, but also – and this may help to meet the point that not all works of genius are equally suited to express such particular ideas – the idea of morality, or its supersensible substrate, itself. Our experience of the sublime points in the same direction. It combines a feeling of displeasure at the domination of nature over us, or at our inability to grasp infinite magnitudes, with the pleasurable feeling of the excitation within us of a supersensible rational faculty which is dominant over sense and the shortcomings of our understanding. Finally, in contemplating natural beauty we come to see nature as if it were designed for human purposes; in this way, too, we are led to the idea of a supersensible substrate.

For Kant, a logical link between the aesthetic and the moral is important for metaphysical reasons. Having divided human nature, he needs to show how the two parts can operate together. In particular, there must be some way in which our rational faculties as moral beings are exercised in the world of sense experience. Aesthetic experience has a central place in Kant's overall architectonic because it provides this bridge. It is only through claiming that beauty is the symbol of morality that Kant can seek to justify the demand for universal agreement that aesthetic judgements bring with them – that is, the demand that we all *ought* to agree in them.

Kant's way of linking the moral with the aesthetic will cut little ice with those who do not accept his presuppositions about the two worlds in which we live. Someone who *did* accept the metaphysical assumptions, however, was Schiller. In one way his theory is importantly different from Kant's. While the latter confines himself to metaphysical and epistemological enquiries about the relation between the aesthetic and the moral, Schiller adds a temporal and educational thesis: that aesthetic experience is a necessary feature of the individual's progress towards moral goodness.

Schiller takes over from Kant the idea that we have sensible and non-sensible, or moral, faculties. In his terms this becomes the thesis that we are powered by both a 'sensuous drive' and a 'formal drive'. The former presses us back into all the diversity of our experiences, while the latter urges us towards the freedom to bring harmony into this diversity. The two drives need to be kept in balance, so as to prevent the one-sided development of our natures – towards passivity and multiplicity, or towards activity and abstraction, defects that Schiller associates particularly with the modern age. In order to keep each drive within its proper bounds, a third drive is necessary. Schiller calls this the 'play drive', its object being 'living form' or beauty. The state of aesthetic freedom which we experience in play is necessary for our transition from passivity to activity. 'There is no other way of making sensuous man rational except by first making him aesthetic' (Schiller, 1967, letter 23, p. 2).

On this view, the end of aesthetic education, as for Plato, is moral goodness. This seems to suggest a subordination – again, as in Plato, and also, for reasons given above, in Kant – of aesthetic value to moral value. But there is also another, very different, strain in Schiller. When he tells us that it is play alone that makes man whole and unfolds both sides of his nature at once, or that 'he is only fully a human being when he plays' (letter 15, p. 9), or that beauty is 'the consummation of his humanity', the aesthetic seems to become of independent significance to us. Schiller's apparent ambivalence over the relative value in our lives of the aesthetic and the moral seems to indicate that he is breaking away

from the Kantian framework towards a position in which aesthetic experience is of central importance to human flourishing. In this he belongs not to the Enlightenment, but to the Romantic reaction against it.

If 'morality' is taken out of its Kantian context and given its very widest interpretation, as having to do with living a flourishing human life as a member of a community, then Schiller can also be said to make aesthetic experience a necessary aspect of the moral. He writes of the communal benefits of the aesthetic (letter 27); it is beauty alone that can confer on man a social character. 'Only the aesthetic mode of communication unites society, because it relates to that which is common to all.'

Both Kant and the Kantian Schiller claim that one cannot understand the aesthetic except via the moral: in Schiller the concept of the play drive is parasitic on that of the formal drive. For the non-Kantian Schiller, as we have seen, the aesthetic is a necessary part of human well-being and of the moral in a very broad sense. For other philosophers, not least during the twentieth century, the aesthetic domain is not logically connected with the moral or with personal well-being in these or in any other ways, since it constitutes an autonomous realm of its own. Beardsley, for instance (1958, p. 462), sees the objects of aesthetic experience of works of art as confined to certain perceptible features of them, to do with their unity, their complexity, and the intensity of (equally perceptible) human regional qualities in them. Links with other human interests thus become contingent. There are two such contingent ways in which Beardsley's version of aesthetic experience can have moral effects (in some sense of the term) or can contribute to well-being: these things may happen via the experience itself – that is, 'inherently'; or as a side-effect of acquaintance with a work, independently of any aesthetic experience (Beardsley, 1958, p. 558).

An example of the latter would be the claim that reading a certain novel is likely to be morally corrupting. (We will come back briefly to side-effects when we look at Plato's position.) Among the positive inherent effects that Beardsley claims for aesthetic experience in his sense are (1) the relief of tension and the promotion of inner harmony; (2) the refinement of perception; (3) the development of the imagination and the ability to put oneself in others' shoes; and (4) the fostering of mutual sympathy and understanding. Of these, claim (1) depends on empirical evidence which is not provided, while (2), (3) and (4), despite appearances, do not imply transfer from the domain of aesthetic experience to other purposes in life. The mutual sympathy in (4), for instance, is only among aesthetic connoisseurs.

Philosophers like Beardsley, for whom the aesthetic is an autonomous domain, are encompassed in Stuart Hampshire's remark that, for them, 'the enjoyment of art, and art itself, is . . . a detached and peculiar pleasure, which leads to nothing else. Its part in the whole experience of man is then left unexplained' (Hampshire, 1959, p. 246). This comment might also apply to G.E. Moore, whose view of the connection between meeting one's moral obligations and aesthetic enjoyments is that the former is a means to the latter as well as to personal affection, both of which ends are the greatest intrinsic goods (Moore, 1971, ch. 6). A difference between Moore and Beardsley is that, while it is not clear whether Beardsley is claiming that aesthetic activities are necessary to *everyone's* flourishing, as distinct from that of connoisseurs, Moore does seem to want to defend this (unless he would hold that some people can put all the weight, with regard to intrinsic goods, on personal affection and none on the aesthetic). A difficulty with Moore's account is that it rests on an appeal to intuition, thus failing to give us any reasons why aesthetic experience has so large a place in his account of human flourishing.

On a broader account of the aesthetic experience of art than autonomous views of it provide, its objects are not limited to features picked out by our perceptual faculties alone, still less to such formal features as Beardsley describes, like complexity and unity. On one such view, the work of art is not always a completed entity requiring only our trained aesthetic perception to yield its aesthetic fruit.

On the contrary, for the latter to be possible, we must often make an imaginative contribution of our own, especially by experiencing the work 'from within', as if we were participants in its world, or entering into intimate communion with its characters or creator (Elliott, 1966–7). If one conceives aesthetic experience as not only of perceptual features, but also of imagined human feelings and situations, this helps to provide some kind of non-contingent link between the aesthetic and other human interests.

Among modern writers, Savile (1982, ch. 5) and O'Hear (1988, chs 4–7), both influenced by Schiller, have explored the contributions that aesthetic experience in this larger sense can make to human flourishing, including its moral aspects in a broad sense. Savile stresses the role of the arts in helping to prevent ossification in our assumptions about the world and our affective response to others. The arts help us, as Schiller saw, to feel our way into the situations of others in all their subtlety (Savile, 1982, pp. 96–7). Savile does not go so far as to claim that the arts are *necessary* for this moral end (and indeed this would be hard to show, seeing that such sympathetic involvement could come about through ordinary social intercourse and conversation). But he draws attention to certain advantages that the arts have in this area: they allow us to stand back from the immediate business of life and reflect; they are public objects and thus enable us to share experiences and help to bind us together within a culture; and their sensuous basis gives them an immediacy of appeal (Savile, 1982, pp. 99–100).

Can the aesthetic experience of art help to make us morally better people? We have to tread carefully here. The issue seems in part to depend on empirical evidence which philosophers do not tend to provide. But we also need to be clear about what is at issue. Is it that art can help to turn the egoist into an altruist? Or, since engaging with it often depends on one's *already* possessing a capacity for sympathetic involvement, does it, rather, *reinforce* our altruistic dispositions in us individually and collectively? Prima facie, the second suggestion seems more plausible than the first; but the issue is, finally, an empirical one. There is, perhaps, one *non*-empirical link that can be suggested between the aesthetic and the moral in this area. If it is a precondition of aesthetic experience of the arts on this broader (unlike the narrower) view that one is able sympathetically to enter into others' feelings and situations, then a *constituent* of moral goodness (as the possession of altruistic dispositions) is necessary for such aesthetic engagement. One cannot go further to claim that moral goodness itself is necessary, since one can be capable of sympathetic involvement without being altruistically inclined. Whether this whole argument is sound depends on the supposed link between aesthetic experience and sympathetic involvement.

Savile also draws attention to our need to impose order on our world, not least to integrate our different desires into the overall picture we have of ourselves. The role which Schiller ascribes to form is important in this connection: the formal features of a work cannot be divorced from the multiplicity of the phenomena whose tensions and contrasts they help to order within a unity. Is there more than this *parallel* between a work of art and a flourishing human life? Can experience of the arts help in *promoting* our inner order? We have already seen this issue raised in Beardsley. O'Hear writes about art's ability to resolve certain fundamental tensions in our existence, such as those between the self and the objective world, between feeling and reason and between the individual and the community. He follows Nietzsche (1966, § 7) in advocating the redemptive powers of art, its ability to save us from 'gazing into the horrors of the night' (O'Hear, 1988, p. 140).

Once again, whether art can resolve fundamental tensions is partly an empirical question. O'Hear's talk of redemption seems to accord to art powers once ascribed to religion, and is an instance of the wider, post-Nietzschean, claim that art has replaced religion in modern society. Whether O'Hear brings art *too* close to religion is another question. Should one accept his assumption that a harmonious inner unity is desirable?

Some would argue that conflict and tension are ineradicable from human life, and that we would do better to learn to live intelligently within them than seek an illusory harmony. From this perspective, one role of the arts may be to help us to express and explore our basic tensions, rather than to resolve them. On these issues, a lot may turn on what one is writing into 'resolve' and 'harmony'.

We have been considering conceptual and to some extent empirical relationships between aesthetic experience, largely of the arts, on the one hand and moral goodness and flourishing on the other. Our conclusion that there are some legitimate ways in which non-contingent connections can be established in these areas does not impugn the proposition that aesthetic engagement with a work is something pursued for its own sake. We do not, for instance, read poems as aesthetic objects *in order to* reflect on the ethical life, where the latter is a further goal to which the former is a means; but in choosing so to read them we may well have such ethical ends in mind, accruing as part of our intrinsic experience of the work.

We need, finally, to say a word about moralistic theories of art. Tolstoy (1960, ch. 5) first defines art as a human activity in which 'one man consciously, by means of certain external signs, hands on to others feelings he has lived through' and in which 'other people are infected by these feelings and also experience them.' Later (ch. 8) he writes that 'art is a human activity having for its purpose the transmission to others of the *highest and best* feelings to which men have risen' (italics added). This slide enables him to argue that 'true art' must help to unite people into one universal brotherhood, and allows him to reject as real art works based on the mere enjoyment of beauty. In his application of moral criteria to rate the value of works of art, Tolstoy echoes Plato, who includes in the aesthetic part of his scheme of education in *the Republic* (bks 2 and 3) engagement only with those works which foster the virtues. Tolstoy is even closer, in his socialist sentiments, to Marxist views of art, which rate its value in terms of its contribution to the progress of communism.

That there are, as was argued earlier, various ways in which art may be connected with morality does not justify the stronger claim that the purpose of art, or of 'true art', is to promote moral ends. Moralistic views often bring with them appeals for the censorship of works that go against the favoured moral criteria. To what extent censorship is justified outside a moralistic framework is a further question.

See also 'ART FOR ART'S SAKE'; CENSORSHIP; FUNCTION OF ART; KANT; PLATO; RELIGION AND ART; SCHILLER; TOLSTOY.

BIBLIOGRAPHY

Beardsley, M.: *Aesthetics* (New York: Harcourt Brace & World, 1958).
Elliott, R.K.: 'Aesthetic theory and the experience of art', *Proceedings of the Aristotelian Society*, 67 (1966–7), 112.
Hampshire, S.: *Thought and Action* (London: Chatto & Windus, 1959).
Kant, I.: *Kritik der Urteilskraft* (Berlin: 1790); trans. J.H. Bernard, *Critique of Judgment* (New York: Hafner, 1951).
Moore, G.E.: *Principia Ethica* (Cambridge: Cambridge University Press, 1971).
Nietzsche, F.: *Die Geburt der Tragödie aus dem Geiste der Musik* (Leipzig: E.W. Fritzsch, 1872); trans. W. Kaufmann, *The Birth of Tragedy* (with *The Case of Wagner*) (New York: Vintage Press, 1966).
O'Hear, A.: *The Element of Fire* (London: Routledge & Kegan Paul, 1988).
Plato: *Republic*, in *Collected Dialogues*, ed. E. Hamilton, trans. H. Cairns (New York: Pantheon, 1961).
Savile, A.: *The Test of Time* (Oxford: Clarendon Press, 1982).
Schiller, F.: *On the Aesthetic Education of Man* (1795); trans. E.M. Wilkinson and L.A. Willoughby (Oxford: Clarendon Press, 1967).
Tolstoy, L.: *What is Art?*; trans. A. Maude (Indianapolis: Bobbs-Merrill, 1960).

JOHN WHITE

museums Despite its evident centrality to the modern experience of art, the museum is almost entirely absent, as idea or institution, from the contemporary literature of aesthetics. The word scarcely appears in texts of the most different philosophical persuasions, and a quick survey of the *British Journal of Aesthetics* and the *Journal of Aesthetics and Art Criticism* turns up not a single article devoted to the subject. This is due, fundamentally, to the reigning orthodoxy in aesthetics, which identifies the autonomy of art with a transcendence of social and historical context. And yet it is in large part the museum that, by providing an institutional (and physical) form for art's autonomy, has created the possibility of aesthetic experience as conceptualized by aesthetic theory.

The transformative effect of the museum on the nature of art objects was noted in 1815 by Quatremère de Quincy, for whom the display of works removed from their original political, religious and moral uses would lead inevitably to art 'conceived without passion, executed without warmth, and viewed without interest'. For the collection of artworks without regard for their social functions could mean nothing 'but to say that society has no use for them' (Quatremère de Quincy, 1989, pp. 31, 37). Yet, even while protesting against Napoleon's removal of classical statues from Rome in 1796, Quatremère saw that city as itself a museum: a prototype of history museums, theme parks and allied forms of display that aim at presenting an experience to which the viewer, distanced by history and cultural difference, can only have a spectator's, an aesthetic, relation.

Quatremère's complaint was echoed by John Dewey, who contrasted his own understanding of art as enhanced experience with 'the museum conception of art'. The museum, by separating artworks from their indigenous status, had given them a new one, 'that of being specimens of fine art and nothing else'. By the same token, Dewey was careful to note, it also set these objects 'apart from common experience' and enabled them to 'serve as insignia of taste and certificates of special culture' (Dewey, 1980, pp. 6–9). Although he identified the museum and the notion of art associated with it as peculiar to modern, originally Western, society, Dewey followed the chief convention of aesthetic theory in constructing a theory of art in abstraction from historical specificity and so without further mention of museums.

However, it can well be said that without the museum the idea of art as a cross-cultural, trans-historical phenomenon, which underpins even Dewey's account, would not have come into existence. It is no coincidence that the onset of what has been called the Museum Age coincided, in the later eighteenth century, with the development of the modern system of the arts, as a domain of objects and practices sharing what were now called 'aesthetic properties'. The museum's role in this development was to represent, in the display of the objects collected in it, their essential character as 'works of art'. Its organization came to embody the classification of artworks, by nationality and period, and as between 'high' and 'decorative' arts; over time its inclusion of ever more types of object – ancient Middle Eastern, Asian, 'primitive', 'folk', and so on – actualized the extension of the label 'art' over an expanding domain.

The princely art gallery, from which the museum evolved, typically aimed at dazzling and impressing visitors with the power and wisdom of the prince. Accordingly, the collection was used decoratively; in the hanging of pictures, 'size, colour and subject matter determined the arrangement, and paintings were often cut down or enlarged to fit into the ensemble' (Duncan and Wallach, 1980, p. 455; see Bazin, 1967, ch. 7). In contrast, museums early on made the works displayed the centre of attention. For example, the transformation of the Royal Collection in Vienna into a public museum in 1776 involved the rehanging of paintings in simple, uniform frames, with clear labels, grouped by national schools and art-historical periods.

The official in charge of this installation, Chrétien de Mechel, described his aim in the institution's catalogue as the construction of 'a Repository where the history of art is made visible'. This aim was criticized at the time (in von Rittershausen's commentary on the Vienna collection, 1785) as an elevation of science over aesthetic sensibility (Bazin, 1967, p. 159). An ideal of the museum as an institution dedicated to purely aesthetic experience is visible also in such texts as Goethe's description of the Dresden Gallery in 1768 as a 'temple', a 'place consecrated to the holy ends of art' (Bazin, 1967, p. 160). The conflict between historical knowledge and aesthetic contemplation – a conflict inherent in the modern idea of art, which seeks transcendent meaning in an historically diverse range of objects – has structured debate in the museum field ever since. The former seems the clear victor in the practical terms defined by the average visitor, who rarely pauses in contemplation of an individual work but tends to be drawn by the architecture of the institution towards a survey of the entire collection. None the less, the museum remains at once the repository of art history and a testimony to the supposedly non-historical character of art's meaning.

Whether instituted under royal, papal, parliamentary or revolutionary auspices, the museum was from the start 'one of the fundamental institutions of the modern state' (Bazin, 1967, p. 159). Indeed, as Duncan and Wallach (1980, p. 449) observe, 'in common with ancient ceremonial monuments, museums embody and make visible the idea of the state', often 'by the use of a Roman-derived architectural rhetoric'. On the one hand, the claim of the modern ruling classes to be the rightful heirs of the rulers of the past is expressed by the exhibition of a set of paragons (masterpieces) defining social power in terms of aesthetic value. On the other, aesthetic experience cannot in practice be separated from the social and political meanings imposed by this institution. Just as the state appears as the guardian of culture, art in this context appears as the highest embodiment of the values that modern society calls its own.

R.G. Saisselin has noted resemblances between the museum and that other institution of the modern era, the department store, 'an anti-museum of modern, productive, dynamic capitalist production in which *objets d'art* [are] but one possible line of goods'. Taking the place occupied in earlier European society by the church, palace and villa, these two spaces define the nature of art in modern society, as they 'correspond to the internal contradictions of bourgeois aesthetics which are founded on idealism in a world that in its daily business is anything but ideal' (Saisselin, 1984, pp. 42, 47). Analogously to the way in which the state is supposed to incarnate the social interest in contrast to the competitive conflict of wills that structures civil society, the realm of art signifies the claim of capitalism's higher orders to rise above the confines of commerce as worthy inheritors of the aristocratic culture of the past. Involvement with the autonomous artwork represents detachment from the claims of practical life, even while its ownership and enjoyment require both money and the time made possible by money, and so signify financial success along with cultural superiority.

While the store displays the world of (mass-produced) commodities, the museum presents an array of (unique) items not for sale, but none the less bearing the high prices earned by being objects 'beyond price'. It was the new uses that these items, stripped of any original functions, acquired in the museum – as elements of history and as materials for the construction of a mode of sensibility characterized by distance from material necessity and so free to cultivate responsiveness to experience – that appeared as the autonomy of art. Since the 1970s the museum has changed, with the destabilization of the concept of art visible in the increasing frankness with which the commodity character of artworks is recognized and even celebrated. Museums have responded by such means as their self-promotion as locales for social affairs and their use of space for shops and restaurants. Despite such developments, the museum still both celebrates the innovative individual central to bourgeois ideology and proclaims the freedom of art from the constraints of social history.

With this it also asserts the eternal validity of the modern concept of art as a matter of pure aesthetic appreciation, thus defining human history in terms peculiar to capitalist society. Beginning most notably with the dislocation of art in Europe during the French Revolution and the Napoleonic wars, the great museum collections were shaped by way of conquest and purchase, and today bear testimony to such political–economic processes as imperialistic expansion and the rise of economic powers in North America and Japan. While its omnivorous collecting exemplifies the unique openness of bourgeois culture to the practices and products of other societies, the museum also embodies the redefinition of all cultures in terms of its own. In particular, by exhibiting works of many types and from many disparate cultures in the same space, the museum activates the modern concept of art and so implicitly proclaims the essential, timeless character of modern social constructs generally.

An exhibition space open to all, the museum not only created new modes of object-display but also called for a new collective subject to experience them.

> This new collective in the face of which all future art will exist and agonize is 'the public'. It is for the public that society in the new democratic age retraces in social space – through the creation of zoos, libraries, parks, museums, and concert halls – the amenities of leisure and privilege once held by a few within the private space of moneyed or aristocratic property. (Fisher, 1975, pp. 598–9)

As a public institution, the museum suggests the idea that aesthetic experience is in principle universal; variations in the understanding and appreciation of art seem, then, to be a matter of individual ability, of the 'eye'. But this ability – 'artistic competence', as Bourdieu and Darbel call it – depends on possession of a store of knowledge derived from the formal and informal education in general reserved for the upper classes. Given the class character of culture, the love of art – or the capacity for aesthetic experience – serves to legitimate privilege, in a differentiation of haves from have-nots that renders its social and economic basis invisible. This is why 'in the tiniest details of their morphology and their organization, museums betray their true function, which is to reinforce for some the feeling of belonging and for others the feeling of exclusion' (Bourdieu and Darbel, 1990, p. 112). The possibility that the powers of subjective response called for by the museum's appropriation of aristocratic pleasures could truly become the property of all remains to be realized by a future social transformation.

See also ART HISTORY; CULTURE; DEWEY.

BIBLIOGRAPHY

Bazin, G.: *The Museum Age* (New York: Universe, 1967).

Bourdieu, P. and Darbel, A.: *L'Amour de l'art. Les musées d'art européens et leur public* (Paris: 1969); trans. C. Beattie and N. Merriman, *The Love of Art* (Stanford: Stanford University Press, 1990).

Dewey, J.: *Art as Experience* (New York: 1934); (New York: Perigree, 1980).

Duncan, C. and Wallach, A.: 'The universal survey museum', *Art History*, 3 (1980), 448–74.

Fisher, P.: 'The future's past', *New Literary History*, 6 (1975), 587–606.

Quatremère de Quincy, A.-C.: *Considérations morales sur la destination des ouvrages de l'art* [Moral considerations on the purpose of works of art] (Paris: 1815); (Paris: Fayard, 1989).

Saisselin, R.G.: *The Bourgeois and the Bibelot* (New Brunswick, NJ: Rutgers University Press, 1984).

PAUL MATTICK, JR

musical composition *See* COMPOSITION, MUSICAL.

N

narrative The distinctive mode of discourse that we use when we tell a story, the terms *narrative* and *story* being more or less synonymous as names for the end-product of such discourse. In practice, a completed narrative will nearly always contain other than narrative discourse: in a short story or novel, for example, narrative passages will alternate with descriptive or analytical ones, and with passages of dialogue, all of which form part of a narrative whole but might be analysed into their distinct discursive modes. Pure narrative, every sentence of which takes a narrative form and could be construed as advancing the story nearer to its conclusion, is uncommon; only in the most economical kinds of narrative – jokes are perhaps the best example – are we likely to meet with it.

Narrative is a universal phenomenon, to be found in one form or another in every culture of which we have knowledge, both pre-literate and literate. In societies without writing, oral narratives extend all the way from local fables or legends to cosmological myths and racial epics, which may be memorized and recited by itinerant storytellers. In societies with writing, narrative pervades the whole of culture, and can be found in brief, elementary forms such as the obituary inscription on a gravestone, or in immensely elaborate ones, such as multi-volume works of historiography or of fiction. Our daily lives contain a more regular exposure to narrative than we sometimes notice: we tell or are told anecdotes, rumours, dreams and jokes; we read or watch newspaper and television 'stories'; we fantasize crude narratives to ourselves when we are idle or frustrated; we read or make up stories for children; and so on.

The prevalence of narrative in casual conversation, when speakers give narrative form to some recent or remote experience that they adjudge to be deserving of it, demonstrates the powerful place that it has among us as a means of attracting and keeping the attention of others. Narrative is a strongly sequential form of discourse which creates the expectation in anyone reading or listening to it that a story once begun will be carried on to a satisfying end or resolution. By imposing an order or logic on the events it narrates, it gives meaning to them; narrative indeed may be claimed as the principal means any of us have whereby to 'make sense' of our experience. A life narrated is a life made meaningful.

The events recounted in narrative may be true or invented, or a mixture of the two; narrative discourse itself is neutral in respect of truthfulness. It is the context in which we meet with a particular narrative that determines whether we take it to be true or fictional. The 'story' narrated by a television journalist during a news bulletin we assume to be true; these events have actually happened, and have happened to real people. The story narrated in a novel we assume to be fictional, for we have learnt in childhood that these 'stories' contain make-believe people and events, not historical ones. Much narrative, however, is neither certifiably true nor self-evidently invented. Such frequently are the narratives we recount to one another socially, in the course of which we knowingly 'embroider' certain facts – and in so doing cast doubt on the authenticity of all narrative, inasmuch as it is a form of discourse expressly fashioned so as to influence its hearers or readers, and always liable therefore to sacrifice an austere factuality to rhetorical effectiveness.

A narrative may be characterized, at the simplest level, as a sequence of events extended in time and registering an alteration in some original state of affairs. These events may be narrated either as having happened in the past or, much more rarely, as happening simultaneously with their narration – a running commentary on a sporting event would be an example of instant narrative; or, again rarely, as happening in some hypothetical future. Some narratologists, or theorists of narrative, argue that a single narrated event constitutes a complete narrative: for instance, the narrative sentence, 'The tree fell across the roadway.' This one event registers an altered state of affairs, but hardly seems sufficient on its own; we surely need at least two consecutive events to have what we intuitively recognize to be a story: for instance, 'The tree fell across the roadway. My neighbour drove his new car into it.' The mere collocation of these two sentences suffices to form a narrative, even if in practice a narrator would almost certainly introduce some logical connective in order to tighten the link between them: for instance, 'The tree fell across the roadway and/then/so my neighbour drove his new car into it.'

Mere sequence does not guarantee us a narrative, however; the two (or more) consecutive sentences must have referential elements in common: for instance 'The tree fell across the roadway. The German army marched into Poland' are two consecutive sentences recording events so disparate in location, personnel and magnitude as to fail to form a narrative; though it is worth observing that, once logically connected – for instance, 'The tree fell across the roadway and the next day the German army marched into Poland' – they cohere into at least a parodic form of narrative, which we find comic because of the incongruity between its two conjoined elements. Humour of this kind trades on our assumption that, in narrative, event B does not merely follow event A but follows *from* A: that in narrative, unlike in life or in logic, *post hoc* is invariably *propter hoc*.

When we analyse narrative, a distinction often needs to be made between narrative and narration, or between a story and its telling, as when we say to someone: 'You ruined that story the way you told it.' Such a comment seems to imply that stories exist independently of their telling, that the 'same' story might be told in different ways. But this is a mistaken view. Rather, a particular story might be seen as the sum-total of all its tellings, from which a 'core' narrative common to them all might be derived. Because of the high cultural value we accord to narrative, stories once read or heard invite retelling, and so undergo constant transformation, with new stories being generated by old. Some theorists believe that the 'core' narratives of any culture might be reduced to a few dozen or less, from which all other narratives could be shown to have derived. Narrative is open both to reduction and to potentially endless expansion in retelling, by the removal of existing, or the insertion of fresh, events.

A story may be narrated either in the first person, as in autobiographical writing, or in the third, as in the writing of history or of most fiction; or in a mixture of the two, as in those novels where the perspective on events shifts from chapter to chapter. (Narration is also feasible, though very rarely practised, in the second person, as when fictional detectives tell their fictional suspects: 'You climbed through this window here, and went across to the safe.') The normal narrative tense in English is that known as the 'simple' past, or else 'past definite', which narrates events as being temporally discrete from the moment of their narration: for example, 'I climbed through the window, I went across to the safe.' Narration is possible also in the so-called 'historic present' tense: for example, 'I climb through the window, I go across to the safe' – a narrative device valued for its apparent immediacy.

All narration is the work of a narrator, whether such a figure be explicitly present or not. In first-person narrative, the narrator is the 'I' figure who is telling the story; in third-person narrative, the narrator is only 'implied', since in this case we are being told a story but we never find out who by. And, corresponding to a narrator, present or implied, there has also to be a narratee, present or implied, or someone to whom the story is addressed, narrative being essentially a contractual performance between two or more individuals.

The term 'narrative' is often extended – dubiously, some would say – to describe art forms which are either only partly verbal or not verbal at all: to strip cartoons, church murals or movies, for example. These are held to be narrative because they 'tell' a story, except that they contain little or no narration. A cinema film, for example, is a sequence made up of images and their attendant dialogue, and is only actually narrated on the rare occasions when a 'voice-over' is introduced, to establish certain otherwise unrepresentable narrative connections. For the rest, these quasi-narrative forms might be better classed with drama, where 'stories' are enacted or *shown*, and seldom if ever narrated. The true narration in such cases will be done by ourselves, when we subsequently transform the spectacle we have witnessed into a verbal account for others, and thereby assist in that circulation of narrative which is a principal engine of culture.

See also HUMOUR; TRADITION.

BIBLIOGRAPHY

Booth, Wayne C.: *The Rhetoric of Fiction* (Chicago and London: University of Chicago Press, 1969).
Genette, Gérard: *Figures III* (Paris: 1972); trans. Jane E. Lewis, *Narrative Discourse* (Ithaca, NY, and London: Cornell University Press, 1980).
Mitchell, W.J.T., ed.: *On Narrative* (Chicago and London: University of Chicago Press, 1981).
Scholes R. and Kellogg, R.: *The Nature of Narrative* (New York and London: Oxford University Press, 1966).
Stanzel, F.K.: *Theorie des Erzählens* (Göttingen: 1982); trans. Charlotte Goedsche, *A Theory of Narrative* (Cambridge: Cambridge University Press, 1986).

JOHN STURROCK

Nietzsche, Friedrich (Wilhelm) (1844–1900) German philosopher and poet; at first a champion of Wagner, but later his bitterest critic. Unrecognized during the sane years of his life, he has exerted a huge influence in the twentieth century, for example on existentialism and postmodernism. Nietzsche's thought about art (indeed, his philosophy in general) may be divided into four sharply contrasting periods: an early period centred on *The Birth of Tragedy* (1872); a 'positivistic' period centred on *Human, All-too-Human* (1878); the period of *The Gay Science* (1882–7) and *Thus Spoke Zarathustra* (1883–6); and his last year before the onset of madness, 1888, the central work of which is *Twilight of the Idols*. (It must be added, however, that this opinion, as with almost everything to do with Nietzsche, is highly controversial.)

'THE BIRTH OF TRAGEDY'

Nietzsche's interest in art is marked by an intense seriousness, an attribute he shares with his mentor, Schopenhauer. Fundamentally, he asks but one question: what can art do for life? How can it help us flourish, or at least survive? And he possesses but one evaluative criterion: good art is art which 'promotes' life, bad art that which 'hinders' it. At some stages in his career he sees art as, literally, a life-saving activity, our only salvation from 'nausea and suicide'. At others, he sees it as useless, hostile even, to the promotion of life. At these moments, with the radicalism of a Plato, he does not hesitate to demand its elimination from our culture.

The sense of life as deeply problematic is something Nietzsche took over from the self-confessed pessimist, Schopenhauer. In *The Birth of Tragedy* (alternatively titled *Hellenism and Pessimism*) he emphasizes that the radical insecurity of the individual in the face of the 'terror and horror' of (Darwinian) nature belongs inalienably to its metaphysical essence: 'Socratism', the conviction that science is capable of knowing and even 'correcting' being, is a destructive illusion. History is a mere flux of generation and destruction to which we are powerless to impart direction or significance.

Faced with such nausea-inspiring 'absurdity', we cannot do better than learn from the Greeks. They, though deeply sensitive to the 'wisdom of Silenus' – 'best of all is not to be born, not to be, to be nothing. But the second best for you is to die soon' – not only survived but also constructed a culture the like of which has never since been seen. The Greeks, Nietzsche holds, survived through their art: more specifically, through their two types of art – 'Apollonian', the art of, for example, Homer, and 'Dionysian', the later art of the great tragedians Sophocles and Aeschylus. (The claim that the music dramas of Richard Wagner represent a rebirth of Dionysian art constitutes the main propaganda point of *The Birth of Tragedy*.)

Nietzsche describes Apollonian art as a 'radiant glorification' of the phenomena of human existence by means of which the Greeks 'overcame . . . or at any rate veiled' (Nietzsche, 1966a, § 3) from themselves the horrors of life. In the 'dream-birth' of their gods and heroes they produced a beautiful, 'transfigured' portrait of *themselves* that 'seduced' them into a favourable evaluation of life as such. Typically, Nietzsche elucidates transfiguration in terms of 'illusion' and even 'lies'. But we cannot understand Apollonian seduction as sentimentality, a simple censoring of the horrible, for he also says that in Apollonian art *'all* things, whether good *or evil* [*böse*] are deified' (Nietzsche, 1966a, § 3; italics added). The way to understand this idea of a beautiful illusion that is yet in some way truthful is to think of Uccello's *Battle of San Romano* or of that modern epic, the Western. In art (or, more generally, consciousness) of this kind, war, pain and death exist yet are 'overcome', swamped, by our sense of the power and magnificence, the *style* of its heroes. Dazzled by their beauty, we are desensitized to the horrors they confront.

What now of the Dionysian solution to the problem of living? To understand this, we have to take account of the fact that *The Birth of Tragedy* takes over, assumes as given, Schopenhauer's version of Kantian idealism. According to this, the everyday world of plurality and individuality is mere appearance or phenomenon. Beyond or behind the *principium individuationis* lies reality itself, the monistic thing in itself called by both Schopenhauer and Nietzsche 'the will', and

by the latter also 'the primal unity'. According to the metaphysics in question, this is what constitutes our true identity.

Nietzsche's account of Dionysian art comes as an answer to Aristotle's question as to the nature of the 'tragic effect'. Why is it that we voluntarily subject ourselves to depictions of the terrible in life, the downfall and destruction of human beings of more than usual power and quality? Presumably, we must derive some kind of satisfaction. But what is its nature?

Schopenhauer had classified the tragic effect as the highest species of the 'feeling of the sublime', the feeling of fearless exultation that we sometimes experience when confronting the normally fearful – for example, a storm or waterfall. He, following Kant, explains this as a becoming alive to the 'supersensible', supra-individual aspect of one's being. And Nietzsche does the same: the 'artistic taming of the horrible' is, he says, 'the sublime' (Nietzsche, 1966a, § 7). In tragedy, though forced to witness the destruction of its hero, 'we are not to become rigid with fear: a metaphysical comfort tears us momentarily from the bustle of changing figures. We really are, for a brief moment, the primordial being itself' (Nietzsche, 1966a, § 17). In Greek tragedy this effect is achieved through the singing of the chorus. Though we partially empathize with the tragic hero, our primary identification is with the chorus. This leads us to view the action from a Dionysian, metaphysical perspective, and through this we experience an exultant affirmation of our supra-individual identity. Tragedy has the quasi-religious function of 'redeem[ing] us from the greedy thirst for this existence'. With an 'admonishing gesture' it 'reminds us of another existence and a higher pleasure' (Nietzsche, 1966a, § 21).

'HUMAN, ALL-TO-HUMAN'

In 1876, unable to sustain his friendship with Wagner any longer, Nietzsche abruptly departed from Bayreuth in the middle of its first festival. This dramatic change in his personal life was the outward manifestation of a profound change in philosophical outlook, a change that found expression in *Human, All-too-Human*. *The Birth of Tragedy*, dominated by Schopenhauer's pessimistic transcendentalism and its musico-dramatic expression in Wagner's *Tristan and Isolde*, had been the product and expression of Romantic alienation from worldly reality in general, and from the materialism and scientific optimism of the nineteenth century in particular. But in *Human, All-too-Human* all such 'untimeliness' disappears. The idea of a 'metaphysical world' relative to which nature is mere appearance is held up to ridicule. All that exists is material reality. Moreover, it is a reality in principle capable of being understood, even controlled, by human beings. In short, the hitherto despised position of Socratism comes now to be *occupied* by Nietzsche.

In line with this new-found optimism, art comes to be seen as useless – an object, even, of contempt. Its function, as conceived in *The Birth of Tragedy*, was to *protect* us from the horrors of human reality. But now we need no such protection or 'narcoticizing'. On the contrary, we need to look at reality as unflinchingly as possible. The more we look, particularly, to the metaphysical comforts of art, the less we are inclined to change that in the world which disturbs us. Art, like religion, is the opiate of the neurotic. (Indeed art *is* religion: the *feelings* served and promoted by religion are able to survive because, submerged in the vagueness of art, they have been severed from those cognitive claims that have become ludicrous to the post-Enlightenment thinker.) Thankfully, however, concludes Nietzsche, we are moving into a post-artistic culture. We live in the 'evening twilight of art': 'the scientific man is the further evolution of the artistic' (Nietzsche, 1986, §§ 222–3).

'THE GAY SCIENCE'

Here we confront yet another abrupt shift in Nietzsche's stance towards life and towards art. As 'aesthetic phenomenon', we are told, 'existence is still *bearable* for us.' But without the aestheticization of life, the realization that 'delusion and error are conditions of human

knowledge' would lead us to 'nausea and suicide' (Nietzsche, 1968a, § 107). We are back, in short, with the failure of Socratism: the brief reconciliation is over. We face, once again, our powerlessness ultimately to know and hence to impose significant form upon the world. Its character is 'in all eternity chaos' (Nietzsche, 1968a, § 109).

Faced with this terrible knowledge brought by that intellectual 'honesty' which defines the scientist in general and the philosopher in particular, we must turn from science to art, that 'cult of the untrue' (Nietzsche, 1968a, § 107) – not, or not primarily, the art of artworks, but art, rather, which has our own life as its product. We must learn from artists, learn in particular to utilize 'artistic distance' (Nietzsche, 1968a, §§ 78, 107) so that by standing back from an object 'there is a good deal that one no longer sees and much the eye has to add if we are still to see [anything] . . . at all.' Yet we must be 'wiser' than they. For their subtle powers of transfiguration usually stop with the artwork, whereas 'we want to be poets of our lives' (Nietzsche, 1968a, § 299). We want and need to write for ourselves, in particular, not the suicide-threatening life of honesty, but, rather, a 'mocking, light, fleeting, divinely untroubled, divinely artificial' kind of life that 'like a pure flame licks into unclouded skies'. Above all, we must learn from the Greeks, who knew that to live requires one to 'stop courageously at the surface', to be 'superficial – *out of profundity*' (Nietzsche, 1968a, § 4).

It is not difficult to recognize here a return both to the pessimism of the *The Birth of Tragedy* and to the Apollonian solution of redemption through illusion. As in *The Birth of Tragedy*, however, Nietzsche contemplates a *second* art-solution to the predicament of living. This crucially involves the idea of willing the 'eternal recurrence' of *everything* in one's life (Nietzsche, 1968a, § 341), an idea which may be seen as equivalent to the injunction to *amor fati*, to *love* everything that has happened in one's life – indeed in the world.

How is such 'redemption' of the totality of the past possible? By discovering a 'personal providence' even in the most problematic events in one's past; through seeing 'how palpably always everything that happens to us turns out for the best' (Nietzsche, 1968a, § 277). But to do this one must be an artist: one must script for oneself such a personality that the vicissitudes of one's past acquire a cumulative value rather like a well constructed *Bildungsroman*. Construing one's life so that one can will its eternal recurrence, unlike 'profound superficiality,' is entirely 'honest': one wills, loves *all* of one's life, and there is none of the 'looking away', evasion, falsification, self-deception and repression that is involved in the life of artifice. But it is an honesty achievable only by that ideal fiction, the *Übermensch* (overman). Only such a being would have the 'overflowing' psychic health necessary to incorporate the horrors of the world into a lovable, beautiful whole. We, like Nietzsche's alter ego Zarathustra, remain 'convalescents', unable to will the eternal recurrence. Lacking *übermenschlich* health, *we* cannot but retreat into profound superficiality.

'TWILIGHT OF THE IDOLS'

The idea of the beautifying illusion as a solution to the predicament of living continued to have a powerful hold over Nietzsche in the last year of his productive life: 'Truth is ugly. We possess *art* lest we perish of the truth' (Nietzsche, 1968b, § 822), runs an unpublished note from 1888. But what distinguishes *Twilight of the Idols* from *The Gay Science* is a renewed interest in the tragic effect. What the tragedian communicates, Nietzsche says, is a state of '[being] *without* fear in the face of the fearful . . . courage and freedom of feeling before a powerful enemy, before a sublime calamity' (Nietzsche, 1966b, § 9, p. 24). What is this freedom of feeling? It is 'the will to life rejoicing over its own inexhaustibility . . . be[ing] oneself the eternal joy of becoming'. And, he points out, 'herewith I again touch the point from which I once went forth: *The Birth of Tragedy*' (Nietzsche, 1966b, § 10, p. 5). There is, that is, a cyclical quality to Nietzsche's thought about art: at the end of his career, as at the beginning, he offers us not merely the beautiful but also the

sublime as solutions to the problem of living: not merely the transfiguration of the world of individuals, but also its transcendence.

Different though they are, Nietzsche's Apollonian and Dionysian solutions share with each other (and with Schopenhauer) the desire to escape the actuality of human life. Though he would not wish to admit this, they are both species of – to use his own language – 'romanticism'. For all his tough talk about honesty, courage and facing up to life as the 'will to power', Nietzsche's thought about art is, at the end as at the beginning, the product of a wounded consciousness.

See also FUNCTION OF ART; SCHOPENHAUER; WAGNER.

WRITINGS

All of Nietzsche's works have something to say about art. None are exclusively about it. I list below an (inevitably personal) selection of what seem the chief works from the point of view of art.

The Birth of Tragedy (1872); trans. W. Kaufmann (New York: Vintage Press, 1966a). This volume also contains *The Case of Wagner*.

Thus Spoke Zarathustra (1883–5), *Twilight of the Idols* (1888) and *Nietzsche contra Wagner*, all in *The Portable Nietzsche*, trans. and ed. W. Kaufmann (New York: Vintage Press, 1966b).

The Gay Science (1882); trans. W. Kaufmann (New York: Vintage Press, 1968a).

The Will to Power (1901); trans. W. Kaufmann and R. Hollingdale (New York: Vintage Press, 1968b).

Richard Wagner at Bayreuth (1876); vol. 4 of *Untimely Meditations*, trans. R. Hollingdale, (Cambridge: Cambridge University Press, 1983).

Human, All-too-Human (1878); trans. R. Hollingdale (Cambridge: Cambridge University Press, 1986).

BIBLIOGRAPHY

Heller, Erich: *The Importance of Nietzsche* (Chicago: University of Chicago Press, 1988).

Higgins, Kathleen: *Nietzsche's Zarathustra* (Philadelphia: Temple University Press, 1987).

Nehamas, Alexander: *Nietzsche: Life as Literature* (Cambridge, Mass.: Harvard University Press, 1985).

Schacht, Richard: *Nietzsche* (London: Routledge & Kegan Paul, 1983).

Silk, M.S. and Stern, J.P.: *Nietzsche on Tragedy* (Cambridge: Cambridge University Press, 1981).

Young, Julian: *Nietzsche's Philosophy of Art* (Cambridge: Cambridge University Press, 1992).

JULIAN YOUNG

notation Music has a notation. Painting does not. Ballet could use a notation. Printmaking needs none. Where works of art admit of multiple instances whose identity is not settled by their history of production, a criterion is necessary to determine what qualifies diverse items as instances of a single work.

The need may be most pressing in the performing arts. No two performances are exactly alike. Nor should they be. To be instances of the same work, performances need agree only in certain respects; elsewhere they are free to diverge. A work's score specifies the respects in which its performances are required to agree. However else they may differ, performances that comply with a single score are instances of the same work. Performances that do not, are not. A score, then, constitutes a criterion of work identity. Its primary function is the authoritative identification of a work from one instance to the next.

Authoritative identification requires that scores be both accurate and adequate. A score is accurate only if its verdicts accord for the most part with our antecedent judgements about work identity – only if, that is, it tends to count as instances of a given work performances that we already consider instances of that work, and to exclude as instances of that work performances that we already exclude. It is adequate only if it

provides a suitable basis for deciding what performances are and what performances are not instances of the work – only if, that is, it enables us to decide hitherto undecided cases. Accuracy turns on fit with precedent. The role of notation is to ensure adequacy.

SYNTAX

A symbol system consists of characters, some of them denotational. If no mark is an instance of more than one of its characters, the system is syntactically disjoint. In that case, all marks belonging to the same character are interchangeable without syntactic effect. They are tokens of the same type. Typically, of course, characters can combine to form other characters, elementary characters being components of complex ones. Such combination occasions no violation of disjointness, for part and whole are not freely interchangeable. C is part of CDE, but is not the same character as, because not freely interchangeable with, CDE. If, for each mark, it is possible to ascertain which, if any, of the system's characters that mark belongs to, the system is syntactically differentiated. We can then tell whether two marks belong to the same character – whether, that is, they are tokens of the same type.

Notations must be syntactically disjoint and differentiated. A score cannot authoritatively identify a work unless it is determinate and decidable whether divergent inscriptions are copies of the same score.

SEMANTICS

If performances of distinct works complied with a single score, that score would be ambiguous. In that case, compliance with a particular score would not settle the question of work identity. For from the fact that two performances complied with the same score, it would not follow that they were instances of the same work. If scores are to perform their primary function, notations must be unambiguous. Performances of at most one work can comply with any score.

If a single performance complied with

distinct (inequivalent) scores, it would be an instance of more than one work. It would be the same work as each of several performances that were not the same work as each other. In that case, a single performance, or indeed any sample class of performances, would be insufficient to fix the identity of the work performed. To preclude this possibility, a notation must be semantically disjoint: its compliance classes must not intersect. Then a performance cannot comply with divergent scores, nor, therefore, be an instance of more than one work. Redundancy, however, is permissible. A performance in a redundant notation complies with several scores. But because the scores in question are coextensive, it belongs to only one compliance class. Since all and only members of the one class comply with the several scores, work identity remains determinate. All and only members of the class are instances of the work.

A notation's compliance classes must be differentiated. It must be possible to ascertain which, if any, of a notation's characters a given performance complies with. Otherwise we cannot tell whether a given performance answers to a particular score or whether two performances answer to the same score. Semantic differentiation mandates a lower bound on the differences a system is prepared to recognize. In a system that admits of infinite precision, we can never fully settle whether an element corresponds to a given character or to one of its infinitely close neighbours. Were scores symbols in such a system, we could never tell what score a performance complied with, hence never tell what work a performance was an instance of.

In sum, a notation is syntactically disjoint and differentiated, semantically disjoint, differentiated, and unambiguous. Because scores are characters of a notation, it is determinate and decidable what constitutes being the same score, determinate and decidable what constitutes complying with the same score. A score defines a work. It provides, moreover, a privileged definition. Each performance determines a unique score (or class of coextensive scores) and each score a unique class of performances. Every chain from performance to score to performance to

score links the same class of inscriptions with the same class of performances. The inscriptions are instances of the score; the performances, instances of the work.

MUSIC

Traditional Western musical scores are largely, but not fully, notational. The syntactic requirements are clearly met. No mark belongs to more than one character; and no mark is counted part of a score unless it is possible to identify the character it belongs to. But complications arise in the semantic realm. The same piano tone complies with C-sharp and D-flat. Different violin tones comply with the two notes. This threatens semantic disjointness. For evidently some C-sharps are D-flats and some are not. If, however, instrumentation is construed as part of the score, the difficulty evaporates. Since no piano tone complies with any violin note, the compliance classes of piano C-sharp and violin C-sharp do not intersect.

Although the full range of musical sounds is dense, it does not follow that musical scores lack semantic differentiation. For differentiation turns on the way those sounds are classed as compliants of a single note, not on whether there are discernible or indiscernible differences among compliants. Music scored for piano recognizes but one pitch between C and D; music scored for violin, two. The sounds from a dense realm are thus forced into a limited number of compliance classes. So long as it is possible to identify the note with which any given tone complies, pitches are semantically differentiated.

Notes specify relative duration as well as pitch. If there is no lower bound on the differences in relative duration that musical notation recognizes – if the sequence: whole note, half note, quarter note . . . is endless – semantic differentiation of relative duration is lost. In practice, of course, no score mandates infinitely fine differences in duration. By elevating this limit in practice to one of principle, differentiation can be preserved.

Notes, rests, key and time signatures can, evidently, be construed as notational. But scores contain some symbols, such as verbal indications of tempo and volume, that resist a notational reading. The terminology is semantically non-disjoint, for a single passage can comply with several non-coextensive terms. Since tempo and volume can be prescribed to any degree of precision, the terminology is non-differentiated as well. And some of the terms are ambiguous. 'Andantino', for example, sometimes denotes a slower tempo than 'andante', sometimes a faster one. From a given performance, then, it would be impossible to tell what the score's verbal indications of tempo and volume were.

Notationality is preserved if such symbols are construed not as constituents of the score proper, but as recommendations as to how it is to be performed. In that case, however, otherwise correct performances that do not conform to the score's verbal indications will still be performances of the work. Other signs are handled similarly. Where possible, they are construed so as to comply with the requirements of notationality. Otherwise, they are considered extrinsic to the score, and consigned to an advisory position.

Not all so-called scores are notational. Where there is no minimal unit of significance, where every difference in certain respects marks a different compliance class, as is evidently the case in musical graphics, the 'scores' are non-notational. It is impossible to tell whether a performance complies with, or merely approximates, such a score.

DANCE

Like music, dance works admit of multiple performances distant in time and space. So dance, too, would presumably benefit from the determinacy and decidability a notation provides. In the absence of a notation, a dancer learns a role from someone who already knows it. He learns, that is, to copy his mentor's performance. But not every aspect of the mentor's performance is part of the dance proper. Some features belong to the mentor's interpretation of it. Without a notation, however, a student has no way to distinguish constitutive from contingent properties of the performance. There is no telling what features of a performance must be replicated to perform the same work, or whether the student's performance agrees closely enough in the proper respects.

A number of dance notations have been formulated. None has gained the hegemony of standard musical notation. As yet, conformity with a score is not the accepted criterion of identity for works in the dance.

See also PERFORMANCE; SYMBOL.

BIBLIOGRAPHY

Benesh, Rudolf and Benesh, Joan: *An Introduction to Dance Notation* (London: Adam & Charles Black, 1956).
Elgin, Catherine Z.: *With Reference to Reference* (Indianapolis: Hackett, 1983).
Goodman, Nelson: *Languages of Art* (Indianapolis: Hackett, 1976).
Karkoschka, Erhardt: *Das Schriftsbild der Neuen Musik* (Celle: Herman Moeck, 1966).
Laban, Rudolf: *Principles of Dance and Movement Notation* (London: Macdonald & Evans, 1956).

CATHERINE Z. ELGIN

O

ontology of artworks Branch of aesthetics which examines the kind(s) of existence possessed by works of art (including literary and musical works). Not until the twentieth century did the ontology of artworks become a regular and sustained topic of discussion among philosophers. Of course, one finds remarks on the topic in the writings of earlier philosophers; but those remarks were either undeveloped or, as in the case of Hegel, not picked up by other philosophers. In this century, Roman Ingarden has been far and away the most prominent figure on the Continent and, after him, Benedetto Croce. By contrast, in the Anglo-American tradition contributions have come from many different quarters, and no one thinker has stood out from the others in the way that Ingarden has stood out among Continental philosophers.

The phenomena which a satisfactory ontology of art must organize and account for are extraordinarily rich and diverse. Let us begin with a quick survey, couched in ordinary language, of those phenomena; and then move on to look at some of the theories.

In several of the arts – music, dance and drama, for example – we regularly work with the distinction between a performance of something and that which is (or can be) performed. Let us call the latter a *performable*. In music, at least, one may have either of two quite different entities in mind when speaking of a *performance*. One may have in mind an *act of performing* the work. Or one may have in mind an *occurrence* of the work performed. Let us regiment our use of the language a bit, and call only the latter a *performance*.

That we do in fact operate with the distinction between performables and performances is clear from the following three considerations (of which the second and third are, strictly speaking, applications of the first).

First, a performance will always diverge in certain of its properties from the work of which it is a performance; and often, where it need not diverge, it will in fact diverge. Thus it comes about that critics make such remarks as 'All the energy of the first movement of the concerto was missing in last night's performance.' To speak thus is to work with a performable/performance distinction, and to claim that, though the first movement of the performable has the property of being energetic, the first movement of last night's performance lacked that property.

Second, our way of using the language of identity and diversity indicates that we are working with the performable/performance distinction. For we speak of the *same* work as having *distinct* performances (occurrences). But in general, two distinct things cannot both be identical with some one thing. That leaves open the abstract possibility that one of the performances is identical with the performable and the other is not; but that just seems incoherent. The conclusion must be that our way of using the concepts of identity and diversity in speaking of the performance arts indicates that we do indeed operate with a distinction between performables and performances.

Third, our way of using the concept of *existence* indicates the same thing. We often speak of works as existing *before* any performance of them has taken place. Then, after the work has existed for some time, a performance of it takes place; after a while, the performance is over, while the work endures. Here too, then, we assume the distinction. It is worth adding that in dance and drama we regularly find reason to introduce an entity which comes in between the work and its performances. We speak of a *production*. And a certain production of a work is neither the work itself nor is it a particular performance. (It is, in fact, another sort of performable.)

In certain of the non-performing arts we work with distinctions closely similar to the performable/performance distinction. When dealing with graphic art prints, for example, we regularly distinguish between a particular *impression* and the *work* of which it is one of the impressions. When dealing with cast sculpture, we distinguish between a particular casting and that work of which it is one of the castings. And now and then in architecture we find need for a counterpart distinction – between, say, an example of one of Frank Lloyd Wright's usonian houses, and that Usonian House itself of which the house is one of the examples.

The considerations which compel these distinctions are, in their structure, exactly the same as those which compelled the distinction between performables and their performances. A given impression of a print may well have come into existence after the print itself had been created, and may well go out of existence before the print does. We speak of two *different* castings of the *same* sculpture. And a particular usonian house may, to cope with the high rainfall of its climate, have a drain spout where the Usonian House itself, of which it is an example, has none. In literature and film we also work with such distinctions. For most works of literature, there are many *copies* of the same literary work – and when there are not in fact many copies, always there could be. And in film there are many copies of the same work of cinematic art – or, once again, if there are not, that is purely accidental; there could be.

It will be convenient to have one set of terms to mark all these different, but parallel, distinctions. Let us follow an increasingly common practice, and borrow from C.S. Peirce the terms 'type' and 'token'. Peirce introduced these terms to mark the distinction between a word understood as something which can be repeatedly inscribed or pronounced, and a word understood as an inscription or sounding out. The former he called a *type* and the latter he called a *token*. We will call an impression of an art print a

token, and the work of which it is an impression, a *type*; a performance of musical work a *token*, the work of which it is a performance, a *type*; and so on.

One notices a tendency, in those who first begin reflecting on the ontology of artworks, to think that the performed work in music is the same as its score, when there is a score – as there is a tendency to think of the performed work in drama as identical with its script and the built work in architecture with its drawing. But, quite clearly, this is mistaken; and our ordinary distinction between a work of music and its score, a work of drama and its script, and so on, is to be honoured. For not only may a work of music exist without ever having been scored; all the score impressions may be destroyed and the work still endure – by virtue, for example, of being lodged in people's memories. It may be added that the type/token distinction also has applications to scores, scripts and drawings.

We speak of paintings and non-cast sculptures differently. Here we do not operate with anything like the type/token distinction. Of course, there are reproductions of paintings and copies of non-cast sculptures. But these are not originals in the way in which impressions of prints and castings of sculptures are originals. In the field of graphic art prints we distinguish between an impression and a reproduction of the impression; this is exactly like the distinction between a painting and a reproduction of the painting. What is missing in our talk of paintings is that other distinction which we work with in the field of graphic arts – the distinction between an original impression of a print and the print of which it is an impression.

The type/token distinction has even more pervasive application in the arts than so far indicated. And where it does have application, it is often worth reflecting on the subtle differences in how the distinction finds application. So the above must be taken as an *indication* of the phenomena which an ontology of artworks must take into account, not as an ample and suitably qualified *description* of the phenomena.

In my statement of the phenomena I have

highlighted the distinction between those arts in which we make use of one or another version of the type/token distinction, and those arts such as painting in which we do not make use of any such distinction. Some of those who have written on the ontology of art have regarded this distinction as not ontologically significant, and have gone on to develop ontologies of artworks which are uniform across the distinct arts. We may call them *uniform* theories – in distinction from non-uniform theories. Of course, there may be uniformity across the arts with respect to the type/token distinction and non-uniformity in respect to other ontologically significant distinctions; for example, some of the arts are obviously temporal in ways that others are not. Unfortunately, it will be necessary here to exclude those other distinctions from consideration. In turn, a good many of the uniform theories which have been developed in our century have also been *unitive*, in the sense that they deny any fundamental ontological distinction as that between types and tokens. Let us begin by considering some of these uniform and unitive theories.

In the first half of the twentieth century, *mentalistic* theories of the ontological nature of artworks enjoyed a good deal of popularity. We can take the theory of R.G. Collingwood as representative. In *The Principles of Art*, Collingwood observed that one can compose tunes and poems in one's head; he went on from there, and from a few other considerations, to conclude that the work of art *is* a mental object. He conceded, of course, that musicians make sounds with instruments, that painters cause viscous pigment to adhere to canvas, that sculptors chisel away at marble and wood, and so forth. But no such physical entities are works of art, insisted Collingwood; they are devices which serve, when perceived with appropriate imagination, to communicate a work of art from one mind to another – from the creator's mind to the minds of members of the public. On this view, performances, impressions, castings, copies and the like are not works of art – as paintings are not. They are, all of them, 'mere' devices for transmitting the work of art from the mind of the artist to the minds of his or her public.

Collingwood's theory has a rather large number of consequences which, in combination or singly, have by most thinkers been regarded as a *reductio ad absurdum*. Among such are these: on this view one can, in principle, create a 'painting' entirely in one's head, without ever making pigment adhere to surface; and the object which one hangs on a wall and puts in a crate for shipping to an art show is not a work of art. What is called 'Van Gogh's *Starry Night*' does not hang on any wall. Furthermore, on this view, a work is not in existence when no one has it in mind. Works typically go in and out of existence; they exist intermittently.

Nominalistic theories of the ontology of artworks deny that there are any such entities as those we have singled out as *types*; there are only tokens. Thus they too are unitive uniform theories. Of course, as indicated above, it certainly *appears* that in our discourse about the arts we commit ourselves to the existence of types. Thus, to make his theory plausible, the nominalist has to make it seem plausible that we do not thus commit ourselves – for example, by making it seem plausible that reductive analyses can be given of all true sentences which appear to commit their users to the existence of types – a 'reductive analysis' of such a sentence being another sentence which asserts the same proposition but clearly does not commit its users to the existence of types. It is probably fair to say that no nominalist theorists have in fact made it seem plausible that reductive analyses can be given of all such sentences. Nelson Goodman is the most aggressively nominalistic of all those who have written about the arts. But nominalism functions for Goodman more as ideal than as project; and, certainly, it is not in his hands a *completed* project. In his *Languages of Art* Goodman makes clear his commitment to a nominalistic ontology. But he says that in the book he will speak with the 'vulgar' rather than with the 'learned'; and he offers very few suggestions as to how vulgar talk might be replaced with learned.

A complex variant on the more or less

standard nominalism to which Goodman is attracted has been developed by Joseph Margolis. On Margolis's view, works of art are all tokens of a special sort; namely, they are 'culturally emergent entities' which, though embodied in physical objects, are not to be identified with those objects. Margolis concedes that in our discourse about the arts we also refer to types; but in his ontology he insists that there exist no such entities. As he realizes, this commits him to the position that it is possible to refer to entities that do not exist – indeed, to entities that in no sense whatsoever 'are'.

The observation that the nominalist tries to achieve a unitive uniform theory by denying the existence of types leads one to wonder whether anyone has tried to achieve a unitive uniform theory by moving in the opposite direction – denying tokens rather than types. Exactly such a theory has recently been proposed by George Currie in *An Ontology of Art*. Currie thinks that an artist, in composing or creating, discovers a certain structure – of words, of sounds, of colours, or whatever. He adds that the artist always does this in a certain way; and he insists that not only is *what* the artist discovers relevant to aesthetic appreciation, but also some features of *how* he discovers it are relevant. He calls those features that are thus relevant the artist's *heuristic path*. And his ontological proposal is that works of art are action types of the following sort: someone's discovering a certain structure via a certain heuristic path. Discoveries of the same structure via different heuristic paths are instances of different works, as are discoveries of different structures via the same heuristic path. The structures as such are not works at all.

Currie is led to this unusual view from his conviction that 'distinct works may possess the same structure.' For example, though it is theoretically possible that Beethoven and Brahms should independently have discovered and composed the same musical structure, their works would none the less have different properties – for instance, Brahms' might be Liszt-influenced, Beethoven's would not be. But one and the same entity cannot both have and lack a certain property. 'In cases like that,' says Currie (1989, p. 65), 'what differentiates the works is the circumstances in which the composer or author arrived at the structure.'

But is it decisively clear that the property we wish to attribute to what Brahms composed is *being Liszt-influenced*? May it not rather be the relational property of *being such that this composing of it was Liszt-influenced*? Obviously, one and the same entity may have both that property and this other one: *being such that that composing of it was not Liszt-influenced*. Thus is is questionable that the argument even gets off the ground. To this we may add that the theory has a good many counter-intuitive consequences; for example, since on this view a work of music is a *composing*, and composings are not the sorts of things that can be heard, it follows that works of music cannot be heard.

The views that we have considered are all *unitive* uniform theories. A *dualist* uniform theory, by contrast, would contend that, though our ordinary ways of speaking do not reveal it, the type/token distinction does in fact have application in the arts of painting and non-cast sculpture. It is rather often said, for example, that we might well have a technology for making *copies* of paintings – not reproductions, but copies – looking as much like the 'original' as you please. All those copies would then be 'originals', in the same way that all the impressions of a print are 'originals'; and it is purely accidental, of no ontological significance, that we have no such technology – or that we do have it but do not use it.

But the argument is fallacious, in an interesting way. What brings it about that a set of print impressions are all impressions of the same print is not that they are indiscernibly alike; they may be very far from that. So, too, what brings it about that a series of musical performances are all performances of the same work is not that they sound indiscernibly alike; they may sound very different indeed. Two performances are performances of the same work if they are brought about under the guidance of the same set of rules for correctness in performance. And they

313

may satisfy that condition, while yet sounding very different. Our practice of painting might have been such that painters ordained rules for correctness of instances; but in fact it is not like that.

A *non-uniform* theory of the ontology of artworks will regard the type/token distinction as present in some of the arts and not in others. It turns out that the main work of accounting for this difference will have to be done by an appropriate theory of the nature of artistic types. Ingarden on the Continent, and I myself in the Anglo-American tradition, have developed the most elaborate theories of artistic types. Taking as my cue the phenomenon just mentioned of *rules for correctness*, I argue that artistic types are a special sort of *kinds*; I call them *norm* kinds. It is typical of natural kinds that there can be both well formed and malformed examples; there are, for instance, malformed examples of the horse. In a similar way, there are incorrect performances of musical and dramatic works, defective castings of sculptures, and so on. Thus, artistic types are not *sets*; for a set cannot have different members from those it does have, whereas artistic types can have more or fewer tokens than they do have. Artistic types are instead *kinds*; for kinds can have more or fewer examples than they do have. But, more specifically, they are *norm kinds*. One composes a work of music by selecting a set of rules for correctness of (musical) performance; thereby one selects a certain norm kind. That, then, is the work that one has composed, which is then available for performance.

Many significant positions staked out during the twentieth century in the extraordinarily rich discussion concerning the ontology of artworks have not been presented here; many significant contributors to the discussion have not been cited. The above is merely an indication of the structure of the options that have been developed concerning the most fundamental issue in the ontology of artworks.

See also COLLINGWOOD; CROCE; DEFINITION OF 'ART'; INGARDEN; PERFORMANCE.

BIBLIOGRAPHY

Collingwood, R.G.: *The Principles of Art* (Oxford: Oxford University Press, 1970).
Currie, George: *An Ontology of Art* (New York: St Martin's Press, 1989).
Goodman, Nelson: *Languages of Art* (New York: Bobbs-Merrill, 1968).
Ingarden, Roman: *The Literary Work of Art* (Evanston, Ill.: Northwestern University Press, 1973).
Levinson, Jerrold: *Music, Art, and Metaphysics* (Ithaca, NY: Cornell University Press, 1990).
Margolis, Joseph: *Art and Philosophy* (Atlantic Highlands, NJ: Humanities Press, 1980).
Wollheim, Richard: *Art and Its Objects* (New York: Harper & Row, 1971).
Wolterstorff, Nicholas: *Works and Worlds of Art* (Oxford: Clarendon Press, 1980).

NICHOLAS WOLTERSTORFF

oriental aesthetics *See* CHINESE AND JAPANESE AESTHETICS; INDIAN AESTHETICS.

originality An influential segment of the literature that deals with originality in the arts treats 'original' as a synonym for 'authentic', as in 'the authentic *Portrait of Madam Cézanne* by Roy Lichtenstein'. Intimately allied with issues of authenticity are ontological questions regarding if and when copies, for example, are tokens of originals. Neither the notion of originality involved in discussions of authenticity, nor the notion of originality required by the view that nothing is art unless it is original, will be discussed here. This latter view must either employ a notion of originality so weak as to be uninteresting, or admit that there are vastly fewer works of art than ordinarily thought. (There may, indeed, be far fewer works of art than most people think, but this is not at issue here either.) What will be considered here are notions of originality compatible with the view that a work of art can be authentic without being original. These notions of originality occur in questions about the relevance of a work of art's originality to its artistic value.

In one sense, acknowledging a work of art's originality is necessarily according it positive artistic value merely in virtue of its being original. Francis Sparshott suggests a rationale for this practice by introducing an analogy between a work of art's originality and the special sort of uniqueness a loved one has for his or her lover. Sparshott explains that someone is loved for the special way he or she does the things that we all do. Unfortunately, this explanation tends to undermine the essentially romantic and non-rational notion initially invoked by the analogy. It does this by overlooking the fact that what is compelling about the analogy is its recognition that we possess a notion of the loved one for which he or she is irreplaceable in our affections, even by an exact replica (a notion we hold independently of any philosophical concern with whether such a replica is possible). It is this notion of highly romanticized irreplaceability that is central to one sort of artistic virtue that people accord works of arts when they see them as being true originals. (A critique of the weight that philosophers should give to the romantic notion of originality would have to address the question of the notion's non-rationality.)

Less romantic versions of the notion of originality assume either that some measure of artistic value accompanies an object's being the first of its kind, or that being the first of its kind is necessary to the possibility that something has artistic value. Depending on which version you prefer, an object is original if it is the historically first token of a design type; or is the first object to present previously unknown information; or is the first object to show its content in the way that it does (which content may be something widely known); or is the first object to contain specific (exhibited or non-exhibited, positive or negative) artistic properties; or is a member of a set of objects that is the first set of objects in a specific style created by a specific artist. The question is, why should an object's merely being the first of its kind in any of these ways count as an artistic virtue (or as something necessary to an object's having artistic value)? With two exceptions, it is obvious that we cannot answer this question by appealing to the artistic value that a work would possess were it not the first

of its kind, so it seems that what often is valued by those people who cherish originality is the mere fact of a work of art's being the first of its kind.

The first exception to this is the case where a work of art's being the first of its kind is held to imply, for one theory-specific reason or another, that the object is the only possible instance of its kind (see Goodman, 1968, ch. 3, for example). In such cases originality amounts to de-romanticized irreplaceability. But it is not clear why any degree of artistic value should follow from the fact that a work of art merely is of a unique kind that cannot be replicated.

The second exception is the view that something is art only if it has a unique place in art history, a place something has only if it constitutes a turning point in art history. On this view the value of an object's being the first of its kind is clear enough, since the value of originality is the value something has because it constitutes a turning point in art history. However, this view is one version of the approach dismissed earlier because of its unreasonable implications regarding how many of the objects in art galleries, and so on, really are works of art. So the question remains, what is the artistic value merely of something's being the first of its kind for the very large number of works that, while not turning points in art history, none the less are first in one of the ways listed above?

The significance that an original work of art has for thoroughly knowledgeable, up-to-date art viewers as a source of something not previously experienced is genuine enough, whatever the work is like; but by itself this kind of significance seems insufficient to ground even the weakest of positive artistic judgements. First, this value is too often fleeting, and thus cannot account for the staying power of some works of art that critics seek to explain by emphasizing these works' originality. Second, since this sort of significance is shared by all objects that provide knowledgeable people with novel experiences, it is questionable whether this sort of originality should be held to contribute to an object's artistic value, as opposed to some other, more generic, sort of value.

Suppose that the significance of a work of art's being the first of its kind ultimately rests in the role the work plays in providing access to an artist's creative acts, such as design acts that are the first of their kind, for example. In this case, what is held to be of artistic value is the *artist's* originality. Artistic value derives from someone's being the first person to accomplish creative acts of this or that kind. Here it is again questionable whether this sort of originality should be held to contribute to an object's artistic value, as opposed to some more generic sort of value. But the deeper question is why someone's being the first person to perform a given sort of action matters at all to the value of the action or to the person performing it. If we are not to indulge in the romantic notion of originality suggested earlier, perhaps the best explanation left of why originality is counted an artistic virtue in its own right involves an equally romanticized notion of competitiveness.

It may be that in concerning ourselves with works of art we engage in a long-standing practice that counts as a genuine achievement someone's being the first person to accomplish anything whatsoever (where 'achievement' imputes virtue to the person whose achievement it is). An account of why this practice exists might attempt to track our development as highly competitive creatures, and might explain our valuing originality in art and artists as a consequence of the value we find in the ability of someone or something to dominate any situation. This value, which is deeply embedded in the love of athletic contests, for example, may well be the basis for the value that originality in art has to people in certain art-making cultures (just those cultures that place special value on a work of art's originality). If so, the importance of originality in art does not differ significantly from the importance of winning in athletics. Nor, more generally, does this value differ signficantly from what is acknowledged by our respect and admiration for people who can dominate other people and situations.

But if this account, or one relevantly like it, does reveal the basis for the popular view that originality in art either confers or at least is necessary to artistic value, it also calls into question a key working assumption of this discussion: that artistic value in the form of originality is something to be sought and praised.

See also AUTHENTICITY OF THE ARTWORK; CREATIVITY; FORGERIES.

BIBLIOGRAPHY

Goodman, Nelson: *Languages of Art* (Indianapolis: Bobbs-Merrill, 1968).

Hoaglund, John: 'Originality and aesthetic value', *British Journal of Aesthetics*, 16 (1976), 46–55.

Janson, H.W.: 'Originality as a ground for judgment of excellence', *Art and Philosophy*, ed. Sidney Hook (New York: New York University Press, 1966).

Lessing, Alfred: 'What is wrong with a forgery', *The Forger's Art*, ed. Denis Dutton (Berkeley, Calif.: University of California Press, 1983), pp. 58–76.

Levinson, Jerrold: 'Aesthetic uniqueness', *Journal of Aesthetics and Art Criticism*, 38 (1980), 435–50.

Sparshott, Francis: *The Theory of the Arts* (Princeton, NJ: Princeton University Press, 1982).

Sparshott, Francis: 'The disappointed art lover', *The Forger's Art*, ed. Dennis Dutton (Berkeley, Calif.: University of California Press, 1983), pp. 246–63.

GEORGE BAILEY

P

perception   It is virtually truistic that our experience of artworks (or of non-linguistic artworks, anyway) has something essentially to do with our perception of them. David Prall, for example, writes that 'aesthetic experience [is] the experience of the surface of our world directly apprehended, and this surface is always, it would seem, to some degree pleasant or unpleasant to sense in immediate perception' (Prall, 1967, p. 20). In order to cast as wide a net as possible over the subject of perception in the arts, the present discussion is divided into three sections, each devoted to an issue of broad significance. The first section treats the contested relationship between perception and cognition in the apprehension of a work of art; the second considers some respects in which the character of perceptual processing determines what we can *understand* or *make sense of* in a work; and the third considers a respect in which the character of perceptual processing determines what we can *say* about a work of art.

PERCEPTION AND COGNITION IN THE APPREHENSION OF AN ARTWORK

A dispute of central importance in the philosophy of art concerns the relationship between perception and cognition; specifically, it concerns the extent to which perception is 'cognitively penetrable'. Inspired by so-called new-look psychological theories of the 1950s and 1960s, Nelson Goodman and Ernst Gombrich (among others) have argued that the way an object looks is inevitably influenced by the ways we believe or expect or want it to look. Goodman writes:

> The catch here, as Ernst Gombrich insists, is that there is no innocent eye. The eye comes always ancient to its work, obsessed by its own past and by old and new insinuations of the ear, nose, tongue, fingers, heart, and brain, . . . Not only how but what it sees is regulated by need and prejudice. It selects, rejects, organizes, discriminates, associates, classifies, analyzes, constructs, . . . reception and interpretation are not separable operations. (Goodman, 1968, pp. 8–9)

On this ground, Goodman attacks the traditional view that an artwork (for instance, a painting) pictorially represents an object in virtue of *copying* or '*mirroring*' the way it looks. (Gombrich takes a similar line.) Any seeing of an object is inevitably a cognition-laden 'seeing-as', and, among other problems, seeings-as are not the sort of thing that can be copied; in other words, the idea of copying the way an object looks involves a category mistake:

> Something is wrong with the very notion of copying any [aspect of an object]. For an aspect is not just the object-from-a-given-distance-and-angle-and-in-a-given-light; it is the object as we look upon or conceive it, a version or construal of the object. In representing an object, we do not copy such a construal or interpretation – we achieve it. . . . To ask me to copy x [construed] as a so-and-so is a little like asking me to sell something as a gift. (Goodman, 1968, p. 9)

Rather, Goodman contends, a work of art is representational (as opposed to, say, descriptive) primarily in virtue of its membership in a symbol system possessing certain syntactic and semantic properties; specifically, a representational work belongs to a syntactically and semantically *dense* or *analogue*

317

symbolic system (see Goodman, 1968, pp. 226–7, for instance). Furthermore, such a work is *realistic* not in virtue of resembling ('looking like') its object nor, generally speaking, in virtue of affording a visual experience relevantly similar to that afforded by its object, but rather in virtue of the *familiarity* of the symbolic conventions it employs. To take an extreme example, a painting of a red hat, done in red paint, is more realistic than an otherwise identical painting in green paint, not because the former looks more like the hat, but because we are habituated to the convention of using red paint to depict red objects. If artists typically produced colour-reversed paintings, these would eventually come to be more realistic than the colour-normal ones (see Goodman, 1968, pp. 35–6, for instance).

Subsequent research in psychology has called the new-look approaches seriously into question, however. A body of data has emerged indicating that a significant portion of our perceptual processing may be sealed off from deeper cognitive processes – 'encapsulated', as Jerry Fodor puts it. Assembling evidence from a variety of perceptual domains, Fodor (1983) shows that at least some relatively 'shallow' perceptual representations (for example, of the shapes, colours, pitches, and timbres of objects, as well as the logico-syntactic forms of linguistic utterances) may be largely impermeable to the influence of cognitive systems like belief, memory, and decision-making. (A crude but clear illustration is provided by the persistence of certain visual illusions; for instance, the arrows in the Muller–Lyre illusion continue to look different in length even when we know they are identical.) In addition, there is evidence to suggest a variety of species-wide structures in human perception. Just for example, there appear to be eleven 'basic' or 'universal' colour categories (see Hardin, 1988, pp. 155–69); local stresses are probably heard as strong beats (*ceteris paribus*) by any normal human listener, and there appear to be roughly twelve basic musical interval categories. In the musical realm, E.M. Burns and W.D. Ward have found that

observers are not, in general, able to categorize [melodic intervals] to a finer degree than chromatic [semitones], . . . The inability to categorize the isolated intervals more precisely is also true of Indian musicians . . . whose scales theoretically include microtonal variations of certain intervals, . . . the use of a relatively small number of discrete pitch relationships in music is probably dictated by inherent limitations on the processing of high information-load stimuli by human sensory systems (Burns and Ward, 1982, pp. 249, 264).

None of this is meant to deny that perception 'selects, rejects, classifies, constructs', and so forth. Consider, for instance, the results of an experiment by Roger Shepard and Daniel Jordan (1984). Shepard and Jordan found that certain logarithmically uniform frequency steps between successively sounded tones were heard as non-uniform; in other words, although the tonal stimuli were separated by equal frequency steps, listeners heard them as unequally spaced. Moreover, the pattern of perceived 'inequalities' strongly suggested that the tones were being mapped into a mental template or schema representing the (non-uniform) steps of a diatonic musical scale. It is plausible to suppose that similar operations are implicated in real-time music perception. The important point at present, however, is that such perceptual 'classifications' are likely to be cognitively impenetrable; for example, it is likely that listeners will continue to hear the sounded intervals as non-uniform in size even after being told they are identical. So although perception is doubtless cognitively penetrable at many places – your (explicit) knowledge that a painting is a full figure portrait can visually sift a human form out of an otherwise chaotic *mélange* of colours, and your (explicit) belief that a tune has one time signature rather than another can radically alter the metrical pattern you hear – it is unlikely to be *as* plastic, or *as* permeable to deeper cognitive processes, as Goodman and others have supposed it to be.

Not surprisingly, Goodman's conventionalist platform has been called into question as well. For example, if colour perception is more or less impermeable to cognitive processes, then one's visual perception of a red hat, and one's visual perception of a painting of the hat, done in red paint, will be relevantly similar; in an obvious sense, the painting will 'look like' the hat. If that is so, then it seens entirely reasonable to suppose that what makes the red painting more *realistic* than an otherwise identical green painting is just its resemblance to the hat. Flint Schier (1986, p. 187) has recently forwarded the plausible thesis that a picture S 'resembles its depictum O [in so far as] there is an overlap between the recognitional abilities triggered by S and O'. On Schier's view, the colour-normal painting of the red hat is more realistic than the colour-reversed one because, in the colour-normal case, anyone capable of visually recognizing the colour of the hat itself is *ipso facto* capable of recognizing the colour of the hat depicted. That is, he is *ipso facto* capable of correctly *interpreting* the painting: 'Once you have succeeded in an initial pictorial interpretation, perchance [but never necessarily] as the result of some tuition, you should then be able to interpret novel icons without being privy to additional stipulations given only that you can recognise the object or state of affairs depicted' (Schier, 1986, p. 43). *Contra* Goodman, no learning of pictorial *conventions* is required.

PERCEPTUAL PROCESSING: WHAT CAN BE *UNDERSTOOD* IN AN ARTWORK

The nature of perceptual processing also significantly determines what we can 'understand' or 'make sense of' in a work of art. A musical example is especially vivid here. According to a currently popular cognitivist theory (Lerdahl and Jackendoff, 1983), the perception of a piece of tonal music consists in the computation of a series of increasingly abstract mental representations of an acoustic stimulus, a substantial number of which are generated according to grammatical rules. As the stimulus is heard, the listener's (unconscious) knowledge of these rules guides him in the assignment of an analysis or *structural description* of the music, much as unconscious grammatical knowledge is thought to guide the competent speaker–hearer in the structural description of utterances in his natural language. The motivating insight is that it is because we assign such structural analyses to a musical signal that we hear downbeats and melodies and harmonies and cadences as opposed to mere jumbles of undifferentiated sounds. As Lerdahl and Jackendoff put it, the assignment of these analyses to heard tonal works constitutes our *understanding* of them. Such a view may help to explain the apparent failure of certain musical idioms – for example, so-called twelve-tone or serial music of the twentieth century – to win a substantial audience. If, as is likely in the case of twelve-tone compositions, the structure of a musical work violates principles mobilized in real-time music perception (in particular, the principles embodied in the hypothesized musical grammar), then such a work is likely to be difficult for a perceiver to understand or make sense of. (See Lerdahl, 1988, for illuminating discussion of the potential schisms between compositional and listening 'grammars'.) Similarly, *ceteris paribus*, musical and visual works that adhere to certain *gestalt* principles of good grouping are apparently easier to understand than those that do not (see, for instance, Lerdahl and Jackendoff, 1983, pp. 40–2), and it may be that visual works that accommodate certain hemispheric attentional asymmetries are easier to understand than those that do not. Countless other examples could be provided; see, for instance, Rentschler, Herzberger and Epstein, 1988, for an introduction to many of the psychological, neurophysiological and anthropological data bearing on perception in the arts.

PERCEPTUAL PROCESSING: WHAT CAN BE *SAID* ABOUT AN ARTWORK

Finally, let us consider a respect in which the character of human perceptual processing constrains what we are able to *say* about a work of art. It turns out that, along many perceptual dimensions, our ability to *discrimi-*

nate or *compare* values considerably exceeds our ability to *identify* or *recognize* them. For example, although the average listener can discriminate roughly 1400 steps of pitch difference across the audible range, he can (learn to) recognize or identify pitches (by ear) only as instances of the roughly eighty-seven chromatic categories instantiated on the piano keyboard. Similarly, although the average viewer can discriminate roughly ten million different shades of colour, the number of identifications he can make (by eye, as it were) is far smaller (see Hardin, 1988, pp. 182–3). The point is that our mental schemas for pitch and colour (among other things) are evidently much less fine-grained than the pitch and colour differences we can perceive. As a result, since our ability to *name* the pitches and colours we perceive is limited by our ability to identify them (here, naming is just the reporting of a type identification), our ability to say what we hear or see in a work of art will be correspondingly limited. For instance, although a trained listener will be able to report that he hears an A-natural in a performance of a musical work, and perhaps even that it is a slightly high or 'sharp' A-natural, he will not be able to report precisely which 'determinate' A-natural he hears. This (psychological) impossibility of reporting what we hear and see may be partly what philosophers have meant by their talk of an *ineffable* knowledge of artworks: in respect of the fine-grained differences in pitch, colour, loudness, shape and so forth that we perceive in a work of art, it seems we know more than we can say. (See Raffman, 1988, for further development of this conception of ineffable artistic knowledge.)

See also GOMBRICH; GOODMAN; INEFFABILITY; REALISM; RESEMBLANCE.

BIBLIOGRAPHY

Burns, E.M. and Ward, W.D.: 'Intervals, scales, and tuning', *The Psychology of Music*, ed. D. Deutsch (New York: Academic Press, 1982), pp. 241–69.

Fodor, J.A.: *The Modularity of Mind* (Cambridge, Mass.: MIT, 1983).

Gombrich, E.: *Art and Illusion* (New York: Pantheon, 1960).

Goodman, N.: *Languages of Art* (Indianapolis: Bobbs-Merrill, 1968).

Hardin, C.L.: *Color for Philosophers* (Indianapolis: Hackett, 1988).

Lerdahl, F.: 'Cognitive constraints on compositional systems', *Generative Processes in Music*, ed. J. Sloboda (Oxford: Oxford University Press, 1988), pp. 231–59.

Lerdahl, F. and Jackendoff, R.: *A Generative Theory of Tonal Music* (Cambridge, Mass.: MIT, 1983).

Prall, D.W.: *Aesthetic Judgment* (New York: 1929); Apollo edn (New York: Crowell, 1967).

Raffman, D.: 'Toward a cognitive theory of musical ineffability', *Review of Metaphysics*, 41 (1988), 685–706.

Rentschler, I., Herzberger, B. and Epstein, D., eds: *Beauty and the Brain: Biological Aspects of Aesthetics* (Basel: Birkhauser Verlag, 1988).

Schier, F.: *Deeper Into Pictures: An Essay on Pictorial Representation* (New York and Cambridge: Cambridge University Press, 1986).

Shepard, R. and Jordan, D.: 'Auditory illusions demonstrating that tones are assimilated to an internalized musical scale', *Science*, 226 (1984), 1333–4.

DIANA RAFFMAN

performance Within the major performing arts of the Western tradition – drama, ballet, opera, both instrumental and vocal music and, possibly, narrative forms of poetry – performance need not involve the presentation of an independently identifiable work; that is, performances may be improvised, as is often the case with mime, for example. Moreover, within these arts, some works do not require performance; a musical work may consist of taped natural sounds. Usually, though, the performing arts involve the presentation of works which are independent of their instances, and which derive that independence either through the existence of notated specifications for performances (such as scripts, or musical scores), or through the creation of model instances, faithfulness to which is preserved within the performance tradition. Ballet typifies this latter case.

Works in the performing arts have been identified sometimes with their notations (or with classes of performances compliant with their notations). But notations need not be involved in the creation of such works. More to the point, emphasis on notations underplays the role of conventions, both as they affect the reading of notations and as they exist within the performance tradition in general. Where written specifications for the performances of works exist, they must be read in terms of the conventions which apply to them. In some cases, the performer will be expected to depart from what is notated – to embellish, to fill in the figured bass, to introduce an accidental. In other cases, what is written has the status of a recommendation to the performer, without determining properties constitutive of the work. For example, metronome indications for tempo need not always be followed precisely. Whether all constitutive aspects of the work are notated, and whether everything which is notated is constitutive, depends on the background of conventions against which the piece's creator works.

Works in the performing arts admit of multiple instances and frequently involve notations, but these features do not distinguish them from many works in the other arts. For example, novels may have multiple instances; statues may be produced on the basis of sketches and models. In the performing arts, the work is conceived for performance and is completed when a specification for performance, or model instance, is produced. The work is not identical with the script or score, but comes into existence through, and usually at the same time as, the production of the specification. As a result, a play is completed when it is scripted, even if it is destined never to be performed. A novel must exist in at least one instance, but a performing work need have no instances. And, while a statue may be produced from the plans, the existence of the work relies on the execution of the plan. That is, the plan in these cases is a plan for the *creation* of the work itself; whereas, where the performing arts use notations,

those notations specify not how the work is to be created, but, instead, how the created work is to be instanced. In terms of the distinction drawn here, cinema is not a performing art as such, though dramatic (and musical) performance usually is involved in the *creation* of the cinematic work.

Specifications of works intended for performance are frequently minimal, leaving considerable freedom to the performer in the realization of the work. Typically this is the case with jazz, for example. Even where the specification is detailed, it under-determines vital aspects of any performance. For instance, playwrights do not usually notate the timing and nuances of phrasing to be employed by the actors. To the extent that performers, in presenting the work, must go beyond that with which they are provided by the work's creator, performance is essentially creative. At this minimal level, creativity in performance is consistent with dull, mechanical rendition. If we value the performer's creativity, we value those skills which breathe life into the work, a well as those involved merely in its bare transmission.

Where performance takes at its point the presentation of an artist's work, accuracy must be its first goal. One can perform a Beethoven symphony only if one attempts to preserve that which constitutes the work as the particular piece that Beethoven composed. Audiences are interested in works, generally, as the works of artists. Given this, it is reasonable to regard performers as having a duty to the audience to do what is in their power to render the work accurately. Performances have other goals to serve, though. They should be stimulating, revelatory, and so on. A first performance should aim for as much clarity of form and content as is consistent with the artist's instructions. If a work is already well known, there is room for adventurous and idiosyncratic approaches to its interpretation, but accuracy remains of primary importance.

How should inaccuracies in performance be regarded? One might deny that a performance which differs in the smallest detail from what is constitutive of the work is a performance of it. Such a denial aims to check the first step down the slippery slope created by the transitivity of the identity relation. But this approach is counter-intuitive, given that performances often remain identifiable as renditions of a given work despite many inaccuracies. A normative approach to the issue is more reasonable. An inaccurate rendition is a performance of a given work if it is the performer's intention to perform that work and if the work remains recognizable within the performance. A performance is the worse for inaccuracies, but it may be a fine performance for all that, because accuracy is not the sole criterion of value for performances. Given human fallibility, it would be churlish to condemn a live performance which achieves spontaneous vibrancy at the cost of minor errors.

Within music, since the 1960s there has been a marked move towards 'authentic' performance. The goals and achievements of this movement are hotly debated. Two lines of argument should be distinguished.

1. There is disagreement about the ontic character of musical works, with some authors seeing them as 'pure' sound structures and others viewing them as including among their constitutive elements the instruments and performance practices known to and specified by the composer or mandated by the conventions of the time. What one takes to be required of an accurate performance depends on one's view of the ontic character of the work. Authors in the first camp, who see musical works as thin in properties, regard the authenticity movement as going beyond that which can or should be required in the name of accuracy. 'Authentic' performances have no more claim to legitimacy than do many 'inauthentic' performances. By contrast, those who take the view that musical works are thick with properties regard the pursuit of accuracy as requiring the approach adopted by the authenticity movement. But it should be noted that what composers can determine as constitutive of their works varies considerably from place to place and time to time, in a way which suggests that musical works display considerable ontic variety. If authenticity is mainly a matter of accuracy, then the authentic performance of jazz or fifteenth-century masses is far less restrictive of performers than is the authentic performance of Berlioz.

2. There is also dispute over the desirability of authenticity in musical performances of works of the past. If the aim of authenticity is to provide access to the experience of the music which the composer's contemporaries should have had, and if historical and cultural differences between us and them prevent our sharing that experience, then the pursuit of authenticity is pointless. On this view, works are reconstituted through time so that, strictly speaking, it is not Beethoven's symphonies (as he would have recognized them) that we appreciate. But I believe that we can narrow the gap that separates us from the past and from other cultures, and that our interest in the art of past eras could survive as it does (as an interest in the works produced by creative artists) only if the extreme version of the view presented above were false.

A final, different issue: sometimes it is said that the critic is like the performer in generating the work's properties through his or her interpretation of it. Now, there are obvious parallels between the two activities – both the performer and the critic must understand the work if they are to perform their jobs convincingly, even if the performer's understanding is more practical and may be difficult to articulate. But if the suggestion is that critics and performers do essentially the same thing, the distinction between the performing and non-performing arts drawn above is obliterated. Yet that distinction does seem to be widely acknowledged, and on the following grounds.

The playwright and the composer create works for performance. The contribution of the performer is anticipated and desired by the work's creator. The performer mediates between the artist and his or her public, most of whom would otherwise lack access to the artist's work. By contrast, the critic's efforts, useful and interesting though they may be, are unnecessary if the work is to reach its audience and, in that sense, are uninvited. Moreover, criticism concerns itself with performances of works, as well as with the works themselves, but we would not normally consider the presentation of the critic's views as a performance of the performance.

See also AUTHENTICITY AND THE ARTIST; NOTATION; ONTOLOGY OF ART-WORKS.

BIBLIOGRAPHY

Davies, Stephen: 'Authenticity in musical performance', *British Journal of Aesthetics*, 27 (1987), 39–50.
Davies, Stephen: 'The ontology of musical works and the authenticity of their performances', *Noûs* 25 (1991), 21–41.
Dipert, Randall R.: 'The composer's intentions: an examination of their relevance for performance', *Musical Quarterly*, 66 (1980), 205–18.
Dipert, Randall R.: 'Toward a genuine philosophy of the performing arts', *Reason Papers*, 13 (1988), 182–200.
Godlovitch, Stan: 'Authentic performance', *Monist*, 71 (1988), 258–77.
Kenyon, Nicholas, ed.: *Authenticity and Early Music* (New York and Oxford: Oxford University Press, 1988).
Kivy, Peter: 'On the concept of the "historically authentic" performance', *Monist*, 71 (1988), 278–90.
Leppard, Raymond: *Authenticity in Music*, (London: Faber & Faber, 1988).
Levinson, Jerrold: 'Evaluating musical performance', *Journal of Aesthetic Education*, 21 (Spring, 1987), 75–88.
Young, James O.: 'The concept of authentic performance', *British Journal of Aesthetics*, 28 (1988), 228–38.

STEPHEN DAVIES

perspective In the pictorial arts, the term 'perspective' generally refers to the system of artificial perspective, whereas 'aerial perspective' refers to the depiction of the loss of clarity in form and colour in the far distance. Artificial perspective, the subject of this article, is the method for depicting space which was invented by Filippo Brunelleschi in Florence in the 1420s and perfected by writers and artists in the course of the fif-teenth century, notably Leon Battista Alberti, Lorenzo Ghiberti and Piero della Francesca. The invention of artificial perspective marks a watershed in the history of changing attitudes towards images, their use and their manufacture in Western Europe, dividing the mystery of the icon from the secular magic of illusionism. For this reason, it has always fascinated historians of art. However, it has become the subject of philosophical controversy only in the twentieth century, as a result of an article published by Erwin Panofsky in 1927.

Panofsky's ideas were partly influenced by the German mathematician Guido Hauck, who had elaborated a curvilinear alternative to the system of artificial perspective some fifty years earlier. But the influence of the neo-Kantian philosopher Ernst Cassirer was more important. Following Kant, Cassirer believed that the mind imposes a form on the ultimate material of experience, that this is an absolute and invariable prerequisite for cognition, and that the form itself is determined not by the objects we apprehend, but by the structure of human sensibility and understanding. However, Cassirer argued that human knowledge and experience are conditioned in this way not only by the fixed and unalterable canons of space, time and causality, but also by the variable 'symbolic forms' of language, mythology, art and science (Cassirer, 1923–9).

Panofsky's article, entitled 'Die Perspektive als "symbolische Form"', presents the case for regarding artificial perspective as a symbolic form. It cannot, Panofsky argues, claim to be a uniquely valid method for representing space as we see it because it is based on two important assumptions: 'first, that we see with a single motionless eye; and second, that the plane section through the cone of sight is an adequate reproduction of our visual image. The fact is, however, that these assumptions involve an extremely bold abstraction from reality (if, in this context, we may call the subjective visual impression "reality").' (Panofsky, 1927, p. 260.)

The first assumption is evidently false; the second, Panofsky argues, is no closer to the truth than the first. His argument is obscure and somewhat confused. However, he claims that perspective pictures represent the visual field as if it were flat, whereas in fact it is shaped like a sphere; that the system of perspective records the influence of distance on apparent size in a way which accords more closely with the images on our retinas than with our visual impressions, where the influence of distance is compensated for by psychological mechanisms; and that the system of perspective is designed to produce pictures on flat surfaces and represents straight lines as straight, whereas the retina is concave, and so straight lines are represented on its surface by curves. It follows, Panofsky argues, that artificial perspective is – to borrow a phrase that Cassirer used (1946, p. 137) to describe language – 'a magic mirror which falsifies and distorts the forms of reality in its own characteristic way' and which influences our perception and our imagination accordingly.

Since the publication of Panofsky's paper, many distinguished theorists of art, psychologists and philosophers have addressed the question of whether the system of artificial perspective is best regarded as an elaborate code or as a discovery about the form of visible space. Following Panofsky, Read claims (1956, p. 67) that 'the theory of perspective . . . is a scientific convention; it is merely one way of describing space and has no absolute validity.' Goodman argues that 'the bundle of light rays delivered to the eye by the picture [of a building] drawn in standard perspective is very different from the bundle delivered' by the building itself, and he therefore maintains, like Read and Panofsky, that 'the behaviour of light sanctions neither our usual nor any other way of rendering space' (Goodman, 1981, p. 19).

On the other hand, Gombrich describes (1977, p. 205) artificial perspective as 'the most important trick in the armoury of illusionistic art'. The trick is turned by applying a set of rules, but the impression it causes in a spectator proves that artificial perspective is far from being an arbitrary code. 'What may make a painting like a distant view through a window . . . is the similarity between the mental activities that

both can arouse' (Gombrich, 1973, p. 240), and therefore 'the goal which the artist seeks . . . [is] a psychological effect' (Gombrich, 1982, p. 228). Artificial perspective, he argues, tends to produce this effect. Pirenne argues (1970, p. 10) in a similar vein that a picture painted in perspective will 'produce visual percepts in the observers . . . which resemble those which would be given by the (actual or imaginary) scene represented'.

As these quotations reveal, not only is the status of artificial perspective disputed, it is also uncertain what would settle the matter. In order to prove that artificial perspective has or does not have a singular authority, independent of custom and convention, should we attempt to measure the geometrical differences between a picture painted in perspective and a retinal image? Should we compare the pattern of light reflected by such a picture with the pattern reflected by the scene depicted? Or should we investigate the psychological episode that the picture is apt to cause?

I suspect that none of these strategies is the right one. In order to decide whether Brunelleschi and his followers devised an ingenious code or discovered a method for reproducing the visible form of space, we must first appreciate that the system of artificial perspective is a synthesis of the various techniques for depicting non-planar spatial relations that already existed – namely, overlapping, foreshortening and perspective diminution. (No special techniques for depicting planar spatial relations – above, below, to the left of, to the right of – are needed, for they can be reproduced on the painted surface.) If we can explain what these relatively primitive techniques accomplish, and how they accomplish it, we shall find it easier to understand their harmonious integration into a unified system, and the awkward puzzle that Panofsky created may be solved more easily.

Overlapping, which is the simplest technique for depicting non-planar spatial relations, was already used by Egyptian artists in the Old Kingdom to depict the partial occlusion of one object by another. The object which is partly hidden from sight is only partly depicted, and the part of the painted or carved surface which would otherwise depict this hidden part depicts instead the part of the object in front which hides it.

Foreshortening and perspective diminution are more sophisticated techniques, but they serve essentially similar purposes. Foreshortening allows a painter to depict what philosophers have misleadingly called 'apparent shape' – that is, an object's outline or silhouette. 'Occlusion shape' is a less tendentious term. A circular plate viewed obliquely has an elliptical occlusion shape: it will occlude an elliptical patch on a plane perpendicular to the line of sight. An object's occlusion shape is a function of its actual shape and its orientation relative to the line of sight of a spectator, and so foreshortening allows a painter to depict not only the shape of an object, but also its orientation. Thus, a panel by Uccello in the National Gallery, London, which depicts the battle of San Romano, includes a fallen knight lying along a line orthogonal to the picture plane. Needless to say, this is a feat of artistry which was beyond the powers of the artists who depicted the many fallen warriors on the Bayeux tapestry or the Narmer palette.

Perspective diminution allows a painter to depict relative occlusion size. If I hold out my hands in front of me, and extend one arm further than the other, my hands will not appear to differ in size, but the greater occlusion size of the nearer hand will be evident: the nearer hand will occlude a larger patch on a plane perpendicular to my line of sight. The relative occlusion size of two objects is a function of their relative size and their relative distance from the spectator, and so perspective dimunition allows a painter to make a picture in which one object is further from the spectator than another without depicting partial occlusion. (It seems likely that painted scenery employing perspective diminution was introduced by Sophocles, and that the technique was perfected by Agatharcus of Samos, when he painted a back-cloth for a revival of a play by Aeschylus in the 430s BC.)

Many philosophers have mistakenly supposed that occlusion shape and relative occlusion size are not visible properties of the physical world, but features of our subjective visual impressions. To take a recent example, Christopher Peacocke writes as follows:

> Suppose you are standing on a road which stretches from you in a straight line to the horizon. There are two trees at the roadside, one a hundred yards from you, the other two hundred. Your experience represents these objects as being of the same physical height and other dimensions; that is, taking your experience at face value you would judge that the trees are roughly the same physical size . . . Yet there is also some sense in which the nearer tree occupies more of your visual field than the more distant tree. This is as much a feature of your experience itself as is its representing the trees as being the same height. (Peacocke, 1983, p. 12)

In Peacocke's view, this shows that visual experience has certain features that do not 'represent the environment of the experiencer as being in a certain way', because 'no veridical experience can represent one tree as larger than another and also as the same size as the other' (Peacocke, 1983, pp. 5, 12). I do not intend to say anything about Peacocke's view that visual experience involves mental representations. What is relevant for present purposes is the idea, plainly present in this passage, that the relative occlusion size of the two trees is not actually a feature of the visible environment but of the visual impressions of the person who sees the trees.

This idea is mistaken. Their relative occlusion size is a visible property of two trees, no less than their relative size. (And the occlusion shape of a plate is a visible property of the plate, no less than its shape.) This is clear from the fact that I can mistake the relative occlusion size of two trees, and my mistake can be corrected by measurement and geometrical calculation. For example, I might guess that the nearer tree has double the occlusion size of the further tree, and be surprised to discover that the correct ratio is three or four to one. By and large, painters with a traditional academic training will be good at giving accurate reports of occlusion shape and relative occlusion size, and the rest of us not so good.

Perhaps the temptation to deny that occlusion shape and relative occlusion size are visible features of our physical environment is due to the fact that the shape of an object's outline will change as we move around it, although the object itself does not undergo any change; and the relative occlusion size of the two trees in Peacocke's example will change as we move from one end of the avenue to the other, although the trees do not change or move. However, it does not follow that occlusion shape and relative occlusion size are not visible features of our physical environment, or that when we describe them we are talking about our visual impressions (let alone about features of these impressions 'which do [not] in themselves represent the environment of the experiencer as being in a certain way'. After all, the distance between me and the door changes as I walk towards it, without the door moving; but this does not show that the changing distance between me and the door is not really a feature of my physical environment, but is in some peculiar way merely a feature of my subjective experience.

Relative occlusion size, like partial occlusion, is relative to a point of view, and occlusion shape is relative to a line of sight; but this does not impugn their objectivity in the least, or imply that they are nebulous, merely apparent, or unreal. Nor does it imply a contradiction to suppose that two trees appear to be (and actually are) the same height whilst their occlusion size, relative to my point of view, appears to be (and actually is) different. Despite what Peacocke says, this is no more contradictory than the fact that a single object may be big relative to one thing and small relative to another.

The notion that occlusion properties are merely apparent, subjective or unreal is one of the commonest errors in the philosophical canon, and its influence on the theory of painting is unmistakable. For if we imagine that the elliptical occlusion shape of a circular plate viewed obliquely belongs in the metaphysically subordinate category of mere appearance, or that it is a feature of the subjective visual experience of a person looking at the plate, then we are bound to conclude that a painting which depicts a plate foreshortened shows the plate *as it appears to us* rather than *as it is*, or that the technique of foreshortening aims to reproduce a feature of our subjective visual experience. Indeed, this conclusion was already drawn by Plato, in the *Sophist* (235d–236c). Twenty-three centuries later the same notion, but given a Kantian inflexion, led Panofsky to suppose that artificial perspective aims at 'an adequate reproduction of our visual image'. (There is an important ambiguity here, since in this context 'reproduce' can mean either 'make a copy of' or 'produce artificially'. This ambiguity, which recapitulates an ancient ambiguity in the meaning of 'mimesis', has had its own repercussions, but they are beyond the scope of this article.)

Once the mistake has been corrected, we can see overlapping, foreshortening and perspective diminution for what they are: techniques for depicting non-planar spatial relations. Overlapping allows the painter to make a picture in which one object is further from the spectator than another, in the manner described above. (However, their relative distance from the spectator will be indeterminate.) Foreshortening allows the painter to depict orientation relative to the line of sight of the spectator, by making the shape of the part of a picture which depicts an object the same as the object's occlusion shape. Perspective diminution allows the painter to depict relative distance from the spectator, by making the relative size of the parts of a picture which depicts various objects the same as the objects' relative occlusion size. (Shading is a close cousin of foreshortening: it allows an artist to depict orientation relative to the source of illumination.)

Before the invention of artificial perspective, these techniques for depicting non-planar spatial relations were used independently. They were also used inconsistently. For example, in the panel from Duccio's *Maestà* which depicts the flagellation, Pontius Pilate appears to be standing both behind and in front of a column. The invention of artificial perspective was a systematizing achievement: it integrated the existing techniques for the depiction of non-planar spatial relations into a harmonious unity, and thereby guaranteed a consistent pattern of spatial relations between the parts of a depicted scene.

What conclusions should we draw about the debate which was initiated by the publication of Panofsky's paper? Panofsky himself was right to deny that 'we see with a single motionless eye', but wrong when he maintained that artificial perspective is based on the assumption that we do; and wrong when he stated, in the concluding paragraph of his paper, that artificial perspective is 'an ordering of visual appearance . . . transforming *reality* into *appearance*'. Goodman was right to insist that 'the bundle of light rays delivered to the eye by the picture [of a building] drawn in standard perspective is very different from the bundle delivered' by the building itself; but wrong to conclude that artificial perspective is merely a conventional method of projection which has been sanctioned by habit. Gombrich was right to deny this, but wrong to base his view on the claim that 'what may make a painting like a distant view through a window . . . is the similarity between the mental activities that both can arouse.' Alberti was closest to the truth when he stated (1966, p. 47) that 'the function of the eye in vision need not be considered in this place', and confined his discussion of perspective to geometry.

See also DEPICTION; GOMBRICH; GOODMAN; LANGUAGE AND PICTORIAL ART; REPRESENTATION; RESEMBLANCE.

BIBLIOGRAPHY

Alberti, Leon Battista: *Della Pittura*; *On Painting*; trans. J.R. Spencer (New Haven, Conn.: Yale University Press, 1966).
Cassirer, E.: *Die Philosophie der symbolischen Formen*, 3 vols (Berlin: Bruno Cassirer, 1923–9); trans. R. Manheim, *The Philosophy of Symbolic Forms*, 3 vols (New Haven, Conn.: Yale University Press, 1953–7).
Cassirer, E.: *Sprache und Mythos*, (Leipzig: Teubner, 1925): *Language and Myth*, trans. S. Langer (New York: Harper, 1946).
Gombrich, E.H.: 'Illusion in art', *Illusion in Nature and Art*, ed. E.H. Gombrich and R.L. Gregory (London: Duckworth, 1973, 193–243).
Gombrich, E.H.: *Art and Illusion*, 5th edn (Oxford: Phaidon, 1977).
Gombrich, E.H.: 'Experiment and experience in the arts', *The Image and the Eye* (Oxford: Phaidon, 1982), 215–43.
Goodman, N.: *Languages of Art* (Brighton: Harvester, 1981).
Kemp, M.: *The Science of Art* (New Haven, Conn.: Yale University Press, 1990).
Panofsky, E.: 'Die Perspektive als "symbolische Form"', *Vorträge der Bibliothek Warburg*, 1924–5 (Leipzig: Teubner, 1927), 258–330.
Peacocke, C.: *Sense and Content* (Oxford: Oxford University Press, 1983).
Pirenne, M.H.: *Optics, Painting and Photography* (Cambridge: Cambridge University Press, 1970).
Read, H.: *The Art of Sculpture* (London: Faber and Faber, 1956).
White, J.: *The Birth and Rebirth of Pictorial Space*, 2nd edn (London: Faber & Faber, 1967).

JOHN HYMAN

picturing *See* DEPICTION; REPRESENTATION.

Plato (c.427–347 BC) Greek philosopher; Socrates' follower and Aristotle's teacher. His dialogues are, arguably, the most influential philosophical works ever written, containing the first extended discussions of many of the central issues of metaphysics, ethics, politics, and art.

Plato can be regarded, with perhaps equal reason, as both the founder of philosophical aesthetics and the fiercest critic of aesthetics' right to an autonomous existence. Issues of aesthetic significance, predominantly applying to art (poetry, music, painting, dance) though sometimes framed around larger questions of beauty, are approached from diverse angles throughout Plato's works; but the unifying thread is an insistence that artistic values be subject to the sovereignty of truth and morality, and that they justify themselves in relation to the needs of psychology, politics and (ultimately) metaphysics.

Behind Plato's concerns with art lies a conviction of the unity of all value, as seen in the dissatisfaction with functional and relativist definitions of 'beauty' or 'fineness', and the assumption of the latter's inseparability from goodness (*Hippias Major*). But, from the earliest dialogues, there are tensions visible in Plato's attitudes to art, especially poetry. Working in a culture in which poetry was a serious influence on beliefs and ideas, not least through education (*Protagoras* 325e–326b), Plato disputes the ethical wisdom and religious insight traditionally ascribed to poets. He inherited this distrust from earlier philosophers such as Xenophanes and Heraclitus, as well as from his mentor, Socrates (*Euthyphro* 6b–c).

Yet Plato evinces a strong fascination for poetry, emulating its dramatic and verbal qualities in his own writings. His Socrates often expresses deep respect for poetry, as well as a range of doubts about its credentials. Most consistently challenged is the idea that poets possess a rationally explicable 'craft' or 'artistry' (*technē*), though the practitioners of the visual arts *are* granted this status (for instance *Gorgias* 503e). Set against *technē*, if sometimes disingenuously, is the traditional concept of inspiration (*Apology* 21–2; *Ion*; *Meno* 99c–d). If poets are inspired, they may offer valuable experiences which cannot be scrutinized with consistent clarity, or expected to conform to predeterminable standards. If, however, poets do not know how or what they create, their status as guides to life (cf. *Lysis* 214a1–2) must be suspect, and the powerful emotions which they undoubtedly evoke (*Ion* 535) may be psychologically dangerous. The pleasure of art stands in an uneasy relation to ethical aims (*Gorgias* 501–2). Yet Plato is also able to allow for 'internal' aesthetic principles, such as those of form, organization and coherence (for example, *Phaedrus* 268–9; *Republic* 4.420c–d).

The strands of thought so far mentioned are variously elaborated throughout Plato's 'middle' period, which culminates in the *Republic*. But the latter also furnishes much more sustained arguments of aesthetic relevance, and ones which are influenced by an increasingly systematic and ambitious philosophical outlook. A turning point seems to have been the *Cratylus*, where for the first time Plato focuses his questions about art on the concept of mimesis (whose Greek senses include 'imitation', 'representation' and dramatic 'enactment'). Part of the importance of this new angle is that poetry, the visual arts and even music can now be treated as analogous in their representational relation to the world. In *Cratylus* itself artistic mimesis is cited chiefly as a reference point for complex arguments about linguistic signification, but in the *Republic* we are given two major discussions of the mimetic dimensions of poetry and art themselves.

The first, in books 2–3 (376–403), presents a critique of the false and harmful views which the poets, especially Homer and the tragedians, allegedly express; and then of the powerful way in which poetry's dramatic mode (here called 'mimesis') invites an insidious act of psychological identification on the part of actor, hearer or reader. Although ostensibly concerned with the education of the young, Plato is here effectively constructing an aesthetic scheme (and a challenge to aesthetics) which judges art by three main criteria: truthfulness, which need not exclude fiction, and which Plato, like Tolstoy, interprets in a normative sense; ethical quality of content; and psychological benefit.

Plato's case looks, at times, severe to the point of doctrinaire narrowness. But his purpose is to press questions about the underlying justification of art – its place in the life both of the individual and of the city. Despite occasional and ironic talk of aesthetic 'play' (for instance, *Republic* 3.396e), Plato refuses to allow that art can be a self-sufficient pursuit; its power to 'enter the soul', and to influence the life of a culture, is too great for that. One by-product of this stance is an inclination towards artistic conservatism: changes in the styles of music will entail changes in the laws of politics (*Republic* 4.424c). Moreover, it is made clear (*Republic* 3.400–2) that Plato's principles apply to a very wide range of artistic experience. His position, though prescriptive and in some respects puritanical, still deserves to be regarded as an aesthetic philosophy: its goal is 'a passion for beauty' in all its forms (*Republic* 3.403c).

Plato returns to art in *Republic* 10, now with the entire psychology and metaphysics of the work behind him. His concern is again chiefly with poetry, but he is prepared here to question the value of verisimilitude in other representational art, especially painting. All art, *qua* mimesis, is now impugned as mirror-like image-making – the creation of mere 'appearances' that fall short even of sensible reality, and are 'twice removed' from the transcendent truth (the plane of the Forms) posited by Plato's metaphysics. Yet poetry, in particular, is a more formidable force than this suggests, for it has the power to 'bewitch' the soul and to compel the responses of those whom it affects; Plato speaks here, as throughout his work, from personal knowledge of the experiences he criticizes (*Republic* 10.605c). The potency of poetry can be analysed, on the *Republic*'s model of the soul, as a subversion of reason's control by intense arousal of the emotions. It is this which makes it something to be either proscribed or at least subjected to political control. Yet Plato completes his indictment with a final, wistful admission of poetry's lingering attractions (*Republic* 10.607c–d).

The combination of arguments in *Republic* 10 is thus deeply ambivalent: contempt for the artifice and pretence which serves a merely superficial realism, alongside a troubled awareness of art's capacity to touch deep psychic roots. Such paradoxes continue, moreover, to be compounded by the activities of Plato the artist. The *Republic* itself ends with an eschatological myth that both emulates and offers to replace some of the myths of the poets. Like all Plato's myths, it attests to a faith in the emotive and persuasive value of narrative and of imagery. Here lie clues to a very different Platonic aesthetic, which links the imagination with higher truths and with a vision of ideal beauty – an aesthetic eventually elaborated by neo-Platonism in antiquity and in the Renaissance.

After the *Republic* there are no radically new departures in Platonic aesthetics. But continuing challenges to art's credentials, on grounds that range over psychology, ethics and epistemology, appear right up to Plato's final work, the *Laws*. The *Sophist* echoes *Republic* 10's condemnation of mimetic image-making, but here the main target is rhetorical sophistry, not art. *Timaeus* shows how Plato's thinking about images and mimesis had expanded well beyond the arts, providing hypothetical concepts for the interpretation both of human thought in general and even of the world itself (as an 'image' of some eternal model). *Philebus* (47e–50b) includes a brief but intricate account of the psychological experiences of both tragedy and comedy, and a passage which adumbrates a kind of hedonistic aestheticism based on the notion of the pleasure of 'pure' forms, colours and musical tones (*Philebus* 51b–d). The *Laws* contains dozens of passages of aesthetic bearing, some of them complex, obscure yet deeply interesting (and still rather neglected). The richest are in bks 2 (653–71) and 7 (796–817): they encompass ideas about art and cultural recreation; the psychological roots of aesthetic form and order; the importance of moral feelings in art; the value of certain types of artistic tradition; the nature of representation in poetry, music, dance and visual images; and much besides.

Nowhere does Plato relinquish his demand that artistic beauty and value be grounded in a goodness that is essentially ethical; the beauty of art is a reflection of moral beauty (*Laws* 2.654b). Yet the *Laws* occasionally intimates a latent awareness of the need to make allowance for principles that are 'internal' to the arts and to the experiences they afford. The integration of this awareness with his overarching moralism is something that Plato finally, one may feel, falls short of achieving; the relationship between pleasure and other criteria of artistic value remains problematic (*Laws* 2.667).

Plato is the only great moral questioner of art and aesthetic experience who can also be regarded as a profound lover of art; even Tolstoy was not, unlike Plato, both of these things simultaneously and throughout his life. As late as the *Laws*, Plato was impelled to call his own work 'the truest tragedy'

(7.817b): there is a vital sense, therefore, in which his aesthetics is embodied in the entirety of his philosophical creativity.

See also MORALITY AND ART; REPRESENTATION.

WRITINGS

Republic, trans. H.D.P. Lee (Harmondsworth: Penguin Books, 1955), bks 2, 3, 10.
Laws, trans. T.J. Saunders (Harmondsworth: Penguin Books, 1970), bks 2, 7.
Ion, trans. D.A. Russell, in *Ancient Literary Criticism*, D.A. Russell and M. Winterbottom (Oxford: Oxford University Press, 1972).
Hippias Major, trans. P. Woodruff (Oxford: Basil Blackwell, 1982).

BIBLIOGRAPHY

Ferrari, G.R.F.: 'Plato and poetry', *Cambridge History of Literary Criticism* vol. 1 (Cambridge: Cambridge University Press, 1989), pp. 92–148.
Halliwell, S.: *Plato Republic 10: with Translation and Commentary* (Warminster: Aris & Phillips, 1988).
Halliwell, S.: 'The importance of Plato and Aristotle for aesthetics', *Proceedings of the Boston Area Colloquium in Ancient Philosophy*, 5 (1991), 321–48.
Moravcsik, J. and Temko, P., eds: *Plato on Beauty, Wisdom and the Arts* (Totowa, NJ: Rowman & Littlefield, 1982).
Nehamas, A.: 'Plato and the mass media', *Monist*, 71 (1988), 214–34.

STEPHEN HALLIWELL

pleasure, aesthetic   When is pleasure in an object properly denominated 'aesthetic'? The characterization of aesthetic pleasure is something that almost every theorist of the aesthetic has attempted. A number of background desiderata, it seems, must be satisfied for such a characterization to be accounted a success:

(1) that it illuminate the relation between aesthetic pleasure and the taking of an aesthetic attitude to works of art;

(2) that it address the possible difference between aesthetic pleasure in works of art or other artefacts, and aesthetic pleasure in natural phenomena;

(3) that it represent aesthetic pleasure as in some fashion distinct, on the one hand, from purely sensory or sensual pleasures, and, on the other, from purely cognitive or intellectual ones;

(4) that it represent aesthetic pleasure as somehow immediate, its own justification, and not a matter of ulterior purposes or future rewards;

(5) that it exhibit aesthetic pleasure as individualizing, appreciating, an object for what it most distinctively, if not uniquely, is.

(6) (perhaps the desideratum most difficult to meet) that it make intelligible how aesthetic pleasure can be taken in what are usually labelled non-aesthetic aspects of a work of art – for instance, its cognitive content, moral import or political message – without thereby turning into pleasure of a non-aesthetic, or art-inappropriate, sort.

Before venturing a proposal which might answer, as far as possible, to these desiderata, I review briefly some of the prominent suggestions that the tradition of aesthetic thought has thrown up so far. In Kant's influential treatment, aesthetic pleasure is characterized as the by-product of a non-conceptual and disinterested judging, whose focus is exclusively the formal purposiveness of the object judged. In being non-conceptual it is distinguished from pleasure taken in an object as good, since such a judgement always presupposes a concept of the object as of some kind or other. In being disinterested – that is, not grounded in the subject's personal desires, needs or susceptibilities – it is distinguished (or so Kant believed) from sensory pleasures such as those of a warm bath or the taste of raspberry. In deriving from an impression of purposiveness, independent of actual purpose, which an object's mere pattern or structure sustains – an impression which, in stimulating imagination and understanding to an unaccustomed free play, directly gives rise to the pleasure in question – aesthetic pleasure is shown to reside in forms or appearances *per se*, and not in an object's real-world status or connections.

Different strands of this complex conception have been stressed by subsequent writers. Schopenhauer agreed with Kant that the pleasure in beholding an object aesthetically is a disinterested one, but claimed that its focus is not an object's pure form as such in relation to the cognitive faculties, but rather some metaphysical *idea* inherent in an object – a grade of the universal will's objectification – which, in drawing the subject's attention, lifts him temporarily out of the painful striving to which he, as a spatio-temporally bound individual bundle of will, is ordinarily condemned. In a similar vein Bullough, varying the notion of the disinterestedness of aesthetic pleasure, proposed that such pleasure issues upon the subject's metaphorically *distancing* any object of perception, in the sense of bracketing all of its life implications, thus putting the subject's practical self 'out of gear' and clearing a space for rapt absorption. Others, such as Eliseo Vivas and Jerome Stolnitz, have emphasized the *intransitivity* of the mode of attention that yields aesthetic pleasure, by which is meant its not going beyond the object but instead terminating on it.

The formalist strand in Kant's conception has been taken up in different ways by Clive Bell, J.O. Urmson and Monroe Beardsley. Bell claimed that pleasurable aesthetic emotion is the result of contemplation of an object's *significant form*, and that pleasure derived from attention to any other aspect of an artwork – for instance, its representational content – is *ipso facto* non-aesthetic; it is unclear, however, whether Bell had any intelligible, non-circular account to give of when a form is significant, and so the cash value of Bell's pronouncement seems to be just that form, narrowly construed – that is, the pure arrangement of elements in a medium – is the sole legitimate object of aesthetic experience. More liberally, Urmson has suggested that specifically aesthetic pleasure is pleasure deriving from a concern with appearances as such, with how things look or sound or seem, rather than with how they actually are; on such a suggestion the aesthetic includes, but is not restricted to, the narrowly formal. Relatedly, Beardsley has proposed that aesthetic pleasure be defined as pleasure taken in either an object's formal qualities (for instance, balance, unity, tension) or its regional qualities – that is, *Gestalt* qualities of character or expression which attach to structured wholes (for instance, vivacity, serenity, gloominess, grace).

That aesthetic pleasure derives from a wholly non-conceptual engagement with an object, as Kant would have it, has not been as readily accepted as some other parts of his theory. What the balance of thought and feeling in aesthetic experience is or should be has been a prominent topic for critical discussion in the twentieth century. David Pole has proposed that involvement with a work of art is aesthetic when the emphasis is on experiencing more intensely some aspect of the work, be it formal, expressive, or moral, rather than on reaping some detachable good such as information or explanation; but as Pole observes, many such work aspects – for example, political meaning – will be of an irreducibly conceptual, and not simply perceptual, sort. Roger Scruton has urged even more strongly that aesthetic experience and the satisfaction inherent in it is necessarily permeated by thought or imagination – that such experience always involves conceptions of objects, of their features, under certain descriptions. An object not consciously construed in one fashion or another cannot, for Scruton, be an object in which one is finding aesthetic, as opposed to merely sensational or instinctive, satisfaction.

In the light of the foregoing abbreviated history of the notion, and bearing in mind the desiderata detailed above, I propose the following characterization of aesthetic pleasure. *Pleasure in an object is aesthetic when it derives from apprehension of and reflection on the object's individual character and content, both for itself and in relation to the structural base on which it rests.* That is to say, to appreciate something aesthetically is to attend to its forms, qualities and meanings for their own sakes, but also to attend to the way in which all such things emerge from the particular set of low-level perceptual features which define the object on a non-aesthetic plane.

We do not apprehend the character and content of an artwork – including formal, aesthetic, expressive, representational, semantic or symbolic properties – as free-floating, but rather as anchored in and arising from the specific structure which constitutes it on a primary observational level. Content and character are supervenient on such structure, and appreciation of them, if properly aesthetic, involves awareness of that dependency. To appreciate an object's inherent properties aesthetically is to experience them, minimally, as properties of the individual in question, but also as bound up with and inseparable from its basic perceptual configuration. Features aesthetically appreciated are features thought of as qualified by, or even internally connected with, their underlying bases.

Especially if a characterization of aesthetic pleasure is to be adequate to our interest in art, it will have to be roughly of the sort I have sketched. This is because of desiderata 5 and 6 given at the outset. Aesthetic pleasure is supposed to be both individualizing and capable of being taken in an object's cognitive and moral aspect, without becoming *a fortiori* purely cognitive or moral satisfaction. Now, it seems that what is most distinctive about an artwork, and possibly the only thing for which uniqueness might be claimed, is not its artistic character or content *per se*, in the sense of the totality of its noteworthy properties – any or even all of which might be encountered in other artworks – but the specific complex of the work's character and content with the particular perceptual substructure which supports it. So, in so far as that is what is attended to, interest in an object carries to what is maximally distinctive about it, and so desideratum 5 is satisfied. And where a work has a prominent intellectual or moral or political content, pleasure in this remains recognizably aesthetic when it results not so much from acquisition of some portion of scientific knowledge or ethical insight or political

wisdom *per se*, but from appreciation of the *manner* in which – the work being viewed in its proper historical context – these are embodied in and communicated by the work's specific elements and organization. So desideratum 6 is taken care of as well.

Aesthetic satisfaction in Thomas Mann's *Death in Venice*, for instance, is to be derived from more than its beauty of language, the strikingness of its images, or even the downward curve of its sad narrative; it is had as well in its moral mediation of life and art, and in its symbolism of death and disintegration. But the satisfaction is properly aesthetic in these latter cases precisely when such symbolic or moral content is apprehended in and through the body of the literary work itself – its sentences, paragraphs and fictive events – and not as something abstractable from it. Aesthetic pleasure in Matisse's *The Red Studio* is not exhausted in delectation of its shapes, planes and colours; it includes, for one thing, delight in the originality of Matisse's handling of space. But such delight is inseparable from a conception of what that handling amounts to, and how it is based in, or realized by, the particular choices of shape, plane and colour before one.

Aesthetic appreciation of art thus always acknowledges the vehicle of the work as essential, and never focuses merely on detachable meanings or effects. It is a signal advantage of the characterization outlined here that it ensures both that aesthetic pleasure is individualizing or work-centred, and that aesthetic pleasure can be taken in what are, on a traditional reckoning, non-aesthetic aspects of a work, without thereby becoming non-aesthetic.

Desiderata 1 and 4 are also easily satisfied. To take an aesthetic approach to an artwork is, if anything, to approach it in a disinterested fashion with a concern not only for its resultant, high-order qualities, meanings and effects, but also for the way these intertwine with and rest on the work's lower-level perceptual face. And to derive aesthetic pleasure from apprehending a work's content and character in relation to its concrete construction is to obtain a satisfaction then and there, not merely to invest in one for the future.

Desideratum 3 asks for a differentiation of aesthetic pleasures from sensory and from intellectual ones. When is pleasure in a flavour, for example, aesthetic rather than merely sensory? It seems natural to suggest that what is required is some grasp of the flavour for the quality it is, perhaps in opposition to other flavours not then present, and of the flavour as itself founded on other discriminable qualities. To appreciate the taste of raspberry aesthetically is to register not only the brute taste, but also, so to speak, its form – that is, its relation to other, simpler qualities in the taste, or to ones it contrasts with in imagination. A purely sensory pleasure in raspberry taste, in so far as this is possible, will neither focus the flavour for what it is nor involve awareness of relationships and dependencies within the experience as a whole. On the other hand, as already remarked, since aesthetic pleasures always involve an appreciation of contents-in-relation-to-vehicles-or-supports, then although necessarily involving thought of a kind, they do not collapse automatically into pure intellectual pleasures, in which satisfaction is grounded in the acquisition of knowledge or insight as such, for themselves, independent of how they are conveyed.

This leaves desideratum 2: that aesthetic pleasure in art be related intelligibly to aesthetic pleasure in nature. Putting aside, for the moment, what may importantly distinguish these pleasures – in a Romantic landscape painting, on the one hand, and in the actual vista of the Alps, on the other – we can ask what might tie them together. What would make them both aesthetic? I suggest it is this: that the pleasure in both cases is taken in experienceable aspects of the respective things, coupled with a vivid awareness both of the interrelations of such aspects and of their groundedness in the object's observable structure. Aesthetic pleasure in natural objects, like aesthetic pleasure in works of art, is typically a multi-level affair, involving reflection not only on appearances *per se*, but on the constitution of such appearances and the interaction between higher-order perceptions. The shapes, colours and expressivenesses of natural objects are appreciated in

their complex relation to one another and to the concepts under which we identify such objects. Even to enjoy aesthetically something as simple as the luminosity of the sun's colour at sunset is to enjoy such luminosity as the upshot of a particular shade and brightness of yellow, and as somehow appropriate to the heavenly body which is the source of all life.

Some theorists, such as Arthur Danto and Nelson Goodman, have stressed the great difference in kind between aesthetic response to nature and aesthetic response to art, while other theorists, such as Richard Wollheim and Anthony Savile, have even proposed that the aesthetic interest in art is logically prior to that in nature, the latter being properly analysed in terms of the former. While recognizing that there may be two species of aesthetic response here, I suspect there is no priority either way. In any event, my concern has been only to characterize aesthetic satisfaction in such a way as to visibly cover both.

It is clear that aesthetic pleasure as characterized in this article comprises more than pleasure in aesthetic qualities *per se* – that is, those that Frank Sibley has famously identified – and, equally, more than pleasure in mere appearances. Of course, when one is after aesthetic gratification one is interested in appearances, but one is equally interested in how, on a phenomenological plane, such appearances are generated; or, alternatively, how aesthetic qualities emerge from an object's structure. Somewhat legislatively, I have sought a notion which would make aesthetic pleasure, where works of art are concerned, something closer to pleasure proper to something as art – that is to say, art-appropriate pleasure. In this broader, art-conscious sense that I have attempted to profile, the relationship of substructure and superstructure in the total impression that an object affords is necessarily of concern when an object is approached aesthetically.

Of course, we can still acknowledge, in deference to tradition, a narrower notion of aesthetic pleasure restricted to pleasure taken in aesthetic and formal properties as such, immediately experienced. But in the light of the wider range of contents that much art

PLEASURE, AESTHETIC

aims for and boasts of – for instance, emotional, moral, religious ones – and which can presumably be made the object of art-appropriate attention, and in the light of the entrenched connection between aesthetic appreciation and the appreciation of art, it seems useful to have articulated a notion of aesthetic satisfaction with respect to which such contents are not automatically excluded. So long as the complex of a work's embodying and conveying a formulable content or meaning, and not that content or meaning in isolation, is the focus of appreciation, then the associated pleasure can, on this more liberal conception, be accounted aesthetic – no matter what the variety of content or meaning in question.

Two last points. First, though implicit in my proposal regarding aesthetic pleasure is a notion of aesthetic appreciation which approximates, where artworks are concerned, more closely to that of artistic appreciation than does the traditional notion of aesthetic appreciation, it is not wholly equivalent to it. In order to have a notion of aesthetic appreciation applicable to artworks and natural phenomena alike, none of the ingredients specific to the appreciation of art, such as concern with style, personality, intention and design, could be invoked. The result, though, is a notion which seems to fit what goes on when we regard a natural phenomenon as more than just a source of sensation, but without necessarily treating it as artwork *manqué*. Aesthetic appreciation of nature requires, at a minimum, not only attention to manifest effects but a concern with their perceptual and conceptual underpinnings.

Second, the proposal has the virtue, ironically, of preserving a connection between the aesthetic and the formal in art, reminiscent of Kant, but without reducing the aesthetic to the formal narrowly construed – for instance, as pattern in space or time. For in deriving gratification from the unique *manner* in which a work's content and character, whatever they might comprise, are rooted in and emerge from the work's form *sensu stricto* – the particular arrangement of elements (colours, sounds, words, movements, gestures) through which it conveys whatever else it does – one is focused on something which could fairly well be described as formal, in a wide sense.

Pleasure in an artwork is aesthetic when, whatever aspects of it are attended to, be they psychological or political or polemical, there is also attention to the *relation* between content and form – between what a work expresses or signifies, and the means it uses to do so. This relation, which I have made the *sine qua non* of the aesthetic, is quite obviously a kind of higher form – which means that Kant, in an oblique fashion, was right about aesthetic pleasure after all.

See also ATTITUDE, AESTHETIC; FORM; JUDGEMENT, AESTHETIC; KANT; PROPERTIES, AESTHETIC.

BIBLIOGRAPHY

Beardsley, M.: *The Aesthetic Point of View*, ed. M. Wreen and D. Callen (Ithaca, NY: Cornell University Press, 1982), chs 1–3.

Bell, C.: *Art* (London: Chatto & Windus, 1914).

Bullough, E.: '"Physical distance" as a factor in art and as an aesthetic principle', *British Journal of Psychology*, 5 (1912), 87–98.

Kant, I.: *Kritik der Urteilskraft* (Berlin: 1790); trans. W. Pluhar, *Critique of Judgement* (Indianapolis: Hackett, 1987).

Levinson, J.: *Music, Art, and Metaphysics* (Ithaca, NY: Cornell University Press, 1990), chs 6, 7.

Levinson, J.: 'Pleasure and the value of works of art', *British Journal of Aesthetics*, 32 (1992).

Meynell, H.: *The Nature of Aesthetic Value* (London: Macmillan, 1986).

Pole, D.: 'When is a situation aesthetic?', *Proceedings of the Aristotelian Society*, suppl. vol. 31 (1957), 93–106.

Savile, A.: *The Test of Time* (Oxford: Oxford University Press, 1982).

Schaper, E.: *Pleasure, Preference and Value* (Cambridge: Cambridge University Press, 1983).

Schopenhauer, A.: *The World as Will and Idea*, bk 3; trans E.F.J. Payne (New York: Dover, 1966 [1819]).

Scruton, R.: *The Aesthetics of Architecture* (Princeton, NJ: Princeton University Press, 1979).

Stolnitz, J.: *Aesthetics and Philosophy of Art Criticism* (New York: Houghton-Mifflin, 1960).

Urmson, J.O.: 'When is a situation aesthetic?' *Proceedings of the Aristotelian Society*, suppl. vol. 31 (1957), 75–92.

Vivas, E.: 'Contextualism reconsidered', *Journal of Aesthetics and Art Criticism*, 18 (1959), 222–40.

Wollheim, R.: *Art and Its Objects: An Introduction to Aesthetics* (New York: 1968); 2nd edn (Cambridge: Cambridge University Press, 1980).

JERROLD LEVINSON

Plotinus (204–c.270) Greek philosopher of the Christian era; the best-known Neoplatonist thinker, and a major influence on Western mysticism.

Born in Egypt and educated at Alexandria, Plotinus joined the Emperor Gordian III on an expedition to Persia in 242, hoping to learn about Persian mystical philosophy. In the event, Gordian was killed and Plotinus travelled to Rome, where he established an academy and came to be favoured by the Emperor Gallienus. He was regarded as a spiritual master, known for gentility and kindness and reputed to be a mystic.

One of Plotinus' students in later life was Porphyry, who wrote the biography of his teacher and edited his works. These are known collectively as the *Enneads*, and consist of six books each of nine chapters (*ennea*: 'nine'). Chapter 6 of bk I, entitled 'On beauty', contains Plotinus' most systematic treatment of this issue. Unusually in the history of philosophy, aesthetics is prominent within Plotinus' entire system, and from this single chapter one may learn much of his general philosophical outlook. Indeed, for the many centuries during which his philosophy was influential, the essay 'On beauty' was the only known part of the *Enneads*.

Plotinian philosophy is essentially Platonistic, and this provides a key to understanding his emphasis on the importance of aesthetic experience in advancing from miserable ignorance to mystical transcendence. From the earliest speculative philosophers (the pre-Socratics) Plato had inherited a belief in the possibility of comprehending reality by relating apparently disparate phenomena to some deeper ordering and unifying principles. The general character of this ancient idea is captured by a formula associated with Pythagoras, another mystic in whose philosophy aesthetics plays a significant part. According to this, the existence of an ordered reality (*kosmos*) is due to the imposition of limit (*peras*) upon the unlimited (*apeiron*) to produce the limited (*peperasmenon*). Plotinus follows Plato in taking the ordering principles to be *forms* which organize quantities of matter into intelligible unities. Variants on this basic theme are common within ancient and mediaeval philosophy, and are important to the aesthetic theories of these periods, which generally treat the experience of beauty as a mode of knowledge of (or identification with) reality.

Plotinus' version of the 'philosophy of form' is esoteric but recognizably related to aspects of Christian theology, which it deeply influenced. At the heart of things is a transcendent divine reality which escapes all categories of description. None the less, it has three modes, or aspects (*hypostases*). First and foremost it is ultimate unity (*the one*); second, it is both intellect and what intellect knows (*mind* or *thought*); and, third, it is the source of life (*the soul*). Emanating out of this 'primal core' is the remainder of things, ordered according to their degree of existence or participation in the nature of innermost reality. All entities seek union with the divinity, and strive to move inwards towards it, seeking to realize their potential for perfection and aspiring to the condition of pure, self-originating, matterless *form*.

Aesthetic experience plays an important role in this process of self-perfection. In 'On beauty', Plotinus pursues the Socratic quest after essential definitions. He wonders what precise conditions are necessary and sufficient for beauty, and first considers the suggestion that the essence of beauty is *symmetry* (*Enneads* I.6.1). This is dismissed, however, because some beautiful things, such as single colours and musical notes, are simple (without parts) and hence lack symmetry; while some symmetrical things, such as some faces, lack beauty. Also, Plotinus assumes a principle of composition according to which a complex entity can only have a given property if its parts have it independently of their membership of the whole. Instead, beauty is taken to be *unity* or oneness, by which he means formal unity: 'In what is naturally unified, its parts being all alike, beauty is present to the whole' (*Enneads* 1.6.2). This is a comprehensive notion covering both simples and complexes. Different answers to the question 'What is it? – for instance, 'red', 'middle C', 'a square', 'a horse', and so on – all introduce unifying forms which impose an integrated nature upon the matter in which they inhere. When we experience such forms we derive pleasure from this perceived unity, and the soul is also awakened to its co-natural affinity with the source of empirical and other forms – namely, divinity in its aspects of *oneness, mind* and *soul*.

Beauty is generally a *supervenient* quality – that is to say, one which results from the organization of matter by formal principles. The beauty of a (near) perfect pattern, say, consists in the ordering of stuff (wood, paint and so on) according to a geometrical ideal, and this is true also of the constituent parts of the pattern, such as lines and curves, considered in their own right. Since it does not identify empirical beauty with any particular form, this view allows for indefinitely many kinds of beautiful things – beauty is 'variably realizable'. Equally, however, it raises the question of non-empirical beauty, such as that of a proof, or a virtuous character. Plotinus not only recognizes the aesthetic quality of these, but regards non-sensible beauty as being of a higher order, and claims that the ascent through the hierarchy of beauty-inducing forms is the pathway to mystical union with *the one*, an aspect of which (in its hypostasis as *mind*) is the dazzling self-existent form of beauty:

> Like anyone just awakened the soul cannot look at bright objects. It must be persuaded to look first at beautiful habits, then the works of beauty produced not by craftsmen's skill but by the virtue of men known for their goodness, then the souls of those known

for beautiful deeds . . . Only the mind's eye can contemplate this mighty beauty . . . So ascending, the soul will come first to Mind . . . and to the intelligible realm where Beauty dwells. (*Enneads* 1.6.9)

These ideas may strike us as extravagant and even unintelligible. But Plotinus is worth reading, both in order to make sense of work in mediaeval and Renaissance thought, and to see how aesthetics could have a central place within a well built philosophical and religious system.

See also BEAUTY; INEFFABILITY; MEDIEVAL AND RENAISSANCE AESTHETICS; PLATO.

WRITINGS

Ennead VI, ed. and trans. A.H. Armstrong, Loeb Classical Library, Plotinus, vol. 6 (London: Heinemann, 1988).

Enneads, ed. and trans. E. O'Brien, *The Essential Plotinus* (Indianapolis: Hackett, 1989).

BIBLIOGRAPHY

Anton, J.P.: 'Plotinus' refutation of beauty as symmetry', *Journal of Aesthetics and Art Criticism*, 23 (1964), 233–7.

Beardsley, M.: *Aesthetics from Classical Greece to the Present Day* (Montgomery, Ala.: University of Alabama Press, 1975).

Gurtler, G.M.: 'Plotinus and Byzantine aesthetics', *The Modern Schoolman*, 67 (1989), 275–84.

Miller, C.L.: 'Union with the one, *Ennead* 6, 9, 8–11', *New Scholasticism*, 51 (1977), 182–95.

JOHN HALDANE

popular art The main aesthetic issue is whether popular art really deserves artistic status and is indeed capable of genuine aesthetic merit, or whether it is intrinsically and necessarily an aesthetic failure and a corruptive danger to high art. Though never a central concern of traditional philosophical aesthetics, popular art has since the 1970s become a very much contested topic through the increasing dominance of mass-media culture and the growing alienation of much of the public from contemporary avant-garde forms of high art.

The controversy over popular art extends even to its name. While those sympathetic to popular art call it such, those who oppose it prefer to label it 'mass art' (the term 'mass' signifying an undifferentiated and possibly subhuman conglomerate), and they distinguish true popular art as traditional folk art which developed and exists apart from mass-media technology and 'the culture industry' (an influential term coined by Horkheimer and Adorno, 1986). Since such folk art is no longer a very serious force to be reckoned with, while mass-media arts are no doubt the most popular forms of our aesthetic consumption, I think the term 'popular art' is justified for them. My position on such art (elaborated in Shusterman, 1992) lies between the condemnatory pessimism shared by reactionary high-culture elitists and left-wing Marxists of the Frankfurt school, and the celebratory optimism of popular culture enthusiasts. It is a position of *meliorism*, which recognizes popular art's grave flaws and abuses, but also its merits and potential. It holds that popular art should be improved because it leaves much to be desired, but that it can be improved because it can achieve real aesthetic merit and serve worthy social goals.

Though we shall concentrate on the aesthetic arguments against popular art, it is important to note that perhaps the most damaging indictments are not directed at popular art's aesthetic status but at its pernicious sociocultural influence. Yet these more general indictments seem to involve and rest on aesthetic considerations. For example, the charge that popular art corrupts high culture by borrowing from it and by luring away potential artists and audiences presumes that popular art's borrowings are to no good aesthetic purpose (since works of high art borrow from each other with no consequent complaint), and that creative talent and appreciative attention can be put to no good use in popular art since it is intrinsically worth-less aesthetically. Similarly, the charges that popular culture is emotionally destructive because it produces spurious gratification, and is intellectually destructive because of its superficiality and escapism, rest on the presumed aesthetic inability of popular art to produce genuine aesthetic pleasure through meaningful form and content. Further, the charges that popular art 'not only reduces the level of cultural quality . . . ' but also encourages totalitarianism by creating a passive audience peculiarly responsive to the techniques of mass persuasion' (Gans, 1974, p. 19) rest on the assumptions that popular art's products are invariably of negative aesthetic value and so necessarily lower taste, and that they necessarily require a mindless, passive response because they can neither inspire nor reward any aesthetic attention beyond uncritical passivity.

In considering the arguments against the aesthetic legitimacy of popular art, it would be futile to attempt a total whitewash, for much of popular art is lamentably unaesthetic and socially noxious. What philosophers need to consider, however, is the validity of arguments claiming to show that popular art is necessarily an aesthetic failure – that, in the words of Dwight Macdonald (1957, p. 69). 'there are theoretical reasons why Mass Culture is not and can never be any good.' We shall consider six such charges.

1. Popular art fails to provide real aesthetic satisfaction but only spurious ones, which are 'washed-out', vicarious, escapist and ephemeral. There are several problems with this charge, apart from the problem of knowing what is 'spurious' satisfaction. For most of the public, the pleasures of popular art (such as movies and rock music) are surely as intense and real and direct as those derived from high art, which also has an escapist dimension. Nor do high and low art always differ with respect to the ephemerality of their pleasures. But even if our pleasure from a pop song is briefer than that from a sonnet, this does not entail this pleasure's illegitimacy or irreality. Moreover, the argument that popular art can produce only ephemeral pleasures is flawed in forgetting that many of the great classics of high art (for

instance, Greek and Shakespearean drama) were originally produced and consumed as popular art.

2. It is argued that popular art can provide no real aesthetic pleasure because it requires no effort but only passivity. As Horkheimer and Adorno remark (1986, p. 137), its 'pleasure hardens into boredom because it must not demand any effort . . . No independent thinking must be expected from the audience'; anything 'calling for mental effort is painstakingly avoided'. One of the problems with this argument is that it equates all effort with 'mental effort' or 'independent thinking'. Critics of popular art tend to forget that there are forms of aesthetically rewarding activity other than intellectual exertion – dancing, for example. Moreover, these critics too often make the mistake of assuming that because some popular art can be enjoyed without intellectual effort it can never sustain or reward intellectual interest. But from the fact that something can be enjoyed on a shallow level, it does not follow that it must be so enjoyed and has nothing else to offer.

3. The charge of popular art's intellectual shallowness typically breaks down into two subcharges. First, that it cannot deal with the real problems of life in a serious way because it is aimed to distract the masses and keep them in a false contentment by showing them only what they can easily understand and accept. But this argument falsely assumes that consumers of popular art are just too stupid to understand more than the obvious, and that they are incapable of appreciating views with which they disagree. Empirical studies of television watching (see Fiske, 1987) show this is false. Second, there is the charge that popular art's products necessarily lack sufficient complexity, subtleties and levels of meaning so that they may be comprehensible to the large audiences that popular art seeks to please. But again, the argument presumes the inability of popular art's audience to appreciate any intellectual complexity, and again, empirical evidence shows that they do. Intellectualist critics typically fail to recognize the multi-layered and nuanced meanings of popular art, either because they are unwilling to give it the sympathetic attention needed to reveal such complexities or simply because they lack the specific (pop) cultural knowledge to understand them (for instance, the inversions, techniques, slang and intertextual allusions of rap music).

4. The common claim that popular art is necessarily uncreative relies on three lines of argument: its standardization and technological production preclude creativity because they limit individuality; its group production and division of labour frustrate original expression because they involve more than one artist's decision; the desire to entertain a large audience is incompatible with individual self-expression, hence with creativity. All these arguments rest on the premiss that aesthetic creation is necessarily individualistic – a questionable romantic myth nourished by liberalism's ideology of individualism, and one which belies art's essential communal dimension. In any case, none of these arguments is compelling; nor will they isolate popular works from high art.

The sonnet's length is just as rigidly standard as the TV situation comedy's, and the use of technology is present in high as well as popular art, where it serves less as a barrier than as a spur to creativity. As for the second argument, we can grant no contradiction between collective production and artistic creativity without thereby challenging the aesthetic legitimacy of Greek temples, Gothic churches and the works of oral literary traditions. The third argument, that popular art cannot be creative because it must offer homogenized fare to meet an average of tastes, involves a number of errors. It confuses a 'multitudinous audience' with a 'mass audience'. Popularity requires only the former. A particular taste group sharing a distinct social or ethnic background or specific subculture may be clearly distinguishable from what is considered the homogeneous mass audience of average Americans or Britons, and yet still be numerous enough to constitute a multitudinous audience whose satisfaction will render an art sufficiently popular to count as popular art and achieve mass-media coverage.

Moreover, popular artists are also consumers of popular art and form part of its audience, often sharing the tastes of those towards whom their work is directed. Here there can be no real conflict between wanting to express oneself creatively and wanting to please one's large audience. Finally, the argument that popular art requires conformity to accepted stereotypes rests on the empirically falsified premiss that its consumers are too simple-minded to appreciate views that are unfamiliar or unacceptable to them.

5. A fifth charge often levelled at popular art is that it lacks the autonomy necessary for true artistic status (see Adorno, 1984; Bourdieu, 1984). Popular art forfeits this status by its desire to entertain and serve human needs rather than purely artistic ends. Such inferences rest on defining art and the aesthetic as essentially opposed to life and reality. But, though a hoary dogma of aesthetic philosophy, why should this view be accepted? Originating in Plato's attack on art as doubly removed from reality, and reinforced by Kant's aesthetic of disinterestedness (defined as indifference to real existence and praxis), the view has been sustained by a philosophical tradition which has always been eager, even in defending art, to endorse its difference from the real so as to ensure philosophy's sovereignty in determining reality.

But surely art forms part of our reality and can belong to practical life? Music is used to lull babies to sleep. Poetry is used for prayer and courtship, fiction to inculcate moral lessons, architecture to create living and working spaces. Though it is true that the deep integration of art and life characteristic of premodern cultures (particularly the Greek) was eclipsed in the nineteenth century by the 'separatist' idea of 'art for art's sake', this ideology of radical autonomy was largely the product of the artist's loss of traditional forms of patronage. Moreover, today's developments in postmodern culture suggest the disintegration of this purist ideal, and the increasing implosion of the aesthetic into all areas of life.

6. Finally, popular art is condemned for not achieving adequate form. Usually it is not unity but formal complexity that is denied to popular artworks, and used to distinguish them from genuine art. For Bourdieu popular art involves 'the subordination of form to function' and 'content', and thus cannot achieve the complex formal effects of high art, 'which are only appreciated relationally, through a comparison with other works which is incompatible with immersion in the ... [content] given' (Bourdieu, 1984, pp. 4, 34). But this formal complexity of intertexuality is also often present in works of popular art, many of which self-consciously allude to each other. Nor are these allusions and their formal aesthetic effects unappreciated by the popular art audience, who are generally more literate in their artistic traditions than are the audiences of high art in theirs. The formal quality of popular art can only be properly assessed by examining concrete examples, and the reader is referred to Cavell (1981) and Shusterman (1992, chs. 7 and 8).

See also AUTONOMY, AESTHETIC; CULTURE; MORALITY AND ART; PLEASURE, AESTHETIC.

BIBLIOGRAPHY

Adorno, T.W.: *Aesthetic Theory* (London: Routledge & Kegan Paul, 1984).

Bourdieu, Pierre: *Distinction* (Cambridge, Mass.: Harvard University Press, 1984).

Cavell, Stanley: *Pursuits of Happiness* (Cambridge, Mass.: Harvard University Press, 1981).

Fiske, John: *Television Culture* (London: Routledge & Kegan Paul, 1987).

Gans, Herbert: *Popular Culture and High Culture* (New York: Basic Books, 1974).

Horkheimer, M. and Adorno, T.W.: *The Dialectic of Enlightenment* (New York: Continuum, 1986).

Macdonald, Dwight: 'A theory of mass culture', *Mass Culture: The Popular Arts in America*, ed. B. Rosenberg and D. White (Glencoe, Ill.: Free Press, 1957).

Shusterman, Richard: *Pragmatist Aesthetics:*

Living Beauty, Rethinking Art (Oxford: Basil Blackwell, 1992), chs 7, 8.

RICHARD SHUSTERMAN

pornography Etymologically, the word means writing associated with the brothel, and it applies most specifically to a genre of fiction which draws its materials from sexual fantasy and consists almost exclusively of detailed descriptions of sexual activity, tireless and sometimes elaborately perverse. It typically lacks any interest of character or plot. In its 'ideal type', developed by the Marquis de Sade (1740–1814) in such works as *Justine* and *The 120 Days of Sodom*, the apparatus also includes, for instance, an isolated, luxurious château, and silent servants. Such features are now less common, though they can still sometimes be found in examples with more literary pretension, such as *The Story of O*, published under the pseudonym Pauline Réage, a well known book which also preserves the Sadean emphasis on cruelty. In recent times the strictly sadistic aspect has generally been more cultivated in other media.

Written pornography seems to have first appeared, at any rate in Europe, in the middle of the seventeenth century. The first original English prose pornography (as opposed to translations), and also the first to take the form of a narrative rather than a dialogue, was John Cleland's *Memoirs of a Woman of Pleasure* (1748) – better known as *Fanny Hill*. However, visual representations with an explicit sexual content go back to ancient times and appear in almost all cultures, and some of them (such as murals at Pompeii and some Attic vase painting) seem designed to elicit the same kind of interest as written pornography. The word 'pornographic' is now applied to works in any medium, and by far the largest proportion of pornography current in the 1990s consists of material in mechanically reproduced visual forms, such as photographic magazines, cinema films and video tapes.

Particularly in relation to this visual material, a distinction is often drawn between 'hard-core' and 'soft-core' pornography. The distinction has a complex structure, but roughly speaking the subject-matter of soft-core pornography excludes violence, and if males are represented at all, they are not visibly aroused. It is interesting for the psychology of pornography that magazines of the kind standardly for sale in respectable newsagents in Europe and North America, which have soft-core illustrations, often contain written text which, if the distinction is applied to text, must count as hard-core. In the case of films, soft-core pornography may possess more ambitious production values than hard-core, sometimes aiming for distribution in ordinary cinemas as opposed to specialist porno houses.

Although the term 'pornography' is applied to works in any medium, it may still be taken to refer to what is, in a very broad sense, a genre. A pornographic work is one that combines a certain content, explicitly sexual representation, with a certain intention, sexual arousal. (Pornographic material is, of course, often sold in sex shops and used in connection with sexual activity, particularly masturbation). A feature of this definition, as opposed to more wide-ranging or, again, evaluative proposals for the use of the word, is that it leaves open questions about the relation of pornography to other notions – in particular, those of the *obscene* and the *erotic*. Even leaving aside its technical use in English law, 'obscene' in its ordinary use is a strongly negative term, suggesting the hideous, repulsive or unacceptable; 'erotic', on the other hand, has more positive connotations in contemporary society. Pornography is sometimes taken to be necessarily associated with obscenity; sometimes it is contrasted with the erotic. If pornography is defined merely in terms of a certain content and a certain intention, it will remain for discussion whether all pornography is obscene, or to what extent it can be erotic.

Such discussions naturally bear on a further question – whether there can be a pornographic work of art. It is not disputed that most pornography is of no aesthetic or artistic interest at all, but there is disagreement as to whether this is so merely because it is not worth anyone's while to make it more interesting, or because it is inherent in the content and intention of pornography. It has been argued in favour of the second view that the one governing aim of pornography, to arouse its audience sexually, necessarily excludes the more complex intentions and expressive features necessary to aesthetic interest. Against this, there are some visual works which it is hard to deny are pornographic in terms of their content and (it is reasonable to suppose) their intention, but which have been widely thought to have merit, such as the series of illustrations to Aretino's works by Giulio Romano (1492–1546), and prints by Utamaro and other eighteenth-century Japanese artists. There are also writings, for instance by Georges Bataille, which are assertively pornographic at least in terms of content and structure, and which possess literary interest.

There is strong pressure to use 'pornographic' in an unequivocally negative way, to imply condemnation on moral and social grounds, or aesthetic grounds, or both. In this sense, the pornographic is often contrasted with art. It may also be contrasted with the erotic, pornography being specially associated with cruelty and violence, particularly against women, while the erotic is taken to imply sexual relations that are both gentler and more equal. If the term is used in this way, there is a danger that different issues may be run together, and some important questions begged: it may be harder, for instance, to separate, intellectually and politically, the question of whether some objectionable work has merit from the question of whether it should be rejected (for instance, banned) whatever its merit.

It would be naïve to suppose that in this area definitional issues could be uncontentiously settled without ideological implications. For one thing 'pornography' is a candidate for legal use in regulating, and perhaps trying to suppress, objectionable material. More generally, and more deeply, the nature and definition of pornography are necessarily at issue when it is asked what exactly is objectionable about such material. Pornography is found in varying degrees offensive by many people, and some of it is deeply offen-

sive to almost everybody. Is this best explained by general psychological theory, or in cultural (and therefore perhaps more local) terms? To what extent can any such questions be discussed without bringing in considerations that are in a broad sense political?

The most radical cultural analysis of pornography since around 1980 has come from feminist critics. Most pornography is intended for and used by men, and consists of representations of women and of heterosexual activity serving male fantasies. Most pornography involving same-sex activity between women is also intended for men (there is usually at least one sequence of this kind in the standard pornographic film.) However, pornography is not exclusively related to men's fantasies about women. There is a great deal of male homosexual pornography intended for male homosexuals, and also pornography which is used by women and on an equal basis by heterosexual couples. Moreover, it is not necessarily true that the more extreme or the 'harder' a piece of pornography is, the more sexist it is. Much of the most extreme pornography indeed expresses violence against women; but, with more widely available material, it is significant that the distinction between hardcore and soft-core, mentioned above, is itself drawn on sexist lines: it is soft-core pornography that exclusively offers women to the view of a male figure who is either outside the representation or unaffected within it.

The radical feminist thesis is that not just the fantasy but also the reality of male domination is central to pornography, and that sadistic pornography involving women is only the most overt and unmediated expression of male social power. Moreover, the objectifying male gaze to which pornography offers itself is thought to be implicit not only throughout the commercial media, but in much high art. This outlook reinterprets the relation of pornography to other phenomena. Traditional views, whether liberal or conservative, are disposed to regard pornography as a particular and restricted phenomenon, and extreme sadistic pornography as even more so; but a radical feminist approach is likely to see the overtly sadistic varieties of pornography, and the phenomenon in general, as merely less reticent versions of what is more acceptably expressed elsewhere.

This approach leads to new emphases in the definition of pornography, but they involve a conflict. On the one hand, it should be less significant in this perspective to pick out a class of works distinguished by the extremity of their sexual content – or indeed, at the limit, by their having explicit sexual content at all. On the other hand, a radical feminist critique is likely to want to distance itself from conventional puritanism, and to encourage the expression of some rather than other kinds of sexuality and eroticism. It is thus involved, just as much as are traditional approaches, in making discriminations between kinds of sexual content – discriminations which inevitably run into familiar ethical, psychological and (if enforcement is proposed) legal complexities of separating some kinds of sexual representation from others.

See also CENSORSHIP; FEMINIST CRITICISM; MORALITY AND ART.

BIBLIOGRAPHY

Dworkin, Ronald: 'Do we have a right to pornography?', *Oxford Journal of Legal Studies* (1981), reprinted in *A Matter of Principle* (Cambridge, Mass.: Harvard University Press, 1985).
MacKinnon, Catherine A.: *Feminism Unmodified* (Cambridge, Mass.: Harvard University Press, 1987), pt 3.
Obscenity and Film Censorship: Report of a UK Government Committee (Cmnd 7770 HMSO, 1979, reprinted Cambridge University Press), pt 2.
Peckham, Morse: *Art and Pornography* (New York: Basic Books 1969).

BERNARD WILLIAMS

postmodernism *See* MODERNISM AND POSTMODERNISM.

poststructuralism *See* STRUCTURALISM AND POSTSTRUCTURALISM.

properties, aesthetic A definition or analysis of aesthetic properties may best be approached by first listing those properties and types of properties that are typically thought to be aesthetic when ascribed to works of art (we may then see what, if anything, they have in common):

(1) what might be called pure value properties: being beautiful, sublime, ugly, dreary;

(2) emotion properties: being sad, joyful, sombre, angry;

(3) formal qualities: being balanced, tightly knit, loosely woven, graceful;

(4) behavioural properties: being bouncy, daring, sluggish;

(5) evocative qualities: being powerful, boring, amusing, stirring;

(6) representational qualities: being true-to-life, distorted, realistic;

(7) what might be called second-order perceptual properties: being vivid or pure (said of colours or tones), dull or muted;

(8) historically related properties: being original, bold, conservative, derivative.

Is there any common characteristic of these various properties by which they are all recognized as aesthetic qualities? Several proposals may look initially promising, but may be dismissed by counter-example. It might be thought, for example, that these are all phenomenal or perceptible properties of the works themselves. It is often pointed out that the emotion properties do not simply refer to ordinary emotions of persons: they must be perceived in the works – for example, in musical pieces – themselves. But not all the qualities listed above can be perceived in the works themselves. One could not perceive whether a representational work was true-to-life without knowing the model or type of model represented; one could not know that a work was original without knowing the tradition. Aesthetic properties have also been called regional qualities (Beardsley, 1973), qualities of complexes that emerge from qualities of their parts, but vividness of colour and purity of tone are not such. They can qualify single colours or tones. Many of the properties in the above list – for example, the emotion and behaviour properties – are ascribed literally to humans and perhaps only metaphorically to artworks. But this is not true of the formal or representational properties, for example.

Another influential suggestion has been that aesthetic properties are those that require taste to be perceived (Sibley, 1959). Ordinary perceivers do not see sadness, balance, power and realism in artworks as readily or automatically as they perceive redness or squareness. It seems that they must be more sensitive or knowledgeable to see the former qualities; hence the suggestion that they require taste. But the traditional concept of taste has suggested a special faculty akin to moral intuition. Without some independent description of such a faculty and how it is supposed to work, its existence is no more plausible in the one case than in the other. Furthermore, there are qualities in our list that do not seem to require taste to be perceived – vividness in colour, for example.

Those qualities that do seem to require taste for their appreciation need not lead us to posit a special faculty. The apparent need for taste can be explained, first, by the fact that many of the qualities in question appear to be complex relations. We may require considerable exposure, or in some cases training, before we become capable of recognizing such complex relations in works of art. Second, most of the qualities mentioned in our list are at least partly evaluative. To call an artwork tightly knit, daring, powerful, or vivid is to suggest a positive evaluation of it. To call it sluggish, boring, drab or derivative is to suggest or express a negative evaluation.

Thus, ascription of these properties expresses some set of aesthetic values. This fact points to a more plausible general criterion for identifying aesthetic properties: they are those which contribute to the aesthetic values of artworks (or, in some cases, to the aesthetic values of natural objects or scenes) (Beardsley, 1973). It has also been plausibly suggested that aesthetic properties are those which make artefacts works of art, or which help to determine what kinds of artworks

they are (Sparshott, 1982, p. 478). These two criteria may well be related, if, as seems likely, 'work of art' is itself a partly evaluative concept, so that to call something a work of art is to imply, for example, that it is worthy of sustained perceptual attention. (To propose such criteria is not to imply that aesthetic properties can always be clearly distinguished from others, that there are no borderline cases.)

We might conclude that works of art are objects created and perceived for their aesthetic values, and that aesthetic properties are those which contribute to such values (using 'aesthetic' in the broad sense indicated by the variety of properties on our list). In considering this analysis, however, we must not forget that there are negative evaluative properties on the list as well. If being ugly, boring, distorted or dull contribute to an object's value, they normally contribute only to negative value (though not always, since a work's ugliness may contribute to its power or realism, for example). There are also qualities, such as emotion qualities like sadness, that seem to be evaluatively neutral. It will be argued below, however, that such properties do contribute to aesthetic value, albeit more indirectly or less obviously than some of the others listed.

If we restrict attention to the positively evaluative properties, it might seem that artists would intend to build as many as possible into their works, and that their works would be better the more such properties they have. But this idea is too simple, since many of these properties do not blend well in particular contexts (more on the implications of this later). In the case of both positive and negative evaluative properties, it is part of the task of critics to point them out and to justify their claims in this regard. This may also be part of our criteria for identifying such properties.

Most of the qualities listed, it was noted, are both relational and (partly) evaluative. In principle, it should be possible to analyse particular references to such properties into evaluative and non-evaluative (descriptive or objective) components. A crucial question concerns the relation between these components. The properties on our list differ among themselves in the degree to which they always include (in their instantiations) specific evaluative or objective aspects.

These distinctions can be brought out by analyses of the following form: 'object O has aesthetic property P' means 'O is such as to elicit response of kind R in ideal viewers of kind V in virtue of its more basic properties B'. If P is evaluative, then R will be positive or negative, often involving pleasure or displeasure. V will almost always include characteristics such as being knowledgeable of the kind of artworks to which O belongs, being unbiased or distinterested, and being sensitive enough to react to properties of type B. B, as noted, may be more broadly or narrowly specified. Although the evocative qualities on the initial list most clearly involve reactions of observers, this analysis views many of the other properties there as having similar structure. Ascribing such properties expresses a positive or negative response, suggests that others ought to share the response (ought to approximate to the ideal viewer), and points to certain more or less specific objective properties of the object.

Beauty, for example, is non-specific on the objective side, but always elicts a pleasurable response in sensitive observers. Philosophers have not always agreed that the objective side of beauty cannot be specified. Perhaps the best-known attempt to do so was that of Hutcheson, who held that it is always uniformity amidst variety that causes aesthetic pleasure expressed in ascriptions of beauty. But all such attempts fall easily to counterexamples, in this case ordered complex objects that do not appear beautiful. Although B (from the above formula) is therefore unspecified in the case of beauty, there will always be some properties – usually, but not always, formal relations – in virtue of which an object is beautiful. Sometimes these more basic properties will themselves be evaluative properties. For example, an artwork may be beautiful in virtue of its grace or power. It may in turn be powerful in virtue of its piercing pathos or graceful in virtue of its smooth lines. The properties of power and grace, while still

evaluative, are more specific on their objective sides. 'Graceful' always refers to formal qualities that elicit positive responses, and formal qualities of certain kinds. Squat objects with sharp, jutting edges and angular, broken planes cannot be graceful. 'Powerful' generally refers with approval to more basic expressive qualities. A piece of music for the harp that is pianissimo and legato throughout cannot be powerful.

Ascriptions of more broadly evaluative and less specifically objective properties, when challenged, are always defended by appeal to less broadly evaluative and more specifically objective properties. Ultimately, a critic or viewer should defend evaluations by pointing to non-evaluative properties of the works in question. These will be formal, expressive, representational or historical properties of the work (relations of the work to its tradition) that lack evaluative dimensions in themselves. For example, while to say that a painting's composition is balanced may be to evaluate it positively, to say that it is symmetrical is not evaluative; similarly for 'poignant' and 'sad' when predicated of musical works. Ultimately, appeal may be always to non-evaluative formal properties, but this claim is more controversial.

Sibley (1959) raised the question of how aesthetic qualities relate to non-aesthetic properties, and he claimed that the latter are never sufficient conditions for the former. Given our different criteria for aesthetic properties, the more interesting question is how the more basic or less (broadly) evaluative relate to the less basic and more (broadly) evaluative. Appeal to evaluative properties at a certain level may always support evaluative claims at a higher level. Grace, for example, might always contribute to beauty, and vividness to power. This is because these properties involve similar evaluative responses. But can the same be said of the relation between non-evaluative or basic aesthetic properties and evaluative properties? It seems not. The same objective formal properties – for instance, gentle curves and pastel colours – that make one artwork graceful might make another simply insipid. The same harmonies that make one piece of music powerful might make another strident, or, indeed might make the same piece strident to a different (but equally knowledgeable) listener.

From the point of view of a single critic, it would seem that evaluative aesthetic properties must supervene on non-evaluative qualities of artworks: that is, there can be no difference in evaluative properties without some differences in objective qualities. This amounts to a constraint on rational aesthetic judgement: given all the same objective properties, evaluative judgement must remain constant, at least for those with fully developed tastes. But the apparent principle of supervenience fails when we compare judgements across equally competent or even ideal critics. The examples noted in the previous paragraph suggest two reasons why we cannot specify interesting principles of aesthetic evaluation, why non-evaluative or basic aesthetic properties do not always contribute in the same way to evaluative properties.

First, aesthetic properties of parts of artworks are altered or transformed, often in unpredictable ways, when juxtaposed with other aesthetic properties in other works. A curve that is graceful in one sculpture may be insipid in another. Second, there remain irreconcilable differences in taste, even when we consider the aesthetic judgements of only ideal critics (again, this does not imply different faculties, but only different evaluative responses to the same objective properties).

The literature in aesthetics is replete with debates about the nature of the particular kinds of aesthetic properties included in our list. It seems quite clear, for instance, how the complex formal properties that determine the structure of whole works are built up from simpler formal relations. The latter include repetitions, variations, contrasts and closures among elements such as melodic phrases or harmonic chords in musical works. Problems here are not philosophical but critical – it can be a complicated task indeed to isolate all the hierarchical and overlapping structures in complex pieces of music, for example.

When it comes to expression and representation, debates on the nature of aesthetic properties become philosophically more interesting. Debates about the nature of representational properties focus on the visual arts. They concern both the questions of necessary and sufficient conditions for elements of paintings to represent particular objects, as well as criteria for judging certain works to be more realistic or true-to-life than others. Regarding the first question, proposed criteria include intentions of artists (they represent what they intend to represent), conventions (paintings represent as symbolic systems do), resemblance and causal criteria. Certainly none of these seems sufficient in itself. The first two are not sufficient because paintings fail to represent what viewers cannot see in them, whatever the intentions of the artists and the conventions determining reference at the time. The last two are not sufficient in themselves, either, since resemblance can be accidental and paintings often do not represent their models. The debate on the second question centres on whether realism is a matter of resemblance or convention, or both (and in what proportion).

Debates about the nature of expression focus on music, the expressive art form *par excellence*, where the central question is how mere sequences of sounds can be sad, joyous or angry (express sadness, joy or anger). According to one side of this debate, they do so by causing these or related emotions in listeners. According to the other side, they do so by mimicking human expression of the emotions, in voice, demeanour, or behaviour. It may be that both sides are correct, and, furthermore, that these two methods reinforce one another in the recognition of musical expressiveness. We might be affected emotionally by the recognition of structural features of human emotional expression in music; and we might in turn recognize such features more readily when we begin to feel their effects.

In literature and painting, the more standardly representational arts, expression is more closely tied to representation. Literature, of course, can simply describe emotional states directly, while paintings can represent persons in the grip of the emotions or scenes seemingly suited to these experiences. The

345

latter is again more complex, since such scenes might either once more evoke emotional states in viewers or express emotions by looking the way scenes would look to persons in those states.

There is also considerable debate across the arts on a topic regarding expressive aesthetic properties that originates with Aristotle – namely, how audiences can enjoy experiencing expressions of negative or painful emotions in art. Explanations include Aristotle's idea of catharsis, the claim that what we enjoy is the artistic skill involved in the expression, the idea that we enjoy the lack of real objects or threats connected with these emotions in real life, and that we gain reassurance in our own sensitivities from such experiences. None of these is without problems. The first and last lack evidential support. The second fails to explain enjoyment of junk horror movies, and the third explains only why we endure such experiences, not why we seem to enjoy them.

This last topic takes us back to the central issue of value and aesthetic properties. Aesthetic properties have been identified here primarily as those which contribute to the aesthetic value of artworks (or, in some cases, natural objects), and as those which provide reasons for aesthetic judgements or evaluations. Many of these properties are themselves evaluative, consisting in relations between objective basic properties and evaluative responses of observers (the evidence for this being that ascriptions of such properties necessarily express approval or disapproval). Others have been characterized here as non-evaluative basic properties that ultimately ground evaluations. It remains to explain briefly how and why these basic properties are ultimate sources of aesthetic value.

Complex formal properties constitute principles of order among the elements they structure. They enable perception and cognition to grasp such elements in larger wholes and to assign them significance in terms of their places and functions within such structures. This recognition of order, especially after being challenged by complexity, is pleasing to those faculties that seek it (although, as noted above, it is not always

constitutive of beauty). Likewise, representational and expressive properties engage the imagination and affective capacities in satisfying ways free of the costs and dangers often associated with the latter in real life. Of significance too is the way that these distinct aesthetic properties interact in the context of artworks. Formal properties help to determine expressive behavioural and representational qualities, which may in turn enter formal structures at higher levels, and so on. Since elements within works are grasped in terms of their contributions to aesthetic properties and to such complex interactions among them, this makes for an intensely meaningful and rich experience of these elements as they are perceived. (What were called second-order properties refer directly to such properties as intensity in the perception of elements, while historical properties refer to order of a different kind that relates whole works to each other.)

At best, complexes of aesthetic properties in artworks can so engage all our cognitive and affective capacities as to seem to be distinct worlds, intentionally designed to challenge and satisfy these uniquely human capacities or faculties. Basic aesthetic properties create value ultimately by contributing to the constitution of such alternative worlds in which we can become fully and fulfillingly engaged.

See also BEARDSLEY; BEAUTY; EXPRESSION; FORM; REPRESENTATION; SIBLEY; TASTE.

BIBLIOGRAPHY

Aagaard-Mogensen, L.: 'Aesthetic qualities', *Essays on Aesthetics*, ed. J. Fisher (Philadelphia: Temple University Press, 1983), pp. 21–34.
Beardsley, M.: 'What is an aesthetic quality?', *Theoria*, 39 (1973), 50–70.
Beardsley, M.: 'The descriptivist account of aesthetic attributions', *Revue Internationale de Philosophie*, 28 (1974), 336–52.
Goldman, A.: 'Aesthetic qualities and aesthetic value', *Journal of Philosophy*, 87 (1990), 23–37.
Hutcheson, F.: *An Inquiry into the Original of Our*

Ideas of Beauty and Virtue (London: 1725); (New York: Garland, 1971).

Isenberg, A.: 'Critical communication', *Philosophical Review*, 58 (1949), 330–44.

Mitias, M., ed.: *Aesthetic Quality and Aesthetic Experience* (Amsterdam: Rodopi, 1988).

Sibley, F.: 'A contemporary theory of aesthetic qualities: aesthetic concepts', *Philosophical Review*, 68 (1959), 421–50.

Sparshott, F.: *The Theory of the Arts* (Princeton, NJ: Princeton University Press, 1982).

ALAN H. GOLDMAN

psychoanalysis and art Psychoanalysis is a field of inquiry into the human mind and mental development, aimed at therapy for mental disorders. It thus has a different fundamental focus from aesthetics, which is concerned with the abstract nature of beauty, aesthetic experience and the evaluation of art. Psychoanalysis is committed to the premiss that unconscious motives are the fundamental impetus and determinants of form for human productions and behaviour. It seeks to translate the obvious import of everyday human activities into their hidden, unconscious messages. Art figures in psychoanalytic discussion primarily as a product of human creation, to be decoded into the unconscious motives that it represents.

A number of psychoanalytic theorists, however, provide suggestions regarding the pleasure the audience takes in artworks. In addition, psychoanalytic theory has served as the starting point for certain twentieth-century schools of art and art criticism. Thus, while psychoanalysts' accounts of art rarely amount to aesthetic theory as such, their writings touch on many matters of relevance to aesthetics.

SIGMUND FREUD

The founder of psychoanalysis, Freud (1856–1939) elaborates a theory of mind that treats the human psyche as comprising multiple dynamic components. An entirely unconscious segment, which Freud calls the 'id', comprises basic instinctual drives. Another, largely conscious, component, called the 'ego', attempts to reconcile the demands of the instincts with the demands of the larger world. In the course of the ego's efforts, a part of it branches off into a third component of relative independence. This component is called the 'superego'. It internalizes parental and social demands, and it serves as an internal control and censor over the ego's activities.

Freud analyses mental disorders in terms of disharmony among these components. Disorders arise, for example, as the result of a conflict between the id's demands – usually sexual – and the ego's and the super-ego's efforts to steer the mind into conformity with socially imposed criteria for respectability. They may also result from the ego's inability to maintain some autonomy from the super-ego or external reality. Normal childhood development involves a series of stages in which the id's demands are gradually brought under the control of the ego. The route involves numerous conflicts among the elements of the psyche and external reality, conflicts which may be only partially resolved and may continue to plague an individual throughout adulthood. One particularly difficult conflict that usually has some effect on adult behaviour is the Oedipal situation, in which the (male) child comes to view his father as a rival for his mother's attention and hence wishes to kill (or be rid of) him. Traumatic experiences in childhood may also hinder development into maturity, fixating an individual's control over and expression of instinctual desires at an early stage of development.

The conflicts between instinctual desires and the demands of society and the super-ego lead to many desires becoming repressed – that is, exiled into unconsciousness. Similarly, memories of experiences which conflict with the psyche's internalized notions of acceptability tend to be repressed. Psychoanalysis attempts to recover and treat the motives for neurotic behaviour by unburying repressed ideas, memories and desires. Among the techniques that psychoanalysis employs in this effort are the analysis of dreams (which are believed to express repressed ideas in a disguised way) and free association (in which a patient freely says to the analyst whatever comes to mind, in the hope that these may trigger forgotten but significant memories).

Although he describes his own artistic sensitivity to form and artistic methods as deficient, Freud contends that psychoanalysis can legitimately approach artworks in the same manner as it approaches dreams or neurotic symptoms. 'The product itself after all must admit of such an analysis, if it really is an effective expression of the intentions and emotional activities of the artist' (Freud, 1966–74, vol. 13, p. 212). Freud's writings on the artists and artworks are, consequently, focused on the artist's psychobiography and its relation to his or her artworks. Among these are 'Delusions and dreams in Jensen's "Gradiva" ' (1907), 'Creative writers and daydreaming' (1908), *Leonardo da Vinci and a Memory of Childhood* (1910), 'The Moses of Michelangelo' (1914), 'A childhood recollection from "Dichtung und Wahrheit" ' (1917), and 'Dostoevsky and parricide' (1928).

Freud approaches the creative work and products of artists with the full arsenal of his psychoanalytic methodology. In artworks as in dreams, he takes the surface or 'manifest content' to be a deceptive camouflage for underlying, 'latent' meanings. He also seeks the formal determinants of an artwork, as of all products of human making, in the artist's personal biography. The form of Michelangelo's Moses, for example, is motivated, according to Freud, by his long-standing irritation over many inconsiderate outbursts made by the pope whose grave the sculpture adorns. Michelangelo depicted Moses as one who overcomes rage, Freud argues, in order to achieve a posthumous criticism of the dead pope, who lacked the dignified restraint of the sculpture.

Michelangelo's alleged wit notwithstanding, Freud's account of the artist's psychology is unlikely to charm many artists. He compares artists to children, their activity to neurosis, and their achievements to symptoms of narcissism. Artists, according to Freud, are 'people who have no occasion to submit their inner life to the strict control of reason' (Freud, quoted in Spector, 1972, p.

33). Through art, they indulge desires that most adults have put aside. The original motivation of psychic life, in the Freudian account, is satisfaction of the 'pleasure principle', which directs the individual to pursue pleasure. Maturation involves the individual's recognition that pleasure is more certain if one submits to the constraints of reality – and a constraining 'reality principle' emerges, to which the pleasure principle is subordinated. The artist, however, unlike the average adult, continues through creative activity to gratify the pleasure principle without accepting limitation by the reality principle.

Freud's 'Creative writers and daydreaming' compares artistic activity directly to immature behaviour. He considers both daydreaming and literary art to be psychologically akin to children's play. All three are motivated by unconscious desires. Children's play is motivated by the wish to be grown up. But the overriding wishes of adults are more embarrassing desires of an erotic and ambitious nature. The average adult, therefore, does not freely display his or her motives in public, as the playing child does, but satisfies them only in imagination, in the form of fantasies. The artist, by contrast, is a kind of exhibitionist who publicly displays his or her fantasies.

That literature serves the same function as fantasy is suggested, Freud claims, by the number of works that have a hero who is the centre of the reader's interest and sympathy, and whose survival and security are preserved throughout the work. He concludes that the hero of all novels is 'His Majesty the Ego' – the very hero of daydreams (Freud, 1966–74, vol. 9, p. 150). The ego is the hero even in novels that treat several characters with similar sympathy. In such cases, the ego is simply divided into several component egos.

The artist's creativity is, in Freud's view, primarily motivated by repressed sexual desires. He sees the artist as an introvert whose erotic desires are more powerful than those of the ordinary human being. These impulses are diverted, however, into the non-sexual activity of art. Artistic activity might be taken as the paradigm for what Freud labels 'sublimation', a process in which sexual urges are given an indirect outlet for their expression. All forms of cultural achievement, according to him, are products of sublimation. Those who appreciate beauty, too, are sublimating. Freud writes in *Three Essays on Sexuality*. 'There is to my mind no doubt that the concept of "beautiful" has its roots in sexual excitation and that its original meaning was "sexually stimulating"' (Freud, 1966–74, vol. 7, p. 156n.).

Artists, then, are sufficiently in control of themselves to be able to sublimate their raging desires. Despite their relative developmental immaturity, a good artist is, in Freud's view, sufficiently connected to inter-subjective reality to communicate with his or her audience. None the less, the artist's motivations are personal and fundamentally narcissistic. The audience might be repelled were it not for what Freud describes as 'the essential *ars poetica*'. This technique involves the artist's use of disguises to conceal the work's egoistic character in the aesthetic form offered in the presentation. Freud considers the latter to be akin to sexual forepleasure, for he claims that it is an incentive, providing an increment of pleasure in order to provoke the release of greater pleasure. In the literary case, the reader's ultimate enjoyment is a release of mental tensions, perhaps resulting from a context of which his or her own daydreams can be enjoyed without shame.

Although Freud does not analyse the techniques utilized by artists in giving form to their work, his analysis of the formative principles at work in dreams (and jokes) is suggestive in this connection. Among the formative principles active in what Freud calls 'the dreamwork' are 'condensation' (which conjoins elements of two or more constituent images into a composite image); 'displacement' (in which the psychological significance of one object is assumed by a substitute); 'representation' (in which thoughts are translated into images); and 'secondary revision' (a vaguely described process that renders the disparate elements comprising the dream into a coherent, intelligible whole).

Assuming that one accepts the psychoanalytic premises that dreams represent the fulfilment of unconscious wishes that can be stated as thoughts, and that artworks similarly satisfy unconscious desires, one might expect the process involved in the dreamwork to resemble the psychological processes involved in the formation of artworks. However, the processes of the dreamwork resemble certain principles of traditional Western aesthetics. The dreamwork gives coherent form, establishes closure, and ensures the meaningfulness of material that the mind absorbs from the environment. One might reverse the direction of the analogy, therefore, and consider traditional aesthetic principles to be suggestive in interpreting Freud's analysis of dreams.

OTTO RANK

Rank (1884–1939) explicitly set out to extend Freudian psychoanalytic theory to illuminate art, myth and creativity. He initially attracted Freud's attention with his study *The Arts*, which elaborates a psychology of the artist's personality on the basis of Freudian theory. Rank analyses the artist as intermediate between the dreamer, as described in Freud's *Interpretation of Dreams* (1990), and the neurotic. Like dreamers and neurotics, artists are described by Rank as motivated by repressed sexual wishes.

Rank's later work, *Art and Artist: Creative Urge and Personality Development* (1932), departs from Freudian theory in emphasizing will as the guiding force in the development of the creative personality, and in analysing artistic creation as a function of the interaction of both individual and collective factors. The latter stem from social environment and societal ideology, and ensure the intelligibility of the artwork's form. Rank does not completely abandon his earlier comparison of the artist and the neurotic. Analysing all human creative impulses as aimed at the 'constructive harmonization' of the independent individual and the collective, he contends that the creative person succeeds where the neurotic fails. None the less, Rank dignifies the artist's role by claiming that he or she triumphs over biology, mastering his or her ego to a greater degree than most individuals. He postulates that the collective factor involved in artistic creation is a spiritual principle – 'genius' – working in the artist. He also considers a spiritual presupposition – the belief in the possibility of a kind of immortality through art – to be essential to artistic creation.

Rank does, however, follow the lead of Freud's biologism (that is, Freud's belief that psychological processes can be reductively explained in terms of physiological ones) in his analysis of artistic form. Rank, who speculates on the significance of the birth trauma for the individual's psychological life, considers artistic form to refer back to the primal form of the mother's body. The mother's body is also the content of much art, according to Rank, albeit presented in an idealized form.

CARL G. JUNG

The approach of Jung (1875–1961) to art is premissed on his general critique of Freudian psychoanalytic theory. Freud, Jung argues, is too reductivist in his theorizing. Freud attempts to explain all psychic phenomena by means of personal psychobiography, and in terms of the vicissitudes of the individual's repressed sexual desires. Jung denies that sexual desire can account for all varieties of psychic phenomena (unless one broadens the definition of 'sex' to the point of vacuity). Moreover, he denies that personal psychobiography is the ground on which all psychological structures develop. Jung argues that Freud's analysis does not do justice to the real significance of art, either as a psychological phenomenon or as an aesthetic one.

While eager to distance himself from Freud, Jung follows him in distinguishing the psychoanalytic approach to art from an aesthetic approach. The former can give an account of art as a phenomenon derived from psychic motives, claims Jung; but aesthetics alone considers art in its essential nature. The two approaches ought, Jung contends, to complement one another. But the influence of Freud's psychoanalytic theory has led many to the erroneous expectation that Freudian analysis can explain art. This Jung considers particularly pernicious in the light of the fact that Freud treats art on a par with a psychopathological symptom. In Jung's view, this strategy leads him to miss the deeper significance of art.

Jung distinguishes two different types of artistic creation, the psychological and the visionary. The psychological type involves a calculated project on the part of the artist. Such creation draws from conscious life, and deals with matters assimilated by the poet's psyche. The material is the stuff of human experience generally, and the artist offers the audience a greater depth of insight into ordinary matters than they typically have. Nevertheless, the resulting artwork remains within the sphere of what is psychologically intelligible to the artist and (presumably) to his or her audience.

Visionary artistic creation, by contrast, involves an imagistic richness that outstrips the artist's capacity for expression. The material is unfamiliar and surpasses understanding. The work disturbs its audience; none the less it is pregnant with meaning. Jung describes this kind of art as 'sublime', and compares the act of its creation to Nietzsche's Dionysian experience. We might be reassured, Jung tells us, if we could find a striking personal experience in the artist's biography to account for the work. But the experience behind such work is not personal, but collective. The images provided by the work represent archaic psychic structures that are commonly active in the unconscious of every individual.

Such structures populate what Jung describes as the 'collective unconscious', a psychic layer that exists along with, but deeper than, the personal unconscious. The basic structures inhabiting the collective unconscious are what he calls 'archetypes'. Archetypes are deeply rooted, nearly automatic patterns of instinctive behaviour that are aroused when an individual's circumstances correspond to a typical, universal human experience (for instance, losing a loved one, becoming a parent). The archetypes themselves are unconscious, but they appear to consciousness in the form of images that represent instincts. The characters of the world's mythologies, for example, are particular images for archetypes. The provocative images of visionary art, too, are archetypal images.

Art, according to Jung, is indispensable for culture. Just as he contends that dreams provide compensatory images to correct the errors of consciousness, he argues that art provides compensation for the errors of nations and eras. Art serves this role only in so far as it is a symbol – that is, only in so far as primordial images are active behind artistic ones. By definition, visionary art serves this role. Jung grants, however, that psychological art, too, may be symbolic. In such cases, the symbolic content is outside the range of the artist's understanding. The reader may have similar difficulty recognizing this content. Sometimes, though, such art becomes the focus of a revival in a later epoch, when the consciousness of the age has grown to such a point that it can recognize what an earlier era missed.

Whichever mode of creation is involved in the making of the work, the creative impulse is an autonomous complex, a split-off part of the psyche that leads its own life outside the control of consciousness. The difference between the two modes of creation depends on the artist's conscious relation to the complex. The psychological artist, who feels at one with the creative process, has acquiesced to the unconscious orders of the complex from the beginning; the visionary artist, who has not acquiesced in this way, has been caught unawares.

Jung emphatically denies that artistic activity is comparable to psychopathology, but he does contend that artistic activity makes artists, as a group, more susceptible to certain kinds of psychopathological conditions. Any autonomous complex draws energy away from consciousness. Thus, the energy that fuels the unconscious direction of creative work is drawn away from conscious control of the personality. For some artists, this diversion of energy results in 'the instinctual side of the personality' prevailing over the ethical, 'the infantile over the mature,

and the unadapted over the adapted' (Jung, 1966, p. 79).

OTHER ALTERNATIVES TO FREUD'S APPROACH

Many other psychoanalytic theorists have deviated from Freud's views, while none the less building on elements of his model. Among them is Ernst Kris, author of the influential work *Psychoanalytic Explorations in Art* (1952). Kris describes the process of artistic creation as 'regression in the service of the ego'. He is convincd, *contra* Freud, that art is considerably more controlled than is fantasy, and that the ego plays the role of critic and director for the material that emerges from the unconscious. Ernest Schachtel grants the ego's role in directing unconscious material, but claims that the artist has greater than average access to unconscious material because he or she is unusually open to the world. Trusting in his or her own perception, the artist is less in thrall to convention than most of his or her contemporaries. Jack J. Spector argues that Freud might have developed a more comprehensive aesthetic theory had he developed further his concept of 'ideational mimetics', the tendency to form mimetic representations of concepts that one is entertaining, often as a consequence of observing others' behaviour or receiving communications from others. Spector believes that an elaboration of this concept might have led to an aesthetics based on empathy, which would be particularly illuminating with respect to performance.

THE IMPACT OF PSYCHOANALYSIS ON ART AND CRITICISM

Virtually every educated person in the twentieth century is aware of Freud. Consequently, much twentieth-century art is informed by Freudian themes (for instance, the Oedipal complex, the psychological significance of dreaming, the importance of the unconscious). Indeed, the impact of Freudian theory on the populace at large is so pervasive that the burden of proof would rest on anyone who claimed that a given artwork or school was completely uninfluenced by psychoanalytic thought.

Certain schools of art have explicitly drawn inspiration from Freud. Most notorious among these are the surrealists. Growing out of the Dada movement, which was not unified in its responses to Freud, surrealism employed Freudian concepts to its own purposes. Drawing on Freud's theory of the importance of free association for therapy, surrealist poets employed free association (a method they valorized as a form of 'automatism') as a means of tapping the unconscious. They enlisted the resulting dream-like imagery in their poetry. Aesthetically, they hoped to jar and provoke their audience into an altered state of responsiveness. 'Beauty' was not their ideal. Surrealist theorists, notably André Breton, also attempted to expand Freud's theories regarding the importance of sexuality into a new collective mythology, focused on achieving the heights of sexual satisfaction with a mythic female principle. Hence Breton developed images of a number of female love deities, who were to supplement the collection of psychologically significant figures (such as family members) so important to Freud's theory.

The surrealists took issue with Freud on many points, particularly on matters concerned with therapy. Unlike Freud, they aimed to liberate the id, giving it dominant control over the psyche. They also valued mental disorder as a means of breaking down the barriers between art and life. The surrealists' interest in spiritualism also clashed with Freud's clinical, biologistic approach to aberrant mental phenomena. Freud himself took issue with his surrealist followers; and in general, he disliked modern art. He rejected the products of another school motivated by his theories, the expressionist movement, which attempted to represent the primitive processes of inner life. A more recent artistic trend that Freud's theories partially inspire is the post-Second World War tendency in some American painting to work with mythic elements. Perhaps this phenomenon draws greater inspiration from Jung, whose concept of the archetypes provides a means of

theoretically bridging personal images and collective themes.

Many twentieth-century art and literary critics have seen in the theories of Freud and other psychoanalytic theorists (among them Jacques Lacan and Julia Kristeva) tools for unpacking the significance of art. Critics have employed psychoanalytic theory in diverse projects, such as

(1) seeking repressed content in manifest artworks and in the characteristic aims of given schools of art and literature;

(2) interpreting the behaviour of literary characters in psychoanalytic terms;

(3) decoding the art of movements whose techniques were inspired by Freud;

(4) analysing aspects of a work in terms of the artist's biography;

(5) analysing the relationship between the works of different artists in terms of the Oedipal complex (the project of Harold Bloom); and

(6) utilizing Freudian concepts (such as 'displacement' and 'condensation') as fundamental terms in criticism.

While formalists and others have opposed the Freudian emphasis on the artist's biography as a key to the artwork, the range of employments of psychoanalytic theory in criticism suggests that it will continue to be a major catalyst for art and literary criticism, as well as a stimulus for art.

See also CREATIVITY; CRITICISM; PLEASURE, AESTHETIC; SYMBOL.

BIBLIOGRAPHY

Bersani, Leo: *The Freudian Body: Psychoanalysis and Art* (New York: Columbia University Press, 1986).

Freud, Sigmund: *The Standard Edition of the Complete Psychological Works of Sigmund Freud*, trans. and ed. James Strachey, 24 vols (London: Hogarth Pres, 1966–74). Vol. 7, *A Case of Hysteria, Three Essays on Sexuality, and Other Works*; vol. 9, *Jensen's 'Gradiva' and Other Works*; vol. 13, *Totem and Taboo and Other Works*.

Jung, C.G.: *The Collected Works of C.G. Jung*, trans. R.F.C. Hull, Bollingen series, 24 vols.

of such a character is perfectly possible), her actions in the novel flow naturally from the situations in which she finds herself; her actions are uniformly consistent with her character, and comprehensible in the light of it.

Finally, we might say that, in addition to typicality of character, *typicality of situation* is relevant to an assessment of realism in a literary work. For example, Dickens's novels are often held up as exemplars of realism because they seem to describe the life of typical people in nineteenth-century Britain – in contrast, say, to the lives of the gentry described by Jane Austen. Grinding poverty was a fact of life for many people, one that is not ignored, but also not explored, in Austen. Here again, realism is in some sense tied to verisimilitude; however, in literature the connection is much more difficult to be precise about.

See also ABSTRACTION; GOODMAN; ICONOCLASM AND IDOLATRY; ILLUSION; REPRESENTATION; RESEMBLANCE; WOLLHEIM.

BIBLIOGRAPHY

Freedberg, David: *The Power of Images* (Chicago: Chicago University Press, 1989).
Goodman, Nelson: *Languages of Art* (Indianapolis: Hackett, 1976).
James, Henry: 'In Holland', *Transatlantic Sketches* (Boston: Houghton Mifflin, 1868).
Pole, David: 'Goodman and the "naive" view of representation', *Aesthetics, Form and Emotion* (New York: St Martin's Press, 1983).
Wollheim, Richard: 'Reflections on *Art and Illusion*', *On Art and the Mind* (Cambridge, Mass.: Harvard University Press, 1974).
Wollheim, Richard: *Painting as an Art* (Princeton NJ: Bollingen Press, 1987).
Zuccari, Federico: 'Idea dei scultori, pittori e architetti' (1607); trans. Joseph J.S. Peake, in *Idea: a Concept in Art Theory*, Erwin Panofsky, (New York: Harper & Row, 1960).

CRISPIN SARTWELL

relativism This doctrine assumes variant forms, the most common being (1) dogmatic relativism, which denies either the existence or the knowability of ahistorical, universal or eternal truths about art's alleged intrinsic nature or the qualities of aesthetic appreciation, concluding that all truth claims about art and our modes of understanding it are unverifiable and, consequently, equivalent to each other; and (2) a pragmatic or common-sense relativism, which simply recognizes an evident plurality of criteria between cultures concerning what counts as an artwork, as the beautiful or as meaning in the interpretation of art, without claiming, as dogmatic relativism does, that 'anything goes'. Pragmatic relativism recognizes the possibility of talking about 'truths' within distinct cultural horizons, without laying claim to a universality other than that which constitutes a specific cultural community.

Dogmatic relativism is commonly associated with a belief in the absence of, or loss of faith in, immutable critical standards in aesthetics and art criticism. It is allied with similar pessimistic convictions in epistemology and moral theory. Nietzsche is often taken to be one of the most modern sources of contemporary dogmatic relativism, in so far as from the pronouncement that 'everything is false' he drew the conclusion that 'everything is permitted' (Nietzsche, 1968, § 602). Such extreme relativism is associated with a form of nihilism which denies the possibility of any lasting foundation to either epistemological or interpretative principles, and which historical pessimists such as Paul Johnson have seen as the dominant *Weltanschauung* of the twentieth century: 'a world adrift, having left its moorings in traditional law and morality' (Johnson, 1983, p. 48). Similar sentiments have been repeatedly echoed across twentieth-century Europe, as avant-gardism. Dadaism, modernism and abstract expressionism and, more recently, deconstruction have challenged every supposed critical verity and boundary between different modes of artistic and cultural practice. Yet dogmatic relativism in both its aesthetic and epistemological forms is far from a contemporary phenomenon, having its roots in both the pluralist outlook of Michel de Montaigne (1533–92) and the scepticism of Pyrrho of Elis (c.360–270 BC).

Dogmatic relativism is, arguably, doubly inconsistent. First, the conviction that the absence or unknowability of universal truths about art and artistic interpretation implies that *all* views about the nature of art or aesthetics are as good as one another, self-defeatingly proclaims precisely the universalism that it denies. Second, all views about art's character or the qualities of aesthetic response are equivalent only in so far as they fail to match up to the supposed universal criteria of artistic and aesthetic truth. Yet to claim this is inadvertently to lay down what such criteria are or ought to be; which, in turn, is to contravene the premiss of the argument – namely, that there are no such criteria or that, even if there are, they are unknowable. Dogmatic relativism can consequently be accused of an inverted absolutism and an attitude of *ressentiment* – that is, it implicitly lays down the conditions whereby all truth claims would not be equivalent and, in so far as it is forced to realize that such universal conditions are unattainable, it closes its eyes to the rich plurality of truth claims in variant artistic traditions by consigning all to an indifferent equivalence.

Whereas dogmatic relativism defines itself in relation to a yearning for an albeit unattainable universal standard of truth and appraisal in the arts, pragmatic aesthetic relativism does not. It simply recognizes the *de facto* existence of a plurality of modes of appreciation and idioms of truth claim, not only in a culture but also between cultures. The possibility of rival, if not contradictory, practices and conceptual employments is accepted, and an attempt to formulate a general theory of art which might sublate such difference is eschewed. Most important, pragmatic or cultural relativism is not wedded to the pernicious indifference of the 'anything goes' doctrine, but, on the contrary, defends the possibility of localized truth claims integral to different artistic and cultural horizons. Whereas dogmatic relativism inadvertently endorses the foundational in truth claims (that is to say, because no universal foundation can be established, no

universal truth can be endorsed), pragmatic relativism does not. It perceives truth claims to rest on and be relative to distinct cultural practices. In other words, pragmatic relativism is not prepared to deny *all* local artistic or aesthetic truths because of the absence of a universal foundation, whereas dogmatic relativism is. Pragmatic relativism is plainly not a variant of subjectivism, but is consistent with appeals to intersubjective criteria for aesthetic appraisals within distinct aesthetic communities.

David Hume recognized that the denial of universal truth claims about art's essential nature does not lead to the conclusion 'everything is permitted'. Although the proposition that beauty 'exists merely in the mind that contemplates' things and not in things themselves 'seems to have attained the sanction of common sense, there is . . . [also] a species of common sense which opposes it' (Hume, 1965 [1757], pp. 86–7). That 'species of common sense' recognizes that established critical consensus, shared practices of critical discernment, comparative knowledge of different artistic traditions and the suppression of overt personal or cultural prejudice, all serve the attainment of a 'standard of taste by which the various sentiments of men may be reconciled' (Hume, 1965 [1757], pp. 86–7). Though the judgements legitimated by such standards will not have the binding force of *a priori* reasoning, Hume recognizes the solid consensus and experiential reasoning which sustains them; and he understands, furthermore, how aesthetic education is dependent upon the recognition and acceptance of such argumentation.

Though belonging to a very different philosophical tradition, Gadamer presents a similar line of reasoning. He shares Hume's scepticism regarding *a priori* claims to fixed epistemological foundations, and yet is vehemently opposed to any form of subjectivism. In *Truth and Method* he argues that all truth claims by and about art are inevitably preconditioned by the norms and values of the cultural horizon that shape them and are, in a foundational sense, relative. Nevertheless, the localized cultural claims to truth that Gadamer defends gain their authority from what can be argumentatively validated by a community of interpreters whose experience is such as to substantiate and re-endorse their warrant. Gadamer does not suggest an ahistorical or transcultural platform from which conflicting truth claims in aesthetics can be appraised. On the contrary, we can only attempt to reconcile any 'conflict of interpretation' by appeal to those standards forged in the course of a culture's development. Pragmatic relativism in effect attempts to bypass or neutralize the issue of the absence of objective foundations, by showing that truth claims in and about the arts gain their warrant from the competence of those practices which forward them. Thinkers such as Habermas and Apel have consequently examined the parameters of such competence in order to establish intersubjective criteria for such truth claims, whilst recognizing that such criteria are historically malleable and to an extent renegotiable within a given community. Nevertheless, though the truth claims of different cultural practices never have the force of universal claims, they are not made on subjectivist grounds. The weight of the traditions and practices which support them is such as to make them relatively objective – that is, in Gadamer's phrase, 'beyond our willing and doing' (Gadamer, 1960, foreword).

Pragmatic relativism is therefore wedded to the view that no work of art possesses a universal property that makes it universally a work of art, and recognizes that works of art are only what they are within specific cultures. Furthermore, it holds that how works of art are perceived, evaluated, interpreted, described and judged depends upon the norms and practices of different cultures. The plurality of such practices does not, on a critical level, imply a crude subjectivism, as each culture can establish its own intersubjective criteria for truth claims and aesthetic evaluation.

Of the problems associated with pragmatic relativism, three stand out:

(1) The position cannot be formally substantiated without self-contradiction. Pragmatic relativism cannot simultaneously declare itself to be *the* most appropriate way of looking at the arts *and* advocate a plurality of interpretative values.

(2) Consequently, the pragmatic relativist can only 'show' rather than demonstrate his commitment. Nietzsche and Derrida recognize in quite different ways that perspectivism and stylistic pluralism (both variants of pragmatic relativism) can be merely insinuated rather than proved. It is for this reason that pragmatic relativism has been treated with such ridicule in some academic communities.

(3) Though pragmatic relativism can successfully challenge subjectivism on the grounds that the truth claims relative to a given tradition are not arbitrary but gain their warrant from an historically established consensus, it can do little when a consensus and the norms which sustain it are challenged by competing values. Reasoned arbitration is possible only when the disputants within a tradition agree as to the identity of their tradition. When what constitutes a tradition is in question, appeal to shared norms or practices to warrant a given claim is obviously impossible.

Despite its difficulties, pragmatic relativism is both plausible and persuasive. First, it is essentially a modest position, seeking not to impose the truth claims of, say, the Western tradition of aesthetics over the *rasa* (taste) doctrine of India, but to recognize and learn from the nature and conceptual parameters of both. Second, pragmatic relativism is primarily an open-spirited stance which, by being receptive to the truth claims of other traditions and cultures, places great emphasis upon understanding through difference rather than similarity. Third, pragmatic relativism entails presuppositions which, in effect, allow it to add to our understanding of an artwork. If there are fixed truths about art and the norms of its appreciation, the task of criticism would merely be to identify their concrete exemplifications. Interpretation would be replaced by descriptive typology. However, the lack of universal foundations implies that what is accepted as an artwork is differently determined by different interpretative traditions. Changes and alterations to those interpretations will, historically speaking, cumulatively expand our understanding of art. Pragmatic relativism not only recognizes, but extends, the knowledge-constitutive role of interpretation, whereas commitment to any form of foundationalism limits interpretation to the mere rendition of the art's alleged timeless essence.

See also GADAMER; HUME; TASTE; TRADITION.

BIBLIOGRAPHY

Bernstein, R.J.: *Beyond Objectivism and Relativism* (Oxford: Basil Blackwell, 1983).
Gadamer, H.-G.: (*Wahrheit und Methode* (Tübingen, 1960); trans. J. Weinsheimer and D.G. Marshall, *Truth and Method*, 2nd rev. edn (New York: Crossroad, 1989).
Hermeren, Goran: *The Nature of Aesthetic Qualities* (Lund: Lund University Press, 1988), ch. 2.
Hollis, M. and Lukes, S.: *Rationality and Relativism* (Oxford: Basil Blackwell, 1982).
Hume, D.: 'Of the standard of taste' (1757); in *Aesthetics*, ed. J. Stolnitz (London: Macmillan, 1965).
Johnson, P.: *A History of the Modern World, from 1917 to the 1980s* (London: Weidenfeld & Nicolson, 1983).
Margolis, J.: 'The reasonableness of relativism', *Philosphy and Phenomenological Research*, 42:1 (1982), 93.
Margolis, J.: *Pragmatism without Foundations, Reconciling Realism and Relativism* (Oxford: Basil Blackwell, 1986).
Nietzsche, Friedrich: *The Will to Power*, trans. W. Kaufmann and R. Hollingdale (New York: Vintage Press, 1968).

NICHOLAS DAVEY

religion and art In the Middle Ages art, science, philosophy, history and practical life were all offshoots of religion, and so regarded theoretically. Nowadays, they are usually treated as separate universes of discourse. The most sustained attempts to chart their boundaries have been made within the idealist tradition. Here each is assumed to be a particular mode, or phase, of *Geist* ('mind' or 'spirit'). Typical idealist thinkers in this respect are Kant, Schiller, Hegel, Croce, Collingwood, Michael Oakeshott and (up to a point, since he also has naturalistic leanings) Santayana.

The key tenet of idealism is that reality is first and foremost mental. (Nature and the physical world are merely abstract aspects of it.) That is, it belongs to consciousness, from whose contents, or possible contents, it is scarcely to be distinguished. Anything wholly transcendental – that is, permanently inaccessible to consciousness – might as well, at least for a strict Hegelian, not exist. A thing exists, ultimately, only so far as it can exist *for us*.

Nevertheless, for many idealists the phenomenal world (the world as it appears to consciousness) is shot through with intimations of transcendence. For Kant, since the transcendental is *ex hypothesi* inscrutable, traditional theology is impossible. The divine (which, whatever else it may be, is normally thought of as transcendental) cannot be known, 'proved' or reasoned about. At best it can be intuited from the manifest facts of ethical and aesthetic life.

Judgements in both spheres ('this is good', 'that is beautiful', and so on) possess a peculiar subjective immediacy which seems to confirm their implicit claim to objective, universal validity. The self is necessarily their focus, but their intrinsic structure is such as to point away from it, towards the transcendental. The reality of the transcendental is underwritten by the fact that the experiencing self must logically belong to it, since it cannot simultaneously be an object of its own observation.

In ethical life, according to Kant, we feel ourselves to be governed by an imperative which no naturalistic or utilitarian considerations can fully explain. No doubt the cohesion of society, like our aggregate self-interest, is furthered by observance of the moral law, but that is not the reason, subjectively speaking, why we observe it. We observe it simply because we know we must; and that undeniable 'must', though (or perhaps because) it is inscrutable, points to a transcendent source. A command cannot issue from nowhere.

Aesthetic judgement similarly legislates for all observers. A thing can be pleasing, but it cannot be beautiful, for me alone. If it really is beautiful, you too are in a sense 'obliged' to see it as such. The beautiful, like the good, is not independent of the observer's subjectivity, since a thing's beauty, though objective, must be subjectively experienced. It cannot simply be taken on authority or accepted as a piece of information. It is, however, independent of the observer's self-interest. This makes it apprehensible only by those, the good, who have the capacity to suspend their self-interest. On the other hand, unlike goodness, it is also independent of the observer's moral interests and enthusiasms. It is not its goodness which makes a thing beautiful, but its appearance of 'free' or self-governed purposiveness. (Not, be it noted, its appearance of serving some *extraneous* purpose. The latter is the principle behind the so-called 'functionalist' aesthetic, where beauty is not 'free', but dependent on function.)

Kant was notoriously indifferent to art, and has little to say about it, since he invariably regards its beauty as inferior to that of nature. But what he says about the relation of the aesthetic and the moral to the transcendental is clearly suggestive in respect of any joint consideration of art and religion, particularly in the case of his remarks on the sublime. Our response to the sublime in nature (or, one might add, in art, so far as art reflects nature) prefigures the religious attitude. It consists in the awareness of an awesome limitlessness and unbounded power, but one in which the subject's natural fear of such a power is qualified by his sense of his own righteousness and innocence when confronted by it.

In this respect the awe provoked by the sublime differs from the superstitious, self-abasing terror of the savage. The civilized man's fortitude and self-respect – that is, his own sublimity of character – at once enable him to triumph over a threatening nature (or his terror in the face of it) and reconcile him

with it (quite how is unclear), so that he not only participates in its power, but also gathers from it the intimation of an underlying, and ultimately benevolent, divinity.

Schiller's account of the sublime, as of the aesthetic generally, has much in common with Kant's. Hegel's aesthetics, however, like his metaphysics, are different. They are art-rather than nature-centred. Art is superior to nature as a vehicle of the divine, because, like the absolute mind (or Idea) of which the universe as a whole consists, and unlike nature, it too is self-conscious, or a product of self-consciousness. The divine, however, is not transcendent, since there is no transcendence. Hegel's 'God', therefore, is more or less a figure of speech, being simply the immanent absolute risen to self-consciousness in the world which it has itself created or 'posited'. A prime medium through which it rises to self-consciousness is art, defined as 'the sensuous embodiment of the Idea'.

In primitive or 'symbolic' art the absolute fails to achieve full articulation, being overwhelmed by the 'crassness' (as Hegel calls it) of the sensuous or natural world. This is because man, or incarnate mind, is yet undeveloped, and is hence still too deeply enmeshed in that world. At the other extreme, in modern or 'Romantic' art, form has been outstripped by content. Mind is now so self-aware that representations of nature (which is not self-aware) are inadequate fully to embody it. Art has finally been superseded by philosophy (most notably by Hegel's own), in which alone the absolute is completely realized, and of which even religion is a mere shadow. (This is inevitable, and no cause for regret.) Only in 'classical' art, epitomized by Graeco-Roman sculpture, are form and content wholly in balance, since only then was the evolving idea precisely matched to the natural forms available for its representation – that is, the human body, used to depict the gods.

Hegel's aesthetics, like his ethics, is a branch of his metaphysics. The beautiful is essentially an 'appearance' of the true, of ultimate reality. The aesthetic ideal is the idea in sensible form. If it be asked why the real should manifest itself in beauty, the reason lies in its essential organic harmony, or unity in diversity, which is also the principle of the beautiful.

The earlier Collingwood, like Hegel, sees religion as a more 'advanced' phase of spirit than art. For religion, though defective, deliberately aims at truth, while art (like primitive man) is indifferent to truth, making no distinction between fact and imagination. Religion is the prototype of science, history and philosophy. The later Collingwood and other thinkers (including Santayana) have seen art as superior to religion, precisely because, in its purest or most mature form, it actively asserts nothing. 'The poet nothing affirmeth,' said Sir Philip Sidney, 'and therefore never lieth.'

The idea that art (or the highest art) is essentially non-declarative points in two directions. On the one hand it leads to aestheticism, the view, central to the so-called aesthetic movement (exemplified by Pater, Whistler, Wilde), to Bloomsbury aesthetics (as in Fry and Bell) and to Oakeshott, that aesthetic experience, and thus art, is *sui generis*. A wholly distinct and autonomous province of experience, it is reducible to no other and is valuable precisely on that account, as satisfying a similarly unique human need.

On the other hand, art's non-declarative character is taken by some (mostly critics, such as Matthew Arnold and F.R. Leavis, rather than philosophers) merely to indicate that, unlike religion (or at least, dogmatic religion), it recognizes the limits of the sayable. Nevertheless, what cannot be said can still be suggested; and art's suggestiveness, for all that its medium is fiction, is actually truer to the complexities of experience than the cut-and-dried factual claims of religion or philosophy. A tacit presupposition of this view (which is essentially a secular Kantianism, disengaged from any explicit metaphysical theory) is that all art, even non-realist art, is in some sense representational. (So-called 'expressive' art may be thought to represent inner, 'subjective' experience, which eludes one-to-one pictorial or linguistic articulation.) Art points beyond itself to a reality apprehensible by no other means. It elicits meaning and coherence from experience. It reconciles us to life by exposing some of its mysteries as superficial, and persuading us humbly to accept the rest. In short, it does what religion offers to do, only better, because more honestly. It achieves symbolic 'truth' precisely by forswearing any claim to literal veracity.

All this raises the question as to whether religious art can be called art at all, unless religion itself is somehow to be regarded as an imperfect form of art. Clearly, on the idealist view, both art and religion endeavour, by imaginative means, to discover structure and meaning in the cosmos. The difference is that art knows itself to be fictional (at least in form), whereas religion claims to be true. It demands active belief, where art demands at most Coleridge's 'willing suspension of disbelief'.

Excluding jokes such as *trompe-l'oeil*, where the delight lies in the illusion's being detected, art which invites literal or near-literal belief is fantasy art (what Plato supposed most art to be). Its aim is to excite pleasurable emotions by constructing, and sustaining, an illusory world more submissive to the subject's self-indulgent desires than the real one can be. Accordingly, it will usually employ more surface verisimilitude, and less obvious stylization, than art which has no such extraneous purpose, or whose purpose is simply to focus attention on the object for its own sake.

Hence there arises the paradox that fantasy art often seems more 'real' than what Collingwood called 'art proper', or even than nature. An obvious example is pornography, which has come overwhelmingly to rely on photographic images. For a photograph seems to present the object directly, rather than depict it; to be not art, but fact. It thus exacts a minimum of imaginative effort from the spectator.

Collingwood stigmatized pornography as typical of 'amusement art', while regarding religious art as 'magical art'. Amusement art excites emotions simply in order that we may enjoy the sensation of having them without the responsibilities involved in acting upon them. It is, in Collingwood's view, a substitute for action. This conviction is shared, incidentally, by many who defend pornography as harmless, because supposedly cathartic. The question is not usually addressed as to whether the emotions concerned would stand in need of catharsis if they had not first been stimulated to an unnatural degree; nor whether, since the whole point of pornography is to obliterate the distinction between fantasy and reality, the user can be relied upon to discharge them solely in fantasy; nor whether, even if he could, his craving for fantasy ought to be indulged.

These reservations, of course, could apply equally to sentimental or any other amusement art. Following Mill's somewhat erratic train of thought in his *On Liberty* and *Utilitarianism*, I.A. Richards suggested that any 'impulse' might legitimately be satisfied so long as its being so did not thwart the satisfaction of 'superior' impulses. Ignoring the question as to what 'superior' might mean, though, it may be felt in general that amusement art is tolerable, or even valuable, so long as the consumer himself understands it to be such, and is therefore in no danger of being mastered by his fantasy – that is to say, of mistaking it for reality.

But, clearly, we have to do here not with fantasy in a pejorative or debilitating sense, rather with something like play (a category central to Schiller's aesthetics). Play may be considered either as a necessary liberation from the serious business of life, or as a rehearsal for it. (Indeed, *both* seem on reflection to be intrinsic to the idea.) In the first capacity it recalls the aestheticist view of art, in the second the Arnold–Leavis view, of art as a means of grasping and mastering a complex reality, which will include the appropriate emotions. But either option must render dubious the distinction between amusement art and 'art proper'. The real distinction is between 'art proper' and fantasy art as previously defined.

Magical art stimulates emotions (martial, patriotic, revolutionary, religious, acquisitive, moral, and so on) with a view to their being discharged in the appropriate actions. Its value, therefore, will depend entirely on that of the ends it serves. The sole aesthetic criterion, if it can truly be called aesthetic, will be technical or pragmatic, concerning the efficiency with which a given artwork stimulates the required emotion. Beauty might conceivably do this (though not on Kant's view), but will otherwise be incidental. For crudity, either of execution or of the emotion demanded, will not matter so long as the emotion is, in fact, evoked and acted upon. A vulgar advertisement may sell a product better than a sophisticated one. A sentimental religious print may conduce to piety as effectively as an artistic masterpiece, and more. From a religious standpoint, as from any other of a primarily purposive character, 'good' art, or 'art proper', is superfluous, except as a lexicon of proven techniques of emotional stimulation.

Indeed, in and for itself, 'art proper' might even be harmful. The object of religion is to open the mind to the possibility of transcendent things, and thereafter to close it. In the religious view the complexities of experience, transcendent or otherwise, to which 'art proper' exposes us are at best irrelevant, and at worst a return to the chaos and doubt from which, in virtue of its affirmative or even dogmatic character, religion rescues us.

It might be said, nevertheless, that 'art proper' is itself insufficiently distinguishable, except on pure aestheticist premisses, from magical art. The attitude to the world which Arnoldians believe it to promote, and prize it for promoting, is effectively moral, even quasi-religious, and can scarcely fail to find expression in behaviour. Certainly nineteenth-century realists such as George Eliot, Trollope and Tolstoy claimed to be writing with a moral purpose, revealing the hidden order of things, and extending human sympathies. How much difference is there between an art which professes (and achieves) such aims, and explicitly didactic (that is, magical) art?

The answer might be that whatever the authors themselves may have claimed, and whatever moral effects their work actually had, what made it 'art proper' was the fact that in practice it did not subordinate the immediate aesthetic aim (truth to the object, or fidelity to the integrity of the artistic creation as such) to any prior goal, moral or otherwise. This patient refusal to jump to conclusions, or to bend the artistic process into premature conformity with them, would itself constitute a moral phenomenon and a moral example.

Science and history present parallel cases. How far religion also does so – and here obvious political analogies suggest themselves – will depend on whether we see religion primarily as a 'world-open' receptivity to the transcendent, or as a 'world-closed' claim finally to have captured it in doctrine. If the first, how is religion to be distinguished from art, or from its supposed effects? These are questions that can be answered neither simply, nor here.

See also AUTONOMY, AESTHETIC; BEAUTY; CATHARSIS; HEGEL; INEFFABILITY; KANT; PORNOGRAPHY; SCHILLER.

BIBLIOGRAPHY

Collingwood, R.G.: *Speculum Mentis: Or the Map of Knowledge* (Oxford: Clarendon Press, 1924).

Collingwood, R.G.: *The Principles of Art* (Oxford: Clarendon Press, 1938).

Croce, Benedetto: *Aesthetic: As Science of Expression and General Linguistic* (Milan: 1902); trans. D. Ainslie (London: Macmillan, 1922).

Hegel, G.W.F.: *Introduction to Aesthetics* (Berlin: 1835); trans. T.M. Knox, ed. C. Karelis (Oxford: Clarendon Press, 1979).

Kant, Immanuel: *The Critique of Judgement* (1748); trans. J. C. Meredith (Oxford: Clarendon Press, 1969).

Leavis, F.R. and Wellek, René: 'Literary criticism and philosophy', *Scrutiny*, vol. 5, no. 4 and vol. 6, nos. 1, 2; reprinted in *The Importance of Scrutiny*, ed. Eric Bentley (New York: New York University Press, 1964).

Santayana, George: *The Life of Reason* (London: Constable, 1922).

Schiller, Friedrich von: *Naïve and Sentimental Poetry* (1800) and *On the Sublime* (1801); trans. J.A. Elias (New York: Frederick Ungar, 1966).

Schiller, Friedrich von: *On the Aesthetic Education of Man* (1802); ed. and trans. E.M. Wilkinson (Oxford: Clarendon Press, 1967).

Scruton, Roger: *The Philosopher on Dover Beach* (esp. title essay) (Manchester: Carcanet Press, 1990).

R.A.D. GRANT

Renaissance aesthetics *See* MEDIEVAL AND RENAISSANCE AESTHETICS.

representation The relation of a depiction to what it is a depiction of, in virtue of which it is a depiction of that item.

As defined thus, and as predominantly used in aesthetics, 'representation' generally refers to *pictorial* representation. In this sense, Raphael's *Portrait of Pope Leo X* represents Pope Leo X. So representation is a relation of a picture to the thing of which it is a picture (the *object* of the picture). (I use the term 'depiction' (above) to try to capture the fact that there are representations that are not, strictly, pictures, such as figurative sculptures and, perhaps, works of programme music.) But, of course, pictures bear many relations to their objects. For example, it may have been true at some time that Raphael's portrait was located to the south of the pope. The relation of representation, then, is more specifically the relation of a picture to its object in virtue of which it is a picture of that object.

The first philosophical text that appears to give a full-fledged account of this relation is Plato's *Republic*. In book 10 Socrates describes a craftsman who can make what every other craftsman can make, and in addition can make 'all plants and animals, including himself, and thereto earth and the gods and all things in heaven and Hades' (*Republic* 596.C6). When his interlocutor expresses incredulity, Socrates says that in fact anyone can be such a craftsman, if he carries a mirror about with him, which contains a reflection of the objects around him. And, he says, a painter is a craftsmen of this kind. So, first of all, a picture is held here to be like a mirror image of its object; painting is a process of *mimesis*, or imitation. (However, as Hans-Georg Gadamer, among many others, has pointed out, the translation of 'mimesis' as 'imitation' is problematic, and at the least too narrow. 'Mimesis' has the sense of 'making the absent present', which at once allows the relevance of sheer imitation and makes more sense of the ontological upshot of Plato's treatment.)

Of course, the sense in which a painter can create animals and artefacts is attenuated. As Socrates argues, the painter produces not, say, a real bed, but the mere appearance of one. In Plato's epistemology, mere appearance is to be shunned in favour of reality. This forms the basis of Plato's notorious exclusion of the mimetic artist from the ideal state. The painter seduces us with appearances and tempts us to confuse image with reality. But this position has been rejected by many thinkers, and also many artists, who have held that the elucidation of appearances through mimesis can be valuable, and in fact can help guide us to and through reality. At any rate, whether pictorial mimesis was condemned or celebrated, it quickly became the standard account of representation in the Western tradition, and in fact the standard account of the overall activity of the artist. The notion was held more or less as common sense at least through the Renaissance. In a remark about Masaccio, Vasari writes that 'painting is simply the imitation of all the living things of nature with their colours and designs just as they are in nature' (Vasari, 1978 [1568], p. 46).

Nevertheless, it is possible to become extremely puzzled about how a flat picture can be an imitation of a three-dimensional object, and the notion of imitation has remained for the most part unexplicated. Let us, then, characterize imitation as the intentional creation of a situation in which one item (the imitation) comes to resemble another – for instance, in which a picture comes to resemble its object. Resemblance, in turn, may be characterized in terms of shared properties. Each property that two things share is a respect in which they resemble one another. It follows from this that each thing resembles each other thing in indefinitely many respects; and for precisely this reason Nelson Goodman views ascriptions of resemblance as vacuous, and terms the notion itself

'a pretender, an impostor, a quack' (Goodman, 1972, p. 437).

For example, on the present account, garbage and the good resemble one another because they share the properties of being referred to in the present sentence, of being self-identical, of being created by man, and so forth. Nevertheless, it seems that we would like to say that garbage and the good are not very similar at all. Now I freely admit that, on the present account, each thing resembles each other thing in indefinitely many respects. But on the face of it, the promiscuity of a relation should not impugn its legitimacy. For example, the relation of distinctness is displayed by any pair of things. The relation of resemblance as I describe it, however, also holds between any thing and itself. But there are some other relations that also display this peculiarity. For example, if everything is contained in one universe of discourse, then each thing stands to each other thing in the relation of being in the same universe of discourse as that thing, including itself.

It should at once be admitted that the context and conventions within which an ascription of resemblance is deployed fix, in a rough way, the respects of resemblance that are relevant for enumerating the truth conditions of the ascription. This sensitivity to context is obviously not unique to resemblance. (Consider the relation of being far from.) In short, for each utterance of an ascription of resemblance there is a relevant *configuration of shared properties* – relevant, that is, for fixing the truth conditions of the ascription on that occasion.

The imitation view of representation, then, is that it is a necessary condition for one item to represent another that the first be an imitation of the second in the specified sense.

A variety of objections have been brought to this view, but they can be grouped roughly under two heads. First, some thinkers have argued that the sheer imitation of things in the real world is literally impossible. Ernst Gombrich holds that the history of art shows that people cannot simply sit down and paint what they see; that they always proceed by an interpretative process he terms 'schema and correction' (Gombrich, 1983, introduction and pt 1). They start with a vocabulary of pictorial conventions to which they graft the particular demands of the object that they are trying to represent. The slow development of such schemata is in large part the history of artistic styles. The way a painter in the sixteenth century made a portrait is obviously different from the way portraits are made in the twentieth century, though *people*, the subjects of portraits, have not changed so dramatically. Goodman makes a similar, though much more radical, objection; he says that the very demand to copy an object the way it is is incoherent, for 'the object before me is a man, a swarm of atoms, a complex of cells, a fiddler, a friend, a fool, and much else' (Goodman, 1976, p. 6). That is, one cannot imitate the way an object is, because there *is* no particular 'way an object is'. Thus there is, strictly, nothing *in particular* to be imitated.

A second style of objection is that, even if it were possible to achieve imitation, an imitation of the real world has no value, is a mere redundancy. Eugene Véron writes that 'if the artist were really able to reduce himself to the condition of a copying machine' his work would be 'a servile reproduction' and 'inferior to reality' (Véron, 1879, § 2). That is, roughly, a modern version of the ancient Platonic criticism that mimetic representation is worthless in comparison to the real things represented. Many artists and theoreticians have felt the force of such an objection, and have concluded that the task of representative arts is not to imitate but to idealize their objects. This view was originally associated with the Neoplatonism of Plotinus and the Renaissance Neoplatonists. Such thinkers asserted that, if pictures represented their objects not as they were but as they should have been, representative art would lead not away from but towards a high reality. A version of such a view was held by Hegel, who maintained that 'the sensuous is *spiritualized* in art', and that 'from the wealth of [its] own resources [art] brings into being works of fine art as the primary bond of mediation between that which is exclusively external, sensuous, and transitory, and the

medium of pure thought' (Hegel, 1975, p. 2). And the art historian Kenneth Clark writes: 'In our Diogenes search for physical beauty our instinctive desire is not to imitate but to perfect' (Clark, 1956, p. 424).

Many works of art instantiate such a programme of idealization. The works of Raphael, for example, are clearly not *mere* imitations of external objects; they are exquisitely composed; and the faces of, for example, his madonnas clearly embody idealized beauty rather than specific features of real models. Nevertheless, it is hard to see how idealization could provide an account of representation in our defined sense. It is hard to see how the *Portrait of Pope Leo X*, for example, could possibly represent the pope *in virtue* of idealizing him; a portrait might well represent its sitter even if it is no more idealized than the sitter himself, or even if it is uglier. Thus, idealization is best seen as a normative programme for how representational artists ought to proceed, rather than as a full-fledged theory of representation.

Furthermore, misgivings have arisen about a basic metaphysical picture on which both the imitation and the idealization views have been asserted to rest. Such views, it is claimed, rest on an ontological distinction between real things (the world, bits of which serve as objects of representations) and conceptualizations of the world and its constituents (including representations). It has been asserted by Dewey, Heidegger, Gombrich, Gadamer and many others that the world does not sit there passively waiting to be imitated or idealized, that the world is at least in part articulated or even created by the act of representing it. (Such a view surely has its origins in Kant.) 'Through art,' Dewey writes, 'meanings of objects that are otherwise dumb, inchoate, restricted, and resisted are clarified and concentrated . . . by creation of a new experience' (Dewey, 1934, pp. 131, 132). It must be remarked that on Dewey's view there remains something distinct from the representation that is clarified in the work, though the work is no mere reflection of an antecedent reality.

Gombrich shares this view. But even this qualified metaphysical realism is jettisoned by Heidegger and Gadamer. Heidegger (1971, p. 42) writes that 'the work sets up a world and keeps it abidingly in force.' Gadamer (1975, p. 125) remarks; 'There must be almost a reversal of the ontological relation of original and copy.' And he goes on to say: 'Word and picture are not mere imitative illustrations, but allow what they represent to be for the first time what it is' (Gadamer, 1975, p. 126). Or, to put what I shall term the articulation view at its baldest: life imitates art.

The last quotation from Gadamer raises the spectre of an overall theory of representation which is associated with the articulation view, but which could be held independently. For Gadamer there conflates the function of word and that of picture. Goodman is the most prominent advocate of what we may term the denotation view of representation. He writes: 'A picture that represents – like a passage that describes – an object refers to and, more particularly, *denotes* it. Denotation is the core of representation' (Goodman, 1976, p. 5). On such accounts, the relation of a picture to its object is similar in some respects, if not identical, to the relation between a name and what it names – or, perhaps better, between a description and what it describes. Goodman in fact holds an articulation view of the function of both pictures and descriptions (and of pictorial systems and languages as wholes); but, again, a denotation view is in principle open to anyone who would like to relate pictorial representation to linguistic denotation.

However, one widely drawn implication of the denotation view (certainly it is drawn by Goodman) is that the relation of depiction to depicted object is mediated by a conventional symbol system. Thus, talk of any 'intrinsic' or 'natural' relation (paradigmatically, resemblance) between depiction and object would seem to be out of place. Pictorial artists operate with a conventional 'vocabulary', and interpreters of such pictures must be competent in that vocabulary in order to interpret successfully. Gombrich, in *Art and Illusion*, gives a long list of examples of conventional symbolic modes of depiction that drive the history of art – for example, conven-

tionalized ways of treating the figure that appear in instruction books for artists (Gombrich, 1983, e.g. p. 127).

However, it is obvious that there are many differences between pictorial and linguistic symbol systems which must be accounted for by proponents of a denotation view of representation. Goodman asserts that what distinguishes pictorial sytems is that they are *dense* and *replete*. Roughly, a symbol system is dense when between any two characters in the system it is possible to produce a third. Analogue systems are dense in this sense, while digital systems are not. The more replete a symbol system is, the more aspects of the symbol are relevant to its interpretation. Thus, though the typeface in which a description is set makes no difference in the interpretation of a description, such factors as thickness of line or fine gradations of colour can be quite relevant in interpreting a picture.

Nevertheless, Goodman seems to ignore other differences between pictures and linguistic items which render the denotation view problematic. For example, linguistic systems must be learned painstakingly as one masters their symbolic elements, such as words, one by one. Pictorial systems are mastered, as it were, all at once. Given the ability to interpret one picture in the system, one thereby gains the ability to interpret many others. This suggests that depiction is not a symbol system in Goodman's sense at all.

Flint Schier has recently developed an account of representation that builds on the insight just mentioned. He holds that what is characteristic of 'iconic' or pictorial systems is that 'once someone has interpreted any arbitrary member of it, they can proceed to interpret any other member of the system, provided only that they are able to recognise the object depicted' (Schier, 1986, p. 44). Schier terms this characteristic of pictures 'natural generativity'. For example, if I know what Jane looks like, then if I am competent in interpreting photographs (a competence that can be demonstrated in a single correct interpretation of a photograph), I can successfully interpret photographs of Jane as depicting Jane. Schier takes the fact that pictorial interpretation displays natural generativity to show that pictures call up the same 'recognitional capacities' as typical experiences of seeing items in the world. This is obviously not true of linguistic systems, which do not display natural generativity. For example, if I am learning English, and I know what 'cat' refers to, I am not enabled thereby to interpret the word 'dog'. This suggests that pictorial systems are much less conventional than linguistic systems, though Schier admits that there are conventional elements in pictorial systems.

Now, Schier argues that his view is in a sense a return to imitation accounts of representation. The property that picture and depicted object share in virtue of which one is a representation of the other is that 'there is an overlap between the recognitional abilities' that they trigger (Schier, 1986, p. 186). I think that Schier's view is roughly correct, but that it can be used (despite Schier's own protestations) to support a much more traditional version of the imitation view. For it seems plausible that the reason two items (for instance, Jane and a picture of Jane) trigger the same recognitional abilities is that they display deeper similarities – for example, similarity in colour or relations of colour, and similarity in shape. If our recognitional capacities were triggered *arbitrarily* – that is, not in virtue of any deeper similarities – they would be adaptively counter-productive. If my recognitional capacity for persons, for example, is triggered by a mannequin, it is surely in virtue of a set of properties shared by persons and mannequins. And, of course, a mannequin is a representation of a person in the relevant sense.

Some of the objections to the imitation view mentioned above can now be dealt with. For example, we noted that Goodman held that since there is no single 'way an object is', it is impossible to imitate the way an object is. But, of course, it is perfectly possible to imitate some of the features that allow one to recognize an object, and no imitation theorist has ever held that a picture must imitate all the ways an object is (whatever that might mean), or any one of

them in particular. Nor does the view require that no interpretation take place in the act of depiction. For example, the selection of properties of the object that are to appear in the depiction obviously gives scope to interpretation. And if experience of objects in the world itself involves interpretation, then the same types of interpretation are involved in depicting those objects. As to the deeper metaphysical claim that there is no world to be imitated, that obviously cannot be addressed here. But the metaphysics on which it is based may be said to be massively implausible.

Thus, after a long excursion, I think the most ancient view of the matter is roughly correct, and that a picture represents its object in virtue of being an imitation of it.

See also DEPICTION; GOMBRICH; GOODMAN; PLATO; RESEMBLANCE; SYMBOL.

BIBLIOGRAPHY

Clark, Kenneth: *The Nude* (Princeton, NJ: Bollingen Press, 1956).

Dewey, John: *Art as Experience* (New York: Minton, Balch, 1934).

Gadamer, Hans-Georg: *Wahrheit und Methode* (Tübingen: 1960); trans. J. Weinsheimer and D.G. Marshall, *Truth and Method* (New York: Crossroad, 1975).

Gombrich, E.H.: *Art and Illusion* (Oxford: Phaidon, 1983).

Goodman, Nelson: 'Seven strictures on similarity', *Problems and Projects* (Indianapolis: Bobbs-Merrill, 1972).

Goodman, Nelson: *Languages of Art* (Indianapolis: Hackett, 1976).

Hegel, G.W.F.: *Vorlesungen über die Ästhetik*, ed. H.G. Hothe (Berlin: 1838); trans. T.M. Knox, *Aesthetics* (Oxford: Clarendon Press, 1975).

Heidegger, Martin: 'Der Ursprung des Kunstwerkes' (Frankfurt: 1950); trans. Albert Hofstadter, 'The origin of the work of art', *Poetry, Language, Thought* (New York: Harper & Row, 1971), pp. 17–87.

Plato, *Republic*, in *Collected Dialogues*, ed. Edith Hamilton and Huntington Cairns (Princeton, NJ: Bollingen Press, 1963).

Schier, Flint: *Deeper into Pictures* (Cambridge: Cambridge University Press, 1986).

Vasari, Giorgio: *Lives of the Artists* (2nd edn, Florence, 1568); trans. George Bull (London: Allen Lane, 1978).

Véron, Eugene: *L'Esthétique* (Paris: 1878); trans. W.H. Armstrong, *Aesthetics* (London: 1879).

CRISPIN SARTWELL

resemblance Nothing would seem more obvious than the idea that a painting of a bowl of flowers represents a bowl of flowers because it looks like a bowl of flowers. In the middle of the development of Greek naturalism, Plato accused the artist of simply holding a mirror to nature: a painting was simply a copy of appearance. But Greek painting never simply looked like the world; it offered a selective and narrow vision. And any number of different kinds of painting may represent a bowl of flowers, from a child's, to a seventeenth-century Dutch master's to Odilon Redon's. Artists have also shown great sensitivity to the world's looks and persuaded others of their visions: as Oscar Wilde said, there was no fog in London before Whistler painted it.

Ernst Gombrich's *Art and Illusion* (1960) marked a major breakthrough in addressing the complexities of what were previously regarded dismissively as illusions/imitations/ copies of nature. He drew attention to psychological and technical achievements involved in the production of convincing pictures of the world, and also to the role which conventions play in the process of representation.

It was Nelson Goodman's *Languages of Art* (1968) that effectively started the philosophical debate over resemblance, addressing itself to the conventionalist issues raised by Gombrich. In a declaration geared to provoke the greatest possible argument, he wrote: 'The most naive view of representation might perhaps be put somewhat like this: "A represents B if and only if A appreciably resembles B", or "A represents B to the extent that A resembles B." Vestiges of this view, with assorted refinements, persist in most writing on representation' (Goodman, 1968, p. 3). Against this view he assembled a string of arguments. Representation cannot be equivalent to resemblance because resemblance, unlike representation, is reflexive and symmetrical: I resemble, but do not represent, myself to a maximal degree; if *A* resembles *B*, *B* resembles *A*, but a landscape does not represent a painting of that landscape. Resemblance can occur without representation (as in twins, which resemble but do not represent each other). Furthermore, a painting of a landscape resembles another painting more than it does a landscape.

Goodman's fusillade against resemblance was motivated by a desire to replace a realist theory of representation with a conventionalist theory:

> The plain fact is that a picture, to represent an object, must be a symbol for it, stand for it, refer to it; and that no degree of resemblance is sufficient to establish the requisite of reference. Nor is resemblance *necessary* for reference; almost anything may stand for anything else. A picture that represents – like a passage that describes – an object refers to and, more particularly, *denotes* it. Denotation is the core of representation and is independent of resemblance. (Goodman, 1968, p. 5)

His onslaught also built upon contemporary arguments over the ontological status of the work of art, the problem of the relationship between the physical object which was the painting and its perceptual features which were both, seemingly, the characteristics of the paint out of which the image was made and the image itself. *Languages of Art* launched a significant critical debate.

Critics replied that resemblance is not a matter of similarity of substance. No one expects the physical object which is a painting to resemble the physical object which is its subject. But the picture which the painting presents can, however, resemble the appearance of its subject. Thus the Duke of Wellington can look like his picture and vice versa: if one wanted to find out what the Duke of Wellington looked like one would rather look at his portrait than read his description. Even better, one would rather look at a photograph. The arguments can be multiplied (see Manns, 1971). Goodman (1968, p. 4) felt that such a line of thought would 'resign a large part of the question: namely what constitutes a representation'.

A primary difficulty, as a number of writers agree, is that the terms 'represent', 'picture', 'depict' and 'portray' are often treated synonymously and can be applied to descriptions as much as to paintings. Another difficulty occurs over the notion of representation, which applies equally to words, pictures and things. Furthermore, one can refer to mediaeval and Renaissance representations of Christ, though the historian would want to describe medieval art as pictographic and Renaissance art as representational.

Imagine a naturalistic artist painting a *Baptism of Christ*, the chances are that he would use a model (M). The most scrupulous rendering of M would not be a portrait of M but, say, a picture of Christ. There is an analogy with acting: the specific visual features of an actor would not count as the specific features of, say, Macbeth; the actor simply plays the part of Macbeth. Portraits constitute a pictorial genre, like *Baptisms of Christ*, *Last Suppers* and so on. Of course, it is possible that we may, for historical reasons, be interested in the appearance of M, in which case we would be interested in any pictures of M; but the picture of M is not a representation of M but a representation of Christ. How, then, could the representation of Christ be said to resemble Christ? In the same way that an actor plays Macbeth by assuming the role, and he is a good actor to the extent that he plays his role well, the representation of Christ is recognized to be such by the conventions governing his depiction. The representation is successful to the degree that it is convincing; no one ever complains of not having met Macbeth, or Christ.

To take a real example: Leonardo's depiction of an angel in his *Baptism of Christ* may be admired by comparing it with Verrocchio's. Verrocchio's angel looks rather wooden in comparison with Leonardo's and the anatomical structure of St John leaves a lot to be desired. It is theoretically possible,

but irrelevant, that Verrocchio used bland and disfigured models; it requires a greater stretch of the imagination to believe that human appearance improved from the time of Duccio to Leonardo's – what improved was representational success.

The success of my analogy between acting and picture-making depends upon my example, drawn from the Italian Renaissance. In the nineteenth century, Gustave Courbet refused to paint an angel on the grounds of his never having seen one, and his own representational ambitions can be seen in *A Burial at Ornans*, where the roughness and crudity of his painting is intended to match the physiognomies of his characters. By contrast, medieval artists did not use live models but were well aware of the appearance of angels, as they inherited pictographic stereotypes which they could individuate through inscriptions or symbols. Specifically valued features of resemblance are ultimately dictated by the requirements placed upon visual imagery by the culture in which it is produced.

The fact that a picture resembles the appearance of its subject does not solve the problem of representation, however. Titian's portrait of Pietro Aretino may look strikingly like my next-door neighbour dressed up to look like Aretino, but it does not represent him. Furthermore, a cloud may resemble a face but it does not represent one (unlike Mantegna's painting of a face-in-the-cloud, in *Virtue chasing Vice*, which was a representation of a face in a cloud). We may see X as if it were a Y, but this does not make it a representation of a Y. Late mediaeval sculptures like the figures of the founders at Naumburg Cathedral attracted attention as actors in a story, out of desire to read expressions into their individuated figures; but the sculptors had not reached the point where they could engage in the kind of narrative read into their images by later Ciceroni.

Clearly, representation entails intentionality and the successful realization of intentions: if an artist declared his intention to paint a picture of the Forth Bridge, and the result looked nothing like it, one would be inclined to refuse to declare it a representation of the Forth Bridge (one might weakly say that his intention was to paint the Forth Bridge). A purely abstract painting inspired by and titled *The Forth Bridge* would not be described as a representation of the Forth Bridge, either, as it was not intended to look like the Forth Bridge. The idea of a black painting being a representation of a black cat in a coal-cellar at night is a standard joke. On the other hand, Wassily Kandinsky's early abstract water-colours, which set out to veil appearances but in which the spectator was intended to grasp those appearances, could be said to be representational in so far as one can, actually, grasp those appearances.

There is, of course, the problem that if a photographer took a picture of the Forth Bridge in the middle of the night, and only a part of it were discernible, one would have to accept that it was a picture of the Forth Bridge. One may wonder about its status as a representation of the Forth Bridge, but this would form part of a more general question about the status of photographs as representations (see Scruton, 1981). One might be inclined to say that photographs show, rather than represent, or that they offer, re-presentations.

At this point, one would say that for P to function as a visual representation of X there has to be some resemblance to X in appearance: but what counts as a representation of X, rather than Y or Z, does so in virtue of conventions governing the recognition of X as X. Resemblance is a matter of degree; representation, in the sense of signification rather than depiction, is not. Both a child's drawing of a man and Leonardo's represent a man unequivocally; when placed in the context of a work of art, the representational significance may be determined through the appropriate conventions.

There is a further, more interesting, problem which needs to be solved, and that revolves around the notion of the subject's appearance:

Ludwig Richter relates in his reminiscences how once, when he was in Tivoli as a young man, he and three friends set out to paint part of the landscape, all four firmly resolved not to deviate from nature by a hair's-breadth; and although the subject was the same, and each quite credibly reproduced what his eyes has seen, the result was four totally different pictures, as different from each other as the personalities of the four painters. (Wölfflin: 1950, p. 1)

All four pictures must have resembled the scene, but the same four pictures did not resemble each other. How could any one of the four be described as a successful, or unsuccessful, representation of the scene? Can one talk about the look of the Duke of Wellington if he looked differently in different paintings? The problem posed by Wölfflin's example is that of artists who possessed similar representational skills. None of them would have made any horrendous mistakes, but in getting their images right they arrived at different results: wherein lie the resemblances?

Artists' media present them with possibilities for visual construction which they have to use in relation to the scene in front of them. A piece of charcoal does not offer the same possibilities of use as the HB pencil; a predilection for one palette over another will open and close a variety of possibilities: small brush-strokes have a different effect from large; the artist has to look for features in the scene which will enable him to use his medium to maximum effect. In Gombrich's formulation, representations resemble objects and environments not by being copies, or mirror images, but by being relational models. The artist depicts a ray of sunlight penetrating gloomy shadows by matching the depicted light against the depicted gloom; the resulting illusion of apparent glaring brightness contributes towards the persuasive power of the image (Gombrich, 1986, fig. 27). Anyone can turn a schematic smiling face into a sad one by reversing the direction of the line of the mouth.

The artist whose concern is with producing paintings which look like the world cannot create those images on the basis of what he sees. The story goes that when one of his students said to Whistler, 'I paint what I see', he replied, 'Yes, but just wait till you see what you have painted!' Distant objects appear to be larger than their appearances are when measured; conversely, close objects appear smaller: if objects were drawn the size they appeared to be, the drawing would never actually match the visual experience (Gombrich, 1986, ill. 228). Similarly, as colours brought into close proximity with each other transform each other's appearance, any attempt to match the appearance of coloured objects with colours on the palette would be doomed to failure once they had been placed next to each other on the canvas.

All representational art depends upon the artist's ability to create persuasive models which appeal to an imaginative perceptual response on the part of the spectator, from the ritual mask to Constable's *Wyvenhoe Park*. The restricted range of naturalistic painting which exists on the historical and cultural map must be the result of an experimental investigation into the world of visual experience. The best that the naturalistic artist can achieve is a depiction of what he saw from a given spot, or what could be seen if one went there, but it cannot possibly convey the experience one would have in looking at the motif in real life (Gombrich, 1988). The artist's portrayal is necessarily selective, and there is always more in the visible world to occupy one's attention and response to it than there could be in its picture; this would account for the variety of successful resemblances of the same scene.

See also DEPICTION; GOMBRICH; GOODMAN; REALISM; REPRESENTATION.

BIBLIOGRAPHY

Gombrich, E.H.: *Art and Illusion* (London and New York: 1960); 5th edn (Oxford: Phaidon, 1986).
Gombrich, E.H.: 'Voir la nature, voir les peintures' [Seeing nature and seeing paintings], *Les Cahiers du Musée national d'art moderne*, 24 (1988), 21–43.
Goodman, N.: *Languages of Art* (London: Oxford University Press, 1968).
Manns, J.W.: 'Representation, relativism and resemblance', *British Journal of Aesthetics*, 11 (1971), 281–7.
Novitz, D.: *Pictures and their Use in Communication* (The Hague: Martinus Nijhoff, 1977).
Pitkänen, R.: 'The resemblance view of pictorial representation', *British Journal of Aesthetics*, 16 (1976), 313–23.
Pole, D.: 'Goodman and the naïve view of representation', *British Journal of Aesthetics*, 14 (1974), 68–80.
Schier, F.: *Deeper into Pictures* (Cambridge: Cambridge University Press, 1986).
Scruton, R.: 'Photography and representation', *Critical Inquiry*, 7 (1981), 577–603.
Wölfflin, H.: *Principles of Art History* (Munich: 1915); trans. M.D. Hottlinger (New York: Dover, 1950).

RICHARD WOODFIELD

restoration *See* CONSERVATION AND RESTORATION.

Ruskin, John (1819–1900) English art critic, educator, economist, and social reformer. Ruskin is Britain's greatest critic of art and society. His aesthetics is grounded in his thinking on the morality of art (his refusal to separate aesthetics from ethics is always in evidence), and focuses upon three relationships:

(1) between art (man's creation) and nature (God's creation);
(2) between art (including architecture, 'the distinctively political art') and the values of the society in which it was created;
(3) between the viewer and the object.

To teach people how to 'see clearly' was the project that shaped Ruskin's life-work, as reflected in his writing on a vast range of topics, from Turner and the pre-Raphaelites to Tintoretto and Carpaccio, from Venetian Gothic architecture and the Alps to minerals and birds. (The Library Edition of the *Works* extends to 39 volumes.)

Three problems associated with defining Ruskin's aesthetics actually help to explain its nature. First, he is contradictory, not only from work to work, but sometimes within a single work. Ruskin himself claimed that he was never satisfied that he had 'handled a subject properly' until he had contradicted himself 'at least three times'. (R.G. Collingwood compares Ruskin with Hegel, both 'historicists', in this regard: see Hewison, 1976, p. 206.) Second, although there are many continuities in Ruskin's aesthetics (and these might be called 'Ruskinian'), his individual observations must always be read in relation to the immediate context in which they were first made. Much of his writing – particularly in the middle and late periods – was for a specific purpose, and was addressed to a specific audience or readership. Ruskin enjoyed working against the grain, and was a master of irony that is easily missed when read out of context. Third, although he stated that no true disciple of his would ever be a 'Ruskinian', we find that not only his admirers, but also many Victorian public buildings that he himself hated, were frequently described as 'Ruskinian', both during and after his lifetime.

Ruskin's mind can in certain respects be compared to that of Coleridge: both are multifaceted, encyclopaedic, dynamic, religious. Unlike Coleridge's concept of the imagination, however, Ruskin's is based upon what he understood to be the truth of 'fact' (including such Old Testament 'facts' as the Fall). As Hewison summarizes Ruskin, the 'penetrative imagination' deals with external fact and the inner truth it reveals, seeing the object or idea in its entirety; the 'associative imagination' expresses the artist's thought, conveying the vision of the penetrative imagination; the 'contemplative imagination' deals with remembered or abstract ideas, and acts as a metaphor-making faculty. This last became increasingly important in practice from the 1860s, when Ruskin's interest in myth deepened, but contemplation (Greek: *theōria*) had been central to his thought since *Modern Painters*, vol. 2 (1846): 'Now the mere animal consciousness of the pleasantness [the pleasures of sight] I call Aesthesis; but the exulting, reverent, and grateful perception of it I call Theoria. For this, and this only, is the full comprehension and contemplation of the Beautiful as a gift of God' (Ruskin, *Works*, vol. 4, p. 42).

The 'theoretic faculty' perceives two kinds of beauty. 'Typical Beauty' is that external quality of bodies which 'may be shown to be in some sort typical of the Divine attributes', while 'Vital Beauty' is 'the appearance of felicitous fulfilment of function in living things, more especially of the joyful and right exertion of perfect life in man'. Landow (1971, pp. 178–9) argues that, unlike vital beauty, the idea of typical beauty lost its force when Ruskin's religious beliefs changed.

Unlike Coleridge, the evangelical Ruskin makes no claim for the creative power of the imagination, guarding against the danger that the self might usurp God's role as creator. He invented the term 'pathetic fallacy' (in *Modern Painters*, vol. 3) to describe the 'error' of projecting on to external things attributes of the perceiving mind under the influence of emotion. Charles Kingsley's 'They rowed her in across the rolling foam – /The cruel, crawling foam' evokes from Ruskin the dry comment, 'The foam is not cruel, neither does it crawl.'

The work that first made a great impact on the artworld when Ruskin was only twenty-four – the anonymous first volume of *Modern Painters* – proclaimed the undervalued Turner to be the greatest English artist because he painted the facts of nature truthfully. Its subtitle reflects the youthful ambition of its author, who was ignorant of the German founders of modern aesthetics: *Their Superiority in the Art of Landscape Painting to all the Ancient Masters, proved by examples of The True, The Beautiful and The Intellectual, from the Works of Modern Artists, especially from those of J.M.W. Turner, Esq., R.A.* Having developed his aesthetic theories in vol. 2, Ruskin interrupted his work on *Modern Painters* in order to study architecture, defining its 'Seven Lamps' as those of sacrifice, truth, power, beauty, life, memory and obedience, and writing his history of *The Stones of Venice*, from an apocalyptic perspective in which the city is seen as being under judgement after the 'fall' that was the Renaissance. The famous chapter in vol. 2 on 'The

Nature of Gothic' had a separate and influential afterlife as a key text for the Working Men's College Movement, and for William Morris, who reprinted it in the beautifully designed Kelmscott edition.

Having completed *Modern Painters* in the years immediately before and after his 'unconversion' from evangelical dogma (1858), Ruskin developed the social ramifications of his thought (already present in *The Seven Lamps of Architecture* and *The Stones of Venice*) in a series of books and lectures in the 1860s. (A statement from *Unto This Last* is characteristic: 'There is no wealth but life.') In the subsequent decade two new platforms became available to him: the newly founded Slade Professorship of Fine Art at Oxford, and his monthly *Fors Clavigera: Letters to the Workmen and Labourers of Great Britain*. Much autobiographical writing is woven into the latter, and then reworked in *Praeterita*, written in the 1880s in increasingly difficult circumstances associated with his mental decline in retirement at Brantwood, in the Lake District. *Praeterita* is the autobiography of a brilliant draughtsman, art critic and social critic, for whom theory and practice, art and society, are interrelated rather than separate entities.

See also COLERIDGE; IMAGINATION.

WRITINGS

The Seven Lamps of Architecture (London: Smith, Elder, 1849); Library Edition vol. 8.

The Stones of Venice, vol. 1 (London: Smith, Elder, 1851); vols 2, 3 (1853); Library Edition vols 9–11.

The Two Paths (London: Smith, Elder, 1859); Library Edition vol. 16.

Modern Painters, vol. 1 (London: Smith, Elder, 1843); vol. 2 (1846); vols 3, 4 (1856); vol. 5 (1860); Library Edition vols 3–7.

Fors Clavigera: Letters to the Workmen and Labourers of Great Britain (Keston: Allen, 1871–84); Library Edition vols 27–9.

The Works of John Ruskin, ed. E.T. Cook and A. Wedderburn, Library Edition, 39 vols (London: Allen, 1903–12).

BIBLIOGRAPHY

Hewison, R.: *John Ruskin: The Argument of the Eye* (London: Thames & Hudson; Princeton, NJ: Princeton University Press, 1976).

Hilton, T.: *John Ruskin: The Early Years, 1819–1859* (New Haven, Conn., and London: Yale University Press, 1985).

Ladd, H.: *The Victorian Morality of Art: An Analysis of Ruskin's Esthetic* (1932; New York: Octagon, 1968).

Landow, G.P.: *The Aesthetic and Critical Theories of John Ruskin* (Princeton, NJ: Princeton University Press, 1971).

Rosenberg, J.D.: *The Darkening Glass: A Portrait of Ruskin's Genius* (1931; London: Routledge & Kegan Paul, 1963).

MICHAEL WHEELER

S

Santayana, George (1863–1952) Spanish philosopher and novelist; for many years at Harvard University. Santayana somewhere notes that philosophers come to aesthetics through opposite routes – as metaphysicians who need to complete their systems, and as artists who need to generalize about their experiences. He belonged in both camps, with emphasis on the latter. He was an obvious literary artist in his poetry and fiction, but he was a poet-philosopher all the time, even when he was a metaphysician. While he wrote *about* art intermittently, particularly in *The Sense of Beauty* and *Reason in Art*, he sought to be artful in all of his writings, including his 'theoretical' ones.

His central work in aesthetics is that early and most remarkable book, *The Sense of Beauty*; its subtitle is *Being the outline(s) of aesthetic theory*. Santayana reveals his hand, and his approach, when he says at the very outset: 'The sense of beauty has a more important place in life than aesthetic theory has ever taken in philosophy.' And, indeed, the stylistic beauty of this treatise is as telling as its philosophical or theoretical side, and must properly be seen as part of its 'statement'. Santayana also says: 'To feel beauty is a better thing than to understand how we came to feel it.' He certainly feels it, and might even be said to explain how he comes to feel it. But, as always, he explains it more as a literary critic than as a metaphysician. He addresses himself to the task of creating literary art as surely as he works at discovering any principles of art in a theoretical fashion.

Santayana is cavalier about distinctions, even the distinction between theory and art, between comprehension and inspiration: 'But the recognition of the superiority of aesthetics in experience to aesthetics in theory ought not to make us accept as an explanation of aesthetic feeling what is in truth only an expression of it.' This might be seen as a form of self-scolding, or a way of guarding against the neglectful obliteration of an important distinction. But the distinction that he makes does not actually mark out different phases or moments of experience, or different sections of his own texts.

As further indication of his way with distinctions, Santayana objects, on theoretical grounds, to calling beauty a 'manifestation of God to the senses'. Such an observation is obscure and beyond truth or falsehood, albeit high-minded. But then an analysis of what is meant by God, an unpacking of the metaphor, reveals how and why the attributes of God are indeed an appropriate way to reach an understanding of beauty. In a word, a good metaphor can give a scrawny theory some divine afflatus and some cognitive force. Art and philosophy always were one enterprise! The presumed structure of Santayana's 'theoretical' work is the barest skeleton upon which various comments, or 'little essays', are hung. The parts of the treatise, which *The Sense of Beauty* might be said to be, are quite incidental to a process which is fundamentally critical, literary and ironic. The dynamic of making and unmaking distinctions, the play of perspectives – not the semblance of structure which these distinctions might have been thought to have created – constitute the essential quality of Santayana's presentation.

The organization of the book, such as it is, consists of part 1 on the nature of beauty; parts 2, 3 and 4 on matter, form and expression. In part 1 Santayana distinguishes the moral and the aesthetic, or work and play. He teases the distinction and accords it some initial and conventional deference. But then he undermines it and shows in effect how any adequate value theory must ambiguously embrace both the moral and the aesthetic.

Beauty is defined in part 1 as 'objectified pleasure', or 'pleasure regarded as the quality of an object'. It suggests a psychological tendency or process in us, whereby we attribute or affix our feelings to things. It is a provocative definition, but leaves the locus of pleasure somewhat problematic. The lower senses, taste and touch, are mostly bodily and not objectifiable. Smell seems mildly but vaguely objectifiable. Hearing and seeing take us entirely from the organs whereby we perceive, to the objects out there which we esteem and enjoy. Santayana was never entirely satisfied with this approach, and at a later date wrote self-critically of his tendency to 'skirt psychologism'.

Part 4, on the concept of expression, is most startling and unusual. Expression is an evocation of memory, the bringing of some association to mind, in the presence of sensed matter and form. The memory may be vague; some emotion may persist, with the details of its occasion forgotten. Indeed, vagueness sometimes helps make possible the fusion of present and past. Santayana's theory of expression, if it can be called a theory, undermines any clear and traditional notions about the fixity of the art object. In principle, any sensation or idea or concept can conjoin or fuse with any other, and this is what his 'theory' asserts. But in practice, as we know from the associations we attempt in the making of metaphors, not everything tossed into the air can be said to fly. Theory cannot quite account for art, or substitute for it.

Santayana's concept of expression, one might say, is the general case of which certain late-twentieth-century and radical views about art are so many special instances. Theories can attach to sensuous objects as surely as sentimental memories can. That an object is offered for appreciation by the artworld demonstrates an 'expressive value' in it. Expression allows any association – a previous sensuous memory, a mood, a thought, a theory – to attach itself to the presently perceived object. More exactly, San-

tayana's notion of expression allows this, and our experience of art confirms that such things happen. But it is a question of sensibility, and criticism, as to whether an association 'works', and whether or not it succeeds effectively in affiliating with a sensuous object.

Santayana's *The Sense of Beauty* fits into no clear tradition of aesthetic writing, yet is rich in historical antecedents. It has no clear influences and effects, yet shows remarkable anticipation of what is happening in aesthetic theory and criticism one hundred years after its appearance. It is at once *sui generis* yet full of perennial wisdom.

See also EXPRESSION.

WRITINGS

The Sense of Beauty (New York: Scribner, 1896); ed. W.G. Holzberger and H.J. Saatkamp, jun. (Cambridge, Mass. and London: MIT Press, 1988).
The Life of Reason, vol. 4, *Reason in Art* (New York: Scribner, 1905; 1955).

BIBLIOGRAPHY

Schilpp, P.A., ed.: *The Philosophy of George Santayana* (New York: Tudor, 1951).

MORRIS GROSSMAN

Jean-Paul Sartre (1905–80) French novelist, playwright, journalist, literary critic, political activist and philosopher, and one of the most influential intellectuals of the twentieth century. Sartre's voluminous writings never included a 'philosophy of art' in the traditional sense, although a case can be made (and he himself insisted) that aesthetics is implicit in everything he wrote (Schilpp, 1981, p. 15).

Sartre is best known for his philosophy of 'existentialism' – the view that in human being 'existence precedes essence', that humans first come on the scene and only then define who they are or who they ought to be. In early writings, such as the novel

Nausea (1938), the wartime plays *The Flies* (1943) and *No Exit* (1945), and up through the massive philosophical work *Being and Nothingness* (1943) and the lecture 'Existentialism is a humanism' (1946), he develops a view of freedom according to which each human being, facing whatever 'coefficient of adversity' in his situating conditions, is completely responsible for the fundamental values he or she chooses to follow.

Sartre described this 'human condition' as similar to the challenge confronting an artist – to invent without being given any standards in advance. However, he thought, as people invent, they should strive to avoid forms of 'bad faith' in which they cover up their freedom; they should assume full responsibility for their actions and act so as to recognize and promote freedom for everyone. In the case of the French writer after the Second World War, Sartre argued that this meant a new kind of literature, an 'engaged' literature. So in 1945, with a group of friends, he founded a literary magazine, *Les Temps Modernes*, to encourage writers who would recognize their social role and work 'to change simultaneously the social condition of man and the concept he has of himself', (Sartre, 1988, p. 255). On this basis, he criticized 'art for art's sake' and the cult of 'genius', and he indicted a number of earlier writers, including Baudelaire, for elaborate efforts to hide their freedom and social responsibility from themselves.

In later years, Sartre seemed to judge less and interpret more. In plays such as *The Devil and the Good Lord* (1951) and *The Condemned of Altona* (1960), in critical studies like that of the criminal literary figure Jean Genet, and the never completed study of the novelist Flaubert, *The Idiot of the Family* (1971–2), Sartre recognized far greater complexity and force of circumstance in human life, and in the creative artist's life in particular. He came to believe that human values are largely interiorized from one's family history and one's situating institutions and practices. Still, he thought that we never simply return what we have been given. There is always an element of freedom. Indeed, in a figure such as Genet, Sartre thinks one can come to see

this freedom at grips with destiny, crushed at first by its mischances, then turning upon them and digesting them little by little ... [one can learn] the choice that a writer makes of himself, of his life and of the meaning of the universe, including even the formal characteristics of his style and composition, even the structure of his images and of the particularity of his tastes. (Sartre, 1963a, p. 584)

As Sartre saw it, a work of literature, and any work of art, is a free, imaginative creation addressed to other freedoms. It has a kind of autonomy and offers aesthetic enjoyment simply in arousing the reader's (viewer's, listener's) free response. At the same time, it discloses the world in some of its aspects and, often, for a determinate audience. The function of literary (or art) criticism is to exhibit, in the work, the interplay between freedom and situation which constitutes the creator's distinctive view of things; and also, since the work is 'an act of confidence in the freedom of men' (Sartre, 1988, p. 67), the critic must assess its import for the human situation of freedom and unfreedom in which it speaks. In his essay 'Black Orpheus' Sartre admires African poetry for its dynamism and because it makes blackness a symbol of openness, of freedom ('Black Orpheus' (1948) in Sartre, 1988, pp. 289–300). He praises the sculptor Giacometti's embodiment of the forces of repulsion and attraction which keep people at a distance while together; and he prefers Tintoretto to Titian because he sees in the former's expressiveness and violence a rejection of the Venetian establishment which Titian, with his smooth and idealized figures, served so slavishly (Sartre, 1963b).

The theoretical basis for Sartre's view of the work of art lies not only in his ontology of freedom, but in his early phenomenological analysis of the imagination in *Psychology of the Imagination* (1940). Here he describes imagining not as 'having images' somehow internal to consciousness, but as a distinctive way of having a world – a way of intending an object, of making it present, but in a mode of absence, or as '*irréel*'. In imagining the Parthenon, he says, one takes a certain sensuous content or physical object (perhaps a sketch) *as* something which is not, *as* the Parthenon which is elsewhere. One conjures the world not present.

One may also conjure a world that is not real at all. This is what happens on seeing a performance of *Hamlet*, on hearing a performance of Beethoven's Seventh Symphony, or when viewing a Matisse. One picks up the solicitations of the perceived thing (the actor's voice and movements, the scraping of strings and hooting of horns, the coloured shapes on canvas) and transforms them into an imaginative consciousness of the Prince of Denmark, the symphony or a dancing woman – with all the feelings appropriate to those things.

All works of art are, in this sense, beyond the real, not anywhere. 'Aesthetic contemplation is an induced dream', Sartre says, and 'Beauty is a value which applies only to the imaginary and which entails a negation of the world' (Sartre, 1948, p. 282). This is its seductive power. The artist is, in a way, an escapist (Sartre thinks Flaubert was almost neurotically so). None the less, the sort of imaginative negation at stake not only in creating, but in responding to, a work of art, may also *disclose* the world as it is – through *Hamlet*, the symphony and the flying figure, we are afforded a fresh perspective on ordinary things. This is particularly true for literary texts. And, Sartre points out, our own freedom is inevitably engaged with the freedom of others, and with the freedom of the artist, in the aesthetic response we make to such works and in the moral and social response we make to them as well.

See also COMMITMENT AND ENGAGEMENT; IMAGINATION; TRUTH IN ART.

WRITINGS

L'Existentialisme (Paris: Nagel, 1946); trans. Bernard Frechtman, *Existentialism* (New York: Philosophical Library, 1947). Includes 'Existentialism is a humanism'.

L'Imaginaire: Psychologie phénoménologique de l'imagination (Paris: 1940), trans. Bernard Frechtman, *Psychology of the Imagination* (New York: Philosophical Library, 1948).

Saint-Genet, comédien et martyr (Paris: 1952); trans. Bernard Frechtman, *Saint-Genet, Actor and Martyr* (New York: G. Braziller, 1963a).

Essays in Aesthetics; trans. and ed. Wade Baskin (New York, Philosophical Library, 1963b).

'*What is Literature?' and Other Essays*; intro. Steven Ungar (Cambridge, Mass.: Harvard University Press, 1988). Includes 'Black Orpheus', pp. 289–330.

BIBLIOGRAPHY

Kaelin, E.F.: *An Existentialist Aesthetic* (Madison, Wis.: University of Wisconsin Press, 1966).

Schilpp, P.A.: *The Philosophy of Jean-Paul Sartre Library of living Philosophers*, vol. 16 (La Salle, Ill.: Open Court, 1981).

JOHN J. COMPTON

Schelling, Friedrich Wilhelm Joseph von (1775–1854) German idealist philosopher. The first philosopher to write a philosophy of art, Schelling was educated together with Hegel and Hölderlin in a Tübingen seminary. He occupied various chairs of philosophy, in, for example, Jena, Würzburg, Munich, finishing his career in what had been Hegel's chair of philosophy in Berlin, which he took on in 1841 and occupied until his death. His *Philosophy of Art* (1802–3) attempts a systematic philosophical articulation of the arts, in which art has a status equal to philosophy.

In his earlier *System of Transcendental Idealism* (1800) he saw art as the 'organ of philosophy', because it can show what philosophical concepts cannot: the absolute. By the middle of the nineteenth century such ideas, which had been the foundation of Romantic art and philosophy, often came to be regarded, particularly in the English-speaking world, as mere mystical hyperbole. They did live on in artistic movements such as symbolism, but they played less and less of a role in the dominant strands of philosophy. Behind the ideas of the early Schelling lies the notion that art has truth status, a notion which lost currency in the light both of the advances of the natural sciences and of the clarification of the truth status of propositions in analytical philosophy.

The notion of the truth of art was revived in a philosophically viable way by the work of T.W. Adorno, as well as by Hans-Georg Gadamer, on the basis of the work of his teacher, Heidegger, and plays a subterranean role in poststructuralism (Bowie, 1990). If we take account of these approaches we are now in a better position to understand why Schelling's early work gave such importance to art than if we rely upon philosophical approaches orientated towards the natural sciences as the sole arbiters of truth. This article concentrates on the *System of Transcendental Idealism* as it is Schelling's most important and influential contribution to the understanding of art's importance to philosophy: despite some remarkable insights into art's relationship to mythology and into some of the specific arts, especially music, the *Philosophy of Art* does not have the same degree of importance.

The work of the early Schelling is part of the flowering of philosophy in Germany initiated by Kant's critical philosophy. In common with many of his contemporaries, and J.G. Fichte in particular, Schelling regarded Kant's division of the world into 'representations' and 'things in themselves', and the concomitant division between theoretical and practical reason, as a failure to achieve Kant's own stated aim. As Kant had made clear, philosophy had to arrive at an explanation of the world and our place in it with its own means, without using theology as a basis. This could not, though, be done at the expense of separating thought and being. The desire to avoid this separation led to an orientation towards monism, and its key exponent, Spinoza. At the same time the fear was that Spinoza's philosophy led, as F.H. Jacobi saw it, to 'nihilism', to the world of reductionist conceptions of modern science.

This reductionist view was precisely what Kant's insistence on practical reason was meant to overcome, in the name of reason, the capacity to have purposes which are not determined by natural causality. Fichte made

Kant's practical philosophy primary: even the subject's cognitive relationship to the world was grounded in its 'activity'. This activity, which Kant himself saw as a 'spontaneity', in that it could not be explained in terms of the law of causality, Fichte made into the very principle of reality. Without the cognitive activity of the subject there would not be a world to know (though there might still be a world). The reason the world is intelligible has to lie, as Kant had shown, in the subject. Fichte dealt with the problem of the resistance of the 'external' world by making it the reflection back into the subject of its own activity. If this were not the case it would, he claimed, be impossible to understand how it is that we can feel the resistance of the world: without an identity between what can feel and what is felt one is stuck with the Cartesian problems which Kant had not fully escaped. The prior factor has to be that which allows one to be *aware* of even the most mechanical phenomena, which, for Fichte, was self-consciousness.

How is it that Schelling's version of these ideas leads him to privilege art over philosophy? The linking factor between Spinoza and Fichte is, for Schelling, the notion of that which is the cause of itself. In Spinoza, this is 'God', in Fichte the 'I' (as a spontaneity). Schelling's early key idea was that, instead of being the inaccessible thing in itself that Kant made it in the *Critique of Pure Reason*, nature in itself was 'productive'. Kantian synthetic judgements deal with the world as 'product', as that which appears at a particular moment; *Naturphilosophie*, in Schelling's sense, deals with the 'productivity', which gives rise to transient 'products' by opposing itself to itself, like the flowing molecules of a stream when they form an eddy. The very need for synthetic judgements derives from the fact that what is being synthesized is split within itself: objects are determined by their not being other objects; they cannot be fully themselves without the other objects from which they are separated. Nature must, then, unite itself because it is divided within itself.

If the objects of scientific knowledge are to be subsumed under general laws which interrelate, they must, as Kant had realized in the

Critique of Judgement, ultimately share the same status. The model of this is the organism, whose parts cannot be themselves without each other. This notion of the relation of parts to whole made Kant link the natural organism to the artwork. Schelling went beyond Kant by suggesting that, as we ourselves are part of nature, what knows in us must have an organic relationship to what is known: there can be no ultimate division between the two. This is what he means by the absolute. The question is how philosophy can explicate this link between knowing and being known.

Schelling suggests, with prophetic consequences, that the forces of Fichte's conscious philosophical 'I' have an 'unconscious' history, which it is the task of transcendental philosophy to retrace. The structure of this argument prefigures both Hegel's genetic account of self-consciousness in the *Phenomenology of Spirit*, and psychoanalysis. How can it be, though, that philosophy should have access to what is unconscious? Schelling argues that we will never understand the forces that give rise to self-consciousness if we try to do so in terms of conceptual knowledge. How can *unconscious* forces appear as themselves to the *conscious* mind? Freud will later make it clear that we do not have cognitive access to drives, only to their 'representations', though he still thinks we can make psychoanalysis into a positive science. Schelling is led to the idea of the object which cannot be conceived of merely as a causally determined natural object, in order to suggest how we can understand 'unconscious activity' via 'conscious activity'. This object is a product of spontaneity: the work of art.

The artwork begins with the conscious intention of the artist, but it must be the result of more than conscious reflection and technique if it is to achieve aesthetic status. A work of art is not art because it shares the same determinable attributes as some other objects, but rather because it reveals the world in a way which only it can: a chemical or physical analysis of a Rembrandt painting tells us nothing about it as a work of art. There is no cognitive criterion which allows us to judge whether something is art or not. The work of art is what unifies 'unconscious' production – the productivity which gives rise to natural products – with 'conscious' production, which allows us to know nature as an object of science. As such, the work of art is the only means of direct access to the absolute, because it overcomes the division between the conscious subject and the object world by revealing the ground they both share. Philosophy cannot represent this ground because this would entail making it into an object of reflexive knowledge by saying what it is (matter, mind, energy, or whatever). As soon as one attempts to do this one is forced to *relate* the absolute to what it is not, and it thereby loses any possibility of being absolute.

Talk of the absolute makes everyone uneasy. However, what Schelling means becomes clear in the way he claims that both science and art are means of revealing the absolute. Science, though, is faced with an endless task, in that each new revelation is arrived at via the exclusion of other possibilities: successive networks of interdepending theories, as modern science shows (and as Kant realized in the *Critique of Judgement*), do not allow one to arrive at something non-contingent. In art this failure is constitutive: the very fact that artworks are 'capable of an infinite interpretation', and our *awareness* of this fact, demonstrate the real nature of being, as that which cannot ever be known in its entirety. Each interpretation may disclose an aspect of the work, but at the same time it hides other aspects.

Science and art depend upon the same activity, which we can regard, in the light of Heidegger (who relies on Schelling to a far greater extent than he ever admitted), as ways of disclosing the world which share the same source. Many of these ideas were the common property of the Jena Circle of Romantic thinkers, which included Friedrich Schlegel and Novalis, and to which Schelling belonged for a time, before moving away, after the beginning of the century, from the Romantic position. In the *Philosophy of Art* he moves towards the position of his identity philosophy, which, like Hegel's after it, claims to be able to show the absolute in philosophy by articulated insight into the finitude of particular knowledge. This leads him to a systematic philosophical presentation of the various forms of art, of the kind more familiar from Hegel's *Aesthetics*.

The hopes invested in art as the means of communicating a 'mythology of reason', that will reconcile the contradictions in modern societies between sensuousness and reason, which are present in the *System of Transcendental Idealism* (and, in a different way, in the work of Schiller), give way in the work of the later Schelling to a conviction that great art depends upon the right social conditions to flourish and thus cannot really help create these conditions. At the same time, the key philosophical thought of the *System of Transcendental Idealism*, that philosophy has to come to terms with a ground of reflexive thinking which transcends it, remains central to the later Schelling, particularly in his critique of Hegel, and has a significant influence on thinkers like Schopenhauer, Kierkegaard, Nietzsche and Heidegger, all of whom see art as vital to philosophy.

See also AUTONOMY, AESTHETIC; HEGEL; HEIDEGGER; SCIENCE AND ART.

WRITINGS

Sämmtliche Werke, ed. K.F.A. Schelling (Stuttgart: 1856–61).
System of Transcendental Idealism (1800); trans. Peter Heath, intro. Michael Vater (Charlottesville: Virginia University Press, 1978).
Ideas for a Philosophy of Nature; trans. E.E. Harris and Peter Heath, intro. Robert Stern (Cambridge: Cambridge University Press, 1988).
Philosophy of Art (1802–3); (Minneapolis: Minnesota University Press, 1988).

BIBLIOGRAPHY

Bowie, Andrew: *Aesthetics and Subjectivity: from Kant to Nietzsche* (Manchester: Manchester University Press, 1990).
Frank, Manfred: *Einführung in die frühromantische Ästhetik* [Introduction to early romantic aesthetics] (Frankfurt am Main: Suhrkamp, 1989).
Jähnig, Dieter: *Schelling. Die Kunst in der Philosophie* [Art in Philosophy], 2 vols (Pfullingen: Neske, 1966, 1969).

ANDREW BOWIE

Schiller, (Johann Christoph) Friedrich von (1759–1805) German dramatist, poet, and philosopher; a major figure in the *Sturm und Drang* movement and in the Weimar culture of the late eighteenth century. All Schiller's philosophical writings, with the exception of an early dissertation on the mind–body problem, were devoted to aesthetic topics and are in the form either of letters or of essays. His reputation as a philosopher rests largely on his major work, *On the Aesthetic Education of Man* (1795), a series of twenty-seven letters written to his patron, the Duke of Augustenburg, and sometimes called his *Aesthetic Letters*.

His aesthetics has often seemed enigmatic. Its character is apparent from the dictum, 'It is only through beauty that man makes his way to freedom' (Schiller, 1967 [1795], letter 2, para. 5), which sets the practical concept of freedom alongside the theoretical concept of beauty, crossing boundaries between ethics, politics and aesthetics. Why Schiller elected to treat aesthetics in this dynamic manner requires explanation. His dictum, which has the ring of a political slogan, presupposes that man is in a condition of unfreedom, which, Schiller believed, resulted both from social and economic divisions, devised by the human intellect, and from crude sensuality encouraged by materialism. The way he envisaged that this condition could be corrected depended on his theory of human nature, that 'the will is the specific character of man, and reason itself is only the eternal rule of his will' ('On the Sublime' (1793)). Thus a powerful means for changing the will was needed. Schiller identified this as beauty.

He describes his inquiry as 'concerning art and beauty' (Schiller, 1967 [1795], letter 1, para. 1), but does not discuss these concepts, being primarily concerned with their effects upon moral character and action. What effects works of art have, if any, is a contingent matter and the concern of psychologists and sociologists; but Schiller was claiming an *a priori* connection between beauty and freedom. He defines beauty as 'freedom in appearances', and also speaks of it as the necessary means for attaining freedom. The claim 'freedom only through beauty' can be taken in different senses – practical, as saying that a liberal society requires the development of aesthetic sensibility; and also theoretical, as attempting to bridge the Kantian gulf between the worlds of nature and freedom. The dual nature of his thesis is the expression of the duality of his own make-up as poet and philosopher. This complexity does not make for easy understanding. But his relentless defence of his thesis presents a refreshing challenge.

Although he is generally regarded as a Kantian, he endeavoured to correct Kant's formalism and criticized his treatment of beauty in a correspondence with C.G. Körner, between January and March 1793, that was intended as the basis of a dialogue that never materialized (the book was to be titled 'Kallias'). He attacked the subjectivity of Kant's theory, which treated the aesthetic as yet another compartment in an already over-compartmentalized theory of mind; and rejected his distinction between free and dependent beauty, because the formality of the former notion was unacceptable, and the linking of beauty with perfection of a kind in the latter was too rational. Instead, he advanced his own view of beauty as objective, as pertaining to objects in the world of appearances, which linked beauty to the senses, as opposed to the intellect or subjective pleasure. He saw his theory as resolving the controversy between rationalist, empiricist and idealist theories of beauty. But his tactics ignore the fact of aesthetic disagreement, and endow beauty with a mystical power to create harmony.

His ambiguous concept of aesthetic education, refers not to an education in the fine arts, but to his interest in an ideal humanity that can only be achieved through beauty and art. For Schiller, the ideal was not beyond the world of sensible appearances, as it was for Kant. It referred to wholeness in which reason and the senses are in tandem. It had already been exemplified in the rounded humanity of the ancient Greeks, and he believed that in order to correct 'barbarian' and 'savage' tendencies in human nature it must re-emerge. But this leaves open the question of whether his main interest was the concept of beauty or the perfectibility of human nature. His definition of beauty as 'living form' (Schiller, 1967 [1795], letter 15, para. 3) not only characterizes beautiful objects, but, he also claimed, creates beautiful human beings, showing how closely the public world of appearances was associated by him with the realms of consciousness and moral character – which prompted Hegel to comment (favourably) that Schiller's aesthetics was one of 'totality and reconciliation'.

His strategy for proving this large claim is cumbersome, for he employs two methods: one relating to evolution, which pertains to the world of nature; and the other to transcendental deduction, which is the tool of reason. By the latter method, two fundamental and necessary drives in human nature – the formal (*Formtrieb*), representing the rational, abstract aspect, and the sensuous (*sinnliche Trieb*), which represents the concrete aspect of experience – are shown to be capable of being brought into an ideal equilibrium. From this state of psychological harmony the play drive (*Spieltrieb*) emerges.

Although this concept is derived from Kant's view of aesthetic judgement as the free play of the cognitive faculties, the idea that human beings reach their fullest potential when 'playing' with beauty is Schiller's unique contribution. It introduces the notion of an aesthetic attitude as detachment from practical or intellectual concerns. The play drive is also treated as evolving from animal play (Schiller, 1967 [1795], letter 26), which is the result of a superfluity of energy; but the essence of aesthetic play is that it employs both sense and reason in a recreative harmony. Schiller's argument becomes convoluted because he not only argues that beauty is necessary for human well-being, but also shows how our psychological make-up can be conditioned by the effects of two kinds of beauty, energizing and melting, so that ideal beauty will be attained. But causal accounts do not establish anything of importance for aesthetics. Furthermore, psychological conditioning is inimical to education.

A more plausible account, showing that the development of aesthetic sensibility is essential for a liberal society, is given in terms of semblance (*Schein*). Aesthetic semblance, which is distinguished from illusion (Schiller, 1967 [1795], letter 26, para. 5), has to do with our ability to distance ourselves from matter through the special aesthetic senses of sight and hearing, and to create appearances by giving form to what is formless. Although it can be argued that touch and smell are also aesthetic senses, Schiller rightly implies that in an aesthetic context we are not concerned with physical properties of objects such as weight, volume and so on, but with appearance of colour, shape, texture and sound. For Schiller, an interest in semblance is the hallmark of a liberal society, in which the conditions for egocentricity to flourish have been eradicated. Within the 'joyous Kingdom of play' the Kantian virtue of dignity has been replaced by grace, which is a kind of beauty, applying to character as well as appearance and implying spontaneity and lack of constraint. Only the sketchiest outline of the ideal society is given (Schiller, 1967 [1795], letter 27).

Whether Schiller succeeds in showing that beauty can bridge the gap between the worlds of nature and freedom depends upon the sense in which these terms are taken. The thrust of his argument is to establish the priority of the aesthetic dimension in human development. But he is inconsistent, sometimes speaking of the aesthetic as a transitional stage between nature and morality or freedom, and at others as the ultimate achievement for humanity. With regard to his aim of showing that beauty creates beautiful human beings, the difficulty of proof is considerable and too much is uncritically assumed. For example, aesthetic education takes it for granted that emotions can be trained. There are times in his argument when an ideal human nature takes priority. For instance, his concern to show that the

ability to instil a mood of serene disengagement from any proclivity to action or intellectual activity is the mark of aesthetic excellence, leads him to overlook differences between art forms (Schiller, 1967 [1795], letter 22).

Schiller occupies a rightful place in the development of post-Kantian idealist aesthetics, although he was an eclectic thinker who drew on the theories of Goethe, Herder, Fichte and Wilhelm von Humboldt, as well as those of Kant. His theory of beauty has been seminal. Croce's expression theory defends the priority of the aesthetic over other areas of human activity; and the concepts of living form, semblance and aesthetic education have had an extensive influence on twentieth-century aesthetics.

Schiller's aesthetics also provides an introduction to standard problems – the definition of beauty; the question of an aesthetic attitude; what constitutes aesthetic excellence; the relation between art and morality. He has become a focus of interest for late-twentieth-century British and Continental philosophers, especially the hermeneutic philosopher, Gadamer, whose defence of a liaison between philosophy and poetry is after Schiller's own heart.

See also EDUCATION, AESTHETIC; KANT.

WRITINGS

'On the Sublime' (1793); in *Two Essays by Friedrich von Schiller: Naive and Sentimental Poetry and On the Sublime*, trans. J.A. Elias (New York: 1966).

On the Aesthetic Education of Man (1794–5); trans. and ed. Elizabeth M. Wilkinson and L.A. Willoughby (Oxford: Clarendon Press, 1967).

BIBLIOGRAPHY

Gardiner, P.: 'Freedom as an aesthetic idea', *The Idea of Freedom*, ed. A. Ryan (Oxford: Oxford University Press, 1979), pp. 27–39.

Miller, R.D.: *Schiller and the Ideal of Freedom* (Oxford: Clarendon Press, 1970).

Savile, A.: *Aesthetic Reconstructions: The Seminal*

Writings of Lessing, Kant and Schiller, Aristotelian Society Series, vol. 8 (Oxford: Basil Blackwell, 1987).

Schaper, E.: 'Towards the aesthetic: a journey with Friedrich Schiller', *British Journal of Aesthetics*, 25 (1985), 153–68.

MARGARET PATON

Schlegel, August Wilhelm von (1767–1845) German poet, critic and scholar. By the time of his death, with his younger brother Friedrich, August Schlegel was recognized as a founder of the modern romantic school of German literature. In the classical–modern debate he generally favoured the modern over the classical. He is important for his success in clarifying the meaning of romanticism via his distinction between classical (or ancient) and Romantic (or modern) forms of literature.

He was born into a literary family. His father, Johann Adolf, a high official in the Lutheran church, was a religious poet and a friend and associate of Gottlieb Rabener, Christian Gellert, and Friedrich Klopstock. His uncle, Johann Elias, was a dramatist. His brother, Friedrich, was a well known poet and thinker, regarded as the most penetrating mind among the founders of German Romanticism. August studied theology and then philology at the University of Göttingen. After three years as a tutor in a private family, he lectured on aesthetics in Jena beginning in 1798, where, with his brother, the philosopher and poet Novalis, and Ludwig Tieck he laid the critical foundations of Romanticism. While in Jena, his wife left him for the well known idealist philosopher, F.W.J. Schelling. From 1804 to 1817 he travelled in the entourage of Mme de Staël, whose *De l'Allemagne* ['On Germany'] expands many of his views. He also studied Oriental languages and became, in 1818, the first professor of Indology in Germany. He became professor in Berlin in 1819.

August Schlegel wrote dramas in the classical style and much verse, though without great success. He was a critic, producing his *Lectures on Dramatic Art and Literature* – widely recognized as a crucial statement of

Romanticism – in 1809, and a translator: he translated *Bhagavadgita* (1823), the dramas of Calderón and the poetry of Petrarch and Dante. With Tieck, he is most important for his translations of Shakespeare's plays.

The term 'romantic' emerged in the second half of the seventeenth century in both England and France. It then meant 'as in the romances', with special reference to medieval romances and Ariosto and Tasso. When the term arrived in Germany in the late eighteenth century, it was used as a synonym for 'Gothic'. It appears that Novalis invented the words *Romantik* and *Romantiker* at the end of the eighteenth century. For Novalis, the former meant someone who composed romances and fairy-tales, and the latter was synonymous with *Romankünstler*. Friedrich Schlegel defined romantic poetry as 'progressive *Universalpoesie*'. Slightly later he connected the term 'romantic' with Shakespeare, Cervantes and Italian poetry. He considered that in his unromantic age only the novels of Jean-Paul (Richter) were romantic. He also claimed that all poetry must be romantic.

Statements of August's in several series of lectures, especially those delivered in Vienna in 1808–9, were more influential in fixing the image of Romanticism. (The contrast of the classical and the romantic is implicit, but not yet explicit, in the lectures on aesthetics given in Jena in 1798.) In the lectures that he gave in Berlin from 1801 to 1804, he compared the difference between the classical and the romantic with that between ancient and modern poetry. In this formulation, the romantic is progressive and Christian. In his account of romantic literature, he distinguished between form and content. He described the great Italian writers Dante, Petrarch and Boccaccio as the founders of modern Romanticism; despite their admiration for classical literature they struck out on their own, and their own form and expression were unclassical. Thus Dante, who admired Virgil, produced something different from and better than the *Aeneid*. This is also the case with Michelangelo and Raphael in the field of art. In Schlegel's typology, examples of Romantic literature include the *Nibelungenlied* and other German heroic poems, the King Arthur and Charlemagne romances, and Spanish literature from *El Cid* to *Don Quixote*. Schlegel took up the theme again in his Vienna lectures, published in 1809–11, which were quickly translated into the major European languages.

The object of the Vienna lectures is both a general survey of drama in different periods and nations, and the exposition of a series of general ideas in order to evaluate their true artistic merit. Schlegel insisted that it is for the philosophical theory of poetry and of the fine arts to establish the fundamental laws of the beautiful. He associated the romantic–classical antithesis with those of the organic–mechanical and the plastic–picturesque. He opposed ancient literature and its neo-classical successor, a form of poetry allegedly representing perfection, to the romantic drama of Shakespeare and Calderón, that is supposedly representative of so-called infinite desire.

The influence of Schlegel's identification of Romanticism with modern literature, as opposed to classical or ancient literature, was spread by other writers, especially through the efforts of Mme de Staël. Her *De l'Allemagne* appeared in 1813 in London, and was then republished in Paris in 1814, several months after a French translation of Schlegel's *Lectures on Dramatic Art and Literature*. Her restatement of his parallels of classical and sculpturesque, romantic and picturesque, helped to popularize his view. In this way, Schlegel's ideas exerted a decisive influence, first in France, where Stendhal was the first to declare himself a Romantic, and then throughout Europe – particularly Italy, Spain, Portugal and Poland. In Russia, Pushkin labelled his *Prisoner of the Caucasus* a Romantic poem; and Coleridge, in England, made use of Schlegel's ideas in his lectures delivered between 1808 and 1818 and published later as *Shakespearean Criticism*.

See also CRITICISM; SCHLEGEL, FRIEDRICH VON.

WRITINGS

Vorlesungen über dramatische Kunst und Literatur

(1809); trans. J. Black, *Lectures on Dramatic Art and Literature* (London: Bell, 1884).
Vorlesungen über schöne Kunst und Literatur (Heilbronn: Henniger, 1884).

BIBLIOGRAPHY

Haym, R.: *Die Romantische Schule* (Darmstadt: Wissenschaftliche Buchgesellschaft, 1972).
Welleck, René: *A History of Modern Criticism*, vol. 2 (New Haven, Conn.: Yale University Press, 1955).

TOM ROCKMORE

Schlegel, Friedrich von (1772–1829) A many-sided cultural figure, Schlegel is best known with his brother, August, as one of the leaders of the German Romantic movement. He made contributions to the theory and practice of painting and to the evaluation of Gothic architecture; and he established Sanskrit studies in Germany. He lectured on philosophy and history; and on literature, of which he published an important history. He was also active as a diplomat. The son of a Lutheran minister, he was the youngest of five brothers. For more than a century he was less well known than his elder brother, August, but he is now generally regarded as a more significant figure. Many of the views that August later popularized were either restatements or modifications of Friedrich's ideas.

Friedrich initially studied law in Göttingen and Leipzig, but quickly abandoned it for literary pursuits. In 1804 he married Dorothea Viet, the daughter of Moses Mendelssohn. His novel *Lucinde* (1799), advocating free love – written while he was courting his future wife, who was married to someone else at the time – caused an enduring scandal. Both he and Dorothea converted to Roman Catholicism in 1808 – a change that was to be important for the later evolution of Schlegel's thought. Although his conversion was sometimes seen as the indirect result of the failure of August's marriage and his own subsequent break with his brother, Schlegel understood it as part of a continuous process. The conversion later led him away from certain of his early concerns, including his interest in the East arising out of his study of Sanskrit, and his pantheism. His religious views subsequently coloured all his later writings.

As a lecturer at the University of Jena, Schlegel studied the ideas of Kant (which he rejected); those of Fichte, which remained a basic influence on his thought; and those of Schelling. In Berlin, he studied Schleiermacher, Spinoza, Leibniz, and Schiller. Like Schelling, Schlegel knew Fichte, whom he regarded as the greatest living metaphysical thinker even though objecting to the abstract character of Fichte's thought; the parallels between the views of Schlegel and of Schelling, in so far as both were influenced by Fichte's, led each to accuse the other of plagiarism.

With August, Friedrich founded and edited the journal *Athenäum* (1798–1800), which laid the conceptual foundations of German Romanticism and was regarded by his contemporaries as the organ of the Romantic school. In 1802 he went to Paris, where he studied Sanskrit and Persian, lectured on philosophy, and edited the journal *Europa*. In 1808 he published *Über die Sprache und Weisheit der Inder* [On the language and wisdom of the Indians]. He was appointed court secretary to Archduke Charles in 1809 and, after the peace of 1814, Metternich's representative from the Viennese Court in Frankfurt. In Vienna, he lectured on modern history in 1810 and on ancient and modern literature in 1812. From 1820 to 1823, with Adam Müller he edited the review *Concordia*. His *Philosophie des Lebens* [Philosophy of life] appeared in 1828.

After Novalis, Schlegel was the outstanding literary theoretician of the first phase of Romanticism (the *Frühromantik*, c.1795–1801), and as philosopher and historian he was one of the main representatives of later Romanticism. His Romanticism evolved from what was initially an entirely classical approach to literature. The term 'romantic' was employed beginning in about 1810 by the opponents of this tendency; the term 'Romantic school' was popularized by Heine in 1836. Schlegel's theory, never stated in

systematic form, can be deduced from his writings. Here we can look to a series of important articles published in *Athenäum*, in which the term 'romantic' was understood in an imprecise sense as 'not classical'. As well as the Schlegels, the contributors to this journal included Novalis, Schleiermacher, Ludwig Tieck and the *Naturphilosoph* ['philosopher of nature'] Hülsen.

The typical Romantic mixture of idealistic philosophy and romantic poetry reflects an alienation from contemporary society that is exemplified by Friedrich Schlegel's writings. He was concerned to find a way to take up the difference between the ancient and the modern, or the classical and the romantic, into a wider unity. He wrote essays entitled 'Athenaeum Fragments', 'On Goethe's Wilhelm Meister', 'Ideas' and 'Conversation on Poetry'. In the *Athenaeum Fragments* Schlegel commented on philosophy and politics and formulated his literary theory. His main ideas are illustrated in the following, frequently cited, passage:

Romantic poetry is a progressive universal poetry. Its destiny is not merely to unite all the separate genres of poetry and to put poetry into contact with philosophy and rhetoric. Its aim and mission is, now to mingle, now to fuse poetry and prose, genius and criticism, the poetry of the educated and the poetry of the people, to make life and society poetic, to poeticize wit, to fill and saturate the forms of art with matters of genuine cultural value and to quicken them with the vibrations of humor. It embraces everything that is poetic, from the most comprehensive system of art ... to the sigh or kiss which the poetic child expresses in artless song. It can lose itself so completely in its subject matter that one may consider its supreme purpose to be the characterization of poetic individuals of every kind, and yet there is no form better suited to the complete self-expression of the spirit of the author, so that many an artist who merely wanted to write a *Roman* willy-nilly portrayed himself. It alone can, like the epic, become a mirror of the whole surrounding world, a portrait of the age. And yet it can, more than any other art form, hover on the wings of poetic reflection between the portrayed object and the portraying artist, free from all real and ideal interests ... [The] essential nature [of the romantic genre is] that it is eternally becoming and can never be perfected. No theory can exhaust it, and only a divinatory criticism could dare to attempt to characterize its ideal. It alone is infinite, as it alone is free; its supreme law is that the caprice of the author shall be subject to no law. The romantic genre is the only one that is more than a genre, but is, as it were, poetry itself, for in a certain sense, all poetry is or ought to be romantic. (Quoted in Eichner, 1970, pp. 57–8)

Writing in the wake of the French revolution, Schlegel here regards romantic poetry, like Fichte's *Wissenschaftslehre* [Theory of knowledge] and Goethe's *Wilhelm Meister*, as corresponding to the spirit of the times and as surpassing all limits. What he calls progressive universal poetry is intended to unite all the different forms of poetry that it will bring into contact with philosophy and rhetoric. The aim in view is to be reached through irony and wit. Irony surpasses every limit and wit is understood as a fragmentary expression of genius that knows no bounds. Unlike other types of literature, that have already attained fixed form and, hence, can be described, Romanticism is and will remain in a state of becoming. It follows that a Romantic work of art, be it philosophical or poetical, must retain a fragmentary character. Schlegel finds in Romantic poetry the literary equivalent of the idealist conception of the subject as unlimited and, hence, as free.

See also IRONY; SCHLEGEL, AUGUST VON.

WRITINGS

Kritische Friedrich Schlegel Ausgabe, ed. E. Behler (Paderborn: Schöningh, 1966).

Kritische und Theoretische Schriften, ed. A. Huyssen (Stuttgart: Reclam, 1978).

BIBLIOGRAPHY

Eichner, Hans: *Friedrich Schlegel* (New York: Twayne, 1970).
Wellek, René: *A History of Modern Criticism*, vol. 2 (New Haven, Conn.: Yale University Press, 1955), pp. 5–35.

TOM ROCKMORE

Schopenhauer, Arthur (1788–1860) German philosopher; one of Kant's greatest critics, and a major influence, especially in ethics and aesthetics, on later writers, including Nietzsche and Wittgenstein.

Schopenhauer is unusual among the great philosophers in according to the arts a central place in his philosophical system. Schopenhauer saw himself as a disciple of Kant in his general philosophy, with the crucial difference that he thought it possible to know the nature of the reality which lies beyond sensuous experience, without resorting to the elaborate jiggery-pokery that Kant indulged in in his metaphysics of morality. Schopenhauer believed that the ultimate reality is will – more precisely, the will-to-live – ubiquitous and undifferentiated.

In our own everyday activity of willing we come into contact with this ultimate reality, though in a deceptive form, since each of us believes that he is a separate will; this is the fundamental error of the *principium individuationis*, but if we accept his arguments on the subject, Schopenhauer believes, we shall grasp that in fact we are all parts of the single will. This leads him directly to his most celebrated view, his pessimism. Since in willing, which we do all the time, we are trying to change the state we are in, it follows that that state is felt to be unsatisfactory. But as soon as we achieve what we were willing (something that occurs less often than we would wish), we are propelled into willing something else, that being our essential nature. But it is also the essential nature of everything else, so the world is a scene of

387

perpetual frustration, with brief respites of boredom.

This drastic account of things would seem to leave no room for any consolation or mitigation, and our general unwillingness to acknowledge our plight adds a strong element of delusion to the already gloomy picture. But there is help at hand, and in a form sufficiently impressive to compromise Schopenhauer's pessimism considerably. For under certain circumstances we are able to suspend, if only temporarily, the activity of willing; and those circumstances are, in the first (and, for most of us, the only) place, when we are having an aesthetic experience. Accepting Kant's aesthetic theory as enthusiastically as he rejects his moral theory, Schopenhauer argues that in the presence of beauty we can practice 'disinterested contemplation', seeing objects for their own sakes and not having, as we always otherwise do, any palpable designs on them.

But to this he adds an element which makes his theory of the visual arts and literature (music is altogether different, as we shall see) radically different from Kant's. It is one of the surprises of his philosophy that he announces a belief in Platonic ideas, though they have only the ontological, and not the normative, status that they possess for Plato. What this amounts to is that, in the contemplation of a work of art, its content ceases to be particular and assumes universality. So Schopenhauer combines a Kantian account of aesthetic experience with an Aristotelian account of its objects. His account of art is thus essentially cognitive, not perceptual, since perception is of particulars, while art is concerned with universals. Why this should make us eager to have aesthetic experiences remains unclear, however, since the Schopenhauerian universe is quintessentially undesirable. If it is painful to experience any emotion, for instance, it is not clear why it should be pleasurable to contemplate any emotion in its universal form. The fact that we are briefly released from wanting to act seems insufficient to account for the delight we take in art, granted what its subject-matter is bound to be.

It could be claimed that Schopenhauer is in no worse a position than other theorists of art when they deal with 'negative states', such as jealousy and betrayal: it is just that he does not admit that there are any positive states, such as fulfilled love – or, indeed, any kind of fulfilment. So it could be said that for him the whole of art presents the kind of problem that tragedy has traditionally presented for everyone.

It is no surprise that Schopenhauer puts a very high value on tragedy, but not for any of the traditional reasons. He finds in it the portrayal of the nothingness of life, so that it can serve to prepare us for our own cessation – indeed, make that cessation seem something devoutly to be wished for. In other words it preaches, in Nietzsche's contemptuous term (for this very theory), 'resignationism'. It helps to detach us from life, which we otherwise so absurdly cling to, despite its pervasive wretchedness. Whatever may be said against this theory, at least it avoids the usual glibness about 'tragic affirmation'. On the other hand, given Schopenhauer's general metaphysical views, it is not clear that the enticing prospect of ceasing to exist is one that we can actually accomplish. Since our usual view of ourselves as separately existing beings is radically mistaken, my ceasing to exist can come to no more than my no longer having the illusion that I exist in the sense that I normally think I do. It is as if we are all – to use an image which is Schopenhauerian in spirit though not in letter – pimples on the ocean of cosmic pus which constitutes the will, and resignation to my non-existence is acquiescence in rejoining the rest of the undifferentiated ocean. What that would come to is, of course, unimaginable, but it would hardly be the same as simple non-existence.

The paradoxes that lie just beneath the surface of Schopenhauer's account of the visual and literary arts become much more striking when we consider his account of music, to which he accords a uniquely exalted status. Whereas the other arts involve representations and concepts, music dispenses with both of these, with the minor exception of onomatopoeic music (for instance, the bird-calls at the end of the second movement of Beethoven's 'Pastoral' Symphony). Not being mimetic or expressive in any ordinary sense, music is, according to Schopenhauer, a direct *presentation* of the will, and is therefore to be prized uniquely. He even writes of 'music or the world', and means what he says. This certainly puts music in a remarkable ontological position, while at the same time it renders Schopenhauer's eulogies of it all the more puzzling. In the first place, he regards his claim as true of all music (with the exception mentioned above), so that comparative qualitative assessments of different works are out of place – which seems strange. But that is a minor point compared with the further point that music is esteemed for presenting a reality which, in the rest of his work, Schopenhauer so comprehensively condemns.

The mixture, in his philosophy, of traditional and innovative elements here emerges as something very close to contradiction. Since, with remarkably few exceptions, western philosophers have taken a view of reality which has led them to place a positive value upon it, something which repesents it accurately would automatically inherit the favourable estimate of what it depicts. An alternative way in which mimetic art may be prized is in that it somehow transforms what it imitates, giving value to something that lacks it – or even, in the case of tragedy, to something that is acutely painful or has an otherwise negative value. But since Schopenhauer makes it the special glory of music that imitation or transformation is sidestepped – and so music is, as Nietzsche was later to put it, 'the truly metaphysical activity of mankind' because it gives us the actual movements of the will – how does it come about that he is so ecstatic about it? Music certainly cannot be accused of misleading us if Schopenhauer is right, but why should we not want to be misled over such a sordid matter? To this question, it seems, he has no answer except the traditional one – which he should certainly have queried – that it is better to know the truth.

It appears that what Schopenhauer did was to make an attempt, in itself praiseworthy, to account for the extraordinary power that music has over us, or at any rate over many people – though in general, it would seem, not over philosophers. But in accounting for this power he overplays his hand badly, and produces nonsense on at least two levels: in the first place, it is wholly unclear how music can be identified with will, whatever interpretation we put on that term or concept, which is both central to Schopenhauer's metaphysics and extremely vague in the context of it. In the second place, granted that the claim is meaningful, he has not succeeded in his task of explaining the value of music: on the contrary.

If he did have a plausible answer, it would no doubt be related to his Kantian insistence that in aesthetic experience our own wills are in abeyance, even if we are contemplating the single will itself. But this seems to be putting far too great an emphasis on the concept of disinterested contemplation – or, rather, getting it to do work for which it was not designed. It may be that in aesthetic experience 'we keep the sabbath of the penal servitude of willing ', as Schopenhauer put it with characteristic colour. But it does not follow that not willing is in itself pleasurable or worthwhile, irrespective of what we contemplate when we are in this condition. *A fortiori*, it does not follow that will-lessly contemplating the will is pleasurable, but that must be Schopenhauer's view. Perhaps it would be most plausible if he claimed that, from that vantage point, life became a farce, but he does not; though, were he to, his fervent admiration for Rossini would thereby be explained. For in the works by which Rossini is best remembered, especially his *Barber of Seville*, we have a kind of parody of the will-to-live. His characters are puppets, animated by nothing more than a vague demonic energy; but the fact that in these works Rossini taps a vein of malicious humour which is peculiar to him gives the lie to the general claim about music.

It has been argued, above all by Erich Heller in his book on Thomas Mann, *The Ironic German*, that it is because, and not in spite, of the profound confusions and ambiguities in his metaphysics, and especially in his aesthetics, that Schopenhauer has had so powerful an influence: not indeed on philosophers, who have for the most part ignored him since he died, as they did while he was alive – to his immense chagrin. But the list of artists who have been influenced by him, to whom reading him has come with the force of a revelation, is uniquely long and impressive. At their head is Richard Wagner, who read him first in 1854, and incessantly thereafter.

But Tolstoy, an utterly different artist, also praised him in the most abandoned terms, and began to translate his *magnum opus*, *The World as Will and Representation*. Turgenev, Zola, Maupassant and, especially, Proust were other European novelists on whom he made a lasting impression. And for Thomas Mann he was part of the constellation whose other members were Wagner and Nietzsche, under whose light he wrote his entire output. Among writers in English, Hardy and Conrad are the most notable figures who admired him. Less often mentioned is his impact on the remarkable Brazilian novelist Machado de Assis, whose masterpiece *Epitaph of a Small Winner* is clearly written under his aegis. In all these cases it can be argued that it was Schopenhauer's elevation of art at the expense of existence that had the greatest impact. The incongruity of this elevation was something that they overlooked: what may well have excited them was his pessimism, refreshing among philosophers, combined with the idea that they were equipped, as artists, with the means of offering consolation, or even escape. The more appalling the world, the more heroic the achievement of art in effecting its transfiguration.

There are two philosophers on whom Schopenhauer made an impression, though in neither case did it last. The first was Nietzsche, for whom, as for Wagner, en-countering him was a revelation. His first book, *the Birth of Tragedy*, was written under their joint spell; he soon rejected both of them, though not before writing to them panegyrics of a strange kind. But Schopen-hauer's 'Romantic pessimism' was some-thing that Nietzsche soon felt he had to tran-scend, though his replacement of the will-to-live by the will-to-power shows a residual influence. In the case of Ludwig Witt-genstein, the effect of Schopenhauer is most striking in the *Notebooks 1914–1916* and in the concluding passages of the *Tractatus*. But by the thirties he had come to feel that 'where true depth begins, Schopenhauer's runs out', and that may be taken as a harsh but finally just estimate of his work.

See also FUNCTION OF ART; KANT; NIETZSCHE; WAGNER.

WRITINGS

The World as Will and Representation, 2 vols; trans. E.F.J. Payne (New York: Dover, 1969).
Parerga and Paralipomena, 2 vols; trans. E.F.J. Payne (Oxford: Clarendon Press, 1974).

BIBLIOGRAPHY

Gardiner, P.: *Schopenhauer* (Harmondsworth: Penguin Books, 1967).
Hamlyn, D.: *Schopenhauer* (London: Routledge & Kegan Paul, 1980).
Heller, Erich: *The Ironic German* (Cambridge: Cambridge University Press, 1981), ch. 2.

MICHAEL TANNER

science and art While science, no more than art, can be thought to have one single aim, one crucial aspect of successful scientific investigation provides the basis on which any comparison of the two activities must rest. Although science and art are both human activities, and respond in various ways to human interests, our interests in scientific activity will be directly and successfully served only by theories which correspond or approximately correspond to the way the world is, at least in their observational conse-quences.

Our interests in pursuing scientific activity are not, of course, confined to representing the world. We may pursue science in order to manipulate the world, build bridges, fly planes, produce energy, and so on. We may be interested in scientific theories in order economically to summarize a mass of data. We may – as, arguably, Newton was – be interested in science for religious or metaphysical or ideological reasons. We may also – as Karl Popper and some of his followers do – see the progress of science in terms of the ever speedier elimination of false theories. Nevertheless, it remains true that each of these interests will be best served by theories which, at the observational level at least, fit the facts, or are judged in terms of their successes and failures in this respect. Even the investigator who wishes to use science to subserve some grander ideological scheme will come to grief, if others can show that the empirical facts fail to confirm his scientific theories.

There are many well canvassed difficulties in seeing scientific theories wholly in representational terms. In most theories there are elements which go beyong our powers to verify or check. In this and other respects there will always be an element of construction in the postulation of scientific theories, of imaginative leaping beyond the data. But checkable data must always support a theory if it is to be deemed successful scientifically, and it would be a justifiable criticism of a scientific theory if it rested on no checkable facts. Whatever difficulties there are in analysing the relationships between scientific theories and the facts which support or fail to support them, the reason for the need for an embedding of science in fact is clear: science is concerned with the description, explanation and manipulation of a world which has an objective existence apart from anything we might believe or feel about it. In scientific activity, then, our beliefs and feelings and imaginings must always be seen as responsive to the way the world is independently of our beliefs, feelings and imaginings.

In dealing with the world as it is, apart from our beliefs, desires and imaginings, science will tend – and has tended since the seventeenth century – to abstract from the way things appear to us as human perceivers. The search for casual regularities in the world, central to the scientific aims of explanation and manipulation of physical phenomena, may well go hand-in-hand with a downplaying of aspects of phenomena which are important to us as perceivers and

agents in the world. It is not coincidental that, in its search for an observer-independent view of the world, science has demoted the qualities of colour, sound, feel, taste and touch, with which our phenomenal world is filled, to the status of 'secondary' qualities: qualities which arise only in the interaction of object and observer, and which can be ignored in those descriptions of the causal networks in which things operate, in which there is no reference to perceptible effects.

Together with the displacement of the perceptual, the scientific drive for an observer-independent account of the world will characteristically tend to reductionism. That is, in probing beneath the perceived surfaces of things, it will tend to see what appear to be many different things in terms of smaller numbers of fundamental entities and processes. Where what we are interested in is causal explanation and manipulation of the world, successful reductions of this sort will represent considerable intellectual advances, in that we will thereby be enabled to ignore those aspects of reality which are important only at a human or perceptual level, and which are not crucial to the way things happen in this physical world – again, apart from effects on perceivers.

Science, then, attempts to investigate the world as it is in itself. It prescinds from observer-relative properties, it seeks theories of far-reaching application which abstract from differences at the phenomenal level, and the success of its theories is judged in terms of the way they are empirically borne out. In all these respects there are significant differences between art and science.

Artistic activity and expression are characteristically directed to stimulating experiences and reactions of various sorts in perceivers. They work, in the first instance, in so far as they succeed in doing this in the manner intended by the artist. Contemplating a Turner canvas, let us say, evokes the swell and pull of the sea. A Bach fugue may combine a sense of beauty of the theme with one of an imposing quasi-architectural structure. The exterior of a Georgian house conveys a sense of calm simplicity and order together with an unostentatious grandeur.

Baudelaire at once consoles and transforms the meaning death might have for the poor:

C'est la gloire des Dieux, c'est le grenier
mystique
C'est la bourse du pauvre et sa patrie
antique
C'est le portique ouvert sur les Cieux
inconnus.

It is the glory of the Gods, the mystic
granary
It is the purse of the poor and his ancient
fatherland
It is the gate opening on to unknown
skies.

With a work of art, then, success is bound up with the responses, thoughts and attitudes it evokes or might evoke in those who perceive it. By contrast, a scientific theory faces the tribunal of a nature which is quite impervious to the perceptions or reactions of human beings.

A work of art is an attempt to express some vision or attitude to the world from a consciously human perspective, and it will communicate this vision through the way it works on the perceptions or sensibility of its audience. From this fundamental difference between the theories of science and works of art, it obviously follows that artists cannot overlook the effects of secondary qualities. As far as our perception of the world goes, it is hardly possible to draw a justifiable distinction between primary and secondary qualities. That distinction arises only when our perspective is that of natural science.

As the world of art is first and foremost the world of human experience, it is arguable that artists should not seek the type of beneath-the-surface simplification and generalization pursued, and rightly pursued, in scientific inquiry. Human experience and activity, once clothed in cultural forms, develop new complexities and meanings. Thus, a rude hut is transformed into a Doric building, with columns and capitals, porticoes and plinths. New possibilities of balance, of proportion, of light and shade, of surface and depth are thus opened up (and in this context it is notable that in the Parthenon, the most famous of all Doric buildings, the effect of balance and harmony is achieved by deviating from the mathematical identities and lines that a scientific theory might favour in order to give the observer the impression of harmony and balance).

To the reductionist mind, any building is the same: a shelter from the elements. In one sense this is correct: beneath the appearances, all buildings are the same, just as any meal is just a way of assuaging hunger. But to emphasize the deep way in which all buildings and all meals are the same is to overlook the superficial way in which they are all different, the way in which human experience focuses so much on the surfaces of things, on the way things appear to us, affect us, delight us, matter to us, give pain to us.

As artists operate in the world of human meaning and experience, they cannot avoid the superficial richness, complexity and diversity of that experience, or the way in which cultural practices endow our experience with values and meanings. There can naturally be forms and styles of art which ape the reductionisms and simplifications of science, which purport to show the skull beneath the skin and the universal animal lurking behind the performances and rituals of civilization. But the decision to take this direction – like the closely linked decision to adopt a strictly functionalist approach to architecture – will be an aesthetic decision, and not, as in scientific inquiry, something forced on us by the nature of the discipline. And, as with other aesthetic simplifications, it is a decision which leaves the artist open to criticism on the grounds that he is failing to do justice to the full richness and complexity of human experience. At any rate, it would not be a decision which could be justified by any direct appeal to some analogy between art and science, since the justification of the reductionism of science appeals to a respect in which science is significantly different from art.

The fact that works of art operate at the level of the *Lebenswelt* and at the level of the world as experienced, rather than at the level of deep scientific reduction, shows the Pythagoreanism which underlies certain aesthetic theories to be the result of another misplaced analogy between art and science. Thus, we are told by some theorists of art and of human psychology alike that the reason a certain building or painting gives us satisfaction is because it is based on some mathematical formula, such as the golden section, to which our mind or brain naturally responds. While it is certainly true that the bays of the upper storey of the Palazzo della Cancelleria in Rome involve repeated examples of the golden section, it is not, however, true to say that for the majority of those who admire the building the golden section is any part of their conscious experience of it, for the majority will never have heard of the golden section. Even though it may be true that it is a figure which is disposed to induce in the perceiver a sense of order, the mathematical figure itself provides at most the framework for the full aesthetic experience offered by a particular building or painting. A Mexican palace, a Greek temple, the Cancelleria, a sketch by Le Corbusier and a figure in a Euclidean textbook may all be examples of the golden section, but, from the point of view of the experience of the perceiver, just as important as what they have in common are the differences between them, and the different feel that each thing will have for a perceiver, which patient attention to surface detail can articulate and explain.

Much the same can be said about attempts to analyse paintings in geometrical terms, as when someone speaking about Piero della Francesca's *Baptism of Christ* starts to trace out geometrical lines and shapes over the canvas. Even if it were true that Piero and other artists were – like Schoenberg and his followers in the twentieth century – influenced by mathematical considerations in their work, to treat and conceive works of art simply in terms of some hidden mathematical essence is to obliterate the human and aesthetic meaning that they will in any case have. In the case of the *Baptism of Christ*, emphasizing formal relationships at the expense of the rest of what is on the canvas will be to downplay or overlook altogether its tenderness, its peace, its religiousness, its poignancy, and its human and religious meaning generally. Similarly, analysing the Cancelleria as just an example of the golden section will be to leave out of account pretty well everything that contributes to the actual experience the building offers. As L.B. Alberti observed (and as Le Corbusier and other modernists have overlooked), the beauty of architecture requires the addition of ornament to the harmony of proportion. And, as already remarked in dealing with the Parthenon, what counts even in the harmony of proportion is perceived harmony, which may actually require deviation from strict mathematical or scientific harmony.

The differences between science and art, then, will lead us to take up different attitudes to reductions and simplifications in the two fields. Naturally, the fact that science is so important a part of our life and civilization will mean that artists will have to respond to science and its discoveries in various ways, but there is nothing in the nature of science or of art which implies that the only or best way of doing this is by means of an art which apes the simplifications and reductions of science.

There is, finally, one further important respect in which science differs from art, which again arises directly from science's aim of representing a world which exists independently of human response. In the light of this central aim of science, it is possible to speak of scientific progress, which will be measured by the increasing adequacy of succeeding theories in representing, revealing and predicting parts of the physical world. Thus, without any of us being better observers or theorizers of the natural world, we can all be said to have better scientific knowledge than Aristotle or Priestley. We all know, simply because science has progressed, that the earth is not the centre of the universe and that there is no such stuff as phlogiston. But it would not be possible to say that we are better poets than Homer or Shakespeare – or, indeed, that poetry has made progress since Homer or since Shakespeare. Part of the reason for this is that in poetry, as in the other arts, there is no external goal which remains constant over time, in terms of which success can be judged.

It is true, as T.S. Eliot remarked, that there is a sense in which we know more than the dead writers knew, but knowing more in Eliot's sense is not in any straightforward way knowing better. For Eliot, part of what we know is the dead writers and their works, and in so far as we see ourselves as operating within a particular tradition, knowledge of authorities within the tradition will be very important to us – later artists and critics – in order to learn the expressive potential of the tradition. Of course, this too is a difference between art and science. Contemporary scientists are interested in the truth or the empirical adequacy of theories as this appears to them, and to discover this they do not have to know about Aristotle or Copernicus or Priestley. By contrast, in the human world, of which art is a significant part, judgement of works is not performed by an ahistorical nature, but rather by the response they evoke among those schooled in the tradition to which artists and audience alike belong.

See also ATTITUDE, AESTHETIC; FUNCTION OF ART; PROPERTIES, AESTHETIC.

BIBLIOGRAPHY

Goodman, N. and Elgin, Catherine Z.: *Reconceptions in Philosophy and Other Arts and Sciences* (London: Routledge & Kegan Paul, 1988).
Leavis, F.R.: *Nor Shall My Sword* (London: Chatto & Windus, 1972).
O'Hear, A.: *The Element of Fire: Science, Art and the Human World* (London: Routledge & Kegan Paul, 1988).

ANTHONY O'HEAR

Scruton, Roger (1944–   ) As well as being a noted political theorist and commentator on political events, Scruton has written widely on aesthetics and on matters of taste in architecture and the arts.

In his inaugural lecture as Professor of Aesthetics at the University of London, Scruton attempted to restore the subject of aesthetics to the place of philosophical eminence once accorded it by Kant and Schiller, and from which it has been deposed by generations of analytical philosophers. Scruton's view stems from a bifurcation between the world revealed by scientific inquiry, and that in which we live our daily lives, the *Lebenswelt* of the phenomenologists. In the scientific paradigm, the human subject is, as far as possible, eliminated; Scruton agrees with many contemporary analytic philosophers and philosophers of science in seeing science as aiming at an impersonal and absolute view of the world as it is in itself, and not necessarily as it is revealed to us in everyday experience. But unlike, say, Quine, Scruton is concerned to stress what is absent from the scientific paradigm and its construal of objective knowledge.

What is absent is precisely that 'intentional understanding' by which we describe, criticize and justify the world as it appears. Intentional understanding fills the world with the meanings implicit in our aims, actions and emotions. The concepts and explanations generated in this understanding have evolved in answer to the needs of generations, and cannot be replaced by the deeper-level scientific accounts of the world, which, in their abstraction from appearance, can lead to an estrangement of the human subject from the world of appearance in which, perforce, he lives his life.

In his earlier books, *Art and Imagination* and *The Aesthetics of Architecture*, Scruton developed an analysis of aesthetic judgement, grounding that judgement in the imaginative experience of the perceiver and stressing the ways in which works of art have to be experienced in order to communicate. This fundamentally psychological approach to the aesthetic led him to reject accounts of works of art which locate their significance in some message hidden beneath or outside the surface of their appearance, or which postulate the need for some quasi-linguistic decoding of the aesthetic. Aesthetic experience is, for Scruton, on the level of our shared everyday recognition of the fitting, the beautiful, the funny, the tragic, the bizarre, and so on. In works of art we have some kind of disinterested manifestation of the sensibility of the everyday; they and the criticism of works of art can be seen as the refinement of our understanding of the everyday. Aesthetic experience, indeed, is for Scruton as for Kant that which reveals the sense of the world.

In *The Aesthetics of Architecture*, Scruton was concerned to demonstrate by means of examples what the sense of particular given buildings is to the perceiver; how, by means of detail (or lack of it), a given building may come to appear serene or balanced or lively or theatrical or pompous, and so on. On one level, then, aesthetics is the systematic study of such experience; in turning its attention to specific works and scenes it might be said to reveal the sense of the world. But in his subsequent writings, Scruton makes grander claims for aesthetics, linking it to religion and the decline of religion.

Placing himself in the tradition of Kant, Arnold, Ruskin and Leavis, Scruton wants aesthetics to reveal the sense of the world in the way natural theology tried to do and failed. It is through aesthetic contemplation that we feel the purposiveness and intelligibility, and even the personality, of everything that surrounds us; in it we get those imitations of the transcendental, of the world as somehow grounded, which men once found in religion. It is precisely because they cannot accommodate this sense that Scruton rejects both the imperialistic claims of science to explain everything, and the tenets of moral systems such as utilitarianism, which would treat human beings in accordance with some norm of scientific detachment and objectivity, and analyse their actions in abstraction from the contexts and contents which make them meaningful for their agents.

While many readers would accept Scruton's analysis of aesthetic experience at what might be called the lower level, the quasi-religious role he claims for aesthetics and for works of art is likely to cause considerable problems. For one thing, it is not clear how works of art can restore meaning of a religious sort to the world in the absence of any religion or natural theology to frame them. Just what are the intimations of the transcendental intimating if, as Scruton says,

the idea of God is something we can grasp only negatively? Moreover, the relationship between the world of science and the *Lebenswelt* is more difficult to understand than Scruton's simple bifurcation suggests. None the less, many will admire his successive attempts to link the analysis of aesthetic experience and judgement with the experiences that perceivers of works of art actually have, and to place aesthetics firmly within the *Lebenswelt*. They will also admire his attempt to bring thinkers such as Arnold, Ruskin and Leavis within the scope of contemporary philosophy – which normally neglects such figures, and even the problems they wrestled with; philosophy's neglect notwithstanding, the problems that they and Scruton address are central to the future of our culture.

See also IMAGINATION; RELIGION AND ART.

WRITINGS

Art and Imagination (London: Methuen, 1974).
The Aesthetics of Architecture (London: Methuen, 1979).
The Aesthetic Understanding (Manchester: Carcanet Press, 1983).
The Philosopher on Dover Beach (Manchester: Carcanet Press, 1990).

ANTHONY O'HEAR

Shaftesbury, Lord [Anthony Ashley Cooper, 3rd Earl of Shaftesbury] (1671–1713) English moral philosopher and man of letters; prevented by ill-health from the political life usual in his family. Shaftesbury has some claim to the title of founder of modern aesthetics. He was brought up in the household of his grandfather, the 1st earl, who was actively involved in the politics of the Restoration. His education was placed in the hands of the 1st earl's friend and supporter, John Locke, though it took a more classical pattern than Locke's own model. Shaftesbury acknowledges this debt, though he later qualifies its extent:

From the earliest infancy Mr. Locke

governed according to his principles ...
I was his more peculiar charge, being as
eldest son taken by my grandfather and
bred under his care, Mr. Locke having
the absolute direction of my education,
and to whom next my immediate
parents, as I must own the highest
obligation, so I have ever preserved the
highest gratitude and duty. (Shaftesbury
1900 [1705], p. 332)

One of the interesting questions about Shaftesbury concerns the way in which his classicism is modified by Lockean empiricism, even
though Shaftesbury himself specifically
rejects Locke's ideas.

Shaftesbury was fundamentally a moralist.
Three factors shaped his moral theory. He
was a country Whig who defended both the
rights and the obligations of his class. He was
an opponent of Hobbes, and attempted to
establish a public interest in place of the self-
interested egoism that he attributed to Hob-
besians. And he was a sentimentalist who
found the basis for moral judgement in a
moral sense.

In practice, Shaftesbury advocated a Neo-
platonic form of classicism. His first published
work was an introduction to a collection of
sermons by Benjamin Whichcote, and he was
familiar with the Cambridge Platonists. The
internal sense that Shaftesbury introduces
into his Neoplatonism is not bare sense perception, and it undoubtedly retains something of earlier, Augustinian, connotations.
Augustine, also, spoke of an interior sense
which 'is in some kind of way a ruler and
judge among the other senses ... The interior
sense judges the bodily senses, approving
their integrity and demanding that they do
their duty, just as the bodily senses judge
corporeal objects approving of gentleness and
reproving the opposite' (Augustine, 1973
edn, p. 37). Augustine subordinates the
interior sense to reason, however, and Shaftesbury likewise distrusts mere sense. The
difference between them lies in Shaftesbury's
conversion of interior sense into a moral
source, so that virtue is known by the feelings
that it is capable of producing under the influence of a moral sense. Thus Hobbes's total

reliance on egoistic self-interest is countered
by a natural impulse for the good which is
non-egoistic, according to Shaftesbury. One
has direct empirical verification of that good
through the moral sense.

The connection between virtue and beauty
is close. It begins with a typical Neoplatonic
equation: 'I am ready enough to yield there is
no real good beside the enjoyment of beauty.
And I am as ready, replied Theocles, to yield
there is no real enjoyment of beauty beside
what is good' (Shaftesbury, 1964 [1711], p.
141). That identity is explicated in terms of
an immediate sense response, which can be
taken as an aesthetic sense paralleling the
moral sense:

[The mind] feels the soft and harsh, the
agreeable and disagreeable in the affections; and finds a foul and fair, a harmonious and a dissonant, as really and
truly here as in any musical numbers or
in the outward forms or representations
of sensible things. Nor can it withhold its
admiration and ecstasy, its aversion and
scorn, any more in what relates to one
than to the other of these subjects. So
that to deny the common and natural
sense of a sublime and beautiful in
things will appear an affectation merely,
to any only who considers duly of this
affair. (Shaftesbury, 1964 [1711], pp.
251–2)

Thus Shaftesbury moves from a harmony
between the intelligible and sensible worlds
to a harmony within the senses themselves.
In so doing, he shifts aesthetic judgement in
the direction of Locke, no matter how much
his own classicism leads him to distrust
Locke's bourgeois reliance on mere sense.
Francis Hutcheson sees the possibilities
implicit in this shift, and develops them into
a full theory of aesthetic sensibility.

Shaftesbury is also given credit for introducing 'disinterestedness' into modern
aesthetics (Stolnitz, 1961). For example,
Shaftesbury claims: 'In all disinterested cases,
[the heart] must approve in some measure of
what is natural and honest, and disapprove
what is dishonest and corrupt' (Shaftesbury,

1964 [1711], p. 252). But the case is complex. Shaftesbury is not concerned to eliminate interest, but to guide and correct it so that one's true interests are discovered. In an essay entitled 'Plastics', i.e. plastic form, he explains that 'the great business in this (as in our lives, or in the whole of life) is "to correct our taste". For whither will not *taste* lead us?' (Shaftesbury, 1914 [1711], p. 114). Neither the aesthetic sense nor taste can be relied upon, in the absence of reflection. Disinterestedness is a possibility in contrast to pure self-interest, but both must be corrected by a number of practical tests, including the approval over time of an educated public and correction by discourse and even raillery. Shaftesbury's use of 'disinterestedness' does not denote a special aesthetic attitude, therefore, and it is not opposed to moral and critical examination.

Shaftesbury's place as a founding father of modern aesthetics rests on his practical concern with art and the education of taste more than on any single theoretical innovation. His influence on Hutcheson and Hume is clear. He writes unsystematically, but there is a coherent view of aesthetics as a harmony of the person with the values of beauty and taste, which is often far more persuasive in Shaftesbury's way of approaching problems than it is in his largely traditional Neoplatonic language.

Before Shaftesbury, harmony is the music of the spheres; after Shaftesbury, it is the soul's sensory response to art and style. Taste in its aesthetic mode is naturalized and added to the five external senses. Shaftesbury's overt debt to Locke is not large, but in subtle ways he relies as heavily on his own experience and his ability to use that experience as a basis for judgement as does Locke. That spirit is absorbed into eighteenth-century aesthetics, even as Shaftesbury's own writings come to seem mannered and his patrician classicism is replaced by a more egalitarian aesthetic sense.

See also HARMONY AND SYMMETRY; HUTCHESON; TASTE.

WRITINGS

The Life, Unpublished Letters and Philosophical Regime of Anthony, Earl of Shaftesbury, ed. Benjamin Rand (London: Swan & Sonnenschein, 1900).
Second Characters (1711); ed. Benjamin Rand (Cambridge: Cambridge University Press, 1914).
Characteristics (London: 1711); ed. John M. Robertson (Indianapolis: Bobbs-Merrill, 1964).

BIBLIOGRAPHY

Augustine: 'On free will', *Philosophy in the Middle Ages*, ed. Arthur Hyman and James J. Walsh (Indianapolis: Hackett, 1973).
Kivy, Peter: *The Seventh Sense* (New York: Burt Franklin, 1976).
Stolnitz, Jerome: 'On the significance of Lord Shaftesbury in modern aesthetic theory', *Philosophical Quarterly*, 43 (1961), 97–113.
Townsend, Dabney: 'Shaftesbury's aesthetic theory', *Journal of Aesthetics and Art Criticism*, 42 (1982), 205–13.
Voitle, Robert: *Anthony, Earl of Shaftesbury* (Baton Rouge: Louisiana State University Press, 1984).

DABNEY TOWNSEND

Sibley, Frank Noel (1923–   ) British philosopher of art, for many years at the University of Lancaster. Although perhaps cited most often as the author of the seminal paper, 'Aesthetic concepts' (1959), that work is only one of a lengthy set of essays, some (at the time of writing) yet to be published, which fit together to give a systematic view of a central set of aesthetic problems.

The first part of 'Aesthetic concepts' begins with instances of aesthetic concepts used in judgements of taste. These are contrasted with what are called 'non-aesthetic concepts' – examples of which would be 'red', 'curved', 'square', and 'in iambic pentameters'. Examples of aesthetic concepts are 'graceful', 'balanced' and 'tightly knit'. The distinction is offered in the expectation that the reader will recognize that the ability to apply aesthetic concepts requires a power to discriminate ('taste') that goes beyond an ability merely to say that something is square, or curved or possessed of a certain pattern of rhymes and stresses.

The features designated by aesthetic concepts depend on and emerge from the non-aesthetic features that a work possesses. Thus the aesthetic balance in a painting may depend on and emerge from such non-aesthetic features as a patch of red in a certain position. Although anyone possessed of normal eyesight could see the position of this colour patch, it takes something more to see that it contributes to the balance in the work. 'Aesthetic concepts' and its related 'Aesthetic and non-aesthetic' (1965) explore the relationships between aesthetic and non-aesthetic concepts. The central, and much debated, claim is that aesthetic concepts are not positively condition-governed by the non-aesthetic concepts upon which they depend and from which they emerge. No description of the work in non-aesthetic terms (for example, a description of a painting in terms of the position of colour patches) will entail the conclusion that it has an aesthetic feature, such as balance, even though it is the position of those colour patches that is responsible for the possession of an aesthetic feature, such as balance. By contrast, the description 'is a closed figure with four sides and four equal angles' will entail that the figure in question is a square. Another way of putting this is that one could see that a painting had colour masses in a certain configuration without thereby seeing that it had balance.

This account has profound implications. First, a certain kind of proof will not be possible in cases of aesthetic dispute. If someone doubts a figure to be a square, a *conclusive demonstration* is possible, for squareness is positively condition-governed. But no non-aesthetic description of a picture (to which the contending parties are likely easily to agree) will entail the conclusion that it is aesthetically balanced. This has to be seen. For aesthetic judgement is *perceptual* (Sibley, 1965).

The second part of 'Aesthetic concepts', which has important implications for aes-

thetic education, describes how we might bring someone to see what we see by way of aesthetic qualities in a work of art. In 'Aesthetic and non-aesthetic', too, important conclusions are drawn about criticism. Criticism will not be a matter of demonstration but of perceptual proof, bringing someone to see something. This goes hand in hand with critical explanation, in which, having seen the aesthetic qualities of a work, one points to the non-aesthetic features which are responsible for the aesthetic features. Thus, knowing that a poem, say, has a certain rhyme pattern will not guarantee that we will see its aesthetic unity: but once we have perceived the unity, we may point to the rhyme scheme as the factor upon which that unity depends.

It might be asked whether criticism, in the sense of the activity of pointing to the perceptual aesthetic features of a work, can be objective. This question is addressed in the two papers 'Colours' (1967–8) and 'Aesthetics and objectivity' (1968). The former investigates the conditions that underpin our propensity to say that certain things are, say, red or green. The latter argues that a case can analogously be made for saying that things are, say, graceful or delicate. For our language, which imputes colours to objects, depends in the last resort upon an agreement in judgements, and it is argued that that sort of agreement holds, with variations, in the aesthetic case as well.

Criticism is dealt with further in 'General criteria in aesthetics' (1983). (And see, here, Dickie, 1988.) In this paper Sibley addresses the question of whether reasoning is possible in aesthetics. The traditional problem here is that a reason, to be a reason, must be *general*: if courage is to be a reason for praising one person, it must be a reason for praising anyone who shows it. The difficulty in aesthetics is that what seems to be a reason for saying that this picture is, say, balanced (as when we say that the reason it is balanced is this patch of red in this position) might be the very thing that makes another picture unbalanced. Here Sibley distinguishes between 'merit' features, such as grace and balance, and neutral features, such as the possession of a red patch in a certain position. Those who focus on the latter are right that the presence of such features cannot constitute general reasons for saying that the work has merit. But the former are general in the sense that they prima facie count only for a judgement of merit (although in some cases, carefully described by Sibley, their pro-judgement force may be neutralized).

The claims of 'Aesthetic concepts' are central to Sibley's work. And they have been vigorously contested. Thus, Meager (1970) has maintained that concepts other than aesthetic concepts display the property of being non-positively condition-governed. Provided, however, that some indubitably aesthetic concepts do display this property, Meager's claim does not undermine the claims that Sibley makes about the nature of aesthetic judgement and its non-demonstrative perceptual nature. But it will still leave open the question of what makes a non-positively condition-governed concept an aesthetic one. Others (for instance, Cohen, 1973) have attempted to show that there are positively conditioned-governed aesthetic concepts, thus striking at the roots of Sibley's account. Cohen has further asked whether the initial distinction between aesthetic and non-aesthetic concepts, upon which everything in Sibley's 'Aesthetic concepts' rests, can be non-circularly drawn.

These controversies continue, their existence testifying to the important bearing that Sibley's work is seen to have on questions about the nature of aesthetic appreciation and criticism.

See also EDUCATION, AESTHETIC; CRITICISM; PROPERTIES, AESTHETIC.

WRITINGS

'Aesthetic concepts', *Philosophical Review*, 68 (1959), 421–50.
'Aesthetic and non-aesthetic', *Philosophical Review*, 74 (1965), 135–59.
'Colours', *Proceedings of the Aristotelian Society*, 68 (1967–8), 145–66.
'Aesthetics and objectivity', *Proceedings of the Aristotelian Society*, suppl. vol. 42 (1968), 31–54.
'General criteria in aesthetics', *Essays on Aesthetics*, ed. J. Fisher (Philadelphia: Temple University Press, 1983), 3–20.

BIBLIOGRAPHY

Cohen, T.: 'Aesthetic and non-aesthetic', *Theoria*, 39 (1973).
Dickie, G.: *Evaluating Art* (Philadelphia: Temple University Press, 1988).
Meager, R.: 'Aesthetic concepts', *British Journal of Aesthetics*, 10 (1970).

COLIN LYAS

'significant form' *See* BELL; FORM.

structuralism and poststructuralism Structuralism is an aesthetic theory based on the following assumptions: all artistic artefacts (or 'texts') are exemplifications of an underlying 'deep structure'; texts are organized like a language, with their own specific grammar; the grammar of a language is a series of signs and conventions which draw a predictable response from human beings. The objective of structuralist analysis is to reveal the deep structures of texts. The roots of structuralism lie mainly in structural linguistics, in particular the theories of the Swiss linguist, Ferdinand de Saussure (1857–1913), whose *Course in General Linguistics* provides structuralism with its basic methodological model. Other major sources of structuralist aesthetic theory have been Russian formalism (a school of literary theorists who flourished in post-Revolutionary Russia) and structural anthropology (Claude Lévi-Strauss being a key figure in this area).

Poststructuralism is a broad-based cultural movement embracing several disciplines, which has self-consciously rejected the techniques and premises of structuralism, particularly the notion that there is an underlying pattern to events. Nevertheless, it owes a great deal to the earlier theory, and has been variously described as 'neo-structuralism' and 'superstructuralism'.

For Saussure, language is a self-regulating

system, in the sense that a game like chess can be considered as self-regulating:

> In chess, what is external can be separated relatively easily from what is internal. The fact that the game passed from Persia to Europe is external; against that, everything having to do with its system and rules is internal. If I use ivory chessmen instead of wooden ones, the change has no effect on the system; but if I decrease or increase the number of chessmen, this change has a profound effect on the 'grammar' of the game ... everything that changes the system in any way is internal. (Saussure, 1960 [1915], pp. 22–3)

Chess is a whole system, with its own specific rules and procedures ('grammar') that prescribe what can happen during the game. Language is similarly held to be a self-contained, self-regulating system with an underlying structure of rules which allow a certain degree of freedom to the individual language-user; the rules specify general principles and practices which can be varied (or 'transformed') at local level by the individual. It is in the *structure* of the language, rather than in the utterances made within it, that Saussure's interest lies, and he distinguishes sharply between the former (*langue*) and the latter (*parole*). Jean Piaget has noted that 'the notion of structure is comprised of three key ideas: the idea of wholeness, the idea of transformation, and the idea of self-regulation' (Piaget, 1971, p. 5), and these will remain primary considerations for structuralist theorists and critics in their analyses of phenomena.

Saussurean linguistics is based on a series of critical distinctions which have been taken over by structuralists: in particular, *langue/parole*, signifier/signified, synchronic/diachronic, and syntagmatic/paradigmatic. Signifier/signified refers to the distinction between a word, spoken or written, and the mental concept lying behind it. The union of signifier and signified, word and concept, in an act of understanding, creates what Saussure calls the 'sign'.

The study of language is for Saussure the study of signs and how they work. He subsumes such a study within the wider discipline of 'semiology', which takes all sign systems as its field of inquiry. The connection between signifier and signified is described as being arbitrary, which means that it is subject to change over time as long as there is general agreement as to that change within a given linguistic community: 'The principle of change is based on the principle of continuity', as Saussure (1960, p. 74), puts it, thus introducing the distinction between synchronic and diachronic. Synchrony deals with the totality of a phenomenon over time, whereas diachrony deals with some particular aspect of that totality at a given point in time. In chess terms, the game plus its grammar is a synchrony; an actual move of any of the pieces within the game itself is a diachronic event. Diachronic events must always be examined in terms of their relationship to the whole system.

Saussure's theory of relations involves the distinction between syntagmatic and paradigmatic. A syntagm is a combination of words consisting of two or more consecutive units, constructed according to the rules of syntax of the relevant language: 'God is good', 'If the weather is nice we'll go out' (Saussure, 1960, p. 123). Each word is linked to the next word in the sequence, as it unfolds, in linear relationship. Paradigmatic (or, as Saussure originally termed them, 'associative') relations are more akin to John Locke's notion of 'association of ideas', and fall into no predictable pattern since they depend on the particular mental processes and experience of the individual; in Locke's words, 'there is another connexion of ideas wholly owing to *chance or custom*. Ideas that in themselves are not at all of kin come to be so united in some men's minds that it is very hard to separate them; they always keep in company' (Locke, 1964 [1690], pp. 250–1). Deconstruction relies heavily on the notion of paradigmatic relation, which it interprets in a particularly radical way in its critical theory and practice.

Saussure's theory of value has had important implications for the development of structuralism. He equates value with function: units have value only in the sense that they can be compared, or exchanged, with other units in their own sign system. There is no such thing as intrinsic value in Saussure, and he takes a purely formal, function-orientated approach to the question of value. Structuralism is similarly form- and function-orientated.

Structuralists have adopted the bulk of the terminology and methodology of Saussure's *Course in General Linguistics*. The basic concerns of a structuralist critic are to identify the boundaries of the system under analysis, to establish the nature of its syntax and the relations obtaining between its syntactical elements, and then to view her findings in both synchronic and diachronic perspective where transformations of the syntactical elements can be traced in detail. Russian formalists like Vladimir Propp have shown how a range of folk-tales could vary subtly from one example of the genre to another by the transformation of basic narrative units. The supernatural, for example, might appear in every case, but in a different form each time around, to different effect, and at a variety of points in the plot.

The study of transformation can lead to some very sophisticated comparative analysis of narratives within and across genres, and that is one of structuralism's great strengths. Lévi-Strauss's work on primitive myth is a model of how to catalogue transformations within a genre for the purposes of comparative cultural analysis. In *The Raw and the Cooked*, his analyses of a range of South American Indian myths are directed towards proving that, 'in all these instances we are dealing with the same myth', and that 'the apparent divergences between the versions are to be treated as the result of transformations occurring within a set' (Lévi-Strauss, 1969, p. 147). Unity remains an overriding concern of structuralists. The major virtue of structuralist analysis for Lévi-Strauss is that its 'unique and most economical coding system' enables the critic to 'reduce messages of a most disheartening complexity' to a determinate order in terms of their deep structures. Roland Barthes is similarly concerned with coding in narrative but, as his reading of Balzac's novella *Sarrasine* in S/Z suggests, he is committed to demonstrating how *complex* rather than how economical such coding can be: 'the codes it mobilizes', he remarks of the literary text, 'extend *as far as the eye can reach*, they are indeterminable' (Barthes, 1974, pp. 5–6).

As an aesthetic theory, structuralism has been criticized on a variety of counts, most notably as being mechanical in operation, ultra-formalist, committed to determinism and idealism, and lacking in evaluative power. It can easily decline into a highly predictable form of analysis in which codes are checked off, signs catalogued and comparisons made on a formal level which says little about content or psychological effect. Since it stays at a formal level, structuralism tends to avoid evaluation, the critic's concern being with the way a text and its units are organized rather than with what it might be saying. The notion of deep structure seems to deny human agency (deep structures work *through* individuals), and has deterministic connotations: structuralists are notorious for claiming the 'death of the [individual] subject'.

Structure remains a highly problematical concept, and in practice most structuralists have tended to analyse individual artworks in terms of an assumed ideal structure, which suggests an underlying Platonism to the enterprise. Derrida, amongst others, has been particularly critical of this aspect of structuralist methodology (see 'Force and signification', Derrida, 1978, pp. 3–30). Structuralism is a superbly efficient theory when it comes to describing and comparing phenomena in formal terms, but arguably seriously deficient when it comes to evaluating them.

Evaluation has traditionally been a central concern of criticism, and structuralism's weakness in this respect has been heavily criticized by, for example, Marxists, who see the refusal to evaluate almost as a dereliction of a critic's duty towards readers. So-called 'structuralist Marxists' have tried to have the best of both worlds by adapting structuralist methodology to Marxist political purposes; but although Pierre Macherey's 'reading against the grain' techniques, in which the text is ransacked for evidence of ideological contradictions and 'false' authorial resolutions of 'real' sociopolitical debates, has had a considerable vogue in recent years (see particularly Macherey, 1978; Eagleton, 1976), the respective theories are generally felt to be largely incompatible, given their differences on value.

Structuralism's implicit determinism has exercised poststructuralist thinkers considerably. Many poststructuralists, drawing on developments in modern science, stress the importance of chance and indeterminacy in human affairs. Whereas structuralists invariably seek to find an underlying unity in texts or events, poststructuralists search out instability. Derrida has described structuralism as being authoritarian and totalitarian in operation, as forcing artworks to conform to pre-established schemas. The emphasis in poststructuralist analyses is on the contingent, the different, the unsystematic and unsystematizable. Poststructuralism is a wide-ranging movement which encompasses not just Derrida and deconstruction, but also Foucault-inspired 'discourse theory' and the postmodernism of theorists like Jean-François Lyotard and Jean Baudrillard. In general it can be said that poststructuralists reject the certainties of structuralism, the idea that structure can be pinned down and all textual 'messages' ultimately reduced to pre-existing codes.

Discourse theory studies the way that discourses (of aesthetics, for example) arise in a society, and how they construct notions of value and make claims to power. Foucault rejects the idea of history as a teleological process, and emphasizes difference and discontinuity instead. In *Madness and Civilisation* he explores how the discourse of 'madness', as a recognizable phenomenon with its own set of social practices and institutions, arose in seventeenth-century Europe as a method of social control and how it represented a break with past practices. Foucault sees no pattern or reason to history, and resists totalizing theories and analyses (both structuralism and Marxism would be so describable). His 'archaeological' investigations into

history often concentrate on bringing to the surface hidden or subjugated discourses – as in the case of his studies of sexuality – in order to illustrate just how lacking in rational pattern or teleological progress history actually is.

Lyotard's postmodernism involves a wholesale rejection of large-scale, all-embracing theories of explanation (in Lyotard's terminology, 'grand narratives' or 'metanarratives'), such as Marxism or Hegelianism. Once again, as in Derrida and Foucault, the reaction is against 'authoritarian' theories – that is, theories which assume an underlying pattern to events. Postmodernism is less a coherent movement than a set of attitudes towards authority. Lyotard regards all theoretical discourses, including philosophy, as forms of narrative and as having no ultimate purchase on truth or knowledge. Ordinary narrative is taken to be just a fact of human existence requiring no further justification or licence from any grand narrative: 'it certifies itself in the pragmatics of its own transmission' (Lyotard, 1984, p. 27). He supports the cause of 'little narrative' (*petit récit*), which he identifies with the individual, over that of 'grand', which he identifies with systems and institutions. He sees the world as being made up of a multiplicity of little narratives, all of which have their own particular integrity and sense of importance, but none of which can be considered to take precedence over any of the others. Grand narrative is held to dominate and suppress little narrative, and is therefore to be resisted. There is a libertarian strain to Lyotard's thought.

The postmodernist adopts what Lyotard (1984, p. xxiv) calls an attitude of 'incredulity towards metanarratives', refusing to acknowledge their authority. In aesthetic terms of reference this had led to a rejection of programmatic theories like modernism. Postmodernist artists are quite happy to rework older styles and forms, seeing no need for a break with tradition in the manner of their modernist counterparts. In architecture the result has been the reintroduction of older architectural features – often in the guise of ornamental additions to existing modern buildings – and a turning away from the more brutal forms of modern architecture. In literature postmodernism has encouraged a return to linear narrative, and in art to figurative painting. One of the criticisms of postmodernism has been that it is innately conservative, although postmodern artists often use older forms in an irreverent and even cynical way. Irony and pastiche, it has frequently been pointed out, are the staples of the postmodernist repertoire.

Jean Baudrillard espouses an even more radical attitude to signs and systems than Lyotard, completely rejecting the idea that signs communicate the deep structure of artefacts or phenomena, or exemplify the workings of pre-established codes. Indeed, signs do not seem to communicate anything much at all in Baudrillard's world, where image has taken over from reality ('the cinema and TV are America's reality', he remarks at one point (Baudrillard, 1988, p. 104)). His work registers as an updated version of Marshall McLuhan: 'the medium is the message' stated in apocalyptic terms. We live in a 'hyperreality' surrounded by simulacra and simulations, in Baudrillard's view, and there is no longer any point in trying to engage in interpretation of texts or events. He might more correctly be dubbed an anti-aesthetician than an aesthetician, but he has nevertheless inspired an art movement in America ('simulationist' art) which has claimed to provide visual equivalents of his theories. Ironically enough, Baudrillard has proved not to like the art that his theories have generated, and has dissociated himself from the group's efforts.

What all of these poststructuralist thinkers share is a distrust of totalizing theory and of notions of unity. They bequeath to criticism a commitment to contingency and discontinuity, and it is a commitment that has provoked considerable debate. Given that they have rejected the notion of authority in general, it is hard to see on what grounds poststructuralists can claim authority for their own theories (a problem that traditionally plagues relativists and anti-foundationalists). Neither is it clear how we are even to understand their theories, if signs really are as unstable as they are arguing. Perhaps poststructuralism is more successful in drawing attention to the excesses of structuralism than in offering a truly viable alternative to traditional ways of going about criticism and aesthetic theory.

See also BARTHES; CRITICISM; DECONSTRUCTION; DERRIDA; IRONY; MARXISM AND ART; MODERNISM AND POSTMODERNISM; NARRATIVE.

BIBLIOGRAPHY

Barthes, Roland: *S/Z* (Paris: 1970); trans. Richard Miller (New York: Hill & Wang, 1974).
Baudrillard, Jean: *America* (Paris: 1986); trans. Chris Turner (London and New York: Verso, 1988).
Derrida, Jacques: *Writing and Difference* (Paris: 1967); trans. Alan Bass (London: Routledge & Kegan Paul, 1978).
Eagleton, Terry: *Criticism and Ideology* (London: New Left Books, 1976).
Lévi-Strauss, Claude: *The Raw and the Cooked: Introduction to a Science of Mythology I* (Paris: 1964); trans. John and Doreen Weightman (London: Jonathan Cape, 1969).
Locke, John: *Essay concerning Human Understanding* (London: 1690); ed. A.D. Woozley (London and Glasgow: Fontana/Collins, 1964).
Lyotard, Jean-François: *The Postmodern Condition: A Report on Knowledge* (Paris: 1979); trans. Geoff Bennington and Brian Massumi (Manchester: Manchester University Press, 1984).
Macherey, Pierre: *A Theory of Literary Production* (Paris: 1966); trans. Geoffrey Wall (London and Boston, Mass.: Routledge & Kegan Paul, 1978).
Piaget, Jean: *Structuralism* (Paris: 1968); trans. Chaninah Maschler (London: Routledge & Kegan Paul, 1971).
Saussure, Ferdinand de: *Course in General Linguistics* (Paris: 1915); eds Charles Bally, Albert Sechehaye and Albert Reidlinger, trans. Wade Baskin (London: Peter Owen, 1960).

STUART SIM

style The concept of style can seem simple

enough. We can think of style merely as a way of doing things, or a way in which something is made. But this captures little of the complexity of the relevant issues. It is by no means a straightforward matter to identify precisely what qualities should properly be considered stylistic, nor indeed to what sorts of things such qualities should properly be applied. Generally, style applies to those sorts of artefacts and performances which communicate partly by inviting our conscious recognition that they are to be regarded as artefacts or performances.

Stylistic qualities invite our attention, legitimately or otherwise, to the maker's or performer's activity in producing the object or performance – what in art we think of as a 'work'. To ascribe stylistic qualities to a natural object is at best metaphorical: neither a volcano nor a potato can have a style (though a picture of either might). Much the same applies to activities and actions that are not performances: to refer to the style of someone's sweeping a room or running to catch a bus is to imply that somehow they are making a performance out of the business, but one might refer with propriety to the style in which someone greets another or serves a meal; and, similarly, one might properly talk of the style of a highly domesticated, artefact-saturated landscape. Hence to refer to the style (or stylishness) of what we normally suppose should not be a self-conscious performance, nor a self-consciously produced artefact, is normally pejorative. It is, for example, not normally a compliment to refer to the style in which someone makes love, or to the style with which a student explains the lateness of an essay; to the style of a mechanic's cleaning rags, or an academic's rough notepaper. Style in the wrong place can be meretricious.

Yet even this is not a straightforward idea; there is a central tradition of aesthetic judgement that places the highest value on the forms of useful artefacts following their 'unselfconscious' fitness for their function, as if their very absence of 'style' in this pejorative sense were itself a style. Similarly, an ability to apologize, or to show affection to another naturally, without any sense of 'making a

performance' out of the business, may be regarded as a style, a natural manner of the highest order – a sign of integrity. Evaluative disputes about style tend inevitably to look towards concepts of integrity and honesty (in design, performance or in unperformed behaviour), and to their polar opposites. Our concepts of stylishness, of the mannered or the naturally simple (whether in art or outside art), inevitably take us to the brink of some of our subtlest moral concepts. For they have to do with our sense of how we may, or may fail to, see through the ways in which something is made or performed to deeper matters of the agent's thought and intention.

To suppose that style can be thought of as a manner, or a characteristic manner, of doing or making something that might have been done differently, is as if one might 'peel off' the external manner of production from an inner kernel that could be given a different casing. In this sense it can be an intelligible exercise to rewrite a poem or a musical piece in the style of another or of another period. Thus we might construe the concept of style as 'signature'. Individual artists, authors, composers, types of people and identifiable periods and movements have their characteristic styles. The recognition of such stylistic signatures, therefore, may be the central skill of a certain kind of connoisseurship, a highly saleable skill for antique dealers, a taught skill in many English literature courses, an examined skill in 'dating' documents; and a rich source not only for the forger's art, but, more importantly, for a high variety of fictional devices, elegantly discussed by Walton (1987). Such identifications of style and of stylistic change are, moreover, central to the fact that art inevitably has a history, the dynamic traces of which are those of stylistic development. For style-as-signature announces, and may thus misannounce, whose mind, thought, intention one is to be properly receptive to in responding to the work.

However, a sharp distinction between a stylistic skin and an inner kernel is unconvincing, for much of the content of a work inevitably resides in a celebration of how it is made or performed, a content that is essentially stylistic. Goodman (1978) objects to those for whom such a concept of style requires thereby some concept of synonymy that distinguishes between different works having the same 'content' and different styles. Partly his point rests on a general scepticism over the concept of synonymy, but it might, equally, rest firmly enough on any reasonably applicable idea of aesthetic content.

This requires a concept of style which the idea of style-as-signature alone is inadequate to capture. The development of an artist's style is essentially linked with the development of the work's communicative authority. In this sense style is a 'direction of salience', similar to what Wollheim (1987a, pp. 19–26) calls 'thematisation': stylistic devices invite us to attend to those features of a work *as* central that are central to that response to the work that the artist demands of us. When an artist's use of style achieves this sort of authority our responses flow, as it were, in the direction the work demands, not – or not unless we have misresponded – merely as our whim as beholders, audience or readers dictates.

This is best illustrated by examples from particular arts. Let us start with painting. A representational painting presents to us a set of objects depicted for our imagination such that they, and the masses of colour and form they invoke, are arranged in a certain way within the depicted space defined by the frame of the picture. It thus presents a pictorial space. Also, given familiar forms of perspective, we may think of the depicted space as if it had a limit like the view beyond the plane of a framed window. It may then invoke this as a picture plane. And all of this will be achieved by an elaborately and carefully marked, handled, pigmented surface. Thus a painting may present us with a pictorial space, a pictorial plane, and a depicting surface (these last two are notoriously easy to confuse if we are inclined to think of a picture as like a glass window through which we can look, but at an imaginary landscape rather than at a real one some distance beyond the glass).

Gombrich, notoriously, has argued (1960,

especially, but also subsequently) that the 'illusion' of the pictorial requires that we cannot attend simultaneously to the depicting surface of a painting or drawing and to what is depicted by it. But as Wollheim (1987a; 1973), Podro (1987) and others have insisted, it is essential to any proper response to pictures that we should attend to each in terms of our attention to the other: any understanding of pictorial style that goes beyond the mere concept of 'signature' must require this. For the capacity of style in painting and drawing to communicate to us derives from how we may be led, by various ways of depicting, to attend simultaneously to a wide variety of quite different types of topics of aesthetic and imaginative interest: to the objects as depicted, to the balance and structure of their pictorial space, sometimes to the picture plane with its magical sense of the celebration of optical phenomena; and, in the case of pictures that celebrate their painterly qualities of touch and graphic vigour, to the depicting surface itself. The control of pictorial style – what gives an integrated, dominant authority to the picture as a coherent expression of an artist's visual intelligence – requires that the direction of our attentive interest traverse this terrain in ways that cohere with the absorbed attention of the artist's own thought in making the work.

It is central to any idea of stylistic development that, as an artist's style matures, the demands that the works make on our attention and judgement – their imaginative authority – will be more firmly insistent. But a meretricious development of style may also occur. For it is all too easy for a certain sort of facility on the part of an artist to be engaged in the mere production and reproduction of style-as-signature. Then it is all too obvious who, or what type or 'school' of artists, produced the work or the performance; all too easy for an individual artist or performer to engage in facile self-imitation, or for a teacher to encourage a facile academicism. The difference seems to be that mere signature need pay little attention – and thus demand none – to the integrity of a work's levels of significance and interest: then it may be depressingly easy to 'disintegrate' the work or performance, to 'peel off' a skin of manner of 'performance' from a kernel of 'content'.

Much the same can be said about each of the arts. In the design of useful objects (see Dormer, 1990) stylistic excellence can also be best thought of as being about salience – with how our attention may be controlled by the interrelation of forms, qualities of finish (or the lack of it), patterns of decoration or of noticeable plainness to what may in consequence be regarded as more or less important. This might be function alone, or the celebration of grandeur, of modesty or simplicity or, perhaps, pride in possession. Here, notoriously, therefore, while the concept of style itself is not a moral concept, discussion of style – whether it be the style of a Shaker chair, a grandiose sideboard, a slot machine, or a Coca Cola bottle – leads us inevitably towards such concerns either in terms of stylistic integrity itself or of the integrity of what the style may be taken to imply. Antique dealers apart, mere style-as-signature is again inadequate to deal with these facts.

An actor or musician may perform with a style that is manifestly, and all too dismally, recognizable as the style of that performer, but the stylistic integrity of a performance must achieve more than that. What is required is a kind of seriousness that controls the direction of our attention to the salient elements in the work, so that each aspect of what we are shown (often at quite different levels of attention) can be understood by us in terms of how it is understood by the performer. Integrity of style makes the concentrated thought of the performer *to* the work manifest *in* the performance. Inevitably, as with style in painting, this form of understanding must involve a grasp of the complexity of the different 'levels' in a work (the 'formal' structure of the work, its patterns of narrative, of themes, of dramatic developments and interactions, together with the 'texture' of a performer's 'patterns' of expressive stress and emphasis) and at the same time integrate them into a whole for our attention.

Similarly, in literature, it is notoriously easy to imitate (as pastiche) the style of another writer. Mock Shakespeare, mock Milton, T.S. Eliot or Henry James is disturbingly easy to achieve. It is a dull skill to learn the trick of writing merely in the manner of such authors. Occasionally they may even do it themselves; few great writers are ever quite free from the faults of self-imitation. But, as the tradition of rhetoric and literary criticism has always insisted, this is not stylistic integrity. Integrity of style both celebrates the differences between, say, metre, stress, emphasis and the literal and metaphorical meanings of the words and phrases, and, at the same time, needs to 'orchestrate' these distinct elements into an authoritative unity, so that an apparently simple distinction between literary form and content becomes, paradoxically, out of place.

Concepts of style enter in when we embrace what can seem to be two paradoxical features of art. The first is that art both communicates and celebrates the fact of its ways of communication, yet must, with stylistic honesty (as with other forms of honesty), eschew self-conscious posturing: the second is that the responses that stylistic integrity demands of us require that we distinguish radically different aspects of a work and of our attention to a work, yet respond at the same time to the work as an ordered unity. Style resolves the first apparent paradox in terms of the second.

See also FORM; GENRE; PERFORMANCE.

BIBLIOGRAPHY

Akerman, James S.: 'Style', *Aesthetics Today*, ed. Morris Phillipson (Cleveland: World Publishing, 1961).

Dormer, Peter: *The Meanings of Modern Design* (London: Thames & Hudson, 1990).

Gombrich, E.H.: *Art and Illusion* (New York, London: Phaidon, 1960).

Gombrich, E.H.: 'Style', *International Encyclopedia of the Social Sciences*, ed. David L. Sills (New York: Macmillan, 1968).

Gombrich, E.H.: 'Mirror and map: theories of pictorial representation', *Philosophical Transactions of the Royal Society*, 270 (1975), 119–

49; reprinted in his *The Image and the Eye* (London: Phaidon, 1989).

Goodman, Nelson: 'The status of style', *Critical Inquiry*, 1 (1975); reprinted in his *Ways of Worldmaking* (Hassocks: Harvester Press, 1978), pp. 23–40.

Podro, Michael: 'Depiction and the golden calf', *Philosophy and the Visual Arts: Seeing and Abstracting*, ed. Andrew Harrison, Royal Institute of Philosophy (Dordrecht: Reidel, 1987).

Walton, Kendall L.: 'Style and the products and processes of Art', *The Concept of Style*, ed. Berel Lang (Philadelphia: 1979); expanded edn (Ithaca, NY: Cornell University Press, 1987), pp. 72–103.

Wollheim, Richard: *On Art and the Mind* (London: Allen Lane, 1973).

Wollheim, Richard: *Painting as an Art* (London: Thames & Hudson, 1987a), esp. pp. 26–36.

Wollheim, Richard: 'Pictorial style: two views', *The Concept of Style*, ed. Berel Lang (Ithaca, NY: Cornell University Press, 1987b).

ANDREW HARRISON

sublime Defined by the Concise Oxford Dictionary as 'so distinguished by ... impressive quality as to inspire awe or wonder, aloof from ... the ordinary'; but used by Kant and others in the special, though closely related, senses discussed below.

The world of letters has its own dialect, one that reflects and at the same time serves to fix the stylistic preferences of a particular place and time. The vocabulary of criticism mirrors the history of taste. Fifty years ago someone who wanted to join a discussion of poetry or fiction would have to have mastered such terms as 'objective correlative', 'ambiguity', 'existential', 'paradox', 'symbol'. Nowadays you can get along quite well without them. The lexicon is born in the classroom. Students and grown-up beginners need guidance: What do you look for? What should you appreciate? What needs to be analysed? The key terms offer answers, and when the answers begin to seem inadequate, the terms become obsolete. Such terms are characteristically ill defined; they have to be to serve their purpose. Philosophers and grammarians can say pretty clearly what

makes a word ambiguous, but what they say will not replace William Empson's *Seven Types of Ambiguity*, where definition is all by way of example. And then, since it is easier to ape your elders and master the lexicon than it is to come to grips with the examples, the key terms come to carry less and less information: they become clichés, and outsiders make fun of the critics' jargon. It is in this company that we find 'the sublime'.

By the second third of the eighteenth century, the term was firmly entrenched, both as an adjective and as noun. Every man of taste (another stock phrase) had at his finger-tips a catalogue of examples – volcanoes, raging seas, towering cliffs, the pyramids, ruined castles, blasted heaths and so forth. That there is an interesting and subtle distinction to be drawn between the true and the false sublime was taken for granted. Curious intellects pondered the question of how to make psychological sense of that 'agreeable horror' (Addison's phrase) that marks an encounter with the sublime. By the middle of the nineteenth century the term 'sublime' had largely disappeared from the critical vocabulary, and had begun to sound archaic. Late-twentieth-century students have to have it explained, and it survives only in mock-literary writing – in restaurant guides, for example, where it is applied to pastries and rich desserts.

The story of the sublime begins with Longinus, a second-century Greek rhetorician, if it was indeed he who was the author of *Peri Hupsos* (meaning 'on impressiveness of style'; it went into Latin as *De Sublimitate*, from Latin to French, and thence to English; Dr Johnson's *Dictionary* (1755) says of 'the sublime' that it is 'a Gallicism now naturalized'). Longinus provides a handbook for orators who want to develop their speaking skills, but later audiences were not much interested in his helpful hints: on such technical matters, they had Cicero and Quintilian, not to mention Aristotle, as mentors. What captured their attention was what Longinus has to say in passing about content rather than about style, and the poetic examples he gives. Here are some Longinian dicta that were endorsed and elaborated by every subsequent exponent of the sublime.

(1) The grand style is suited only to subjects that are in themselves lofty, magnificent and astonishing. For ordinary topics, everyday language is good enough.

(2) The grand style may, but need not be, ornate: the sublime often calls for extreme simplicity, as in the Mosaic account of creation. Sometimes stupendous effects are achieved just by mention and display, without any oratory at all. The silence of Ajax in the eleventh book of the *Odyssey* is an example.

(3) The grand style has great emotional force: it not only persuades, but 'ravishes and transports' the hearer. It is irresistible.

(4) The speaker who succeeds in presenting an exalted subject in a suitably elevated style thereby reveals an inward greatness of soul.

(5) The products of a lofty mind (what would later be called works of genius) are often rough-hewn and imperfect in detail. That is to be excused and not blamed: it is part of their intrinsic grandeur.

(6) Nature as well as art affords instances of the sublime: mighty rivers, in contrast to little streams; Mount Etna in eruption, the sun, the stars – all are astonishing.

(7) Since the sublime, wherever it occurs, is like a force of nature rather than a product of skill, it is destined to please all men, everywhere and at all times.

Translations of *Peri Hupsos* appeared in the sixteenth century without attracting much notice. The real inauguration came in 1674, when Boileau produced both *L'Art Poétique* [Poetic Art] and *Traité du Sublime ou du Merveilleux dans le Discours Traduit du Grec de Longin* [Treatise on the sublime or the marvellous in the discourse translated from the Greek of Longinus]. Neither Boileau nor his audience was much taken by the sublimity of natural wonders – that came later with the English and then with the Germans. His

French readers were more interested in the arts and with the idea that great art, especially tragedy, has power to stir the deepest passions. In the protracted and tiresome debate about the comparative merits of the ancients and the moderns, Boileau, a champion of the ancients, frequently draws on Longinus. But the other side could use him too: it depends on who you think is more sublime.

Longinus' views were also put into play by both parties to the dispute about French and English drama. Corneille was sublime in his laconic understatement, Shakespeare was sublime in his roughness and grandeur. (*King Lear* was a favourite example of an awe-inspiring though 'irregular' work.) On an even broader scale, Longinus was pressed into service both by neo-classical critics who deferred to Aristotle and believed in the 'rules', and by the avant-garde who thought that Milton, especially in *Samson Agonistes* and the descriptions of Satan in *Paradise Lost*, teaches, by precept and by example, iconoclasm and the need to transcend the rules. The competition was bitter, although in retrospect it is hard to see what was at issue. The neo-classicists always allowed space for genius to take liberties, and their opponents, the forerunners of Romanticism, were willing to grant that where stupendous effects were achieved, following the rules was all right. (Pope's *Essay on Criticism* (1711) presents an elegant set of balanced oppositions in compromise.)

Once the sublime had taken root, nobody paid attention to Longinus. Not everyone was an enthusiast, though. Dr. Johnson, who disliked the wilder aspects of nature and thought enthusiasm for the Scottish highlands was absurd – almost as bad as approving of the landscape of Norway or Lapland – had a low opinion of poetic evocations of the natural sublime. Satirists such as Swift and Pope, in the meantime, had a field day at the expense of the enthusiasts. Belief in a kind of experience that ravishes and transports and at the same time ennobles and elevates is certainly appealing, and many people said silly things and at great length. Numerous comedies caricatured pretentious persons (mostly women) who expatiate on the sublime.

In an influential series of articles in *The Spectator* (1711–12), Joseph Addison studies Milton more carefully than anyone before him, pointing out the 'beauties' and the 'blemishes' and arguing the Longinian point that, since the poetry is sublime, readers should be indulgent towards the blemishes. Addison was the first to suggest a distinction, that rapidly caught on, between the beautiful and the sublime. He is not consistent: 'beauty' is still the genus, and 'sublime' is the word for the greatest pre-eminent beauties. But he does hold that there is a difference, not just of degree but in kind. 'Beauty', which properly applies to what is regular, pleasing, well constructed, is ceded, as it were, to Boileau and his party. The sublime – Addison's actual term is 'elevated' – is a different genre. Beauty and sublimity are two varietal species of artistic excellence. Addison was also one who encouraged his readers to appreciate the sublime in nature – he favoured 'a vast Desert, a huge Heap of Mountains'. The Alps he found a source of 'agreeable Horror', and his oxymoron was echoed and paralleled in many contemporary writings. (Kant, who knew, at least at second hand, the whole literature, says that our response to the sublime is a 'negative pleasure'.)

For those given to reflection on their encounters with the sublime, there were questions. How are we to explain the fact that we enjoy what we find frightening and hence painful? Why, in confrontation with large and menacing things, should we feel elevated and somehow above it all? These are old questions, raised before sublimity was invented. The phenomena had been noted by Plato, who observes that we are repelled and yet somehow drawn to look at decaying corpses, that we *enjoy* the enactment of horrible and disgusting deeds on the stage.

In 1757 Edmund Burke published *A Philosophical Enquiry into the Origin of our Ideas of the Sublime and the Beautiful*. Burke really liked popular graveyard poetry and Gothic fiction with all their stock props – the screeching owls, the ravenous beasts, the ghosts, the ruined battlements and the like. He stipulates a distinction between 'positive' or 'independent' pleasure on the one hand, and on the other, 'delight', which signifies relief from pain and danger and is therefore 'relative'. Delight is connected in some way that is not explained with the instinct for self-preservation. It is with delight, not pleasure, that we respond to the sublime. This sounds more like a rephrasing of the question than an answer. One's general impression is that Burke thinks that violent and unfocused emotions, negative as well as positive, have intrinsic value (which means that no explanation is either necessary or possible).

Kant's treatment of the sublime is of great interest, but difficult to summarize without assuming knowledge of his overall philosophical project – knowledge not easy to come by. Kant's initial foray, *Observations on the Feeling of the Beautiful and Sublime*, appeared in 1763, eighteen years before his first *Critique*, and his developed position is presented in the first part of the *Critique of Judgement* in 1790. The *Observations* are informal and discursive, rather in the manner of Hume's essays. They offer little that is new, and no arguments, but seem rather to be a compendium of currently received opinion. Kant writes:

> Finer feeling … is … of two kinds: the feeling of the *sublime* and that of the *beautiful*. The stirring of each is pleasant, but in different ways … The description of a raging storm, or Milton's portrayal of the infernal kingdom, arouse enjoyment but with horror; on the other hand, the sight of flower-strewn meadows … or Homer's portrayal of the girdle of Venus, also occasion a pleasant sensation but one that is joyous and smiling … Night is sublime, day is beautiful … The sublime *moves*, the beautiful *charms* … The sublime must always be great; the beautiful can also be small. The sublime must be simple; the beautiful can be adorned and ornamented. (Kant, 1960 [1763], pp. 46–9)

Two of the four sections of the *Observations*

are devoted to sexual differences – men are sublime, women beautiful; and to national characters – English, Spanish and Germans have an affinity with the sublime, French and Italians with the beautiful. The Dutch, who care for neither, go in for being neat and making money. The effect of this parade of popular prejudice and illiberal bias is somewhat mitigated by a point that *is* original with Kant and anticipates the developed views of the third *Critique*. It is that virtue based on benevolence, though variable and not to be depended on, is beautiful and inspires love, while virtue based on adherence to principle is sublime and commands respect. Previous authors had assumed that only exceptional persons can aspire to sublimity – great works of art argue a lofty mind; works of genius transcend the rules. But Kant claims that the sublimity that supervenes on acting from principle is open to every human being – even women and savages. (The Indians of Canada get particularly high marks.)

Kant's final word on sublimity comes twenty-seven years later. In the *Critique of Pure Reason* he had argued that, while we cannot know the future in detail, there are none the less certain things we *can* know with complete certainty, such as that whatever comes our way will be spatio-temporal and describable under causal laws. The price to be paid for such certainty is that we have to acknowledge that the world of science, the world we live in, is a world of appearance, not the really *real* world. What Kant calls 'the noumenal world' has somehow got to *be* there, but we can know nothing about it. Attempts to find out, for instance, whether God exists, or whether the will is free, are futile: just raising such questions leads to a series of contradictions, symptoms of the breakdown of our intellectual apparatus. In the *Critique of Practical Reason* Kant argues that, while we cannot know anything about the real, noumenal world, we have a foothold in it; and so, even though everything we do can be explained scientifically, we are subject to the moral law and, as such, endowed with a capacity for acting on principle no matter how great the temptations to be selfish or greedy may be. The categorical imperative, which says that human beings have dignity and must be treated with respect, overrides every ignoble impulse that would lead us to use and exploit other people for our own ends.

In the third *Critique* Kant again distinguishes the beautiful from the sublime, but now he is much more systematic and has dropped all the chatty bits about national character and sexual difference. The beautiful is what is found to be a source of pleasure by someone who is not concerned with satisfying his appetites, or with classification, or with utility, or with the moral good – in short, someone who is disinterested, who responds to the item in question, whether natural phenomenon or work of art, not for what it stands for but for what it is. Beauty is not, on Kant's view, a *property* of objects, but we talk – and not incorrectly – as if it were. The sublime is different. When we confront something so vast, so powerful and potentially dangerous as to defeat our attempts to grasp it, we incline to say that the object – a storm at sea, for instance – is sublime: but that is a plain, though understandable, mistake. A storm is only a storm: what moves us is the reminder of something in ourselves – our unique status as centres of moral authority in the noumenal world. We try, and necessarily fail, to imagine infinity:

> Still the mere *ability even to think* the given infinite without contradiction is something that requires the presence in the human mind of a faculty that is itself supersensible ... Therefore the feeling of the sublime in nature is respect for our own vocation which we attribute to an Object of nature by a certain subreption (substitution of a respect for the Object in place of one for the idea of humanity in our own self – the Subject); and this feeling renders, as it were, intuitable, the supremacy of our cognitive faculties on the rational side over the greatest faculty of sensibility (Kant: 1964 [1790], § 27)

An interesting idea, even if not very persuasive. To see why Kant was so taken with it, we need to consider the project of the third

Critique as a whole. He thought he had finished, but two considerations led him to think there was something more to be done. First, he discovered an anomaly in aesthetic judgement – what he calls the 'judgement of taste'. To say seriously of some individual that it is beautiful is not just to confess that one likes it but to claim that it merits admiration, that everyone *ought* to like it. Kant also saw that such a claim cannot be backed by a generalization, since there are not and cannot be laws or principles of taste.

The second consideration that moved him is more difficult to describe: having made a point of distinguishing the world of nature, what science studies, from the moral realm where freedom reigns, he complained (perhaps unreasonably) that there is too little connection between the two and that a 'bridge' is needed. He thought that an explication of the beautiful and the sublime could provide such a bridge. What he meant to do and the extent to which his efforts are successful are questions in dispute, but here is a tentative suggestion: Kant was committed to rejecting all arguments for the existence of God, since they pretend to say something about ultimate reality, but he seems to have been haunted by the so-called 'argument from design', according to which God is not only all-powerful but intelligent and just. If that argument were valid, then life would have coherent meaning, morality would comport with science, virtue would be rewarded. A telling observation of Kant's is that when we find some natural object, such as a wild flower, beautiful, we see it as having a purpose although we know that it does not; and that when we find a work of art beautiful, we imagine it as having just grown, like a wild flower, rather than having been made, as we know it to have been, with a purpose. Therefore, if we find beauty in the universe as a whole, we see it *as if* it were the creation of an artist. There is no reason to think that the world *has* been planned, but it is cheering and invigorating to think that it *might* have been. What gap is the sublime supposed to bridge? Perhaps it is the division, again one established by Kant himself, between the moral realm where action accords with principle and the aesthetic realm where there is perception and feeling but no principle, On Kant's view, an action has moral worth only if the agent is moved by respect for the moral law rather than by any hope of reward, here or in the afterlife. The sublime is marked by feelings of awe and respect, but remember that it is also a source of *pleasure*. Kant's idea may be that a correct interpretation of my response to mountains and storms will provide me with an incentive to do my duty. Vast and powerful forces give me a sense of elation: I think, 'They can crush me and yet I am still (like Pascal's "thinking reed") superior to them.' Then I realize that the storms and mountains represent or symbolize my strong inclinations to act as I wish without reference to the moral law, and that I have the power to triumph over such temptation. ('My strength is as the strength of ten because my heart is pure.')

If the foregoing speculations are correct, then Kant's motive in the third *Critique* is not to bridge gaps and achieve unity: the distinctions insisted on in the first two *Critiques* are *a priori* and necessary, not to be overridden. His wish is, rather, to make the whole system less austere and more congenial. That, one might argue, is a retrograde step: it is not the philosopher's job, any more than it is the scientist's, to come up with results that are attractive and inspiring. In Longinus the sublime is a matter of style and feeling and so, despite Kant's efforts, it remains. You can master the grand style and pick sublime topics, and yet write something that is no good at all. You can be thrilled in a storm by fantasies about your own omnipotence, and yet remain a selfish and inconsiderate person. The sense of spiritual elevation is not an indication of actual spiritual elevation.

See also BEAUTY; BURKE; KANT; PLEASURE.

BIBLIOGRAPHY

Addison, Joseph: *The Spectator*, 4 vols, ed. Gregory Smith (Dutton, NY: Everyman, 1966).

Burke, Edmund: *A Philosophical Enquiry into the*

Origin of our Ideas of the Sublime and the Beautiful (London: 1757); ed. Boulton (London: Routledge & Kegan Paul, 1958).

Kant, Immanuel: *Beobachtungen über das Gefühl des Schönen und Erhabenen* (Königsberg: 1764); trans. J.T. Goldthwait, *Observations on the Feeling of the Beautiful and Sublime* (Berkeley, Calif.: University of California Press, 1960).

Kant, Immanuel: *Kritik der Urteilskraft* (Berlin: 1790); trans. J.C. Meredith, *The Critique of Judgement* (Oxford: Clarendon Press, 1964).

Monk, Samuel H.: *The Sublime* (Ann Arbor, Mich.: University of Michigan Press, 1960).

MARY MOTHERSILL

symbol A semantic construct which substitutes one term or entity for another. At this level of generality it can easily be equated with a sign, usually a broader category, or a metaphor, which is a narrower one.

Indeed, one of the more difficult facets of using the term 'symbol' results from the lack of agreement as to whether all signs are symbols or all symbols are signs. If one regards all signs as symbols, one usually turns 'symbolizing' into a variety of semantic or rhetorical operations, most of which involve substitution or 'standing in for'. In this case, symbolizing has little specific aesthetic meaning, as when, say, a representation of parched earth symbolizes a drought. But if all symbols are understood as a subcategory of signs, this generally involves treating symbolizing as a special instance of the semiotic. In aesthetics, symbols are often treated as a special or privileged case of the semiotic. Indeed, there are those who claim that the symbol is central to works of art, and is therefore more than merely a matter of the substitution of one semantic term for another or the generation of sign-making possibility. Instead of being a special case of semiosis, the symbol is understood in this context as inherently an aesthetic entity or act.

For those who make this larger claim, the symbol partakes not only of the semiotic realm but also of the psychological and even of the ontological. Symbols are, then, not what make art but rather what make art possible. This larger claim rests on a tradition most importantly developed in the Romantic era, a tradition that culminated in the symbolist art of the later nineteenth century. But even before this tradition developed its complex genealogy, the understanding of the concept of sign was influencing the possible meanings of 'symbol'. In Augustine's hermeneutics, for example, the ancient distinction between natural and conventional signs is extended into at least an incipient understanding that the entire created world can be a symbol – or a repository of usable symbols – since it is seen as the incarnate word of God. Though Augustine more often uses the term 'sign' instead of 'symbol', his larger claims about the symbolic (as opposed to the literal) meaning of sacred scripture make most sense if read as the foundation of much medieval aesthetics.

But it was at the end of the eighteenth century and the beginning of the nineteenth that the symbol began to play the most crucial role in aesthetics. In 1801 August Schlegel argued that 'making poetry (in the broadest sense of the poetic that is at the root of all the arts) is nothing other than an eternal symbolizing' (in Todorov, 1984, p. 198). The symbol for Schlegel was the way (the semantic structure, if you will) by which the infinite was able to appear in finite expression. Todorov (p. 198) argues convincingly that this is the cornerstone of Romantic aesthetics and that all modern meanings of symbol flow from this understanding.

But part of the understanding of the Romantic symbol is involved in knowing what it is not, what it is being defined against: allegory. Allegory, for Romantic writers such as Goethe, was a lesser aesthetic form because it represented the spiritual world in a way that was too literal (paradoxically reversing the medieval sense of allegory, which meant all that went beyond the literal). For Goethe, the 'allegorical differs from the symbolic in that what the latter designates indirectly, the former designates directly.' For him, works of allegory 'destroy our interest in representation itself' (in Todorov, 1984, p. 199); in other words, allegory betrays or fails adequately to convey spiritual meaning. In part, what is being used here is the distinction between natural and conventional signs; allegory is too reliant upon convention, whereas symbol is more expressive of natural forms and truths.

Also at least partly reminiscent of Augustine's notion of the world as constituted as a symbolic rendering of divine will is the Romantic emphasis on the flux involved in the Romantic symbol, as opposed to allegory's static structure. One property of the symbol for Wilhelm von Humboldt is that 'the representation and what is represented [are] in constant mutual exchange', an exchange which can 'incite and constrain the mind to linger longer and to penetrate more deeply' (in Todorov, 1984, p. 215). This sense of the symbol is connected with a notion of delay, which suggests that the symbolic meaning occurs only through temporal unfolding; furthermore, it begins to suggest that symbols have a mystical dimension which surpasses their natural semiosis but builds upon it. These two features of the symbol, its diachronic and its supra-rational dimensions, are what usually mark it off from signs in the broad or common sense. Allegory, like conventional signs, usually involves an intentional and one-to-one correspondence that is regulated and codified. Symbolism, like natural signs, takes its force from laws and an understanding that cannot be so easily limited or contained within definable concepts.

The mystical aspects of Romantic aesthetics were encouraged by writers such as Swedenborg, who said that nature is a system of correspondences between the heavenly and the human, and these correspondences are manifest through symbols. However, it was more from Swedenborg's many expositors that the symbol came to be thoroughly aestheticized. Emerson, reading Swedenborg in the middle of the nineteenth century, lamented his lack of a developed poetics and went on to supply one for him, in *Nature* (1836). The symbolists in France were also heavily indebted to Swedenborgian mysticism. Mallarmé's claim that to name a thing is to destroy it, while to suggest it is to give it life, is an extension of the idea that symbolic expression is necessary to establish and uncover connections that are otherwise lost to merely rational cognition.

Another major development in the aesthetic use of the symbolic came about through Freud, whose model of the psyche, with its language of condensation and displacement, can be seen as a semiosis which makes considerable use of symbolic substitution. Indeed, it is possible to see Freud as offering a thoroughly secularized view of the correspondence theory of meaning, as the semiotic processes of projection and introjection establish connections between the realms of objective existence and subjective experience. The landscape of the psyche is filled with symbols, usually in the form of images, that are invested with emotion and contain the residue of traumatic events. One of Freud's main expositors, Jacques Lacan, went so far as to use the term 'symbolic' to refer to the whole realm of language and semantic meaning, a realm in which the real and imaginary are mediated. Since in the Freudian scheme the unconscious can be imagined as a place of immeasurable depth, and a place where the 'normal' sense of logical identity does not apply, it can be regarded not only as a locale, but as a source of symbolic forms or symbolizing energies.

Such psychological adaptations of the complex uses of symbols and symbol-making are themselves part of a larger development in what is called 'the problematic of language'. This very complex set of ideas, interrelated and also contradictory, questions the assumption that language is 'merely' a transparent medium through which meaning passes unobstructed. Language, especially its symbolizing properties, is more accurately seen as constituting meaning rather than merely reflecting it. The problematic developed in the nineteenth century, partly in tandem with Romantic aesthetics, and culminated in a sense with Nietzsche, who saw most concepts or ideas as tropes or metaphors that have become calcified by long use; thus all ideas are symbolic transformations whose changes are now hidden from view. But this problematic also involves a cross-fertilization with many writers on myth. For example, Herder's notions of the relations between language and national or ethnic identity add to the sense of languages as containing certain crucial pre-logical truths that are best expressed in symbolic form. For such writers, mythological thinking is a special case of the symbolizing activity where an otherwise ineffable meaning, such as national identity, can be embodied in, or at least expressed through, a collective activity such as the development of a vernacular literature. Here, the symbolic is at once natural and conventional.

The consideration of the symbol as a special instance of condensation also shows up in a poet such as Pound, whose theory of imagism, which defines an image as a complex of emotional and intellectual truth in an instant of time, is related to late Romantic, anti-allegorical notions. Pound also said that 'the natural object is always the adequate symbol', thus bringing to a peak the bias in favour of natural over conventional signs. In very broad terms, the symbol is used frequently in post-Romantic thought to convey either a realm or a construct of meaning in which more is compressed that can be 'spelt out'. Wherever an aesthetician needs to discuss an experience or a meaning in which both the substitution of terms and the compression of meaning occur, then there is likely to be some reference to the concept of the symbol.

See also INEFFABILITY; LANGUAGE, ART AS; METAPHOR; PSYCHOANALYSIS AND ART; SCHLEGEL, AUGUST VON.

BIBLIOGRAPHY

Adams, Hazard: *The Philosophy of the Literary Symbolic* (Gainesville, Fla.: University of Florida Press, 1986).
Balaikian, Anna: *The Symbolist Movement* (New York: New York University Press, 1973).
Emerson, Ralph Waldo: *Selected Essays* (Harmondsworth: Penguin Books, 1982).
Todorov, Tzvetan: *Théories du symbole* (Paris: 1977); trans. Catherine Porter, *The Theory of the Symbol* (Ithaca, NY: Cornell University Press, 1984).

CHARLES MOLESWORTH

symmetry *See* HARMONY AND SYMMETRY.

T

taste In aesthetics, 'taste' generally refers to the capacity to discern the aesthetic features of objects, especially beauty. As such, it played a central role in eighteenth-century aesthetic thought, but is no longer much used except in the broad sense of aesthetic preference.

Early writers on the subject, like Shaftesbury and Hutcheson, thought that aesthetic judgement depended on a special 'inner sense' akin to the moral sense, in which they also believed. Later writers, like Kant, were content to explain our capacity for aesthetic discrimination as the special operation of our ordinary cognitive faculties. Those who speak of taste as a form of aesthetic perception or intuition mostly agree that it is some sort of inner feeling that enables us to judge whether or not an object is beautiful or sublime, or whatever. This is usually identified as a highly distinctive feeling of satisfaction or pleasure. Sometimes it is spoken of as an aesthetic emotion, as when Clive Bell wrote that 'the starting point of all systems of aesthetics must be the personal experience of a peculiar emotion' (1914, p. 6).

Another commonly held view is that it is necessary to adopt the correct aesthetic attitude in order to experience this feeling. This is usually characterized as one of disinterestedness in which we contemplate the object without regard to its possible use, its moral significance or its private emotional associations. This idea finds its fullest expression in Kant's *Critique of Judgement*.

A third area of general agreement amongst the faculty of taste school is that it is the formal features of an object, such as unity, balance and harmony, that are most apt to elicit an aesthetic response, although such non-formal features as novelty, intensity and brilliance of colour are sometimes also included. According to Kant, no judgement of taste that addresses itself to the content as opposed to the spatial or temporal form of the object, whether it be a work of nature or a work of art, can be truly disinterested. Such a response would be sensuous, and so private and personal.

The problem which confronts all those who treat taste as a quasi-perceptual faculty is how to account for the enormous differences in taste that exist not only between one culture and another but between one human being and another. This suggests that taste cannot be other than purely subjective and that judgements of taste, unlike perceptual judgements, cannot be either correct or incorrect, valid or invalid. On the other hand, it is easy to think of judgements with which virtually all who took a serious interest in such matters would concur and which it would seem ridiculous to deny: for example, the Lake District is a very beautiful region of Britain, Milton is a greater poet than Pam Ayres, the Grand Canal in Venice is more beautiful than the Manchester Ship Canal, Rembrandt is a greater painter than Annigoni. How can this seeming antinomy be resolved? This is the problem of taste.

Whereas idealist philosophers such as Schopenhauer, Schelling and Hegel have tried to objectify beauty by identifying it with some higher truth, the usual procedure amongst empiricists has been to settle for intersubjective validity, as the best that can be hoped for. Thus Hume, the leading eighteenth-century empiricist, happily admits that since no mere feeling can represent what is really in the object, 'to seek the real beauty or real deformity is as fruitless an inquiry as to ascertain the real sweet or the real bitter' (Hume, 1965 edn, p. 235). Nevertheless, in both cases intersubjective agreement is possible. In the latter case, all that is required is to ascertain that the organ of taste is in a sound state, since its physical constitution is the same in all human beings.

In the case of aesthetic taste, what is required, according to Hume, is the discovery of universal standards of taste that will reflect the intersubjective agreement that already exists. He thinks these can be discovered empirically, since they will be no more than 'general observations concerning what has been universally found to please in all countries and all ages' (Hume, 1965 edn, p. 236). The unstated assumption here is that whatever pleases is good, so whatever pleases universally is universally good. This does not mean that good taste is the same as popular taste, which is in any case subject to the dictates of fashion, since Hume firmly rejects the principle of the natural equality of taste in favour of the idea of the competent judge. Rather, good taste is that which, over time and across cultures, coincides with the taste of the most competent judges. Most writers since Hume have tended to agree that some people are better qualified to make aesthetic pronouncements than others, and popular taste – except, for example, in deconstructionist theory – has generally been despised.

The competent judge, or man of taste, must satisfy three conditions:

(1) He must possess delicacy of taste: that is to say, his sensory and intellectual faculties must be sufficiently highly developed to enable him to discern every feature of the object which is capable of eliciting an aesthetic response.
(2) His judgement of the object must be made under the most favourable conditions. These coincide to a large extent with what is required for the disinterested contemplation of the object, although this is not developed to anything like the same extent that it is in Kant. This includes freedom from all prejudice, a perfect serenity of mind and a due attention to the object.
(3) He must possess a wide experience of the sort of beauty being judged, because only with practice can one learn to discrimi-

nate the relevant features of the object. Moreover, in the end, judgements of taste are always comparative. 'By comparison alone we fix the epithets of praise and blame, and learn how to assign the due degree of each' (Hume, 1965 edn, p. 243).

An obvious weakness in this approach lies in its bald assumption that judges who are equally competent by whatever criteria one chooses will be more likely to agree than disagree in their judgements. This is based on the quasi-physiological thesis, frequently advanced but never proved, that just as there are certain qualities in objects that are fitted by nature to produce the subjective sensation of taste and smell, say, so there are certain qualities in objects that are fitted to produce aesthetic feelings. The only evidence that can be adduced that this might be so is that those objects which have come to be regarded as great works of art often do seem to possess an appeal that is both timeless and cross-cultural. The survival test could perhaps be applied without reference to the idea of the competent judge, but then there would be the problem of weeding out those works which, like the writings of the Marquis de Sade, survive for the wrong reason.

However, even if universal agreement about the merit of some art could be secured, it must seriously be questioned whether this could be expressed in terms of universally applicable standards or principles of taste. According to Kant, these cannot exist, because every true judgement of taste is a singular judgement, applying only to that particular object; and no reasons, in the form of universal principles, can be given in its support as they can in cases of moral disagreement. Fortunately, it is not necessary for there to be universally applicable standards of taste in order for there to be universal, or at least general, agreement about the beauty of specific objects and works of art. That such agreement is possible is quite surprising, and constitutes a prima facie objection to both relativism and subjectivism.

Art is a highly complex cultural phenomenon, and yet taste is not necessarily culture-bound. It is not even true that most people prefer the art of their own time and society. For example, the modern brutalist style of architecture is highly unpopular. It is even possible to have a lively appreciation of the art of societies which are as different from our own as it is possible to be and about which virtually nothing is known – for example, the wall paintings at Lascaux – 'the Sistine Chapel of the Palaeolithic age' – which were painted about 20,000 years ago. What, of course, is difficult and sometimes impossible to know in the case of alien art is what significance it had for the people who produced it, because many of the objects which now afford us aesthetic delight were produced for a purpose other than what we would term aesthetic. Nevertheless, the presumption must be that if a society or culture consistently produced work that has a strong aesthetic appeal for other societies and cultures, then they too were endowed with aesthetic taste.

It may be true that certain aesthetic values are inextricably linked to the values of a particular culture at a particular time. This might be the truth that lurks behind the common observation that great art somehow reflects the spirit of the age. It might help to explain why even those artists who return to an earlier style of art for their inspiration invariably produce work that is quite different in spirit from their originals. One thinks of Renaissance classical sculpture, Victorian Gothic architecture, pre-Raphaelite medievalism and so on. However, even if aesthetic values are tied as closely to a particular culture at a particular time as is sometimes claimed, that certainly does not render them inaccessible.

An obvious objection to the faculty of taste theory is that there is no such thing as *natural* good taste. All taste has to be acquired, so that to some extent our aesthetic preferences are a product of our training and unbringing, in which we come under social and educational pressures to admire what others admire. Thus, there was far greater agreement in taste amongst the leisured classes of the eighteenth century, with their common social and educational background, than

there could possibly be in our own far more diverse society. This is why it seemed feasible to Hume, as it does not to us, to fix and make explicit the standards by which agreement in taste could be secured.

Moreover, in stressing the timeless and cross-cultural appeal of at least some art, one must be careful not to minimize the extent to which there is, and always must be, a purely personal element in one's aesthetic tastes and preferences. As Hume pointed out, 'we choose our favourite author as we do our friend, from a conformity of humour and disposition' (1965 edn, p. 250). It is not, for example, surprising that our tastes change as we grow older. Such variations are readily explicable and do not seriously dent the intersubjectivity thesis, although it greatly increases the likelihood of aesthetic disagreement amongst equally competent and sensitive judges.

But this is perhaps only a problem for those who think that if *informed* taste is ultimately based on comparing art objects, then this obliges us to place them in order of merit, as if in competition for a Booker prize. To have good taste is no more, and no less, than to admire those things which are worthy of admiration on the basis of one's ability to discern their aesthetically relevant properties. It does not require us to grade one work higher than another, or to prefer one particular style of art over all others. That really is a matter of personal taste.

See also ATTITUDE, AESTHETIC; BEAUTY; BELL; CULTURE; EDUCATION, AESTHETIC; HUME; JUDGEMENT, AESTHETIC; KANT; PLEASURE, AESTHETIC.

BIBLIOGRAPHY

Bayley, S.: *Taste: The Secret Meaning of Things* (London: Faber & Faber, 1991).

Bell, C.: *Art* (London: Chatto & Windus, 1914).

Dickie, G.: *Evaluating Art* (Philadelphia: Temple University Press, 1988).

Hume, D.: *'Of the Standard of Taste' and Other Essays*, ed. J.W. Lenz (New York: Bobbs-Merrill, 1965).

Kant, I.: 'Analytic of the Beautiful', *Critique of*

Judgement [*Kritik der Urteilskraft* (1790)], trans. J.C. Meredith (Oxford: Clarendon Press, 1964).

Mothersill, M.: *Beauty Restored* (Oxford: Clarendon Press, 1984).

Saville, A.: *The Test of Time* (Oxford: Clarendon Press, 1964).

Sibley, F.: 'Objectivity and aesthetics', *Proceedings of the Aristotelian Society*, suppl. vol. 42 (1968), 31–54.

Vivos, E. and Krieger, M., eds: *The Problems of Aesthetics*, (New York: Rinehart & Winston, 1965), § 6.

DAVID A. WHEWELL

text A term very widely and differently used in contemporary aesthetics. Its denotation ranges from a specific concrete verbal inscription or utterance (existing as a particular spatio-temporal object or event) to an abstract verbal entity manifested in different concrete texts, and still further to any object, event or action that is construed or interpreted as meaningful. In this way the world itself can be seen as a text, and deconstruction's textualism with its denial of an *hors-texte*, or referent outside of language, can be linked to this usage (Derrida, 1976, p. 158).

The meaning of 'text' is best understood in its particular theoretical context through its relationship and contrast to the notion of 'work' (such as literary work, artwork). Roughly speaking, Anglo-American aesthetics has concentrated on the move from text to work, where textual identity was regarded as something clearer, more determinate and more precise through which we could determine the more problematic and vague identity and meaning of the work. In contrast, poststructuralist Continental aesthetics has concentrated on the move from work to text, where it is the work, instead, that is regarded as the clear, determinate and fixed entity from which we must be liberated into text, conceived now much more broadly and dynamically as the activity of creatively constituting meaning through reading and interpreting. This is a move away from reified meanings and fixed and closed objects of criticism to the flux of textual creation and the play of language – a move sometimes linked (for instance, in Barthes) with a shift of criticism's goal from the truth about the work to the pleasure of the text. Understanding the notion of 'text' requires looking more closely at these two contrasting moves.

FROM TEXT TO WORK

Criticism is interested in determining the correct meaning and value of works of art; but this, it is argued, requires determining their identity. We cannot properly judge the meaning or value of a novel by a bad translation or a drastically abridged version that does not represent the work's crucial features and aesthetic qualities. But how do we determine the work's identity, without already engaging in interpretation and evaluation which were themselves supposed to require identity for their criterion of correctness? One way traditional theory could avoid this problem was to posit the identity of the work in the artist's intention, which, even if it was practically unavailable, provided a fixed intentional object with which the work could be identified. This option lost its appeal once the authority of authorial intention was challenged by New Criticism's doctrine of the intentional fallacy (see Beardsley, 1973, p. 16) and poststructuralism's doctrine of the death of the author (Barthes, 1977).

It thus became increasingly convincing to identify the literary work with its text, and to view the meaning of the work as the meaning of the text. As Beardsley insisted (1973, pp. 32–4), not only is there the epistemological argument that textual meaning is more available than authorial intention, being determined by public rules of linguistic meaning, but it is in the text (rather than in the intentional state of the author) where we readers and critics find or realize the aesthetic value of the work. Finally, identifying the work with the text rather than with an authorial intention allows the meaning of the work to change over time while still maintaining its identity. For the very same text can change its meaning if its words acquire new meanings over time through linguistic change.

What, then, is the identity of a text? First,

a Peircean distinction must be made between different 'token' texts and the same 'type' text that they manifest. The former are concrete spatio-temporal particulars, the latter a more abstract entity that they exemplify or manifest. While two copies of *The Waste Land* and an oral declamation of it constitute three different token texts, they manifest the same type text or work, if they present the very same words in the same order. Nelson Goodman, one of the most rigorous in defining literary work-identity as textual identity, defines textual identity more precisely in terms of two features (Goodman, 1969, p. 209): syntactic identity (by which he means identity of all the characters of the text including punctuation marks) and identity of language (to avoid the problem that the same string of characters can mean different things in different languages).

Most aestheticians find Goodman's criterion of textual identity far too strict, since it rejects as illegitimate or as different texts all sorts of texts which critical practice normally accepts as representing the text or work in question. Not only are translations and variant versions excluded, but even texts which have a single unimportant misprint or omit an inconsequential punctuation mark. Moreover, the criterion is obviously inadequate to deal with the important critical question of the comparative authenticity of rival texts of a given work (for instance, whether the folio or second quarto text of *Hamlet* best conveys that work's identity), since for Goodman different type texts mean different works. To avoid this difficulty, some aestheticians (such as Stevenson (1957) and Margolis (1965)) have proposed viewing the work not as a type text, but as a megatype which can embrace different type texts having the same general design or meaning, and thus can include translations and even adaptations to different media.

But with this greater flexibility of textual identity, there is much greater vagueness. How do we determine similarity of design or meaning, and what is the semantic standard from which similarity must not depart? At this point, we encounter an intentionalist backlash, which argues that work identity and even textual identity require an appeal to authorial intention. For, as Hirsch (1978) argues, if the same syntactic text can embody different meanings or designs (hence different semantic texts), we obviously need more than textual identity to give us the identity of the work, or indeed to establish the identity of the text itself as a meaningful piece of language. Other intentionalists (Knapp and Michaels, 1985) further insist that since all meaning is intentional, textual meaning is logically identical with authorial meaning. But this has been shown to involve a false identification of all meaning-giving intentions with those of the historical author (see Shusterman, 1992, pp. 96–7).

The latest response in Anglo-American theory to the demand to fix the identity of the text through authorial intention has not been to resurrect the syntactic standard, but, rather more radically, to question the need for defining or securing a fixed textual identity. We see one form of this strategy in Stanley Fish, who insists that since texts are constituted only through interpretations, different interpretations entail different texts, and since the goal of interpretation or explanation is to say something new, there can be 'no distinction between explaining a text and changing it' (Fish, 1989, p. 98). This view conflates the identity of the text with its interpretative meaning, and thus does not adequately account for the possibility that different interpreters or interpretative communities can differ in interpreting the same text. But if interpretative debate is to be meaningful, the same text must be able to sustain different interpretations and be re-identified through different accounts of its meaning.

To resolve this problem and avoid the conflation of textual identity and interpretation, one can distinguish between a text's logical or referential identity – that which allows us to refer to or re-identify it for predication or interpretation – and, on the other hand, its substantive identity, the essential nature or full meaning of what we have identified in the first sense (see Shusterman, 1992, p. 94). And as Rorty points out, to secure the first sort of identification there is no need to posit a fixed textual identity or essence of the text; all we need is agreement on a reasonable number of propositions. And as the particular group of propositions can change over time, so can a text's identity. But the importance of a permanently fixed identity wanes once we are confident that in any situation we can agree on (or assume) enough identifying propositions to agree on which text we are talking about. Rather than trying to ensure permanent sameness, 'we should dissolve . . . texts . . . into nodes within transitory webs of relationships' (Rorty, 1985, p. 12). This vision converges with the poststructuralist move from work to text heralded by Barthes.

FROM WORK TO TEXT

The poststructuralist theory of the text, developed in France in the late 1960s and early 1970s by Barthes, Kristeva and Derrida, aims to replace the fixed work with the changing text as the object of literary study and source of aesthetic pleasure. While the work is viewed as a closed and permanent unity, a 'computable' finished product having certain limits of meaning and bearing the authority of its author, the text is instead conceived as an open, transgressive process and an endless field of meaning-production. It is a practice rather than an object, 'a methodological field . . . experienced only in the activity of production'; and it 'cannot stop' its productive activity (Barthes, 1981, p. 157). Text is thus limited neither to literature nor to verbal artefacts, but involves the entire realm of meaning. 'All signifying practices can engender text: the practice of painting pictures, musical practice, filmic practice, etc.' (Barthes, 1981, p. 41).

In contrast to the sign and the work which suggest a determinate signified, text 'practises the infinite deferment of the signified'. Rather than a fixed signification, text involves a perpetual play of *signifiance* (a term introduced by Kristeva), which involves associative movements, overlappings and connections of meaning – an idea that can be associated with Derrida's theme of the irreducible play and generativity of *différance*

(Derrida, 1976, p. 93). Thus the text is radically plural, and not constrained by filiation to the author (as the work presumably is). 'It is not that the Author may not come back in the Text, in his text, but then he does so as guest' (Barthes, 1981, p. 160). If the work is produced by an author for consumption by the reader, the text is not consumed as an object but creatively produced as an activity of play and practice. The text is like a score which 'asks of the reader a practical collaboration' (Barthes, 1981, p. 163). While the work directs the reader to uncovering the truth of its meaning or to consuming the pleasure its author has provided, the text aims neither at such truth or pleasure but rather at a more powerful *jouissance*, 'a pleasure without separation'; as the text plays out its play of *signifiance*, the reader loses himself in this play as he also erotically plays with it in the production of textual meaning (Barthes, 1981, p. 164).

Apart from *signifiance*, Barthes's theory of the text employs three other concepts derived from Kristeva: phenotext, genotext and intertextuality. The phenotext is 'the verbal phenomenon as it presents itself in the structure of the concrete statement' (Kristeva, 1972, p. 335), and thus represents the sense of text that is closest to work or, indeed, is close to the meaning of 'text' in Anglo-American thought. The genotext is the structuring background for the phenotext, and includes both verbal dimensions and psychological drives. More important is the idea of intertextuality: 'any text is an intertext; other texts are present in it, at varying levels, in more or less recognizable forms: the texts of the previous and surrounding culture' (Barthes, 1981, p. 39). This notion captures the etymological root of 'text' as a tissue or woven texture. Finally, intertextuality allows us to assimilate all language into the text, which, on the premiss that our reality is always linguistically given, leads to ontological textualism, or the view of the world as text.

See also BARTHES; DERRIDA; INTENTION; INTERPRETATION; KRISTEVA; ONTOLOGY OF ARTWORKS.

BIBLIOGRAPHY

Barthes, Roland: 'The death of the author' and 'From work to text', *Image–Music–Text* (London: Fontana, 1977), pp. 142–8, 155–64.

Barthes, Roland: 'Theory of the text', *Untying the Text: A Poststructuralist Reader*, ed. Robert Young (London: Routledge & Kegan Paul, 1981), pp. 32–47.

Beardsley, Monroe C.: *The Possibility of Criticism* (Detroit: Wayne State University Press, 1973).

Derrida, Jacques: *De la grammatologie* (Paris: 1967); trans. G. Spivak, *Of Grammatology* (Baltimore, Md: Johns Hopkins University Press, 1976).

Fish, Stanley: *Doing What Comes Naturally* (Durham, NC: Duke University Press, 1989).

Goodman, Nelson: *Languagues of Art* (Oxford: Oxford University Press, 1969).

Hirsch, E.D.: *The Aims of Interpretation* (Chicago, Ill.: University of Chicago Press, 1978).

Knapp, S. and Michaels, W.B.: 'Against theory', *Against Theory*, ed. W.J.T. Mitchell (Chicago, Ill.: University of Chicago Press, 1985).

Kristeva, Julia: 'Sémanalyse: Conditions d'une sémiotique scientifique', *Semiotica*, 5 (1972).

Margolis, Joseph: *The Language of Art and Art Criticism* (Detroit: Wayne State University Press, 1965).

Rorty, Richard: 'Texts and lumps', *New Literary History*, 17 (1985), 1–16.

Shusterman, Richard: *Pragmatist Aesthetics: Living Beauty, Rethinking Art* (Oxford: Blackwell, 1992).

Stevenson, Charles: 'On "What is a poem?"', *Philosophical Review*, 66 (1957).

RICHARD SHUSTERMAN

theories of art Attempts to understand the 'essence' of art in terms of a single key concept, such as 'expression' or 'representation'.

ART AS REPRESENTATION

By 'the representational theory' is meant here a historically persistent complex of views which see the chief, or essential, role of the arts as imitating, or displaying or setting forth aspects of reality in the widest sense.

A typical representational account sees art as portraying the visible forms of nature, from a schematic cave drawing of an animal to the evocation of an entire landscape in sun or storm. The particularity of individual objects, scenes or persons may be emphasized, or the generic, the common, the essential. The scope of representation can involve perspectives, slants on the world, ways of seeing the world – perhaps as created and sustained by an all-good, fecund deity, or as grimly devoid of any divine presence or glory.

A representational artist may seek faithfulness to how things *are*. He or she may dwell selectively on the ugly and defective, the unfulfilled; or on the ideal, the fully realized potential. The artist may see the ideal as reached by extrapolating from the empirical, 'correcting' its deficiencies; or by contemplating the alleged idea or form to which empirical objects approximate and aspire. As this suggests, a representational theory may derive its account and evaluation of the arts from a metaphysic. Representational theories thus give the arts a distinctive *cognitive* role. The artist opens our eyes to the world's perceptual qualities and configurations, to its beauties, uglinesses and horrors.

At the level of detailed philosophical analysis, what exactly it is to represent, although it may have seemed to us an intuitively straightforward notion, is a problem of some complexity (see Wollheim, 1987, pp. 76ff.)

However we analyse it, it is very doubtful that representation possesses the explanatory power it would need in order to yield a one-concept theory of art. Clearly, there is art that is not at all representational: music is seldom and very inessentially representational; painting and sculpture can be abstract as well as figurative. Although in prose a subject may often be important, in poetry its importance can be much reduced and the poem be appreciated as an artefact in its own right rather than as a window on the non-art world. The work of representing may seem insufficiently ambitious. As the *re*-presenting or imitating of what nature or God has already created, it can at its best be technically notable, but must always be derivative and repetitious. The beauties of art are very seldom transcriptions, into a medium, of pre-existing natural beauties.

The representational theory, say its critics, must deflect attention from the work of art and its distinctive values, to what is always other than itself. Artworks, however, call attention upon their own unique forms, lines, colours, images, meanings, patterns of sound. What we encounter in them we have not encountered and cannot encounter elsewhere in the world. Revelatory or not, an artwork does not become 'disposable' once we have extracted from it a message, a way of looking, a perspective.

On the other hand, however, why may we not understand music as representing the life of feeling, the flowings and checkings of vitality? Even abstract artists have often seen their work in revelatory terms – displaying hidden laws of nature, or metaphysical ideas. Could we not claim that art is always a mimesis of nature: if not of nature's visible appearances, then of its fundamental energies and their endless transformations?

We could: but at a price. The concept of representation may be over-extended in a way that unhelpfully conceals what would be better seen as distinct and different (even at times conflicting) aims of art. Even with a clearly representational painting we may say, 'The objects are represented – in such a way as heightens their crucial *expressive* qualities.' Or again, we may say, 'The forms of nature have no more than stimulated the artist to create a *new* world.' Often, too, we shall say, 'The formal ordering of the artwork does not reproduce nature's order; it has its own distinctive order – invented, not discovered'. (*See also* DEPICTION; PLATO; PLOTINUS; REALISM; REPRESENTATION; RESEMBLANCE; SCHOPENHAUER; TRUTH IN ART.)

ART AS EXPRESSION

Supposing we were to start again, this time putting *expression* at the centre, some of our problems would certainly be alleviated. Music expresses feelings, emotions, moods, their conflicts, triumphs, defeats. A painted landscape may engage us as expressive of peace, melancholy or menace; so too a lyrical poem, a semi-abstract sculpture, a scene or situation in drama. What is more, they may express highly particularized modes of feeling, even new emotions. Romantic theorists and others down to our own day have indeed argued for expression theories of art. In R.G. Collingwood's account, the artist struggles to clarify and articulate his initially unfocused feeling. Coming to grasp it and to express it by way of the fashioning of an artwork constitutes a single task.

It is not only sensations, feelings, moods and emotions that may be expressed, but also attitudes, evaluations, atmospheric qualities, expectation, disappointment, frustration, relief, tensings and relaxings . . . : not only brief bursts of lyrical feeling evoked by specific, intensely felt events, but also the inner quality of a whole life-world. Even when art argues a case, its real interest is always to express the felt experience of arguing: and when it depicts or describes, its concern is with the human affective analogues of the objects and events of the outside world that make up its ostensible subject-matter. Its real subject is always the human subject.

But what exactly am I reporting when I say, 'I find this phrase for clarinet poignantly expressive' or, 'The harmonic twist in the final cadence expresses foreboding'? Not necessarily that I am emotionally excited – I do not need to be, in order to 'read' the emotional quality – nor that I am necessarily directly sharing the artist's emotions. I may certainly have reason to hope that my experience will be related to the artist's intentions, if these are well realized in his work. It is the work of art itself that is the primary locus of relevant emotional qualities, their development and transformations. The *music* is tender; the *painting* is tranquil. We seem driven to say that, although, as works of art are not themselves sentient, we are well aware that there must be metaphor in the claim.

A critic of the expression theory, however, will argue that, important though expression may be, there are other factors no less essential to the creating and appreciating of art. Clive Bell, for instance (1914, p. 132), wrote,

'If art expresses anything, it expresses an emotion felt for pure form': and form must be our primary concern. Or one may argue that the expressive qualities we value are those which steer clear of clichéd, stereotyped or trite forms of feeling; innovative qualities, perhaps exclusive to a single work of art. But if we say that, we are showing our allegiance to a criterion of creativity or originality, and not to expression alone. (*See also* COLLINGWOOD; EMOTION; EXPRESSION.)

FORMALIST THEORIES: 'ORGANIC UNITY'

Art, it can be argued, is not a window upon the world: it is on the artwork itself that appreciative attention must primarily be focused, particularly on its distinctive structure, its design, unity, form. Discrete episodes of expressive intensity are not enough: 'Does the work *hang together?*' is always a relevant and surely a vital question, a question that shows the primacy of formal unity. Concepts of form and of unity applicable to works of art have been developed over the centuries from suggestions first made by Plato and Aristotle.

We distinguish different kinds of wholes: some, like a pile of stones, are no more than loose aggregates; others, like a plant or animal, are tightly integrated ('organic') complexes, where each part exists only to serve the whole. A work of art is, characteristically, a complex (of notes, instrument timbres, brush-strokes, colour patches, words, images, speech rhythms, and so on) whose elements do not impinge on us as isolated units, but are determined in their perceived qualities by the context of all the *other* elements and their relationships. The character of the whole, as a function of the individual components and their inter-relationships, in turn modifies, controls these components as we perceive them. The spectator's 'synoptic' grasp of the unity will be quite vital: the parts are not perceived as vignettes, cameos, musical miniatures (see Osborne, 1955; 1968).

In the unities that, on this theory, the arts seek to provide, our efforts towards synoptic perceptual grasp are neither defeated nor gratified on the instant. The very intricacy of an artwork's structure can challenge and stimulate our perceptive powers, making its appreciation both a strenuous and a rewarding activity. Not only do works of art achieve formal unity in individually different ways within a single type of art form (such as sonata form); but these generic forms themselves are constantly open to creative revision. It is not enough (nor indeed necessary) that the unifying principles be rationally intelligible: but they must be *perceivable* in the work – audible, visible, or, in literature, discernible in the meaning and sustainable interpretations of the actual text.

Why should we attach high value to formal unities of this kind? Basically, because of the quality of consciousness they make possible. Where the items of a complex lend themselves to perception because of their thematic interconnections, as do those of a successful work of art, we are enabled to synthesize a far greater totality than in any other context. Whereas consciousness can often be attenuated, meagre, sluggish, here it is at its most active and zestful. Again, as finite beings, we are necessarily always vulnerable to the threat of diminished personal integration, of being fragmented – as we are, finally and literally, in death. We are seldom further from that state of lost personal unity than when we are rapt in enjoyment of a well integrated work of fine art. Elements of experience normally disparate and distanced are brought into a vivid relation, and our experience is given new unity.

The temporal arts, although presenting motifs, brief melodies, rhythms, phrases of poetry which constantly pass into silence, effect a partial transcendence of that evanescence in time, precisely on account of their formal structuring whereby early notes (or images) are retained, remain active, ingredient in the total experience, recalled even as a movement (or poem) comes to its close. Something parallel happens in spatial art also, where the mutual connectedness and formal contribution of every represented object overcome the normal mutual 'indifference' of objects in space.

Can formalism, then, constitute a single all-sufficient theory of art? Defenders have not wanted to deny that art can perform additional functions – to instruct, represent, express: but none of these is the essence of art. Even so, there are many cases where one may justifiably question whether a work's formal structure is so decisively the essential thing that its other features must be given subordinate place. The formal structure of a work of art may be valued for its controlling, its focusing, of the work's unique *expressive* qualities – for which we ultimately treasure it. In other cases we may say that the expressive and the formal properties are co-equally important. There are putative works of art – including, notably, some later twentieth-century art – whose structure is so remote from traditional instances of 'configurational unity', that the claim that their form is their essential feature, *qua* artwork, becomes drastically attenuated. Other critics have argued that the theory has most plausibility with regard to *complex* works of art, but has little power to illuminate in the case of *simple* ones – where the concepts of synthesizing, interconnecting, mutual modifying gain no hold. Or is simplicity always deceptive, illusory, in significant works of art?

Even more elusive is precision in defining the 'formal unity' that is thought proper to works of art and to them only. Too loose definitions may extend to the unity of a living organism, the features of a face or a mathematical formal system; too narrow definitions will demand that in a fine work of art, nothing could be altered but for the worse (Alberti, 1988 [1486]), or that to damage any part is to destroy the character of the whole. In fact, some incomplete or fragmentary works testify, rather, to the resilience of their overall character.

Notoriously, there can be no once-and-for-all pinning down of necessary and sufficient conditions for the formally satisfying or the aesthetically 'right'. Often, like Wittgenstein on designing a door, we can do no more than say, 'Higher, higher . . . *there*, thank God!' (Wittgenstein, 1966, p. 13, variant n. 3). (*See also* BELL; COLERIDGE; COMPOSITION, MUSICAL; FORM; HARMONY AND SYMMETRY; HUTCHESON.)

ART AS CREATION

Representation theorists and expression theorists do, of course, allow that art can be innovative – reworking nature's materials in a 'new' nature, or drastically modifying life experiences in the fashioning of expressive art. The formalist or organic unity theory makes the artist's innovative role more central: the unities of art are nowhere paralleled in nature. But why not, then, make quite explicit the work of the artist as the creation of the new? *Creation* is surely well suited to be the leading concept in a theory of art. And it has indeed been made central by a variety of theorists and artists. To some, 'creative imagination' is that power by which, in a display of freedom that echoes the divine prerogative of creation *ex nihilo*, we summon up to actuality possible worlds – worlds that God has not created but has, as it were, left for us to create.

Obvious implications follow for artistic practice and for criticism. Art should be freed from dependence on appearances. The development towards abstraction in the visual arts can be proclaimed as a 'purifying away' of objective reference. Originality and individuality become criteria of high merit. We may particularly value indications of the creative process within an artwork itself: the growth of a musical subject from fragments in the earliest moments of a piece, the progressive incorporation of material that at first seems alien.

So: does 'creation' yield a complete theory of art? When I try to develop such a one-concept theory, I find that my concept of creation has to undergo progressive enrichment, if I am to accommodate within it the full freight of meaning and criteria of value it would require for this role: it must mean 'new *and* aesthetically valuable, rewarding'. Even for the God of Genesis, after the work of creation (in the narrower sense of *making*, calling into being) there remained a question of evaluating what had been done: a question favourably answered – 'Behold, it was very good.' For the human artist, the possibility surely exists that he make something from (nearly) nothing, but . . . behold, it is very bad – unless we pack into the concept, from the start, that an artefact counts as a creation only if it has artistic merit. Novelty is not enough: an object can be original, in the sense of a perceptually distinct, unique addition to the beings already in the world, and yet be unrewarding to contemplate, fail to sustain attention.

Among products of high creativity we must include some scientific theories, mathematical calculi and theorems, philosophical systems. But they are not art. However creative my daydreams, they are not art, either: they are not worked in a medium, intersubjective, shared. Conversely, not every movement, style or period in art sets a high evaluation on the particularized and original. We should also be cautious in accepting that ideal of 'purifying' art from all dependence on natural appearances. To purify can be to attenuate, if it means to cut oneself off from any allusion to the world beyond the canvas. Such allusion can add immensely to the wealth of meanings in a work of art.

Even if we reject a theology of man as co-creator with God – perhaps particularly if we reject it – the creation theme rightly spotlights the artist's distinctive dignity. His imagination continues, intensifies, perfects and on occasion transfigures nature's own doings. It is not merely a fanciful metaphor to speak of the artist as bringing into being 'what nature has not created, and awaits creation'. (*See also* CREATIVITY; IMAGINATION; ORIGINALITY).

DEVELOPING TRADITIONS

Emphasizing the free-standing character of works of art as created objects encourages us to see them as autonomous, independent and self-explanatory. For countless individual works of art, that statement needs correction, however. We shall not understand or appreciate them without at least an outline knowledge of the tradition in which they stand, the genre to which they belong – and thus some understanding of whether they simply continue or modify or rebel against tradition and genre as so far developed. Indeed, it is tempting for an aesthetician, who despairs of

any of the unified theories of art to fulfil their promise, to abandon all such theorizing and urge instead that we take those ongoing developing traditions, genres and media (and the complex actual vocabulary or criticism) as the basic data for reflection on the arts in all their diversity.

Further, we have only to consider some twentieth-century movements in art (Dada, conceptual art, ready-mades, for instance) to realize that none of the favoured unifying categories or key concepts is in the least likely to illuminate their nature and role. (*See also* TRADITION).

THE INSTITUTIONAL THEORY

One strategy for coping with these last-mentioned issues (and with other problems too) is that of the 'institutional theory of art'. In a strong form it takes the unifying factor to be not the possession of common perceptual ('manifest') features by artworks, but the conferral on certain objects, by representatives of the 'artworld', of the status of 'candidate for appreciation' as works of art (Dickie, 1985, p. 34). The artworld is thought of, roughly, as the set of art critics, organizers of exhibitions, owners of galleries and others with relevant experience and authority. It may, however, provide me with little illumination, when bewildered before an object like Duchamp's *Fountain* (a ready-made urinal) or Carl Andre's *Equivalent VIII* (a rectangle of bricks), to be told that the artworld representatives have indeed conferred art status upon it. I cannot prevent myself asking by what criteria, on account of what features (manifest, once more), has this status been conferred? Either we must look for an answer that will render needless the artworld's conferral – that is, by appeal to 'reasons' or to criteria for their decisions, reasons which may be made open and public and applied by all. Or, if no disclosable reasons are relevant, the artworld's decisions, in being detached from any of the characteristics which we may look for or become aware of in contemplating a putative work of art, cannot be defended from arbitrariness or waywardness (see Wollheim, 1987, ch. 1).

Being deemed a work of art, given space in a gallery, publication by a reputable publisher, performance by a respected orchestra, imply judgements that the work will reward the attention solicited for it. But, again, we have a legitimate interest in knowing the features of the work that have led to its selection and promotion.

A later version of the institutional theory drops the notion of conferral, and claims that a work of art is to be understood as an artefact made for presentation to an 'art-world public' (Dickie, 1989). The artworld becomes the totality of 'frameworks for the presentation of a work of art by an artist to an art-world public', a public prepared to understand such objects. But what this leaves altogether unclarified is the point and value of these activities.

It may be said that we need a theory that can be of help with those recent putative art objects that have not been held to have *any* aesthetic qualities. But objects that fail to meet any criteria for aesthetic interest or excellence are no less a problem to an institutional theory if it accepts the challenge of explaining *why* the artworld's representatives confer art status on them, or of explaining the point of presenting these works to an 'understanding' public. (*See also* 'ARTWORLD'; DANTO; DICKIE.)

ART AS PLAY

Various other concepts have been proposed as bases on which to construct theories of art. The concept of play is one such. That aesthetic activity is a kind of play was a seminal claim of Kant. The concept appears in several contexts in his aesthetic writing. A judgement of taste arises in a 'free play' of imagination and understanding, where a perceptual complex is grasped and synthesized, and we are aware of order and purposiveness, but without the application of classificatory concepts. To Kant, art can be described as play, 'i.e. an occupation . . . agreeable on its own account' (Kant, 1961 [1790], §§9, 43). Gratuitousness, spontaneity and freedom are emphasized; the aesthetic objects are a delight to explore and rewarding to contemplate. In Friedrich Schiller's writing on aesthetic education, a concept of play is central and highly elaborated. In rough outline: we can locate a zone between, on the one hand, feeling and desire in their immediacy, and, on the other, the domain of abstract, impersonal, formal reason. In that (aesthetic) zone, the 'play impulse' and its products draw upon both the sensuous and the rational, and intimately connect or fuse them. In this way, the otherwise conflictful elements of human nature are brought into unity. (*See also* KANT; SCHILLER.)

INEXHAUSTIBILITY AND DENSITY OF MEANING

'The heresy of paraphrase' is a familiar phrase expressing the fact that a significant work of literary art cannot be reduced to a summary of its plot or 'message'. No more can a painting be reduced to an inventory of the objects it represents. From a single metaphor up to a complex art work, inexhaustibility of interpretation is a mark of authentic art. The coexistence of multiple levels or layers of meaning gives a sense of richness and 'depth'. There is also a kind of 'aesthetic transcendence' where the expressive quality, say, of a passage of music, far surpasses in gravity or poignancy the unconvincing human situation (say, an operatic plot) to which it ostensibly refers, or where a deceptively commonplace still-life has a resonance beyond the reach of analysis.

In each of the arts there occurs the fullest possible assimilation of its symbolic materials and other constituents. In poetry the sound and the rhythm matter as well as the sense; in a painting the picture plane and the traces of brush-strokes, as well as the represented depth. The notes of a chord are heard each as continuing a 'horizontal' line of music, as well as 'vertically' as constituting a chord, with its distinctive harmonic quality, and as moving towards or away from some moment of tension; and, again, as a composite of the timbres of the individual instruments that are playing it. Together, such features furnish the basic materials for yet another – and a promising – communicational theory of art. (*See also* INTERPRETATION.)

KEY CONCEPTS AND THEIR INTERRELATIONS

Supposing that none of the germinal concepts of the theories considered above can function by itself as sole key concept generating a complete unitary theory of art, we should not be left with an unrelated plurality of notions. Some of the most interesting work in aesthetics lies in exploring the interconnections among these concepts. Resisting the temptation to extend some preferred concept so as to cover the whole field, we can remain sensitive to aesthetically important creative and appreciative tensions between them. Representational artworks are sometimes judged to fall below, or to rise to, expressiveness: my appreciation of sculpture may develop from the easier beauties of representation to those of three-dimensional formal structures.

A theory must do justice to the fact that certain media and materials lend themselves to our doing several significantly different things simultaneously in and through them. It is a happy contingency that we can at once represent and express and construct new configurational unities in and through the skilled handling of paints, inks or crayons, carved wood or chiselled stone. Some of our appraisals of artworks draw explicitly on these multiple possibilities, challenges and tensions. For instance, we marvel at a composer's success in managing a demanding and potentially cramping form, while yet attaining a high degree of expressiveness and inventiveness within it; or at a novelist who represents a wide range of human activity and experience, and whose work thoroughly assimilates it, with unimpaired unity.

Some writers have seen the history of theorizing about the arts as a gradual realization that works of art are to be properly appreciated as 'objects in their own right'. Other concerns – with truth to human nature and experience outside art, with moral or political or religious impact – are to be relegated to the inessential. If, however, representational art fashions an image of human life, it cannot be of indifference whether in particular cases it is an adequate, defensible image or a grotesquely reduced parody. This question can obviously be raised only where a work, or an *oeuvre*, does set out to characterize human experience as such, the human life-world rather than a selected fragment. Major works of art do typically attempt something close to this. Art can be one main source of a culture's view of itself, its members and their world. We cannot properly rule out a moral scrutiny and appraisal as irrelevant to such works, even though we should be equally misguided to judge any works of art solely by their moral quality.

Furthermore, in its exploration of the widest range of human experience, art cannot fail to be particularly concerned with the boundaries and *limits* of experience, where the expressible begins to yield to the inexpressible. To attach high importance to these is not to demand of art that it labour in defence of particular religions or particular beliefs, but only that, where some approach to a comprehensive image of the life-world is attempted, neither the seeming bounds of that world, nor the peculiar ability of the arts to bring them to vivid awareness in a transcending movement of the mind, be ignored.

THE STATUS OF THEORIES OF ART

Philosophy tries to be as self-conscious as possible about its own practice and aims: it is bound to raise the question of the status of what we have been calling theories of the arts. Are these, in fact, definitions of 'art'? Or are they better seen as philosophical analyses of concepts used in discourse about art? Or are they theories proper – systematic, explanatory accounts? Is their function descriptive, or prescriptive as well?

The multifariousness of the arts, their traditions, developing genres, idioms and media, their self-transcending *nisus*, make definition an unrealistic, perhaps even undesirable, goal. To seek it obstinately results in oversimplification and distortion. But it is equally important for the writer on aesthetics not to lurch too far in the opposite direction, stressing complexity and difference, and prematurely to give up any attempt to see an intelligible structure of relationships among the phenomena of the arts.

A substantial amount of theorizing about the arts involves conceptual and linguistic analysis. The analyses of the concepts of representation, expression and form are all crucial and all contested. Aesthetics involves analyses also of the role of the artist's intention and imagination, of the nature of metaphor, symbolism, beauty, sublimity, and the whole range of critical discourse. Nevertheless, the philosophical study of art is analysis not only of discourse, but (no less legitimately) of description, of phenomenology, of the appreciative experiences which largely prompt the discourse. Although the philosopher must be respectful of the art critic's expertise, that does not mean that he or she must be altogether dependent on the critic to speak or write before the philosopher may break his silence. Philosophers of art must reserve the right to find a body of criticism, or a critical theory, incomplete or even confused. They must themselves function as critics – for instance, in their choices of what they see as revealing examples or counterexamples from the arts by which to examine and test critical theories. And when an avant-garde innovator proposes some objects as artworks – objects which, if admitted to the category, would overturn an otherwise very broadly based theoretical understanding of the arts – it should not be taken for granted that theory should immediately and necessarily capitulate.

The aspiration to produce a unitary theory, even if it fails to result in one, remains legitimate and often fruitful. We may enhance our understanding of art by seeing how much work a given key concept can do for us, and finding where it ceases to be as illuminating as some alternative concept. If we are forced towards a theory with several fundamental concepts rather than one, the phenomena in their complexity may well be better understood, and the interrelations and tensions within and among the key concepts

may illuminate the inner dynamics of creation.

If, in my theorizing, I am one-sidedly neglectful of some major function or feature of art, I am very unlikely to do appreciative justice to manifestations of it in individual works of art. I may need a theoretical reminder, even if it in turn exaggerates, that there is more to the arts than I have been allowing. A normative role certainly cannot be denied to aesthetic theory. For example: although we are most unlikely to find a complete and adequate theory in Clive Bell's account of 'significant form', that account helped to make possible the shift in sensibility needed for acceptance of post-impressionist painting – a shift from excessive concern with certain sorts of represented subject to much greater concern with plastic and painterly values and with formal relationships in general.

BIBLIOGRAPHY

Alberti, L.B.: *De Re Aedificatoria* (Florence: 1486); trans. J. Rykwert, N. Leach and R. Taverner (Cambridge, Mass. and London: MIT Press, 1988).

Beardsley, M.C.: *Aesthetics: Problems in the Philosophy of Criticism* (New York: Harcourt, Brace, 1958).

Bell, C.: *Art* (London: Chatto & Windus, 1914).

Charlton, W.: *Aesthetics* (London: Hutchinson, 1970).

Collingwood, R.G.: *The Principles of Art* (Oxford: Clarendon Press, 1938).

Dickie, G.: *Art and the Aesthetic* (Ithaca, NY and London: Cornell University Press, 1974).

Dickie, G.: *The Art Circle* (New York: 1985).

Dufrenne, M.: *Phénoménologie de l'expérience esthétique* (Paris: 1953); trans. E.S. Casey, A.A. Anderson, W. Domingo and L. Jacobson, *The Phenomenology of Aesthetic Experience* (Evanston, Ill.: Northwestern University Press, 1973).

Kant, I.: *Kritik der Urteilskraft* (Berlin: 1790); trans. J.C. Meredith, *Critique of Judgement* (Oxford: Clarendon Press, 1961). Part 1 of the work is Kant's 'Critique of aesthetic judgement', to which section numbers refer.

Osborne, H.: *Aesthetics and Criticism* (London: Routledge & Kegan Paul, 1955).

Osborne, H.: *Aesthetics and Art Theory* (London: Longman, 1968).

Schiller, F.: *Über die ästhetische Erziehung des Menschen* (1794–5); ed. and trans., with intro., E.M. Wilkinson and L.A. Willoughby, *On the Aesthetic Education of Man* (Oxford: Clarendon Press, 1982).

Sharpe, R.A.: *Contemporary Aesthetics* (Brighton: Harvester, 1983).

Tilghman, B.R.: *But is it Art?* (Oxford, Basil Blackwell, 1984).

Wittgenstein, L.: *Lectures and Conversations on Aesthetics, Psychology and Religious Belief*, ed. C. Barrett (Oxford: Basil Blackwell, 1966).

Wollheim, R.: *Art and Its Objects*, 2nd edn (Cambridge: Cambridge University Press, 1980).

Wollheim, R.: *Painting as an Art* (Princeton, NJ, and London: Thames & Hudson, 1987).

RONALD W. HEPBURN

Tolstoy, Leo [Lev Nikolayevich] (1828–1910) Russian novelist, educator, and social reformer; one of the great moral influences in his own and the following century. Nearly all Tolstoy's writings on art appeared during the last, 'messianic', phase of his life. These include a number of short articles on individual artists, his philosophical essay *On Art* (c.1895–7), his notorious attack on Shakespeare in *Shakespeare and the Drama* (1906), and his only major work on aesthetics, *What is Art?* (1898).

Shortly after completing *Anna Karenina* in 1877 Tolstoy underwent a spiritual crisis, and he became preoccupied with moral and religious questions. This is evident not only in his overtly didactic writings, including those on art, but in all his later fiction. It has been more common in Russia than elsewhere for the writing of fiction to be seen as a high moral calling. The novelist as moralist, religious or political teacher and even prophet has been a recurring phenomenon in Russian literature, from Gogol through Dostoevsky and Tolstoy to Solzhenitsyn. Whatever the historical or cultural reasons for this attitude, its justification requires some sort of theoretical underpinning, and this is what Tolstoy's theory of art provides.

He assumes, without argument, that if art is to be an activity worthy of the very highest respect then it must be possible to justify it on moral grounds, since moral values have supremacy over all others. He is therefore opposed, on principle, to the idea that art is self-justifying or that its value is in any way self-evident. His approach to all human activities and institutions is similarly moralistic and practical. He is just as opposed to the doctrine of science for science's sake, for example, as he is to that of art for art's sake. This was the principal reason for his hostility to the eighteenth-century view of art as the creation of beauty. Beauty, he insists, has no objective worth and should never be placed above the demands of morality. There is, in any case, no common standard of beauty as there is of morality.

In Tolstoy's view, to justify art in terms of beauty is to treat mere enjoyment as the ultimate criterion of aesthetic merit. The enormous sacrifices in men, money and materials made in the name of art over the centuries could only be justified if art were more than just entertainment and served some high moral or religious purpose, as it was intended to do in the Middle Ages. That purpose, he insists, must be looked for in the meaning and purpose of life itself. This, for Tolstoy, was what religion, stripped of its supernatural and superstitious accretions, was ultimately about. 'Religions', he says 'are the exponents of the highest comprehension of life accessible to the best and foremost men at a given time in a given society; a comprehension towards which all the rest of that society must inevitably and irresistibly advance' (Tolstoy, 1930, p. 127). On this view, the value of individual works of art will depend, as far as their content is concerned, on the extent to which they are in conformity with the highest religious perceptions of the age. In our time, this is the Christian ideal of the union and brotherhood of man. Conversely, art which is socially divisive or elitist is failing in its true function and so is bad or counterfeit art.

Relatively few works since the Renaissance, when artists reverted to the hedonistic values of Greece and Rome for their inspiration, manage, in Tolstoy's estimation, to survive this test, although he sees some improvement in his own day. His list of failures includes Shakespeare's *King Lear*, Michelangelo's *Last Judgement*, Wagner's *Ring of the Nibelungs* – and even his own two masterpieces, *War and Peace* and *Anna Karenina*. Many commentators have seen the apparent absurdity of this conclusion as sufficient grounds for rejecting the theory. However, any theory which proceeds rationalistically from first principles, as Tolstoy's does, cannot be overturned simply on account of the unwelcome nature of its conclusions.

Unlike most writers on aesthetics, Tolstoy does not assume that somehow we already know what is good or bad in art, but sets out to discover the principles by which we should judge. Moreover, disagreements about first principles are notoriously difficult to resolve without resorting to *ad hominem* arguments. There can be no common ground between Tolstoy and his opponents unless the latter are at least prepared to concede overall supremacy to moral values, but to do that is to give the moralist approach to art a firm foothold.

It has been argued (Diffey, 1985, p. 134) that whilst Tolstoy's attempt to justify art as a human activity or institution in terms of religious perceptions is perhaps defensible, he is clearly mistaken in using this as a criterion for evaluating individual works of art, since 'the reasons why something in general is valuable may not be the reasons why an individual thing of that kind is good.' One might, for instance, value cricket as an activity on the grounds that it promotes physical fitness and is character-building, but it would be absurd to claim that one particular game of cricket was better than another because it produced more fitness or nobler characters.

This is clearly an important distinction, and one which Tolstoy patently ignores, but it is not entirely clear-cut. For there has to be some connection between the overall justification of an activity and particular evaluations made within it. For instance, one could not consistently place a high value on the character-building potential of cricket and rate highly a particular game that was dogged by bad sportsmanship. Similarly, if the most exalted function of art is to unite mankind in common bonds of feeling, then socially divisive works cannot be rated as masterpieces. It has to be admitted, however, that Tolstoy's moralistic approach fails to yield the sort of criteria that an art critic might find useful. This is partly due to the fact that Tolstoy, the theorist, has very little interest in what are normally regarded as the formal or aesthetic properties of a work of art – or, indeed, in the work of art itself apart from its effect on the audience. Critics, by contrast, tend to interest themselves chiefly in the internal properties of a work.

Tolstoy is of course untroubled by this because for him the aesthetic properties have value only as a means to an end, the immediate artistic end being the transmission of feelings from artist to audience, and the ultimate moral end being the transmission of feelings that unite us. Thus, if a work fails in its proper effect then it is worthless, and nothing the critics can say in its defence will alter the fact.

Since Tolstoy's moralistic approach rides on the back of an expression theory of art, it is indirectly vulnerable to attacks on his version of that theory, which he summarizes as follows:

> To evoke in oneself a feeling one has once experienced and having evoked it in oneself then by means of movements, lines, colours, sounds or forms expressed in words, so to transmit that feeling that others experience the same feeling – this is the activity of art.
>
> Art is a human activity consisting in this, that one man consciously by means of external signs, hands on to others feelings he has lived through, and that others are infected by these feelings and also experience them. (Tolstoy, 1930, p. 123)

Aesthetic experience for Tolstoy is the experience of being united with the artist, and others affected by the work, in a common bond of feeling. When in this state, the recipient feels as if the work is his own and that what it expresses is what he has longed to express. This quality of infectiousness is what distinguishes true art from its counterfeit, and 'the stronger the infection the better is the art, as art' (Tolstoy, 1930, p. 228).

Works that fail in expressiveness, as do 'brain-spun or invented works' (Tolstoy, 1930, p. 196), are necessarily counterfeit. Other works will be limited in their capacity to infect others, especially where the feelings involved are only accessible to people of a certain class, creed or culture; for instance, art which appeals to patriotic, aristocratic or sectarian feelings. Such art is 'exclusive', and is morally bad rather than counterfeit. The best art must be accessible to all and must therefore appeal to feelings that are common to all.

This criterion of universal accessibility devalues all art that makes any real demand on the audience's intelligence, learning or powers of concentration. Any work that needs to be explained is a failure, for 'to say that a work of art is good but incomprehensible to most men, is the same as saying of some kind of food that it is very good but most people can't eat it' (Tolstoy, 1930, p. 176). Thus arises Tolstoy's preference for simple folk-art over sophisticated metropolitan art.

According to Tolstoy (1930, p. 228), the infectiousness of a work depends on three conditions: first, the degree of sincerity of the artist – that is, the artist should be impelled by an inner need to express his feelings; second, the degree of individuality of the feelings transmitted; and third, the beauty (that is lucidity) of their expression. The first condition, to which Tolstoy attaches particular importance, contradicts the modern view that the genesis of a work is irrelevant to its evaluation. The second makes it improbable that exactly the same effects could be produced in some other way – something that instrumentalist theories are often accused of making possible. The third condition draws our attention to the work's internal organization, but it is a characteristic weakness of Tolstoy's theory of art that he has nothing of interest to say about that.

See also EXPRESSION; FUNCTION OF ART; MORALITY AND ART; RELIGION AND ART.

WRITINGS

What is Art? and Essays on Art, trans. Aylmer Maude (Oxford: Oxford University Press, 1930).

BIBLIOGRAPHY

Diffey, T.J.: *Tolstoy's What is Art?* (London: Croom Helm, 1985).
Garrod, H.W.: *Tolstoy's Theory of Art*, Taylorian Lecture (Oxford: Clarendon Press, 1935).
Gifford, H.: *Tolstoy* (Oxford: Oxford University Press, 1982).
Redpath, T.T.: *Tolstoy, Studies in Modern European Literature and Thought* (London: Bowes & Bowes, 1960).

DAVID A. WHEWELL

tradition In considering the relevance to aesthetics of traditions and of the knowledge embodied in artistic traditions, we can begin by looking at aesthetic reactions in terms of practical knowledge. Practical knowledge is knowledge of how to act, and, by extension, of how to feel. It is knowledge of the responses and feelings that are called for by specific circumstances. Practical knowledge is, in other words, the sort of knowledge that underlies moral activity and aesthetic appreciation.

A man who responds to circumstances or to objects on impulse or at random and with no consistency manifests his lack of such knowledge. With him there is, it would seem, no room for the application of any notion of appropriateness between the stimulus and his response. There is only a causal connection between the two, with no room for any normativity. But though we are creatures with impulses and animal needs, as human beings we are also endowed with self-consciousness. We cannot avoid reflecting on the rightness or wrongness, the appropriateness or inappropriateness, of what we do. To the extent that we do this, we separate ourselves from the immediacy of our impulses. We transform them into *intelligibilia*, according them meaning, seeing them as appropriate or inappropriate reactions, as reasonable or unreasonable springs of action. In so doing, we imply an ability to harness and transform our biological nature.

Practical knowledge, then, is a knowledge of the appropriate action or feeling in a given situation. As knowledge of what is appropriate to the ends we *should* aim at and of the means we *should* use to realize our aims, it is knowledge which characteristically actually issues in action or feeling. If we did not feel it prompting us to act, we could not be credited with a full understanding of the appropriateness of the action or feeling.

The ability to give a theoretical account is neither necessary nor sufficient for practical knowledge in either moral or aesthetic realms. What is required is that one should actually act or respond. Nevertheless, this requirement raises the question of how one acquires this knowledge; how, in the case of a perceiver, aesthetic responses are formed; and how, in the case of an artist, the likely reactions of perceivers to a work can be judged in advance, as he is working – something that is a precondition of intelligent activity on his part. Shared practical knowledge on the part of artist and perceiver alike, then, forms the basis of communication in the aesthetic realm. It is plausible to suggest that upbringing or schooling, formal or informal, in a tradition of expression is what grounds the practical knowledge in question.

Our aesthetic responses, like our moral practices, are certainly rooted in our existence as biological beings, and in various ways constrained by our physical nature. Sounds we cannot hear can never form part of a musical tradition, nor could a musical tradition be based on intervals too close for us to distinguish. It is arguable, too, that our taste for certain types of harmony, say, or colour contrasts has roots in biology. Nevertheless, it is also clear that a great deal of our aesthetic knowledge and perception is learned. Westerners find the rhythms of Tchaikovsky's ballet scores so obvious as to appear entirely natural, but students in the Chinese school of ballet have to be taught what the rhythms are before they can pick them up. No doubt the response of Westerners to the 'natural' elements of Chinese music would stand in analogous need of in-

struction. Studies of the psychology of perception and their application to art by Gombrich and others have shown the extent to which the perception of what appear to us to be realistic images also depends on upbringing in the relevant traditions and cultures. Obviously, too, judgements of the worth and success of particular works of art will depend on the critic or perceiver having some understanding of the tradition from which they stem. It is only when he is armed with this knowledge that he will begin to be able to appreciate just what is communicated, and what aimed at, by the works in question.

It is important to appreciate the extent to which the knowledge embodied in an artistic or moral tradition is not something of which those brought up in the tradition are explicitly aware. (It is for this reason that they regard as quite natural forms and responses that the foreigner might find puzzling and unnatural.) But the untheoretical readiness of an audience to respond in specific ways to what they are presented with forms the basis on which an artist can plan his work: he puts himself in the position of perceiver or audience, and plans on the basis of his untheoretical responses to what he does.

There have been periods in the history of art in which artists have been bent on dispensing with tradition and starting afresh. The most notable example of this trend is artistic modernism in the twentieth century, and along with the composer Schoenberg the most notable theorist and proponent of modernism is Le Corbusier. Le Corbusier explicitly advocated an architecture based on engineering and mathematics. In *Towards a New Architecture*, he advocates the elimination of all 'dead' concepts with regard to the house. In their place we are to build from a 'critical and objective' point of view, so as to arrive at the geometrical and mathematical purity of the 'house machine'. Despite the pretension and the rhetoric, Le Corbusier was not dispensing with traditional knowledge altogether. His architecture, though devoid of ornament, is still based on geometrical forms which men have, through the centuries, found pleasing to the eye – as Le Corbusier himself implicitly admitted in his efforts to show that his buildings were based on the forms underlying classical architecture.

But Le Corbusier was dispensing with, and intentionally dispensing with, much of the architectural knowledge embodied in more recent traditions of architecture, and it was because of this that his architecture aroused, and continues to arouse, such strong passions. He certainly offended against what most of his contemporaries had grown up to think of as familiar and fitting in buildings, although he and his followers stress what they regarded as the moribund state of those traditions (as did Schoenberg in the case of music and Herbert Read and others in the case of the visual arts). Even here, though, the modernists achieved much of their effect initially precisely by the contrast with what had gone before. Even, and perhaps especially, in breaking with tradition, an artist is still parasitic on it. And in the 1990s, some sixty or seventy years after the first stirrings of artistic modernism, and when in some fields the initially revolutionary view has become the established policy, we are perhaps in a better position to consider the inherent strengths and weaknesses of just what was being proposed by the anti-traditionalists.

In the case of architecture, at least, and in the face of the continuing widespread unpopularity of modernist architecture, the traditionalist will emphasize the cost of wiping away too much of a tradition at any one time. Echoing Burke and Hayek in politics, the traditionalist will point to the way a traditional style encompasses a vast pool of implicit knowledge, of styles, designs and solutions, which have survived because they have turned out to respond to human needs and desires. In doing this, and in becoming established, they have then in turn become constitutive of the needs and desires of succeeding generations. Until one disturbs a traditional order, one may not know just what the role of any particular element in it may be. This is because much of what is in any tradition will not have been explicitly planned, or even retained, with any precise knowledge of its significance. It will have endured through a process resembling biological natural selection, shaped invisibly by its actual, but often unseen, responsiveness to some need or taste.

The concept of a tradition as a spontaneously developing order, much of whose value is implicit rather than explicit, can certainly be applied with profit in many fields, including the aesthetic. It is true that traditional knowledge, often of an unformulated kind, plays a major role in aesthetic understanding. And it is not hard to find examples of the unforeseen costs, even in the aesthetic field, of going against traditional practices. An obvious example of this sort of cost is the way many supposedly functional modern buildings have proved less well adapted to the functions they serve than their Victorian or Edwardian counterparts, particularly if function is taken in a wide sense to include the contentment or otherwise of the users of the buildings. A less obvious, but no less pertinent, example would be the way a strongly developed tradition in the arts may allow for nuances of expression, and even for shock and inventiveness, in a way which the abrogation of that tradition will destroy. As the Canadian pianist Glenn Gould has pointed out, the straight-laced Mendelssohn can surprise the listener by the gentlest movement, whereas the technically crude Mussorgsky has to hit the listener over the head with a forte–piano contrast or a quasi-modal moment to make an effect felt.

However, even accepting that in various ways individual expression in the arts depends on the prior existence of traditions of expression, it does not follow that the only viable or possible response of an artist is blindly to follow what has gone before.

Again, to take an obvious example, Palladio, Hawksmoor and Schinkel were all great architects, and great classical architects. But none of them simply copied classical models, and none built in the same way. Simply to repeat what has gone before can seem insipid, or worse. But once one allows that individual creativity and expression and originality are important artistic values, it becomes impossible to say in advance just which departures from tradition are to be sanctioned at any given moment. Like everything else in a tradition, the success of an innovation or a departure from a rule is something to be judged on its own merits, in terms of its success or otherwise in appealing to an appropriate audience. On the other hand, recognizing the importance of traditional styles and orders, the way in which originality depends on their existence, and the unpredictability of the costs of disturbing them, would seem to be a strong argument for teaching newcomers to a field of art the tradition relevant to them and their field.

See also ART HISTORY; MODERNISM AND POSTMODERNISM; ORIGINALITY.

BIBLIOGRAPHY

Bantock, G.M.: *Education, Culture and the Emotions* (London: Faber & Faber, 1967).
Hayek, F.A.: *The Fatal Conceit* (London: Routledge & Kegan Paul, 1988).
Oakeshott, M.: *Rationalism in Politics* (London: Methuen, 1962).
O'Hear, A.: *The Element of Fire* (London: Routledge & Kegan Paul, 1988).

ANTHONY O'HEAR

truth in art Question 1: Are there true statements in works of art? Question 2: Does truth matter to the aesthetic value of a work of art? To answer these questions let us focus on literature, where true statements are more likely to be found, then briefly note how other arts may express truths. A true statement is expressed by a sentence whose terms (a) refer to something and (b) describe it rightly. So do artworks include terms that refer to something?

First, consider fictional names like 'Hamlet'; does 'Hamlet' refer to Hamlet? Hamlet does not exist in the real world, but I say that he *occurs* (not 'exists') in other possible worlds. *Actualists* (such as Kripke, 1980) deny that; they hold that things that *do* not exist *cannot* exist either. Let us examine some of their arguments.

1 *The causal argument* A name and the thing it names are related by a causal chain that begins in a dubbing ceremony where a namer encounters the named. 'Hamlet' does not so interact with Hamlet, nor does 'mermaid' interact with mermaids. Therefore it is not only that Hamlet and mermaids do not exist: they cannot exist, either; there can be no such things. Is that true? In Kripke's semantics 'Plato' denotes not only Plato's occurrence in this world but his occurrences in other possible worlds as well; yet no causal chain links the real dubbing of Plato with other-worldly occurrences of Plato. So, in these other worlds, 'Plato' names something that cannot be causally linked to its real namer; 'Hamlet', too, may then name something that cannot be causally linked to Shakespeare. Indeed, Plato-in-the-other-world ($w1$) is causally linked to a dubbing ceremony in $w1$, but then Hamlet-in-$w1$ is causally linked to his naming by his parents in $w1$.

2 *The uniqueness argument* Shakespeare's description of Hamlet is satisfied not by one, but by infinitely many possible beings in many possible worlds. A person *a* that satisfies that description in $w1$ may also occur in world $w2$, where another man, *b*, satisfies that description (suppose that, in $w2$, *a* is a grave-digger, not a prince). Who then is Hamlet? This argument moves Wolterstorff (1980) to say that Hamlet is not an individual but a universal, a kind-property (a property instantiated by every individual of a given kind). That would make nonsense of all that we say of Hamlet: no property can mourn, love, fight and die. To rebut the argument, ask: do we know who of the denizens of $w1$ is Plato? Plato in $w1$ need not resemble the real Plato; so how do we tell who is Plato in $w1$?

Kripke says there is one property that Plato-in-$w1$ must share with the real Plato: coming from the same gametes. But how do we identify those gametes in $w1$? They too may be very different in $w1$ from what they are in reality. The answer is that we cannot identify Plato in $w1$. As Kripke says, we do not train a telescope on $w1$, searching for one who satisfies certain conditions there. That Plato occurs in some world $w1$ is assumed, not discovered. Who on $w1$ is Plato? He who is identical with Plato, that's who. Identity cannot be empirically established. The same applies to Hamlet. Who in $w1$ is Hamlet? Not whoever satisfies the Hamlet description in some world, but Hamlet: no one else. We need not postulate a special property, Hamletiety, that enables us to locate Hamlet after all. That Hamlet occurs in some worlds is assumed, not discovered. We cannot recognize him; so what? Transworld telescopes do not have a very good resolution anyway.

3 *The incompleteness argument* For everything x and every predicate F, 'x is F' is either true or false, but that Hamlet was tall is neither true nor false; thus with respect to tallness Hamlet is ontologically incomplete (vague). Suppose that Wiggins (1980) is right, and that vague objects cannot exist; then 'Hamlet' fails to refer. Is Hamlet a vague object? Margolis (1980) says no, for the above is but an epistemological vagueness; we just do not know how tall Hamlet is. That is implausible, for even an all-knowing God cannot tell whether Hamlet is tall or not; so the problem is not of knowledge. A better answer is that Hamlet is not vague, because he is tall in some worlds and not tall in others. Here we get to truth: say that 'a is F' is true if and only if a has the property F in the *target world* of that statement.

The target world of 'Cigarette-smoking causes cancer' is the real world; therefore that statement is true, for in reality cigarette-smoking does cause cancer. Were its target world one in which tobacco does not cause cancer, the statement would be false. Now, statements about Hamlet have a *set* of target worlds. A statement about Hamlet is true when satisfied in *all* the worlds of that set, false if satisfied in none, and truth-valueless if satisfied in some of them only. All of *Hamlet*'s target worlds satisfy 'Hamlet is a Dane'; none satisfies 'Hamlet married Ophelia'; and some (but not all) satisfy 'Hamlet is tall.' There is a world where Hamlet is a husband (for Hamlet might have married Ophelia), but that world does not belong to the set of target worlds defined by *Hamlet* as Shakespeare wrote it. The same truth conditions apply to all statements about non-existents: 'The present king of France is a king' is true, for in all its target worlds that king is a king, but 'The present king of France is bald' is truth-valueless, because he, that king, is bald in some worlds in that set and hirsute in others.

The description of the object referred to may be explicit, implicit or metaphorical. What *Hamlet* tells us is mostly not stated by any protagonist; it is implied by the total drama – that is, by the nature of *Hamlet*'s target worlds. Hamlet does not say that fatalists tend to be cruel; we learn that by observing him in $w1$. In much of literature, mostly in poetry, descriptions are metaphorical. Literally construed, such works can have no target worlds, for they entail logical impossibilities (cf. oxymorons); yet we can understand what worlds comply with the metaphorical description. Of course, metaphors cannot be reduced to literal descriptions, but this is not extraordinary. Many other features of an artwork cannot be reflected in its target worlds: its style, the order of narration, and so on. No artwork is exhausted by the target worlds it specifies, just as not *all* its merit comes from its truth. In abstract art, metaphorical description is the main way for a work to express true statements: architecture and music, while literally non-representational, can portray a world metaphorically: its atmosphere, dynamic structure, and general 'feel'. A painting can be both literally and metaphorically true of its target worlds.

We now have a positive answer of sorts to question 1: we have seen that artworks do express true statements; but that is not a very interesting kind of truth. We wish to know whether artworks express statements that are true, not of some possible world $w1$, but of the real world ($w0$). Does *Hamlet* say something true about reality? The above discussion has answered that question too. If there is something, a, that occurs in world $w1$ as well as in reality, then if we know that it is F in $w1$, we know that in reality it could be F, for possible worlds are the various possibilities of the real world. To let art instruct us about the real world we should therefore seek those entities that occur both in the world depicted in an artwork, and in reality.

Are there such entities? So far we have discussed only things that do not occur in reality, such as Hamlet and the present king of France. What about names like 'Rome' that occur in works of art? Do they denote the real things known by these names, or not? Ingarden (1973) has denied that in Sienkiewicz's novel *Quo Vadis?* the word 'Rome' refers to the real city, Rome. Reference, some say, is an intentional act, and in writing a novel one does not intend to refer to anything real, nor say anything about it. But that cannot be right. If the terms 'Rome', 'Caesar', 'the Christians' and so on in the said novel do not refer to what we refer to by these names, then the novel is incomprehensible. The novel does not explicitly say that Caesar was a man and not a machine, that the laws of nature in Rome are those that prevail in the real Rome. We can assume all these facts, without which nothing in the novel makes sense, only on the basis of our acquaintance with the real Rome and the real Caesar. Indeed, Rome as depicted in the novel is different from the real Rome; for instance, it is the home of some people that did not exist. I conclude that in the novel the term 'Rome' refers to Rome, the city we know, but not as it is in reality; the Rome that the novel describes is an occurrence of Rome in another possible world. It retains all the properties of the real Rome except those that the novel explicitly modifies, and those that these imply. Things occur in the real as well as in other possible worlds, fiction describes them as they are in those worlds, and thus we learn how they could be in reality.

These truths about reality may still sound trivial, but that depends on what things we are willing to acknowledge as genuine transworld individuals. Most writers admit only things like Rome and Caesar, but that is too restrictive. Kripke and Putnam also treat 'natural kinds' (water, gold, elm, raven, and so on) as individuals, but this is still not enough. Nominalists may construe all predicates as names of individuals (Zemach, 1982). If that is so, then *Hamlet* is about Hamlet, and about Denmark, but also about love, melancholy and the quest for truth. The latter are things that occur not only in *Hamlet*'s target worlds but, as we know, in reality too. We know that the quest for truth

of Hamlet caused (in *Hamlet*'s target worlds) the death of all those who loved him, and delivered his country into the hands of a blood-thirsty tyrant (Fortinbras); therefore, we also know what that quest *can* cause in *reality*.

A truth about a possible world is a possible truth about the real world, and as such it is highly interesting to us: *Hamlet* teaches us not only what happens in *w1*, but also what can happen here. Furthermore, we can discover the essence of a thing by examining an occurrence of it in one world; for example, by examining the occurrence of water in the real world we find that its essence, a property it has in all possible worlds, is H_2O.

Now the world at which a thing is examined may be a possible one: that is the procedure known as *Gedankenexperiment*, whereby we gain insight into the nature of some thing by imaginatively envisaging how certain actions and initial conditions will influence that thing. That method is used by historians, generals and social planners, but its best example is in works of fiction that deal with human nature. So by examining the quest for truth that occurs in *w1*, we may reach the conclusion that the catastrophe that this quest leads to in *w1* is not an accidental but an essential feature of it. If so, if it is necessary to that quest that it leads to calamity, then that quest will end in a bloodbath in every possible world (including the real one) that has the relevant features. Such a truth that we learn by reading *Hamlet* is extremely important to us, for it tells us what the quest for truth, so typical to our culture, *will* lead us to. Thus, important truths can be gleaned from works of art.

Question 2 asked whether there is a connection between the truthfulness of an artwork and its aesthetic value. Classicists considered that connection self-evident, while formalists held it to be impossible, for the excellence criteria in art are alien to those pertaining to information-gathering and science. Romantic thinkers were divided: under the influence of Kant's distinction between phenomena (objects known to science) and noumena (things in themselves), some thought that art can gain us access to the latter (Schopenhauer, 1961; Heidegger, 1971) or to pure uncategorized-by-reason intuitions (Croce, 1909). Others rejected all claims of art to knowledge, stressing the freedom of art from didactic strictures of morality and fact (Valéry, 1958; Beardsley, 1958). The latter view seems well supported, for the work of some great artists is permeated by heinous moral views (Gogol, Dostoevsky, Griffith, Pound) or radical factual errors (Homer, Dante).

Moreover, factual and moral excellence do not guarantee aesthetic merit – Robert Nozik has versified Newton's laws, to show that great science can be atrocious poetry! Yet some philosophers (including Hospers, 1960) rightly protest that the said divorce of excellence criteria flies in the face of common practice: we praise great art for providing insight into reality, mainly into human nature, and we censure a work for lack of deeper knowledge of social and personal phenomena. How can that be explained? If artists describe possible worlds, why do they have to discover new and important facts about our neighbours or our emotions? Should that task not be left to scientists, who are better equipped for it?

We said that much of a work's target world overlaps the real world. No writer, fantasy writers included, can forgo borrowing from reality. An utterly fictitious work will be too enormous to write; if it is given us by aliens we shall find it irrelevant and boring. An artist's target world may differ from reality in detail, but not in basic features: the kind of beings in it, their beliefs and desires, what motivates them, the emotions they have, and most laws of nature, cannot but be those that occur in wo. Now if a work has considerable aesthetic value, its world (say, $w1$) is well organized; it is unified yet variegated, revealing a new, exciting kind of unity in a multifarious world. Since $w1$ is mostly wo, the significance and unity that emerge in $w1$ is relevant to us in wo. An author is a world-sculptor, who mostly works on borrowed material. We, who are that material, are keenly interested in what is done with it, for the features salient in the target world may fashion our own life. Of course, the aesthetic achievement may be due to those elements in $w1$ that are not taken from wo. In that case our aesthetic admiration is not due to the work's truth. Such works, however, must be rare.

Here is why. Suppose that a novel is based on a shallow view of some people and presents them falsely. In principle, this is no problem; we just assume that in $w1$ these people are not as they are in wo. But, then, what else is different in $w1$? If the trait is deep and pervasive, we cannot isolate it from its conceptual environment in wo: that is inconsistent. Reading a racist novel, we cannot simply assume that the Jews in $w1$ are malevolent, and go on aesthetically to appreciate the work. If we cannot import our beliefs about Jews into $w1$, some other changes must be made in it to keep it consistent. Those concepts that take on a novel significance are connected to other beliefs we have, which now we realize are all false in $w1$.

Withholding our real beliefs from $w1$ may spread like cancer, so in the end $w1$ collapses: it is not cohesive enough. Thus, just as a discovered truth about wo often makes $w1$ beautifully structured, violating a basic truth about wo may make $w1$ either so inchoate, or else so meagre (since many beliefs must be excised to keep it consistent), that its aesthetic value becomes nugatory.

See also AUTONOMY, AESTHETIC; FICTIONAL ENTITIES; JUDGEMENT, AESTHETIC; METAPHOR.

BIBLIOGRAPHY

Beardsley, M.: *Aesthetics* (New York: Harcourt, Brace, 1958).
Croce, B.: *Estetica come scienza dell'espressione e linguistica generale* (Milan: Sandron, 1902); trans. *Aesthetics* (London: Macmillan, 1909).
Heidegger, M.: 'Der Ursprung des Kunstwerkes' (Frankfurt: 1950); trans. A. Hofstadter, 'The origin of the work of art', *Poetry, Language, Thought*, (New York: Harper & Row, 1971).
Hospers, J.: 'Implied truths in literature', *Journal of Aesthetics and Art Criticism*, 29 (1960), 36–46.
Ingarden, R.: *Das literarische Kunstwerk* (Halle:

1931); trans. G.G. Grabowicz, *The Literary Work of Art* (Evanston, Ill.: Northwestern University Press, 1973).

Kripke, S.: *Naming and Necessity* (Oxford: Basil Blackwell, 1980).

Margolis, J.: *Art and Philosophy* (Atlantic Highlands, NJ: Humanities Press, 1980).

Schopenhauer, A.: *Die Welt als Wille und Vorstellung* (1818); trans. *The World as Will and Idea* (Garden City, NY: Doubleday, 1961).

Valéry, P.: *Poésie et pensée abstraite* (Oxford: Clarendon, 1939); *Poésie, essais sur la poétique et la poète* (B. Guégan, 1928); trans. *The Art of Poetry* (New York: Random House, 1958).

Wiggins, D.: *Sameness and Substance* (Oxford: Basil Blackwell, 1980).

Wolterstorff: *Works and Worlds of Art* (Oxford: Oxford University Press, 1980).

Zemach, E.: 'A plea for a new nominalism', *Canadian Journal of Philosophy*, 12 (1982), 527–37.

EDDY M. ZEMACH

V–W

value, aesthetic *See* JUDGEMENT, AESTHE-TIC; RELATIVISM; TASTE.

Wagner, Richard (1813–83) German composer (most famously of the four operas in *The Ring* cycle), poet, revolutionary, and author of books on art, religion, and politics. Wagner is unique among the greatest artists for having theorized a great deal, his topics ranging from vivisection and vegetarianism to the nature of art and its relations to religion and to revolution. This speculative work took the form of substantial books and essays, short fiction, and a copious corres-pondence (12,000 letters survive, some as long as fifty pages). Although not much of what Wagner wrote comes under the heading of aesthetics as such, he was not averse to philosophizing about it. He composed his prose mainly under the stress of needing to work out his position on the fun-damental issues involved in composing operas, or, as he increasingly preferred to call them, 'music dramas'.

After composing his first three operas, *Die Feen* ('The Fairies'), *Das Liebesverbot* ('Forbid-den Love') and *Rienzi*, which are highly com-petent and in some ways original works broadly in the German, Italian and French traditions respectively, he began to realize that contemporary operatic forms and fashions, as well as operatic life and standards of performance, were unacceptable to him. For an artist destined to be more revolutionary than any other in his century, his awareness of his mission came to him slowly; he was not a precocious composer, and the main thing in common between these three early works and his subsequent ones is that he wrote his own libretti from the outset – something that had rarely been done by his predecessors.

Like Verdi, his exact contemporary, Wagner never felt inclined to write substan-tial non-operatic works; but, unlike Verdi, he was heir to an immensely impressive tradi-tion of symphonic and instrumental composi-tion, and Beethoven was always his greatest idol. By the time he was in his late twenties, and living in Paris, he was beginning to have ambitions to bring closer together the achievement of the Austrian symphonists and the possibilities of operatic composition, contemporary examples of which he viewed with increasing distaste. Because he was living in acute poverty he turned to journal-ism, and it was at this time that he produced his first substantial body of prose, consisting of short stories strongly influenced by E.T.A. Hoffmann, and reports on ˉthe Parisian musical scene. Most of these pieces make lively and enjoyable reading, unlike his later prose works; and in them there are the first signs of what became his lifelong obsession with the development of opera as a leading artform. In the story 'A Pilgrimage to Beet-hoven', he presents the great composer on his death-bed giving expression to proto-Wagnerian ideas on the relationship between music and words, and on the kind of opera he would like to write: '[It] would contain no arias, duets, trios, and all the other things with which an opera is patched together these days.'

Beethoven's Ninth Symphony was always a talismanic work for Wagner, and his returns, throughout his life, to writing about it might be said to reflect his developing thoughts on his deepest aesthetic concerns. In the explanatory programme that he wrote when he gave the work what was probably its first exemplary performance in Dresden in 1846, he claimed that the celebrated in-troduction to the last movement – in which, in passages of powerful and expressive recitative, the themes of the previous three movements are tried out and found wanting by the lower strings – was Beethoven's embodiment of the idea that purely instrumental music was not enough. So Beethoven introduced voices singing Schiller's 'Ode to Joy', in order to complete a work which had, up to that point, been the greatest of all examples of a purely instrumental artform. Meanwhile, Wagner was himself producing operas in which the music and the drama were on ever more intimate terms, though he did not yet feel the necessity for working out the relationship between them at any great length. The three works of this decade, *Der fliegende Holländer* ('The Flying Dutchman'), *Tannhäuser* and *Lohengrin*, are characterized by growing mastery in musical–dramatic presentation; but there was nothing here to alarm the operatic world of the time.

In 1848–9 Europe was shaken by a series of revolutions, and Wagner participated, to an undetermined extent, in that of May 1849 in Dresden. The result was that he narrowly escaped arrest and imprisonment, and was exiled from Germany for the next twelve years. He had already begun to think about various mythological subjects for a new work, but came to realize that he would not be able to accomplish anything without drastic speculations on the whole nature of his work as an artist, and as a member of a society which he had come to regard as fundamentally corrupt. The first fruits of this were his major theoretical works, *Art and Revolution* (1849), *The Art-Work of the Future* (1850) and *Opera and Drama* (1851) – this last is the most important treatise in the history of operatic aesthetics. His basic premise in these works is that art has to reclaim the social function that it fulfilled in the classical Greek *polis*, and decisively reject its function as entertainment, which it has lapsed into in the decadent modern world. To achieve its proper aim, it must deal with the 'purely human', that which is common to people of all times and places. Its subjects must therefore be mythological, not historical. And it must represent a new synthesis of the arts, which Wagner characterized as the

Gesamtkunstwerk, perhaps best translated as 'the total work of art'. The focus of this kind of art was to be drama, to which the other arts, which had developed autonomously to their disadvantage, must all contribute.

In particular, the role of music in this new collective art must be reversed from that which Wagner alleged it had played in traditional opera, where it had been the end, the so-called drama having been the means. Music had to be subordinate, he declared, to make more powerfully expressive what was being enacted in the drama – which consisted, of course, not only of the text, but also of the action. A great deal of what Wagner wrote, in his historical reconstruction of the history of the various artforms, is to be taken with a pinch of salt. What matters is that, without indulging in extensive special pleading – in which he borrowed heavily from Feuerbach, among many other, mostly German, thinkers – he would not have been able to return finally to his creative work, the composition of the *Ring*. He came to see that as he had originally conceived it, as a single music–drama called *Siegfrieds Tod* ('Siegfried's Death'), it was not sufficiently a drama, because of the amount of narrative and explanation of former events that it contained. He therefore set about filling out the action, and the result was four dramas – or poems, as he called them – which he would not finish composing until 1874. The first, whose function was largely to clear the ground, is *Das Rheingold*, and in it he stuck very closely to the prescriptions he had set out in *Opera and Drama*. Because it is primarily an expository work, the theory goes remarkably smoothly into practice. But it is in the second of the dramas, *Die Walküre* ('The Valkyrie'), that his prodigious musical gifts begin to reassert themselves.

It so happened that at this time (1854) he was introduced by a friend to the works of Schopenhauer, and the effect of reading him, especially his *magnum opus*, *The World as Will and Representation*, was immediate and lasting. It also involved what amounted to a *volte-face* on the relationship of music to the other arts, but this was something that Wagner never explicitly acknowledged. It was left to Nietzsche, in *Towards a Genealogy of Morals* (1887), to point it out with typical firmness. For Schopenhauer, music was by far the most important of the arts, because unlike the others, which have an oblique relationship to the will – which is the sole reality, all else being appearance – music is the direct presentation of the will.

Wagner's conversion to this view was a smooth affair, as was his general acceptance of Schopenhauer's pessimistic evaluation of existence. Wagner's disillusionment with political events during the mid-century, and his paradoxical combination of exuberant vitality with a yearning for death, found what he took to be their ideal working-out in Schopenhauer's philosophy. After writing two acts of the up-beat *Siegfried* he broke off work on the *Ring* for twelve years, during which he wrote *Tristan und Isolde*, which he conceived in the spirit of Schopenhauer, whose influence is manifest in its text. But the philosopher would have been horrified by the lovers' achievement of 'nothingness' by taking erotic love to a previously unimagined extreme. Wagner's next work, the ostensibly cheerful *Die Meistersinger von Nürnberg* ('The Mastersingers of Nuremberg'), is in fact far more imbued with pessimism. And by the time Wagner returned to the *Ring*, Schopenhauer's influence is pervasive, if elusive – it is more a matter of the overall tone of the work than of its conclusion, which is notoriously ambiguous.

During his later years Wagner continued to write prose works, though short ones. To celebrate the centenary of Beethoven's birth, in 1870 he produced a monograph on the composer in which his view of music is most explicitly Schopenhauerian. After the first performance of the *Ring* in 1876 he devoted himself to *Parsifal*, his 'stage consecration festival drama', in which he put into practice the formulation at the opening of his essay 'Religion and art' (1880):

It could be said that at the point where religion becomes artificial, it is reserved to art to salvage the kernel of religion, inasmuch as the mythical images which religion would wish to be believed as

true are apprehended in art for their symbolic value, and through ideal representation of those symbols art reveals the concealed truth within them.

The clumsy expression, combined with depth of insight, in this piece of Wagnerian prose is typical of his mature thought on aesthetic matters.

See also NIETZSCHE; SCHOPENHAUER.

WRITINGS

Opera and Drama (1851); trans. Edwin Evans (London: Wm. Reeves, nd).

BIBLIOGRAPHY

Borchmeyer, Dieter: *Richard Wagner: Theory and Theatre* (Oxford: Oxford University Press, 1991).
Skelton, Geoffrey: *Wagner in Thought and Practice* (London: Lime Tree Books, 1991).

MICHAEL TANNER

Wilde, Oscar (Fingall O'Flahertie Wills) (1854–1900) Irish playwright, poet, and man of letters; a luminary of late nineteenth-century cultural life, his career was cut short by imprisonment during the 1890s and consequent ill-health.

Various factors have stood in the way of appreciating Wilde's significance as a theorist of art – personal notoriety, a primary reputation for sparkling comedies of manners, and a penchant for paradox. Then there is the difficulty of telling when he is being serious; for, as he warns at the end of 'The truth of masks', he may be merely representing a certain 'artistic standpoint' which he 'entirely disagrees' with. It is possible, however, to discern a coherent and challenging aesthetic informing the themes treated by his three main essays, 'The decay of lying', 'The critic as artist', and 'The soul of man under socialism' (all published during 1889–90): the themes of art's imitation by life and nature; of the role of criticism; and of the relation between art, politics and morality.

Sounding a note that was to become dogma in the following century, Wilde proclaims that 'art never expresses anything but itself', and so is 'not to be judged by any external standard of resemblance' (Wilde, 1983, pp. 987, 982). This is not intended to criticize representational art and plead for abstraction, but to point out that even the most 'realistic' art acts only as a 'veil, rather than a mirror'. And in so far as imitation takes place at all, it is life and nature which imitate art, not vice versa. Part of Wilde's meaning here is, of course, that people's behaviour is influenced by painting and literature. 'The nineteenth century . . . is largely an invention of Balzac' (1983, p. 983). He is indicating, as well, the idea later developed by Ernst Gombrich that an artist's perception of nature is partly a function of the artistic tradition to which he belongs. It is Turner and the impressionists, he suggests, who are responsible for London looking so foggy.

But Wilde is also making a more philosophical point. Nature, he writes, 'is our creation. It is in our brain that she quickens to life. Things are because we see them' (1983, p. 986). Life and nature are in themselves a chaos, lacking in form and structure until human beings impose these. And they impose them, not least, through the self-consciously form-giving activity of the arts. Art cannot, therefore, be answerable to an 'external standard of resemblance'; for, prior to the constructive contribution of art, there exists nothing determinate for works of art to resemble. For Wilde, as later for Nelson Goodman, art is 'a way of world-making' and not a mirror of something already in place.

This theme is continued through Wilde's contention, in 'The critic as artist', that not only does the critic have a vital role to play but that his calling is actually a higher one than that of the artists whose works he criticizes. (Needless to say, the 'true' critics Wilde has in mind are not the writers of hack columns in newspapers.) This would be an absurd contention, of course, if the critic's job were simply to describe works of art or to fathom the artist's intentions. But, for Wilde, the job is not at all to be a 'fair, sincere and rational' commentator. In what has now

become a familiar belief, he holds that 'criticism is itself an art', no more to be judged by fidelity to the works discussed than these works are by any 'external standard of resemblance' (Wilde, 1983, p. 1026). Criticism should 'treat the work of art simply as a starting-point for a new creation' (p. 1029), a peg on which the critic hangs his own reflections. Such criticism, indeed, is 'more creative than the [artist's] creation', primarily because the critic goes to work on superior materials. Artists are confronted by life, which is 'deficient in form' and 'incoherent in its utterance'. The advantage which critics enjoy is that they 'gain their impressions almost entirely from what art has [already] touched' and given form to (p. 1034).

Wilde was a great admirer of Plato, but in these claims we can discern his divergence from, as well as his debt to, Plato. Wilde's contemplative critic, like Plato's philosopher, is superior to the artist, and for a similar reason – his acquaintance with forms. But whereas for Plato the artist is simply a poor imitator of reality – the forms – for Wilde he is the creator of forms, which then provide the cool, contemplative critic with the materials for a more self-conscious and refined intellectual creation.

This elevation of the critical thinker above the artist should give one pause before classifying Wilde, in the usual manner, as a full-fledged member of the 'art for art's sake' school. After all, if art is to provide material for the thinker, it would seem to have a 'sake' beyond itself. Many of Wilde's aphorisms, to be sure, ape the pronouncements of Théophile Gautier, Walter Pater and other disciples of aestheticism – 'All art is quite useless', 'Art is the only serious thing in the world', 'All art is immoral', and so on. But these need to be taken in context, and allowance has to be made for Wildean irony and a desire to épater les bourgeois. Moreover, it is easy to find 'one-liners' which suggest a different attitude – for example, 'the arts are made for life and not life for the arts', and 'all beautiful things are made by those who strive to make something useful' (quoted in Ellmann, 1987, pp. 256, 246).

'Art for art's sake' is, anyway, a slogan that can be taken in various ways. Minimally, it proclaims that the only criteria which should govern the production of, or judgement upon, a particular work are aesthetic ones. Wilde seems generally to have subscribed to this. He would also accept the dictum read as a way of berating those artists whose works are motivated by commitment to social reforms. Not only does this tend to result in bad art or literature, as with Zola, but most social remedies for man's ills 'do not cure the disease: they merely prolong it' (Wilde, 1983, p. 1079). However, he explicitly rejects 'art for art's sake' if interpreted as a pronouncement on 'the final cause of art' – or, rather, its lack of such a 'cause' (see Ellmann, 1987, p. 249). And despite the 'immoralist' ring to some of his remarks, it is clear that the mature Wilde had a deep concern for the moral condition of man and believed that art had a vital role to play in improving it. As already implied, care must be taken with these remarks. Thus, having written that 'the virtues of the poor . . . are much to be regretted' (Wilde, 1983, p. 1081), he then explains that these alleged virtues – obedience, say, and gratitude for charity – are nothing of the sort, but the symptoms, rather, of a degraded and crushed personality. More generally, his jibes at 'the ethical' are attacks on what passes for morality in a society he despises.

'The soul of man under socialism' is, in fact, a thoroughly moral manifesto for Wilde's ideals of freedom, individualism and self-realization. Like Kierkegaard and Marx, he perceives the lives of people in his century as becoming increasingly mechanistic and anonymous. In part, the cure will be through radical economic and political change: the abolition of private property, for example, and guarantees against the tyranny of both government and public opinion. (This is a long way from Gautier's readiness to welcome the return of a tyrant, provided 'he brings me back a hamper of Tokay' (Gautier, 1981, p. 39).) But the main vehicle of these ideals is art. 'Art is the most intense mode of individualism', since it embodies a person's 'unique temperament', thereby offering an

escape from 'tyranny of habit, and the reduction of man to the level of a machine' (Wilde, 1983, pp. 1090–1). Not only is artistic endeavour a particularly valuable route towards self-realization, but it provides a model for every person's proper relation to himself. For, like Nietzsche, Wilde urges us to view our own lives as works of art to be constructed. Society is tending to 'make men themselves machines . . . whereas we want them to be artists, that is to say men'. Indeed, 'to become a work of art is the object of living' (quoted in Ellmann, 1987, pp. 184–5, 292).

Fully to appreciate Wilde's position here, we must recall once again his persistent contrasting of the incoherent chaos of life and nature with the structured order of the artist's and critic's 'worlds'. Humans are distinguished from other beings by their capacity, which largely owes to language, for imposing form on chaos; and one individual is distinguished from his fellows by the particular style with which this capacity is exercised. And it is in this capacity that the possibilities for true freedom and self-realization reside. 'We are never less free than when we try to act': the free man, rather, is one who 'creates the age' by forging his own perspective, by the artistic and contemplative construction of 'a world more real than reality itself' (Wilde, 1983, pp. 1040, 1021, 1049).

It would be quite wrong, argues Wilde, to regard this aesthetic individualism as a philosophy of selfishness. It is, in fact, the only effective antidote to egotism, for the person whose 'primary aim is self-development' is content 'letting other people's lives alone', in contrast with the egotist who manipulates their lives for his own advantage (1983, p. 1101). There is something here of the optimism of Socrates that the person whose soul is just will simply have no inclination to wrong others. As Wilde puts it, truly free and realized individuals will not sin, 'not because they make the renunciations of the ascetic, but because they can do everything they wish without hurt to the soul' (1983, p. 1058).

See also AESTHETICISM; ATTITUDE, AES-

THETIC; CRITICISM; FUNCTION OF ART; MORALITY AND ART.

WRITINGS

Complete Works of Oscar Wilde, ed. Vyvyan Holland (London and Glasgow: Collins, 1983).
Aristotle at Afternoon Tea: The Rare Oscar Wilde, ed. J. Wyse Jackson (London: Fourth Estate, 1991).

BIBLIOGRAPHY

Ellmann, Richard: *Oscar Wilde* (Harmondsworth: Penguin Books, 1987).
Gautier, Théophile: *Mademoiselle de Maupin*, trans. J. Richardson (Harmondsworth: Penguin Books, 1981), preface.
Gide, André: *Oscar Wilde* (Paris: Gallimard, 1938).

DAVID E. COOPER

Wittgenstein, Ludwig (1889–1951) Austrain born, and later naturalized British, philosopher; regarded by many as the 20th C.'s most important philosopher, whose later philosophy is as influential as the earlier one of which it is so critical. Youngest child of Karl Wittgenstein, the iron and steel magnate and patron of the arts, Ludwig Wittgenstein wrote two philosophical masterpieces, *Tractatus Logico-Philosophicus* (1921) and the posthumously published *Philosophical Investigations* (1953). Neither has much to say about art, which did not lie at the centre of his philosophical concerns.

But Wittgenstein had a deep and abiding interest in certain of the arts, and, though only briefly, practised two of them, architecture and sculpture. In 1925 he assumed control of the project assigned to his friend Paul Engelmann, a pupil of Adolf Loos (whom Wittgenstein at one time admired), to design a house in Vienna for Wittgenstein's sister Gretl, applying himself to the task with characteristic fanatical zeal. The house still stands, at 19 Kundmanngasse, although its interior, to which Wittgenstein gave special attention, has been greatly altered. The house is a stark monument to his functional, anti-decorative architectural ideal, which is perhaps most appealingly realized in the doors, radiators and windows that enliven the otherwise drab appearance, and which he insisted were constructed to the precise millimetre. He also modelled a bust, which Gretl, who sat for it, displayed in the Kundmanngasse house. But Wittgenstein believed that he possessed only artistic taste, understanding and good manners, rather than creative ability, and thought of his architectural work as merely the rendering of an old style into a language appropriate to the modern world. These were, therefore, isolated forays into artistic practice.

Perhaps his two favourite art forms were music and literature. He had a fairly extensive, although unsystematic and idiosyncratic, knowledge of literature, made more accessible by his mastery of German, English, Norwegian and Russian, and he immersed himself so intensely in his favourite works that he knew them almost by heart. He had a very good musical memory and an acute ear, and frequently played music in his head; he played the clarinet and was unusually adept at whistling music, sometimes performing complete works. He thought of music as having come to a full stop with Brahms. He confessed that it was impossible for him to say in *Philosophical Investigations* one word about all that music had meant in his life, so that it would be difficult for him to be understood. He seems to have had little interest in painting, his one recorded remark on Michelangelo being banal. When, after the First World War, he gave away the fortune inherited from his father, part of it was distributed to impecunious Austrian artists.

In his early philosophy are to be found a few gnomic utterances about art: 'Ethics and aesthetics are one', 'The work of art is the object seen *sub specie aeternitatis*'. These show the influence of Schopenhauer, for whom the aesthetic attitude was one of pure will-less contemplation in which the subject's entire consciousness is filled by a single perceptual image, so that the object he contemplates becomes for the duration of his contemplation his whole world. But they do not invite prolonged thought, especially in the light of Wittgenstein's view at the time that what is of value in art must elude the net of language and therefore can never be spoken about.

The situation is not so bleak, however, if we turn to his later thoughts about art. Even here, though, the lack of an extended treatment of aesthetics in his writings means that an interpretation of the way in which he would have applied his new method of thinking to the philosophy of art must be largely speculative. But the lecture notes taken by students who attended his classes at Cambridge confirm that he had strong opinions about aesthetics; and these notes, and remarks in various writings, make it possible to identify a number of themes in his treatment of art, although the diversity of his thoughts precludes a comprehensive account, and many of these were not considered and carefully articulated opinions but spontaneous remarks.

The least surprising feature is the application of one of the leading ideas of his later thought to the concepts of art and beauty. What do the arts have in common, in virtue of which they are all forms of art? What do all beautiful things have in common, in virtue of which they are beautiful? In both cases Wittgenstein rejects the supposition that the reason the items concerned fall within the concept is because they share a property common to and distinctive of them; but the alternative account that he offers appears to be different in the two cases. The reason the various art forms are all forms of art is not because they possess a distinctive common property, but because of the criss-crossing and overlapping of many resemblances: the arts form a 'family'. But the reason why the beauty of one kind of thing (a face, say) is very different from the beauty of another kind (a chair, for example) is because 'beautiful', like 'good', is an attributive, rather than a predicative, adjective, so that it needs to be taken together with the substantive it qualifies, the nature of the judgement of beauty being determined by the kind of thing being judged.

Two of the most prominent themes concern the effects that the arts have on us. The first emphasizes the autonomy of artistic value against theories that deny works of art any distinctive value. There is a temptation, in reflection upon the nature of art – one to which Tolstoy succumbed – to conceive of the appreciation of any work that we value as consisting in the work's inducing in us a rewarding experience, and, then, to conceive of this experience in abstraction from the work that gives rise to it. The result is that the value of a work of art is thought of as residing in its effects, and these effects are thought of as possessing a nature independent of the work that causes them. So the value of a work of art stands to the work in much the same relation that the value of a medicine stands to the medicine: just as the valuable results of the medicine can be fully characterized without mentioning the nature of the medicine that causes them, so the value of a work of art is located in an independently specifiable effect.

But, as Wittgenstein insisted, this is certainly a misrepresentation of artistic value. For if this conception were correct, the appreciation of a work of art would consist of two experiences – the experience of the work and another experience to which this gives rise; and the value of the work would be determined by the nature of the second, not the first, experience. But the experience of a work of art does not play a merely instrumental role in artistic appreciation. On the contrary, the value of the work is determined by the nature of the experience of the work itself, rather than any other experience it happens to generate. The only way of appreciating a work of art is to experience it with understanding – to read, listen to, imagine, look at, perform the work itself. When we admire a work, it is not replaceable for us by another that creates the same effect, for we admire the work itself; its value does not consist in its performing a function that another work could perform just as well. (As Wittgenstein pointed out, there is a similarity between, on the one hand, the doctrine that the value of a work of art is a function of an experience produced by the experience of the work and, on the other hand, the idea – one of the principal targets of *Philosophical Investigations* – that the sense of a sentence is a process that accompanies the utterance or perception of it.)

The second salient theme concerning the effects of works of art is opposition to the alleged relevance of psychological experiments to the solution of certain kinds of aesthetic puzzlement. When we are puzzled by our reaction to a work of art, our puzzlement, Wittgenstein insists, cannot be removed by a psychological investigation aimed at determining the cause of our reaction. For our reaction is 'directed' or intentional, taking some aspect of the work as its object; the puzzlement will be removed only by identifying the reason why we react in this way to the work, rather than by identifying the cause of our reaction; and the criterion for a successful resolution of the puzzle is that we should *accept* or *agree with* the offered explanation – a clear mark that what is sought is a reason, not a cause.

This position is more difficult to evaluate, since there are different kinds of aesthetic puzzlement and Wittgenstein's examples are something of a medley. Moreover, it appears to rest on the contentious doctrine that the intentionality of an aesthetic impression is not susceptible of a causal analysis. The principal forms of aesthetic puzzlement that Wittgenstein seems to have had in mind concern what it is about a work of art that makes it so impressive, or impressive in a particular way; or what is wrong with a certain work or a performance of it; or why a work has just the distribution of features that it does. In such cases, what is needed to remove the puzzlement is, Wittgenstein claims, a certain kind of description of the art object. Such a description draws attention to the features that give the work the character in question, but does so in such a manner that we can now perceive these features in the work, with the result that our perception of it is modified.

One way in which this can be achieved is by placing side by side with the work other items that possess or lack these characteristics, or by indicating an analogy between the work and something else. So – to take one of Wittgenstein's favourite examples – one way

of removing puzzlement about the particular pattern of variation in loudness and tempo in a musical theme would be to draw a comparison by pointing out that, at this point in the theme, it is as if a conclusion were being drawn; or that this part is, as it were, in parenthesis; or that it is as if this part were a reply to what came before. The explanation is persuasive, rather than diagnostic, effecting a clarification or change in the perception of the work; it differs from the causal diagnosis of a headache, where the sufferer's acceptance of the diagnosis is unnecessary and leaves his headache unchanged.

This example makes it clear that the principal focus of Wittgenstein's interest in aesthetic puzzlement is the enhancement of artistic appreciation: the kind of explanation that dissolves the puzzlement must further the understanding and appreciation of the work of art. This explains his emphasis on comparisons; the requirement that, if the proposed solution is to remove the puzzlement, the puzzled subject should agree with a proposed solution to his problem; and the resultant transformation of the subject's experience. But unless Wittgenstein's opposition to the relevance of psychological experiments to the solution of aesthetic puzzlement is narrowly restricted in this way, it is open to obvious counter-examples (Cioffi, 1976).

This second theme is linked with another observation that Wittgenstein makes. Psychological experiments designed to determine which musical or pictorial arrangement produces the more pleasing effect on a particular person or set of people are irrelevant to aesthetics. For aesthetic appreciation is concerned, not with liking or disliking a work of art, but with understanding it and experiencing its features as right or wrong, better or worse, close to or distant from an ideal. This normative element in the appreciation of a work of art is misrepresented if artistic appreciation is thought of as merely a matter of what gives pleasure to the listener or spectator. In fact, artistic appreciation can be made sense of only by locating it in the cultural context to which it belongs and from which it derives its distinctive shape; different cultures determine different forms of artistic and aesthetic appreciation; and any description of a culture that illuminates the nature of aesthetic judgements within that culture will be a description of a complicated set of activities from which the words used to express those judgements draw their life.

See also EXPRESSION; INEFFABILITY; SCHOPENHAUER.

WRITINGS

Philosophische Untersuchungen (Oxford: 1953); trans. G.E.M. Anscombe, *Philosophical Investigations* (Oxford: Basil Blackwell, 1953).
Tractatus Logico-Philosophicus, trans. C.K. Ogden (London: Routledge & Kegan Paul, 1922); trans. D.F. Pears and B.F. McGuinness (London: Routledge & Kegan Paul, 1961).
Wittgenstein, Lectures and Conversations on Aesthetics, Psychology and Religious Belief, ed. C. Barrett (Oxford: Basil Blackwell, 1966).
Notebooks 1914–1916, 2nd edn, trans. E. Anscombe, (Oxford: Basil Blackwell, 1979).
Wittgenstein's Lectures, Cambridge 1932–1935, ed. A. Ambrose (Oxford: Basil Blackwell, 1979).
Vermischte Bemerkungen (Frankfurt: 1977); trans. P. Winch, *Culture and Value* (Oxford: Basil Blackwell, 1980).

BIBLIOGRAPHY

Cioffi, F.: 'Aesthetic experience and aesthetic perplexity', *Acta Philosophica Fennica*, 28 (1976).
Moore, G.E.: 'Wittgenstein's lectures in 1930–33', *Philosophical Papers* (London: Allen & Unwin, 1959), pp. 312–15.
Tanner, M.: 'Wittgenstein and aesthetics', *Oxford Review*, 3 (1966).

MALCOLM BUDD

Wollheim, Richard (1923–) British philosopher, for many years Grote Professor at the University of London; best known for his writings on psychoanalysis and on the visual arts. Most of the themes of Wollheim's work in aesthetics – the ontology of art, representation, expression, the understanding and interpretation of art – were introduced in his first major book on aesthetics, *Art and Its Objects* (1968), a work in the analytic tradition which was amongst the first to relate the later writings of Wittgenstein to the subject. Two things unusual from within that tradition particularly distinguish his work. The first is his attention to painting. The nature of painting is the subject of his later work, and his intimate knowledge of paintings permeates his writings.

The second distinguishing feature of Wollheim's work is his deep commitment to Freud and his indebtedness to the work of the Kleinian art critic, Adrian Stokes. This influence manifests itself both in writings on Freud and art and in the fact that he brings to his study of the experience of art a conception of mind which catches the way we never shake ourselves totally away from the early fantasy that assimilates the mind to the body, mental activity to bodily functioning, and mental contents to the parts of the body. These are processes essential to his accounts of artistic expression.

In the preface to his collected essays (1973), Wollheim speaks of his impatience with any form of culture that turns its back on history, complexity or melancholy – a remark that indicates the dominant preoccupations of his work. The regard for history is evident in his attention to the ways in which the past informs the present, both culturally in the form of tradition, and in personal psychology. His regard for complexity is manifest in his recognition of tensions and forces, in both life and art, which have no simple resolution. He endorses Freud's statement that the artist is particularly adept at patterning those vicissitudes of feeling and impulse to which we are all subject. The third element, melancholy, is revealed in his acknowledgement of Stokes's regard for the sense of loss, the feeling for order and the desire to restore, as the perennial subject-matter of art. (One of Wollheim's deepest loves in painting is Poussin.)

However, he does not equate art with neurosis, and he rejects psychoanalytic accounts of art, modelled on such processes as dream interpretation, which seek to reveal

447

a hidden or latent content in art. Rather, he speaks of art as a form of externalization or embodiment of the inner world, through visual conceptions and metaphors of the body. This position is worked out most richly in Ch. 6 of his major later work, *Painting as an Art*. Wollheim's interest in the relationship between psychoanalysis and art is phenomenological. In this, and in other contexts, he explicitly rejects attempts to found the study of art on linguistics. His insistence that the intentional nature of art presupposes a universal human nature also sets his work apart from other work in art theory derived from structural linguistics.

It is not the work on psychoanalysis and art, however, but that on ontology, identity and representation, that has received most attention from analytic philosophers. *Art and Its Objects* is structured on the belief that, if issues of the ontology of works of art can be clarified, then the clarification of many other issues in aesthetics will follow. This work explores the ramifications of the view that works of art are physical objects. Although he marshals the arguments against this view, he is unwilling to relinquish it totally – at least in the case of artworks that he describes as 'individuals'. For the significance of the material embodiment of art is an essential part of his accounts of creativity, interpretation, representation and style.

Wollheim argues that there are two categories of artworks: *individuals* such as paintings, sculpture and, possibly, architecture, which are present to us as unique and particular objects; and those which involve performance or notation, such as music, drama and literature, which he claims are *types*. For the resolution of the question of whether those artworks which are individuals can be identified with physical objects, Wollheim refers us to the metaphysical complexity of the subject. It is at this point that the unexamined tension between the empiricist and the phenomenological grounds of his work is most apparent. However, his immediate reasons for refusing to relinquish completely the physical object hypothesis are significant. For the most likely alternative views involve the claim that artworks are characterized by the possession of peculiarly aesthetic qualities. Wollheim objects that this both distorts the nature of criticism and limits the scope of interpretation. For if the view that there is a clear and general distinction between aesthetic and non-aesthetic properties of art were correct, then there would not be an internal connection, as he insists there is, between the medium and its expressive or representational effects.

Wollheim analyses representation, for example, in terms of 'seeing-in' – that is, the psychological capacity for seeing the marks on a stained or painted surface, and seeing the figurative effects of those marks, as two parts of one and the same simultaneous perceptual experience. It is this feature of art, the fact that artist and spectator are required to attend to the role of the medium, both in making and responding to the work, that opens it to criticism and interpretation. For Wollheim it is essential that any feature of artworks can, in principle, become aesthetically relevant.

To elucidate the nature of those artworks which depend on performance or notation, he introduces the logical distinction between type and token. For the issue depends on the criterion of identity for such works. They are, he argues, types. This also has direct relevance to his position on the ineliminability of interpretation. For there are no properties that cannot pass from token to type; for instance (with suitable exceptions for features of time, place etc.), anything that can be predicated of a performance of a piece of music can also be predicated of the music itself. However, as not every property of the token *ipso facto* belongs to the type, performance essentially involves interpretation. It is an essential feature of both categories of art, individuals and types, that the experience of art is always and necessarily interpretative.

Wollheim explicates criticism as the retrieval of the creative process. The creative process, however, is not to be identified narrowly with the artist's intentions. It also includes such things as chance and the conventions and traditions in which the artist is working. Knowledge of such things depends on the critic's cognitive stock, and the artist might only become aware of them as he becomes spectator to his own work during or after its making. Furthermore, the critic might bring to bear resources from his own times, unavailable to the artist. The only limitation to the information relevant to critical experience is the requirement that it shall enable the spectator to experience some part of the content of the work which otherwise may have been overlooked. Thus here, as throughout, the experience of a work of art is shown to be analogous to the process of the psychological understanding of oneself.

See also CRITICISM; EXPRESSION; INTERPRETATION; ONTOLOGY OF ARTWORKS; PSYCHOANALYSIS AND ART; REPRESENTATION.

WRITINGS

On Art and the Mind: Essays and Lectures (London: Allen Lane, 1973).

Art and Its Objects: An Introduction to Aesthetics (New York: Harper & Row, 1968; London: Pelican Books, 1970); 2nd edn, with 6 supplementary essays (Cambridge: Cambridge University Press, 1980).

Painting as an Art (the A.W. Mellon Lectures in the Fine Arts, 1984) (London: Thames & Hudson, 1987; Princeton, NJ: Princeton University Press, 1987).

On Painting and the Self (Boston, Mass.: Harvard University Press, 1992).

CAROLYN WILDE

Index

COMPILED BY MEG DAVIES

Note: Page references in **bold** type indicate chief discussion of major topics. Where names of contributors to the *Companion* are indexed, the references are to citations in articles other than their own articles.